1996
DESKBOOK ENCYCLOPEDIA
OF
AMERICAN SCHOOL LAW

"This publication is designed to provide accurate and authoritative information in regard to the subject matter covered. It is sold with the understanding that the publisher is not engaged in rendering legal, accounting or other professional service. If legal advice or other expert assistance is required, the services of a competent professional person should be sought."—from a Declaration of Principles jointly adopted by a Committee of the American Bar Association and a Committee of Publishers and Associations.

Published by
Data Research, Inc.
P.O. Box 490
Rosemount, Minnesota 55068

OTHER TITLES PUBLISHED
BY DATA RESEARCH, INC.:

Students with Disabilities and Special Education
Private School Law in America
U.S. Supreme Court Education Cases
Deskbook Encyclopedia of American Insurance Law
Deskbook Encyclopedia of Public Employment Law
U.S. Supreme Court Employment Cases
Deskbook Encyclopedia of Employment Law
Statutes, Regulations and Case Law Protecting
  Individuals with Disabilities

ISBN 0-939675-52-8
ISSN 1058-4919

The Library of Congress has cataloged this serial title as follows:
Deskbook Encyclopedia of American school law.— 1980/81—Rosemount, Minn.:
Informational Research Systems, 1981-

          v.; 23 cm.
Annual.
Published 1996   by: Data Research, Inc.
Prepared by the editors of: Legal Notes for Education,
1980/81-
1. Educational law and legislation—United States—Digests. 2. Educational law and legislation—United
States—Periodicals. I. Informational Research Systems (Washington, D.C.) II. Data Research, Inc.
(Rosemount, Minn.) III. Legal Notes for Education. IV. Title: Encyclopedia of American School Law.
KF4114.D46   92-054912
                              344.73'07'02638—dc19
                                  [347.304702638]
                                                    AACR 2#M#MARC-S

Library of Congress [8704r86]rev

PREFACE

The *1996 Deskbook Encyclopedia of American School Law* is a completely updated encyclopedic compilation of state and federal appellate court decisions which affect education. These decisions have been selected and edited by the editorial staff of Data Research, Inc., publishers of *Legal Notes for Education*. Topical classifications have been revised and edited to reflect rapid changes in education law and many cases reported in previous editions have been re-edited or reclassified.

This edition contains a brief introductory note on the American judicial system and updated appendices of recent U.S. Supreme Court cases and recently published law review articles. Also included are portions of the U.S. Constitution which are most frequently cited in education cases. This publication is intended to provide educators and lawyers with access to the most current available cases in education. We believe that you will find this edition even more readable and easier to use than previous editions.

EDITORIAL STAFF
DATA RESEARCH, INC.

INTRODUCTORY NOTE ON
THE JUDICIAL SYSTEM

In order to allow the reader to determine the relative importance of a judicial decision, the cases included in the *1996 Deskbook Encyclopedia of American School Law* identify the particular court from which a decision has been issued. For example, a case decided by a state supreme court generally will be of greater significance than a state circuit court case. Hence a basic knowledge of the structure of our judicial system is important to an understanding of school law.

Almost all the reports in this volume are taken from appellate court decisions. Although most education law decisions occur at trial court and administrative levels, appellate court decisions have the effect of binding lower courts and administrators so that appellate court decisions have the effect of law within their court systems.

State and federal court systems generally function independently of each other. Each court system applies its own law according to statutes and the determinations of its highest court. However, judges at all levels often consider opinions from other court systems to settle issues which are new or arise under unique fact situations. Similarly, lawyers look at the opinions of many courts to locate authority which supports their clients' cases.

Once a lawsuit is filed in a particular court system, that system retains the matter until its conclusion. Unsuccessful parties at the administrative or trial court level generally have the right to appeal unfavorable determinations of law to appellate courts within the system. When federal law or constitutional issues are present, lawsuits may be appropriately filed in the federal court system. In those cases, the lawsuit is filed initially in the federal district court for that area.

On rare occasions, the U.S. Supreme Court considers appeals from the highest courts of the states if a distinct federal question exists and at least four justices agree on the question's importance. The federal courts occasionally send cases to state courts for application of state law. These situations are infrequent and in general, the state and federal court systems should be considered separate from each other.

The most common system, used by nearly all states and also the federal judiciary, is as follows: a legal action is commenced in district court (sometimes called trial court, county court, common pleas court or superior court) where a decision is initially reached. The case may then be appealed to the court of appeals (or appellate court), and in turn this decision may be appealed to the supreme court.

Several states, however, do not have a court of appeals; lower court decisions are appealed directly to the state's supreme court. Additionally, some states have labeled their courts in a nonstandard fashion.

In Maryland, the highest state court is called the Court of Appeals. In the state of New York, the trial court is called the Supreme Court. Decisions of this court may be appealed to the Supreme Court, Appellate Division. The highest court in New York is the Court of Appeals. Pennsylvania has perhaps the most complex court system. The lowest state court is the Court of Common Pleas. Depending on the circumstances of the case, appeals may be taken to either the Commonwealth Court or the Superior Court. In certain instances the Commonwealth Court functions as a trial court as well as an appellate court. The Superior Court, however, is strictly an intermediate appellate court. The highest court in Pennsylvania is the Supreme Court.

While supreme court decisions are generally regarded as the last word in legal matters, it is important to remember that trial and appeals court decisions also create important legal precedents. For the hierarchy of typical state and federal court systems, please see the diagram below.

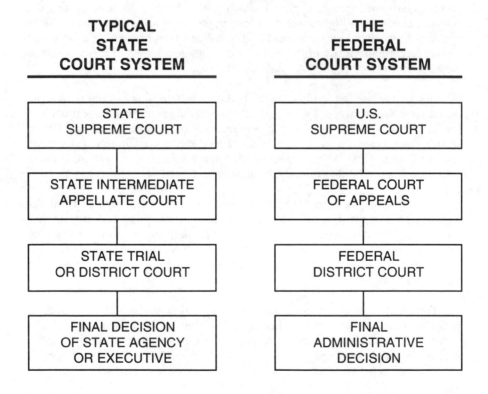

TYPICAL STATE COURT SYSTEM	THE FEDERAL COURT SYSTEM
STATE SUPREME COURT	U.S. SUPREME COURT
STATE INTERMEDIATE APPELLATE COURT	FEDERAL COURT OF APPEALS
STATE TRIAL OR DISTRICT COURT	FEDERAL DISTRICT COURT
FINAL DECISION OF STATE AGENCY OR EXECUTIVE	FINAL ADMINISTRATIVE DECISION

Federal courts of appeals hear appeals from the district courts which are located in their circuits. Below is a list of states and the federal circuits in which they are located.

First Circuit — Puerto Rico, Maine, New Hampshire, Massachusetts, Rhode Island

Second Circuit — New York, Vermont, Connecticut

Third Circuit — Pennsylvania, New Jersey, Delaware, Virgin Islands

Fourth Circuit — West Virginia, Maryland, Virginia, North Carolina, South Carolina

Fifth Circuit — Texas, Louisiana, Mississippi

Sixth Circuit — Ohio, Kentucky, Tennessee, Michigan

Seventh Circuit — Wisconsin, Indiana, Illinois

Eighth Circuit — North Dakota, South Dakota, Nebraska, Arkansas, Missouri, Iowa, Minnesota

Ninth Circuit — Alaska, Washington, Oregon, California, Hawaii, Arizona, Nevada, Idaho, Montana, Northern Mariana Islands, Guam

Tenth Circuit — Wyoming, Utah, Colorado, Kansas, Oklahoma, New Mexico

Eleventh Circuit — Alabama, Georgia, Florida

District of Columbia Circuit — Hears cases from the U.S. District Court for the District of Columbia.

Federal Circuit — Sitting in Washington, D.C., the U.S. Court of Appeals, Federal Circuit, hears patent and trade appeals and certain appeals on claims brought against the federal government and its agencies.

TABLE OF CONTENTS

TABLE OF CASES

TABLE OF CASES

COLORADO

CONNECTICUT

NEW MEXICO

NEW YORK

NORTH CAROLINA

NORTH DAKOTA

CHAPTER ONE

ACCIDENTS, INJURIES AND DEATHS

I.   NEGLIGENCE

Negligence refers to acts or omissions demonstrating a failure to use reasonable or ordinary care. Negligence may refer to inadvertence, carelessness, or the failure to foresee potential harm. There is some overlap in the cases between negligence and intentional misconduct. A pattern of negligence by school districts which shows a conscious disregard for safety may be deemed "wilful misconduct," a form of intentional conduct discussed in Section V of this chapter.

A.   Elements

The essential elements of a negligence lawsuit are 1) the existence of a legal duty to conform conduct to a specific standard in order to protect others from unreasonable risks of injury, 2) the breach of that duty that is, 3) the direct cause of the injury, and 4) damages. Simply put, negligence consists of a duty of care, followed by a breach of that duty which causes injury and damages.

An Idaho student enrolled in a weightlifting class. The instructor decided to cancel weightlifting one day and to hold a softball game instead. Students were not told about the game until they reported to the weight room. The instructor supervised the game from behind a backstop. The student slid into first base and broke his ankle. He claimed that the instructor was negligent in requiring the class to play softball, failing to properly supervise students, failing to instruct students on how to play softball and not inspecting their footwear. He filed a lawsuit against the school district and instructor in an Idaho trial court, which granted summary judgment motions by the district and instructor. The student appealed to the Court of Appeals of Idaho, which determined that the student had failed to show a sufficient causal connection between the alleged negligence and his injury. There was no evidence that inspecting the student's shoes would have made any difference and no evidence that the use of running shoes, as opposed to baseball shoes, made a difference. The student could not show that there was a duty to inspect shoes or to instruct students in how to play softball and the trial court had properly granted summary judgment to the district and instructor. *Sanders v. Kuna Joint School Dist.*, 876 P.2d 154 (Idaho App.1994).

A New York student was shot to death near his junior high school during the lunch hour. The student's mother sued the City of New York and other defendants in a New York trial court alleging that the school had failed to adequately supervise the lunch recess. The court set aside a jury verdict for the mother and dismissed the complaint. The New York Supreme Court, Appellate Division,

First Department, affirmed the trial court's order, agreeing that the evidence was insufficient to support a finding of lack of supervision. Although New York schools owed a special duty of care to their students, they could not be held liable for injuries not proximately related to the absence of supervision. *Maness v. City of New York*, 607 N.Y.S.2d 325 (A.D.1st Dept.1994).

A student at a Delaware university suffered severe chemical burns in a fraternity hazing incident. The student sued the fraternity, its national affiliate, the university and a fellow student who poured chemicals on him. A jury awarded him damages against the university and the other student in the amount of $30,000. However, after trial, the court relieved the university of liability stating that there was no legal duty owed by the university to the student. The student appealed that decision to the Supreme Court of Delaware. The supreme court stated that the student-university relationship was not sufficient by itself to protect its students from the actions of third parties. However, the university's policy to prevent hazing as well as its overall commitment to provide security on campus, constituted an assumed duty toward students. Furthermore, since the fraternity was located on university property, the university had a duty as an owner to protect students against foreseeable dangers. Since the university knew hazing was occurring, such action was foreseeable. The supreme court remanded the case for an apportionment of liability. *Fureck v. Univ. of Delaware*, 594 A.2d 506 (Del.1991).

B. Defenses

There are several defenses which may shield school districts and employees from liability in a negligence lawsuit. Traditionally, the doctrine of governmental (or sovereign) immunity protected any state agency, such as a school district, from liability. In states where the doctrine is retained, immunity is typically waived up to the amount of any liability insurance purchased by the defendant school district. In some states where the doctrine has been abolished, *in loco parentis* or *"save harmless"* laws have been implemented to shield school employees from some types of personal liability for injuries.

A California statute protected school districts and their employees from liability for injuries to participants in "hazardous recreational activities," which were defined as recreational activities conducted on public property which created a substantial risk of injury. A member of a high school gymnastics team died as the result of an accident on the high bar at a supervised practice during the off season. His estate filed a lawsuit against the school district in a California trial court, claiming negligence. The jury determined that the gymnast had been engaged in a hazardous recreational activity and that the coach was not grossly negligent. The estate filed motions for a new trial, judgment notwithstanding the verdict and to vacate the judgment. The court granted the motion for a new trial to determine whether the injury resulted from a school-directed activity but denied the other motions. The parties filed appeals from unfavorable parts of the trial court decision.

The California Court of Appeal, Second District, held that the matter of governmental immunity should never have gone to the jury because "hazardous recreational activities" did not include school-sponsored extracurricular athletic activities that were supervised by school personnel. The accident had occurred during a structured training drill supervised by the coach, but not as part of a school-sponsored team practice. Because the immunity statute did not protect school districts from liability resulting from the negligent supervision of extracurricular activities, the trial court had committed error by failing to grant the estate's motions for judgment notwithstanding the verdict and a new trial. *Acosta v. Los Angeles Unif. School Dist.*, 37 Cal.Rptr.2d 171 (Cal.App.2d Dist.1995).

Traditional common law principles held that if a plaintiff's own negligence contributed to his or her injuries, the plaintiff could not hold the defendant liable. It was irrelevant that the plaintiff's negligence was slight or that the defendant's negligence was extreme; any amount of negligence on the plaintiff's part would completely bar his or her recovery of money damages. The defense of contributory negligence is retained in a minority of states. Most states have replaced this defense with the doctrine of comparative negligence.

In comparative negligence states, a plaintiff whose negligence contributes to the injury is not barred from recovering damages. Rather, the negligence causing the plaintiff's injury is apportioned by the court between the plaintiff and defendant on the basis of their degrees of fault. For example, in a student injury case, a jury may find that a student who slipped on a bar of soap while running down the stairs was 40 percent negligent, and that the school district whose agent left the bar of soap on the stairs was 60 percent negligent. Assuming the student's damages amount to $10,000, the student would be entitled to recover $6,000 from the district. In some comparative negligence states, the plaintiff may not recover if his or her negligence is the same as or greater than the defendant's negligence.

An 18-year-old Louisiana special education student allegedly raped a 13-year-old special education student in a storage shed behind their school. He later pleaded guilty to juvenile court charges and was given a probationary sentence. The victim's parents removed their daughter from school and began teaching her at home. They alleged that she suffered psychological injuries because of the incident and filed a lawsuit against the perpetrator and the school district in a Louisiana trial court. Testimony at trial conflicted, and the court found that the victim had consented to having sex and had instigated the incident. However, it determined that the victim's consent was meaningless because of her status as a minor. The court ruled that the school board had not breached any duty to supervise its students and had not negligently maintained the shed in which the rape had occurred. The parties appealed to the Court of Appeal of Louisiana, Third Circuit. The court of appeal affirmed the trial court's factual finding that the board had not failed to supervise its students. It also affirmed the finding that the board's maintenance of the storage shed had not been a contributing cause of any of the victim's damages. The school board was not liable for any of the damages. Although the trial court had apparently ruled correctly given the conflicting testimony, it should have applied principles of comparative fault instead of ruling that the victim's age alone invalidated consent. Applying principles of comparative fault, the court of appeal reduced the $25,000 damage award against the perpetrator by five percent. *L.K. and L.K. v. Reed*, 631 So.2d 604 (La.App.3d Cir.1994).

An Illinois high school student drowned in the school swimming pool. His body was discovered by the class instructor after students had exited the pool at the conclusion of a class. The student's estate sued the board of education and instructor in an Illinois trial court for wrongful death. At trial, two students testified that they had seen the student exiting the pool. Testimony was also presented that no rope was provided to separate the deep end of the pool from the shallow end and that the deceased student was afraid of water. The jury returned a verdict for the estate of almost $1 million, despite its finding that the student had been comparatively negligent for reentering the pool. The court refused to award judgment notwithstanding the verdict to the board of education. It appealed to the Appellate Court of Illinois, First District, which stated that the operation of the school swimming pool constituted a government function and that those using the pool were owed no special duty. The evidence was speculative that the placement of a rope to separate the deep from the shallow end of the pool could have prevented the drowning. The rope requirement provision contained in Illinois law could not be construed to create a duty of the school board to have the rope placed in the pool at all times. Because the estate's theory was speculative, the jury's verdict had been incorrect and the case was reversed. *Williams v. Chicago Bd. of Educ.*, 642 N.E.2d 764 (Ill.App.1st Dist.1994).

A California school employed a woman part-time to feed horses twice a day at its two campuses. The employee's work was divided into two shifts. One day, after her morning shift, she left one campus to take her lunch break. Later, as she was headed toward the other campus for her afternoon shift, her truck struck an automobile, killing the driver. In addition to the employee and automobile manufacturer, the driver's family sued the school, claiming that it was vicariously responsible for the death of the driver. The school asked the court for summary judgment, contending that since the employee was not engaged in her work at the time of the accident, it could not be responsible. The trial court granted the school's request, and the driver's family appealed to the California Court of Appeal. The court of appeal stated that employers are vicariously liable for the torts of their employees committed within the scope of the employee's employment. However, an employer is not liable for torts committed by an employee who is going to or coming from work. Further, the California Supreme Court has held that an employee, while taking a lunch break, is not in the service of his employer. The employee was not engaged in any school business at the time of the accident. Therefore, the school could not be held liable. *Tryer v. Ojai Valley School*, 12 Cal.Rptr.2d 114 (Cal.App.2d Dist.1992).

II. SCHOOL ATHLETICS

Generally, courts hold that student athletes assume the risks incidental to participation and, absent a showing of negligence by the coach, league or

school, may not recover damages for their injuries. For more cases on athletics, please see Chapter 14.

A. Participants

1. **Duty of Care**

The cases indicate that where a participant is injured, but through ordinary care and common sense could have avoided the injury, the school and its agents will not be held liable. Further, some states require a showing that the school or its agents acted recklessly or willfully as a prerequisite to overcoming the defense of governmental immunity.

A Maryland high school junior was the first female football player in her county's history. She participated in weightlifting and strength training exercises and participated in contact drills. However, in the first scrimmage with another team, the student was tackled while carrying the football and suffered multiple internal injuries, including a ruptured spleen. She was hospitalized and her spleen and part of her pancreas were removed. Three years later, the student and her mother sued the school board claiming that the board had a duty to warn them of the risk of serious, disabling and catastrophic injuries. A Maryland trial court granted the board's motion for summary judgment, finding no such duty to warn of the risk of varsity football participation. The student and her mother appealed to the Court of Special Appeals of Maryland. On appeal, the student and her mother claimed that the lower court had erroneously ruled that the board had no duty to warn of catastrophic risks and that the student had assumed the risk of injury by participating. The court found no case from any jurisdiction holding that a school board had a duty to warn varsity high school participants that severe injuries might result. The dangers of varsity football participation were self-evident and there was no duty to warn of such an obvious danger. The court affirmed the order for summary judgment. *Hammond v. Bd. of Educ. of Carroll County*, 100 Md.App. 60, 639 A.2d 223 (1994).

A New York high school student claimed that his football coach struck him on the head 13 or more times with a foam rubber tackling dummy. He alleged that he suffered "devastating permanent neurological injuries" that left him learning impaired, depressed and socially withdrawn. A two-month trial was held at which conflicting testimony was received from teammates, friends, teachers and doctors. The jury returned a $25,000 damage award to the student for past pain and suffering, but refused to award damages for future pain and suffering or economic loss. The court denied the student's motion to set aside the verdict as inadequate and he appealed to the New York Supreme Court, Appellate Division, Third Department. The court held that the jury could have reasonably found from the conflicting evidence that the student had not been materially or adversely affected by the incident and that he might have exaggerated his injuries. Because the student had not made a compelling case for future pain and suffering, the appellate division court affirmed the trial court's decision. *Raucci v. City School Dist. of the City of Mechanicville*, 610 N.Y.S.2d 653 (A.D.3d Dept.1994).

A New York high school student was injured while participating in a junior varsity soccer game. She had played organized soccer for four years prior to her injuries and had undergone the required physical examination. The student brought a personal injury action against the school districts involved. The court denied the school districts' motions for summary judgment and they appealed to the Supreme Court, Appellate Division. The duty of care owed a student who voluntarily participates in school athletics is ordinary reasonable care. There was no evidence to indicate that the school districts had breached this duty. Therefore, the court held for the school districts and granted them summary judgment. *La Mountain v. South Colonie Central School Dist.*, 566 N.Y.S.2d 745 (A.D.3d Dept. 1991).

2. Governmental Immunity

The doctrine of governmental immunity applies when the school district or its employees act within the scope of their employment and such immunity has not been abolished by the courts of that state.

A student manager of an Illinois school volleyball team wheeled a volleyball stand onto the gym where the stand separated and landed on a spectator's foot. The spectator sued the student manager and the school district in an Illinois trial court for her injuries. The trial court granted the district and the student a motion to dismiss the lawsuit because the student manager was an employee of the school district covered by the Illinois Local Governmental Employees Tort Immunity Act. The act required civil suits against local governments and their employees to be brought within one year, which the spectator failed to do. The spectator appealed to the Appellate Court of Illinois, Fourth District, claiming that the trial court erred in finding that the student manager was an employee of the school district. The appellate court held that the student manager was an employee of the school district and was entitled to the protection of the one-year statute of limitations. The spectator was barred from bringing a claim against the school district and the student manager. The appellate court affirmed the trial court's decision. *Sunderlend v. Tri City School Dist. 1*, 549 N.E.2d 992 (Ill.App.4th Dist.1990).

A freshman high school football player returning from a game was called to the back of the bus by the older students, who intended to subject him to a hazing ritual known as the "hit line." As a result, he suffered a broken nose and bruised ribs. The student, by his parents, brought a civil rights suit against the school and the football coach under 42 U.S.C. § 1983. In order to prevail on a § 1983 claim, a plaintiff must prove that he was deprived of some right secured by the Constitution by a person acting under color of state law. The court found that school officials were not constitutionally required to protect students from assaults by fellow students and even if such a duty did exist, the football coach was protected by the doctrine of qualified immunity. The court entered summary judgment in favor of the school district and the football coach. *Reeves by Jones v. Besonen*, 754 F.Supp. 1135 (E.D.Mich.1991).

3. Assumption of risk

Many courts have determined that when a participant has assumed the risks of playing in sports, the school district will not be held liable for injuries suffered as a result.

A star high school football player suffered a broken neck in a varsity football game between two New York high schools. The athlete's school had been upgraded the prior season to a more competitive division by the state Public Schools Athletic League (PSAL). The school sought reassignment to the lower division, citing the increased potential for serious injury, but an administrative appeal for reassignment was unsuccessful. Prior to the game in which the athlete was injured, the team's coach advised the school's principal that the game was a mismatch and should not be played. However, the principal decided that the game would go on. The athlete sued the school board and PSAL. Following the trial, the judge instructed the jury to hold the district and PSAL to the same standard of care as a parent of ordinary prudence under the same circumstances. The jury returned a verdict of $1.25 million, reduced by the liability apportioned against the athlete. However, the judge granted the school board and PSAL motions to dismiss the portion of the judgment relating to retention of the school in the higher division, finding that this was a discretionary decision. The remaining parties were liable to the athlete.

The school board and PSAL appealed to the New York Supreme Court, Appellate Division, which affirmed the trial court's decision. On appeal to the New York Court of Appeals, the court held that the trial court's jury instructions had been erroneous. Participation in voluntary athletic events required school districts and officials to exercise only reasonable care, rather than the higher parental care standard. Students who participated in athletic events assumed the risk of reasonably foreseeable injury. In this case, there was no evidence that the school board or its employees had failed to exercise ordinary care to protect the student from an unassumed or concealed risk or that it compelled him to participate. The court reversed the decision and dismissed the case. *Benitez v. New York City Bd. of Educ.*, 543 N.Y.S.2d 29 (Ct.App.1989).

The Florida District Court of Appeal rejected the assumption of risk defense in a case involving a high school student's injury during football practice. The injury occurred during an "agility" drill, when the student's face came in contact with another player's helmet. The injured student had not been issued a helmet because the school lacked a sufficient number of them. The appellate court rejected the school board's argument that the student had assumed the risk inherent in the ordinary play of football stating that no evidence existed that he had assumed the risk of participating in a training drill with insufficient equipment. A new trial was ordered to allow a jury to hear the case. *Leahy v. School Bd. of Hernando County*, 450 So.2d 883 (Fla.App.5th Dist.1984).

4. Insurance Coverage

As noted in Section I.B. above, in many states the defense of governmental immunity is waived to the extent that insurance coverage has been purchased by a school district. The cases below discuss whether a district is obliged to purchase insurance and whether exclusions from coverage are valid.

After a Montana teacher instructed an elementary student to mark the spots where shot-puts would be landing, the teacher threw a shot and struck the girl. The child was injured and sued the school district and the teacher for negligence in a state trial court. The trial court granted summary judgment to the school district and teacher, and the child appealed to the Supreme Court of Montana. On appeal, the child contended that the teacher was not immune from suit and that the school district had waived immunity by purchasing liability insurance. The court noted that the school district was immune from suit for any act of its agent and that the teacher was its agent. Therefore, the teacher was also immune from suit. The court next turned to the question of whether immunity was waived to the extent of insurance coverage. The Montana Supreme Court had previously reached the conclusion that a school district's purchase of insurance in many cases may waive immunity to the extent of the insurance coverage. This was one such case because clearly the school would have no need of liability insurance if it were immune. Therefore, by purchasing such insurance, the school waived immunity. The court remanded the case to determine the extent of the coverage. *Hedges v. Swan Lake and Salmon Prairie School Dist.* 812 P.2d 334 (Mont.1991).

The day after that decision was published, Montana passed a new law amending the governmental immunity law. The amended statute was retroactively applied to the student's case. The trial court stated that the new law changed nothing and once again dismissed the case. The student again appealed to the Montana Supreme Court. The supreme court noted that Montana's new immunity law provided immunity for "legislative acts" or duties associated with "legislative acts." The court had previously interpreted this to mean that a teacher performing official duties was immune from suit since those duties were associated with the legislative acts of the school board. However, the "purpose" section of the new act stated that "legislative immunity extends only to legislative bodies of governmental entities and only to legislative actions taken by those bodies ... governmental entities are not immune ... for nonlegislative actions." The throwing of the shot was not an official duty associated with legislative acts. Therefore, the teacher and school district were not immune. The court remanded the case for further proceedings. *Hedges v. Swan Lake & Salmon Prairie School Dist.*, 832 P.2d 775 (Mont.1992).

A Louisiana student was injured while cheerleading at a football game. The student filed a negligence suit against the school board and its insurer. The insurer moved for summary judgment claiming that its policy contained a provision which excluded coverage for injuries incurred while participating in an athletic exhibition. A trial court granted the motion and the cheerleader appealed to the Supreme Court of Louisiana. On appeal, the cheerleader argued that cheerleading was not a sport or athletic contest. The court examined the exclusionary provision and determined that it was intended to exclude only injuries that are normally encountered in a sporting contest. Accordingly, it concluded that the provision did not bar recovery for the injuries sustained by the cheerleader. The court remanded the case to the trial court for further proceedings. *Garcia v. Bernard Parish School Bd.*, 576 So.2d 975 (La.1991).

B. Spectators, Employees and Parents

A four-year-old girl accompanied her family to a public school gymnasium to watch her older brother play basketball in a department of education league game. The department used the gymnasium under a school board policy promulgated under Maryland education laws that encouraged school boards to use their facilities for community purposes. The girl was severely injured when she either fell from or ran into a piece of damaged equipment. The Court of Special Appeals of Maryland reversed and remanded a trial court decision for the girl's parents. It determined that while the board's policy encouraged public use of the gym, and the girl was entitled to the legal status of invitee, there was evidence in the record that the girl had exceeded the scope of her invitation. *Howard County Bd. of Educ. v. Cheyene*, 99 Md.App. 150, 636 A.2d 22 (1994).

An Illinois man and his son were watching a tennis match standing inside the fence encompassing the tennis court because the spectator bleachers were full. The man's son was hit in the eye with a tennis ball and was injured. The man and his son sued the school district for allowing them to watch the match in an unsafe area. The trial court ruled in favor of the school because the danger of being injured was open and obvious. The student appealed to the Appellate Court of Illinois which affirmed the trial court's decision. It stated that the plaintiffs had voluntarily placed themselves in a position of danger and thus would be unable to establish that they were placed in that area by the school. Under most circumstances, when a danger is obvious the student cannot recover for his injuries. *Chaveas v. Township High School Dist.*, 553 N.E.2d 23 (Ill.App.1st Dist.1990).

A spectator was struck by a football during pregame warm-ups. She sued the school district for damages. The district moved for summary judgment, claiming that governmental immunity barred the spectator's suit. The trial court granted the district's motion. The injured spectator appealed to the Commonwealth Court of Pennsylvania. Under the real property exception a governmental entity may lose its immunity if the injury is due to its negligence in the care, custody or control of its real property. The spectator argued that the district was negligent when it failed to erect a barrier to prevent footballs from striking spectators. The court held that the real property exception applies only when an artificial condition or defect in the land causes an injury. In this case, the spectator's injury was caused by the acts of a third person, so the real property exception did not apply. *Johnson v. Woodland Hills School Dist.*, 582 A.2d 395 (Pa.Cmwlth.1990).

III. OTHER SCHOOL ACTIVITIES

Courts have generally held schools or their agents liable for injuries sustained during the course of regular school events which resulted from the failure to provide a reasonably safe environment, failure to warn partici-

pants of known hazards (or to remove known dangers where possible), failure to properly instruct participants in the activity, or failure to provide supervision adequate for the type of activity and the ages of the participants involved.

A. Physical Education Class Accidents

1. Duty of Care

Courts have ruled that schools and those employees in charge of group activities cannot be held liable for injuries that occur during activities which are well supervised but are the result of conditions of which the school has no prior knowledge or are the result of actions taken by children contrary to instructions. The fact that each student is not personally supervised at all times does not in and of itself constitute grounds for liability.

In 1977, a student (who was then eight years old) was severely injured when watching a flag football game on a field behind his school. The field was adjacent to another football field which was being used by middle school students. An older student ran into the eight-year-old, fracturing his skull and causing serious, permanent injuries. An Illinois trial court dismissed the student's complaint and the student appealed to the Appellate Court of Illinois, First District, Second Division, which affirmed the trial court's action. The Illinois Supreme Court vacated and remanded the appellate court's decision. On remand, the appellate court ruled that the student had stated facts supporting his claim that the nearly adjacent arrangement of the fields created an unreasonable risk of harm to the student. The trial court had improperly ruled that the district had no duty to protect its students from this risk of harm, and the student was entitled to a trial on the matter. However, the evidence did not indicate that the school district, school, school board or its employees should be liable for wilful or wanton misconduct for placing the two playing fields together and for allowing larger students to play in close proximity to smaller ones. The appellate court affirmed the trial court decision in part, reversed it in part, and remanded the case. *Ward v. Comm. Unit School Dist. No. 220*, 614 N.E.2d 102 (Ill App 1st Dist.1993).

A New York student was injured in gym class when he was struck in the eye with a tennis ball. His parents filed a personal injury lawsuit against the school district and a jury awarded him $56,000 for past pain and suffering, $10,000 for future pain and suffering and $20,000 for future medical expenses. The parents moved to set aside the verdict as inadequate and when the trial court refused to do so, they appealed to the New York Supreme Court, Appellate Division, Third Department. The appellate division court affirmed the trial court verdict, reasoning that the award was sufficient to cover future expenses, pain and suffering. There was evidence that recovery was nearly complete, although there was a slightly greater risk for glaucoma in the injured eye. The award was reasonable because the student would continue to need an eye examination every six months. *Levine v. East Ramapo Central School Dist.*, 597 N.Y.S.2d 239 (A.D.3d Dept.1993).

A 14-year-old high school student was injured in a motorcycle accident and was required to undergo surgery to repair damage to his left knee. The doctor instructed the student that he was not to participate in any physical or strenuous activities that could result in further injury to his knee. After the student returned to school, he was instructed by his physical education teacher to go out to the high school football field with his class. The student did not engage in a game of touch football that was being played but stood on the sidelines. While the student was standing on the sidelines a player ran into him, reinjuring his knee. He sued the physical education teacher in an Alabama trial court alleging negligent supervision. The trial court entered summary judgment in favor of the teacher and dismissed the complaint. The student appealed to the Alabama Supreme Court, which stated that the student was not ordered to play in the game, but only to go to the sidelines. Further, the student stated that he felt he was a safe distance away from the action. The teacher did have a duty of reasonable supervision but could not possibly be expected to personally supervise each student in his charge at every moment of the school day. The court further stated that the student was a reasonable age and had a duty to maintain a certain vigilance over his own safety and well-being. Thus, the court affirmed the trial court's decision and dismissed the complaint. *Stevens v. Chestine*, 561 So.2d 1100 (Ala.1990).

2. Governmental Immunity

An overweight teenager attended a Missouri middle school, and sustained injuries when she attempted to jump a hurdle in gym class. The hurdle was apparently placed on a concrete floor which was covered by linoleum. The student maintained that her teacher had urged her to jump the hurdle despite her protest that she could not do so. She brought suit against the school district in a Missouri trial court, alleging that the gym teacher had created a dangerous condition by setting hurdles on a concrete floor and by urging students such as herself to jump over them. The trail court granted summary judgment to the school district, and the student appealed to the Missouri Court of Appeals, Western District. On appeal, the student conceded that the school district was protected by the doctrine of sovereign immunity. However, she maintained that her injury was caused by a dangerous condition of property (which would allow a lawsuit against the school district as an exception to immunity). The court of appeals determined that the injury did not result from a condition of school property, but from the inability of the student to physically jump over the hurdle. If there was fault, it was simply negligence on the part of the teacher in urging an overweight girl to jump a hurdle. Because sovereign immunity protected the school district from claims based on negligence, the court of appeals affirmed the trial court's decision. *Goben v. School District of St. Joseph*, 848 S.W.2d 20 (Mo.App.W.D.1992).

The instructor of a sixth grade gym class demonstrated some basic wrestling maneuvers, and before beginning a practice session ordered the children to use no illegal moves. He then divided the children into groups according to his rough estimation of height, weight, and body structure. The children began to wrestle and a 100-pound boy "body-slammed" an 83-pound boy, causing injuries. The larger boy explained that he had seen Hulk Hogan use the maneuver. The injured boy's father brought suit against the school and officials in a state court. The father alleged that the failure to properly classify the students constituted wilful and wanton misconduct. He also complained that earlier wrestling injury reports should have been more specific and allowed the school to predict the potential for such an injury. The school was granted summary judgment, and the father appealed to the Appellate Court of Illinois. An exception to an Illinois school district's general immunity from suit may be granted if its conduct is found to be wilful or wanton. The father argued that the strict weight classifications, which were established for junior high wrestling programs, should have been implemented in the gym class. The district argued that the procedures taken by the teacher were generally adequate to provide protection for the students, and the court held that they were adequate to qualify for immunity. The father then argued that the inadequacies of the earlier wrestling injury reports led to a failure to predict the injuries and undertake preventive precautions. Though the reports could have been more specific, the district's actions qualified for immunity. The decision was affirmed. *Toller v. Plainfield School Dist. #202*, 582 N.E.2d 237 (Ill.App.3d Dist.1991).

A 14-year-old Detroit student died of a heart attack while running in his physical education class. His mother sued the school principal alleging that he was negligent. She claimed that the failure of the principal to provide emergency procedures and to train his teachers to make emergency calls had contributed to her son's death. The trial court dismissed her claim on the ground that the principal's actions were discretionary and entitled to immunity from liability. She appealed to the Michigan Court of Appeals. The court of appeals held that the principal's decision not to provide emergency procedures or train his teachers to make emergency calls were discretionary actions under Michigan law. Thus, the principal was entitled to immunity from liability. The appellate court affirmed the trial court's decision. *Montgomery v. City of Detroit*, 448 N.W.2d 822 (Mich.App.1989).

B. Shop Class Injuries

1. Duty of Care

Schools are generally held to a standard of care of providing students with a safe environment. Known shop class dangers must be minimized and manufacturers' safety devices should be in place and working. Failure to supervise, to warn students of the dangers, or to keep safety devices installed and in proper working order can result in a finding of school negligence.

A Nebraska student's finger was severed in a shop accident. In his personal injury lawsuit against the school district, the evidence indicated that the shop teacher was negligent in failing to properly instruct the student in the proper use of the power tool. It was also shown that the power tool was unreasonably dangerous, and that the student was contributorily negligent. The court awarded the student over $32,000, even though his medical expenses were only $2,300. It then granted the student's motion for a new trial, stating that the award of damages was inadequate "as a result of a mistake by the court." The school district appealed to the Court of Appeals of Nebraska, which reversed the order for a new trial and reinstated the verdict. There were no grounds for granting a new trial in this case because there had been no showing that the verdict was contrary to law or that the evidence of damages had been insufficient. It appeared that the trial court had merely changed its mind. *Cotton v. Gering Pub. Schools*, 511 N.W.2d 549 (Neb.App.1993).

A Texas student was injured when he used a tablesaw which allegedly lacked a safety guard. The student sued the school district and school officials under 42 U.S.C. § 1983, stating that the district's act of allowing him to use a tablesaw without a safety guard was an act of conscious indifference in violation of his civil rights. The U.S. District Court for the Southern District of Texas held that the district could not be held liable in the civil rights action for the student's injury because the student had not alleged that the unconstitutional act was caused by an official policy of the school district or its employees. The student also could not sustain his action against the school officials since the student had no constitutionally protected right to a safe school environment. The district court dismissed the case. *Grubbs v. Aldine Indep. School Dist.*, 709 F.Supp. 127 (S.D.Tex.1989).

2. Governmental Immunity

A Texas high school student was injured during wood shop class. He sued his teacher in a federal trial court alleging, first, that the teacher was liable under state tort law and second, that the teacher's actions violated the student's rights under the Due Process Clause. The teacher moved for summary judgment on both claims. The trial court found that a Texas statute makes school district employees immune from personal liability for any act committed within the scope of employment. However, the court held that this immunity did not bar the student's claim under the Due Process Clause. To prevail on a due process claim, the student had to show that the teacher's conduct was malicious, egregious or callously indifferent. The student alleged only that the teacher stepped into a small storage room during the class. The court found that this action did not constitute callous indifference to the safety of the student. Therefore, it entered summary judgment on behalf of the teacher. *Moore v. Port Arthur Indep. School Dist.*, 751 F.Supp. 671 (E.D.Tex.1990).

A 16-year-old Michigan student lost his finger in a shop class injury. The machine was not equipped with a guard which normally protects the operator from accidental contact. The student sued the school district in a Michigan trial court. The court granted the district's motion for dismissal, based on the district's assertion of governmental immunity. The student appealed to the Michigan Court of Appeals. On appeal, the student argued that his accident was subject to a Michigan exception to governmental immunity for unreasonably dangerous conditions known to a government entity in a public building. The court of appeals agreed with the school district's assertion that because the machine was not permanently affixed to the floor it was not a "fixture" or part of the building and did not fall within Michigan's public building exception. The student appealed to the Michigan Supreme Court. He argued that because the machine weighed over one thousand pounds it was unnecessary to bolt it to the floor. The supreme court ruled that permanent attachment was not the only way in which the machine could become part of the premises. The machine was heavy, stationary and not bolted to the floor because of its great weight. The defective machinery constituted a dangerous condition of a fixture which might support a claim of liability under the public building exception to governmental immunity. Dismissal was not appropriate and the case was reversed and remanded to the trial court for further consideration. *Velmer v. Baraga Area Schools*, 424 N.W.2d 770 (Mich.1988).

C. Other Supervised Activities

1. Duty of Care

School districts have a duty to use reasonable care to supervise and protect students against hazards on school property which create an unreasonable risk of harm. Liability may also exist where no supervision is provided or where supervision is negligently performed.

A Florida school district conducted an extended day program under which students could remain at school until their parents picked them up. Teachers remained at school to supervise participating students. A fourth grade student who was not an extended day program participant approached a teacher who was supervising the extended day program, and joined the class in viewing a solar eclipse. Although the class was instructed to observe the eclipse by projecting an image using two sheets of construction paper with a small hole punched in one sheet, the student instead looked directly at the sun. He suffered permanent eye damage, and his mother filed a lawsuit on his behalf against the school board in a Florida trial court. The trial court conducted a two day trial resulting in a verdict for the school board. The student's mother appealed to the District Court of Appeal of Florida, Fifth District.

On appeal, the student and his mother argued that the trial court had improperly instructed the jury by preparing a formal verdict question concerning whether the teacher had given permission to the student to participate in extended day program activities. The court of appeal held that the issue of supervision was critical in this case and that the trial court's instruction did not adequately explain Florida law. The school board's policy and state law required school personnel to supervise students as long as they were on school premises, regardless of whether they had permission or whether they were engaged in school-sponsored activity. Because of that policy and state law, the case was reversed and remanded for a new trial. *Versprill v. School Bd. of Orange County Florida*, 641 So.2d 883 (Fla.App.5th Dist.1994).

A Florida seventh grader suffered a broken jaw when she was hit in the face by a classmate while returning to class from the cafeteria. She sued the school board, claiming that her teacher had been negligent in supervising the students because she failed to intervene even though the students were speaking loudly and were not walking in single file as required by school procedures. A Florida trial court directed a verdict for the school board, but this decision was reversed and remanded by the District Court of Appeal of Florida, First District. The court of appeal determined that a jury should be allowed to decide the question of whether the teacher had exercised appropriate care in supervising the students. The intervening intentional act of the other student was foreseeable and did not relieve the school board of liability. *Roberson v. Duval County School Bd.*, 618 So.2d 360 (Fla.App.1st Dist.1993).

A ten-year-old Illinois student injured herself while jumping rope on a cracked and uneven sidewalk. The student's teacher had directed her to skip rope on the sidewalk, which was maintained by the school district. After the student's accident, her mother sued the district, alleging that it was negligent in the maintenance of its property, and that its employee was guilty of wilful and wanton misconduct by directing the student to skip rope on a dangerous sidewalk. The district court dismissed the case and the mother appealed to the Appellate Court of Illinois, Second District. That court reasoned that the school district could not avoid liability for negligence in maintaining its property by asserting that the teacher had been negligent. However, under the state tort immunity act, the school district was immune from liability for ordinary negligence. The court noted that the mother had failed to allege and describe a substantial defect in the sidewalk's surface and it could not be shown that the school district or its employee had acted with wilful and wanton misconduct. The court affirmed the dismissal of the case. *Ramos v. Waukegan Community Unit School Dist. No. 60*, 544 N.E.2d 1302 (Ill.App.2d Dist.1989).

A District of Columbia school began a summer program for gifted and talented eight and nine-year-old students. As part of the program, the school district hired a Ph.D. candidate at American University to teach the students chemistry. The instructor decided to conduct a "hands-on" experiment in which the children made sparklers. The experiment used potassium perchlorate, an unstable and highly volatile chemical, as an oxidizing agent. Commercial sparklers are not made with potassium perchlorate. During the experiment a student's chemicals exploded, burning him. A jury awarded the student $8 million for pain and suffering, $1 million for past and future medical expenses and $1 million to each of his parents for loss of parent-child consortium. The District of Columbia appealed to the District of Columbia Court of Appeals. On appeal, the District argued that it could not be held liable for the student's injuries since they were caused by an independent contractor over whom it exercised no control. The court noted, however, that while the District's argument was perhaps a correct statement of the law, an exception exists when an independent contractor is hired to do work involving a special danger to others which the employer knows to be inherent to the work. It was reasonable for the jury to conclude that the District was aware of the risks involved in the manufacture of sparklers by nine-year-olds. Even if the teaching of chemistry, in and of itself, is not a dangerous activity, the manner in which it was conducted in this case made it so. While upholding the jury award on the issue of liability, the court overturned both the loss of consortium award, noting that such an action did not exist in the District of Columbia, and the award of future medical expenses due to lack of evidence. *District of Columbia v. Howell*, 607 A.2d 501 (D.C.App.1992).

2. Governmental Immunity

An Illinois high school student was injured when a gun concealed in another student's book bag discharged in a classroom. The injured student's mother filed a lawsuit against the education board and school superintendent, claiming that they had failed to install metal detectors or otherwise discover weapons, even though they had knowledge that guns were being brought to school. An Illinois trial court granted the superintendent's motion to dismiss the claim against him as barred by governmental immunity under the state tort immunity act. However, the court denied the board's motion for dismissal, finding that the complaint sufficiently alleged a special duty of the board to protect the student from injury. The board appealed to the Appellate Court of Illinois, First District.

On appeal, the mother argued that the failure of the board to warn students of the presence of weapons in school was a wilful and wanton failure that constituted an exception to the general rule of government immunity. The court determined that in order to find such an exception, there must be a special duty imposed on the government entity that requires knowledge of a particular danger to a particular individual. In this case, the student's mother had only alleged a generalized danger of the introduction of firearms in school and had not alleged that the board had particular knowledge that the student herself was in danger. Because there had been a failure to allege this specific knowledge, there was no reason to invoke the special duty exception to the rule of government immunity. The appellate court reversed and remanded the trial court's decision. *Thames v. Bd. of Educ. of Chicago*, 645 N.E.2d 445 (Ill.App.1st Dist.1994).

An elementary school in New York was struck by a tornado. This caused a wall in the school cafeteria to collapse, killing or injuring 30 students. Earlier that morning, the county had received a "tornado watch" weather statement from the state police. About 40 minutes before the storm struck, the county's emergency manager provided the county public information officer with a copy of the tornado watch report for dissemination. The information officer failed to disseminate the information prior to the time the storm struck. Relatives of the students who were killed sued the county, claiming that since the county had enacted an emergency preparedness plan that provided for direct notification of schools in emergencies, the county had a duty to inform the subject school of the issuance of a tornado watch by the National Weather Service. The trial court denied the county's motion to dismiss and the county appealed to the New York Supreme Court, Appellate Division. The appellate court reversed the denial. It stated that a county is generally immune from liability for acts involving the exercise of discretion. This is in contrast to ministerial acts, which require direct adherence to a governing rule or standard. The emergency preparedness plan did not involve a ministerial act since it stated that schools should be notified "as conditions warrant." Such a provision leaves it open to the county's discretion as to whether a tornado watch warranted implementation of emergency plans. In addition, there was no special relationship between the students and county that required a waiver of the county's immunity. In addition, the county's failure to notify the public in general was an immune exercise of discretion. *Litchhult v. Reiss*, 583 N.Y.S.2d 671 (A.D.3d Dept.1992).

A student at a Texas middle school participated in a chemistry experiment using potassium hydroxide, a dangerously caustic chemical compound. Dry crystals of the compound came into contact with the student's thigh. Because it was in crystalline form, the chemical did not burn her until it interacted with the moisture of her skin. The student did not notice the effects of the burn until later in the day. She went to the school nurse, who allegedly did not have time to treat her. Upon arriving home, the student sought medical treatment. However, she then sued the school nurse and the science teacher, contending that the initial injury and delay in treatment caused severe, permanent, disabling, and disfiguring injury which would require reconstructive surgery. The trial court granted summary judgment to the school employees, and the student appealed to the Court of Appeals of Texas. The court noted that Texas law provides that "[n]o professional employee of any school district ... shall be personally liable for any act incident to or within the scope of the duties of his position of employment, and which act involves the exercise of judgment or discretion on the part of the employee, except in circumstances where professional employees use excessive force in the discipline of students or negligence resulting in bodily injury to students." The court stated that the Texas Supreme Court had held this to mean that school employees could only be held liable in circumstances involving the use of discretion in which they were disciplining a student. Given this precedent, the court stated that the teacher and nurse were immune from negligence claims because they had not been involved in disciplining the student. *Duross v. Freeman*, 831 S.W.2d 354 (Tex.App.1992).

3.   Assumption of Risk

A 19-year-old New York student was injured while participating in a work study program. The student was learning disabled and his mother persuaded him to join a work study program so that he would have enough credits to graduate. He worked with lumber under the direct supervision of a company. During his work study the student severed two of his fingers and injured a third one when using a saw he was familiar with. Alleging negligent supervision, the student sued the school in a New York trial court. The school asserted that it had no duty to exercise control over the student because he was of majority age and because his mother encouraged him to participate in the program. The New York state court held that schools were not insurers for the safety of students. Further, the court stated that a less demanding standard of reasonable care was warranted when a student was 19 years old. The court also stated that there was no evidence that any of the machinery was unfit. Thus, the trial court ruled in favor of the school. *Kennedy v. Waterville Cent. School Dist.*, 555 N.Y.S.2d 224 (Sup.1990).

A seventh grader at a Louisiana junior high school broke his right leg while engaged in a makeshift football game. Although the students knew that they were not permitted to play such rough games, neither the teacher nor the teacher's aide were aware of their activities. On this particular day, the teacher's aide was supervising a class so the teacher could attend a conference with the principal. The student's mother filed suit against the physical education teacher, the teacher's aide, the school board and its insurer alleging negligence and failure to properly supervise the class. A trial court found the school board negligent and awarded the student $200,000 in damages but ruled that neither the teacher nor the teacher's aide were at fault. Both sides appealed. The Louisiana Court of Appeal observed that the teacher had already returned from her meeting with the principal when the student's injury took place. Although the teacher claimed that she would have stopped any "roughhousing" had she seen it, the court stated that she should have noticed what was going on. For this reason, the court ruled that she and her employer, the school board, were equally at fault. On the other hand, the court stated that the students were old enough to understand that tackling each other could cause injury. Moreover, the game was nothing that their parents would not have allowed at home. In light of these factors, the court reduced the percentage of fault attributable to the teacher and the school board to 5 percent. The student's mother would only be allowed to recover $10,000 rather than the $200,000 awarded by the trial court. *Marcantel v. Allen Parish School Bd.*, 490 So.2d 1162 (La.App.3d Cir.1986).

IV. UNSUPERVISED ACCIDENTS

In addition to the duty to supervise students in their daily activities, schools are required to exercise care in maintaining safe grounds and facilities. Schools can be found liable for maintaining or tolerating hazardous structures, fixtures or grounds.

A. On School Grounds

1. Duty of Care

A California elementary school allowed parents to pick up their children after school at a small parking lot which had formerly been used as a bus loading zone. Several children were injured when a car jumped the curb at the loading area. A lawsuit was filed in a California trial court, resulting in a settlement among all parties except the school district and the parents of two injured students. A trial was held at which evidence was presented that the loading zone was overcrowded and chaotic after school, with long lines of cars waiting to pick up students. Evidence also indicated that school employees were aware of the hazardous conditions, although no prior accidents had been reported. The jury found that the lot was dangerous and that the school should be liable for damages. The trial court judge refused to set aside the verdict and the school district appealed to the Court of Appeal, Second District, Division Six.

The court of appeal considered the case in light of § 835 of the California Tort Claims Act, which imposes liability upon public entities which cause dangerous conditions where a complaining party establishes that the injury was reasonably foreseeable and proximately caused by the dangerous condition. It is also required that the public entity have actual or constructive notice of the dangerous condition. In this case, there was evidence that the school district had notice of the dangerous conditions existing in the loading area. The district had allowed the situation to worsen by eliminating staggered class sessions, a policy which had reduced congestion in previous years. Because the district had failed to take reasonable steps to protect students from the danger, the court of appeal affirmed the trial court's decision. *Constantinescu v. Conejo Valley Unif. School Dist.*, 20 Cal.Rptr.2d 734 (Cal.App.2d Dist.1993).

A New York student was injured on an elementary school playground when another child threw a screwdriver which struck her in the eye. The student's parents sued the school district in a New York trial court, claiming that the school had negligently inspected and maintained the playground. No evidence was presented to the trial court concerning how long the screwdriver had been on the playground. The court refused to grant the school district's summary judgment motion. The Supreme Court, Appellate Division, Fourth Department, ruled that the trial court should have granted the district's motion because the district did not create or have constructive or actual notice of the condition causing the injury. The other child's intervening intentional act of throwing the screwdriver relieved the school district of any liability. *Mix v. South Seneca Cent. School Dist.*, 602 N.Y.S.2d 467 (A.D.4th Dept.1993).

After an Ohio high school student was attacked and injured by a pit bull terrier on school property, he and his parents sued the board of education to recover for his injuries. They alleged that the student was attacked by a dog which another student had brought onto school property during the regular school day. They also asserted that the security assistant who was to provide security to the high school, and who had no security training, failed to adequately supervise the parking lot where the attack took place. The trial court granted summary judgment to the board of education, and appeal was taken to the Court of Appeals of Ohio. The court of appeals noted that school officials are only required to exercise that care necessary to avoid reasonably foreseeable injuries. Here, there was no evidence to suggest that either the security guard or the board should have been aware that a student would bring a pit bull terrier to the school. Also, no similar incidents had occurred in the past. Thus, it had not been shown that the board of education had breached a duty of care to the student. Further, no evidence was presented that the security guard was assigned exclusively to guard the parking lot at the time of the attack. Finally, there was no evidence to indicate that the security guard's lack of formal training was the proximate cause of the animal's attack. The court of appeals affirmed the lower court's decision. *Nottingham v. Akron Board of Education*, 610 N.E.2d 1096 (Ohio App.9th Dist.1992).

An eleven-year-old New Mexico student became caught on his bandana in a school cloakroom and died of strangulation. The student's parents sued, alleging that the student had been unsupervised in the cloakroom for approximately 20 minutes. The suit, brought under 42 U.S.C. § 1983, named the teacher for failure to supervise, and the principal for deliberate indifference to training and supervision requirements. A federal district court granted summary judgment to the defendants, and the parents appealed to the U.S. Court of Appeals, Tenth Circuit.

The parents challenged only the district court's judgment with regard to the teacher's liability. However, the court of appeals stated that the teacher had no constitutional duty to protect the student. The U.S. Supreme Court's decision in *DeShaney v. Winnebago County Department of Social Services*, 489 U.S. 189, 109 S.Ct. 998, 103 L.Ed.2d 249 (1989), stated that the Constitution does not impose an affirmative duty on the state to protect an individual's rights except under limited circumstances. These occur when the state takes an affirmative act of restraining the individual's freedom to act on his own behalf through incarceration, institutionalization, or other similar restraint of personal liberty. New Mexico's compulsory attendance laws, however, do not constitute this type of restraint. Although a child may be in the custody of school authorities during school hours, the custody does not amount to restraint that prohibits the child and/ or the child's parents from caring for the basic needs of the child. The court affirmed the district court's grant of summary judgment. *Maldonado v. Josey*, 975 F.2d 727 (10th Cir.1992).

A school in North Carolina placed sand around an exposed tree root in its playground. A student tripped over the root, and sued the school alleging that the playground was unsafe. A state court granted judgment for the school, and the student appealed to the Court of Appeals of North Carolina. The court explained that the duty owed by the school to the student was to use reasonable care to keep the premises safe and to warn of hidden dangers. The duty does not extend to insuring the student's safety. Recovery is usually not granted for injuries suffered by students as a result of common or natural conditions existing in the school ground. In this case, the use of the sand was held to be expected to produce reasonable safety. The trial court decision was affirmed. *Waltz v. Wake County Bd. of Educ.*, 409 S.E.2d 106 (N.C.App.1991).

An Illinois elementary school student was injured when he slipped and fell from a jungle gym on school grounds. The jungle gym was not icy or wet and the student admitted that he knew he could hurt himself if he fell off the apparatus. The student sued the school district seeking damages. The school district claimed that it owed no duty to the student. The Appellate Court of Illinois agreed with the school district. If the owner of land knows that young children frequent the area where a dangerous condition is present, the owner has a duty to remedy the dangerous condition. There is no duty, however, where children would be expected to appreciate and avoid the risk. In this case, the child admitted that he understood the risk involved in playing on the jungle gym. *Cozzi v. North Palos Elementary School Dist.*, 597 N.E.2d 683 (Ill.App.1st Dist.1992).

A Georgia elementary school had two manually-operated merry-go-rounds on its playground. During nonschool hours, the playground was open for public use. A parent took his five-year-old kindergartner and two other children to the playground. The children played on one of the merry-go-rounds until another child was injured on it because a board was missing. The father told them to get off, but did not instruct them not to use the other merry-go-round. He thought the children would recognize its obvious state of disrepair and not go on it. He believed it would not even turn. The children, however, got the merry-go-round to turn, and the kindergartner was injured when she stuck her foot down between the framework and the ground where there was no flooring. The kindergartner's parents sued the county board of education for the injury sustained by their daughter. A Georgia trial court granted summary judgment to the school board, and the parents appealed to the Court of Appeals of Georgia.

The court of appeals stated that where recreational property open to public use was involved, Georgia law provided that the school board was only liable for wilful or malicious failure to guard or warn against dangerous conditions. In order to show that the school board's failure to guard was wilful or malicious, the parents needed to show that the school board had actual knowledge that the property was being used for recreational purposes; that a condition existed involving an unreasonable risk of death or serious bodily harm; that the condition was not apparent to those using the property; and that having this knowledge, the owner chose not to guard or warn. The court stated that the parents could not meet this burden because the father admitted that the danger was apparent both to him and to his daughter. Therefore, the school board was not liable for the kindergartner's injuries. *Edmondson v. Brooks County Bd. of Educ.*, 423 S.E.2d 413 (Ga.App.1992).

A Florida school directed an eleven-year-old girl to be at her elementary school at 6:55 a.m. so that she could be transported to a gifted program at another district. The district received a report of suspicious persons prowling about school grounds, but the school investigator did not inform the girl. The next morning the girl was attacked and raped. The district was sued by the girl and her mother for negligently failing to supervise the girl. A state court granted summary judgment for the school district, and ruled that it had no duty to supervise the girl and protect her against third persons. The girl appealed to the District Court of Appeal of Florida, which held that the school's directive to the girl to wait on school grounds gave rise to a corresponding duty to supervise her. The summary judgment was reversed and the case was remanded for trial. *O'Campo v. School Bd. of Dade Co.*, 589 So.2d 323 (Fla.App.3d Dist.1991).

2. Governmental Immunity

An eleven-year-old Oklahoma student tried to climb to the roof of her grade school to retrieve a personal item. She fell from a metal pipe that held electrical wiring, breaking both ankles. The student and her mother filed a lawsuit against the school district in an Oklahoma trial court. In pretrial proceedings, it was revealed that the school superintendent had knowledge that another student had been injured at the same location and that the superintendent had authorized childproofing the electric service by raising it another five feet. The school district actually made this change after the second incident. The court conducted a trial and returned a decision for the school district. The Oklahoma Court of Appeals granted the mother's motion for a new trial and the district appealed to the Supreme Court of Oklahoma.

On appeal, the mother argued that the trial court had improperly instructed the jury concerning applicable electric codes, the school's later corrective action, and school district immunity under the state tort liability act. The supreme court disagreed, finding that there was sufficient evidence for a jury to determine that the school district had complied with the electric code. The state tort liability act expressly exempted government entities from liability for acts or omissions done in conformance with current, recognized standards. Because this formed a complete defense to liability, the trial court had properly instructed the jury and the mother was not entitled to a new trial. *Juvenal v. Okeene Pub. Schools*, 878 P.2d 1026 (Okl.1994).

A North Carolina high school student was injured when he was struck by a car in a driveway that divided the campus of his school. A lawsuit was filed in a North Carolina trial court claiming negligence by the school board, superintendent, principal and a teacher. The complaint failed to allege the purchase of liability insurance by the board. North Carolina law grants immunity to education boards unless waived by the purchase of insurance. The trial court refused to grant motions by the student to amend the complaint in order to allege the purchase of liability insurance by the board. The Court of Appeals of North Carolina affirmed the trial court order, and held that the superintendent and principal were public officers who were protected from liability in the absence of corruption, maliciousness or bad faith. The claim against the teacher had also been properly dismissed because it failed to state how she had allegedly caused the accident. *Gunter v. Anders*, 441 S.E.2d 167 (N.C.App.1994).

A five-year-old girl fell from a slide on the grounds of an Oklahoma elementary school during the summer recess and sustained head injuries. She and her parents sued the school district for damages, but the trial court granted summary judgment against them. After the court of appeals affirmed, the girl and her parents appealed to the Supreme Court of Oklahoma. They first claimed that the school district had waived its governmental immunity under the Oklahoma Governmental Tort Claims Act by obtaining liability insurance coverage. The court, however, determined that the school district had not waived its immunity by acquiring the policy because the policy specifically limited coverage to any liability "imposed by law." The supreme court held that the girl and her parents could not recover from the school district under any exceptions to the govermental tort claims act. Also, since the only claims brought were under the exemptions, the school district could not be liable for the girl's injuries, and insurance coverage was not available. The risk of falling from a slide is one which children regularly encounter and appreciate on a playground. Since there were no hidden dangers of which the school district had to warn the girl, summary judgment had been properly awarded to the school district. *Brewer v. Independent School District Number 1*, 848 P.2d 566 (Okl.1993).

A student fractured his leg when it was caught in a merry-go-round on the playground of a Pennsylvania elementary school. The student was awarded $30,000 in compensatory damages by a Pennsylvania trial court based on its determination that the merry-go-round was real property and that the school district could not maintain a defense on the basis of governmental immunity. The court found that the equipment was defective and that the school district was negligent in the care, custody and control of its property. The Commonwealth Court of Pennsylvania affirmed the trial court decision, finding that the district had breached its duty of care to protect those using its real estate for a reasonably foreseeable purpose. *Norwin School Dist. v. Cortazzo*, 625 A.2d 183 (Pa.Cmwlth.1993).

A group of people were sledding on a ski hill located on University of Alaska property. Two of the sledders lost control and struck a cluster of trees. One sledder died and the other was seriously injured. The injured sledder and the estate of the deceased sledder sued the university, claiming that it was negligent in maintaining the hill and in failing to protect sledders from a known danger. The university claimed that the ski hill was unimproved land and, according to Alaska law, as the owner of unimproved land which is open to the public for recreational purposes, it was immune to suit for negligence. The trial court agreed that the ski hill was unimproved land, but stated that the recreational purposes immunity granted by Alaska law was only meant to apply to rural land, not urban land. Since the ski hill was in Fairbanks, the university was not immune. The university appealed to the Alaska Supreme Court. The supreme court stated that the law did not apply only to rural land, but to urban land as well. However, it stated that the ski hill was on improved land. The university had cleared trees, mowed grass, and placed lights on or near the hill. The hill was a maintained, landscaped section of the main university campus located next to a gymnasium and hockey rink. Since it was improved, the university was not entitled to immunity. The case would proceed to trial. *Univ. of Alaska v. Shanti*, 835 P.2d 1225 (Alaska 1992).

A five-year-old child collided with a hand railing (located adjacent to a school building) while he was sledding down a hill. He sued the school district to recover for his injuries. A trial court granted summary judgment to the school district, and the child appealed to the New York Supreme Court, Appellate Division. The court noted that a New York statute applied here to insulate the school district from liability because: 1) the character of the property was conducive to the use of sledding and tobogganing, and 2) the child was engaged in that pursuit at the time of the accident, which pursuit was expressly included within the bounds of the New York statute granting immunity. Only if the school district's acts were wilful or malicious could the statute be defeated. Such was not the case here. The court affirmed the trial court's decision. *McGregor v. Middletown School Dist. No. 1*, 593 N.Y.S.2d 609 (A.D.3d Dept.1993).

An Oregon high school student was cut by a knife during a fight in the lunch room. The student sued the school district claiming that it was negligent in failing to exercise proper supervision of students, failing to provide proper security, failing to prevent weapons from being carried into the school building, and failing to stop the attack before the knife was used. The school district moved for dismissal on the grounds of immunity and a jury returned a verdict in its favor. The court of appeals reversed and remanded, but the Supreme Court of Oregon affirmed the judgment of the trial court. The supreme court stated that the school district's choice of the number and allocation of security personnel was a matter of discretion, making it immune from suit under state law. The court also stated that the student's claim that the school district was negligent in failing to break up the fight, an act which would have fallen outside the scope of immunity for discretionary acts, was not supported by the evidence. Because there was no evidence of negligence, the supreme court held for the school district. *Mosley v. Portland School Dist. No. 1J*, 843 P.2d 415 (Or.1992).

A special needs student at a Massachusetts junior high school was injured while fleeing from an altercation with another student. The injury occurred in the presence of the student's teacher in the school cafeteria. At the time of the injury, the student was attending the public schools pursuant to his individualized education plan (IEP). The teacher and school officials were aware that the special needs student was impulsive, erratic, and combative (and thus likely to get into fights). The student sued the city, claiming negligent educational programming and negligent supervision of students. A superior court dismissed the claim and the student appealed to the Appeals Court of Massachusetts. The appeals court noted that the Massachusetts Tort Claims Act exempts from liability any public employee who is exercising a "discretionary function." The court stated that the negligent educational programming claim failed because the adoption of a plan to integrate handicapped pupils into the public schools was purely discretionary. The claim for negligent supervision also failed. The court stated that the management of student imbroglios, student discipline, and school decorum fall readily within the discretionary function exception in the Tort Claims Act. Therefore, the appeals court affirmed the superior court's decision. *Bencic v. City of Malden*, 587 N.E.2d 795 (Mass.App.Ct.1992).

A North Carolina teacher attended an evening fundraiser conducted by an honorary teacher's sorority. The event was held in the school building. While attending the event, the teacher slipped on the waxed floor of a restroom and was seriously injured. North Carolina law provides immunity for local boards of education for bodily injury from negligence, except to the extent that the board is covered by insurance. The teacher sued seeking coverage of her injuries to the extent of the board's insurance, but the Court of Appeals of North Carolina denied coverage. The court stated that North Carolina law also provided absolute immunity to school boards for personal injury suffered during nonschool use of school property. The waiver of immunity to the extent of insurance did not apply in this instance. *Lindler v. Duplin County Bd. of Educ.*, 425 S.E.2d 465 (N.C.App.1993).

B. Off School Grounds

1. Duty of Care

A 15-year-old Georgia student was killed in a car accident after he and a friend left their voluntary summer school session in violation of school rules. The student's mother filed a lawsuit against the board of education, school superintendent, school district and other officials in the U.S. District Court for the Northern District of Georgia, claiming constitutional violations. The court granted summary judgment to the school board and officials, and the student's mother appealed to the U.S. Court of Appeals, Eleventh Circuit. The court observed that the U.S. Constitution did not require the states to guarantee protection of individuals against the threat of third party violence. Compulsory attendance laws did not impose a constitutional duty on schools, and the student's voluntary school attendance during summer session did not create a custodial relationship between himself and the school. The death had resulted from the student's own choice to leave school in violation of school policy. The district court had properly granted summary judgment to the district and officials. *Wright v. Lovin*, 32 F.3d 538 (11th Cir.1994).

A Nebraska school district arranged a ski trip for its students, but more students wished to go than there was room on the chartered bus. A local resident volunteered to transport some of the students in his van if the school district would pay for his gas and lodging. During the drive to Colorado, the van was involved in a single-vehicle accident. It was not clear whether bad weather had caused the accident or whether the driver had fallen asleep while driving the van. One of the students was killed in the accident. Her personal representative sued both the school district and the driver of the van for negligence, and the personal representative and the van driver reached a settlement. The lawsuit against the school district continued, but the trial court granted summary judgment in its favor. On appeal to the Supreme Court of Nebraska, the court noted that even though it had not yet been determined whether the driver had been negligent, the personal representative's claim would fail unless the driver's negligence was imputable to the school district. The court then noted that in settlements involving vicarious liability (where the principal is held liable for the acts of its agent) any settlement with the agent constitutes a settlement with the principal, no matter what the parties may have intended. Here, the settlement with the driver amounted to a settlement with the district and summary judgment was held to have been properly granted to the school district. *McCurry v. School Dist. of Valley*, 496 N.W.2d 433 (Neb.1993).

A Louisiana first grade student ran into the side of a truck traveling about 15 miles per hour as she left school. An eyewitness later testified that the student had run from between two parked cars and that the accident had been unavoidable. The student's parents claimed that the accident had been caused by the absence of a fence around the school and the presence of parked cars, which allowed students to randomly enter the street. A Louisiana trial court dismissed the complaint against the school board. The student and her parents appealed to the Court of Appeal of Louisiana, Third Circuit. On appeal, the school board argued that the Louisiana Discretionary Act Statute immunized it from liability for incidents that occurred off school grounds and after school hours. The court disagreed, finding that school boards in Louisiana had a duty to provide reasonable supervision commensurate with the age of students under its care, and to ensure that young students did not leave school unattended. The school board had authority to implement safety policies, and could have built a fence around the school yard, as it did after the accident. It was not entitled to immunity under the discretionary acts statute because it had breached its duty of care. The court reversed the judgment and awarded the student over $35,000 in general damages, future medical expenses, and past medical expenses. *Gary on Behalf of Gary v. Meche*, 626 So.2d 901 (La.App.3d Cir.1993).

A five-year-old District of Columbia student was struck by a car on the way to school. He had not been escorted by an adult and had crossed several hundred feet from a designated crosswalk. The crosswalk guard arrived late for work that day and was not present at the time of the accident. A District of Columbia trial court judge set aside a jury verdict of over $25,000, ruling that the district owed the student no special duty in this case. The District of Columbia Court of Appeals affirmed the decision, determining that parents and guardians bear the primary responsibility for safely transporting children to school and cannot rely upon school districts to guard against accidents occurring at a substantial distance from designated crossings. *Stoddard v. Dist. of Columbia*, 623 A.2d 1152 (D.C.App.1993).

A car operated by a California motorist struck and severely injured a bicyclist on a public road adjacent to a high school athletic field. A football game was in progress at the time of the accident, and the bicyclist claimed that the driver was distracted by the game and that the school district had created a dangerous condition by failing to erect a barrier to prevent passing motorists from seeing athletic events. The bicyclist sued the driver, school district and city in a California trial court, and the school district filed a motion for summary judgment. The court refused to grant the motion, and the district appealed to the California Court of Appeal, Second District. The court of appeal observed that the school district did not control the street adjacent to its property and that the field was located 140 feet from the sidewalk. The court adopted the reasoning of courts in Michigan, Ohio and Florida in ruling that the district owed no duty to users of an adjacent street to shield an athletic field from view to prevent distractions. Operators of motor vehicles have the express duty to use care in the operation of their vehicles. The court set aside and vacated the trial court's order denying summary judgment. *Lompoc Unif. School Dist. v. Superior Court*, 26 Cal.Rptr.2d 122 (Cal.App.2d Dist.1993).

A part-time custodian at an Ohio university accompanied his supervisor and other employees to an off campus restaurant for lunch. While at the restaurant, the custodian and a coworker allegedly drank alcoholic beverages. There was no university policy prohibiting employees from drinking on lunch breaks, although they were prohibited from working in an intoxicated state and from drinking while on campus. That afternoon, the custodian allegedly drank some rum at work. When he clocked out, coworkers noticed that he was intoxicated. The supervisor confronted him in the parking lot and offered to drive him home. The custodian declined and drove off campus. Fifteen minutes later he was involved in a head-on collision. The driver of the other auto sued the university. The trial court held that the university was not legally responsible and the driver appealed to the Court of Appeals of Ohio. On appeal, the driver argued that the university, as the employer, owed him a duty of care because it had actual knowledge that the employee was intoxicated and contributed to that condition by permitting him to drink during working hours. The court of appeals disagreed, observing that the custodian drank liquor during his lunch break, on his own time, off school property. This violated no school policy. The supervisor had tried to dissuade the custodian from driving by offering to drive him home. However, he had no authority to make him stay at work. Since there was no duty owed to the driver, there could be no breach and hence no liability. *Malone v. Miami Univ.*, 625 N.E.2d 640 (Ohio App.10th Dist.1993).

An Illinois school district posted crossing guards at a particular intersection near an elementary school. The school day began promptly at 8:30 a.m. each morning. At 8:35 a.m., a six-year-old student was injured at the intersection after the crossing guards had left for the morning. The student's parents sued the city, which filed a third-party action for contribution against the school district. The city alleged that the school district was negligent for failing to have a crossing guard present at the time the student was injured. The school moved to dismiss and the trial court granted the motion. The city then appealed to the Appellate Court of Illinois, Third District. On appeal, the city alleged that the school district, with "conscious disregard" and "utter indifference" for the safety of the student, failed to perform its duty of having a crossing guard present at the time of the accident. It also argued that the voluntary provision of a crossing guard at the intersection created a duty to maintain a crossing guard there. The court, however, disagreed. A school board has wide discretion in the exercise of its powers. In order to be liable for actions taken pursuant to that discretion, the act must be done intentionally or committed under circumstances exhibiting a reckless disregard for the safety of others. The city did not allege that the school district intentionally caused the student's injuries, nor did it sufficiently establish the school district's reckless disregard for the student's safety. The school district was not liable for the student's injuries. *Gilmore v. City of Zion*, 605 N.E.2d 110 (Ill.App.2d Dist.1992).

After students were released from a Los Angeles high school for the day, members of the "Bloods" gang shot a student who was waiting for a bus near the school. The gang members had mistakenly identified the student as a member of a rival gang, the "Crips." The student sued the school district, claiming that the school district had negligently supervised the students and the surrounding area. A trial court found for the student and awarded him $120,000 in damages. The school district appealed. The California Court of Appeal held that while a school district may have a duty to supervise the conduct of students on school grounds and to enforce rules and regulations for their protection, it was not liable in this case since it had exercised due care in carrying out this duty. School districts are not insurers of student safety. Schools must be only reasonably supervised, not impenetrable to all gang-related violence. *Brownell v. Los Angeles Unified School Dist.*, 5 Cal.Rptr.2d 761 (Cal.App.1992).

2. Governmental Immunity

A Connecticut town and its school board permitted an American Legion baseball team to use a field adjacent to the high school when school was not in session. A player who was injured in a baseball game sued the town and board of education in a Connecticut trial court for personal injuries. The Supreme Court of Connecticut affirmed the trial court's summary judgment for the town and board, ruling that government entities were entitled to statutory immunity under

Connecticut's Recreational Land Use Act. The court found no merit to the player's argument that the act had no application to developed park facilities and pertained only to injuries on undeveloped property. *Scrapchansky v. Town of Plainfield*, 627 A.2d 1329 (Conn.1993).

Two Texas students asked their bus driver to let them off at a nondesignated stop so that they could ride with another student in a car. The third student later ran into a fixed object, killing one of the students and injuring the other. In the lawsuit which followed, a Texas trial court granted the school district's summary judgment motion and the parents appealed to the Court of Appeals of Texas, Houston. The court ruled that the lawsuit was barred by sovereign immunity, and that the accident had not occurred as a result of the operation of a motor vehicle under the Texas Tort Claims Act. Summary judgment in favor of the school district was appropriate. *Goston v. Hutchison*, 853 S.W.2d 729 (Tex.App.— Houston[1st.Dist.]1993).

A New Mexico high school student was kept after school for detention. Normally, school let out at 2:30 p.m. The installed school zone signals at the east and west end of the campus consisted of signs that flashed from 2:30 to 2:50 p.m. on school days. The student was dismissed at 3:30 p.m., but remained with a friend until 3:55 p.m. Somehow, the student fell into the street and was struck by a vehicle. The signals at both ends of the school zone had stopped flashing before the accident occurred. The student sued the school board claiming that it was negligent by not scheduling the flashing signals to operate for as long as students remained under the school's control, and for not maintaining, or warning of the absence of, the school crossing signs at the crosswalk over the busy street. A New Mexico trial court granted summary judgment in favor of the school board, and the student appealed to the Court of Appeals of New Mexico.

The court of appeals stated that according to New Mexico law, governmental entities are immune from liability for any tort, except as waived by the Tort Claims Act. The student claimed that the school board immunity was waived under the section of the act which provided that immunity did not apply to bodily injury resulting from negligence in the maintenance or existence of any bridge, culvert, highway, roadway, street, alley, sidewalk or parking area. New Mexico law also provided that the state highway commission was responsible for establishing and maintaining crosswalks near school districts, with the advice of the local superintendent of schools. The court of appeals, however, stated that the giving of advice on establishment of crosswalks does not impose responsibility for the maintenance of the crosswalks on the public schools. If the legislature had intended to impose such responsibilities, it would have directly stated so. Therefore, no waiver of immunity was available. *Johnson v. School Bd. of Albuquerque*, 845 P.2d 844 (N.M.App.1992).

3. Comparative Negligence/Assumption of Risk

A New York high school student, who stole an oxidizing agent from his science class, sued his school for personal injury damages when the chemical later ignited in his home. The student alleged that the school was negligent in not providing adequate supervision and allowing access to dangerous chemicals without appropriate warnings or precautions. The school filed a motion for summary judgment, denying the student's allegations and raising contributory negligence as a defense. The trial court denied the motion, and the school appealed to the New York Supreme Court, Appellate Division.

The appellate court relied on the student's own testimony in finding that the school was not negligent. Although the student claimed that the chemical had spontaneously ignited, the police later found matches in the room where the fire had occurred. Additionally, the student admitted that his teacher had gone over the safety procedures and specifically told the class never to remove chemicals from the classroom. The court further stated that even if the school had been negligent, the student's act of intentionally stealing the chemical constituted a superseding force. The court stressed that the student's actions were unforeseeable and went beyond mere contributory negligence. Because of the intentional nature of the student's actions, the school was absolved from any liability. The court thus reversed the trial court's decision and granted summary judgment to the school. *Brazell v. Bd. of Educ. of Niskayuna Public Schools*, 557 N.Y.S.2d 645 (A.D.3d Dept. 1990).

V. LIABILITY FOR INTENTIONAL CONDUCT

The previous cases have involved school negligence. School districts may also be found liable for the intentional acts or omissions of school personnel. Courts often refer to intentional conduct as "wilful or wanton misconduct." Courts have also found school districts liable for intentional acts of third parties on or near school grounds. In those cases, courts may hold that the school district should have foreseen the potential for misconduct. In some cases, a finding of wilful or wanton misconduct will defeat the defense of sovereign immunity.

A. Teacher Misconduct

A Texas high school teacher removed a disruptive student from his class by holding on to his hair and arm. The student had thrown an object at another student and used profanity in the classroom. The teacher took the student to the vice principal's office for discipline, which in this case was assignment to the opportunity center for students for the rest of the semester. The student was later suspended from school for the rest of the year for drawing obscene pictures at the opportunity center. The decision to discipline the student rested with the vice principal and school administrator; the teacher did not participate in the decision to place the student in the opportunity center. The student's parents filed a lawsuit against the teacher in a Texas trial court, claiming that the student had suffered injuries in being removed from the classroom. The court granted summary judgment to the teacher, and the parents appealed to the Court of Appeals of Texas. The court of appeals observed that Texas teachers were protected by absolute immunity from personal liability for any act involving the exercise of discretion with only limited exceptions, including excessive force or negligence during student discipline. The parents argued that the act of removing the student from the classroom constituted discipline under the state education code. The court disagreed, stating that the teacher had not been engaged in disciplinary action but was merely transporting the student to the vice principal's office for the imposition of discipline. The teacher was accordingly entitled to absolute immunity from personal liability and the trial court had properly granted summary judgment in his favor. *Doria v. Stulting*, 888 S.W.2d 563 (Tex.App.— Corpus Christi 1994).

A Louisiana physical education coach removed three kindergarten boys from a film presentation because they were being disruptive. He allegedly told the boys that if they did not stop annoying him he would kill them. The coach then enlisted two of the boys in a prank in which they were to pretend to lay dead in view of the third kindergartner. The coach told the third kindergartner that he had hanged one of the boys with a jump rope. He showed the kindergartner one of the boys, who was lying on the floor pretending to be dead. The kindergartner became very upset and began crying. He later developed symptoms of anxiety and exhibited infantile behavior such as refusing to go to the bathroom alone and refusing to sleep in his own room. The student's parents filed a lawsuit against the school board, resulting in a judgment for the student and parents of over $117,000, including loss of consortium damages of $5,000 for each parent. The school board appealed the damage award to the Court of Appeal of Louisiana, Fifth Circuit.

On appeal, the district argued that the damage award was excessive, that the award of loss of consortium damages was incorrect and that the parents had failed to mitigate their damages. The court of appeal disagreed, finding no abuse of discretion by the trial court in awarding damages to the student and parents. The court rejected the district's argument that the parents were overprotective and that they had made the injury worse by overreacting. The parents had made good faith efforts to seek professional counseling and abide by the recommendations of therapists. Accordingly, the court of appeal affirmed the district court judgment. *Spears v. Jefferson Parish School Bd.*, 646 So.2d 1104 (La.App.5th Cir.1994).

An Arkansas school district hired a bus driver with a previous record of driving while intoxicated and sexual conduct with a minor. The parents of a nine-year-old girl who attended school in the district alleged that the driver sexually molested their daughter on the bus. They filed a lawsuit in an Arkansas trial court, claiming that the district had violated state hiring guidelines for school bus drivers. School board officials argued that they were immune from liability under an Arkansas statute because they were performing "a necessary government function." The court agreed that the directors could only be sued in their official capacities and not as individuals. However, it refused to grant their motion to dismiss the lawsuit, determining that the parents had alleged facts sufficient to establish a claim for negligence and that the directors were not absolutely immune from liability. The directors petitioned the Supreme Court of Arkansas for a writ of prohibition.

The supreme court held that the petition for a writ of prohibition was not a proper remedy for a trial court's failure to grant a dismissal motion. This type of petition could only be granted where the lower court was entirely without jurisdiction. In this case, the statutes under which the directors claimed immunity merely afforded them the defense of statutory immunity and did not wholly deprive the trial court of jurisdiction. The trial court had acted properly and the court denied the petition. *West Memphis School Dist. No. 4 v. Circuit Court of Crittenden County*, 871 S.W.2d 368 (Ark.1994).

A Texas teacher sexually abused a 15-year-old student after cultivating a relationship with her for more than two years. The teacher also showed overt favoritism to female students and engaged in other inappropriate behavior. The principal began receiving complaints from students and parents but took no action. When the victim's parents reported the abuse to the superintendent, he immediately suspended the teacher. The teacher then resigned and pleaded guilty to criminal charges. The U.S. District Court for the Western District of Texas granted summary judgment to the principal and superintendent in a lawsuit filed by the victim and her parents for constitutional violations. The U.S. Court of Appeals, Fifth Circuit, held that a special relationship existed between the victim and school officials, creating a constitutional duty to protect her. The court then vacated its decision and reconsidered the case.

The court adopted a new standard under which supervisory school officials could be held personally liable for violations of student constitutional rights by subordinates in abuse cases. Supervisors could be found liable if they took no action despite a plain pattern of inappropriate sexual behavior by a subordinate, where they demonstrated deliberate indifference toward the constitutional rights of the student. Because the principal had received notice of inappropriate behavior and failed to take any action, he demonstrated deliberate indifference to the student's clearly established constitutional right to bodily integrity. However, the superintendent had responded to his knowledge of the misconduct promptly. He was entitled to summary judgment on the grounds of qualified immunity. The court affirmed the order denying qualified immunity to the principal and reversed the order denying qualified immunity to the superintendent. *Doe v. Taylor Indep. School Dist.*, 15 F.3d 443 (5th Cir.1994).

A California junior high school student alleged that she had been sexually harassed and assaulted by a teacher. She also alleged that the teacher's employment had been previously terminated by another school because of sexual misconduct. In the student's lawsuit against the school district, a California trial court granted the school district's motion for judgment on the pleadings because the student had failed to plead that the district was liable for negligent hiring or supervision. The court also ruled that the district was immune from liability for failing to make a background check of the teacher. The California Court of Appeal, Second District, Division Three, stated that unlike federal courts, California courts recognize a special relationship between school districts and students that imposes an affirmative duty on school districts to take all reasonable steps to protect students. Although sexual misconduct of teachers could not be imputed to school districts to allow recovery under the doctrine of *respondeat superior,* the trial court should have allowed the student to amend her pleadings to properly allege negligent hiring and supervision by the district. The court reversed the lower court's decision. School district employees perhaps should have known of the teacher's prior record. *Virginia G. v. ABC Unified School Dist.*, 19 Cal.Rptr.2d 671 (Cal.App.2d Dist.1993).

The parents of a Georgia first grader sued their board of education, elementary school principal and a teacher in a Georgia trial court for an alleged assault of the child in a restroom by a physical education teacher. There was no evidence that the teacher had a criminal record or that the school or its officials should have known of his alleged criminal propensities. The Court of Appeals of Georgia affirmed the trial court's decision for the school board and officials, ruling that without prior knowledge by school board members of the teacher's criminal propensities there could be no liability for negligent hiring or liability under 42 U.S.C. § 1983. There was no reason for believing that the teacher would commit a criminal act. *Thurmond v. Richmond County Bd. of Educ.*, 428 S.E.2d 392 (Ga.App.1993).

A sociology professor allegedly ordered a student to leave his classroom, then slandered him in a 30-minute tirade to the remaining students. Subsequently, the student entered into a settlement agreement with the college. He then sued the professor for slander. The trial court granted summary judgment to the professor, and the Supreme Court of Montana affirmed. The supreme court stated that the student was statutorily barred in his suit against the professor by reason of his recovery against the college. A state law provided that recovery against a governmental entity barred recovery against the employee whose wrongful act caused the harm. *Stansbury v. Lin,* 848 P.2d 509 (Mont.1993).

A Kansas high school teacher became "involved" with a high school senior. He married the student after she graduated from high school, a fact which was known to the high school principal. Three years later, the teacher was convicted of sexual battery of another high school student, and the state board of education revoked his teaching certificate. The battered student claimed that the school board and its employees had deprived her of her constitutional rights and had acted with deliberate indifference to her rights. She filed a lawsuit in the U.S. District Court for the District of Kansas, which granted the summary judgment motion of the school district and officials. The student appealed to the U.S. Court of Appeals, Tenth Circuit.

On appeal, the student argued that because it was aware of the teacher's prior involvement with a student, the school district had an unwritten policy of condoning or encouraging inappropriate sexual conduct between teachers and students, and that it had failed to thoroughly investigate and discipline such conduct. The school district and officials argued that the other incidents alleged by the student were unknown to school officials at relevant times and that no complaints were made in the three years between the teacher's marriage and the sexual battery incident. The court of appeals held that there was no pattern of deliberate indifference to the student's constitutional rights. In order to advance a successful civil rights complaint, there must be an affirmative link to the complained of acts and the defendant—which was not present in this case. The district court had appropriately granted them summary judgment. *Gates v. Unif. School Dist. No. 449*, 996 F.2d 1035 (10th Cir.1993).

A Florida junior high school teacher visited a 13-year-old student, with whom he had developed a close personal relationship, seven to ten times during summer vacation. On each of those occasions, he fondled her breasts, penetrated her vaginal area, and forced her to perform oral sex on him. The student's parents neither knew of nor consented to the visits. A Florida trial court convicted the teacher of five counts of committing lewd acts upon a child and three counts of engaging a child in sexual activity by a person in custodial authority. The teacher appealed to the District Court of Appeal, which affirmed the convictions, finding that the teacher stood in a familiar or custodial position in relationship to the victim under state child abuse laws. The teacher further appealed to the Supreme Court of Florida. The supreme court held that teachers are not, by reason of their chosen profession, custodians of their students at all times, particularly when school is recessed for the summer. Consequently, the supreme court affirmed the trial court's lewd act convictions but quashed its decision with respect to the convictions for sexual activity by a person in custodial authority. *Hallberg v. State of Florida*, 649 So.2d 1355 (Fla.1994).

An Ohio student transferred to a high school where a teacher stated that the student had been discharged from a drug rehabilitation program and that school administrators would not permit her to return to her former high school. The student filed a complaint against the teacher that was dismissed by an Ohio trial court, and she appealed to the Court of Appeals of Ohio, Montgomery County. It ruled that the trial court had erroneously found that the student's complaint stated no claim upon which relief could be granted. Her allegation that her educational opportunities had been impaired could be legitimately litigated. The student had stated a sufficient complaint for intentional infliction of emotional distress, and the case was remanded. *King v. Bogner*, 88 Ohio App.3d 564, 624 N.E.2d 364 (Ohio App.2d Dist.1993).

B. Student Misconduct

Two New York sisters were assaulted and injured by a group of students and nonstudents as they attempted to leave their high school after classes. Prior to the assault, one of the sisters had been threatened by one of the eventual perpetrators and that incident had been reported to a teacher. The teacher failed to take any action, and when one of the sisters attempted to enter the security department, she found it locked and closed. The sisters filed a lawsuit against the city of New York and the city board of education in a New York trial court, claiming negligent supervision. At trial, there was evidence that no security officers were at their posts during the time of the assault. The jury returned a verdict of $750,000 for one of the sisters, and $50,000 for the other. The court granted the school board's motion to set aside the verdict and dismiss the complaint. The New York Supreme Court, Appellate Division, First Department, reversed this decision. The city and school board appealed to the Court of Appeals of New York.

The court of appeals determined that there was sufficient evidence to establish liability by the city and board for negligent supervision. There was an obvious need for supervision of students when they were dismissed at the end of the day, as this was the time fights were most likely. There was evidence that the school's security policy had not been enforced at the time of the assault. Schools have a duty to adequately supervise students and are liable for foreseeable injuries that are proximately related to inadequate supervision. The court affirmed the appellate division's decision. *Mirand v. City of New York*, 84 N.Y.2d 44, 614 N.Y.S.2d 372, 637 N.E.2d 263 (1994).

A New York third-grade student was sexually assaulted by two older students in a school lavatory. Although there was a lavatory located in her classroom, the student's teacher insisted that her students use the one located in the hallway. One of the older students had previously been identified in some bullying incidents, one of which involved the assault victim. The victim and her guardian sued the school district and teacher in a New York trial court, claiming that the assault had been reasonably foreseeable because of the prior incidents. The trial court set aside a $350,000 jury verdict for the student, but on appeal, the verdict was reinstated by the New York Supreme Court, Appellate Division, First Department. Under New York law, school districts are charged with supervising student activities and are liable for foreseeable injuries related to the absence of supervision. In this case, there had been sufficient evidence for the jury to determine that the school board and teacher breached their duty to provide adequate supervision. Accordingly, the trial court decision was reversed and the jury verdict was reinstated. The New York Court of Appeals affirmed the appellate division court's decision in a brief memorandum. *Shante D. v. City of New York, Bd. of Educ. Local School No. 5*, 83 N.Y.2d 948, 615 N.Y.S.2d 317 (1994).

A nine-year-old fourth grade student was identified as severely behaviorally disabled and was declared eligible for special education after being documented for aggressive and disruptive behavior. A first grade student at the same school stated that the behaviorally disabled student had sexually assaulted him several times in a school restroom. When the school district confirmed the assaults, the disabled student was expelled. The victim's parents sued the school district in a Washington trial court, claiming negligent supervision. The trial court refused to grant full disclosure of a psychological assessment performed by a district psychologist and the court granted the district's summary judgment motion. The student's parents appealed to the Court of Appeals of Washington, Division One.

The court stated that the school district had a duty to supervise students in its custody. The school district could be held liable if the injury was within "a general field of danger which should have been anticipated." Because the school district knew of the aggressive nature of the disabled student, it should have anticipated the possibility of injury to the victimized student. The trial court had mistakenly focused its inquiry on whether the school district had received notice that the disabled student might perpetrate a sexual assault. It reversed the trial court's decision and determined that the school psychologist's records were not confidential. On remand, the victimized student was entitled to full disclosure of the withheld documents. *J.N. by and through Hager v. Bellingham School Dist. No. 501*, 871 P.2d 1106 (Wash.App.Div.1 1994).

A Texas student was allegedly assaulted by a classmate during a vocational education class. The student suffered a broken jaw and claimed that his teacher and principal knew or should have known that the other student was a delinquent minor with known violent propensities. He alleged that the teacher and principal had failed to appropriately discipline the other student and that this failure had led to his injuries. A Texas trial court granted summary judgment to the teacher and principal, and the court of appeals affirmed. It rejected the student's argument that the employee immunity section of the state education code only protected employees from liability for acts and not for omissions. The court stated that the word "negligence" encompassed both acts and omissions. Texas school employees are immune from liability so long as the acts allegedly causing injury are not disciplinary in nature, involve the exercise of professional discretion and occur in the course and scope of employment. The immunity section was intended to protect school employees except where they used excessive force resulting in bodily injury when disciplining a student. *Pulido v. Dennis*, 888 S.W.2d 518 (Tex.App.—El Paso 1994).

An Oklahoma student was shot and killed on school grounds by another student. The deceased student's mother claimed that school employees were aware of the threat of violence to her son. She filed a lawsuit in the U.S. District Court for the Western District of Oklahoma, claiming that the district's failure to respond to the known threat violated the student's constitutional rights. The court dismissed the complaint and the mother appealed to the U.S. Court of Appeals, Tenth Circuit. The court consolidated the appeal with the case of another Oklahoma student who was stabbed on the grounds of his school. The court stated that the Due Process Clause of the U.S. Constitution did not require a state to protect citizens against harm caused by third parties. Compulsory attendance laws did not create an affirmative constitutional duty to protect students, even where a student was the victim of a foreseeable assault. Because no special, custodial relationship existed between students and their schools, there could be no constitutional duty of protection, as the parents claimed. The court affirmed the dismissal of both cases. *Graham v. Indep. School Dist. No. I-89*, 22 F.3d 991 (10th Cir.1994).

Two Louisiana high school students were involved in a fight in their school hallway. One of them was severely injured when they resumed the fight in the assistant principal's office. She sued the school board in a Louisiana district court, which awarded medical expenses and general damages to the injured student, finding a teacher negligent for failing to reasonably supervise the students. The Court of Appeal of Louisiana, Second Circuit, reversed the district court's decision, ruling that the resumption of the fight within the assistant principal's office had been unforeseeable. The teacher had followed school policy by bringing the students there and had returned to his classroom to resume his duties with the situation apparently under control. The court also held that the school board could not be held liable for the other student's attack. Louisiana school boards are not insurers of student safety. *Adams v. Caddo Parish School Bd.*, 631 So.2d 70 (La.App.2d Cir.1994).

A 15-year-old Georgia high school student died from injuries he suffered when he was beaten and kicked by another student in a school hallway between classes. The victim's parents sued the principal and a teacher whose classroom was near the place of the attack, claiming that they were vicariously liable. A Georgia trial court granted summary judgment to the teacher and principal, and the parents appealed to the Court of Appeals of Georgia.

The parents argued that the teacher and principal were not shielded by official immunity because they had merely carried out ministerial duties as assigned by their school board. They also claimed that because the teacher and principal had purchased liability insurance through their professional associations, they waived official immunity to the extent of the insurance coverage that was purchased. The court of appeals disagreed, finding that the purchase of insurance constituted a waiver of official immunity only when purchased by the state on behalf of employees. The court also disagreed with the parents' analysis of the duties of the teacher and principal. Their actions were discretionary in nature, because they were required to decide how to monitor students between classes. Because school officials should not be deterred by the threat of personal liability, they were shielded by official immunity so long as they acted within the scope of their authority, and without wilfulness, malice or corruption. The court affirmed the trial court's award of summary judgment. *Guthrie v. Irons*, 439 S.E.2d 732 (Ga.App.1993).

A California student sexually molested another student who was confined to a wheelchair due to cerebral palsy. The victim's parents sued the school district in a California trial court, but failed to name the perpetrator or his parents as parties. The school district filed a cross-complaint against the perpetrator and his parents, seeking indemnity and alleging a claim against the parents for negligent supervision. After the court ruled for the school district, the parents appealed to the California Court of Appeal. The court of appeal observed that California had recently amended its penal statute to impose criminal liability on parents who failed to make reasonable efforts to control their children, and that the state was clearly expanding parental liability for wrongful acts by children. Parents had the opportunity and duty to control, supervise and train children to behave responsibly. If they failed to do so, the imposition of liability was fair even where, as in this case, the compensation was not due the victim, but rather a third party. The court ruled that the school district was entitled to equitable indemnity from the perpetrator's parents. Under the statute, the parents' liability would be limited to $10,000. *Curry v. Superior Court*, 24 Cal.Rptr.2d 495 (Cal.App.4th Dist.1993).

A 13-year-old Virginia girl was threatened by a boy in one of her classes. The girl told her teacher that the boy had threatened to rape her, and the teacher allegedly advised another teacher of the threat. Three days later, the boy sexually assaulted the girl on school grounds as another student stood watch. The girl sued the school district and teachers in the U.S. District Court for the Eastern District of Virginia under 42 U.S.C. § 1983 and Virginia state law. She alleged that the teachers had failed to discipline the boy or to take any preventive action. She further claimed that a special relationship existed between the school board and its students that created a duty to protect students from harm. The court considered a motion to dismiss the lawsuit advanced by the school board and its employees. According to the court, no special relationship existed between students and the school board or its employees that would create an affirmative duty to protect students. The Due Process Clause does not obligate states to provide protective services to private citizens. The court dismissed the § 1983 complaint. However, it ruled that the girl's state law complaint alleging gross negligence against the teachers warranted further consideration, and a trial if necessary. Other state law complaints advanced by the girl against the school board and teachers for simple negligence were dismissed. *B.M.H. by C.B. v. School Bd. of the City of Chesapeake, Virginia*, 833 F.Supp. 560 (E.D.Va.1993).

Two South Carolina middle school students teased and harassed another student for a period of several months. The two were sent to the school office and disciplined on several occasions and their teacher paddled them once for misbehavior. The harassed student complained one day that the others were throwing spitballs at him and teasing him. Although the teacher instructed the students to stop, a fight broke out at the end of class and the student who had been harassed broke his leg. The student sued the school district in a South Carolina trial court for medical expenses and injuries, and a jury returned a $25,000 verdict for him and $3,000 for his mother. The trial court refused to grant the school district's motion for a directed verdict, finding that there was evidence of gross negligence by the school district. The district appealed to the Court of Appeals of South Carolina. The court of appeals stated that there was evidence in the record that the teacher was aware of the classroom problems and was aware that she could rearrange the classroom for behavior management. The record indicated that the two harassing students sat on either side of the other student and that the teacher had never tried moving them. The court determined that this was sufficient to indicate a failure of school district personnel to exercise slight care. Because South Carolina law defined gross negligence as the absence of care that is necessary under the circumstances, the trial court decision was correct. *Smart v. Hampton County School Dist. No. 2*, 432 S.E.2d 487 (S.C.App.1993).

A Missouri student was injured when a classmate threw a piece of broken asphalt which struck him in the head. The asphalt was taken from deteriorated pavement on school grounds and the incident occurred entirely on school property. The student and his parents sued the school district in a Missouri trial court, claiming that it should have known about the deteriorated pavement, that it should have supervised its students more effectively by denying access to the area, and that it should have known that students would throw broken pieces of asphalt. The court granted the school district's motion to dismiss the matter, finding that the broken asphalt did not create a dangerous condition and that the alleged failure to supervise students was barred by sovereign immunity. It was also found that the classmate's intervening act relieved the district of any liability. The student and parents appealed to the Missouri Court of Appeals, Eastern District, Division Two. The court of appeals stated that public schools and school districts were state entities which were entitled to sovereign immunity in negligence actions. The exception for failure to adequately supervise students was inapplicable in this case because it had merely been alleged that a dangerous property condition existed. The exception for dangerous property conditions was also inapplicable because the complaint failed to allege direct causation of the injury by the school district. The classmate's act of throwing the asphalt was unrelated to any school district function and superseded any action or inaction by the district. The court affirmed the dismissal of the lawsuit. *Patterson v. Meramec Valley R-III School Dist.*, 864 S.W.2d 14 (Mo.App.E.D.1993).

Two female students at a Pennsylvania high school alleged that they were sexually molested by several male students while attending arts class during the 1989-90 school year. The alleged abuse supposedly took place in both a bathroom and a darkroom which was part of the graphic arts classroom. The students alleged that the molestation consisted of offensive touching of their breasts and genitalia, sodomization and forced acts of fellatio. They also claimed they were forced to watch similar acts performed on other students. The students sued the school district and individual officials and teachers under 42 U.S.C. §§ 1983 and 1985(3) for violations of their civil rights. The district court found that the officials were immune and also that the students failed to state a claim against the officials. The students appealed to the U.S. Court of Appeals, Third Circuit. On appeal, the students argued that the school defendants had knowledge of the abuse and maintained a policy of laxity toward such conduct. The school argued that no special relationship of constitutional proportions existed between themselves and the students warranting a duty of care to protect the students from the violence of others. The court of appeals held that no special relationship existed between the students and the school. The state's mandatory attendance laws were not sufficient to establish such a relationship since parents decide whether education is in public or private schools, and the parents remain the students' primary caretakers. The court also found no state-created danger to the students. Finally, there was too little evidence to support a conspiracy theory of deprivation of constitutional rights. The court affirmed the lower court's ruling. *D.R. v. Middle Bucks Area Voc. Tech. School,* 972 F.2d 1364 (3d Cir.1992).

An Illinois high school student was assaulted by another student in the high school parking lot. The victim had warned the principal that his assailant planned to attack him. The principal met with the assailant before the fight and warned him to leave the victim alone. Ignoring the principal's order, the assailant attacked the victim. In the lawsuit which followed, the Appellate Court of Illinois refused to find the school district liable. In Illinois, a school district must engage in wilful and wanton misconduct to be liable. Although the principal's actions may have been somewhat careless, they did not evidence a reckless disregard for the safety of the victim. *Siegmann v. Buffington,* 604 N.E.2d 1038 (Ill.App.3d Dist.1992).

C. Parent Misconduct

A Florida statute makes school teachers and school officials mandatory reporters of child abuse or neglect. A Florida student was subjected to repeated abuse by his stepmother. His teacher reported a series of incidents to the school principal, leading to an investigation by a state agency. The investigation concluded that the abuse reports were unfounded. The abuse continued, and the student's teacher continued to report her observations to school personnel; however, nothing further was reported to the state agency. The stepmother then broke the student's femur, permanently injuring him. Child abuse charges were renewed, resulting in a change of custody to the student's mother. She sued the school board in a Florida trial court, stating that the child abuse statute created a private cause of action for abuse victims. The trial court granted the school board summary judgment, and the student's mother appealed to the District Court of Appeal of Florida, Fifth District. The court of appeal affirmed the trial court's summary judgment for the school board. Although the statute made the knowing and wilful failure to report child abuse a second degree misdemeanor, there was no authority to indicate that the reporting statute created a private cause of action for personal injury damages. *Freehauf v. School Bd. of Seminole County*, 623 So.2d 761 (Fla.App.5th Dist.1993).

An Illinois high school freshman became upset after breaking up with his girlfriend. He began meeting with school counselors, one of whom had the student sign a form in which the student agreed not to physically injure himself. The counselors did not advise the student's parents that he was receiving counseling. During one session, the student said that he did not want to go home because his mother verbally abused him. The counselor took the student to a crisis intervention center. A crisis counselor then contacted the student's mother, and stated that the student would be temporarily placed in an alternative living arrangement. The mother signed a consent for treatment form, but refused to sign a consent for foster care form. The student spent five nights in foster care. The student, parents and a school counselor met and the student was then allowed to return home. The parents filed a lawsuit in the U.S. District Court for the Central District of Illinois, alleging civil rights violations by school officials.

The officials filed a summary judgment motion based on qualified immunity. The court stated that there could be no liability unless the conduct of school officials violated clearly established statutory or constitutional rights of which reasonable persons would have knowledge. Although the school officials failed to contact the parents and excluded the crisis center from the decisionmaking process, they were not on notice that this conduct violated clearly established rights. The student's refusal to go home constituted an emergency. Because the emergency response of the school officials did not violate statutory and constitutional rights, summary judgment was granted. *Pauli v. Bd. of Educ., Farmington Cent. Comm. Unit School Dist.*, 841 F.Supp. 840 (C.D.Ill.1994).

When an eleven-year-old Tennessee student complained of illness, the school was unable to reach her parents. A coworker of the father asked the girl's uncle to take the child home. The uncle went to the school and obtained her custody by signing a sign-out sheet in the school office. He then took her to a secluded place and brutally raped her. The parents sued the uncle, school board and school officials in a Tennessee trial court, which dismissed the claims brought against the school officials and board. The Court of Appeals of Tennessee affirmed the dismissal as to the school board and officials. There was no merit to the parents' argument that they had specifically instructed the school not to release the child into anyone else's custody, and the school officials had no notice that the uncle presented a threat to children. Because the injury was entirely unforeseeable to school officials, they had not breached their duty to exercise ordinary care for the child's safety. *Snider v. Snider*, 855 S.W.2d 588 (Tenn.App.1993).

A referee officiated several matches during a wrestling tournament held at a New York county high school. After watching a match that his son lost, a spectator physically assaulted the referee. The referee sued the board of education, the school district, the high school's principal and athletic director, and the spectator. The board of education and the district brought a motion for summary judgment dismissing them. The trial court held for the referee, and the district and school board appealed to the New York Supreme Court, Appellate Division. The appellate court stated that public entities in New York are immune from tort claims arising out of the performance of their governmental functions, including the provision of security against physical attack, unless the injured party establishes a special relationship with the entity. Although the public high school athletic association handbook delineated several preparations and guidelines made in order to improve safety and control of students and spectators, the handbook did not support a finding that the referee was to be treated any differently from students, or members of the general public. *Perry v. Bd. of Educ.*, 592 N.Y.S.2d 493 (A.D.3d Dept.1993).

D. Unknown Assailant

A Dallas high school student was killed by random gunfire in the school parking lot after a dance. The student's mother filed a lawsuit against the school district, the student who fired the shot and his mother, as well as the school principal. The original petition alleged that the school district was aware that students often carried and fired guns on school property and that the district's security measures were inadequate. The student's mother amended her complaint to include a claim for liability under 42 U.S.C. § 1983. The district and principal filed a successful motion to remove the case from the Texas state court system to the U.S. District Court for the Northern District of Texas. The district court denied the mother's motion to remand the case to state court, and granted a dismissal motion filed by the district and principal. The mother then appealed to the U.S. Court of Appeals, Fifth Circuit.

The court held that the district court had properly refused to remand the case to state court. It had also properly dismissed the case for failure to state a claim under 42 U.S.C. § 1983, because the statute requires showing that a local government unit's official policy or custom deprived the injured party of a constitutional right. This standard also requires the existence of a special relationship between the government actor and the victim. The student's mother was unable to show the existence of a special relationship between the student and district, or that the district had placed the student in peril or acted with disregard for his safety. Because school officials had not shown deliberate indifference to the student's constitutional rights, the district court had properly dismissed the case. *Leffall v. Dallas Indep. School Dist.*, 28 F.3d 521 (5th Cir.1994).

A Louisiana high school security employee observed a small group of youths near a student's car. The employee told the student that his alarm had sounded twice, and when the student observed the youths near his car, he asked the employee to accompany him. The employee responded that she was not responsible for providing security beyond school grounds. The student went to his car alone and was shot twice by one of the youths. He filed a lawsuit in a Louisiana trial court against the school board, security company and employee, claiming negligence. The court found the assailant 80 percent liable and the school board 20 percent liable for the damage award of over $15,000. The school board appealed to the Louisiana Court of Appeal, Fourth Circuit.

On appeal, the school board argued that the incident had been unforeseeable and that the trial court had improperly failed to apportion part of the liability to the student. The court applied ordinary negligence principles in analyzing the case, and found that the school board had assumed a duty to protect students from third party criminal actions by hiring the security employee. The school board's affirmative duty to protect its students extended to adjacent areas. The school security employee had been aware of the presence of the assailant prior to the incident and the trial court had not committed error by finding the board partly responsible for the student's injury due to her inaction. However, the trial court had erroneously failed to assign any liability to the student, and found him five percent negligent for not simply waiting for the youths to leave the area. Accordingly, it reduced the damage award and affirmed the trial court judgment as amended. *Peterson v. Doe*, 647 So.2d 1288 (La.App.4th Cir.1994).

A nonstudent entered a Texas high school during school hours with a concealed handgun that was not discovered by metal detectors. He then caused a disturbance and fired his gun, killing a student. The deceased student's father filed a lawsuit against the school district in the U.S. District Court for the Northern District of Texas, alleging that the district and principal had violated his son's constitutional rights. The court dismissed the case, and the father appealed to the U.S. Court of Appeals, Fifth Circuit. The court of appeals stated that in order to prevail in a case filed under 42 U.S.C. § 1983, the complaining party must demonstrate the violation of an affirmative constitutional right because of the actions, customs or policies of a government actor. In this case, the complaint did not state that the school district had created any danger or risk of serious physical harm to the student. On the contrary, the district had taken affirmative efforts to secure the school. It could not be held liable for a random criminal act and the student had not been victimized by a state-created danger. The court affirmed the dismissal of the lawsuit. *Johnson v. Dallas Indep. School Dist.*, 38 F.3d 198 (5th Cir.1994).

An assistant principal at a New York high school was sexually assaulted in an unlocked room by an unknown armed assailant. She brought this action against the city and the board of education to recover damages for her injuries. The trial court granted summary judgment in favor of the city and the board of education. She appealed to the Supreme Court, Appellate Division. The court noted that the allegations in the complaint did not arise from the defendants' failure to fulfill their proprietary duties. Rather, they arose from the defendants' exercise of discretion (governmental function). Therefore, the grant of governmental immunity was proper. *Porterfield v. City of New York,* 573 N.Y.S.2d 681 (A.D.1991).

VI. SCHOOL BUS ACCIDENTS

Courts have often found school bus operators negligent and their employers liable for injuries received by passengers when the injuries are the result of a failure by the operator to follow generally accepted standards of good judgment in the operation of the vehicle.

A. Duty of Care

A nonstudent entered a bus that was transporting South Carolina high school students and threatened a student who had fought earlier with her sister. The driver reported the incident, and the school's transportation services director warned the students involved against further incidents. School officials were unable to reach the parents of the students, and several days later, the non-student again entered the bus and assaulted with a knife the student she had previously threatened. The injured student filed a lawsuit against the school district in a South Carolina trial court, which granted the district's summary judgment motion. The South Carolina Court of Appeals affirmed the trial court decision, and the student appealed to the Supreme Court of South Carolina. The supreme court stated that South Carolina law protected government entities from liability except where officials were grossly negligent in exercising their responsibilities. Gross negligence was the intentional, conscious failure to do a required duty, and the failure to exercise even slight care. Because school district personnel had made several attempts to remedy the situation in this case, their conduct did not constitute gross negligence, and the trial court had properly dismissed the lawsuit. *Clyburn v. Sumter County School Dist. No. 17*, 451 S.E.2d 885 (S.C.1994).

In another injury case resulting from a school bus fight, the Court of Appeals of Oklahoma determined that a school district was not entitled to summary judgment against the victim of a severe beating by another student on the school bus. The court of appeals reasoned that students were effectively constrained while on school buses, creating a special relationship between school bus drivers and student passengers. Because students had no escape route from an attack on a school bus, it should have been foreseeable to the district that a student could be injured by another student. Although the bus driver was entitled to immunity, the court returned the issue of the school district's liability to the trial court. *Cooper v. Millwood Indep. School Dist. No. 37*, 887 P.2d 1370 (Okl.App.1994).

A Washington school bus driver dropped off a 13-year-old girl on the side of a highway at about 6 p.m. (when it was dark out) without using his stop sign or flashing lights, and without taking any precautions to insure that she crossed the road safely. The girl was killed while attempting to cross the highway. In the lawsuit which followed, two school districts were found to be at fault. The driver of the car that hit the student was found not liable. The Court of Appeals of Washington affirmed the lower court's decision stating that the districts had violated legislative enactments designed to protect students. *Yurkovich v. Rose,* 847 P.2d 925 (Wash.App.Div.1 1993).

Certain Pennsylvania school children sued their school superintendent, the school district and a private bus company under 42 U.S.C. § 1983 alleging that they were sexually molested by their bus driver while being driven to and from school. A federal district court granted summary judgment to the defendants, and the school children appealed to the U.S. Court of Appeals, Third Circuit. The court of appeals found that the bus company and its employees were not acting under color of state law (a prerequisite to liability under § 1983) nor were their actions fairly attributable to the state. Even though the bus company was carrying out a state program at state expense, it was not performing a traditional state function, and there was no state regulation governing the conduct which was alleged to have violated the children's rights. Next, the court stated that even though the school superintendent was a state actor, he did not exhibit deliberate indifference to a policy or custom which directly caused the harm, nor was there a special relationship between him and the children such that an affirmative duty was imposed on him to protect them. The court affirmed the grant of summary judgment to the defendants. *Black by Black v. Indiana Area School District,* 985 F.2d 707 (3d Cir.1993).

A seven-year-old New York student was injured when her school bus overturned. She was treated for a contusion of the head and released from the hospital. Well over one year later, she suffered abdominal and back pain. An orthopedic surgeon removed an osteoid osteoma from her spine. The student's mother asked a New York trial court for permission to file a late claim against the school district. The court agreed and the school district appealed. The New York Supreme Court, Appellate Division, held that it was appropriate to allow the mother to file the late claim since the full extent of the student's injuries were not immediately known. In addition, the school district was not prejudiced by the late filing since it was aware of the accident on the day it occurred. *Lamica v. Malone Central School Dist.,* 580 N.Y.S.2d 93 (A.D.3 Dept.1992).

B.   Governmental Immunity

The parent of a Utah junior high school student complained to his school and a bus driver that the bus stop at which the student was required to catch the bus was dangerous because he had to cross a busy street each morning. The school and driver refused to respond to the complaints. The student was struck and killed by a third party vehicle just before the bus arrived at the bus stop one morning. The parents filed a wrongful death lawsuit against the district and school bus driver, claiming negligent placement of the bus stop and failure to activate the emergency lights of the bus at the time of the accident. The court granted summary judgment to the school district and driver, and the parents appealed to the Court of Appeals of Utah. The court of appeals determined that under Utah law, emergency lights could only be activated when the bus was in a stopped position. Because the bus was still approaching the scene when the student had been killed, the driver had not violated any statute and as a matter of law was not negligent in failing to activate the bus lights. The decision to locate bus stops was made on the basis of the entire school system and required district employees to use basic policy judgment. Accordingly, the district was entitled to immunity from liability in the implementation of its policies. Because the trial court had correctly determined that the district was immune from suit, the court of appeals affirmed the summary judgment order. *Smith v. Weber County School Dist.,* 877 P.2d 1276 (Utah App.1994).

A Texas public school teacher was separately employed as a bus driver by the county transportation department. The transportation department was a separate county agency with a management board comprised of the 13 school district superintendents from the districts to which the department provided transportation. While driving a school bus, the teacher became involved in a traffic accident in which a pregnant woman went into premature labor and gave birth to a child with multiple injuries. The couple alleged that the teacher had caused the accident by failing to obey a stop sign. They sued the school district, county transportation department and teacher in a Texas trial court. The teacher and transportation department settled with the couple and the district filed a summary judgment motion, alleging that it was not the employer of the teacher at the time of the accident. The court granted the motion and the couple appealed to the Court of Appeals of Texas, Texarkana.

The court of appeals determined that in order to create school district liability, an employee must be acting within the scope of general authority at the time of the accident, and acting in furtherance of district business. However, it was possible for an employee to be under the control of two employers at the same time, if service to one employer did not involve abandonment of service to the other. Because there was evidence of joint control of the teacher by both the school district and the transportation department, summary judgment was inappropriate. On remand, the trial court was to determine whether the teacher was under the district's control at the time of the accident, irrespective of her simultaneous employment as a bus driver. *White v. Liberty Eylau School Dist.*, 880 S.W.2d 156 (Tex.App.—Texarkana 1994).

A ten-year-old Michigan student was killed when he was hit by an automobile as he walked to his school bus stop. The student's seven-year-old sister was injured in the same accident. There was evidence that the driver had swerved onto the shoulder, and that the ten-year-old had suddenly stepped into the path of traffic. The student's parents settled claims against the state road commission and the driver of the vehicle in a lawsuit filed in a Michigan trial court. The lawsuit included claims against the school district, the school bus driver and the district director of transportation. The school district and its employees filed a motion for summary judgment which was granted by the trial court. The parents appealed to the Court of Appeals of Michigan. According to the court of appeals, government officials are immune from liability where their "conduct does not amount to gross negligence that is the proximate cause of the injury, or damage." Because the driver of the other vehicle was the proximate cause of the injury, the employees were entitled to statutory immunity, and no liability could be imputed to the school district. The transportation director and the bus driver had not negligently designed bus stop locations or given negligent instructions to students. The trial court decision granting summary judgment for the school district and its employees was affirmed. *Dedes v. South Lyon Comm. Schools*, 502 N.W.2d 720 (Mich.App.1993).

A New Mexico school bus driver picked up students on only one side of a particular road, requiring students who resided on the other side to cross the road each day. A student was struck by a vehicle and injured while crossing the street to reach her bus stop. The bus was not near the site at the time of the accident. The student's parents sued the school district, state board of education, transportation division and other state agencies and officials in a New Mexico trial court, which granted the school and driver summary judgment on the basis of governmental immunity. The parents appealed to the Court of Appeals of New Mexico.

The court of appeals determined that the decision to locate bus stops at particular places was a decision sufficiently related to road maintenance and design so that the school and driver were not entitled to a summary judgment ruling on the issues of immunity and negligent maintenance. The decision to pick up students on only one side of the road conceivably created a dangerous condition which might produce harm at a later time. The driver was not shielded from liability just because the bus was not at the scene of the accident. Because the driver and district might have created a dangerous condition by requiring the student to cross the road, the case was reversed and remanded. *Gallegos v. School Dist. of West Las Vegas, New Mexico*, 858 P.2d 867 (N.M.App.1993).

A Missouri student was injured when he was struck by an automobile after exiting a school bus. The student and his mother sued the school transportation director and the bus company, claiming that the director had negligently failed to designate safe bus stops. A Missouri trial court granted the director's summary judgment motion based upon official immunity and the case was appealed to the Missouri Court of Appeals, Eastern District. The court of appeals held that the director's duties involved the consideration of many factors and required him to exercise professional judgment. Therefore, his duties were discretionary and he was entitled to immunity as a public official. The trial court decision was affirmed and a motion for a rehearing or transfer to the Missouri Supreme Court was denied. *Webb v. Reisel*, 858 S.W.2d 767 (Mo.App.E.D.1993).

A Texas high school student had traveled in a school bus to another school to compete in a marching band contest. After the contest, the student and a friend returned to the empty bus. The bus was parked and the rear emergency door was open. While waiting there, the student attempted to close the door, but in doing so hit her head on the door frame. She sued the school district and the bus driver for damages. A Texas trial court granted summary judgment for the district and driver, and the student appealed. The Texas Court of Appeals, affirmed and the student appealed to the Texas Supreme Court. The supreme court stated that the school district, as a governmental entity, was immune from liability unless that immunity had been waived by the Texas Tort Claims Act (TTCA). The TTCA provides a waiver of immunity if the damage arose from the operation of a motor-driven vehicle; the employee would also be personally liable to the claimant according to Texas law. The court stated that the damages did not arise from the operation of the bus. Here, the bus was parked, empty, and the motor was off. The driver was not aboard, nor were any students aboard. Nor did the student's injury result from the school's practice of loading and unloading students through the emergency door since she was not in the process of doing either when the injury occurred. When an injury occurs on a school bus, but does not arise out of the use or operation of the bus, and the bus is only the setting for the injury, immunity is not waived. Likewise, the bus driver was not personally liable for her injuries. *LeLeaux v. Hamshire-Fannett School Dist.*, 835 S.W.2d 49 (Tex.1992).

VII. WORKERS' COMPENSATION

Employees of school districts are covered by workers' compensation benefits when their injuries result from accidents in the course of employment. Workers' compensation cases are delegated to individual state workers' compensation courts or appeal boards, subject to judicial review.

A mathematics teacher at a Florida junior high school had difficulties with a disruptive student. On one particular day, the student engaged in numerous disruptive activities, including chewing gum, talking to other students, and other unauthorized behavior. The student refused to follow the teacher's order to report to the vice principal. When the teacher attempted to escort the pupil to the office, the student refused. Later, after he had been taken to the disciplinary office, the student returned to the classroom without authorization, and the teacher was forced to remove him to the school's disciplinary room. After returning to the classroom, the teacher suffered a subarachnoid hemorrhage. The teacher made a claim for workers' compensation which was refused. He appealed that determination to the District Court of Appeal of Florida, First District. The appellate court determined that the injury in this case did not arise out of the teacher's employment. In order to show a causal connection between the injury and the employment, the court stated that internal failures of the body must be due to unusual strain or overexertion in a physical sense. Emotional strain is too elusive a factor independent of any physical activity to determine whether a causal connection exists. The court affirmed the denial of benefits. *Zundell v. Dade County School Bd.*, 609 So.2d 1367 (Fla.App.1st Dist.1992).

The court of appeal certified a question to the Supreme Court of Florida concerning the appropriate test for compensation awards in preexisting injury cases involving cardiovascular conditions. The supreme court observed that cases involving cardiovascular injuries were to be analyzed like any other workplace injury. There was no evidence of a preexisting injury in this case. It was inherently unfair to deny the teacher's compensation claim, as it clearly arose from a workplace injury that he would not have encountered except for the disciplinary incident. Because the teacher had suffered a compensable injury that was not attributable to a preexisting condition, the court reversed and remanded the case. In future cases, workers' compensation claimants should have the initial burden of showing no relevant preexisting cardiovascular condition. The burden should then shift to employers to demonstrate the existence of an alleged condition. *Zundell v. Dade County School Bd.*, 636 So.2d 8 (Fla.1994).

A Pennsylvania teacher with over 20 years of experience published a controversial newsletter taking stands on issues including busing, integration, and school discipline. The school principal reprimanded the teacher for using school supplies and copying machines to reproduce his newsletter. After the parents of an African-American student complained about the treatment of their son at a parent/teacher conference, the teacher sent them a newsletter that included comments directed at their son. The school principal reprimanded the teacher and advised him again to quit using school supplies and equipment for his own publication. At the end of the school year, the teacher's position was eliminated because of lack of enrollment in his French class. The district transferred him to another high school. After three years of employment there, the teacher was hospitalized for anxiety. He claimed that the reprimands at his former high school had created an abnormal working environment that caused his mental illness, entitling him to workers' compensation benefits. His claim was denied by the state compensation appeal board based on lack of evidence. The teacher appealed to the Commonwealth Court of Pennsylvania.

The commonwealth court stated that in order to prove a workers' compensation claim on the basis of a work-related mental illness, the claimant had to prove by objective evidence an actual injury caused by extraordinary events or abnormal working conditions. In this case, the teacher's claim was based on his own subjective reaction to appropriate discipline. The transfer to another assignment did not create an abnormal working condition. The court also rejected a claim by the teacher that his First Amendment rights were violated by the reprimands. The court affirmed the compensation appeal board's decision. *Morris v. WCAB*, 647 A.2d 669 (Pa.Cmwlth.1994).

A custodian for a self-insured New Mexico school district suffered a job-related injury and received temporary total disability payments for ten days. She later complained of pain in her shoulder and took medication. An examination over one year later showed a rotator cuff tear. After leaving work, the district paid her total disability benefits for two months. Six months later, the custodian filed a workers' compensation benefits claim and a state compensation judge determined that she had a ten percent physical impairment. However, the statute of limitations began running at the time of her initial claim and had expired by the time she filed her second claim. The judge dismissed her claim, but then awarded the custodian vocational rehabilitation benefits and attorney's fees in excess of the amount she had received in compensation benefits. Both parties appealed to the Court of Appeals of New Mexico.

The court of appeals agreed that the statute of limitations was triggered when an injured employee knew or should have known of the existence of a compensable injury. Because the custodian should have known of her disability prior to initiating her claim, the claim had properly been dismissed. The compensation judge had not abused his discretion in awarding vocational rehabilitation benefits, because these benefits were not subject to the statute of limitations. The legislature intended to treat vocational rehabilitation benefits without a time limitation in the same manner as medical benefits. Even though the award of attorney's fees exceeded the compensation award, there was no abuse of discretion and the court affirmed the compensation judge's decision. *Benavidez v. Bloomfield Mun. Schools*, 871 P.2d 9 (N.M.App.1994).

A Connecticut music teacher was accused of inappropriately touching several elementary students. The accusations were reported in the media and the school board suspended the teacher with pay for four months before terminating his employment. The teacher stated that because of blindness in one eye, he had to lean over students to read music and any touching had been inadvertent. He claimed that the inappropriate touching claims caused him mental distress that led to a nervous breakdown and involuntary hospitalization. He filed a workers' compensation claim, and was awarded benefits by establishing that he had a mental injury that did not flow from his employment termination or result from his own misconduct. The school board appealed to the Supreme Court of Connecticut. The supreme court ruled that the teacher was not legally prevented from receiving a workers' compensation award under the legal doctrine of collateral estoppel, because the hearing officer had not based his decision on any alleged misconduct by the teacher and there was sufficient medical evidence in the record of the teacher's disability. The teacher's injury arose out of and had occurred in the course of his employment, not as a result of his employment termination. It was not necessary for the teacher to prove physical trauma to demonstrate an injury under the act, and the workers' compensation hearing officer's decision was affirmed. *Crochiere v. Bd. of Educ. of Town of Enfield*, 630 A.2d 1027 (Conn.1993).

A Louisiana teacher was struck by a student and received workers' compensation benefits for almost two years before returning to work. She was seen by many specialists, and it was finally determined that she could perform light work. When her eligibility for compensation benefits expired, the teacher returned to work, but within two months, she again alleged that she had been hit by a student. The teacher reported the second injury more than 30 days after the occurrence and resigned at the end of the school year. She then worked for another Louisiana school board for an additional year, and two weeks after the completion of the school year, filed a claim for workers' compensation benefits for both injuries. The state workers' compensation office ruled that the statute of limitations barred a recovery by the teacher, and this result was affirmed by a Louisiana trial court. The teacher appealed to the Court of Appeal of Louisiana, First Circuit.

The court ruled that the teacher's second claim had properly been dismissed because a Louisiana workers' compensation statute barred claims that were filed more than one year after the date of the accident, except where the injury does not become manifest. The teacher had failed to prove that the injuries were not manifest within the one-year period. However, the trial court had incorrectly ruled that the teacher's first compensation claim was barred. This was because the school district had paid her benefits within a three-year period specified in the state workers' compensation statute. The teacher's claim for the first matter nonetheless failed because of a lack of proof of medical expenses. *Lee v. East Baton Rouge Parish School Bd.*, 623 So.2d 150 (La.App.1st Cir.1993).

A Louisiana woman worked as a maid for a school board for approximately four years before a severe mental condition caused hospitalization and subsequent disability. A trial court judge dismissed her claim for workers' compensation benefits because there was "no single precipitating event which could be considered an accident" that caused the disability. The Court of Appeal of Louisiana affirmed the trial court's decision, finding that a mere showing that a mental injury is related to general conditions of employment, or to incidents occurring over an extended period of time, is not enough to entitle a claimant to compensation. Many confrontations and disputes involving the employee had resulted in an accumulation of stress. *Archinard v. Rapides Parish School Board,* 614 So.2d 877 (La.App.3d Cir.1993).

An Oregon school district conducted a program under which students received a free lunch for working in the cafeteria. The district elected to provide workers' compensation coverage to students participating in the program. A fourth grade student who participated in the program was seriously injured while putting away tables in his school cafeteria. He sued the school district for negligence. An Oregon trial court granted the school district's summary judgment motion, ruling that the workers' compensation act was the exclusive remedy for his injuries. The student appealed to the Court of Appeals of Oregon.

On appeal, the student argued that the state workers' compensation act was inapplicable because he was not a covered worker. He argued that since he was under the age of 14, he could not be legally employed under state labor law, and had no ability to enter into a legal contract for employment. The court disagreed, observing that all employed minors, even illegally employed ones, were entitled to coverage under the workers' compensation system. It also ruled that school lunches constituted remuneration under the statute. The student was unable to contradict the school district's evidence that it had elected to make student workers "subject workers" under the statute by filing a written notice with the state workers' compensation director. The court affirmed the summary judgment for the school district. *Clevidence v. Portland School Dist. No. 1*, 866 P.2d 492 (1994).

A bus driver for a public school was injured while driving. He suffered $90,000 in damages, and received partial indemnification from the tortfeasor's insurer and through workers' compensation. A dispute then arose as to whether the school's underinsured motorist (UM) carrier was entitled to reduce benefits paid by the amount received from workers' compensation. A trial court held that the setoff was void as against public policy, and the insurer appealed to the Supreme Court of Nevada. The driver contended that allowing the reduction would permit the insurer to escape paying benefits for which premiums have been paid. The court held that public policy was not violated by the setoff for two reasons: first, the school chose insurance with the setoff provision and thus probably paid less for that coverage. Second, the school was not required to purchase UM coverage. In such an instance, allowing the setoff should lower insurance costs and thereby increase the availability of coverage for public employees. *Continental Casualty Co. v. Riveras,* 814 P.2d 1015 (Nev.1991).

An elementary school teacher in New York volunteered to participate in a donkey basketball game because of the solicitation of the school's principal. She sustained a knee injury while participating in the game, and filed a claim for workers' compensation benefits. The school opposed the claim for benefits, but the workers' compensation board held in favor of the teacher. On appeal to the New York Supreme Court, Appellate Division, the court found that the injury was an accident which arose out of the teacher's employment. The active encouragement by the principal was enough to constitute sponsorship of the game and allow recovery of benefits by the teacher. *Midey v. Romulus Central School District*, 584 N.Y.S.2d 948 (A.D.3d Dept.1992).

A physical education instructor suffered from extensive allergies, including dust, dust mites, weeds, grasses and trees. She also experienced bouts of bronchitis. She then began teaching in a newly constructed gymnasium. Subsequently, she contracted bronchial intrinsic asthma. She filed a claim for workers' compensation benefits, alleging an occupational disability due to "new building syndrome." When benefits were denied, she appealed to the Supreme Court of Kentucky. The court found that the teacher's symptoms had been triggered by substances contained in the environment generally. Since the disability was not work-related, she was not entitled to workers' compensation benefits. *Champion v. Beale*, 833 S.W.2d 799 (Ky.1992).

An attorney officiated at high school football games during the football season. During one game, he broke his leg and sought workers' compensation benefits. The South Carolina Workers' Compensation Commission denied the claim, finding that the official was not an employee because no one had the right to exercise direction and control over the performance of his officiating duties. The official appealed that decision to the Court of Appeals of South Carolina. The court stated that the test to determine whether he was covered was whether the employer had the right to direct the manner or means by which the particular work was accomplished; the method of payment; who furnished the equipment; and the employer's right to terminate the employment. In this case, the school district lacked control of the performance of his work and the method in which he was paid; he furnished his own equipment, and he could not be dismissed once the game began. Therefore, the court affirmed the commission's decision. *Farrar v. D.W. Daniel High School*, 424 S.E.2d 543 (S.C.App.1992).

CHAPTER TWO

FREEDOM OF RELIGION

Page
___

I. ESTABLISHMENT OF RELIGION IN PUBLIC SCHOOLS

The Establishment Clause of the U.S. Constitution's First Amendment provides that "Congress shall make no law respecting an establishment of religion." The Establishment Clause applies to all state government entities, including school districts and universities, through the Fourteenth Amendment. In *Lemon v. Kurtzman*, 403 U.S. 602, 91 S.Ct. 2105, 29 L.Ed.2d 745 (1971), the U.S. Supreme Court devised a three-part test which has since been used in considering whether government practices or enactments violate the Establishment Clause. The *Lemon* test requires that a government practice or enactment must have a secular purpose whose principal or primary effect neither advances nor inhibits religion and does not foster excessive government entanglement with religion. Another important Supreme Court case in this area is *Weisman v. Lee*, 505 U.S. ___, 112 S.Ct. 2649, 120 L.Ed.2d 467 (1992), which prohibits school employees from coercing students to participate in religious programs.

A.   Classroom Religious Activities

1.   Prayers and Bible Readings

A New York board of education directed a principal to have a prayer read aloud by each class in the presence of a teacher at the beginning of each school day. This procedure was adopted on the recommendation of the state board of regents. These state officials had composed the prayer and published it as part of their "Statement on Moral and Spiritual Training in the Schools." The parents of ten students sued the board in a New York state court, insisting that use of this official prayer in the public schools was contrary to the beliefs, religions, and religious practices of themselves and their children. They claimed that the state action violated the Establishment Clause of the First Amendment. The New York Court of Appeals upheld the use of the prayer as long as the schools did not compel any pupil to join in the prayer over the parents' objections. On appeal, the U.S. Supreme Court held that the practice was wholly inconsistent with the Establishment Clause. The Court stated that there could be no doubt that the classroom invocation was a religious activity. Neither the fact that prayer was denomination-ally neutral nor that its observance was voluntary served to free it from the limitations of the Establishment Clause. *Engel v. Vitale*, 370 U.S. 421, 82 S.Ct. 1261, 8 L.Ed.2d 601 (1962).

Following the decision in *Engel v. Vitale*, the Supreme Court struck down two Pennsylvania laws which required scripture reading and prayer at the opening of the school day. In doing so, it formulated the "primary purpose and effects" test, which would later become the first two prongs of the *Lemon* test. Pennsylvania law required that "[a]t least ten verses from the Holy Bible shall be read, without comment, at the opening of each public school on each school day. Any child shall be excused from such Bible reading, or attending such Bible reading, upon written request of his parents or guardian." A family sued school officials to enjoin enforcement of the statute as violative of the First Amendment. A three-judge district court panel held that the statutes violated the Establishment Clause and granted injunctive relief. The school commissioner of Baltimore had also adopted a rule which mandated that at the opening of the school day a chapter of the Bible or the Lord's Prayer would be read without comment. The rule was challenged in the Maryland state court system which eventually reached the conclusion that the rule did not violate the First Amendment.

On appeal, the Supreme Court consolidated the cases and held that both rules violated the Establishment Clause. The Court reiterated the premise of *Engel v. Vitale*, above, that neither the state nor the federal government can constitution-ally force a person to profess a belief or disbelief in any religion. Nor can it pass laws which aid all religions as against nonbelievers. The Court stated that the primary purpose of the statutes and rule was religious. The Court also noted that it was intended by school officials to be a religious ceremony. The compulsory nature of the ceremonies was not mitigated by the fact that students could absent themselves from the ceremonies. *Abington School District v. Schempp*, 374 U.S. 203, 83 S.Ct. 1560, 10 L.Ed.2d 844 (1963).

The U.S. Supreme Court struck down an Alabama statute allowing meditation or voluntary prayer in public school classrooms. The case was initiated in 1982 by the father of three grade school children who filed a lawsuit in U.S. district court challenging the validity of two Alabama statutes: a 1981 statute that allowed a period of silence for "meditation or voluntary prayer"; and a 1982 statute authorizing teachers to lead "willing students" in a nonsectarian prayer composed by the state legislature. The district court declared that the First Amendment to the U.S. Constitution did not prohibit the state of Alabama from establishing a state religion. The father appealed to the U.S. Court of Appeals, Fifth Circuit, which reversed the district court's ruling and held that both statutes were unconstitutional. The state of Alabama then appealed to the U.S. Supreme Court, which agreed to review only that portion of the court of appeals' decision which invalidated the 1981 statute allowing "meditation or voluntary prayer." The Supreme Court reviewed the legislative history of the 1981 statute and concluded that the intent of the Alabama legislature was to affirmatively re-establish prayer in the public schools. The inclusion of the words "or voluntary prayer" in the statute indicated that it had been enacted to convey state approval of a religious activity and violated the first prong of the *Lemon* test and the First Amendment Establishment Clause. *Wallace v. Jaffree*, 472 U.S. 38, 105 S.Ct. 2479, 96 L.Ed.2d 29 (1985).

A Texas school district encouraged recitation of the Lord's Prayer before and after basketball games, during regularly scheduled physical education classes, sporting events, school board meetings, graduation ceremonies, PTA meetings and other events. Bibles were also made available to students, the school choir routinely sang Christian songs, and a history teacher taught the Biblical version of creation. A student who had recently moved to the school district played on the girls' basketball team. She initially participated in the prayers, but her father then complained to school officials, who refused to change school practices. When the student and her parents filed an action for injunctive relief against the school district and its officials, the basketball coach required the student to stand outside the "prayer circle" while the other players and coaches prayed. The student alleged that she was ostracized by other students and alleged that her history teacher called her a "little atheist" during a lecture. The U.S. District Court for the Northern District of Texas granted the student's motion for injunctive relief, restraining the school district from requiring student participation in prayer and religious activities initiated by school officials.

The U.S. Court of Appeals, Fifth Circuit, affirmed the trial court order. The court of appeals then withdrew its opinion and substituted an opinion affirming the temporary injunction, but modifying its prior ruling that a religious group which sought to intervene on behalf of Texas school children should not be permanently barred from intervening at later stages of the lawsuit. (The matter had yet to go to trial and the district court's decision was not permanent.) The district's policy clearly violated the First Amendment's Establishment Clause because the prayers led by faculty members exerted coercive pressure upon students to participate in religion. *Doe v. Duncanville Indep. School Dist.*, 994 F.2d 160 (5th Cir.1993).

2. Other Religious Activities

A 1941 Illinois statute designated Good Friday as a school holiday. A Chicago public school teacher filed a lawsuit in the U.S. District Court for the Northern District of Illinois, claiming that the statute violated the First Amendment to the U.S. Constitution and the Illinois Constitution. The teacher named the state education superintendent, Chicago Board of Education and several officials as defendants, and the parties filed cross-motions for summary judgment. The court observed that Christians observed Good Friday as one of their holiest days. However, members of other religions had to request accommodations for such special treatment on their holy days. Unlike Christmas and Thanksgiving, which have both secular and religious features, Good Friday had no secular aspect and was associated only with Christianity. The recognition of Good Friday as a holiday did more than merely accommodate the Christian religion. Recognition of the holiday conveyed the impermissible message that Christianity was a favored religion in Illinois. Passage of the act recognizing the holiday was primarily motivated as an official endorsement of the holiday's religious message. Accordingly, the court granted summary judgment to the teacher, holding that the holiday designation violated the Constitution. *Metzl v. Leininger,* 850 F.Supp. 740 (N.D.Ill.1994).

Two extension students at UCLA, who were members of the Church of Scientology, instituted a federal court action against the Regents of the University of California, among others, asserting that they had violated the First Amendment of the U.S. Constitution by reimbursing a professor at the university for his participation at a conference which allegedly attacked Scientology. The federal district court examined the Establishment Clause issue and determined that the plaintiffs could not show an Establishment Clause violation. First, they alleged no facts to suggest that UCLA's general policy of reimbursing its professors for certain extracurricular expenses was motivated by a desire to interfere with religion. Rather, the policy encouraged the legitimate secular purpose of fostering academic expression and the free exchange of ideas. Second, they alleged no specific inhibition of religion which resulted from this reimbursement policy. The conference did not inhibit their right to practice their faith. Third, to bar UCLA from reimbursing professors for extracurricular activities which are antireligious or proreligious would require an entanglement of church and state which the Establishment Clause prohibits. Finally, the court stated that any form of relief it could grant would raise insurmountable First Amendment concerns. Accordingly, the court dismissed the taxpayers' lawsuit against the regents. *Van Dyke v. Regents of University of California,* 815 F.Supp. 1341 (C.D.Cal.1993).

In 1990, the U.S. District Court for the District of Rhode Island ruled that prayer at a graduation ceremony violated the Establishment Clause of the First Amendment. When this result was affirmed by the U.S. Court of Appeals, First Circuit, it became apparent that review by the U.S. Supreme Court would be sought. The Utah superintendent of public instruction discussed the possibility of contributing $10,000 from state funds to a Rhode Island school committee to assist it in preparation for Supreme Court review. After receiving input from the governor and several state legislators, the superintendent requested the attorney general's office to file a brief in support of the Rhode Island district's position (in favor of public school prayer). A Maryland nonprofit corporation filed a lawsuit in a Utah trial court, seeking an injunction to prevent the filing of the Supreme Court brief and to prevent any expenditure of public funds on the case. The court dismissed the complaint for failure to state a claim upon which relief could be granted and the corporation appealed to the Supreme Court of Utah.

On appeal, the corporation argued that the disbursement of funds violated the Utah Constitution, which prohibits the expenditure of public money for religious purposes, instruction, or the support of "any ecclesiastical establishment." The supreme court observed that the expenditure requested by the superintendent was in support of litigation to determine the constitutionality of a practice, not in support of prayer in public schools or an ecclesiastical establishment. It was impermissible to rule that the state violated a constitutional provision by defending a law in litigation, even if the law was later found to be unconstitutional. The trial court had correctly dismissed the corporation's complaint. *Society of Separationists, Inc. v. Taggart*, 862 P.2d 1339 (Utah 1993).

A Massachusetts school department rented space for a public school at a Roman Catholic parish center. The lease required that the town not use the rented facilities in any manner which was inconsistent with the teachings of the Catholic church, and required the town to rely upon the authority of the Catholic Archbishop of Boston in making this determination. The students attending public school at the parish center were, at times, exposed to religious symbols and periodically greeted by a parish priest. Two families sued to have the lease invalidated as violative of the First Amendment's Establishment Clause. Prior to a trial on this issue, the parents asked the court for a preliminary injunction ordering the school department to reassign the children. The federal district court granted the injunction. Although the lease had an obvious secular purpose, it had the primary effect of endorsing the Roman Catholic religion because the lease conveyed the impermissible message that Catholicism was preferred. The delegation of authority to the archbishop over the school's use of the facility also excessively entangled church and state. The court ordered the department to reassign the children prior to a trial on the merits. *Spacco v. Bridgewater School Dept.*, 722 F.Supp. 834 (D.Mass.1989).

B. Instruction of Students

1. **Curriculum**

In 1981, the Louisiana legislature passed an Act called "Balanced Treatment for Creation-Science and Evolution-Science in Public School Instruction." The Act provided that any school offering instruction in evolution must provide equal time to instruction in creation science. The Act required that curriculum guides be developed and research services supplied for creation science but not for evolution. The stated purpose of the Act was to protect academic freedom. A group of parents, teachers, and religious leaders challenged the law's constitutionality. After a U.S. district court and the U.S. Court of Appeals, Fifth Circuit, both held that the Act was an unconstitutional establishment of religion, Louisiana state officials appealed. The U.S. Supreme Court addressed the issue of whether the Creationism Act was enacted for a clear secular purpose. It noted that because the Act provided for sanctions against teachers who choose not to teach creation science it did not promote its avowed purpose of furthering academic freedom. The Court ruled that "[b]ecause the primary purpose of the Creationism Act is to advance a particular religious belief, the Act endorses religion in violation of the First Amendment." The Creationism Act was therefore declared unconstitutional. *Edwards v. Aguillard*, 482 U.S. 578, 107 S.Ct. 2573, 96 L.Ed.2d 510 (1987).

Parents of five Colorado high school students sued their board of education, board members, and the Colorado commissioner of education, claiming that the district had a statutory or constitutional duty to teach morality in public schools. They claimed that the curriculum of a world literature class which included the classics should be "offset" with Biblical teachings. A Colorado trial court granted dismissal motions filed by the board, board members and commissioner. It also awarded attorney's fees to the commissioner, finding the lawsuit frivolous. The parents appealed dismissal of the claim against the commissioner to the Colorado Court of Appeals. The court of appeals agreed with the trial court that the parents had failed to make out a legally cognizable claim. The Colorado Constitution called for the "maintenance of a thorough and uniform system of free public schools throughout the state," and did not establish education as a fundamental right or impose duties upon the education board. The parents had relied upon a 1927 Colorado case that was overruled by the U.S. Supreme Court's decision in *Abington School Dist. v. Schempp,* above. The parents presented no rational argument based on existing law and thus the appeal was frivolous. Accordingly, the board of education was awarded its attorney's fees. *Skipworth v. Bd. of Educ. of Woodland Park School Dist., RE-2*, 874 P.2d 487 (Colo.App.1994).

In 1987, the New York State Commissioner of Education promulgated regulations requiring all elementary and secondary schools to provide AIDS instruction to students. In public schools, advisory councils had to be established to make recommendations regarding the content, implementation and evaluation of the instruction. The regulations mandated that representatives from religious organizations sit on the councils. No other segment of the community at large was given this preference. The New York State Boards Association sued the education commissioner in a state court, claiming that the regulations violated the Establishment Clause. The trial court upheld the regulations and the state appellate division affirmed. The association appealed to New York's highest court, the Court of Appeals. The court applied the three-part test of *Lemon v. Kurtzman,* and upheld the regulations. First, the court stated that the regulations had the secular purpose of requiring broad community input into AIDS instruction. Second, the regulations did not impermissibly endorse religion because the councils were merely advisory and would not be perceived as providing an endorsement of religious beliefs. Third, the regulations did not impermissibly entangle government with religion since government was not monitoring religious activity and religious institutions were not exercising discretionary governmental functions. *New York State School Bds. Assn. v. Sobol*, 582 N.Y.S.2d 960 (Ct.App.1992).

2. Content of Textbooks

A California school district language arts task force searched for a new set of elementary textbooks. It publicly displayed six sets of books under consideration for over three months, published a notice in the local newspaper, addressed a school parents' association and held open houses to review textbooks. The board obtained approval from the state board of education to purchase a set of textbooks. The textbook series that was eventually selected was the unanimous choice of grade-level representatives and there was no complaint about the series until halfway through the following school year, when two sets of parents filed complaints resulting in the appointment of a review committee of teachers and parents. When one parent was refused appointment to the committee, she filed a lawsuit in a California trial court, seeking an order that the school board actions had violated her constitutional rights and California state open meetings laws.

The California Court of Appeal, First District, affirmed the trial court's decision that the school board had not violated any constitutional rights of the parents. Evidence indicated that the school board had provided parents with appropriate notice and time to evaluate the textbooks. However, the school board had violated a state open meetings law by privately viewing a videotape on the subject of censorship entitled "Holy Wars in Education." The state law defined meetings broadly to include even informal gatherings that included a quorum of public officials. The court remanded a portion of the complaint for a determination of whether the board's violation of the open meetings act required reconsideration of the board's adoption of the textbook series. *Frazer v. Dixon Unif. School Dist.*, 22 Cal.Rptr.2d 641 (Cal.App.1st Dist.1993).

The U.S. Court of Appeals, Sixth Circuit, has ruled that a group of fundamentalist Christian students in Tennessee had to participate in classroom use of the Holt, Rinehart and Winston basic reading series. The court held that the Free Exercise Clause does not require public school textbooks to be free of conflict with students' religious beliefs. Although the Holt series exposed student readers to a multitude of competing ideas and philosophies, some of which were contrary to the students' religious beliefs, requiring the students to read the series did not place an unconstitutional burden on their free exercise of religion. The court of appeals ruled in favor of the school district. *Mozert v. Hawkins County Bd. of Educ.*, 827 F.2d 1058 (6th Cir.1987).

C. School Programs and Ceremonies

1. Commencement Ceremonies

A student and her father filed suit in a federal court against their school district, seeking to prevent prayer at graduation ceremonies for city public schools. A federal district court held that prayer at public school commencement ceremonies violated the Establishment Clause of the First Amendment. The defendants appealed to the U.S. Court of Appeals, First Circuit. The court determined that prayers at a public school violated the Establishment Clause of the First Amendment, and it affirmed the district court's decision.

On appeal to the U.S. Supreme Court, the Court held that including clergy members who offer prayers as part of an official public school graduation ceremony is forbidden by the First Amendment's Establishment Clause. The government may not coerce anyone to support or participate in religion or its exercise, or otherwise act in any way which establishes a state religion or religious faith, or tends to do so. In this case, state officials directed the performance of a formal religious exercise. The principal decided that a prayer should be given, he selected the religious participant, and through a pamphlet which provided guidelines, directed and controlled the prayer's content. The school district's supervision and control of a high school graduation ceremony placed subtle and indirect public and peer pressure on attending students to stand as a group or maintain respectful silence during the invocation and benediction. The state may not force a student dissenter to participate or protest. The argument that the ceremony was voluntary was unpersuasive. The Court affirmed the lower court decision. *Lee v. Weisman*, 505 U.S. —, 112 S.Ct. 2649, 120 L.Ed.2d 467 (1992).

An Idaho school district permitted student leaders to say a prayer at graduation ceremonies if graduating seniors voted to do so by a majority vote. The district took a number of steps to remove the appearance of official approval of prayers and did not attempt to approve their content prior to the ceremony. Objecting students were allowed to receive diplomas without attending the ceremony. Students and parents who objected to the constitutionality of student-led prayer filed a lawsuit against the school district and education officials in the U.S. District Court for the District of Idaho. The court dismissed the challenge to the graduation policy under the Idaho Constitution, observing that the Idaho Supreme Court had not addressed any public school prayer issue and that this question should be left to the state courts. However, it determined that the school district's policy did not violate the Establishment Clause of the U.S. Constitution. The students and parents appealed to the U.S. Court of Appeals, Ninth Circuit.

On appeal, the parents argued that the graduation prayer policy violated the Establishment Clause under the analysis used by the U.S. Supreme Court in *Lee v. Weisman*, above. The school district argued that the court should adopt the reasoning of the U.S. Court of Appeals, Fifth Circuit, in *Jones v. Clear Creek Indep. School Dist.*, below, which determined that student led-prayer at school assemblies was permissible. The Fifth Circuit encompasses the states of Texas, Mississippi and Louisiana, whereas the Ninth Circuit covers most of the western states. The court held that the school district ultimately controlled graduation exercises by holding the ceremony on school property at times scheduled by district employees and with the use of district finances. School officials could not relieve themselves of their constitutional duties by delegating them to students, and those who were given power over state-sponsored events were required to operate within the same constitutional restraints as state actors. State involvement and the traditionally obligatory nature of student attendance at graduation ceremonies made graduation prayer unconstitutional. The court held that the district's policy violated the Establishment Clause of the U.S. Constitution, and reversed that portion of the district court's decision. *Harris v. Joint School Dist. No. 241*, 41 F.3d 447 (9th Cir.1994).

A Florida school board responded to the U.S. Supreme Court's decision in *Lee v. Weisman*, above, by revising its policy for graduation exercises. The policy vested the graduating senior class with the discretion to choose opening and closing messages of two minutes or less to be given by a student volunteer selected by the senior class. Significantly, the policy required that a student volunteer prepare the message without supervision or review by the school board, school officers or employees. The senior classes at ten of the district's 17 high schools voted for a prayer, while the remaining seven schools voted for a secular message or no message. A group of graduating seniors and a parent filed a lawsuit against the board in the U.S. District Court for the Middle District of Florida, claiming violations of their rights under the Establishment Clause. The parties filed cross-motions for summary judgment.

The court applied the analysis from the *Lee* case along with that of *Lemon v. Kurtzman*, above. The graduation policy did not violate the *Lemon* test because it had a secular purpose that did not have the primary effect of advancing or endorsing religion, and did not excessively entangle the school district with religion. Evidence indicated that the policy had a primarily secular purpose of safeguarding the free speech rights of participating students and refraining from content-based regulations. The policy was entirely neutral on the subject of prayer and did not mention that students should opt for prayer, or for any message at all. The case also complied with *Lee* because it did not involve coercion of students by school officials. The court granted the school board's motion for summary judgment. *Adler v. Duval County School Bd.*, 851 F.Supp. 446 (M.D.Fla.1994).

An American Civil Liberties Union representative sent a letter to Tennessee public school officials advising them that the U.S. Supreme Court's decision in *Lee v. Weisman*, above, prohibited prayers at graduation ceremonies. The letter threatened "that if your school system does sponsor prayer at its graduation ceremonies and we are contacted by students and their families, we will most likely pursue litigation." A high school principal who received a copy of the letter refused to authorize a student request to give a prayer at the school's graduation ceremony. Several students recited *The Lord's Prayer* without permission at their graduation ceremony but the ACLU did not commence a lawsuit. The principal then filed a lawsuit against the ACLU in a Tennessee county court for a declaration that student-led prayers at graduation ceremonies did not violate the state or U.S. constitutions. The ACLU removed the case to the U.S. District Court for the Middle District of Tennessee and filed a dismissal motion. The court stated that federal court jurisdiction extends only to cases and controversies and that the principal was not entitled to an advisory opinion. In this case, it was unclear who the parties would be should the ACLU follow through with its threatened litigation. Because of the hypothetical nature of the controversy, the court lacked jurisdiction to consider the case. The court refused to dismiss the case as requested by the ACLU, instead remanding it to the state court for the resolution of questions of Tennessee law. *Oldham v. ACLU Foundation of Tennessee, Inc.*, 849 F.Supp. 611 (M.D.Tenn.1994).

A Virginia school district permitted student-initiated graduation prayers if the senior classes at its four high schools voted for them. The U.S. District Court for the Eastern District of Virginia granted a preliminary injunction requested by students objecting to the prayer. The U.S. Court of Appeals, Fourth Circuit, lifted the injunction. The parties then submitted stipulated facts and made oral arguments to the court in lieu of a trial. The school board argued that a student-initiated graduation prayer was constitutionally permissible because it lacked coercive, impermissible government involvement. The students argued that any prayer in a graduation ceremony violated the Constitution regardless of the manner in which the prayer was made or selected. The court agreed with the students, ruling that a constitutional violation inherently occurs when a prayer is offered in a high school graduation ceremony, regardless of who makes the decision and authorizes the actual wording. The state's sponsorship of the graduation ceremony was inherent and could involuntarily subject a student to a display of religion that might be found offensive. This would constructively exclude the student from participating in graduation and offend the Establishment Clause. The court issued a permanent injunction forbidding the school board from permitting prayer at its graduation ceremonies. *Gearon v. Loudoun County School Bd.*, 844 F.Supp. 1097 (E.D.Va.1993).

A group of Iowa taxpayers sought a preliminary injunction from a federal district court, seeking to prevent two school districts from permitting their graduating seniors to read invocations or benedictions at graduation ceremonies. The court granted the order and the school districts appealed to the U.S. Court of Appeals, Eighth Circuit. The court ruled that the taxpayers had failed to establish any logical link between their status as taxpayers and the alleged constitutional infringement. The taxpayers did not live within the school districts and were not parents of students attending either district. Because the taxpayers had no standing to bring the lawsuit, the district court's injunction was vacated and the action dismissed. *Friedmann v. Sheldon Comm. School Dist.*, 995 F.2d 802 (8th Cir.1993).

Two Texas High school students brought suit in a federal trial court complaining that the high school's policy and actions permitting invocations consisting of traditional Christian prayer at high school graduation ceremonies violated the First Amendment's Establishment Clause. Three weeks before trial, the school board of trustees drafted a resolution which provided that the use of an invocation or benediction at high school graduation would rest with the discretion of the senior class, be given by a student volunteer, and be nonsectarian and nonproselytizing in nature. The federal district court found for the school district and the students appealed to the U.S. Court of Appeals, Fifth Circuit. Invocations at graduation ceremonies may serve a legitimate secular purpose if they solemnize public occasions. Moreover, the court stated that it was unaware of any exclusively secular equivalent for the solemnization choice. The court determined that the resolution allowed invocations to enhance the significance of graduation while minimizing any governmental advancement of religion. By requiring that invocations be nonsectarian and presented by student volunteers, the resolution effectively excluded religious institutions from its purview. The court of appeals affirmed the decision of the district court.

The students appealed to the U.S. Supreme Court, which granted review and vacated the court of appeals' decision. The Court remanded the case, ordering the court of appeals to reconsider it in light of *Lee v. Weisman*, above. On remand, the court of appeals stated that the Supreme Court's decision in *Lee* did not affect its decision. The seniors at the high school made the decision to give a prayer, not school officials. Because there had been no coercion by school district employees, the court reaffirmed its decision and allowed the graduation prayers. *Jones v. Clear Creek Independent School Dist.*, 977 F.2d 963 (5th Cir.1992).

2. Other Programs

A Mississippi high school principal allowed a student to say a prayer over the school's intercom system. The school district board of trustees voted to suspend the principal for the rest of the school year and part of the following summer for "lack of professional judgment." The principal appealed this decision to a Mississippi trial court, which reinstated the principal with backpay. The court further ordered the district to draft guidelines for school prayer consistent with its opinion. The board appealed to the Supreme Court of Mississippi, and filed motions for stay upon appeal and to stay execution of the trial court order pending appeal. The court stated that the board's motion to stay the award of backpay and costs and to stay the order to draft prayer guidelines should be granted. However, the board had failed to show a strong probability of succeeding on the merits of its decision to suspend the principal. It could not demonstrate irreparable harm if the principal was reinstated pending appeal because his presence at the school would present no harm to the public. The court granted the board's motion to stay execution pending appeal on the backpay, costs and prayer guideline issues, but denied the motion on the issue of reinstatement. *Bd. of Trustees of Jackson Pub. School Dist. v. Knox*, 638 So.2d 1278 (Miss.1994).

Following the public outcry resulting from the suspension and threatened termination of the principal, the Mississippi legislature passed a statute allowing student-led prayer in schools. The statute permitted "nonproselytizing student-initiated voluntary prayer" at all assemblies, sporting events, commencement ceremonies and other school-related events. The American Civil Liberties Union (ACLU) joined students and parents opposed to school prayer in a lawsuit seeking an order to prevent enforcement of the statute. The U.S. District Court for the District of Mississippi considered the ACLU's motion for a preliminary injunction and a motion to dismiss the lawsuit by the state attorney general.

The court commented that the statute failed to define the word "assembly" and extended the right of prayer to students and "others" on school property. The court found little merit to most of the arguments advanced by the attorney general in support of the legislation. By its nature, most prayer on school grounds could lead to the conclusion that the state was approving of the prayer. As written, the statute could disrupt instructional and education activities throughout the school system. Any compulsory event might include a prayer, and with it came the danger of perceived government approval. Because other courts had held that student-initiated invocations and benedictions at high school commencement ceremonies did not violate the constitution, the court upheld the right of students to say prayers at commencement ceremonies. However, it enjoined the enforcement of the statute at all other school-related activities as violative of the Establishment Clause of the First Amendment to the U.S. Constitution. *Ingebretsen v. Jackson Pub. School Dist.*, 864 F.Supp. 1473 (S.D.Miss.1994).

A Florida public elementary school celebrated Halloween by decorating the school with pictures of witches, pumpkins and other typical holiday symbols. Some teachers dressed as witches and other characters. The parent of a student attending the school claimed that the depiction of witches constituted the establishment of a religion by the school. The parent kept his children home on Halloween, and filed a lawsuit in a Florida district court, seeking an order to permanently bar the school from portraying witches in Halloween celebrations. He claimed that Halloween was a religious holiday. The school board argued that it had permitted Halloween activities in a secular manner with no attempt to promote witchcraft. School officials argued that they simply sought to make Halloween a fun day for students and to promote educational purposes by enriching the educational and cultural awareness of students. The court ruled that the use of Halloween symbols did not constitute the establishment of religion. The parent appealed to the District Court of Appeal of Florida, First District.

The court of appeal stated that the public school celebration of Halloween did not violate the Establishment Clause of the First Amendment. Although witches and cauldrons might convey a religious message to some, the context in which the symbols were displayed determined whether a constitutional violation existed. In this case, the symbols were not displayed in a manner that endorsed or promoted religion and there was no danger of any public perception of school endorsement. The district court had properly granted summary judgment to the board. *Guyer v. School Bd. of Alachua County*, 634 So.2d 806 (Fla.App.1st Dist.1994).

The Detroit Board of Education invited Louis Farrakhan to speak at a fundraiser to benefit a public elementary and secondary school known as the Malcolm X Academy. Although the speaking engagement was privately funded, it was to be held at a Detroit public high school. A group opposed to the appearance of Farrakhan filed a motion for a preliminary injunction prohibiting him from speaking at the fundraiser and alleging violations of their First and Fourteenth Amendment rights. The U.S. District Court for the Eastern District of Michigan considered the application under the test developed by the U.S. Supreme Court in *Lemon v. Kurtzman*, above. The court determined that the appearance of the speaker had a primarily secular purpose of discussing self-pride among Detroit's black youth and providing access to an alternative political speaker. The fact that the speaker had a religious affiliation did not defeat the government's secular purpose. Despite Farrakhan's allegedly hostile statements concerning Jews, his appearance was not a constitutional violation. The fundraiser was voluntary and not a required school activity in which participation was coerced. The court refused to grant the preliminary injunction. *S.A.F.E. v. Detroit Bd. of Educ.*, 815 F.Supp. 1045 (E.D.Mich.1993).

A Wyoming school district opened its facilities to the public, so long as the public use did not interfere with school activities. A group of graduating senior class officers arranged for a baccalaureate ceremony which was "sponsored by the community." The ceremony was scheduled to take place in the school gymnasium and the student officers contacted a printer to publish announcements. More than one month after the officers obtained verbal authorization for use of the gym, the school board adopted a new policy which prohibited them from using the gymnasium for the service, because of its fear that the ceremony might violate the Establishment Clause of the U.S. Constitution. The seniors sought declaratory and injunctive relief in a lawsuit filed in the U.S. District Court for the District of Wyoming. The court observed that there was little danger of the appearance of state sponsorship of this privately sponsored ceremony. The board had changed its constitutionally permissible open access policy for one that was applied to the student group in a discriminatory manner and that violated their First Amendment free speech rights. The alteration of the free access policy based on a particular point of view was a constitutional violation. Accordingly, the court granted the injunction and restrained the school district from enforcing its revised policy. *Shumway v. Albany County School Dist. No. 1 Bd. of Educ.*, 826 F.Supp. 1320 (E.Wyo.1993).

D. Use of Public School Facilities for Religious Purposes

1. Noninstructional Hours

A nondenominational religious club met at a Missouri junior high school for four years. Several school district residents then complained about the club's meetings, and the board revised its policy to exclude use of school district facilities to all groups except scouts and school athletic teams between 3 and 6 p.m. on school days. The club filed a lawsuit against the school district in the U.S. District Court for the Eastern District of Missouri, seeking declaratory and injunctive relief. The court held a trial and ordered judgment for the school district. The club members appealed to the U.S. Court of Appeals, Eighth Circuit, which held that the amended school use policy discriminated against free speech rights on the basis of content. In general, where a government entity establishes a public forum, it may not restrict speech on the basis of content. In this case, it was apparent that both the club and scouting organizations were programs concerned with the development and reinforcement of moral values. Accordingly, the amended use policy unconstitutionally denied the club access based on its religious perspective. The court of appeals reversed and remanded the district court's judgment. *Good News/Good Sports Club v. School Dist. of the City of Ladue, Missouri*, 28 F.3d 1501 (8th Cir.1994).

New York Education law authorized local school boards to pass regulations which allowed the use of school property in specified ways. The law did not expressly authorize use of school grounds for religious purposes. A local school board issued regulations allowing social, civic, or recreational uses as well as limited use by political organizations, but provided that the school not be used for religious purposes. An evangelical church sought permission to use school facilities to show a film series on traditional Christian family values. The district denied permission to use its facilities because the film was religious. The church filed a lawsuit in a federal court alleging that the district's decision violated its rights under the First Amendment. The district court determined that the school district's action was "viewpoint neutral" and held for the district. The U.S. Court of Appeals, Second Circuit, affirmed, holding that public school facilities were a "limited public forum" and that the district could exclude certain groups provided that the exclusion was "reasonable and viewpoint neutral." The church appealed to the U.S. Supreme Court.

The Court determined that exclusion of the subject matter because of its religious content would impermissibly favor some viewpoints or ideas at the expense of others. Therefore, the regulation discriminated on the basis of viewpoint. The exclusion of this particular church from using school property was not viewpoint neutral. Next, the Court determined that since the film series was not to be shown during school hours and was to be open to those outside the church, the public would not perceive the district to be endorsing religion. Since use of school facilities by the church did not violate the test articulated by the Court in *Lemon v. Kurtzman*, permission by the school district would not violate the Establishment Clause. The film had a secular purpose, its primary effect did not advance religion and the showing of the film would not "foster excessive state entanglement with religion." Thus, speech about "family and child related issues" from a religious perspective could permissibly be aired on public school grounds. The Court reversed the lower court decisions. *Lamb's Chapel v. Center Moriches Union Free School Dist.,* 113 S.Ct. 2141, 124 L.Ed.2d 352 (1993).

Students at a Washington high school sought permission from school officials to form a religious club and to meet on school grounds before school for prayer, bible study and religious discussion. Even though the school district permitted a number of other student groups to meet on school grounds during noninstructional time, it denied the students' request on the ground that such meetings would violate both the Washington and U.S. Constitutions. The students then brought suit against the school district, claiming that the Equal Access Act required the school to allow them to meet on the same basis as other noncurriculum-related clubs. The district court held that the Equal Access Act did not apply to the school because it did not have a limited open forum. The U.S. Court of Appeals, Ninth Circuit, affirmed, but the U.S. Supreme Court vacated its decision and remanded the case for reconsideration in light of *Board of Education v. Mergens,* 496 U.S. 226, 110 S.Ct. 2356, 110 L.Ed.2d 191 (1990). The district court concluded on remand that the school had created a limited open forum by allowing several noncurriculum-related student groups to meet on school grounds. However, it then held that the Washington Constitution precluded requiring the use of school premises by a religious club. The students again appealed to the U.S. Court of Appeals, Ninth Circuit.

The court of appeals reversed the district court's decision. The district court had held that religious group meetings were unconstitutional within the meaning of the Equal Access Act because such meetings would violate the Washington Constitution, which contained a more restrictive Establishment Clause than the one contained in the U.S. Constitution. The appellate court, however, noted that the Act was most logically understood as authorizing schools to bar meetings that were unlawful for reasons other than their religious content. The Act was clearly intended to prohibit schools from discriminating on the basis of content and gave the students a right to meet on school property on the same basis as other noncurriculum-related clubs. *Garnett v. Renton School Dist. No. 403*, 987 F.2d 641 (9th Cir.1993).

Students at a Pennsylvania high school sought to establish a gospel choir at the school. They asked a school secretary to head and direct the choir. Virtually every song performed by the choir prior to the initiation of the lawsuit at issue contained some reference to God or Jesus Christ. Also, the members of the choir routinely prayed together before practices and performances. The high school's president subsequently wrote a letter to the choir director expressing concern that the current structure of the choir violated the Equal Access Act. A group of student members then sued the school district alleging that their constitutional rights had been violated by school district policy. The U.S. District Court for the Eastern District of Pennsylvania noted that the Equal Access Act provides that no school employee can be present at religious meetings in a participatory capacity and that nonschool persons may not regularly attend religious meetings with students on school premises. Here, although the act entitled students to have access to the premises to engage in choir activities, the activities had to be student-led and initiated. However, the choir here was led by a school employee; thus, the court ordered the choir to either continue its activities without change away from the high school's facilities or to adjust its activities to comply with the Equal Access Act if it wished to have continuing access to the high school. *Sease v. School Dist. of Philadelphia*, 811 F.Supp. 183 (E.D.Pa.1993).

An Indiana elementary school maintained a policy which permitted the distribution of religious literature by any organization. Once a year, the Gideons distributed Bibles to the fifth grade class. Usually, the Gideons sent two representatives to each of the five classrooms of fifth graders, always during regular school hours. They spoke for a minute or two about their organization, encouraged the students to read the Bible, and offered a stack of Bibles placed on a table or desk. During certain years, the Bibles were distributed not in classrooms but in the auditorium or gymnasium. On these occasions the fifth graders were assembled in the auditorium for a short presentation by the Gideons. The father of two elementary school students filed suit in a federal district court alleging that the distribution of the Bibles violated the Establishment Clause. The district court held that the distribution did not violate the Establishment Clause. The father then appealed to the U.S. Court of Appeals, Seventh Circuit.

The court of appeals held that the policy of allowing the Gideons to distribute the Bibles violated the Establishment Clause. The court stated that this was not a case in which a religious group sought access to classroom facilities which had been made available to the general public. Instead, it was access to the children that the Gideons were seeking. The court stated that it was doubtful they would have sought access to the classrooms were they not populated by young children. Further, the mandatory nature of the distributions further put the seal of state endorsement on the distribution. The decision of the district court was reversed. *Berger v. Rensselaer Central School Corp.*, 982 F.2d 1160 (7th Cir.1993).

However, Bible distribution on a public sidewalk was allowed in Illinois. A federal district court noted that while school grounds are generally not considered public forums, sidewalks are. The court found that the sidewalk in front of the school was a public forum since nothing alerted individuals that the sidewalk was school property and nothing was posted that restricted the public's use of the sidewalk. *Bacon v. Bradley-Bourbonnais High School Dist.*, 707 F.Supp. 1005 (C.D.Ill.1989).

Until 1989, an Alabama high school sponsored a religious baccalaureate service for all graduating seniors and their families. The school board then eliminated this service as part of a new policy which prohibited "prayer at a school function." Several local churches organized unofficial services held at local churches. However, the churches proved to be too small, so the organizations applied to the school district, seeking to rent the high school auditorium. The school district denied the request and the church filed this action in a federal district court asking for a preliminary injunction forcing the school board to rent the high school for the spring service. The court concluded that the auditorium had been designated as a public forum. Next, because the auditorium was a public forum, the court had to strictly scrutinize the school board's refusal to make it available to the church. The only justification was that allowing the services to take place might violate the Establishment Clause. The court stated that the board need not prohibit the church's use of the auditorium, but that it should take all additional measures reasonably necessary to disassociate the board completely from the service. The court granted the preliminary injunction and instructed the board to take all additional measures to disassociate itself from the baccalaureate service. *Verbena United Methodist Church v. Chilton County Bd. of Educ.*, 765 F.Supp. 704 (M.D.Ala.1991).

A nonprofit religious organization sought to use a Maine high school cafeteria on a weekend evening in December for a Christmas dinner which was free of charge and open to the public. The organization wished to engage in religious speech during the dinner. The school denied the organization the use of the facilities and it brought suit in a federal district court seeking an injunction requiring the school to lease its facilities. The trial court found for the organization and determined that the school had created a public forum. The school district then appealed to the U.S. Court of Appeals, Fifth Circuit. The school alleged that it was barred by the First Amendment from leasing the school facilities to the religious organization because the organization wished to proselytize Christianity and to encourage those at the dinner to join. The court noted that the school could institute reasonable time, place, and manner regulations, but they had to be narrowly drawn to effectuate a compelling state interest. A recent list of users of the school facilities indicated that many of the groups sought to enlist members. Therefore, the court ruled that the school district had excluded the organization based on the content of speech, resulting in a constitutional violation. The court granted the organization's injunction request. *Grace Bible Fellowship v. Maine School Admin. Dist. #5*, 941 F.2d 45 (1st Cir.1991).

2. Bible Study

A Nebraska high school student wanted permission to begin a Christian Club. The high school permitted its students to join, on a voluntary basis, a number of groups and clubs which met after school. The school required that each of these clubs have faculty sponsors. However, the student who wished to start the Christian Club did not have a faculty sponsor. The principal and superintendent both denied the student's request because she did not have a sponsor and because they believed a religious club at the school would violate the Establishment Clause. After the board of education affirmed their decision, the student sued the school board, the superintendent, and the principal in a federal district court. She alleged a violation of the Equal Access Act, which prohibits public secondary schools that receive federal funding and that maintain a "limited open forum" from denying equal access to students who wish to meet. The district court ruled in favor of the school, holding that the other clubs at the school related to the school's curriculum and thus, the school was not under the Equal Access Act because it did not have an open forum. The student appealed to the U.S. Court of Appeals, Eighth Circuit, which ruled in her favor. The school appealed to the U.S. Supreme Court, asserting that the Act violated the Establishment Clause.

The Supreme Court stated that the other clubs did not relate to any of the school's curriculum. Thus, the school had to provide a limited open forum to all students wishing to participate in groups. The Act provided that the school could limit activities that substantially interfered with the orderly conduct of the school. The Court also stated that the Act did not violate the Establishment Clause because the Act had a secular purpose and because it limited the role of teachers working with religious clubs. The Supreme Court affirmed the court of appeals' decision, holding that the school violated the Equal Access Act. *Bd. of Educ. of Westside Comm. School v. Mergens*, 496 U.S. 226, 110 S.Ct. 2356, 110 L.Ed.2d 191 (1990).

An Ohio elementary Bible study group had met directly after school since its inception in 1970. An elementary school teacher founded the group and continued to play a significant role in its existence. In an effort to avoid the appearance that the club was sponsored by the school, the Superintendent denied the group's request to begin the program at 3:45, but instead offered to allow the program to commence at 6:30. The club then filed this action in a federal district court asserting that the board violated their First Amendment right to the free exercise of their religion. The club argued that the time was unreasonable and relegated the children to the status of second class citizens. The school board, on the other hand, contended that the later meeting time was necessary to clearly distinguish between school and non-school functions. The board asserted that a nexus had developed between the club and the school which had been forged by the teacher's participation in the club. The court found for the school board, stating that elementary school children were impressionable and did not have the cognitive ability to appreciate the difference between their viewpoint and that of another. *Quappe v. Endry*, 772 F.Supp. 1004 (S.D.Ohio 1991).

A group of students in Idaho wished to form a Christian club which would meet on school grounds. The school district disapproved, contending that allowing such activity would violate the Idaho Constitution. The students contended that the refusal was in violation of the federal Equal Access Act (EAA), and they sought relief in a federal district court. The EAA is applicable to schools which receive federal financial assistance and maintain a "limited open forum." It prohibits these schools from denying equal access to students based on the content of the speech at meetings. A provision in the Idaho Constitution forbids the religious use of public school classrooms. The issue in this case concerned whether federal or state law would prevail under these circumstances. The Supremacy Clause provides that when a federal law "made in pursuance of" the Constitution and a state law are in conflict, the federal law will prevail. Therefore, the court held that when a federal law merely permits some activity, a state is free to restrict that activity. However, where a federal law mandates some activity, a state's laws prohibiting such activity are overruled. The EAA mandates equal access. The school district was ordered to allow the meetings on school property. *Hoppock v. Twin Falls School Dist.*, 772 F.Supp. 1160 (D.Idaho 1991).

3. Teacher Proselytizing

A California high school biology teacher claimed that the theory of "evolutionism" was in reality a government-backed religion. He sought the right to teach creationism in his classes and to discuss religious matters with students outside class. He claimed that the school district and certain individuals had conspired to destroy his career and reputation in violation of his constitutional rights. The school district reprimanded the teacher in writing for proselytizing students and teaching religion in his classes. He filed a lawsuit against the district in the U.S. District Court for the Central District of California under 42 U.S.C. §§ 1983 and 1985(3). The court dismissed the lawsuit and awarded the school district attorney's fees, stating that the claims were frivolous. The teacher appealed to the U.S. Court of Appeals, Ninth Circuit.

The court of appeals found no error in the district court's treatment of the constitutional claims. There was no merit to the teacher's argument that the district violated the Establishment Clause by including evolution in the curriculum as a valid scientific theory. While the U.S. Supreme Court has never held that "evolutionism" or "secular humanism" were religions under the Establishment Clause, the Court has held that belief in a divine creator is a religious belief and not a scientific theory. See *Edwards v. Aguillard*, 482 U.S. 578, 107 S.Ct. 2573, 96 L.Ed.2d 510 (1987), above. The restriction on religious speech during nonclass time served an important state interest in avoiding Establishment Clause violations. The district court had properly dismissed the claim of injury to the teacher's reputation, and the district had not deprived him of any constitutional rights. However, the complaint was not entirely frivolous and the court reversed the award of attorney's fees. *Peloza v. Capistrano Unif. School Dist.*, 37 F.3d 517 (9th Cir.1994).

A physiology professor at the University of Alabama occasionally mentioned his religious beliefs during classes. He also scheduled an after class discussion group entitled "Evidence of God in Human Physiology," which several of his students attended. Although he stated that his remarks were his own personal bias, a group of his students complained to the head of the physiology department. The department head, after meeting with the dean and the school's attorney, drafted a memo directing the professor to stop interjecting his personal religious beliefs in class and not to hold the optional classes. The professor petitioned the president of the university for a rescission of the order, but the president affirmed the restrictions. The professor filed suit in federal court under 42 U.S.C. § 1983 seeking an injunction lifting the restrictions placed on his speech. The professor moved for summary judgment. The trial court determined that the university had created a public forum for the exchange of ideas, and that the university's interests were not sufficient to justify restricting the professor's freedom of speech. The court granted summary judgment in favor of the professor. The university appealed to the U.S. Court of Appeals, Eleventh Circuit. The appeals court rejected the district court's determination that a classroom constituted a public forum. It relied on the U.S. Supreme Court's decision in *Hazelwood School Dist. v. Kuhlmeier*, in which the Court stated that "school facilities may be deemed to be public forums only if school authorities have ... opened those facilities for indiscriminate use by the general public." If the facilities, as in this case, have been reserved for other intended purposes, no public forum has been created. Where no public forum exists, school officials may impose reasonable restrictions on the speech rights of students and teachers. Accordingly, the appeals court held that the professor's classroom was not a public forum; therefore, the university could reasonably regulate the professor's speech. In addition, the court held that the university could prohibit the professor from promoting and scheduling optional classes. The court reversed the district court's judgment. *Bishop v. Aronov*, 926 F.2d 1066 (11th Cir.1991).

4. Religious Artifacts

A Kentucky statute required the posting of the Ten Commandments, purchased with private contributions, on the wall of each public classroom in the state. A group of citizens sought an injunction against the statute's enforcement claiming that it violated the First Amendment's Establishment and Free Exercise Clauses. The Kentucky state courts upheld the statute, finding that its purpose was secular, not religious, and that the statute would neither advance nor inhibit any religion, nor involve the state excessively in religious matters. Utilizing the three-part test first announced in *Lemon v. Kurtzman*, the U.S. Supreme Court struck down the statute. The Court concluded that the posting of the Ten Commandments had no secular purpose. Kentucky state education officials insisted that the statute in question served the secular purpose of teaching students the foundation of western civilization and the common law. The Court stated, however, that the pre-eminent purpose was plainly religious in nature. The Ten Commandments undeniably came from a religious text despite the legislative recitation of a secular purpose. The Court stated that the text here was not integrated into a course or study of history, civilization, ethics, or comparative religion, but simply posted to induce children to read, meditate upon, and perhaps, to venerate and obey them. The Court also stated that it made no difference that the cost of posting the commandments was paid for through private funds and that they were not read aloud. *Stone v. Graham*, 449 U.S. 39, 101 S.Ct. 192, 66 L.Ed.2d 199 (1981).

A Michigan secondary school displayed a portrait of Jesus Christ in a hallway near the gymnasium for at least 30 years. A student filed a lawsuit in the U.S. District Court for the Western District of Michigan, seeking an order to remove the portrait on grounds that its display in a public school violated the Establishment Clause of the First Amendment. The court ordered the school to remove the portrait. The school appealed to the U.S. Court of Appeals, Sixth Circuit. Because the student had graduated since the issuance of the district court's decision, the school district argued that the case was now moot because a case or controversy no longer existed between the parties. The court disagreed, finding that the student continued to come to the school for sports events and other activities. The portrait also had the potential of offending other members of the public. Applying the test set forth by the U.S. Supreme Court in *Lemon v. Kurtzman*, 403 U.S. 602, 91 S.Ct. 2105, 29 L.Ed.2d 745 (1971), above, the court determined that the display of the portrait violated all three parts of the *Lemon* test. Display of the portrait had no secular purpose, advanced religion and entangled the government with religion. Because Christ was important only to Christianity, the portrait had a proseletysing effect that was offensive to non-Christians. The court affirmed the district court's order. *Washegesic v. Bloomingdale Pub. Schools*, 33 F.3d 679 (6th Cir.1994).

A Nebraska school board member resigned his position and withdrew his sixth grade son from school when his son received a Bible from the Gideon Society in the hallway of his school building. The distribution was in violation of the school district's unwritten policy, which permitted Bible distribution by the Gideons to fifth graders once a year on the sidewalk outside school. The school's open forum policy left school grounds and facilities (including sidewalks) available to any person or group after school hours. The distribution was noncoercive and a public address announcement prior to the end of school reminded students that they were not obligated to take a Bible. However, on the given day, the student received a Bible in the school hallway. Although there was no evidence that the school district had any part in the violation of its policy, the board member filed a lawsuit against the district in the U.S. District Court for the District of Nebraska under 42 U.S.C. § 1983.

The court considered summary judgment motions advanced by the parties. It observed that the district had not authorized the hallway distribution. The open forum policy was constitutional, because it had a secular purpose which did not advance religion and did not excessively entangle the district with religion. There was no evidence that any group or person was ever denied access to school facilities under the policy and no danger of a student believing that the district approved of the Bible distribution. No district funds were expended and the Gideons had violated a direct order by the middle school principal to keep their activities outside the building. The court granted the school district's motion for summary judgment. *Schanou v. Lancaster County School Dist. No. 160*, 863 F.Supp. 1048 (D.Neb.1994).

A New Jersey school board policy called for sensitivity to different religions in a manner consistent with the U.S. Constitution. The stated purpose of the policy was to teach about religion and its role in the social and historical development of civilization. The policy called for the maintenance of calendars in classrooms and in one central location which displayed cultural, ethnic and religious customs and traditions of various cultures for no more than ten days "during the appropriate season." A group of parents and taxpayers filed a lawsuit against the school board in the U.S. District Court for the District of New Jersey, claiming violations of the First and Fourteenth Amendments to the U.S. Constitution. The parties filed cross-motions for summary judgment.

In considering the summary judgment motions, the court applied the three-part test of *Lemon v. Kurtzman*. It also considered factors such as the age of the children involved, the context in which the government practice appeared, the permanence of the display, whether the symbol was displayed actively or passively, whether the religious holiday has obtained a secular meaning, whether the government practice endorses a particular religion, and whether it is hostile toward religion. The school board's policy passed the *Lemon* test because it had a genuine purpose that did not impermissibly promote religion and did not entangle the government in church-state relationships. Because of the policy's emphasis on religious diversity, it could not be said to favor any particular religion or to favor religion over nonreligion. The use of religious symbols had a genuine secular purpose that emphasized both tolerance and diversity. The court granted the board's cross-motion for summary judgment and denied the parents' motion. *Clever v. Cherry Hill Township Bd. of Educ.*, 838 F.Supp. 929 (D.N.J.1993).

II.   LIMITATIONS ON THE FREE EXERCISE OF RELIGION

The Free Exercise Clause of the First Amendment provides that Congress shall make no law prohibiting the free exercise of religion. This Free Exercise Clause, like the Establishment Clause, applies to state governmental entities such as school districts and universities through the Fourteenth Amendment. Courts have imposed restrictions on the free exercise of religion where such restrictions serve an overriding public interest.

A.   Students

The University of Missouri at Kansas City, a state university, made its facilities available for the general use of registered student groups. A registered student religious group that had previously received permission to conduct its meetings in university facilities was informed that it could no longer do so because of a university regulation that prohibited use of its facilities for the purposes of religious worship or teaching. Members of the group brought suit against the district in federal court, alleging that the regulation violated their First Amendment rights to free exercise of religion and freedom of speech. The court upheld the school's regulation, but the U.S. Court of Appeals, Eighth Circuit, reversed stating that the regulation was discriminatory against religious speech and that the Establishment Clause does not bar a policy of equal access in which facilities are open to groups and speakers of all kinds.

The Supreme Court agreed with the court of appeals' assessment, stating that the university policy violated the fundamental principle that a state regulation of speech must be content-neutral. It is obligatory upon the state to show that the regulation is necessary to serve a compelling state interest and that it is narrowly drawn to achieve that end. The state was unable to do that here. The state's interest in achieving greater separation of church and state than is already ensured under the Establishment Clause was not sufficiently "compelling" to justify content-based discrimination against religious speech of the student group in question. *Widmar v. Vincent*, 454 U.S. 263, 102 S.Ct. 269, 70 L.Ed.2d 400 (1981).

A Florida school district policy vested the superintendent of schools with broad discretion to restrain the distribution at public schools of any material that was not related to school courses. The policy also described appropriate places for distribution of material that was not course-related. An elementary student who attended school in the district brought religious pamphlets to distribute to her classmates. When she asked her homeroom teacher for permission to distribute the brochures, her teacher confiscated them and brought them to the principal. The principal destroyed the brochures, stating that he could not permit the distribution of religious material at school. The student and her mother filed a lawsuit in the U.S. District Court for the Middle District of Florida, seeking a preliminary injunction against enforcement of the policy. The court held that the motion was premature, and that the school had never actually applied the policy. The U.S. Court of Appeals, Eleventh Circuit, affirmed the district court's decision.

The district court then conducted a trial on the student's request for a permanent injunction against enforcement of the policy. The court observed that the policy was a content-based prior restraint on speech that could only be justified by showing that the speech or literature would materially and substantially interfere with school operations or the rights of other students. In this case, the broad powers accorded to the district superintendent could not be supported under law. The Establishment Clause of the First Amendment to the U.S. Constitution prohibited the government from inhibiting the free exercise of religion. The district could not show that religious speech by students would materially and substantially interfere with school operations or the rights of other students. Accordingly, the student was entitled to a permanent injunction against enforcement of the policy. The court also awarded nominal damages and attorney fees. *Johnston-Loehner v. O'Brien*, 859 F.Supp. 575 (M.D.Fla.1994).

The federal Equal Access Act (20 U.S.C. §§ 4071-4074) protects religious speech by student groups in public secondary schools by establishing "limited open forums." Limited open forums are created when schools allow noncurriculum-related student groups to meet on school grounds during noninstructional time. A New Jersey education board established a policy that allowed only clubs and extracurricular activities that were "related to the curriculum" to meet on school grounds. Accordingly, the school board denied official recognition to a student group calling itself the Bible Club. Because of the lack of official recognition, the club could not use bulletin boards, public address systems and other school facilities. The board revised its policy following the U.S. Supreme Court's decision in *Bd. of Educ. v. Mergens*, above. The board reserved its right to sponsor "co-curricular activities and clubs," limiting official sponsorship to those that would "further the educational goals of the district." The board expressly stated that the revised policy was intended to create a closed forum outside the coverage of the Equal Access Act.

The U.S. District Court for the District of New Jersey granted a summary judgment motion filed by members of the Bible Club, ruling that the board's failure to recognize the club violated the Equal Access Act. The court entered a permanent injunction forbidding the board from interfering with the club's access rights under the Act. The board appealed to the U.S. Court of Appeals, Third Circuit. The court held that the prohibition on student-initiated groups did not make the Equal Access Act inapplicable to the district, inasmuch as its policy did not forbid other student service groups such as the Kiwanis-affiliated Key Club. The school district had established a limited open forum and was required to provide equal access to its facilities. *Pope by Pope v. East Brunswick Bd. of Educ.*, 12 F.3d 1244 (3d Cir.1993).

An Illinois eighth-grade student was religiously active. She volunteered to distribute copies of a religious publication at her junior high school, but the school district had a policy which forbade the distribution of written religious material at elementary and junior high schools. The student sued the district in federal court, claiming that the policy violated her First Amendment right to freedom of speech. The U.S. District Court, Northern District of Illinois, agreed with the student and entered an order preliminarily enjoining the school district from enforcing the policy. In response, the district revised its policy. The new policy no longer barred religious materials; instead, it barred the distribution of religious materials that other students could reasonably believe were school-sponsored and materials not primarily prepared by a student or concerning nonschool-sponsored events. The policy also imposed certain time, place, and manner restrictions on the distribution of the materials that were allowed under the policy. These included specified times of distribution at a table specifically set up by the school district for the purpose of distribution as well as limitations on the number of copies that could be distributed without advance notice. The student amended her complaint, challenging this new policy on the ground that it violated her First Amendment right to freedom of speech. The district court held that the new policy failed to satisfy the mandates of the First Amendment. *Hedges v. Wauconda Community Unit School Dist. 118*, 807 F.Supp. 444 (N.D.Ill.1992).

The school district appealed to the U.S. Court of Appeals, Seventh Circuit. The court of appeals ruled that schools may not prohibit students from expressing ideas and that no governmental agency may discriminate against religious speech when other speech is permitted. The Free Exercise Clause of the First Amendment preserves the right of individuals to speak on religious subjects. Schools do not endorse religious speech simply by permitting it and may avoid Establishment Clause violations by establishing content neutral policies. The court affirmed the district court's ruling on the content portion of the school's policy. However, it reversed the district court's ruling on the time and place restrictions for distributing materials. It was permissible for the school district to create a policy limiting the number of copies that could be distributed without prior permission, because the policy did not treat religious materials differently from other subjects. *Hedges v. Wauconda Comm. Unit School Dist. No. 118*, 9 F.3d 1295 (7th Cir.1993).

A Pennsylvania student distributed religious tracts at his high school. Teachers and school administrators complained that the distributions were affecting activities at the school. The school district then formulated a policy regulating the distribution of non-school-written material. The policy required prior approval by school officials of all material to be distributed, and mandated time, place and manner restrictions. It also prohibited certain types of speech outright, including religious material. The student challenged that policy in federal court. The U.S. District Court for the Eastern District of Pennsylvania held that the content-based ban on religious speech was not narrowly tailored to serve a compelling government interest. The time, place and manner restrictions were also found to be too restrictive, as was the prior approval requirement. The court did allow, however, the case to proceed to trial to determine whether the school officials had reason to anticipate substantial interference with work if the distributions continued. *Slotterback v. Interboro School Dist.*, 766 F.Supp. 280 (E.D.Pa.1991).

A second grade student at a Michigan elementary school wanted to show a videotape of herself singing before the congregation at her church. This showing was to be part of her class's show and tell. The student's teacher and principal agreed that she should not be permitted to show the video. The student and her mother sued. Before the U.S. District Court, Eastern District of Michigan, the school district argued that showing the video was inconsistent with the purpose of the show and tell program, which was designed to develop self esteem through oral presentation in the classroom. The school district also expressed concern about the song's message, stating that the context in which it was presented might give students the impression that the school district endorsed the message of the song. The district court stated that school authorities may regulate the content of student speech in any reasonable manner. The limitations placed on the students were reasonable for the reasons the school district had given. Likewise, the student's free exercise claim failed, because the state had not substantially burdened her religious beliefs. The district court granted summary judgment to the school district. *Deenoyer v. Livonia Public Schools*, 799 F.Supp. 744 (E.D.Mich.1992).

B. Teachers

Two Jehovah's Witnesses applied for positions with the California community college district. According to state mandated preemployment procedures, the district required applicants to sign an oath swearing allegiance to the U.S. and California Constitutions. The applicants refused to take the oath based on their religious beliefs, and the district rejected their applications. They then filed suit against the district under the Religious Freedom Restoration Act (RFRA) in the U.S. District Court for the District of California, challenging the validity of the loyalty oath. The parties moved for summary judgment. The court held that requiring the applicants to take a loyalty oath to be considered for public employment placed an undue burden on their right to free exercise of religion. Although employee loyalty was a compelling state interest, the evidence failed to establish that a loyalty oath was an effective way to achieve this goal. An alternative oath directed to an applicant's actions rather than his or her beliefs would be equally effective and less restrictive. Because the loyalty oath could not be justified under the compelling interest test articulated in the RFRA, the court enjoined the district from administering the oath. *Bessard v. California Comm. Colleges*, 867 F.Supp. 1454 (E.D.Cal.1994).

A Connecticut high school teacher belonged to a church which required its members to refrain from secular employment during designated holy days. This practice caused the teacher to miss approximately six school days each year for religious purposes. The teacher worked under terms of a bargaining agreement between the school board and his teachers' union which allowed only three days of leave for religious observation. The agreement also allowed leave for "necessary personal business" which could not be used for religious purposes. He repeatedly asked permission to use three days of his "necessary personal business" leave for religious purposes. He also offered to pay for a substitute teacher if the school board would pay him for the extra days that he missed. These alternatives were turned down by the school board. When all administrative alternatives were exhausted, he filed a lawsuit alleging that the school board's policy constituted religious discrimination. A U.S. district court dismissed the teacher's lawsuit and he appealed. The U.S. Court of Appeals, Second Circuit, said that the school board was bound to accept one of the teacher's proposed solutions unless that accommodation caused undue hardship. The school board appealed. The U.S. Supreme Court decided that the school district was not required to accept the teacher's proposals even if acceptance would not result in "undue hardship." The school board was only bound to offer a fair and reasonable accommodation of the teacher's religious needs. The bargaining agreement policy of allowing three days off for religious purposes was found to be reasonable. Because none of the lower courts had decided whether this policy had been administered fairly, the case was remanded for a determination of that question. *Ansonia Bd. of Educ. v. Philbrook*, 479 U.S. 60, 107 S.Ct. 367, 93 L.Ed.2d 305 (1986).

After several evidentiary hearings, the district court found that providing the teacher with unpaid leave for religious observance beyond the three-day limit constituted a reasonable accommodation of the teacher's religious needs unless paid leave was provided for all purposes except religious ones. The teacher again appealed to the U.S. Court of Appeals, Second Circuit. The court of appeals held that the findings of fact made by the trial court were not clearly erroneous. Therefore, it affirmed the district court's decision. *Philbrook v. Ansonia Bd. of Educ.*, 925 F.2d 47 (2d Cir.1991).

A Jewish high school teacher in Colorado brought suit against a local school district claiming that the district's policy regarding paid leave time for teachers interfered with the exercise of his religion. A U.S. district court dismissed the teacher's claim but the teacher appealed to the U.S. Court of Appeals, Tenth Circuit, arguing that the school year in the district was arranged so that Christian teachers did not need to use their personal leave time or take unpaid leave to observe religious holidays but that he was forced to use unpaid leave days to celebrate Jewish holidays. The court of appeals held that because paid leave time was a subject of collective bargaining and a school district cannot be expected to negotiate leave policies broad enough to suit every employee's religious needs, the teacher did not have a valid claim. The court found the district's policy reasonable even though it meant that some teachers would be required to take occasional unpaid leaves to observe religious holidays. *Hill v. Bogans*, 735 F.2d 391 (10th Cir.1984).

CHAPTER THREE

FREEDOM OF SPEECH AND ASSOCIATION

I. STUDENTS

Generally, speech outside the classroom is protected if it does not disrupt school activities, infringe on the rights of others or endanger the health or welfare of others. The U.S. Supreme Court has ruled that students may be disciplined for engaging in "offensively lewd or indecent" speech.

A. Protected Speech

A male high school student in Bethel, Washington, delivered a speech nominating a fellow student for elective office before an assembly of over 600 peers. All students were required to attend the assembly as part of the school's self-government program. In his nominating speech, the student referred to his candidate in terms of an elaborate, explicit sexual metaphor, despite having been warned in advance by two teachers not to deliver it. Students' reactions during the speech included laughter, graphic sexual gestures, hooting, bewilderment and embarrassment. When the student admitted that he had deliberately used sexual innuendo in his speech, he was informed that he would be suspended for three days and that his name would be removed from the list of candidates for student speaker at graduation. The student brought suit against the school district in U.S. district court, claiming that his First Amendment right to freedom of speech had been violated. The district court agreed and awarded him damages and attorney's fees. The court also ordered the school district to allow the student to speak at graduation. The U.S. Supreme Court, however, ruled that while public school students have the right to advocate unpopular and controversial views in school, that right must be balanced against the schools' interest in teaching socially appropriate behavior. The Constitution does not protect obscene language and a public school, as an instrument of the state, may legitimately establish standards of civil and mature conduct. *Bethel School Dist. No. 403 v. Fraser*, 478 U.S. 675, 106 S.Ct 3159, 92 L.Ed.2d 549 (1986).

In December 1965, a group of adults and high school students, determined to publicize their objections to the hostilities in Vietnam and their support for a truce, wore black armbands during the holiday season and fasted on December 16 and New Year's Eve. Three students and their parents had previously engaged in similar activities and they decided to participate in this program. The principals of the Des Moines schools became aware of the plan and adopted a policy that any student wearing an armband to school would be asked to remove it, and if he refused he would be suspended until he returned without the armband. The three students wore their armbands and were all suspended until they agreed to come back without the armbands. They did not return to school until the planned protest period had ended. The students sued the school district under 42 U.S.C. § 1983 for an injunction restraining school officials from disciplining the students and for nominal damages. A federal district court dismissed the complaint and the Eighth Circuit Court of Appeals summarily affirmed. On appeal to the U.S. Supreme Court, the decision was reversed and remanded. The Court stated that neither students nor teachers shed their constitutional rights to freedom of speech or expression at the schoolhouse gate. In order for the state to justify prohibition of a particular expression of opinion, it must be able to show something more than a mere desire to avoid the discomfort and unpleasantness that always accompany an unpopular viewpoint. Where there was no evidence that an expression would materially interfere with the requirements of appropriate discipline in the operation of the school, the prohibition was improper. The expressive act of wearing black armbands did not interrupt school activities, nor intrude in school affairs. The expression had to be allowed. *Tinker v. Des Moines Community School Dist.*, 393 U.S. 503, 89 S.Ct. 733, 21 L.Ed.2d 733 (1969).

An Indiana elementary student objected to her grades and proclaimed racial bias at her school by wearing T-shirts reading "unfair grades," "racism," and "I hate [this school]." The principal prohibited the student from wearing the T-shirts at school and subjected her to disciplinary action. The student's parents filed a lawsuit against the principal, county school corporation, a social worker and the county and state departments of public welfare for violations of the student's First Amendment rights. The U.S. District Court for the Southern District of Indiana dismissed the lawsuit, and the parents appealed to the U.S. Court of Appeals,

Seventh Circuit. The court held that the state and local departments of public welfare had properly been dismissed from the lawsuit. The district court had properly granted Eleventh Amendment immunity to these entities, and also properly dismissed the social worker from the lawsuit. Municipalities and local governments could be deemed liable under 42 U.S.C. § 1983 only where they had a policy or custom that violated an individual's clearly established constitutional rights. The complaint also failed to allege that the principal was a policymaker who might be held liable under § 1983. There was no clearly established right of a grade school student to wear an expressive T-shirt. Although the U.S. Supreme Court ruled in *Tinker v. Des Moines Comm. School Dist.*, above, that senior high school students had certain speech rights under the First Amendment, there was no case recognizing such a right for elementary school students. The court of appeals affirmed the order dismissing the lawsuit. *Baxter v. Vigo County School Corp.*, 26 F.3d 728 (7th Cir.1994).

Several racial incidents involving fraternities occurred including one in which fraternity members held a "slave auction" where pledges in black face performed skits parroting black entertainers. In response, the University of Wisconsin instituted a rule which prohibited students from directing discriminatory epithets at particular individuals with the intent to demean them and which created a hostile educational environment. University students brought this action in a federal district court challenging the rule as a violation of their free speech rights under the First Amendment to the Constitution. The court noted that the language regulated by the rule was likely to cause violent responses in many cases. The rule, however, regulated discriminatory speech whether or not it provoked such a response. Accordingly, the court determined that the rule was overbroad and found for the plaintiffs. *UWM Post v. Bd. of Regents of Univ. of Wisconsin*, 774 F.Supp. 1163 (E.D.Wis.1991.

B. Student Publications

1. Elementary and High Schools

High school or elementary school administrators may exercise prior restraint over student publications if a reasonable basis exists for the belief that a publication would materially disrupt class work, involve substantial disorder or invade the rights of others.

A Missouri high school principal objected to two articles which had been prepared for publication in the school newspaper. Because the principal believed that there was no time to edit the articles before the end of the school year, he deleted the two pages on which the articles appeared. Former high school students who were members of the newspaper staff filed a lawsuit against the school district and school officials alleging that their First Amendment rights were violated when the pages were removed from the newspaper before publication.

A U.S. district court ruled in favor of the school district. The U.S. Court of Appeals, Eighth Circuit, then reversed, holding that the newspaper was a public forum "intended to be and operated as a conduit for student viewpoint." The school district filed for review by the U.S. Supreme Court, which agreed to hear the case. The U.S. Supreme Court noted that school facilities, including school sponsored newspapers, become public forums only if school authorities have intentionally opened those facilities for indiscriminate use by either the general public "or by some segment of the public, such as student organizations." The Court determined that since the school district allowed a large amount of control by the journalism teacher and the principal, it had not intentionally opened the newspaper as a public forum for indiscriminate student speech. The Court determined that school officials can exercise "editorial control over the style and content of student speech in school-sponsored expressive activities so long as their actions are reasonably related to legitimate [educational] concerns." Because the decision to delete two pages from the newspaper was reasonable under the circumstances, no violation of the First Amendment had occurred. The Supreme Court ruled in favor of the school district and its officials. *Hazelwood School Dist. v. Kuhlmeier*, 484 U.S. 261, 108 S.Ct. 562, 98 L.Ed.2d 592 (1988).

The principal of a New Jersey junior high school censored two film reviews from the school's official student-written newspaper. The films, *Mississippi Burning* and *Rain Man*, were both R-rated and the principal took the action without notice. A student's mother filed a lawsuit against the school board, superintendent and principal in a New Jersey trial court, claiming violations of the student's constitutional rights to free expression. The court held that the principal's action was reasonably related to the school's legitimate educational concerns under the U.S. Constitution. However, the action violated the student's rights under the state constitution, which afforded broad protection to free speech rights. The Superior Court of New Jersey, Appellate Division, substantially affirmed the trial court's judgment, ruling instead that the censorship violated the First Amendment, but not the state constitution. The school board and officials appealed to the Supreme Court of New Jersey.

The supreme court agreed with the appellate division court's decision, and cited portions of it in its opinion. It agreed that the school newspaper was not a public forum and that school officials could exercise editorial control over style and content in a manner that was reasonably related to legitimate educational concerns. In this case, however, the school board's policy was vaguely defined and had no specific rule concerning R-rated films. There was also evidence that the policy was often ignored or inconsistently applied. The school board and officials failed to establish a legitimate educational policy to govern school publications, and the result was a violation of the student's rights under the First Amendment. *Desilets v. Clearview Regional Bd. of Educ.*, 137 N.J. 585, 647 A.2d 150 (1994).

An Oregon high school student distributed an underground publication at school. He was advised by an assistant principal that the distribution violated school policy. The school's official newspaper then prepared an editorial in support of the underground publication. The principal suspended publication of the editorial and later censored it with school board approval. The board then adopted a regulation concerning unofficial publications. A group of high school seniors, including the student who had distributed the underground publication, filed a lawsuit against school officials in a state trial court, claiming state and federal constitutional violations. The students were joined by a junior high school student in seeking declaratory relief, an order barring enforcement of the regulation and monetary damages. The court dismissed all claims based on the Oregon Constitution and statutes, but determined that censorship of the editorial violated the First and Fourteenth Amendments. The court ordered disciplinary records expunged concerning the underground publication. It declared the regulation constitutional, but ordered the district to refrain from prepublication review of nonschool publications and from disciplining students for distributing nonschool publications. The Oregon Court of Appeals held that the students had failed to present a justiciable controversy because the seniors had graduated and the junior high school student's claim was hypothetical.

The Supreme Court of Oregon reversed the court of appeals' decision concerning the state law claims, finding that only the student who had been disciplined for distributing the underground publication had presented a live controversy, since disciplinary records remained in his file. All other state claims should have been dismissed. The junior high school student's claims were dismissed because of her failure to establish that she would be harmed by the regulation. Although the state law claims of the graduated students failed to present a controversy concerning prospective relief and had been properly dismissed, the court of appeals had erroneously determined that their federal claims were moot because they had graduated. The supreme court ruled that the loss of First Amendment freedoms for even minimal periods of time constituted a compensable injury. Therefore, a justiciable controversy existed concerning the past deprivation of federal constitutional rights. The student who had distributed the underground publication was also entitled to bring a federal claim concerning his disciplinary records. The supreme court remanded the case to the court of appeals for reconsideration of his claims and the federal constitutional claims of the former students. *Barcik v. Kubiaczyk,* 321 Or. 174, 895 P.2d 765 (1995).

A Louisiana high school teacher included a section on the First Amendment in her history class. A student group in the class published a newspaper parody stating that bored students should drop out of school, that students should cheat on tests and that students should practice birth control. The school principal confiscated copies of the newspaper and formally reprimanded the teacher. A federal district court affirmed the action and the teacher appealed to the U.S. Court of Appeals, Fifth Circuit. The court affirmed the district court's decision, ruling that the teacher had failed to overcome evidence that she had been legitimately disciplined for inadequate supervision, neglect and violation of school policies. *Moody v. Jefferson Parish School Bd.,* 2 F.3d 604 (5th Cir.1993).

A Nevada family planning organization sought to advertise its services in a high school newspaper. The school had instituted guidelines which reserved the right to deny advertising space to any entity that did not serve the best interests of the school. Based upon these guidelines, the school denied advertisement space to the organization. The organization then brought this action in federal court seeking injunctive relief for the deprivation of its First Amendment right to free speech. The trial court found for the school and the organization appealed to the U.S. Court of Appeals, Ninth Circuit. The court determined that the advertisements were protected speech under the First Amendment. Thus, the question was whether the newspapers were public forums and if so whether the guidelines were reasonable. The appellate court noted that the newspaper was produced as part of a class in which the teacher and principal exercised control over every issue. Therefore, the court found that the school had not created a public forum. Even if the newspaper was considered a public forum, the guidelines were reasonable. *Planned Parenthood v. Clark County School Dist.*, 941 F.2d 817 (9th Cir.1991).

A teacher was employed at a New Jersey school. The school yearbook contained a section entitled "The Funny Pages," consisting of pictures of students and faculty accompanied by humorous captions. One of the pages in this section contained a picture of the teacher sitting next to and facing another teacher. The second teacher had his right hand raised to his forehead. The caption read "Not tonight Ms. Salek, I have a headache." The teacher sued the school in state court, claiming that the import of the photograph was that the other teacher was declining to accept her proposition to engage in a sexual relationship. The trial court held that the photograph was not defamatory and granted judgment to the school. The teacher appealed to the Superior Court of New Jersey, Appellate Division. The appellate court stated that where, as here, the material is susceptible only to nondefamatory meaning and is clearly understood as being parody, satire, humor, or fantasy, there is no libel. Since there was no defamation, none of the teacher's other tort claims, including invasion of privacy, and emotional distress, were valid. *Salek v. Passaic Collegiate School*, 605 A.2d 276 (N.J.Super.A.D.1992).

2.   Colleges and Universities

The Board of Regents of Oklahoma State University (OSU) temporarily suspended the showing by the university Student Union Activities Board (SUAB) of *The Last Temptation of Christ*, a film depicting Jesus descending from the cross to marry, father children and return to the cross. An association of students and faculty members advocating free speech rights filed a lawsuit in the U.S. District Court for the Northern District of Oklahoma, seeking declaratory relief. The regents lifted the suspension, and the film was shown as originally scheduled. The district court held that school officials could not be held liable for damages under 42 U.S.C. § 1983 and the association appealed to the U.S. Court of Appeals, Tenth Circuit. The court remanded the case to determine whether the association was entitled to nominal damages and whether the regents had qualified immunity from liability. The court determined that the association was not entitled to nominal damages and that the board enjoyed qualified immunity. The association filed a second appeal with the Tenth Circuit.

The court rejected the association's argument that the regents had violated the constitutional rights of its members by imposing content-based censorship. The regents had merely imposed a temporary suspension while obtaining a legal opinion concerning OSU's potential liability if it chose to allow the showing of the film. The regents could not be held liable for violating any clearly-established constitutional rights and the regents' action did not violate constitutional restraints on censorship. Because the SUAB and OSU were closely related in funding and staffing, the regents had merely displayed caution in their decisionmaking process. The association was entitled to an award of attorney's fees for work done before the district court's initial order. *Cummins v. Campbell,* 44 F.3d 847 (10th Cir.1994).

Southwest Texas State University had a policy that forbad the distribution of newspapers that contained advertisements. The university did not regulate the distribution of newspapers or literature without advertisements. The regulation also did not apply to the student-run university newspaper, which contained many advertisements. Aside from these restrictions, the university fostered an environment of free expression. A group of students and a small, politically oriented, local newspaper that had attempted free distribution on campus sued the university, claiming that its "no solicitation" policy violated the First Amendment. A federal district court held for the university and the students appealed to the U.S. Court of Appeals, Fifth Circuit. The court of appeals stated that the university was a limited public forum. As such, regulation of expressive conduct was limited. The court of appeals stated that there was no evidence that handing out free newspapers would affect the university's academic mission or crime rate. The regulation was not narrowly tailored to meet the privacy, litter, or congestion interests of the university. Moreover, the fact that the university did not regulate publications without advertisements illustrated the tenuous nature of those arguments. The regulation was declared unconstitutional. *Hays County Guardian v. Supple,* 969 F.2d 111 (5th Cir.1992).

A Michigan student was editor-in-chief of her community college newspaper. She printed an advertisement of a Canadian bar where the drinking age was only 19 and the dancers were nude. The dean restricted her from printing any more of these advertisements. The editor sued the college in a federal district court alleging violation of her freedom of speech rights and intentional infliction of emotional distress. The court stated that if the editor had the authority to run the newspaper the school had to have a compelling state interest to restrict the speech in the newspaper. The court also stated that the newspaper was independent because the editor had the full authority to decide the content, policies and personnel of the newspaper. Further, the school was not promoting a substantial state interest by restricting the advertisement. The prohibitions on the advertisement restricted more speech than was necessary to further the government's legitimate interest. The district court ruled in favor of the editor and awarded her money damages. *Lueth v. St. Clair County Comm. Coll.,* 732 F.Supp. 1410 (E.D.Mich.1990).

A group of student journalists and an organization which promoted the rights of the student press brought a lawsuit against the U.S. Department of Education and the Secretary of Education. They sought to enjoin the government from enforcing a provision of the Family Educational Rights and Privacy Act (FERPA), which allows the complete withdrawal of federal funding from any university which discloses personally identifiable student records. The journalists alleged that this prohibition, as applied to campus security arrest reports, violated their First Amendment right to receive information. The journalists moved for an injunction in a federal district court to immediately halt enforcement of FERPA's prohibition. After resolving numerous procedural matters, the court examined the burdens imposed by FERPA and balanced them against the corresponding governmental interest. The journalists argued that the general arrest reports which are provided by local law enforcement officials do not distinguish which arrestees are students. Further, any attempt at matching those lists to student records is difficult and makes the effort to report campus crime ineffectual. The government maintained that the burden was trivial. The court held that the government's position was "untenable," and that its interests were outweighed by the rights of the journalists. A temporary injunction was issued which prevented the withdrawal of federal funding from any campus which disclosed its arrest reports. *Student Press Law Center v. Alexander*, 778 F.Supp. 321 (D.D.C.1991).

C. Nonschool Publications

A Washington school district adopted a policy requiring its high school students to submit all student-written material to school officials before that material could be distributed on school premises or at school functions. The policy was aimed at student writing that was not contained in official school publications. A group of students published and distributed a newspaper at a school barbecue without submitting it for review. As a result, the students received reprimands on their permanent records. The students sued the school district in a federal district court under 42 U.S.C. § 1983 claiming that the district's predistribution review policy violated their free speech rights. The district court held that the policy did not violate the students' rights. The students then appealed to the U.S. Court of Appeals, Ninth Circuit. The court of appeals contrasted the case to *Hazelwood School Dist. v. Kuhlmeier,* above, wherein the U.S. Supreme Court held that a policy of prior review and censorship of student writing is justified when it is a part of educators' reasonable exercise of authority over school-sponsored publications. In this case the policy was aimed at curtailing communications among students which were unassociated with school sponsorship or endorsement. Therefore, the court held that the policy violated the students' free speech rights guaranteed by the First Amendment. *Burch v. Barker*, 861 F.2d 1149 (9th Cir.1988).

In a Minnesota case, public high school students who produced an "underground" newspaper called *Tour de Farce* asked the federal courts to declare that their school district's written policy concerning distribution of unofficial written material on school grounds violated the First Amendment. The policy allowed school officials to review written materials in advance and prevent their distribution under certain conditions. The U.S. Court of Appeals, Eighth Circuit, upheld the policy's prohibition of obscene material, "libelous" material, "pervasively indecent or vulgar" material, and material advertising "any product or service not permitted to minors by law." The court also upheld a provision which prohibited material that "presents a clear and present likelihood that ... it will cause a material and substantial disruption of the proper and orderly operation and discipline of the school or school activities ...." However, the court invalidated a provision which prohibited material which "invades the privacy of another person or endangers the health or safety of another person ...." It held that such material can be suppressed only when it could result in liability on the part of the school. Because Minnesota law did not recognize lawsuits for invasion of privacy, material that invaded the privacy of others could not be suppressed. *Bystrom v. Fridley High School*, 822 F.2d 747 (8th Cir.1987).

D.   Personal Appearance and Dress Codes

The issue of free speech frequently arises in school district attempts to enforce student dress codes and regulate hair length of students.

Two Massachusetts students tested the limits of acceptable attire by wearing T-shirts to school that could be construed as vulgar, including a number of shirts containing sexual double entendres. The students were sent home for wearing the T-shirts, and their father sent letters to the school committee while it formulated a new policy concerning student attire. The committee voted to amend the dress code, retaining language that personal appearance should not disrupt the educational process, call attention to the individual, violate federal, state or local laws, or affect the welfare and safety of students and teachers. The amended policy forbade "obscene, lewd or vulgar" comments or designs and prohibited clothing "directed toward or intended to harass, threaten, intimidate, or demean an individual or group of individuals," as well as items advertising alcohol, tobacco or illegal drugs. The students and their father filed a lawsuit in the U.S. District Court for the District of Massachusetts, seeking an order that the dress code violated their constitutional rights.

The court agreed with the students that the amended dress code's provision concerning harassing speech violated the U.S. Constitution because it was aimed directly at the content of the speech, not at its potential for disruption or its vulgarity. However, the school district could appropriately restrict expressions of vulgarity and had complete power to determine what speech could be considered obscene. The school district had enforced the dress code in a reasonable manner and was entitled to judgment except as it concerned the harassment portion of the amended dress code, because it restricted speech based on content. *Pyle By and Through Pyle v. South Hadley School Committee*, 861 F.Supp. 157 (D.Mass.1994).

A Texas school district dress code prohibited male students from wearing long hair and earrings. A student filed a class action suit on behalf of himself and male students who were 18 years old or who would turn 18 years old while attending school in the district, seeking an injunction against enforcement of the dress code. A Texas trial court ruled that the code violated student rights to be free from discrimination based upon sex, and was in violation of the Texas Constitution. The Court of Appeals of Texas reversed the trial court decision, ruling that court intervention would be inappropriate. Under the Texas Constitution, the legislature had vested local school district trustees with exclusive powers to manage and govern public schools by adopting rules, regulations and by-laws as they deemed appropriate. *Colorado Indep. School Dist. v. Barber*, 864 S.W.2d 806 (Tex.App.—Eastland 1993).

Fraternity members who attended a Virginia university staged an "ugly woman contest" which was objected to by other university students as racist and sexist. The university determined that the behavior created a hostile learning environment for women and blacks which was incompatible with the university's mission. It suspended the fraternity from many school activities, and the fraternity filed a civil rights lawsuit in a federal district court. The U.S. Court of Appeals, Fourth Circuit, affirmed the district court's summary judgment motion for the fraternity, ruling that the contest was protected by the First Amendment. This was because the contest was expressive conduct intended to convey a message. Although the university had a substantial interest in maintaining an appropriate learning environment, it would have to do so without restricting expression based upon its content. *IOTA XI Chapter of Sigma Chi Fraternity v. George Mason Univ.*, 993 F.2d 386 (4th Cir.1993).

A Texas school district maintained a dress code policy which restricted the hair length of all male students. The policy required boys' hair to extend no further than to the top of a standard dress collar. A group of Native American students and their tribe filed a motion for a preliminary injunction in the U.S. District Court for the Eastern District of Texas contending that the dress code violated their constitutional right to the free exercise of religion. The action resulted from certain students being placed in in-school detention (amounting to a suspension) for wearing their hair long. The only students who were disciplined for violations of the prohibition on long hair were Native Americans.

The court stated that the school district officials had failed to show that the restriction on hair length was a valid means of achieving the objectives of maintaining discipline, fostering respect for authority, and projecting a good public image. The wearing of long hair by Native American students was a protected expressive activity which did not unduly disrupt the educational process or interfere with the rights of other students. Since there was a substantial likelihood of success at trial by the students with respect to the First Amendment claim and the Fourteenth Amendment procedural due process claim and because the threatened injuries would be irreparable, the court granted the preliminary injunction. The potential injury to the students was much greater than the potential injury to the school district. *Alabama and Coushatta Tribes of Texas v. Trustees of Big Sandy Independent School Dist.*, 817 F.Supp. 1319 (E.D.Tex.1993).

A California school district revised its dress code to prohibit all students from wearing clothing with professional or college sports insignia to school or school functions. Students attending district schools who wore college and professional sports emblems were called to the offices of their school principals. They were warned that further violations of the dress code would result in immediate suspension. A number of students and their parents sued the school district for an order declaring the dress code unconstitutional under the U.S. Constitution's First Amendment and a violation of the California Education Code. The U.S. District Court for the Central District of California considered motions for declaratory relief by the parties.

The school board argued that the presence of gangs on school grounds justified the revised dress code. The students and parents presented evidence that there was no gang presence at elementary and middle schools and that gang members at the high school wore white T-shirts and baggy pants rather than clothes bearing sports emblems. The court determined that there was no evidence of any significant gang presence at elementary and middle schools in the district. It issued a decree declaring the revised dress code violative of the students' free speech rights under the First Amendment. However, because there was evidence of a gang presence at the district's high school, school district authorities had shown that the dress code was necessary to prevent disruption of school activities. The court did not restrain the district from enforcing the dress code at the high school. *Jeglin v. San Jacinto Unif. School Dist.*, 827 F.Supp. 1459 (C.D.Cal.1993).

A Virginia middle school student wore a T-shirt that she had purchased at a pop music concert. On the front of the shirt, printed in letters eight inches high, were the words "Drugs Suck!" Several of the student's teachers had noticed the shirt, and one of them took the student to the school's main office. The student was told to turn the T-shirt inside out or borrow a shirt from another student. The student did not comply with the administration's ultimatum. The student's mother was telephoned, but she stated that another shirt could not immediately be brought. The student's father then arrived at school, and the student was suspended. The student missed a day of school and was reinstated the following day. With the support of the American Civil Liberties Union, the student filed a civil rights action in federal court.

The U.S. District Court, Eastern District of Virginia, held that the one-day suspension for refusing to change the shirt did not violate the student's due process rights. The principal had told the student which rule had been violated and the father and the principal had debated the appropriateness of the language on her shirt. The student had received adequate notice of her one-day suspension. The court also stated that the school district's action did not violate the student's First Amendment Rights. The court stated that the word "suck" could reasonably be interpreted to have a sexual connotation by a school administrator. Although the antidrug message itself makes no sexual statement, the use of the word "suck" and its likely derivation from a sexual meaning, is objectionable. Schools thus may limit usage of the word "suck," especially in light of the special characteristics of the school environment. *Broussard v. School Bd. of the City of Norfolk*, 801 F.Supp. 1526 (E.D.Va.1992).

An Oklahoma high school student designed a T-shirt which was intended to portray a typical teenager in 1991—the shirt contained the slogan "The best of the night's adventures are reserved for people with nothing planned." Upon learning that students were wearing the shirts, the school superintendent stated that any student who wore the shirt would be suspended. He also instructed the principal to then give pop quizzes for which the students would receive zeros. Numerous students were suspended, and the superintendent threatened to arrest students or parents who protested his action. No one, however, was actually arrested. The superintendent stated that the slogan on the shirt was from a Bacardi rum ad and constituted an unacceptable advertisement of alcoholic beverages. A number of students and their parents sought a preliminary injunction to enjoin the superintendent from applying school dress code provisions to the T-shirts in question. The case was heard before the U.S. District Court, Western District of Oklahoma. The court granted the preliminary injunction. The students had demonstrated that there was a substantial likelihood of success on the merits of their § 1983 claim for deprivation of their First Amendment rights. The phrase displayed on the back of the T-shirts worn by the students conveyed an idea presumptively protected by the First Amendment. The court granted a preliminary injunction against the superintendent and any agents, employees, or persons acting in concert with him. *McIntire v. Bethel School, Ind. School Dist. No. 3*, 804 F.Supp. 1415 (W.D.Okl.1992).

II. EMPLOYEES

The extent to which school employees may exercise freedom of speech depends on whether the subject matter concerns the public interest. Speech that concerns purely private matters is not protected by the Constitution.

A. Protected Speech

In *Pickering v. Board of Education*, below, the U.S. Supreme Court announced that an employee may not be disciplined for speaking as a citizen upon matters of public concern unless the employee's interest in such speech is outweighed by a reasonable belief on the part of the school district that the speech would disrupt the school, undermine school authority, or destroy close working relationships. The content, form and context of a given statement determine whether an employee's speech addresses a matter of public concern.

An Illinois school district fired a teacher for sending a letter to the editor of the local newspaper. The letter criticized the board and district superintendent for their handling of school funding methods. Voters in the district had voted down a tax rate increase to fund a bond issue for two new schools. The teacher also charged the superintendent with attempting to stifle opposing views on the subject. The board then held a hearing at which it charged the teacher with publishing a defamatory letter. After deeming the teacher's statements to be false, the board fired the teacher. An Illinois court affirmed the board's action, finding substantial evidence that publication of the letter was detrimental to the district's interest. The Illinois Supreme Court affirmed the dismissal, ruling that the teacher was unprotected by the First Amendment because he had accepted the position which required him to refrain from statements about school operations.

The U.S. Supreme Court reversed and remanded the case, finding no support for the state supreme court's view that public employment subjected the teacher to deprivation of his constitutional rights. The state interest in regulating employee speech was to be balanced with individual rights. The Court outlined a general analysis for evaluating public employee speech, ruling that employees were entitled to constitutional protection to comment on matters of public concern. The public interest in free speech and debate on matters of public concern was so great that it barred public officials from recovering damages for defamatory statements unless they were made with reckless disregard for their truth. Because there was no evidence presented that the letter damaged any board member's professional reputation, the teacher's comments were not detrimental to the school system, but only constituted a difference of opinion. Since there was no proof of reckless disregard for the truth by the teacher and the matter concerned the public interest, the board could not constitutionally terminate his employment. The Court reversed and remanded the state court decision. *Pickering v. Board of Education*, 391 U.S. 563, 88 S.Ct. 1731, 20 L.Ed.2d 811 (1968).

An art teacher with 21 years of experience at a Mississippi high school criticized the district superintendent for canceling the art program at a historically black junior high school while retaining the program at a historically white junior high school. The superintendent justified the action by stating that no art instructors could be located for the black school. However, the art teacher soon found candidates for the position. The teacher then joined in ongoing public criticism of the superintendent in the community. He wrote a letter to the editor of a local newspaper, spoke out in public forums, and personally presented the superintendent a "letter of no confidence." The superintendent arranged for the demotion of the teacher to the black junior high school, and the teacher filed a lawsuit against the superintendent, school district and others. The U.S. District Court for the Northern District of Mississippi refused to grant the superintendent's summary judgment motion on the teacher's First Amendment claim, while granting summary judgment to the other defendants on qualified immunity grounds. The superintendent appealed to the U.S. Court of Appeals, Fifth Circuit.

The court of appeals noted that the art teacher had joined in public criticism of the superintendent and was not merely voicing a personal grievance concerning his demotion. His activities could be characterized as protected public speech and the district court could have correctly concluded that there was sufficient evidence to avoid summary judgment. Because the superintendent may have had an unconstitutional reason for reassigning the teacher, the First Amendment claim was properly retained. The court dismissed the superintendent's appeal.*Tompkins v. Vickers*, 26 F.3d 603 (5th Cir.1994).

A Texas school district employed a principal under a series of two-year contracts. She mentioned the possibility of retirement, and the school superintendent interpreted this as a strong possibility. Accordingly, he recommended that the school board renew her contract for only one year. The principal then demanded a two-year contract and filed a grievance with the state teachers' association. The board then unanimously agreed to extend the principal's contract for a second year. When the school board transferred the principal to an administrative position, she filed a lawsuit against the superintendent and school district in the U.S. District Court for the Eastern District of Texas, claiming constitutional violations. The court considered dismissal motions by the district and superintendent.

The principal argued that the transfer was motivated by her discipline of a school board member's child and her open criticism of the superintendent. The court noted that in order to prevail in a retaliatory discharge case based on constitutional grounds, employees had to demonstrate that they were engaged in protected activity and that the protected activity was a motivating factor in the employment decision. In this case, the principal had failed to demonstrate either factor, and summary judgment was appropriate. She could not demonstrate the loss of a property interest when she remained employed by the school board. Further, her expectancy interest in continued employment was only valid for one year at a time. Accordingly, the court granted the motions for summary judgment. *George v. Bourgeois*, 852 F.Supp. 1341 (E.D.Tex.1994).

A substitute teacher employed by a Connecticut school district sought full-time work and felt that the school board failed to use fair procedures for calling substitutes. After the teacher expressed her opinion, the school employee responsible for calling substitutes advised the substitute that she did not intend to call her for further openings. The substitute, who was also a resident of the school district, later met with the school superintendent and board chairman to complain that a vacant position had been filled without posting. These complaints were renewed over the next four years. The substitute then filed a lawsuit against the board and certain employees in the U.S. District Court for the District of Connecticut, claiming that the board's failure to hire her as a full-time teacher and to call her as often as other substitutes violated her First Amendment rights. The board filed a motion for summary judgment, claiming that her speech was not protected.

The court observed that only speech involving matters of public concern was protected by the First Amendment. In this case, the teacher's complaints were not limited to her personal inability to gain employment, they also questioned the board's policy of hiring teachers without posting any notice. The substitute's status as a taxpayer, resident and parent in the district added to the inference that she had acted primarily as a citizen and not merely as an employee. The court denied the board's summary judgment motion because the substitute had raised genuine issues of material fact as to whether she was called less frequently than other teachers despite being available for work and even though there was a shortage of substitutes in the district. *Mazurek v. Wolcott Bd. of Educ.*, 849 F.Supp. 154 (D.Conn.1994).

Because of an impending budgetary crisis, a South Carolina school district announced that instead of paying teachers a lump sum for the summer months, as had been the custom, the school district would pay teachers biweekly. A teacher who had been with the district for ten years responded to the new policy by writing and circulating a letter to fellow teachers in which he expressed his objection to any delay in receiving pay caused by the new policy. He criticized the school district's management of the budget, and encouraged a "sick-out" during exam week. As a result, he was fired. The county school board affirmed the dismissal, and the teacher sued, claiming that his dismissal had violated his First Amendment rights. The district court held for the school district, and the teacher appealed to the U.S. Court of Appeals, Fourth Circuit.

The court of appeals stated that speech by a public school teacher is protected by the First Amendment when the teacher speaks as a citizen about matters of public concern and the teacher's interest in exercising free speech is not outweighed by the countervailing interest of the state in providing the public service the teacher was hired to provide. The court of appeals stated that the letter taken as a whole dealt with matters of public concern. Therefore, it was entitled to some degree of First Amendment protection. However, the letter only dealt with matters of public concern tangentially. The main thrust of the letter was a personal grievance. The First Amendment interest inherent in the letter was outweighed by the public interest in having a public education provided by teachers loyal to that service and in having examinations proctored and completed in a timely fashion. The court of appeals affirmed the teacher's dismissal. *Stroman v. Colleton County School Dist.*, 981 F.2d 152 (4th Cir.1992).

A Phoenix police officer was dispatched to a junior high school to investigate a possible case of child abuse. A student had reported to the school nurse that his stepfather had beaten him the night before. After the police officer conducted his investigation, the school nurse wrote a letter to the school superintendent, the principal, the chief of police, and the mayor of Phoenix, among others. The letter stated that the officer "demanded that the student stand against the wall," that the student "was interrogated as if he, the victim, had committed an illegal act," and that the officer "was rude and disrespectful, and his manner bordered on police brutality." Subsequently, the police officer sued the school nurse alleging that she had defamed him by her statements. The trial court granted the nurse's motion for summary judgment, but the court of appeals reversed. The Supreme Court of Arizona granted review. The supreme court first noted that the nurse's comments involved matters of public concern because her letter criticized a police officer acting in his official capacity. Accordingly, the statement had to be provable as false before a defamation action could lie. The court next determined that the statements were a subjective assessment and that they were not provable as false. The nurse's characterizations were merely her personal impressions of the officer's interview methods. Since her words were not "capable of being reasonably interpreted as stating actual facts" about the officer, they were not actionable as defamation. *Turner v. Devlin,* 848 P.2d 286 (Ariz.1993).

The Chicago Board of Education disciplined two school district employees who had spoken out at board meetings. The employees sued the school board in the U.S. District Court for the Northern District of Illinois for damages and other relief. The court refused to allow the employees to advance a cause of action under a section of the Illinois School Code authorizing district employees to address board meetings. The code did not create an explicit private right of action for damages. The court granted the school board's dismissal motion, but granted the employees leave to file an amended complaint. *Porter v. Bd. of Educ. of City of Chicago*, 837 F.Supp. 255 (N.D.Ill.1993).

A California school administrator served as director of management services, where his duties included demographic planning and liaison with state agencies. After years of service he encountered difficulties with a recently-appointed school superintendent. The two disagreed about the superintendent's inflation of the director's projection for student enrollment. The director spoke with a local reporter, who published an article portraying him as a whistleblower and reporting the inflated enrollment figures. The superintendent and director negotiated resignation terms which included vacation pay, health and welfare benefits, a consulting contract and an agreement for a joint statement to the press concerning the resignation. The superintendent withdrew the resignation offer after the director again spoke with a reporter concerning his resignation. The director sued the school district in a California trial court, which awarded him over $400,000 in damages and over $177,000 in attorney's fees. Appeal was brought to the California Court of Appeal, First District, Division One.

The court of appeal determined that the court had issued erroneous special verdict forms to the jury concerning the director's constitutional complaint. The First Amendment protects employees from retaliatory discharge only when they speak on public issues. In this case, the director had spoken about an individual grievance, which was not a matter of public concern. Nonetheless, the director had an extremely strong case for wrongful discharge under state law, and the inappropriate special verdict form had not prejudiced the school district. This was because the jury would have been likely to reach the same result on the director's alternate theory. The court affirmed the damage award for the director, but reversed the award of attorney's fees. *Weber v. San Ramon Valley Unif. School Dist.*, 25 Cal.Rptr.2d 69 (Cal.App.1st Dist.1993).

Kentucky law prohibited employees of local school districts from taking part in the "management or activities of any political campaign for school board." A group of public school employees sued education officials in Kentucky state court, claiming that the statute deprived them of their right to free speech, free association, free assembly, equal protection, and due process. The employees succeeded at the trial court, and the state board of education appealed to the Kentucky Supreme Court. The supreme court stated that the challenged statute definitely invaded areas of constitutionally protected conduct. In order to support this, the state needed to show that the statute was narrowly drawn to serve a compelling government purpose. The statute also had to be clear enough that ordinary people could tell what actions were prohibited. The court found that the word "activities" was too general. It was not certain what actions were allowed or prohibited. The word "management," however, was sufficiently specific. The court then stated that removal of the word "activities" rendered the statute constitutional, since the statute as modified served the government's compelling interest in running its school districts in an efficient manner. The court severed the unconstitutional term and upheld the rest of the statute. *State Bd. for Elem. Educ. v. Howard*, 834 S.W.2d 657 (Ky.1992).

B.   Personal Appearance and Dress Codes

A Mississippi woman was a member of the African Hebrew Israelites and at times wore a head-wrap as an expression of her religious and cultural heritage. A local school district hired her as a teacher and she wore the head-wrap from time to time without incident. Eventually, she sought and received a transfer to another school closer to her home. However, that school's principal disapproved of the teacher's head-wrap and instructed her not to wear it anymore. Because she was afraid of losing her job, the teacher acquiesced until she attended a district-wide multi-cultural workshop where she discovered that the school district supported multi-cultural diversity. She then resumed wearing the head-wrap. Her principal gave her a written notice of her "inappropriate dress" and when she refused to discontinue the practice, the school district discharged her for insubordination to her principal. She then applied for unemployment benefits, but was disqualified on grounds of misconduct connected with her work. She successfully appealed to a Mississippi trial court, and the state employment commission further appealed the case to the Supreme Court of Mississippi.

The supreme court first noted that schools may enforce dress codes when they support a compelling governmental interest which is reasonably related to their educational mission. However, there was no evidence that the teacher's actions in wearing her head-wrap had any adverse impact on her ability to do her job, nor upon the school's educational mission. Since wearing the head-wrap was grounded in a religious belief which was sincerely held, the teacher's conduct was constitutionally protected as religious and cultural expression. Accordingly, she was entitled to unemployment compensation benefits because her wearing of the head-wrap did not constitute misconduct. The court affirmed the trial court's decision. *Mississippi Employment Security Comm'n v. McGlothin*, 556 So.2d 324 (Miss.1990).

Following a memorandum and discussion with other school officials, the school administration terminated the instructor's employment. The instructor followed the district's grievance procedure, and claimed that she wore her head coverings in compliance with her religious beliefs. The district denied her grievance and she appealed to the U.S. District Court for the Southern District of Mississippi. The court found that although the instructor held sincere religious beliefs, she had failed to communicate them to the school administration at any time until the final stage of her grievance. Because she had failed to timely communicate her religious beliefs to the school district, it was not required to accommodate her beliefs under the First Amendment or Title VII. The district had offered the instructor an opportunity for reemployment following the denial of her grievance if she would agree to remove her head coverings. However, the instructor rejected this offer and the court granted the school district's motion to dismiss the lawsuit. *McGlothin v. Jackson Municipal Separate School Dist.*, 829 F.Supp. 853 (S.D.Miss.1993).

Following a classroom evaluation, a teacher was directed to visit a dentist to improve the condition and appearance of his teeth and visit a physician for help in losing weight. The teacher objected and the New York Commissioner of Education ruled that the school district lacked authority to compel him to visit the dentist or the physician, except to have a physical examination. The teacher then filed a lawsuit against the school district's superintendent alleging that his constitutional rights had been violated. A New York appellate court observed that the school district never took any action to compel the teacher to comply with the directives. The court determined that even if the teacher had a constitutional liberty interest in his appearance, that interest had not been burdened by the school district. The school district had not violated the teacher's constitutional rights. His case was dismissed. *Mermer v. Constantine*, 520 N.Y.S.2d 265 (A.D.3d Dept.1987).

In Massachusetts, a nontenured French teacher was allegedly terminated because of the shortness of her skirts. The school denied that skirt length was the reason for termination and stated that the firing was due to a lack of interest in professional growth, insufficient participation in school activities, unwillingness to work with students after school and poor image. The U.S. Court of Appeals, First Circuit, dealt with the teacher's claim that freedom of choice in matters of personal appearance was a right guaranteed her under the Fourteenth Amendment. In upholding the teacher's dismissal, the court quoted from a previous similar case: "If a school board should correctly conclude that a teacher's style of dress or plumage has an adverse impact on the educational process, and if that conclusion conflicts with the teacher's interest in selecting his own lifestyle, we have no doubt that the interest of the teacher is subordinate to the public interest." *Tardif v. Quinn*, 545 F.2d 761 (1st Cir.1976).

A Tennessee board of education dismissed a teacher for violation of a school board regulation which provided that "no apparel, dress, or grooming that is or may become potentially disruptive of the classroom atmosphere or educational process will be permitted." The teacher was dismissed for wearing a full beard while teaching. The board felt this was disruptive or potentially disruptive of the educational process and in violation of the school board's regulation. The teacher challenged his dismissal in court. The Supreme Court of Tennessee determined that it was within the school board's discretion to determine that the wearing of beards by teachers would be disruptive of the educational process. While the teacher had a right to wear a beard he could be denied that right in the context of the classroom. *Morrison v. Hamilton County Bd. of Educ.*, 494 S.W.2d 770 (Tenn.1973), *cert. denied*, 414 U.S. 1044 (1974).

III. ACADEMIC FREEDOM

School administrators have broad discretion in curricular matters and courts are unwilling to closely scrutinize the reasonable exercise of their discretion. However, decisions involving school library books are subject to First Amendment prior restriant protections. Classroom assignments made by teachers that do not conform to school standards are also subject to close judicial review. See Chapter Seven, Section IV of this volume for cases involving disciplinary action against teachers for using poor judgment in the classroom.

A. Library Materials

The U.S. Supreme Court determined that the right to receive information and ideas is "an inherent corollary of the rights of free speech and press" embodied in the First Amendment. A decision to remove books from a school library is unconstitutional if it is motivated by school officials' intent to deny students access to ideas with which the school officials disagree. The U.S. Supreme Court upheld a U.S. Court of Appeals decision regarding the removal of books from high school and junior high school libraries. The case arose when a board of education, rejecting recommendations of a committee of parents and school staff that it had appointed, ordered that certain books, which the board characterized as "anti-American, anti-Christian, anti-Semitic, and just plain filthy," be removed from high school and junior high school libraries. Students in those schools then brought an action for declaratory and injunctive relief against the board and its individual members, alleging that the board's actions violated their rights under the First Amendment. The U.S. Supreme Court noted that while local boards have broad discretion in the management of curriculum, they did not have absolute discretion to censor libraries and were required to comply with the First Amendment. *Bd. of Educ. v. Pico*, 457 U.S. 853, 102 S.Ct. 2799, 73 L.Ed.2d 435 (1982).

A Louisiana school board placed a book containing voodoo spells on reserve in a junior high school library for reference by eighth grade students having parental consent. The parent of a seventh grade student discovered the book concealed in her home and complained to the school's assistant principal. The school board considered removing the book from the school system at a board meeting and later voted to remove it as offensive, inappropriate or dangerous. Interested parties filed a lawsuit against the school board in the U.S. District Court for the Eastern District of Louisiana, seeking a declaration that the board's action was unconstitutional. The court considered at length the discussions of the school board members and determined that they had taken action because they disapproved of the content and ideas contained in the book. Their action sought to deny student access to ideas because they did not comply with the values, morality and religious beliefs of the board members. Accordingly, removal of the book from the library was unconstitutionally based on content. There was no evidence that any student attempted to act out the spells contained in the book or that any disruption occurred. The board could have taken other, less restrictive action such as limiting circulation to high school students. The court awarded summary judgment to the complaining parties. *Delcarpio v. St. Tammany Parish School Bd.*, 865 F.Supp. 350 (E.D.La.1994).

In a discussion of censorship in school libraries, a New York teacher distributed an article entitled "Better Orgasms," which one of the students in the class of seniors had found in the library. The administration of the school placed a letter in the teacher's personnel file stating that he had used poor judgment. The administration also required approval before the distribution of any other controversial material. The teacher objected to this, but was denied relief in administrative hearings and by a trial court. The issue then came before the New York Supreme Court, Appellate Division. Because the letter did not amount to discipline, the teacher was held not to be entitled to a due process hearing. The letter did not violate the teacher's First Amendment rights because any subsequent distribution of material was not absolutely forbidden. The approval directive was ruled to be an allowable exercise of the administration's right to review instructional materials. *O'Conner v. Sobol*, 577 N.Y.S.2d 716 (A.D.3d Dept.1991).

B. Textbook Selection

A group of parents whose children attended grade school in an Illinois school district filed a lawsuit in the U.S. District Court for the Northern District of Illinois, seeking an order to prevent use of the Impressions Reading Series as the main supplemental reading program for grades kindergarten through five. The parents alleged that the series "foster[ed] a religious belief in the existence of superior beings exercising power over human beings," and focused on "supernatural beings" including "wizards, sorcerers, giants and unspecified creatures with supernatural powers." The court granted a motion to dismiss the lawsuit. The parents appealed to the U.S. Court of Appeals, Seventh Circuit. The court stated that the parents' argument that use of the textbook series established a religion was speculative. Although the series contained some stories involving fantasy and make-believe, their presence in the series did not establish a coherent religion. The intent of the series was to stimulate imagination and improve reading skills by using the works of C.S. Lewis, A.A. Milne, Dr. Suess and other fiction writers. The primary effect of using the series was not to endorse any religion, but to improve student reading skills. Use of the series did not impermissibly endorse religion under the Establishment Clause or the Free Exercise Clause. The parents failed to show that use of the series had a coercive effect that prevented the parents from exercising their religion. The school directors were entitled to judgment as a matter of law. *Fleischfresser v. Directors of School Dist. 200*, 15 F.3d 680 (7th Cir.1994).

A California school district used the *Impressions* reading series for grades one through six. The series contains 59 books with over 10,000 passages from North American literature and folklore. The parents of two students formerly enrolled in the district claimed that 32 passages from the series promoted the practice of witchcraft and that witchcraft was a religion. They claimed that the selections called for students to role play characters including witches and sorcerers in a manner which violated their constitutional rights. The U.S. District Court for the Eastern District of California granted the school district's motion for summary judgment and the parents appealed to the U.S. Court of Appeals, Ninth Circuit. On appeal, the parents argued that it was appropriate for courts to analyze Establishment Clause cases according to the subjective beliefs of school-aged children. The court of appeals disagreed, ruling that the appropriate analysis was whether an objective observer in the position of a student would perceive a message of endorsement of religion by the school district. The contested passages were a very small part of a clearly nonreligious program. It was unlikely that an objective observer would perceive the use of the series as governmental endorsement of religion. The court agreed with the U.S. Court of Appeals, Seventh Circuit, *in Fleischfresser v. Directors of School Dist. 200,* above. The court held that use of the series did not violate either the U.S. or California Constitution. *Brown v. Woodland Joint Unif. School Dist.*, 27 F.3d 1373 (9th Cir.1994).

A Louisiana statute permitted public schools to offer sex education instruction for grades seven and above as part of existing biology, science, or physical education classes. Parents or guardians could instruct that their child be excused from sex education. The statute prohibited the teaching of religious beliefs, practices in human sexuality and subjective moral and ethical judgments in sex education classes, and prohibited testing of students about personal or family beliefs, sexual practices, morality or religion. The statute required the encouragement of abstinence for unmarried persons and prohibited counseling or advocating abortion. A group of parents sued a Louisiana school board to enjoin its use of *Sex Respect: The Option of True Sexual Freedom*, a seventh and eighth grade text, and *Facing Reality: A New Approach to the Real World of Today's Teen*, a tenth grade text. The court ordered the board to obliterate certain passages of the textbooks. One of the publishers refused to let the board obliterate the sections by whiting out the offensive passages and reproducing the amended pages, requiring the board instead to delete the objectionable portions in black ink. The textbooks were then used in class, and a local news report stated that students were able to read parts of the blacked out text. The report also quoted the school board president's sharp criticism of the judge. The court then granted the parents' motions for contempt against the president and board.

The Court of Appeal of Louisiana, Second Circuit, ruled that the trial court had interpreted the statute in a correct manner, but had improperly ruled on a few of the passages in issue. The court had also erroneously granted the motion for contempt, as there was no evidence of any wilful violation of the court's order. The court had correctly found that textual references to "spiritual values" and morality were religious in nature and must be deleted. Passages referring to homosexuality and abortion need not have been deleted as the trial court ruled. The court of appeal reversed the trial court's contempt order, but substantially affirmed its judgment. *Coleman v. Caddo Parish School Bd.*, 635 So.2d 1238 (La.App.2d Cir.1994).

A tenured professor at a public university in Colorado sought an injunction in federal court to prevent the university from distributing standardized teacher evaluation forms in her classes. On cross motions for summary judgment, a federal judge held that the use of such standardized forms did not violate the professor's right to academic freedom under the First and Fourteenth Amendments to the U.S. Constitution. The professor claimed that by being forced to give her students the standardized form, the university was interfering with her classroom methods, thereby violating her right to academic freedom. The court, however, disagreed. Academic freedom refers both to the freedom of the teacher to operate her class without interference from the university and the freedom of the university to operate without interference from the government. Because of these freedoms, the federal judge was reluctant to interfere with the internal operations of a university, unless they conflicted with basic constitutional values. The judge found that although the professor had a constitutionally protected right under the First Amendment to disagree with the university's policies, she did not have a right to fail to perform the duty imposed upon her as a condition of employment. The judge concluded that the evaluation forms were unrelated to course content and in no way interfered with the professor's academic freedom. The court held for the university. *Wirsing v. Bd. of Regents of the Univ. of Colorado*, 739 F.Supp. 551 (D.Colo.1990).

A Florida high school designed a humanities course for its juniors and seniors. Textbooks used in the course had been approved by the Florida Department of Education. One of the textbooks included Aristophanes' *Lysistrata* and Chaucer's *The Miller's Tale*. In response to the sexual content and alleged vulgarity in the textbook, a student's parents filed a complaint with the school board. The school board eventually voted to discontinue use of the text. A group of parents sued the school board in a federal district court complaining that the removal of the text violated the First Amendment. The court ruled for the school board and the parents group appealed to the U.S. Court of Appeals, Eleventh Circuit. The court noted that *Hazelwood v. Kuhlmeier*, above, gave educators greater control over the management of the curriculum than in other areas. Since this was a curriculum decision, the court held that the school board's action was reasonably related to legitimate concerns about the appropriateness of the textbook for a high school audience. The court also noted that the decision not to use the text did not limit the students' freedom of expression since the books had not been banned from the school and copies of the textbook were available in the school library. The appeals court affirmed the district court's decision. *Virgil v. School Bd. of Columbia County, Fla.*, 862 F.2d 1517 (11th Cir.1989).

A teacher in a Michigan public school district taught a life science course using a textbook approved by the school board. He showed movies to his class regarding human reproduction ("From Boy to Man" and "From Girl to Woman") after obtaining approval from his principal. The movies were shown to his seventh grade classes with girls and boys in separate rooms, and only students with parental permission slips were permitted to attend. Both movies had traditionally been shown to seventh grade students in the school. However, after a school board meeting at which community residents demanded that the teacher be tarred and feathered for showing the movies, the superintendent of schools suspended the teacher with pay pending "administrative evaluation." The school board approved this action. The teacher then sued in U.S. district court for violation of his First Amendment freedoms as well as his civil rights. The jury awarded the teacher $321,000 in compensatory and punitive damages against the school board. The damage award was based not only upon actual damages suffered by the teacher, but it compensated him for the "abstract value" of his constitutional rights. A unanimous U.S. Supreme Court reversed the court of appeals' decision and remanded the case to the district court. According to the Supreme Court, an award of money damages may be made only to compensate a person for actual injuries that are caused by the deprivation of a constitutional right. The Court held that damages for violations of the U.S. Constitution should not be allowed to take on an abstract value. *Memphis Comm. School Dist. v. Stachura*, 477 U.S. 299, 106 S.Ct. 2537, 91 L.Ed.2d 249 (1986).

C. Curriculum

A retired filmmaker was a member of the school board of a New York school district. He volunteered to give three lectures to high school mathematics classes on the theme of "the persistence of vision." The lecture included the display of six film clips, one of which included bare-breasted women and a bare-chested man. The school's principal attended the first lecture and asked that the clip showing partial nudity be deleted from the presentation. The board member agreed, and several days later wrote a letter of apology to the class. However, parents and school officials were not satisfied by the apology and the superintendent issued an executive order condemning the board member's action and barring him from visits to the high school during school hours for the rest of the academic year. The school board passed a resolution censuring the board member. The state commissioner of education determined that the superintendent's action was within his authority because it did not interfere with the board member's duties. However, the board had no authority to censure the member and the commissioner annulled the resolution. The board member filed a lawsuit against the district, superintendent and other officials in the U.S. District Court for the Eastern District of New York, alleging constitutional violations under 42 U.S.C. § 1983. The court held for the district, and the board member appealed to the U.S. Court of Appeals, Second Circuit.

The board member argued on appeal that the film clips more closely resembled library resources than school curriculum. Therefore, he had certain First Amendment rights to make the presentation. The court of appeals disagreed, stating that because students were required to attend mathematics classes and the presentation was intended to impart knowledge, it was analogous to curriculum. School boards had the ultimate authority to determine appropriate classroom curriculum and speech, and the district court had properly found that the school administrators had acted out of legitimate educational concern. The district had not violated the board member's First Amendment or due process rights, and the court of appeals affirmed the district court's decision. *Silano v. Sag Harbor Union Free School Dist. Bd. of Educ.*, 42 F.3d 719 (2d Cir.1994).

A California school district contracted with a limited partnership to show current events video productions in its schools. The twelve-minute videos included two minutes of commercial advertising. The contract contained an opt-out feature for students to avoid viewing the production. Although the state board of education adopted a resolution permitting the use of commercial products and services within schools as a discretion of local board authority, the state superintendent of schools strongly objected to commercial programming in schools. The superintendent, a parent, a student organization and two teachers filed a lawsuit against the district seeking an order to void the contract, plus other declaratory relief. The court denied the request for a preliminary injunction, and determined that the mere presence of commercial advertising in public schools was not illegal. Although there had been no evidence of direct coercion in this case, the court retained jurisdiction over the matter and permanently enjoined the showing of commercial broadcasting unless strictly voluntary standards were implemented. The order also required maintenance of the opt-out feature and a supervised alternative activity during times in which the program was shown. Appeal reached the California Court of Appeal, Sixth District.

The court of appeal determined that the decision to permit commercial broadcasting in schools was within the discretion of local school boards. The incidental use of commercial broadcasting within a larger presentation of educational materials was also permissible. The opt-out feature prevented students from being compelled to watch advertising in the classroom. The trial court had correctly found that the school board could enter into a contract for showing commercial broadcasting. However, it was unnecessary for the trial court to issue the injunction establishing procedures for opt-out or to retain jurisdiction. The court affirmed the trial court decision with modifications. *Dawson v. East Side Union High School Dist.*, 34 Cal.Rptr.2d 108 (Cal.App.6th Dist.1994).

The School District of Philadelphia's board of education adopted an adolescent sexuality policy aimed at preventing sexually transmitted diseases. The program included a condom distribution program at school-based health clinics.

Principals at pilot schools sent parents letters advising them that the condom distribution program was to become part of their school health services programs. The letters indicated that parents need not reply if they consented to participation, but that they must respond within two weeks if they wanted their children to opt out of the program. The condom distribution program began 15 days after the mailing. A nonprofit corporation that included many parents of Philadelphia public high school students filed a complaint against the school board in a Pennsylvania trial court, seeking injunctive and declaratory relief. The board filed a summary judgment motion, claiming that the corporation had no legal standing to advance the complaint. The court granted the motion, and the corporation appealed to the Commonwealth Court of Pennsylvania.

The commonwealth court determined that an organization has legal standing as long as at least one member is threatened with a direct, immediate and substantial injury as a result of the challenged action. Because the corporation had many members who were parents of Philadelphia public school students, it was an appropriate entity to assert the rights of its individual members. The requirements of parental consent were time honored and required an expression of approval by the parent. The board's policy lacked the requirement of affirmative parental consent. Because the trial court had erroneously dismissed the corporation for lack of standing, the commonwealth court reversed and remanded the decision for further proceedings. *Parents United For Better Schools, Inc. v. School Dist. of Philadelphia Bd. of Educ.*, 646 A.2d 689 (Pa.Cmwlth.1994).

In 1990, a Pennsylvania school district adopted a graduation requirement that every public high school student, except those in special education classes, complete a total of 60 hours of community service during high school. The goal of the program was to help students gain life skills, and a sense of worth and pride by understanding and appreciating the functions of community organizations. More than 70 approved community service organizations were included in the program. Alternatively, a student could develop his or her own individual community service experience and obtain parental approval, the recommendation of the school counselor and verification by a responsible adult. After completing the 60 hours of community service, each student was required to complete a written experience summary form describing and evaluating his or her community service activity. Subsequently, several students and parents brought suit in a federal district court challenging the constitutionality of the program and seeking a permanent injunction against its enforcement. They claimed that the program was violative of the First and Thirteenth Amendments to the U.S. Constitution. The district court granted summary judgment to the defendants, and appeal was taken to the U.S. Court of Appeals, Third Circuit.

The students and parents argued on appeal that performing mandatory community service is expressive conduct because it forces the students to declare a belief in the value of altruism. Since the First Amendment includes the right to refrain from speaking, being forced to participate in community service is being forced to engage in expressive conduct. The court of appeals, however, noted that the program was not violative of the First Amendment because the program did not require that the students express a belief in the value of community service.

Rather, it seemed that a student could criticize the program in his or her written summary and still receive a passing grade. Next, the court rejected the claim that the program violated the Thirteenth Amendment (which prohibits involuntary servitude). The court noted that the Thirteenth Amendment was limited to slavery. A mandatory community service program in a public high school is simply not like slavery. The court affirmed the district court's decision in favor of the school district. *Steirer by Steirer v. Bethlehem Area School Dist.*, 987 F.2d 989 (3d Cir.1993).

A group of African-American public school students attending New York city schools filed a lawsuit in the U.S. District Court for the Southern District of New York alleging that the city's public school curriculum injured African-American students because of a systematic bias against them. They stated that the curriculum distorted and demeaned the historical role of African-Americans and failed to include their important contributions. The students sought a declaration that the curriculum was discriminatory and an order directing the school board to revise its curriculum to reflect African-American contributions. The school board and other defendants brought a motion to dismiss the lawsuit on the grounds of government immunity and failure to state a claim under 42 U.S.C. § 1983 and other federal statutes.

The court observed that the Eleventh Amendment to the U.S. Constitution did not entitle the state and its agencies, including the school board, to immunity in this case because Congress had explicitly exposed them to suit under Title VI of the Civil Rights Act of 1964. However, in order to prevail in a § 1983 lawsuit, intentional discrimination must be proven and it must be established that the defendants' discriminatory purpose was a motivating factor in its actions. According to the court, no such intentional purpose could be discerned from the school board's actions. It was impermissible for the court to infer discrimination from the alleged failure to incorporate African-American features in the curriculum. The court dismissed the § 1983 complaint for failure to adequately allege intentional discrimination. The court also dismissed the students' Title VI complaint because neither the statute nor its regulations extended to curricular content. *Grimes v. Sobol*, 832 F.Supp. 704 (S.D.N.Y.1993).

A tenured professor at the City University of New York published three writings that contained a number of denigrating comments concerning the intelligence and social characteristics of blacks. The dean of the college tried to prevent the professor from teaching a philosophy class as a result, but when that failed the dean created an "alternative" section of the class to which students could transfer. The dean wrote to the students in the professor's class informing them that they could transfer to the alternative section. Such action was unprecedented. The professor sued claiming that the "shadow class" violated his academic freedom. He also claimed that the school violated his equal protection rights by failing to discipline student protesters who had disrupted his classes. A federal district court found that the shadow class had been established with the intent and consequence of stigmatizing the professor because of the expression of his ideas. The court issued an injunction against the continuance of the practice. The university appealed to the U.S. Court of Appeals, Second Circuit. The court stated that formation of the alternative sections would not be unlawful if done to further a legitimate educational interest that outweighed the infringement on the professor's First Amendment rights. However, it noted that the professor's expression of his theories outside the classroom could not be shown to have harmed the students or the educational process inside the classroom. Therefore, no legitimate educational interest existed. The court also stated that disciplinary proceedings based on the professor's expression of his views would violate his First Amendment rights. However, the school's failure to discipline the student protesters was not an Equal Protection Clause violation, since the school had never disciplined such protesters in the past. *Levin v. Harleston*, 966 F.2d 85 (2d Cir.1992).

A New York school teacher instructed her students to write essays expressing their opinion regarding the firing of a television sports commentator. In the background material she handed out to students, she included a letter to the editor which she had written expressing her views on the subject. The superintendent of the school district felt that the teacher's distribution of her own opinion was improper. The superintendent asked the teacher to rescind the assignment and to turn over her lesson plan and gradebooks. The teacher refused. At a disciplinary hearing, the teacher claimed that the superintendent's actions interfered with her academic freedom. The hearing panel refused to consider the defense. She was suspended for one semester without pay.

The school district appealed to the state commissioner of education, seeking an increase in the penalty to dismissal. The commissioner concluded that the directives concerning the assignment itself encroached on the teacher's right to academic freedom, but that the request to hand over the lesson books did not. The commissioner reduced the penalty to a three-month suspension without pay. A New York trial court affirmed the decision. The district and teacher appealed to the New York Supreme Court, Appellate Division. The court noted that school boards have broad discretion in the management of school affairs. This discretion is limited by the imperatives of the First Amendment. As to the order to rescind the assignment, the commissioner's finding that the district had no legitimate basis for doing so was appropriate. However, since the district retained the ultimate authority to review and assign grades, asking for the grade books did not intrude upon the teacher's academic freedom. Therefore, the commissioner's decision was appropriate. The commissioner's order was affirmed. *Malverne School Dist. v. Sobol*, 586 N.Y.S.2d 673 (A.D.3d Dept.1992).

The concept of freedom of speech also includes the right to refrain from speaking. The U.S. Supreme Court has held that a student may not be disciplined for refusing to recite the Pledge of Allegiance.

In 1979, the Illinois legislature enacted a statute which required that the Pledge of Allegiance "be recited each school day by pupils in elementary educational institutions supported or maintained in whole or in part by public funds." A student who attended an elementary school in Illinois and his father challenged the statute in federal court, claiming that the words "under God" violate the Establishment and Free Exercise Clauses of the First Amendment. They also claimed that the mandatory language of the statute violated *West Virginia State Bd. of Educ. v. Barnette*, 319 U.S. 624, 63 S.Ct. 1178, 87 L.Ed. 1628 (1943). *Barnette* held that students could not be compelled to participate in the recitation of the Pledge of Allegiance. A federal district court granted summary judgment to the school district, 758 F.Supp. 1244 (N.D.Ill.1991), and the student and his father appealed to the U.S. Court of Appeals, Seventh Circuit. The court of appeals upheld the statute. The court stated that any statute which compelled student participation in the recitation of the Pledge of Allegiance was flagrantly unconstitutional. In this case, however, the language of the statute was not necessarily mandatory. The statute could be interpreted to simply mean that the pledge was to be recited by all willing students. In fact, the student in this case had suffered no penalty in refusing to participate in the pledge. The court continued by noting that the pledge could only be banned if the "under God" phrase made the pledge a prayer whose recitation violated the Establishment Clause. The court stated that the phrase was simply ceremonial deism without any true religious significance. The court affirmed the ruling for the school district. *Sherman v. Community Consol. Dist. 21*, 980 F.2d 437 (7th Cir.1992).

A regulation requiring a student who refused to salute the flag to either stand or leave his classroom was declared invalid by the U.S. Court of Appeals. A high school honor student and president of the senior class refused to participate in the pledge because he said there was not liberty and justice for all in the United States. He was offered the option of either standing or leaving the room during the pledge. He chose to do neither, sitting instead. In holding for the student, the court said that the alternatives offered by school authorities could not be imposed over the student's deeply held convictions. The student could not be compelled to participate in the pledge nor could he be punished for refusing to participate. The alternatives offered could be construed as punishment. It was pointed out that the conduct of the student caused no disruption of school activities, a situation which could have changed the decision. *Goetz v. Ansell*, 477 F.2d 636 (2d Cir.1973).

The Governor of the state of Massachusetts asked the state's highest court for an advisory opinion on the constitutionality of proposed legislation requiring all teachers to lead the class in a group recitation of the Pledge of Allegiance. The court, assuming an element of compulsion on the part of teachers to comply with this proposed legislation, held that it would violate their rights to free speech under the First Amendment to the U.S. Constitution. Even if there were no adverse consequences which could be visited upon a teacher for failing to comply, the very existence of a statutory mandate might inhibit a teacher from exercising whatever constitutional right he or she might have to refrain from leading his or her class in the recitation of the Pledge of Allegiance. *Opinions of the Justices to the Governor*, 363 N.E.2d 251 (Mass.1977).

D.   School Productions

Two employees of a New York school district received permission from the school's principal to use school property in filming a portion of a commercial pilot project. A nontenured teacher acted in the film, and a tenured teacher assisted in production. The filming included one scene in which the blouse and skirt was forcibly ripped from the actress, leaving her exposed in her underwear. Upon learning of this scene and viewing the film, the school superintendent ordered the filming stopped. One day later, the nontenured teacher was informed that she would not be rehired and the tenured teacher was suspended. The employees alleged, among other things, that their First Amendment rights had been violated. They sued the superintendent, the president of the board of education, and the board in a federal district court. The First Amendment clearly protects artistic expression such as the film, even when offensive or nonexpressive. Further, the evidence made apparent that the protected speech was the primary motivation leading to the adverse employment action. The school officials failed to show any evidence that the functioning of the school had actually been impaired. Because the tenured teacher was later cleared and reinstated, only the temporary teacher's rights had been violated. Due to immunity protections, only the board of education was held to be liable. *Rothschild v. Board of Educ. of the City of Buffalo*, 778 F.Supp. 642 (W.D.N.Y.1991).

The question of whether a school board may halt production of a school play was decided by a U.S. district court in Ohio. Third graders at an elementary school had an annual tradition of providing entertainment at the final Parent-Teacher Association meeting. In 1985, the teachers decided that the students would perform the musical-comedy play *Sorcerer and Friends*. When the school board was informed of these plans it determined that the play was contrary to the spirit of the school curriculum and voted to halt its performance. The board claimed that the play glorified cowardice, was unpatriotic and disparaging to the elderly. Parents and teachers then filed suit in U.S. district court claiming that the board was violating students' and teachers' First Amendment rights to free expression by suppressing the play. The court agreed and issued an injunction ordering the board to allow the play to be performed. The fact that the play was voluntary, was scheduled after school hours and was not a part of the school's curriculum was crucial to the court's decision. *Bowman v. Bethel-Tate Bd. of Educ.*, 610 F.Supp. 577 (S.D.Ohio 1985).

IV. USE OF SCHOOL FACILITIES

Courts have determined that schools may establish reasonable rules governing the time, place and manner of constitutionally protected speech on school property. The reasonableness of restrictions depends upon the type of forum. A *public forum* exists on property which is generally available for use by the public. Time, manner and place regulations regarding a public forum must be content neutral and narrowly tailored to serve a significant governmental interest. They must also provide for ample alternative channels of communication. A *limited public forum* exists when a school opens part of its campus to expressive activities on the part of groups of certain character. A regulation regarding a limited public forum must allow equal access to all groups that have a similar character. The U.S. Congress has declared it unlawful for a public secondary school which receives federal funds to deny

students the opportunity to hold meetings in a limited public forum on the basis of the religious, political, philosophical, or other content of speech at the meetings. Equal Access Act, 20 U.S.C. § 4071 *et seq.* For additional Equal Access Act cases, see Chapter Two, Section I, part D., and Section II part A. of this volume, above.

A. Time, Place or Manner Regulations

The New York Education Law authorized local school boards to pass regulations which allowed the use of school property in specified ways. The law did not expressly authorize use of school grounds for religious purposes. A local school board issued regulations allowing social, civic, or recreational uses as well as limited use by political organizations, provided that the school not be used for religious purposes. An evangelical church sought permission to use public school facilities to show a six-part film series on traditional Christian family values. The school district denied the church permission to use its facilities because the film was church-related. The church filed a lawsuit in a federal court alleging that the district's decision violated its rights to free speech and assembly under the First Amendment. The district court determined that the school district's action was "viewpoint neutral" and held for the district. The U.S. Court of Appeals, Ninth Circuit, affirmed, holding that public school facilities were a "limited public forum" and that the district could exclude certain groups provided that the exclusion was "reasonable and viewpoint neutral." The church appealed to the U.S. Supreme Court. The Court determined that exclusion of the subject matter because of its religious content would impermissibly favor some viewpoints or ideas at the expense of others. Therefore, the regulation discriminated on the basis of viewpoint. The holding of the court of appeals was reversed. *Lamb's Chapel v. Center Moriches Union Free School Dist.,* 113 S.Ct. 2141, 124 L.Ed.2d 352 (1993).

An Illinois school district published a disciplinary procedure manual that contained an antiloitering rule pertaining to a particular area of a high school campus. Violation of the rule resulted in a three-day suspension. Neighboring residents had previously complained about disregard for property and traffic safety by high school students in the designated area. A freshman at the high school was cited for loitering in violation of the rule and suspended for three days. He requested a formal hearing before a school district hearing officer, who upheld the suspension. The student and his parents appealed to the U.S. District Court for the Northern District of Illinois, which granted the district's dismissal motion. The student and his parents appealed to the U.S. Court of Appeals, Seventh Circuit. On appeal, the student argued that the rule was unconstitutionally vague because it failed to adequately notify students of what conduct was prohibited and failed to define the term "loitering." The court of appeals disagreed, stating that there was nothing unclear about the common use of the word and that the rule gave adequate warning to a reasonable person of the proscribed conduct. The student failed to support his complaint with any allegations of a violation of his free speech rights, and the rule was justified by school district concerns for student safety and prevention of property damage. The rule was drafted with sufficient clarity and the district court had properly dismissed the complaint. *Wiemerslage v. Maine Township High School Dist. 207*, 29 F.3d 1149 (7th Cir.1994).

A Virginia school board rented its facilities to private, community, religious and cultural organizations for use after school hours and on weekends. Its regulations established a noncommercial rate for cultural, civic, educational and governmental groups. A commercial rate was established for private organizations that was five times higher than the noncommercial rate, and was intended to approximate market rental rates. The regulations established a special rate for religious groups, which paid the noncommercial rate for the first five years, but then paid an escalating rate which became equal to the commercial rate after four years. The school board justified the escalating rate as a means of avoiding long rental terms for religious groups, which it believed might violate the Establishment Clause of the First Amendment. A church rented space from the school board over a period of eleven years, and alleged that the escalating rate resulted in rental charges of over $287,000 more than the noncommercial rate that applied to other nonprofit organizations. It sued the school board in the U.S. District Court for the Eastern District of Virginia. The court held that the escalating rental rate violated the First Amendment. However, the court refused to apply its ruling retroactively and denied the church's application for a partial refund. Both parties appealed to the U.S. Court of Appeals, Fourth Circuit.

The court observed that the school board's regulations created an open forum. Accordingly, it was prohibited from denying access to religious groups without showing a compelling state interest. The court found no compelling state interest in this case, because any perceived advancement of religion was incidental to the secular purpose of maintaining an open public forum. The regulations discriminated against religious speech and could not be justified by the board's speculation that continued use of its facilities by religious groups would violate the Establishment Clause. The court affirmed the district court's order concerning the unconstitutionality of the regulations, but reversed its decision concerning retroactive effect. It vacated the judgment and remanded the case for further proceedings. *Fairfax Covenant Church v. Fairfax County School Bd.*, 17 F.3d 703 (4th Cir.1994).

The U.S. Supreme Court determined that the New York state university system could adopt restrictive regulations to prohibit private sales of cookware sold through demonstrations in dormitory rooms on state campuses. In doing so, it reversed a decision by the U.S. Court of Appeals, Second Circuit. It remanded the case for reconsideration of the university system's regulation under a standard that considered not whether the regulation was the least restrictive means of obtaining the objective, but whether it was narrowly tailored to achieve it. By the time the case was remanded to the U.S. District Court for the Northern District of New York, the students who had filed the action had graduated or no longer attended state universities. The court dismissed the lawsuit as moot and refused to grant a motion to amend the complaint by adding students currently attending state schools as plaintiffs. The students appealed again to the court of appeals. The court of appeals agreed with the district court that the graduation of the complaining students left them with no legally cognizable interest in the outcome of the lawsuit. Because there was no longer a case or controversy over which a federal court could exercise jurisdiction, the district court had properly dismissed the case. *Fox v. Bd. of Trustees of State Univ. of New York*, 42 F.3d 135 (2d Cir.1994).

A second-year law student at the University of Minnesota founded a student organization named the "Free Speech Movement." The group's primary purpose was to provide a forum for speech by military and Federal Bureau of Investigation recruiters. Recruitment activity on university campuses was limited by the university's nondiscrimination policy. That policy provided that all persons shall have equal access to its programs, facilities, and employment without regard to race, religion, color, sex, national origin, handicap, age, veterans status, or sexual orientation. As a result, the university barred the military and FBI from recruiting on campus. In fact, the military and the FBI were the only employers affected by the policy. The Minnesota Civil Liberties Union, however, had been allowed to advertise student positions and recruit on campus even though it had limited its employment opportunities to minority students. The university admitted that this violated the policy. The student sued the regents of the university.

The U.S. district court upheld the university's policy. The court stated that recruiting speech proposes a commercial transaction. The First Amendment affords commercial speech less protection than other forms of expression. In order to regulate commercial speech, the government must have an interest that is substantial, and the regulation must directly advance the interest asserted. It must also be no more extensive than is necessary to serve that interest. The university's purpose of assuring equal opportunity to university students was a substantial interest. The nondiscrimination policy furthered the university's interest in assuring equal opportunity. This was true even though the policy had yet to be perfectly implemented. The restriction in recruitment speech by noncomplying employers was narrowly tailored. Moreover, the policy allowed the military access to campus facilities to discuss any other matter of public interest, including the university's nondiscrimination policy and its effect on military recruitment. The court upheld the policy. *Nomi v. Regents for the University of Minnesota*, 796 F.Supp. 412 (D.Minn.1992). On further appeal, the U.S. Court of Appeals, Eighth Circuit, held that the case was moot because the student had graduated. 5 F.3d 332 (8th Cir.1993).

An Ohio statute requires that any publication taking a position on an election or ballot issue must include the name and address of the chairman, treasurer or secretary of the organization or person issuing the publication in a conspicuous place on the publication. A citizen distributed campaign leaflets opposing a school levy that had been placed on an upcoming primary election ballot to persons attending a meeting at an Ohio middle school. The assistant superintendent of elementary education for the city school district advised the levy opponent that the failure to include his name and address on the leaflets violated the statute. However, the advocate distributed more leaflets outside another middle school in the district the following day. The Ohio Elections Commission (OEC) charged the opponent with violating the statute and held a hearing resulting in a $100 fine. The advocate appealed the fine to an Ohio county court, which declared the statute unconstitutional as applied to the advocate. The OEC appealed to the state court of appeals, which reversed the trial court decision, and the advocate appealed to the Supreme Court of Ohio.

The supreme court observed that, in contrast to statutes that required identification of the publisher merely to discourage free speech, the statute had the legitimate purpose of prohibiting persons from making false statements during political campaigns. Other persons were entitled to consider the source and credibility of the publisher. The court found that the statute imposed only a minor burden on publishers of campaign information that did not significantly burden their ability to disseminate information and which was counterbalanced by the state interest in allowing voters to evaluate publications. The act did not violate the First Amendment to the U.S. Constitution or the Ohio Constitution, and the court of appeals' decision was affirmed. *McIntyre v. Ohio Elections Comm.*, 618 N.E.2d 152 (Ohio 1993).

An Illinois school district permitted the Boy Scouts to use school facilities at designated times free of charge. It also permitted the Scouts to distribute fliers and post notices in the school. A number of other secular and religious organizations also took advantage of the school's policy. A fifth grader and his father attended a Boy Scout sign up at the school and objected to the Scout applications, which required affirming a belief in God. The student and his father sued the school district and some of its employees in the U.S. District Court for the Northern District of Illinois, alleging violations of the U.S. Constitution's Establishment and Equal Protection Clauses. The court dismissed the lawsuit and the student and father appealed to the U.S. Court of Appeals, Seventh Circuit.

On appeal, the student and father argued that the school district policy favored religious groups. The court disagreed, observing that all youth organizations using the school's facilities were treated equally. Refusal to let a religious group use its facilities would not demonstrate neutrality, but hostility toward religion. There was no government endorsement of religion by the district in violation of the Establishment Clause. The Scouts' message was sufficiently separated from school district functions to avoid any appearance of district approval. There was no merit to the Equal Protection claim because school facilities were available to all organizations on a first come, first serve basis and it was not alleged that any secular organization had been denied access to school facilities. Boy Scout activities were not attributable to the school district and the organization was not a state actor for constitutional purposes. The court affirmed the dismissal of the lawsuit. *Sherman v. Comm. Cons. School Dist. 21*, 8 F.3d 1160 (7th Cir.1993).

Christian students in a Colorado school believed it was part of their religious duty to distribute the newspaper published by their sect to their fellow students. They engaged in the distribution of the newspapers outside of the school building for several months. They met with the school principal to expand the dissemination of the newspaper to inside the school. The principal applied the school district policy to limit the distribution made by the students to the area outside the school building and to prohibit the sect from distributing their newspaper in the hallways. The students sought an injunctive order in a federal trial court which would allow them to distribute their newspaper in school. The students contended that the school policy was constitutionally void for vagueness, and was based on the open-ended discretion of the school administrator. Because the hallways of the high school are neither a public forum nor a limited public forum the court turned its analysis to the nonpublic forum. In addition to time, place and manner regulations, the state may reserve the forum for its intended purpose, so long as the restriction on speech is reasonable and not an effort to suppress expression merely because of opposition to the speaker's views. The court upheld the school district's policy. *Hemry by Hemry v. School Bd. of Colorado Springs,* 760 F.Supp. 856 (D.Colo.1991).

B. Student Organizations

A gay student association at an Arkansas university registered as a student organization. The group petitioned the university's student senate for funds to finance films and workshops concerning homosexual lifestyles. The group's 1985 request was approved by a school finance committee, but the student senate voted against funding. Despite available funds from the previous year, the group was not funded. It was the only student group not recommended for funding. After failing in appeals within the university, the group brought a lawsuit in a federal district court alleging First Amendment violations. The court agreed with the group that student senate activities were "state action." However, it did not find a First Amendment violation and stated that no student organization had a right to receive funding. The group appealed to the U.S. Court of Appeals, Eighth Circuit, which found that the university and student senate had violated the group's First Amendment rights. The district court had been correct that no group had a right to funding, but once funds were available they had to be distributed neutrally. There was no compelling state interest to protect. Discrimination based upon viewpoint was unconstitutional. *Gay and Lesbian Students Ass'n v. Gohn,* 850 F.2d 361 (8th Cir.1988).

A group of students on the Texas A & M University campus who had formed a group called Gay Student Services (GSS) applied for and were denied official recognition by the university. The reasons given by the university's Vice President for Student Affairs for the denial of the students' request included a quotation from the university regulations handbook to the effect that student organizations may be officially recognized only when formed for purposes which are consistent with the philosophy and goals that have been developed for the creation and existence of the university. In addition, the Vice President noted that homosexual conduct was illegal in Texas and therefore a state institution could not officially support a student organization which would be likely to incite and promote illegal activities. GSS sued the university. The U.S. Court of Appeals, Fifth Circuit, quoted language from a U.S. Supreme Court case, *Healy v. James,* in which a state supported college refused to recognize a group of students who wished to organize a local chapter of Students for a Democratic Society. The *Healy* case held that "the mere disagreement of the President with the group's philosophy affords no reason to deny it recognition. The College, acting here as the instrumentality of the State, may not restrict speech or association simply because it finds the views expressed by any group to be abhorrent." Further, while Texas law prohibits certain homosexual practices, no Texas law makes it a crime to *be* a homosexual. Finding no evidence that any illegal activity took place as a result of GSS's existence in the past the court concluded that the group's free speech rights had been violated. *Gay Student Servs. v. Texas A & M Univ.*, 737 F.2d 1317 (5th Cir.1984).

C. Demonstrations

Generally, students enjoy the same First Amendment protections as all other citizens. This extends to their right to peacefully gather, to demonstrate and to form groups and associations. Balanced against their rights as individuals, however, are the rights of others. Thus, disruptive demonstrations on school grounds may be enjoined if the demonstrations materially disrupt the normal class routine and invade the rights of other students.

The U.S. Supreme Court determined that the New York state university system could adopt restrictive regulations to prohibit private sales of cookware sold through demonstrations in dormitory rooms on state campuses. In doing so, it reversed a decision by the U.S. Court of Appeals, Second Circuit. It remanded the case for reconsideration of the university system's regulation under a standard that considered not whether the regulation was the least restrictive means of obtaining the objective, but whether it was narrowly tailored to achieve it. By the time the case was remanded to the U.S. District Court for the Northern District of New York, the students who had filed the action had graduated or no longer attended state universities. The court dismissed the lawsuit as moot and refused to grant a motion to amend the complaint by adding students currently attending state schools as plaintiffs. The students appealed again to the court of appeals. The court of appeals agreed with the district court that the graduation of the complaining students left them with no legally cognizable interest in the outcome of the lawsuit. Because there was no longer a case or controversy over which a federal court could exercise jurisdiction, the district court had properly dismissed the case. *Fox v. Bd. of Trustees of State Univ. of New York*, 42 F.3d 135 (2d Cir.1994).

Students at Auburn University wished to hold a week-long "camp-out" demonstration at the university's Open Air Forum. The forum was located in a busy part of the campus where the students felt that their demonstration would be most noticeable. The forum was subject to regulations administered by the office of student affairs and the university reserved the right to schedule speakers. Use of the forum was scheduled in time blocks to discourage monopolization. The office of student affairs eventually agreed to open the forum to the demonstrating students during hours which were greatly expanded over normal forum hours. An area in front of the coliseum was made available for nonforum hours. The students decided to hold their camp-out at the forum, where they attracted substantial interest and media coverage. However, the students did not move to the coliseum during nonforum hours as the office of student affairs had directed. Campus police asked the demonstrators to disband when the camp-out continued into the night. When the students refused, their identifications were recorded. Identified demonstrators then received letters to appear before a university disciplinary committee.

The students refused to appear, claiming that their First Amendment rights had been violated.

The students then filed a lawsuit in a federal district court for a temporary restraining order to prevent possible disciplinary proceedings. The university disciplinary committee convened in the meantime. The students refused to appear before the committee. After several delays, the committee recommended a reprimand for each named student. Named students were then reprimanded by letter. The court refused to grant the restraining order and later granted the university's dismissal motion. Restrictions on the forum were content-neutral because they did not unreasonably restrict student speech and applied equally to all. The university also complied with the students' request to extend use of the forum and had reasonably accommodated them by making the forum available at expanded hours. The university had maintained a flexible policy of tolerating freedom of expression in the time, place and manner of the demonstration. The university's regulations were unambiguous and constitutional. *Auburn Alliance for Peace and Justice v. Martin*, 684 F.Supp. 1072 (M.D.Ala.1988).

Students at the University of Virginia challenged a regulation which prohibited the construction of shanties on the university's historic lawn. The lawn regulation was instituted after student organizations constructed wooden shanties in front of the lawn's rotunda to influence the university's policymaking body, the board of visitors, to divest from South Africa. Shanties could not be built within sight of the rotunda, but could be constructed on other parts of the campus. The university argued that the regulations were necessary to protect the aesthetic integrity of the campus. A U.S. district court noted that the shanties that had been constructed before the passage of the lawn regulation had not damaged the lawn in any way. It directed the university not to enforce the lawn regulation against the student organizations. The university's president revised the lawn use policy, and a shanty put up by the student organization was removed from the lawn pursuant to the revised policy. The student organization filed another lawsuit seeking a court order precluding enforcement of the revised policy. A U.S. district court in Virginia noted that ambiguous language in the old policy had been removed and the term "structures" had been defined to make clear what the policy precluded. The court declared that the revised policy was a reasonable time, place and manner regulation of speech. It ruled in favor of the University and the student groups appealed to the U.S. Court of Appeals, Fourth Circuit, which upheld the validity of the new university policies. The new policies were content-neutral and narrowly tailored to protect and preserve the historic integrity of the lawn. Aesthetic concerns constituted a legitimate government interest, and the new policy protected student speech by permitting shanties to be constructed elsewhere on campus. *Students Against Apartheid Coalition v. O'Neil*, 838 F.2d 735 (4th Cir.1988).

A Tennessee group was having a parade to celebrate Martin Luther King's birthday. A group of Ku Klux Klan (KKK) members found out about the parade and wanted to have a parade of their own to express their views. The KKK asked a local school superintendent if they could have use of the area high school for their celebration and parade. The superintendent denied their request because a little league group had already reserved the high school for the same date. The KKK sued the city and the superintendent in a federal district court alleging constitutional violations of their First Amendment rights. The district court stated that all groups must be given equal access to the high school since the school was used for all types of public events. However, the KKK was not discriminated against or denied equal access to the school on an arbitrary basis because the school was being used and had already been reserved for other purposes. The court stated that the guarantees of equal access and freedom from discrimination did not give any group the right of absolute unqualified access. Thus, the district court ruled in favor of the school and refused to give the KKK injunctive relief. *Ku Klux Klan v. Martin Luther King Worshippers*, 735 F.Supp. 745 (M.D.Tenn.1990).

CHAPTER FOUR

STUDENT RIGHTS

I. ADMISSIONS AND ATTENDANCE

The U.S. Constitution does not make free public education a fundamental right. While the Equal Protection Clause does not mandate a program of free public education, the states have enacted legislation for the establishment and enforcement of education laws. The Equal Protection Clause requires that once a program of free public education has been established, the law must be applied equally to any person within the jurisdiction of the state. Thus, children of illegal aliens, children with disabilities, and minority students are all entitled to equal protection of the laws. A school district may, within certain limits, establish health regulations, make minimum age requirements for all students beginning school, require immunization, adopt a curriculum and require that all students meet certain graduation requirements. Students with contagious diseases may not be excluded from class unless they present a medically demonstrable threat to health and safety.

A. Age and Residency Requirements

In May 1975, the Texas legislature revised its education laws to withhold from local school districts any state funds for the education of children who were not legally admitted into the United States. It also authorized local school districts to deny enrollment to children not legally admitted into the country. One group filed a class action on behalf of school-age children of Mexican origin who could not establish that they had been legally admitted into the United States. The action complained of the exclusion of the children from public school. A federal district court enjoined the school district from denying a free education to the children, and the U.S. Court of Appeals, Fifth Circuit, upheld the decision. The legislation was also challenged by numerous other plaintiffs whose cases were consolidated and heard as a single action before a federal district court. The district court held that the law violated the Equal Protection Clause of the Fourteenth Amendment and the U.S. Court of Appeals, Fifth Circuit, summarily affirmed the decision. The Supreme Court consolidated the two cases and granted review.

The state claimed that undocumented aliens were not persons within the jurisdiction of Texas, and were not entitled to equal protection of its laws. The Court rejected this argument, stating that whatever an alien's status under the immigration laws, an alien is a person in any sense of the term. The term "within its jurisdiction" was meant as a term of geographic location and the Equal Protection Clause extends its protection to all persons within a state, whether citizen or stranger. The statute could not be upheld because it did not advance any substantial state interest. The Court stated that the Texas statute imposed a lifetime hardship on a discrete class of children not accountable for their disabling status. There was no evidence to show that exclusion of the children would improve the overall quality of education in the state. *Plyler v. Doe*, 457 U.S. 202, 102 S.Ct. 2382, 72 L.Ed.2d 786 (1982).

The Texas Education Code also permitted school districts to deny free admission to its public schools for minors who lived apart from a "parent, guardian, or the person having lawful control of him" if the minor's primary purpose in being in the district was to attend public free schools. A minor left his parent's home in Mexico to live with his sister in a Texas town for the purpose of attending school there. When the school district denied her brother's application for tuition-free admission, she sued the state in federal court, alleging that the law was unconstitutional. The district court held for the state, noting that the state's interest in protecting and preserving the quality of its educational system and the rights of its bona fide residents to attend school on a preferred tuition basis was legitimate. The Court of Appeals affirmed. The Supreme Court of the United

States upheld the Texas residency requirement. The Court noted that a bona fide residence requirement, appropriately defined and uniformly applied, furthered a substantial state interest in assuring that services provided for its residents were enjoyed only by residents. Such a requirement with respect to attendance in public free schools did not violate the Equal Protection Clause of the Fourteenth Amendment. Residence generally requires both physical presence and intention to remain. The statute stated that as long as the child was not living in the district for the sole purpose of attending school, he satisfied the statutory test. The Court held that this was a bona fide residency requirement and that the Constitution permits a state to restrict eligibility for tuition-free education to its bona fide residents. *Martinez v. Bynum*, 461 U.S. 321, 103 S.Ct. 1838, 75 L.Ed.2d 879 (1983).

Iowa's open enrollment statute allows students to enroll in schools outside their district of residence. The statute requires receiving school districts to bill the sending district for the cost of educating each open enrollment student based upon the cost of educating a student in either of the districts. Iowa's funding system provided for foundation property taxes, state foundation aid and additional tax levies that substantially equalized district expenditures and limited district expenditures per student to 110 percent of the statewide cost per student. Forty students residing in a small Iowa district chose to attend other schools under the open enrollment statute. The sending district claimed that the open enrollment financing system was unconstitutional. It and a number of taxpayers filed a lawsuit in an Iowa trial court, seeking a declaration to prohibit transfer of property tax revenues to receiving districts and a ruling that the open enrollment statute was unconstitutional. The court issued a temporary injunction, but later ruled against the district and taxpayers. The district and taxpayers appealed to the Supreme Court of Iowa.

The court ruled that the school district had no standing to bring a constitutional complaint as it was not a "person" and had no constitutional rights. The state finance system allowed the transfer of local tax revenues in open enrollment cases in order to maintain the same level of funding for students regardless of where they attended school. Access to educational opportunity was a legitimate state goal and the statute rationally achieved its purpose by using a finance mechanism that maintained funding equity for all students. Local property tax revenues were intended to fund the education of resident students, not to support local schools. The finance method simply required districts to fund the education of resident students. The open enrollment legislation had a rational basis and the supreme court affirmed the trial court's decision. *Exira Comm. School Dist. v. State of Iowa*, 512 N.W.2d 787 (Iowa 1994).

Vermont parents notified an elementary school principal that although they were not currently residents of the school attendance area, they would be moving there soon and would enroll their children at the school. The principal stated that they would not be required to pay tuition if they moved to the school's attendance area. Although the students were enrolled in district schools, the family never moved to the attendance area, and the school attempted to collect tuition from the parents. The school district sued the parents in a Vermont trial court, which granted judgment to the school district. The parents appealed to the Supreme Court of Vermont. On appeal, the parents argued that school districts that received nonresident students were required to collect tuition from the student's home school district. The supreme court disagreed, finding that this procedure applied only in cases where the home district had no schools. The legislature had granted school districts the authority to collect nonresident tuition in cases such as this, and the supreme court affirmed judgment for the school district. *Dover Town School Dist. v. Simon*, 650 A.2d 514 (Vt.1994).

A Connecticut parent sought to enroll his daughter in a public school located in the city of New Canaan. His property was on the boundary line of that city and the city of Norwalk and part of the house was located in New Canaan. The New Canaan board and superintendent refused to grant the request because only five percent of the family's property taxes went to New Canaan, while the balance went to Norwalk. The family had previously lived in New Canaan and continued to use a New Canaan mailing address. The family also voted in New Canaan, obtained public library cards there and participated in social and community activities there. The state board of education affirmed the school board's decision, and a Connecticut trial court affirmed. The family appealed to the Appellate Court of Connecticut. On appeal, the family argued that the proper analysis to employ in boundary line cases was not the amount of property tax paid but the family's complete community of interests, including affiliations developed by the student and the family's participation in the community. The court agreed, finding that the lack of definition of the term "residing in" as used in the applicable statute supported taking into account multiple factors, rather than the rigid and arbitrary application of the property tax issue. The court reversed and remanded the trial court's decision. *Baerst v. State Bd. of Educ.*, 34 Conn.App. 567, 642 A.2d 76 (1994).

A North Carolina student's parents moved to Vermont during her senior year in high school. She remained in North Carolina to complete high school. She applied for admission to the University of North Carolina at Chapel Hill and requested classification as an in-state resident. The university's admissions office denied the request for resident status, and two university committees upheld the denial. The Superior Court of Wake County reversed the university's decision, and the university appealed to the Court of Appeals of North Carolina. The court of appeals noted that the admissions committee had improperly relied on the common law presumption that a minor's place of domicile was the same as that of the minor's parents. A North Carolina statute created a specific exception from the presumption of parental domicile in cases where the minor has lived in the state for five consecutive years prior to registering or enrolling at the institution of higher learning for which resident status was sought. The parents' place of domicile did not necessarily determine the domicile of the student. The court remanded the case to the university's resident status committee for application of the appropriate legal standard. *Fain v. State Residence Comm. of the Univ. of North Carolina*, 451 S.E.2d 663 (N.C.App.1995).

The revised Texas Education Code required students to be at least six years old for admission to first grade. The code also granted school boards the authority to make exceptions for students over or under the normal school age. The mother of a student who was five years and ten months old on September 1st of the coming school year lived in a school district in which the board had adopted a policy excluding from first grade all students who were not six by September 1st. Because the student had completed kindergarten at a private school, her mother petitioned the school board to consider allowing her to enroll the student as a first grader. The board denied the petition. The mother sued the school district, superintendent and board in a Texas trial court alleging due process and civil rights violations. She also claimed that the state Gifted and Talented Act, which made no reference to age, created an exception to the requirement that students be at least six for admission to first grade. The court granted the board and superintendent summary judgment, and the mother appealed to the Court of Appeals of Texas, El Paso.

The court of appeals determined that the legislature had vested school boards with wide discretion concerning public school admissions. The school board had discretion to adopt the policy excluding students from first grade who had not attained their sixth birthday prior to September 1st. The trial court had not abused its discretion by granting summary judgment to the school, school board and superintendent. There was no evidence that the Gifted and Talented Act applied in this case. The court affirmed the trial court's decision. *Wright v. Ector County Indep. School Dist.*, 867 S.W.2d 863 (Tex.App.—El Paso 1993).

An Illinois student resided permanently with his maternal aunt. When the aunt attempted to enroll the student in her local high school, the high school refused to allow it. She was told by the school's residency director that school rules required her to have legal guardianship of the student and to have a third-party professional or other governmental agency certify that the student could not reside with his parents due to impossibility or extreme hardship. The Appellate Court of Illinois stated that a child's residence in a school district other than that in which his parents reside is sufficient to entitle the child to attend school tuition-free in the district in which he resides so long as his residence is not established solely to enjoy the benefits of free schools. The school's policy did not meet this standard. *Israel v. Bd. of Educ. of Oak Park*, 601 N.E.2d 1264 (Ill.App.1st Dist.1992).

A Texas girl frequently ran away from home and eventually began living with her boyfriend's parents who lived within another school district. Her parents gave them power of attorney. Further, state agencies determined that it was in the girl's best interest to live with her boyfriend's parents. When they tried to enroll her into the eighth grade, school officials denied admission unless the mother instituted proceedings to install the boyfriend's parents as her daughter's managing conservator. The girl then brought this suit challenging the constitutionality of the admissions policy in federal court. The girl alleged that the policy violated the Equal Protection Clause of the Fourteenth Amendment. In a similar case, *Plyler v. Doe,* above, the U.S. Supreme Court held that children of illegal aliens were effectively prohibited from receiving free public school education because of a residency statute. This was in violation of the Equal Protection Clause because the children were not "accountable for their disabling status." Similarly, the court noted, the girl in this instance was not accountable for her disabling status. Thus, the court determined that the admission policy violated the Equal Protection Clause. *Major v. Nederland Ind. School Dist.*, 772 F.Supp. 994 (E.D.Tex.1991).

The parents of a New York girl presented an altered birth certificate to a school district in order to enroll their daughter in kindergarten the year before she was eligible for a free education. Near the end of the school year, the school discovered the deception, and the district sought to be reimbursed for the cost of the girl's schooling. When the parents refused to pay, the district sued. The trial court held for the school district, and the New York Supreme Court, Appellate Division, affirmed. The district could recover from the ineligible resident just as it could recover from a nonresident who enrolled under false pretenses. Further, the parents were not entitled to offset the amount of school taxes they paid to the district. *Bd. of Educ. v. Marsiglia*, 582 N.Y.S.2d 256 (A.D.2d Dept.1992).

A parent sued a school district after it refused to admit her son to kindergarten. An Illinois statute required that a student be five years of age by September 1st of the year he enrolled in kindergarten. The boy turned five on September 4th. The statute also provided that if a student was not the required age, he could be permitted to enroll in school if an assessment determined that he was ready. The parent requested that her son be assessed. However, the school refused to either enroll or assess the boy. The parent filed a motion for a preliminary injunction requesting that the court order the school to assess her son and claiming his equal rights to education had been violated. The court granted the motion and ordered the school to evaluate the boy. The school assessed and admitted the boy, then appealed to the Appellate Court of Illinois, which found that the trial court erred in requiring the school to assess the boy, since the statute did not require the school to assess students, even if requested to do so. The cut-off on enrollment was a result of studies which showed that the older a child was upon entering kindergarten, the more likely that he would be a successful student. *Morrison v. Chicago Bd. of Educ.*, 544 N.E.2d 1099 (Ill.App.1st Dist.1989).

B. Immunization

Generally, a school district or a state educational agency has a compelling state interest in requiring immunization of all incoming students in an effort to prevent and control communicable diseases.

New York Public Health Law § 2164 requires school-aged children to be immunized against communicable diseases before entering school. Parents holding sincere and genuine religious beliefs against immunization are exempt from the statute. A Jewish family interpreted passages from Leviticus as forbidding immunization and sought exemption from the statute for their twin daughters. When the district determined that the children could not attend kindergarten without being immunized, the parents filed a lawsuit in the U.S. District Court for the Eastern District of New York, seeking a permanent injunction to prevent the district from violating their constitutional rights, a declaration that they were entitled to an exemption from the statute and damages of $1 million. The court issued a temporary restraining order that permitted the children to attend school during the pendency of the action and held a hearing to decide whether to issue a preliminary order.

At the hearing, the school board presented testimony from a Rabbi that nothing in Jewish teachings prohibited the immunization of children, and that the objection of the parents in this case was based on their personal interpretation of scripture. The court determined that their beliefs were genuine and sincerely held and that an examination of medical records indicated that they had opposed all immunizations for at least six years. The court issued a preliminary order restraining the school board from keeping the children out of school. The children could attend school without immunization certificates pending a trial. *Berg v. Glen Cove City School Dist.*, 853 F.Supp. 651 (E.D.N.Y.1994).

A Nebraska school district suffered its first outbreak of measles in nearly a decade. As a result, the school district determined that all unimmunized children should be excluded from the high school at which the confirmed case had arisen for a period of two weeks or until no further cases were reported. Alternately, the students could reenter school upon proof of immunization. Two sisters whose parents had decided not to immunize them based on personal preference, and not for religious or medical reasons, were excluded. The parents sued, stating that the district's decision lacked statutory authority and violated the students' equal protection rights. The Nebraska trial court upheld the district's decision, and the parents appealed to the Supreme Court of Nebraska. The supreme court stated that Nebraska law allowed school districts to exclude students whenever the students' conduct presented a clear threat to the physical safety of the students or others. This "emergency" situation statute took precedence over the general statute which allowed children who were not immunized to attend school. The high communicability of measles justified the exclusion under this section. The court also stated that the parents' equal protection arguments failed. Where a suspect classification is not involved, the statute must merely rationally further a legitimate interest. Here, the state had a legitimate basis for excluding the students. The court affirmed the trial court's ruling. *Maack v. School Dist. of Lincoln*, 491 N.W.2d 341 (Neb.1992).

A New York couple requested a religious exemption from their school district's mandatory immunization requirements for their daughter. They filled out a questionnaire, which was in the form of an affidavit, and denied that they were seeking a medical exemption from immunization. The district denied the petition. The couple then sought to obtain a medical exemption by presenting a note from a doctor. That request was denied. The couple then submitted their second claim for a religious exemption stating that they were now members of the Congregation of Universal Wisdom. The school district again denied the request. The student in question was a six-year-old child who had been diagnosed with Rett Syndrome, which results in severe multiple disabilities in affected children. She had received one dose of oral polio vaccine at approximately three months of age, and was shortly thereafter hospitalized with a viral syndrome. She had not received any other immunizations. Her parents attributed the onset of her present condition to the administration of the oral polio vaccine. The student received home instruction provided by the school district, although evaluations had shown she would benefit from a structured special educational environment. The school district, however, refused to admit the student to its special education school because of the parents' refusal to comply with the mandatory immunization requirements. The parents sued, seeking an injunction and enforcement of their right to free exercise of religion. A federal court denied the religious exemption and refused to hear the parents' claim for a medical exemption. The parents then took that claim before a New York state court.

The New York Supreme Court, Rockland County, held for the school district. The court stated that the district had not acted in an arbitrary or capricious manner. Based on the school district's chief medical officer's own investigation into Rett Syndrome, the school district was able to legitimately determine that there was no medical reason not to immunize a child with the syndrome. The school district was not bound to follow the opinion of the doctor who had given the parents their certificate. Expert testimony at the trial also failed to indicate that there should be no immunization. Since no medically recognized reason existed not to immunize the student, the court upheld the school district's decision. *Lynch v. Clarkstown Cent. School Dist.*, 590 N.Y.S.2d 687 (Sup.Ct.—Rockland County 1992).

C. Gifted Student and Honor Programs

A Connecticut special education statute defined "gifted children" as being "exceptional children" who did not progress effectively without special education. Although this definition coincided with the state law definition of children with disabilities, the statute did not mandate special education for gifted students, as it did for students with disabilities. The parents of a Connecticut student identified as gifted demanded that the school board provide him with special education individually designed to meet his needs. The board refused to provide an individualized education program for the student and the parents filed a lawsuit in a Connecticut trial court for a declaration that he was entitled to special education. The court granted summary judgment motions by the state and local education boards and commissioner of education, finding that gifted children did not have a right to special education under the state constitution. The Supreme Court of Connecticut transferred an appeal by the student and parents from the state appellate court.

The supreme court observed that although the legislature had categorized gifted children within the definition of exceptional children, the statute did not create a right to special education for gifted children. Special education was mandatory only for students with disabilities. Because students with disabilities had different needs than gifted children, there was a rational basis for treating the two groups differently, and there was no violation of the state constitution on equal protection grounds. The court affirmed the trial court's order for summary judgment. *Broadley v. Bd. of Educ. of the City of Meriden*, 229 Conn. 1, 639 A.2d 502 (1994).

A Tennessee elementary school student received perfect attendance awards every year from the first through the sixth grade under an informal program administered by the principal of the school. During the student's seventh grade year, the principals in the county school system decided to change the perfect attendance awards program. Under the new criteria, a student was considered present if he or she was at school for at least three hours and 16 minutes of the class day. During that year, the student received two absences, one of which would have also counted as an absence under the old system. Thus, she did not receive a perfect attendance award. The student and her father unsuccessfully appealed the absences to the local superintendent and then to the county school board. They then filed suit in a Tennessee trial court alleging that the perfect attendance awards program had not been adopted in accordance with Tennessee statutes. The trial court dismissed the complaint. The student and her father appealed to the Court of Appeals of Tennessee.

The court of appeals stated that the Tennessee statutes regarding school attendance gave no indication that the Tennessee legislature contemplated that they would apply to perfect attendance awards programs. The attendance laws were adopted to maintain uniform minimum attendance standards to prevent students from being kicked out of school for poor attendance. They were not intended to regulate and reward good attendance. Since the student would have been absent for at least one day under the old criteria, the court stated that she had been treated in a very fair and reasonable manner. The court affirmed the trial court's decision. *Richardson v. Fentress Co. School Bd.*, 840 S.W.2d 940 (Tenn.App.1992).

A Pennsylvania school district entered into an agreement with other school districts to establish joint schools to provide technical and vocational education. The joint schools operated an area vocational and technical school (AVTS) which had its own admissions policy. The school district in question, however, adopted its own criteria for determining which students could apply to the AVTS, including the requirement of a "C" average. After a student complained, the State Board for Vocational Education conducted an investigation. It concluded that the school district could not apply its own admissions policy. The State Secretary of Education affirmed that result on appeal, and the district asked the Pennsylvania Commonwealth Court to review the secretary's order. The court agreed with the board and secretary. It stated that state regulations did not allow the school district to screen student applicants. An admissions policy must be in force at all times, but such a policy may not be formulated by an individual school district. Only when a school's quota for admissions has been exceeded may a school district formulate its own policy. In addition, the "C" average requirement was invalid since state regulations required that vo-tech programs may not "unfairly penalize students who have not achieved high grades in academic subjects." *East Allegheny School Dist. v. Secretary of Educ.*, 603 A.2d 713 (Pa.Cmwlth.1992).

II. COMPULSORY ATTENDANCE

The states have a compelling interest in seeing that their citizens receive at least a minimal education and they may establish and enforce reasonable

school attendance laws to that end. **For compulsory education cases involving private schools, see Chapter Thirteen, Section II of this volume.**

A. Compulsory Attendance Laws

An emotionally impaired Michigan student was absent or tardy more than 100 days out of a total 182 school days in one year. The IEP proposed by the school district called for placement in a highly structured, self-contained program for emotionally impaired students for most of the day, with mainstreaming in art, music, and physical education. The student's mother attended the IEP conference with an advocate and successfully argued for a full-time regular education program. At a later IEP meeting, the parties approved an IEP calling for 80 percent of the student's time to be spent in regular classes. Less than 60 days after the second IEP meeting, the school's assistant principal signed a complaint against the student's mother for violating Michigan's compulsory education law. A warrant was issued and the student's mother was handcuffed, taken to jail, booked and released on bond. A Michigan state court granted the mother's motion for a directed verdict because of the district's failure to comply with the statutory requirement of submitting proof by an attendance officer. The student's mother then filed a federal district court complaint for violations of the IDEA, 42 U.S.C. § 1983, constitutional violations and personal injuries.

The U.S. District Court for the Western District of Michigan held that the student's mother had failed to exhaust her administrative remedies as required by the IDEA. The student's mother could not advance any federal claim before appropriately exhausting her administrative remedies. There was no equal protection violation by the district. The parent's claims for emotional distress, false imprisonment and malicious prosecution for violating the compulsory attendance law also failed. This was because she had simply failed to send her son to school. There was no merit to her contention that the compulsory attendance law did not apply in cases of disabled students. The case was distinguishable from cases involving expulsion of disabled students because here the school system was attempting to compel the student's attendance. *Torrie By and Through Torrie v. Cwayna*, 841 F.Supp. 1434 (W.D.Mich.1994).

A New York school's attendance policy required students to attend 90 percent of all classes in each course to receive credit, and dropped students from any course from which they were deliberately absent. A group of students brought suit in a state trial court challenging the constitutionality of the attendance policy. The students argued that the denial of credit for a class is equivalent to dropping a student from enrollment, which is contrary to New York law. The school district's motion for summary judgment was granted. The students appealed to the New York Supreme Court, Appellate Division. The court rejected the students' arguments and held that the denial of credit was not equivalent to dropping a student from enrollment since it did not bar a student from attending class or attending make-up classes. The court upheld the lower court's entry of summary judgment on behalf of the school. *Bitting v. Lee*, 564 N.Y.S.2d 791 (A.D.3d Dept. 1990).

B. Home Study Programs

Massachusetts state law grants local school districts the discretion to determine their own standards for home schooling. A public school committee required parents seeking to provide home instruction to their children to give signed consents for home visits by school representatives. The visits were made to observe and evaluate parental instructional methods. The parents of one child who sought to teach the child at home in accordance with their religious beliefs objected to the home visit requirement and refused to sign the consent form. The school committee then voted to disallow home instruction by the parents. The parents sued the school committee in the U.S. District Court for the District of Massachusetts for declaratory and injunctive relief, claiming that the home visit policy violated their First and Fourth Amendment rights as well as their due process right to educate their child. The court granted the school committee's motion for summary judgment and the parents appealed to the U.S. Court of Appeals, First Circuit.

The court of appeals stated that the Massachusetts compulsory attendance law established a state law basis for the parents' claims. The school committee's home visit regulation had been adopted under the statutory authority of the compulsory attendance law, and the specific issue of whether home visits were an essential part of the state's evaluation process had not yet been considered by Massachusetts state courts. Because federal courts abstain from issuing advisory constitutional decisions and seek to avoid intervening in local educational policy issues, it was appropriate for the district court to abstain from ruling on the matter. However, the district court should have retained jurisdiction pending a decision by a Massachusetts court on the compulsory education law. The court of appeals vacated the district court's decision and remanded the case for further consideration. *Pustell v. Lynn Pub. Schools*, 18 F.3d 50 (1st Cir.1994).

A West Virginia couple allowed their son to attend public school through second grade, when he was removed for home schooling. A state statute required the student's composite test results for any single year for English, grammar, reading, social studies, science and mathematics to be at or above the 40th percentile on a national standardized test. At the completion of the student's second grade year, his composite score was at the 62nd percentile. After the first year of home schooling, his composite score fell to the 17th percentile; and after the second year of home schooling, his composite score rose to the 38th percentile. Because the student failed to achieve the 40th percentile at the end of the second "remedial" year of home schooling, his parents were informed that he was no longer eligible for home instruction under the statute. They sued the county education board in a federal district court, claiming that the statute violated the Due Process and Equal Protection Clauses of the Fourteenth Amendment. They sought a preliminary injunction preventing legal action against them for continuing to home school their son. The district court determined that reentry into the public school system would cause little, if any, harm to the student. Also, the court noted that there was no specific fundamental right involved here, and that the parents' liberty interest was subject to reasonable state regulation. The court held that the 40 percent cutoff was rationally related to a legitimate state purpose and that the parents' claims could not succeed. The court granted summary judgment to the school officials. *Null v. Board of Education of County of Jackson,* 815 F.Supp. 937 (S.D.W.Va.1993).

The parents of four North Dakota children began home-schooling their children in 1983. During the relevant six-year period, the parents met the requirements of the private school exception to the state's compulsory attendance laws. Further, the North Dakota Department of Public Instruction approved the parents' home school as a private school. The department set out all the home-schooling requirements under this exception. The North Dakota legislature subsequently amended the compulsory attendance statute to include a home-based instruction exception. The school officials then required the parents to comply. The parents challenged this new requirement in a North Dakota district court. The district court held that the parents could choose between the two exceptions, but if they chose the private school exception they would have to comply with the health, fire, and safety laws applicable to private school buildings. The parents appealed and the school officials cross-appealed to the Supreme Court of North Dakota. The supreme court noted that the amendment was designed to relax compulsory education laws in order to accommodate home-schooling families. Thus, the parents could choose to comply with either the private school exception or the home-based instruction exception and, regardless, did not have to comply with private school health, fire and safety laws and regulations. *Birst v. Sanstead,* 493 N.W.2d 690 (N.D.1992).

A Minnesota couple had their oldest children removed from their custody when they refused, for religious reasons, to allow them to attend public school. The county later sought to place a younger child with protective services. However, a court allowed the parents to keep the child subject to their establishment of a lawful home education program. Minnesota requires that home-schooled children take a standardized achievement examination and perform above the 30th percentile. The child took the first half of the test, but the parents refused to allow her to complete the remainder because they believed that the test should be administered in their home. The parents later refused to allow testing even after the school agreed to administer it in the parents' home. A trial court then ordered the child to be placed with protective services. The parents appealed to the Court of Appeals of Minnesota.

Minnesota courts apply a three-prong test in attempting to balance the parents' interests in freedom of religion with the state's interest in the education of its citizenry. The first prong questions whether the asserted religious belief is sincerely held. The court found that the parents had sufficiently demonstrated their sincerity. The second prong requires that the state have a compelling interest which justifies the imposition of a burden. It is well settled that education amounts to a compelling interest. The third prong requires that the state's interest be pursued through the least restrictive means. When a child fails to perform adequately on a test, the Minnesota home-schooling statutes provide for criminal charges. The court held that it could "discern no rationale" for using harsher sanctions when a parent refuses to allow an examination than when a child fails.

Therefore, removal of custody was found not to be the least restrictive means. The decision was reversed. *Matter of Welfare of T.K. & W.K.*, 475 N.W.2d 88 (Minn.App.1991).

An anonymous informant notified a Maine school board that a local family's children were not attending school. The school district's superintendent wrote to the family to explain the procedure for approval of home schooling programs. The family shared information about the home schooling, but on being notified of official approval, the family replied that they had never asked for approval. The family then announced that they would no longer share information with the school committee if the committee used the information in an approval process. The school district voted to refer the matter to the county district attorney for civil truancy proceedings. On learning of this decision, the family sued the school district in a Maine trial court arguing that the approval process violated the Free Exercise Clause of the First Amendment. The court held for the school district, and the family appealed to the Supreme Judicial Court of Maine. The supreme court held that although the state's prior approval policy for home schooling may have burdened the family's free exercise of religion, the public interest in education outweighed this interest. The court affirmed the superior court's ruling. *Blount v. Dept. of Educ. & Cultural Serv.*, 551 A.2d 1377 (Me.1988).

South Carolina allows home-schooling as an alternative to compulsory school attendance. A state law provides that a request for home-schooling shall be approved if the parent holds at least a high school diploma or equivalent general educational development (GED), and attains a passing score on a basic skills examination to be developed and validated by the state department of education. In order to test instructors, the department sought to use a previously developed test (the EEE) which was used to evaluate the reading, writing, and mathematics ability of entrance level students. The department hired an outside firm to assess the suitability of the EEE to test home-school instructors. The firm assembled a panel to assess the test. The panel examined each question to determine whether it was task-related, or contained a bias which would offend or penalize an examinee based on gender, ethnicity, religion, or socioeconomic status. The results of this panel's assessment led the department to validate the EEE. An association which supported home schoolers alleged that the test was not suitable and challenged the validation process in a state trial court. The trial court held that the test was properly validated, and the association appealed to the Supreme Court of South Carolina.

The association contended that the panelists who were not home schoolers were unqualified to assess the test. Indeed, the educators had not been instructed as to the necessary prerequisites to be a successful home school instructor. The department argued that the use of the test was justified because it tested basic literacy, which is a qualification for an instructor. The court disagreed, and held that the tasks of home schooling were so dissimilar from public school teaching that the use of the same validation test was incorrect. The fact that a high percentage of examinees passed the test was ruled to have no effect on the test's validity. The decision of the trial court was reversed. *Lawrence v. South Carolina State Bd. of Educ.*, 412 S.E.2d 394 (S.C.1991).

C. Truancy

An 18-year-old West Virginia student missed five days of school without an excuse. He was warned that continued absences could result in criminal prosecution. After continuing unexcused absences, the county prosecutor's office filed a criminal complaint against the student in a West Virginia trial court. The student was convicted of violating a state compulsory attendance statute. He then petitioned the Supreme Court of Appeals of West Virginia for a writ of prohibition. The court of appeals observed that the compulsory attendance statute under which the student was prosecuted mandated school attendance for children between the ages of six and 16 and provided enforcement sanctions against parents, guardians or custodians, and not against individual students. There was no possibility of liability under the statute for a nonattending student regardless of age. A different statute applied to cases involving students who were 18 or older, and school boards were allowed to suspend students for improper conduct. For students under the age of 18, the possibility of a delinquency adjudication also existed. The court granted the writ as requested by the student. *State of West Virginia ex rel. Estes v. Egnor*, 443 S.E.2d 193 (W.Va.1994).

Wisconsin's compulsory school attendance statute requires any person having control of a school-aged child to "cause the child to attend school regularly...." The statute cross-references other Wisconsin statutes detailing state procedures for truancy, including a statute which requires each school board to establish written attendance policies. The parent of a student who was absent without excuse eight times during a three-month period failed to respond to repeated notices from the school to meet with officials to resolve the problem. The local district attorney's office brought charges against the student's parent, resulting in a misdemeanor conviction. The parent appealed to the Court of Appeals of Wisconsin. On appeal, the parent argued that the compulsory attendance statute was unconstitutionally vague because it failed to describe the word "regularly." The court determined that the statute was sufficiently definite and understandable to a person of average intelligence to preclude a finding of unconstitutional vagueness. The dictionary definition of "regularly" was not technical and had a common and approved meaning. The compulsory attendance statute sufficiently cross-referenced other statutes so that the full statutory scheme of mandatory attendance was clear. The court also rejected the parent's defense that the student was uncontrollable, because evidence in the record indicated that she had a consistent pattern of unexcused absences dating from her kindergarten year. The court affirmed the conviction and found the statute constitutional. *State of Wisconsin v. White*, 509 N.W.2d 434 (Wis.App.1993).

Two sets of parents objected to the state of Michigan's requirements that nonpublic schools use state-certified teachers. One child's parents argued that the requirement violated their Fourteenth Amendment right to direct the education of their children. The other parents each objected on separate grounds: the mother argued that it was sinful to submit to state authority and hire state-certified teachers. The parents were convicted of violating compulsory attendance laws. On appeal, the Supreme Court of Michigan remanded the case for reconsideration in light of recent U.S. Supreme Court and Supreme Court of Michigan decisions.

The U.S. Supreme Court held that a law of general applicability which is religiously neutral does not violate the Free Exercise Clause. An exception to this ruling is available for "hybrid" claims which allege a burden of the right of free exercise and another fundamental right. Here, the case included claims based on both the Free Exercise Clause and the right to direct the education of children; the case thus fit within the exception. The issue then became whether the regulation was justified by a compelling state interest. At this point the appellate court turned to the applicability of the Michigan Supreme Court decision. That ruling held that a state may not enforce licensing requirements on a preschool director. The court in the present case distinguished it from the earlier Michigan decision because it involved elementary and secondary education as opposed to preschool. The state was ruled to have a compelling interest in the quality of education of children who are old enough to attend school. The convictions were upheld. *People v. DeJonge,* 470 N.W.2d 433 (Mich.App.1991).

Two New York City police officers observed a school-age girl one-half block from a school during school hours. The girl was unable to account for her presence and was forcibly detained. After the girl became violent and struck one of the officers, she was arrested. The girl was adjudicated delinquent and put on probation, but challenged the adjudication on grounds that the police officers had no authority to detain her. The New York Court of Appeals ruled that police have authority to detain suspected truants for violation of noncriminal compulsory education laws enacted for the protection of children. The court also explained that enforcement of the state's compulsory education laws is well within the scope of the traditional authority of the police, and that police officers need not be certain that a student is a truant before detention. *Matter of Shannon B.,* 517 N.E.2d 203 (N.Y.1987).

Two women were charged under Maryland compulsory attendance laws for failing to see that their children attended school or received instruction as required by law. The women each had two children, all of whom were absent from school for at least 70 days during the 1985-86 school year. The women claimed that the law under which they were convicted was unconstitutional because it imposed "strict liability" on them for the actions of their children. The Maryland Court of Special Appeals ruled that the law did not subject parents to prosecution for actions of their children. Rather, the law imposed an affirmative duty on persons who have control over a child to see that the child attends school regularly. Because failure to perform that affirmative duty is a violation of the statute, "[p]assive acquiescence in the child's nonattendance of school is no defense." The women's convictions were affirmed. *In re Jeannette L.,* 523 A.2d 1048 (Md.App.1987).

A Minnesota student's father removed the student from public school for the purpose of providing a home-school education. The county bureau of social services and public junior high school officials became concerned that the student's home education did not meet statutory requirements. Approximately one year later, a school truancy officer issued a citation. The case came before a Minnesota trial court, where both the attorney for the county and the student's attorney stipulated to the court that the student was not attending public school and that by remaining at home he was obeying his father's wishes that he receive an in-home school education. Based on these stipulated facts, the trial court determined that the student was not habitually truant. The county then appealed to the Court of Appeals of Minnesota. The county argued that the recent legislative change which placed habitual truants in the category of "children in need of protection or services" demonstrated an intent to eliminate the volitional element of habitual truancy. The court, however, disagreed. It held that a student absent from school in obedience to his parent's wrongful command should not be stigmatized by an unwarranted truancy label. If a problem existed with the home-school education, the court held that the proper action was against the parent. The court affirmed the trial court's decision, and dismissed the truancy citation. *Matter of Welfare of B.K.J.*, 451 N.W.2d 241 (Minn.App.1990).

III. CORPORAL PUNISHMENT

Many states specifically allow the use of reasonable physical force by school authorities to restrain unruly students, to correct unacceptable behavior and to maintain the order necessary to conduct an educational program. Some states, however, specifically prohibit corporal punishment. Where state law permits, courts generally uphold the reasonable application of punishment and have been reluctant to find that such punishment violates student due process rights.

The U.S. Supreme Court upheld the beating of two Florida students by school administrators in which one student was beaten so severely as to miss eleven days of school. Another student suffered a hematoma and lost use of his arm for one week. The parents sued school authorities on the ground that the beatings constituted cruel and unusual punishment. The Supreme Court upheld the beatings and ruled that the Eighth Amendment prohibition against cruel and unusual punishment did not apply to corporal punishment against students. The Court's reasoning for this decision lay in the relative openness of the school system and its surveillance by the community. The protections of the Eighth Amendment were intended to protect the rights of incarcerated persons. Such surveillance is not so readily apparent in the prison system, and thus the Eighth Amendment safeguards are necessary for convicted criminals but not for students, who have the ability to file civil lawsuits against school districts and employees to vindicate their rights. *Ingraham v. Wright*, 430 U.S. 651, 97 S.Ct. 1401, 51 L.Ed.2d 711 (1977).

An Illinois junior high school teacher separated two students who were shouting at each other in class. One student refused to leave the classroom as instructed by the teacher, who then grabbed her by the wrist and elbow to hurry her along. The student tripped over a desk in the process, and she was taken to the nurse's office to receive ice packs on her wrist and elbow. She later filed a lawsuit against the teacher and school district for claimed violations of her constitutional rights. The U.S. District Court for the Northern District of Illinois considered summary judgment motions by the district and teacher on the student's claims under 42 U.S.C. § 1983.

The court disagreed with the student's argument that the case involved application of Fourth Amendment principles such as a seizure, and rejected the claim for use of excessive force. The court stated that the case was properly analyzed under the relevant case law of corporal punishment and the school's disciplinary code. Corporal punishment has not been ruled by the courts as rising to the level of a constitutional violation except where the punishment is so grossly excessive as to shock the conscience. The teacher's actions in this case could not be construed as a violation of the student's constitutional rights. Under the analysis employed in § 1983 claims, the teacher could not have reasonably expected that the use of corporal punishment violated the student's constitutional rights. The court granted the summary judgment motions and dismissed the student's state law battery claims without prejudice. *Wallace v. Batavia School Dist. 101*, 870 F.Supp. 222 (N.D.Ill.1994).

An assistant principal at an Arkansas middle school paddled three fifth-graders who had been caught smoking on the playground. Following school procedures, the assistant principal had another teacher witness the spanking. The following afternoon, one of the students' mothers noticed bruises on the child's buttocks. The mother contacted school officials and reported the paddling to the county family services office as an incident of suspected child abuse. A case-worker investigated the incident and filed a report for recordation in the State Central Registry. The assistant principal requested an administrative hearing to review the decision. A state hearing officer issued an order in which she found "some credible evidence" to substantiate the occurrence of abuse. The assistant principal appealed to an Arkansas trial court which reversed the agency's decision and directed the assistant principal's name be stricken from the register. The agency then appealed. The Court of Appeals of Arkansas held for the assistant principal. Under Arkansas law, a teacher may use corporal punishment in a reasonable manner against any pupil for good cause in order to maintain discipline and order. However, abuse is any nonaccidental physical injury to a child under one's care. The assistant principal and the witness had testified that the swats were merely "average" and should not have caused bruising. The caseworker also testified that after she had completed her interviews she did not feel that the assistant principal had been abusive, but it was departmental policy to substantiate any allegation of abuse if bruises remain after a 24-hour period. The court stated that such a litmus test, without consideration of the attendant circumstances, is inappropriate. The court upheld the trial court's determination. *Arkansas Dept. of Human Services v. Caldwell*, 832 S.W.2d 510 (Ark.App.1992).

A nine-year-old third grade student at a Kentucky elementary school was paddled on three separate occasions. The first paddling came after the student had been talking in class. The second and third paddlings occurred after she had apparently laughed when another student made a face at her, and she had attempted to join other students who were playing a game. A social worker and police officer later examined the child and stated that bruises on the child were excessive. The child was treated at a local hospital, where a doctor determined that the bruises were the result of excessive force. In response, the school superintendent conducted an investigation and found that the paddlings were consistent with school policy. The student sued the school district and her teachers in federal court under 42 U.S.C. § 1983, alleging that the spankings violated her due process rights. The court stated that the teachers did not violate the student's due process rights. It noted that not every violation of state tort law rises to a constitutional level. The student was not injured to such an extent as to shock the conscience of the court. The court dismissed the student's suit. *Brown v. Johnson*, 710 F.Supp. 183 (E.D.Ky.1989).

Two Texas kindergarten students were snickering in the school hall. The school principal gave the students two swats with a wooden paddle. When the students returned to their classroom, their teacher also saw them snickering and gave them another three swats with the wooden paddle. The students suffered serious bruises. State social workers determined that this constituted child abuse. The students sued the school in a federal district court for violation of due process rights. The district court dismissed the claim and the students appealed to the U.S. Court of Appeals, Fifth Circuit. The court of appeals stated that the spankings did not constitute a due process violation. If the spankings were unreasonable and disproportionate to the offense of snickering, Texas common law was adequate to afford the students due process. The appeals court affirmed the district court's dismissal. *Cunningham v. Beavers*, 858 F.2d 269 (5th Cir.1988).

A fifth grade Georgia student was paddled four times for inappropriate behavior. The student had superficial bruises which had gone away within ten days. Approximately two years later, the student was diagnosed as suffering from post-traumatic stress disorder. The parents sued the school district, seeking to recover for the student's physical and psychological injuries. The trial court dismissed the case and the parents appealed to the Court of Appeals of Georgia. The court of appeals stated that it is to be anticipated that corporal punishment will produce pain and the potential for bruising. However, the court stated that the punishment was not so excessive or severe as to be in violation of state law or school board policy. The court of appeals affirmed the trial court's dismissal. *Mathis v. Berrien County School Dist.*, 378 S.E.2d 505 (Ga.App.1989).

A Florida teacher punished a student by swatting her three times in accordance with the school's corporal punishment rule. A hearing officer determined that the state Department of Health and Rehabilitative Services (HRS) failed to prove that the punishment constituted child abuse under Florida law. The teacher then requested expungement of the investigation. After the HRS denied the request and ordered the report classified as confirmed, the teacher appealed to the District Court of Appeal of Florida. The court ordered the HRS to clear the teacher of all charges. It ruled that the HRS may not reject the hearing officer's fact findings unless it first determines that they were not based upon competent evidence or did not comply with the law. *M.J.B. v. Dept. of Health and Rehabilitative Services*, 543 So.2d 352 (Fla.App.5th Dist.1989).

A third grade female student was called to the principal's office for hitting a boy who had kicked her. The principal allegedly directed a teacher to hold the student upside down by her ankles while the principal struck her with a wooden paddle. Next, the principal allegedly hit the student five times on the front of the leg between the knee and waist. The beating caused a welt on the girl's leg, as well as a two-inch cut that left a permanent scar. Four months later the principal again administered corporal punishment to the student. After the principal had struck the student twice on the buttocks, the student refused to be hit again. The principal called in a male administrative assistant to make the student bend over a chair to receive three additional blows. During the ensuing struggle, the student hit her back on the principal's desk and suffered back pains for several weeks. The student finally submitted to the last three blows. This beating caused severe bruises on the student's buttocks. A nurse who examined the student said that if a child had received this type of injury at home she would have reported it to child abuse authorities. The student sued the principal and other school officials alleging a violation of her liberty interest in personal privacy and bodily security under the U.S. Constitution. A U.S. district court ruled before trial that the school officials could not be held liable for damages because they were protected by "good faith" immunity. The student appealed to the U.S. Court of Appeals, Tenth Circuit. Overruling the lower court, the court of appeals declared that "the law was clearly established ... that some high level of force in a corporal punishment context would violate" a child's right to bodily security. The court decided that this constitutional right is violated by infliction of "punishments that are so grossly excessive as to be shocking to the conscience." Because the beatings alleged in this case were sufficiently brutal, the court ruled that the school officials should have known that such beatings were forbidden by the Constitution. Good faith immunity was therefore not available to the school officials, and the case was remanded for trial. *Garcia v. Miera*, 817 F.2d 650 (10th Cir.1987).

IV. EXPULSIONS AND SUSPENSIONS

School districts and colleges have the power to control student behavior through the use of disciplinary suspensions and expulsions. This power is limited by student constitutional rights to due process. Failure to follow due process requirements can lead to orders reversing suspensions or expulsions, expunging of records of proceedings from student files, and damages against school districts and board members.

A. Academic Expulsions or Suspensions

A student enrolled in the University of Michigan's "Inteflex" program—which was a special six-year course of study leading to both an undergraduate and medical degree—struggled with the curriculum and barely achieved minimal competence. He failed the NBME Part I, receiving the lowest score ever in the brief history of the Inteflex program. The university's medical school executive board reviewed the student's academic career and decided to drop him from registration in the program, and further denied his request that he be allowed to retake the NBME Part I. The student then sued the university in U.S. district court claiming a violation of his due process rights under the U.S. Constitution. At trial the evidence showed that the university had established a practice of allowing students who had failed the NBME Part I to retake the test up to four times. The student was the only person ever refused permission to retake the test. The district court held that his dismissal was not violative of the Due Process Clause. The U.S. Supreme Court upheld the district court's ruling against the student. The Due Process Clause was not offended because "the University's liberal retesting custom gave rise to no state law entitlement to retake NBME Part I." *Regents v. Ewing*, 474 U.S. 214, 106 S.Ct. 507, 88 L.Ed.2d 523 (1985).

The University of Tennessee Board of Trustees' honor code created a violation for failure to report the giving or receiving of unauthorized aid on an examination. Four students reported observing a group of other students who apparently gave or received aid during several examinations. One of the accused students was charged with cheating on five examinations under the honor code. An administrative law judge found the student not guilty on three charges and guilty on two others. He imposed as a punishment one year of probation and the loss of credit for the two classes in which she was held in violation of the honor code. The student appealed the decision to a Tennessee trial court, stating that a 19-day delay by the administrative law judge in issuing his opinion caused her to delay retaking the two courses. The student nonetheless graduated. The court held for the university and the student appealed to the Court of Appeals of Tennessee. The court of appeals found ample evidence in the record that the student had violated the honor code. There was evidence that the student had been looking at another person's examination papers. The administrative law judge's delay did not violate state law and the court affirmed the trial court's judgment for the university. *Daley v. Univ. of Tennessee at Memphis*, 880 S.W.2d 693 (Tenn.App.1994).

A Texas medical school student took a National Board of Medical Examiners test in surgery. Two test proctors observed the student looking at another student's answer sheet. Eighteen days later, the school advised the student by letter that he was accused of cheating on the test. He denied wrongdoing but the school brought formal charges several weeks later and held a hearing on charges of academic dishonesty. The hearing officer and a school official viewed the test site during the hearing. The student was denied permission to view the room. The hearing officer recommended expulsion and changing the student's grade from B to F. A Texas district court held that the university had violated the student's due process rights and the university appealed to the Court of Appeals of Texas, Houston.

The court of appeals observed that the dismissal was for disciplinary reasons, which justified more stringent procedural protection than dismissal for academic reasons. In this case, the university had deprived the student of a meaningful opportunity to respond to the charges against him. It had attempted to discourage him from obtaining legal counsel and had failed to inform him of the charges until it was too late for him to contact witnesses. The test proctors had failed to approach him and escort him outside the examination room and had thus violated university academic policies. The university's actions deprived the student of his procedural due process rights and the court of appeals affirmed the trial court's decision. *Univ. of Texas Med. School at Houston v. Than*, 874 S.W.2d 839 (Tex.App.— Houston 1994).

Three Ohio high school students stole copies of an algebra test from their teacher's file cabinet. They distributed copies to two other students. After they took the test, the teacher noted their identical answers. The school held a disciplinary hearing at which witnesses testified that one of the students acted as a lookout while the other two stole copies. The five students who had cheated on the test were given Fs for the class. The three students who participated in the theft were suspended for ten days in addition to receiving Fs. One of the students who was suspended sued the school district in an Ohio trial court, which abated the suspension, finding it unreasonable. The Court of Appeals of Ohio, Erie County, reinstated the suspension, finding that it was both rational and reasonable. The school had appropriately imposed separate penalties for the separate offenses of cheating and theft. *Reed v. Vermilion Local School Dist.*, 614 N.E.2d 1101 (Ohio App.6th Dist.1992).

A senior at an Indiana high school left school to go to her medical biology class located at a medical center. On the way, she stopped and drank some beer. After admitting this to school officials, she was suspended for five days, and her grades were reduced by 20 percent in each class for the semester. The student handbook provided for a grade reduction of four percent for each class missed each day during the suspension. The student then brought suit against the school in a federal district court, asserting that the grade reduction was violative of her constitutional right to substantive due process. Both the student and the school moved for summary judgment.

The school asserted that a rational relationship existed between the grade reduction and the use of alcohol because the use of alcohol during school hours adversely affected the academic accomplishment of the student user. The student, on the other hand, argued that the use of academic sanctions for nonacademic misconduct constituted arbitrary and capricious action because the penalty was not rationally related to the misconduct and not rationally related to the disciplinary purpose. The court noted that a student's grade or credit should reflect the student's academic performance or achievement, and that reducing grades for misconduct unrelated to academic conduct results in a skewed and inaccurate reflection of the student's academic performance. Here, the court found that the rule was unreasonable and arbitrary on its face. The grade reduction was not imposed for lack of effort in academics, but was imposed as part of a disciplinary action to discourage the consumption of alcohol during school hours. Because the student's misconduct was not directly related to her academic performance, an academic sanction was not warranted. The court granted summary judgment to the student. *Smith v. School City of Hobart,* 811 F.Supp. 391 (N.D.Ind.1993).

A graduate student at a New York state university was charged with academic dishonesty after allegedly cheating on a final examination. The initial charge was based on allegations of a classmate who stated that she saw the student viewing unauthorized notes during the exam. The tribunal found the student guilty and recommended that he be dismissed. The college provost dismissed the student. On appeal, the president of the college approved of the board of appeals' recommendation that the dismissal be upheld. The student then sued the university in a New York state court attacking the hearing procedures and findings. The trial court transferred the case to the Supreme Court, Appellate Division. The appellate court determined that annulment of the dismissal was required. It stated that it is well established that once a public or private college or university adopts rules or guidelines establishing the procedures to be followed in relation to suspension or expulsion of a student, the school must substantially comply with those rules and guidelines. In the instant case, the university had established clear rules to be followed in cases concerning alleged academic dishonesty. In several cases, it failed to follow those rules. The court stated that a new hearing was appropriate. *Weidemann v. State Univ. of New York College at Cortland*, 592 N.Y.S.2d 99 (A.D.3d Dept.1992).

A student at an Ohio medical college experienced personal problems which interfered with his scholastic performance in his pharmacology class. He asked to take a make-up final examination, but was told that he could not do so. He was permitted, however, to substitute his raw score from the pharmacology subsection of the National Board of Medical Examiners (NBME) test for the final examination in the course. He was also aware of a remedial pharmacology course offered during the summer, but he chose not to enroll in the course. After failing the final examination, and after receiving a NBME score of 57 percent, which was a failing grade, the student sought to remedy his failure by sitting for the final examination in the summer remedial course, even though he had not enrolled in or attended that class. The college dismissed him from its program after he failed and he brought suit against the college in the Ohio Court of Claims, seeking both reinstatement and monetary damages for breach of contract. The trial court held in favor of the college, and the student appealed to the Court of Appeals of Ohio. The appellate court noted that the college was not required to give the student unlimited opportunities to obtain a passing grade in pharmacology. Also, it was not arbitrary or capricious for the college to require the student to take both the midterm and final examinations for the remedial course in the time that the other students had to take just the final exam. The court affirmed the trial court's decision in favor of the college. *Bleicher v. University of Cincinnati College of Medicine*, 604 N.E.2d 783 (Ohio App.10th Dist.1992).

B.   Drug and Alcohol Use and Possession

An Ohio high school student was accused of accepting marijuana from another student and selling it to a third student for $5. The school's discipline policy prohibited the selling or distribution of drugs for profit and specified a ten-day suspension plus a mandatory 80-day expulsion. The superintendent of schools expelled the student accused of selling the marijuana for 80 days. However, he suspended the other two students for only three days under a different part of the discipline policy prohibiting possession or use of drugs on school grounds. The expelled student appealed to the board of education, which affirmed the expulsion. An Ohio trial court granted the student's motion for a temporary order staying the expulsion, but later entered final judgment affirming the expulsion order. The student appealed to the Court of Appeals of Ohio, Trumbull County.

On appeal, the student claimed that the school's discipline policy was not in compliance with an Ohio statute directing education boards to adopt suspension, expulsion and removal policies and requiring the posting of these policies in a central location of the school. He also claimed that he was singled out for more severe punishment than the other students even though he was no more culpable in the matter than they were. The court dismissed the first contention, observing that the student had failed to address this issue in the trial court proceedings. It also held that the expelled student's harsher punishment was reasonable. Because there was a basis upon which the board could rely in formulating its discipline policy, the court of appeals affirmed the student's expulsion. *Morgan v. Bd. of Educ. of Girard City School Dist.*, 630 N.E.2d 71 (Ohio App.11th Dist.1993).

A Colorado school district policy prohibited student use of alcohol, marijuana, and other unauthorized drugs during the regular school day and at district-sponsored activities. According to the policy, "an offender of either one of these policies is a student who has sold, used, consumed, [or] *is affected by....*" any of the named substances. A school district employee assigned to monitor a school dance noticed a student under the influence of alcohol. The student admitted drinking alcohol and identified two other students who had attended a party with him. The employee required the two other students to give breath samples, and they admitted drinking beer before going to the dance. The district suspended each student for five days. It also transferred the students to another high school for 90 days. The students sued the school district in a Colorado trial court alleging constitutional violations, and claiming a right to a hearing before transfer to the other school. The court ruled for the school district and the students appealed to the Colorado Court of Appeals.

The court of appeals affirmed the trial court's dismissal of the students' claim that the district employee had violated their constitutional rights. The employee had reasonable suspicion of a violation of school policy and the search was not improper. The trial court had also correctly ruled that the students had no right to a hearing prior to the transfer. However, the trial court misinterpreted the school district's policy as it pertained to students "affected by" the named substances. Student conduct regulations must have a reasonable relationship to education and may not regulate purely private activity. Summary judgment was inappropriate in this case regarding the "affected by" clause. *Martinez v. School Dist. No. 60*, 852 P.2d 1275 (Colo.App.1992).

A Florida high school student consumed alcohol and attended a school football game. He was arrested for relieving himself in a parking lot and admitted to the school's principal that he had been drinking. The school board's student conduct code provided for ten and five-day suspensions. Students could reduce suspensions to three days by completing a treatment program. When the school district suspended the student for five days, he sued it in the U.S. District Court for the Middle District of Florida, seeking damages and declaratory relief. The district and its officials brought a number of summary judgment motions, which were denied in part and granted in part by the court. A material issue of fact existed concerning whether the principal and other school officials had acted in good faith. The student had satisfied the minimal pleading requirements for § 1983 complaints against the school board and its members in their individual capacities. However, the court granted school district dismissal motions on the student's due process claims. The school board could legitimately impose a lesser penalty upon students willing to complete substance abuse treatment programs. *Kubany by Kubany v. School Bd. of Pinellas County*, 818 F.Supp. 1504 (M.D.Fla.1993).

The court then considered summary judgment motions filed by the officials and board concerning other remaining counts. Public officials were entitled to qualified immunity under 42 U.S.C. § 1983 unless it could be demonstrated that they performed a discretionary function which violated clearly established statutory or constitutional rights. On that basis, the court dismissed the student's due process claim because of an alleged lack of evidence that he was under the influence of alcohol. The principal was entitled to immunity in suspending the student. The court refused to grant summary judgment to the school board as a whole concerning the policy that required it to uphold disciplinary decisions of the principal regardless of the merits of the decision. The court granted the summary judgment motions of the officials in their official capacities, granted the board's motion for summary judgment in part, and denied it in part. *Kubany v. School Bd. of Pinellas County*, 839 F.Supp. 1544 (M.D.Fla.1993).

A Delaware student was expelled from school after being arrested for selling drugs to an undercover police officer on three separate occasions. The drug sales took place off school grounds and were not in any way school-related. The student challenged the expulsion, claiming that the state board of education lacked the authority to expel him for off-site nonschool-related drug sales. The Superior Court of Delaware, New Castle County, held that the district's code of conduct (relating to expulsions) was not all-inclusive. The local board was not powerless to act merely because the activity involved had occurred off campus. The court then cautioned that not all off-site nonschool-related activity could subject a student to the threat of expulsion. The expulsion was upheld. *Howard v. Colonial School Dist.*, 605 A.2d 590 (Del.Super.1992).

A Pennsylvania high school senior was accused of selling LSD approximately three weeks before he was to graduate. The school granted the student a hearing approximately one week before graduation to determine what disciplinary action would be taken. The day before the hearing the student developed infectious mononucleosis and the hearing was delayed for several days. Meanwhile, the student was allowed to attend classes and sit for final examinations. The hearing was held on the last day of class for graduating seniors. The student's grades were handed in by his teachers on the same day. On graduation day the school board permanently expelled the student and refused to award him his diploma. The student sued the school board in a Pennsylvania trial court. The court upheld the school board decision finding that the student had been properly expelled for selling LSD. The student then appealed to the Commonwealth Court of Pennsylvania. It overturned the trial court decision, noting that the Pennsylvania Public School Code required high schools to issue diplomas to all students who completed the prescribed coursework. *Schuman v. Cumberland Valley School District Board of Directors*, 536 A.2d 490 (Pa.Cmwlth.1988).

Five students consumed alcohol at a private residence between the end of the school day and their attendance at a football game as members of the band. The principal suspended the students for violating Rule 13 of the Student Guidelines for Reasonable Conduct which stated: "a student shall not possess, use, transmit, conceal, or be under the influence of ... alcoholic beverages ... while under the jurisdiction of the schools." The students appealed the board's decision in an Ohio trial court. The trial court determined that there was no evidence that alcohol had any influence on their conduct and reversed the board's decision. The board appealed to the Court of Appeals of Ohio. The board contended that the court had substituted its interpretation for the board's interpretation of Rule 13. The sole question presented under this assignment was whether the board's construction and interpretation of "under the influence" amounted to an abuse of discretion. The purpose of Rule 13 was to prohibit student alcohol consumption contemporaneous with attendance at school or extracurricular events. The rule was meant to prohibit any alcohol use by any student in conjunction with attendance at school or its events. The board's interpretation of Rule 13 did not amount to an abuse of discretion and the court reversed the trial court's decision. *Rohrbaugh v. Elida Local Bd. of Educ.*, 579 N.E.2d 782 (Ohio App.1990).

C. Misconduct

A California high school senior admitted bringing a gun to school and the school suspended him under a California statute that required the immediate suspension of any student found in possession of a firearm at school. Although the student had never received special education services, the student then requested an evaluation under the Individuals with Disabilities Education Act (IDEA). The school tested and evaluated the student and held an individualized education program meeting, at which it determined that the student was ineligible for special education services. The student requested an IDEA due process hearing to review the IEP meeting findings, and claimed that he could not be suspended from school under the IDEA stay-put provision. The U.S. District Court for the Southern District of California agreed with the student's argument that he was entitled to IDEA procedural safeguards regardless of whether he had been previously diagnosed as a student with disabilities. The IDEA broadly extended protection to all students with disabilities, and necessarily applied to students with undetected disabilities. The court denied the school district's motion to exclude the student from school on the basis of dangerousness. *M.P. by D.P. v. Governing Bd. of Grossmont Union High School Dist.*, 858 F.Supp. 1044 (S.D.Cal.1994).

A California high school student experienced difficulty in changing her schedule. She was required to stand in line, obtain approval from an assistant principal, and then told to return three days later. After the three day wait, a counselor stated that the class she sought was already full. The parties disputed the student's reply. The student alleged that she said, "I'm so angry, I could just shoot someone." The counselor characterized her statement as "if you don't give me this schedule change, I'm going to shoot you!" The counselor reported the incident three hours after it occurred. The assistant principal called the student to her office, and imposed a three day suspension. The student and her parents then filed a lawsuit in the U.S. District Court for the Southern District of California, seeking a declaration that the district had violated the student's free speech rights.

The court observed that the student had not made a threat that justified infringement upon her free speech rights. The evidence indicated that the student's words and physical manner did not present a likelihood of real physical harm to the counselor. The student's overriding interest in free expression prohibited imposition of the suspension. The court further held that the student had received the required notice and hearing concerning the suspension and suffered no due process violation. Although the student did not prevail on all of her constitutional claims, she had succeeded on a significant claim and was entitled to attorney's fees under 42 U.S.C. § 1988. The court limited the attorney's fees award to the free speech violation. *Lovell v. Poway Unif. School Dist.*, 847 F.Supp. 780 (S.D.Cal.1994).

The assistant principal of an Alabama middle school suspended a student for two days because of unexcused absences. Although school district procedures required telephone notification and prompt written notice by mail to parents, the school only sent a notice with the student. He threw away the notice and said nothing to his parents. The student was then accidentally shot and wounded while visiting a friend's house during the second day of the suspension. His parents filed a lawsuit in the U.S. District Court for the Northern District of Alabama, claiming constitutional violations by school officials, including the assistant principal. The court reviewed the basic rule applicable in cases of government liability for private acts of violence by third parties. Many courts have held that there can only be liability where the government official acts with deliberate indifference to and disregard of a clearly defined constitutional right. In this case, there was no duty of the school officials to protect students from other students while off school grounds, for any reason. The suspension was arguably a realistic effort to keep the student under supervision. There was no reason to believe that the suspension created imminent danger for the student and there was no constitutional violation by the school officials. The court granted the school officials' motion for summary judgment. *Thrower v. Barney*, 849 F.Supp. 1445 (N.D.Ala.1994).

A Pennsylvania high school student obtained temporary possession of a set of keys to the high school. Instead of returning them promptly, he violated school policy by making duplicate keys. Several months later, a computer was stolen from the high school and recovered from another student. The school board held a formal hearing at which it considered evidence from both students concerning who actually stole the computer. The board found the student in whose possession the computer was found more credible and voted to expel the student who had duplicated the keys. His parents appealed the decision, claiming that the presence of the superintendent of schools at the hearing was prejudicial. They appealed the board's adverse decision to a Pennsylvania trial court, which vacated the board's decision and remanded the matter for further testimony. The board held another hearing, reached the same result, and the trial court again reversed its decision. The school board appealed to the Commonwealth Court of Pennsylvania. On appeal, the school board argued that the trial court had improperly disregarded the school board's credibility determinations and made its own findings of fact. The commonwealth court agreed, noting that credibility determinations are binding on appeal. Because it was improper for the trial court to have reconsidered the evidence before the board, the commonwealth court reversed and remanded its decision. *Kish v. Annville-Cleona School Dist.*, 645 A.2d 361 (Pa.Cmwlth.1994).

A New York high school student with a learning disability threatened other students and a teacher, and was apprehended while waving an iron bar and threatening to kill someone. The school suspended the student and placed him in homebound instruction pending a psychiatric evaluation by the school district's special education committee. The district petitioned a New York trial court for a temporary order that would permit the district to extend the suspension beyond ten days until an appropriate evaluation and placement could be made. The court entered an order in favor of the school district, based on its showing of a substantial likelihood of injury to the student or others without the suspension and the continuation of home-bound instruction. In making the order, the court discussed the standard established by the U.S. Supreme Court in student expulsion and suspension cases in *Honig v. Doe*, 484 U.S. 305, 108 S.Ct. 592, 98 L.Ed.2d 686 (1988). The case interprets the Individuals with Disabilities Education Act (IDEA) stay-put provision as preventing unilateral suspensions of over ten days without application to a court for approval of longer terms on the basis of the threat of injury to self or others. Finding the school district's actions appropriate, the court granted the requested order pending the district's evaluation and placement proceedings. *East Islip Union Free School Dist. v. Andersen*, 615 N.Y.S.2d 852 (Sup.Ct.—Suffolk County 1994).

An Illinois high school student was suspended from school for 10 days for bringing an ice pick to school. The school board then held a hearing at which it expelled the student from school for the following semester for possessing a weapon on school property. An Illinois trial court entered an order preventing the school board from excluding the student from school the following semester. The Appellate Court of Illinois, First District, affirmed the trial court decision, ruling that the expulsion of the student for an entire semester was an abuse of discretion, given the level of misconduct and the fact that she had already been suspended for 10 days. *Washington v. Smith*, 618 N.E.2d 561 (Ill.App.1st Dist.1993).

A 15-year-old freshman at a Massachusetts high school was suspended for possessing a firearm on or near school premises. Subsequently, the local school committee voted to expel him permanently from the high school. The committee then decided not to provide the student with any educational services. Thereafter, a member of the student's family filed a complaint with the State Department of Education based on the committee's decision. The state Board of Education (which supervises and controls the department of education) interpreted Massachusetts law to require local school committees to provide excluded students between the mandatory school attendance ages with alternative educational services. It filed a lawsuit against the local school committee, seeking to require the committee to comply with the compulsory education statute.

Before the Supreme Judicial Court of Massachusetts, the committee contended that the Massachusetts compulsory attendance law simply directed local school committees to ensure that all children of the proper ages attend school. It did not require, argued the committee, the provision of an educational alternative to a student who had been properly expelled for disciplinary reasons. The court agreed with the committee, finding that the statute addressed only who should attend school and where. It did not include a specific requirement that an educational alternative had to be provided to an expelled child. Further, the board of education did not have the power to require the local school committee to provide an alternative education to the expelled student. Accordingly, the court ruled in favor of the committee and held that the student did not have the right to an alternative education. *Board of Education v. School Committee of Quincy,* 612 N.E.2d 666 (Mass.1993).

A Washington D.C. high school student was arrested at school on a charge that he had raped a 15-year-old classmate. The student was alleged to have been armed during the incident and had a concealed weapon at the time of arrest. Although the student was only 16, he was charged as an adult. The school principal spoke to the student's mother for school arrangements pending the criminal prosecution. He suggested transfer to another school and instruction at home. The student received home instruction prior to a determination by a hearing officer that he should be promptly readmitted to school. The reasons for readmission included the absence of a notice for the involuntary transfer, the criminal presumption of innocence and the absence of a showing that the student was a danger to himself or others. The principal refused to readmit the student in violation of the hearing officer's decision. The board of education later adopted an emergency rule enabling the superintendent to transfer students accused of crimes without first holding a hearing.

The criminal charges against the student were eventually dropped and he graduated with his class. He sued the principal in the District of Columbia Superior Court for constitutional violations. The superior court denied a summary judgment motion by the principal and he appealed to the District of Columbia Court of Appeals. The court of appeals ruled that the informal talks between the principal and the student's mother satisfied minimum constitutional due process requirements. The principal was entitled to qualified immunity in any lawsuit based upon discretionary acts. Accordingly, the principal was entitled to immunity for his decisions prior to the hearing officer's determination, but he was not entitled to immunity for disobeying the hearing officer's order (because he was then simply carrying out his duties.) The case was remanded for entry of partial summary judgment for the principal and for further consideration of the matters for which he had no immunity. *Durso v. Taylor,* 624 A.2d 449 (D.C.App.1993).

During the school lunch period, a student in a California school district went to another campus. Shortly after he arrived, he became involved in an altercation with another student, where he pulled a stun gun and used it to stun the other student. His school district expelled him for the remainder of the school year. The county school board reviewed the decision and determined that the school district lacked jurisdiction to expel him because he was not attending his own school at the time of the incident. According to the county board, his acts were not related to a school activity or school attendance as required by California Law. The school district petitioned a California trial court which granted its petition ordering the board to set aside its decision. The student then appealed to the Court of Appeal of California. The student argued that the prohibited acts had to be related to the school the student was attending. Because he was at another school he contended that the law did not apply. The court, however, disagreed. As long as the prohibited act was related to school activity or school attendance, the school district had jurisdiction. The court affirmed the decision of the trial court. *Fremont Univ. High Sch. v. Bd. of Educ.,* 286 Cal.Rptr. 915 (Cal.App.1991).

An Illinois graduate student was expelled by a school disciplinary committee for violating the university's harassment policy. The student brought a breach of contract action in federal court, claiming that the university had expelled him arbitrarily, capriciously and in bad faith. He sought an injunction compelling the university to rescind his expulsion and to award him an MBA retroactively. After a bench trial, the court determined that the relationship between the university and its students was a contractual one and was governed by the terms set forth in the university's catalogs and manuals. The university was obligated to follow its published standards and procedures when disciplining its students. However, the student was also obligated to abide by the university's rules of conduct. The court held that the committee's determination that the student had engaged in a "systematic, prolonged and premeditated pattern of harassment" against a fellow student was rationally based on evidence and credibility determinations. The student failed to establish that the school breached its contractual obligations to him in conducting its disciplinary proceedings. The court entered judgment on behalf of the university. *Holert v. Univ. of Chicago,* 751 F.Supp. 1294 (N.D.Ill.1990).

Two Illinois students were expelled for the balance of the 1990-91 academic year following an altercation between 4:00 and 4:30 p.m. near the school. The students and their parents sought a state court order restraining the board of education from expelling the students. The trial court granted the injunction and the board of education appealed to the Appellate Court of Illinois. The appellate court noted that school discipline is an area in which school officials normally have broad discretion. Illinois courts have been reluctant to overturn decisions to suspend or expel students. However, the court noted that the testimony was confusing and conflicting. The court determined that the punishment was too harsh, and that the board had abused its discretion in ordering the expulsion of the students involved. The appellate court affirmed the decision of the trial court granting the students an injunction. *Robinson v. Oak Park and River Forest High School,* 571 N.E.2d 931 (Ill.App.1st Dist.1991).

D. Due Process

At the very heart of the American system of criminal law is the concept that due process protections will be enforced and that all people subject to the law will be given fair play. Due process is accorded an individual when the governmental body undertaking the proceeding against that individual adequately informs the accused of the charges, gives the accused enough notice to prepare a proper defense, allows the accused the opportunity to confront witnesses and challenge the testimony given, and permits the presentation of evidence on his or her own behalf.

In *Goss v. Lopez*, the U.S. Supreme Court affirmed the constitutional rights of suspended students to due process protection through notice and hearing. In this case, the students had been suspended from school for up to 50 days for misconduct. Their suspensions were handed down without benefit of a hearing either before or after the school board's ruling. The Supreme Court held that students facing temporary suspensions from a public school have property and liberty interests and are protected by the Due Process Clause of the Fourteenth Amendment. Students faced with suspension or expulsion must be given oral or written notices of the charges against them along with the opportunity at a hearing to present their version of what happened. Recognizing that situations often do not allow time to follow adequate procedures prior to the suspensions, such as in cases where there is a danger to students or property, the court stated that, at the very least, proper notice and hearing should be given as soon after the suspension as is practicable. The Court also stated that if a student is threatened with a suspension longer than ten days, more elaborate procedural safeguards are necessary. *Goss v. Lopez*, 419 U.S. 565, 95 S.Ct. 729, 42 L.Ed.2d 725 (1975).

An Illinois student got into a fight with another student on school grounds. Two teachers were injured while trying to stop the fight. After interrogation by the school dean and by police, the student was suspended from school for ten days. The school sent the student's parents a behavior report that included a statement of the student's rights under Illinois law, including notice of the right to appeal. Four days later, the school held a suspension hearing. The hearing officer upheld the ten day suspension and recommended either expulsion or transfer to an alternative educational facility for the rest of the semester. The student retained an attorney, who appealed the decision. Because the student had refused to attend the alternative educational facility, the school district advised the student that the appeal would be considered an expulsion hearing. The hearing officer, who had also presided over the suspension hearing, recommended expulsion if the student did not attend the alternative school, and his decision was adopted by the school board. The student appealed to the U.S. District Court for the Northern District of Illinois, claiming constitutional and state law violations.

The school district filed a motion for dismissal, which the court considered as a motion for summary judgment. It held that the student had received adequate written notice of all the proceedings, including the expulsion hearing and that the school district had provided the minimal due process required for ten day suspensions. The student had received a meaningful opportunity to contest the charges and was not entitled to further trial-type protections such as a court reporter. The court granted the school district's motion. *Baxter v. Round Lake Area Schools*, 856 F.Supp. 438 (N.D.Ill.1994).

A Florida student was found sleeping in his high school and was taken to a hospital because he was ashen gray and appeared very ill. He was suspended for ten days when it was determined that he had used marijuana during lunch break. He later dropped out of school and told school officials that he had received the marijuana from another student. The school board notified the other student that it was recommending her suspension for distribution of marijuana on the school's campus. At the suspension hearing, the student admitted taking marijuana from her locker and giving it to the other student, but stated that the transaction had taken place off campus. Because the evidence was insufficient to suspend the student on the basis of the rule prohibiting marijuana distribution on campus, the board suspended the student for possession of marijuana on campus. The student claimed that the suspension on different grounds than those originally brought by the school board constituted a violation of her constitutional right to due process. She appealed the school board's decision to the District Court of Appeal of Florida, Fifth District.

The court recited the minimal procedural due process requirements stated by the U.S. Supreme Court in *Goss v. Lopez,* above. The court stated that the school board had not violated the student's constitutional due process rights because the suspension notice adequately informed her of the possibility of suspension for her role in the incident. The actual suspension on different grounds than those stated in the notice did not constitute prejudice in the formal suspension hearing. The court affirmed the school board's suspension of the student for possession of marijuana on campus. *Student Alpha ID No. GUJA v. School Bd. Of Volusia County,* 616 So.2d 1011 (Fla.App.5th Dist.1993).

A Texas student was expelled from school for violating the school drug policy. He was given a hearing but he left when the decision refusing his readmittance was announced. Later that day the assistant superintendent rescinded the expulsion until a second hearing was held. The student was readmitted at the disciplinary facility used by the school district. At the second hearing he was suspended for the rest of the year. He appealed and the assistant superintendent reduced the suspension to 60 days at the disciplinary facility. He appealed the 60-day suspension but the superintendent affirmed it. The school board held a hearing on the suspension and decreased it to 30 days at the disciplinary center. The student then brought suit in a federal district court against the trustees, administrators, and employees of the school district to recover damages for the suspension.

The U.S. Constitution requires that before a student may be suspended the school district must observe procedural safeguards. The court ruled that the student had had an opportunity to introduce witnesses, documents, and to raise arguments in his defense. The district therefore had afforded him due process under the Fourteenth Amendment. Under the Texas statutes, a student may not be suspended unless the board of trustees determines that the student's presence poses a continuing danger of physical harm to himself or others. The court determined that the district's rule allowing suspension had been rational because the presence of illegal drugs was a source of physical harm to students and staff. Also, substantial evidence supported both the initial administrative decision to discipline the student and the final board decision that the student violated the school drug policy. Therefore, the court denied the student any damages. *Salazar v. Luty,* 761 F.Supp. 45 (S.D.Tex.1991).

Following an Alabama high school football game, two groups of students brawled at the stadium. The mother of two of the students in one faction notified the school principal of the altercation. The principal arranged for both groups to meet at separate conferences in his office. While the first group met with the principal, the second faction arrived and remained outside the conference room. As the first faction left the conference room, another brawl erupted. The following day, the principal suspended them for five days and they were recommended for expulsion. At the expulsion hearing which followed, the students whose mother had contacted the principal were expelled. All other students were allowed to return to school on a probationary basis. The expelled students sued in federal court claiming procedural due process violations as well as substantive due process violations. The case was heard before the U.S. District Court, Southern District of Alabama. The court held that the five-day suspension did not violate the students' due process rights, despite the fact that they were not given notice or a hearing before the suspension took effect. In general, students are entitled to oral or written notice of the charges against them and an opportunity to explain their side of the story. However, whenever the student poses a continuing danger or an ongoing threat to disrupt the academic process, no notice or hearing is necessary. Such was the case here. The court further noted that the expulsions did not violate the students' due process rights. The students had been timely informed of the expulsion hearing and their rights. The court granted summary judgment for the school board. *Craig v. Selma City School Bd.*, 801 F.Supp. 585 (S.D.Ala.1992).

An Ohio eighth grader allegedly threatened another student with a knife while walking home from school. After hearing stories of the incident, the principal scheduled a hearing before the superintendent. At the hearing, the student was expelled. His parents appealed the superintendent's decision to the board of education. Another hearing was held and, in accordance with the hearing officer's recommendation, the board affirmed the expulsion. A federal court found that the student had received adequate notice of the charges and evidence against him. It also found that he received ample opportunity to refute the charges in the formal hearings which were held. Accordingly, the district's motion for summary judgment was granted. *Draper v. Columbus Public Schools,* 760 F.Supp. 131 (S.D.Ohio 1991).

The U.S. Supreme Court has addressed the question of whether federal courts may construe school regulations differently than a school board has construed them. A tenth grade Arkansas student left school grounds, consumed alcohol and returned to school intoxicated. He was immediately suspended from school pending a board hearing at which he was expelled. His parents sued for injunctive relief, which was granted by a district court and later upheld by the U.S. Court of Appeals, Eighth Circuit. School regulations provided for suspension or expulsion of any student for "good cause" which was defined as including use or possession of alcoholic beverages or drugs. A subsequent section mandated expulsion for students using or under the influence of drugs or controlled substances. The district court and the court of appeals held that the school board had acted under a section mandating expulsion but held the expulsion violative of substantive due process since the student had not used drugs but alcohol and, in any event, had used the alcohol off campus. For these reasons the lower courts held the student had been unfairly suspended. On appeal to the U.S. Supreme Court, however, the school board's decision was upheld. The high court ruled that it was not within the purview of the district court or the court of appeals to substitute their own view of the facts for that of the school board's. The school board clearly had the authority to suspend and later expel the student for consuming alcohol off campus and returning to school. *Bd. of Educ. v. McCluskey*, 458 U.S. 966, 102 S.Ct. 3469, 73 L.Ed.2d 1273 (1982).

A New York student was suspended for five days for marijuana possession. A hearing officer recommended affirmation of the five-day suspension imposed by the school superintendent but the school board increased the suspension to two months. On appeal to a New York trial court, a board member admitted that he had based his decision upon tape recordings of separate disciplinary hearings involving the student and another student also accused of marijuana possession. The New York Supreme Court, Appellate Division, determined that the reliance on tape recordings was prejudicial to the student because it denied him the opportunity to be fully advised of the evidence against him, and deprived him of the opportunity to cross-examine witnesses and to offer rebuttal evidence. The court ordered expunged any references to the disciplinary hearings from the student's permanent school records. *Ruef v. Jordan*, 605 N.Y.S.2d 530 (A.D.3d Dept.1993).

Six Pennsylvania students were suspected of vandalizing school property with a BB rifle. The school's principal held an informal hearing with three of the students and their parents, at which the students admitted driving by the school and shooting at glass doors. The principal gave the students ten-day suspensions and advised them that a hearing would be held in three days to consider expulsion. The parties presented evidence at the hearing, and the students had the opportunity to present evidence and cross-examine witnesses with the help of counsel. The students again admitted that they had fired shots at glass doors. The school board conducted a second phase of the hearing to determine punishment. The school principal testified that one of the students had vandalized his residence. The board overruled objections to his testimony and expelled two of the students on the basis of the shooting and vandalism at the principal's residence.

One of the students petitioned a Pennsylvania trial court to vacate the expulsion order. The court ruled that the board had improperly considered evidence of the separate acts of vandalism at the principal's residence because they were not part of the expulsion hearing and the student had received no prior notice. The court stayed the board's order and set aside the expulsion. The Commonwealth Court of Pennsylvania affirmed the part of the trial court's order temporarily staying the expulsion, because the failure to grant a stay would have caused the student to miss final exams. However, the trial court had erroneously set aside the board's expulsion order, and should have remanded the case to the board instead. Failure to give the student notice of the charges considered at the expulsion hearing constituted a violation of his due process rights. Accordingly, the case was remanded to the school board. *Yatron v. Hamburg Area School Dist.*, 631 A.2d 758 (Pa.Cmwlth.1993).

A varsity basketball star at the University of Missouri stole $700 from a bookstore. A disciplinary hearing was delayed until after the criminal prosecution was completed. The student entered a plea of guilty to a stealing misdemeanor and received a 60-day suspended sentence, ten days in county jail, and two years of supervised probation. After notice, a conduct hearing was set to commence before a student conduct committee. The committee was convened according to the rules of the university. The student appeared and admitted to the theft and also to hitting a police officer's hand to destroy evidence of the theft. After the hearing, the student was suspended for one semester. He appealed the decision to the university's chancellor, who upheld the suspension. The student then filed suit in a federal district court under 42 U.S.C. § 1983, alleging violations of his constitutional rights. After a one-day trial, the district court issued a preliminary and permanent injunction prohibiting the suspension. The university then appealed to the U.S. Court of Appeals, Eighth Circuit, which stated that the imposed discipline did not result in any constitutional violation. The procedures followed by the university easily met the requirements established for disciplinary proceedings. Accordingly, the court of appeals reversed the decision of the district court. *Coleman v. Monroe*, 977 F.2d 442 (8th Cir.1992).

An Illinois student was expelled from high school for gross misconduct. The specific incidents included fights with fellow students, threatening the principal, and using vulgar language directed towards the principal and other school officials. The principal met with the student's father to serve notice of a hearing on the student's expulsion. This notice was given two days prior to the actual hearing. The student's parents and their attorney attended the meeting at which the expulsion was made final. The student, by his father, filed a petition in an Illinois trial court seeking to prevent the expulsion. The court ruled in favor of the district. The student and his parents appealed to an Illinois appellate court which reversed, stating that the student was not afforded due process. The school district then appealed to the Illinois Supreme Court. The supreme court stated that the claims of due process overlapped with the claims of inadequate notice. Therefore, the hearing must be found to be arbitrary and capricious before the court could overturn the decision. The court then decided that the student was given adequate notice since the principal hand-delivered notice to the student's father. Moreover, the parents were aware of the student's misbehavior; thus, two days was sufficient to prepare for the hearing. The Illinois Supreme Court affirmed the trial court's decision, reversed the appellate court, and ruled against the student. *Straton v. Wenona Comm. Unit Dist. No. 1*, 551 N.E.2d 640 (Ill.1990).

While a Georgia student was participating in an outdoor marching competition, a large insect appeared on his hand. He crushed the insect with his foot and the creature's insides splattered the colorguard instructor's clothing. The instructor then ordered the boy to clean the creature's body from her clothing. The student did not respond to the order. The band director made it clear to the student that he would have to answer to the high school's assistant principal, and that he would then face a disciplinary suspension for insubordination. The assistant principal informed the student that he had been insubordinate and that the punishment would be suspension from school for three days. The student complied with the three-day suspension and missed an important school test as a result. He then sued the board of education alleging that he was denied his due process rights. The board moved for summary judgment which was denied by the trial court, and it appealed to the Court of Appeals of Georgia. The court noted that students facing temporary suspension have interests qualifying for protection of due process. Due process requires that the student be given oral or written notice of the charges against him and an opportunity to present his side of the story. The undisputed circumstances of the case showed that the student was afforded the minimal procedural requirements. He was made aware of the charges against him shortly after the incident occurred and he was also given an opportunity to respond. Therefore, the court reversed the judgment of the trial court and awarded summary judgment to the board. *Wayne County Bd. of Educ. v. Tyre*, 404 S.E.2d 809 (Ga.App.1991).

A 15-year-old student at a Texas high school got in a fight with one of the school's athletic coaches. During the incident, the student punched the coach in the eye. In response to this, the high school conducted a hearing at which the student was expelled from school for two semesters. The coach was not present at the hearing, but he did submit a written statement, setting forth his version of what happened. After the expulsion, the student's parents sued the school district in a federal district court, seeking a temporary injunction to keep their son in school, and claiming that their son was denied his due process rights to confront and cross-examine the coach at the hearing. The court denied the requested relief. It noted that the student had admitted to striking the coach. Even though the coach had not been present at the hearing, the student had also submitted a written statement with his version of the events—and his attorney had been permitted to cross-examine all the witnesses who had presented live testimony. Accordingly, the procedures granted to the student had been fair; the parents' motion for a temporary injunction was denied. *Johnson v. Humble Independent School District*, 799 F.Supp. 43 (S.D.Tex.1992).

The Ohio Sunshine Act requires that all meetings of public bodies, including boards of education, be open to the public. An Ohio board of education suspended three students who allegedly obtained food from the school cafeteria without paying for it. The board called two closed executive sessions, at which the suspensions were discussed. Over two months later, the board suspended the students in a roll call vote at a public session. The students complained that the suspensions violated their constitutional due process rights and the Ohio Sunshine Act. They sued the school board in the Court of Common Pleas of Ohio, Coshocton County. The court of common pleas ruled that the school board had not violated the students' constitutional due process rights, as it had given each student appropriate notice and an opportunity to respond to the charges. However, school board consideration of the suspensions at the two executive sessions in advance of the open board meeting clearly violated the Sunshine Act. The act called for the severe sanction of vacating any action in violation of the act, and the court determined that the suspensions must be vacated as invalid and illegal despite the fact that the students' due process rights had not been violated. The suspensions could not be imposed. *Hardesty v. River View Local School Dist. Bd. of Educ.*, 620 N.E.2d 272 (Ohio Com.Pl.1993).

V. STUDENT SEARCH AND SEIZURE

The U.S. Supreme Court has ruled that under the Fourth Amendment to the U.S. Constitution, searches of students by school officials need not adhere to the strict standard of "probable cause" imposed upon law enforcement officers. Rather, the legality of searches will depend upon the "reasonableness" of the search in light of all the circumstances. There must be reasonable grounds to believe that the search will reveal a violation of school rules or produce evidence of unlawful activity. The states remain free to provide greater protection for students, as Louisiana and California have done. See Chapter Fourteen of this volume for cases concerning student searches in interscholastic athletics.

A. Fourth Amendment "Reasonable Suspicion"

1. *New Jersey v. T.L.O.*

A teacher at a New Jersey high school found two girls smoking in a school lavatory in violation of school rules. She brought them to the assistant vice principal's office where one of the girls admitted to smoking in the lavatory. However, the other girl denied even being a smoker. The assistant vice principal then asked the latter girl to come to his private office where he opened her purse and found a pack of cigarettes. As he reached for them he noticed rolling papers and decided to thoroughly search the entire purse. He found marijuana, a pipe, empty plastic bags, a substantial number of one dollar bills and a list of "people who owe me money." The matter was then turned over to the police. A juvenile court hearing was held and the girl was adjudged delinquent. She appealed the juvenile court's determination, contending that her constitutional rights had been violated by the search of her purse. She argued that the evidence against her should therefore have been excluded from the juvenile court proceeding.

The U.S. Supreme Court held that the search did not violate the Fourth Amendment prohibition against unreasonable search and seizure. Stated the Court: "The legality of a search of a student should depend simply on the reasonableness, under all the circumstances, of the search." Two considerations are relevant in determining the reasonableness of a search. First, the search must be justified initially by a reasonable suspicion. Second, the scope and conduct of the search must be reasonably related to the circumstances which gave rise to the search, and school officials must take into account the student's age, sex and the nature of the offense. The Court upheld the search of the student in this case because the initial search for cigarettes was supported by reasonable suspicion. The discovery of rolling papers then justified the further searching of the purse since such papers are commonly used to roll marijuana cigarettes. The court affirmed the delinquency adjudication, ruling that the "reasonableness" standard was met by school officials in these circumstances and the evidence against the girl had been properly obtained. *New Jersey v. T.L.O.*, 469 U.S. 325, 105 S.Ct. 733, 83 L.Ed.2d 720 (1985).

2. Drug Searches

A Hawaii high school student left school without permission and entered an enclosed culvert that was known as an area used by students for tobacco and marijuana use. A security guard went to the area on instructions from the school's vice principal and detained the student, another high school student and two intermediate school students. The two high school girls were brought to the vice principal's office and asked to empty their pockets and purses. The student's purse contained a small bag of marijuana, and the evidence was used in juvenile court proceedings in which she was convicted of violating drug laws. The student appealed the denial of her motion to suppress the marijuana evidence to the Supreme Court of Hawaii.

The supreme court discussed at length the U.S. Supreme Court's standard in student search cases announced in the case of *New Jersey v. TLO*, above. In that case, the Court determined that while the Fourth Amendment to the U.S. Constitution applied to searches and seizures by public school officials, the search warrant requirement was inapplicable. The appropriate standard in these cases was reasonable suspicion, based on whether a search or seizure was justified at its inception and reasonably related in scope to the circumstances. The Hawaii Supreme Court adopted the *TLO* standard and applied it to the student's case in upholding the conviction. Reasonable grounds for searching her purse existed because of the known reputation of the area for marijuana and tobacco use, the absence of other suspects and the likelihood of storing marijuana in a purse. The search had been reasonably limited in scope and based on individualized suspicion of the student. *In Interest of Doe*, 887 P.2d 645 (Hawaii 1994).

A security officer employed by a Pennsylvania education board entered the boys' lavatory at a public middle school, where he smelled smoke and observed two students. One of the students immediately moved toward a stall, and the officer asked him if he had been smoking. The student admitted smoking and again attempted to enter a stall while fidgeting with his pockets. The officer then patted down the student's pockets and retrieved three packets of crack cocaine. The student was taken to the principal's office and later arrested. At the delinquency proceedings which followed, the student's attorney made a motion to suppress the cocaine evidence as improperly seized in violation of the student's constitutional rights. The court denied the motion and the student appealed to the Superior Court of Pennsylvania.

The superior court analyzed the suppression motion under the standard announced by the U.S. Supreme Court in *New Jersey v. T.L.O.*, above. Under that case, school officials are not bound by the probable cause requirement of the Fourth Amendment, but are instead held to a standard of reasonableness under all the circumstances in conducting a search that is reasonably related in scope to the circumstances which justify the search in the first place. In this case, as in *TLO*, the apprehended student came under suspicion of violating school anti-smoking rules. Once the initial suspicion arose, a further search in a reasonable manner for other evidence was appropriate. Because the officer's search of the student's pockets had been reasonable, the court affirmed the delinquency adjudication. *In re S.K.*, 647 A.2d 952 (Pa.Super.1994).

A teacher's aide at an Illinois high school observed an unusual bulge in a student's groin area. The 16-year-old student had previously been suspected by school officials of possessing illegal substances. When the student was observed on the next day with a similar bulge, two male school officials confronted the student and subjected him to a strip search in the boys' locker room. The search was performed after checking the room for other persons. The faculty members stayed about 15 feet away from the student while he removed his street clothes and put on a gym uniform. No evidence of drugs or contraband was discovered and the student was allowed to go home. The student's mother, who had been telephoned by school officials prior to the search and refused consent to the search, filed a lawsuit in the U.S. District Court for the Northern District of Illinois. The court granted summary judgment motions by the school officials and district, and the mother appealed to the U.S. Court of Appeals, Seventh Circuit.

The court of appeals relied heavily upon the decision of the U.S. Supreme Court in *New Jersey v. T.L.O.*, above. In that case, the U.S. Supreme Court developed a two-part test for evaluating the constitutionality of a student search. First, a search must be justified by some reasonable suspicion that the student violated some regulation or law. Second, the search must be reasonable in scope, and not excessive in view of the purpose of the search. In this case, the school officials had reasonable and probable cause for undertaking a search of the student not only because of the unusual bulge observed for two consecutive days, but because of prior suspicion of marijuana use and possession. It was permissible for school officials to rely upon evidence which had accumulated over a period of time. The strip search was reasonable under these circumstances as a means of revealing concealed drugs or other contraband. The court affirmed the district court's decision for the school district and officials. *Cornfield by Lewis v. Consolidated High School Dist. No. 230*, 991 F.2d 1316 (7th Cir.1993).

A 19-year-old Indiana high school student was involved in an altercation with another student over a marijuana sale. The principal intervened between the students, ordered the 19-year-old to remove his jacket, searched it and found eight marijuana cigarettes. The student was subsequently convicted of attempted sale of marijuana on school property and was sentenced to eight years in prison. On appeal to the Court of Appeals of Indiana, the student maintained that the search of his jacket was an unreasonable search and seizure in violation of the Fourth Amendment. The court held that the search of a student by school officials does not require the same degree of suspicion as the search of an adult. The legality of a search depends simply on the reasonableness, under all the circumstances, of the search. The court found that the search was reasonable. The student's conviction was upheld. *Berry v. State*, 561 N.E.2d 832 (Ind.App.1st Dist.1990).

An Ohio high school teacher detected what she thought was a strong odor of marijuana on a student while she was administering an examination in her classroom. The student was sent to the dean's office. A school security guard and the dean also detected the odor of marijuana about the student. Another security guard arrived, and the student gave his permission for a search of his bag and jacket. The guards then conducted a pat-down search. The student agreed to empty his pockets. None of the searches produced any evidence of possession of marijuana. The female administrators left the office, and the student lowered his pants and pulled the shorts tight around his crotch area. This search also produced no evidence of drug possession. The student subsequently sued the district, contending that the school had violated his Fourth Amendment right to be free from unreasonable searches and seizures.

The school officials moved for summary judgment. The U.S. District Court, Southern District of Ohio, granted the motion. The court stated that in order for the search of a student to be reasonable, the search must be justified at its inception and reasonably related in scope to the circumstances at hand. First, the school officials had reasonable grounds to believe that a search would turn up evidence that the student was violating the law or the rules of the school. The smell of marijuana and the student's sluggish and lethargic manner were consistent with marijuana use. Second, the search had been reasonable in its scope in light of the age and sex of the student, and the nature of the infraction. The student was removed from the classroom and the presence of his classmates. Moreover, the student was asked to remove his jeans only, not his undergarments, and only in the presence of the two male security guards. The student was never threatened in any way, nor touched inappropriately. The court dismissed the student's action. *Widener v. Frye*, 809 F.Supp. 35 (S.D.Ohio 1992).

An Alaska high school student created a disturbance in the school's library. When the school security coordinator confronted the student, he noticed that the student's "eyes were glossy and his face was flushed." The student swayed and bumped into large objects when he walked. The security coordinator asked the student where he had gone for lunch and if he had taken his car, but the student would not answer. The assistant principal was summoned and the student surrendered his car keys to him. The assistant principal had the student sign a consent form to allow the security coordinator to search his car. The car was searched and two grams of cocaine were uncovered. In the criminal proceedings which followed, the student asked the court to suppress evidence of the cocaine. The court refused and the student pleaded no contest. The student then appealed to the Court of Appeals of Alaska. The student argued that the consent given was not voluntary and that the search violated his constitutional rights. The court of appeals held that although the student's consent was not freely given and the consent form did not justify the search, the search was justified because of the defendant's state of intoxication and because the defendant's automobile was improperly parked on school grounds. Therefore, the school security coordinator had a right to search the student's vehicle for intoxicating substances including cocaine. The appeals court affirmed the trial court's decision for the state. *Shamberg v. State*, 762 P.2d 488 (Alaska App.1988).

Three California high school students individually warned the school principal that another student was carrying drugs. The principal confronted the student and asked if he was carrying any drugs. The student denied having any, raised his hands and said, "you can search me if you want to." The principal then searched the student and discovered two bags of cocaine. The student argued that the search was unlawful due to the principal's failure to warn him of his *Miranda* rights. The California Court of Appeal, First District, pointed out that *Miranda* warnings are required only with respect to questioning initiated by law enforcement officers after a person has been taken into custody or otherwise deprived of his freedom of action. The questioning of a student by a principal cannot be equated with custodial interrogation by law enforcement officers. The student's consent to the search was valid, as it was volunteered without even a request for permission to search. *In re Corey L.*, 250 Cal.Rptr. 359 (Cal.App.1st Dist.1988).

After receiving a tip from a student that two girls in her class offered her drugs, the principal questioned the two girls. One of the girls produced a vial of an illegal substance. After the principal found nothing in a search of their lockers, he ordered his assistant principal to strip search one of the girls. The assistant principal found no evidence as a result of the search. The girl's father filed suit in a federal district court seeking damages and an injunction pursuant to 42 U.S.C. § 1983. The district court granted the defendants' motion for summary judgment and the father appealed to the U.S. Court of Appeals, Sixth Circuit. The school board asserted that as an arm of the state the board was immune from suit based upon *Monell v. Dept. of Social Services of New York,* 98 S.Ct. 2018, 436 U.S. 658, 56 L.Ed.2d 611 (1978), which concluded that a municipality may not be held liable under § 1983 on a theory of *respondeat superior.* In the present case, the search and seizure policy was a facially valid policy allowing for the search of a pupil if there was a reasonable suspicion that the student was concealing evidence of an illegal activity. Based on the facts, the board believed the principal was justified in conducting the search. Consequently, the school board could not be held liable for the search in question. The principal and other school officials and board members were also sued in their individual capacities. The principal had possessed reasonable suspicion based upon the tip and the vial that the situation warranted further investigation. In light of the clearly established rights at the time of the search, to order the search was not a violation of the girl's constitutional rights. The appellate court affirmed the decision of the trial court and granted qualified immunity to the school board members and the principal. *Williams by Williams v. Ellington,* 936 F.2d 881 (6th Cir.1991).

A New Jersey assistant principal was informed by a guidance counselor that a student was carrying a bag of marijuana. The assistant principal knew that the student had been caught with marijuana once before, and thus summoned the student to a conference room, asking the student to empty his pockets. The student did so voluntarily. Nothing was discovered. The guidance counselor told the assistant principal to check the student's book bag. The assistant principal returned the student to the conference room with his book bag. The student denied the bag was his. The assistant principal opened the bag and discovered 75 vials of cocaine. Charges were filed against the student, but the evidence was suppressed as unconstitutionally obtained. The state appealed to the New Jersey Superior Court, Appellate Division. On appeal, the appellate court noted that the search was justified at its inception. In addition, the assistant principal did not search the book bag until after the student denied it was his. The court, therefore, found the search to have been reasonable. *State v. Moore,* 603 A.2d 513 (N.J.Super.A.D.1992).

The principal of an Arizona high school dispatched the chief of school security to investigate a reported fight in progress approximately two blocks from school. Staff members observed two students emerging from some bushes, and the chief later testified that one of the students took something from under the bushes and put it in his pocket. The suspect identified himself as a student at the high school by picking a class schedule out of his pocket. The chief observed a portion of a plastic baggy in the student's pocket, which was turned over to the local police department and later identified as cocaine. In criminal proceedings which followed, the student filed a motion to suppress production of the cocaine as evidence in his case. The trial court denied the motion and the student was convicted of cocaine possession. The student appealed to the Arizona Court of Appeals, Division One.

On appeal, the student argued that the security chief's search violated the Fourth Amendment to the U.S. Constitution. The court held that high school security personnel were state actors. Although Fourth Amendment standards of reasonableness apply to all government searches, the state had a substantial interest in providing an adequate learning environment, maintaining discipline and ensuring student safety. Because of the important interest in maintaining school discipline, the usual requirement of probable cause did not apply in school situations. It was only required that school officials be justified in undertaking a search and that their actions were reasonably related in scope to the circum- stances. In this case, the security chief's actions were justified. The court affirmed the trial court's denial of the student's suppression motion and affirmed the conviction. *State of Arizona v. Serna*, 860 P.2d 1320 (Ariz.App.Div.1 1993).

3. Weapon Searches

A random search of automobiles driven by students to a Georgia high school resulted in the seizure of a pistol from the glove compartment of one vehicle. The school's principal suspended the affected student for 10 days, and the county board of education extended the suspension for the remainder of the semester. The Georgia State Board of Education upheld the suspension and the student appealed to a Georgia trial court. The trial court denied the board's motion to dismiss the matter based on the student's failure to appeal to the state board of education. The county board then appealed to the Court of Appeals of Georgia, which held that the state court had been without jurisdiction to consider the appeal. Appeal was properly with the state education board. The trial court had abused its discretion in reversing the state board's decision to set aside the county board's motion. The student's misfiling of the appeal deprived the trial court of a record of the proceedings and constituted an unreasonable delay in filing an appeal under Georgia law. The case was properly dismissed and the court of appeals reversed the trial court's decision. *Elbert County Bd. of Educ. v. Gurley*, 450 S.E.2d 258 (Ga.App.1994).

A 15-year-old New York high school student came to school without proper student identification. The school security officer told him to report to the dean's office to get a new identification card and to leave his books in the school lobby. When the student tossed his book bag on a metal shelf, the officer heard a metallic thud. Because the officer found the noise unusual, he ran his fingers over the outer surface of the bag and felt the outline of a gun. He then called the dean, who also felt a gun from the outside of the bag. The bag was opened in the dean's office and contained a .38 caliber pistol. In juvenile delinquency proceedings in a New York family court, the student brought a motion to suppress the evidence of gun possession, claiming that the search violated his constitutional rights. The court admitted evidence of the weapon and convicted the student of several offenses. The New York Supreme Court, Appellate Division, affirmed the convictions. The student appealed to the Court of Appeals of New York.

The court of appeals stated that the constitutional process of balancing interests heavily favored the governmental interest in keeping weapons out of schools. The student had only a minimal expectation of privacy in his book bag that was clearly outweighed by the governmental interest. The metallic thud was sufficient justification for the officer's touching of the outside of the bag for constitutional purposes. The school authorities had reasonable suspicion of a violation of law that was sufficient to justify the search of the contents of the bag after detecting the shape of a gun. The court of appeals affirmed the adjudication of delinquency. *In the Matter of Gregory M.*, 606 N.Y.S.2d 579 (1993).

A Mississippi eleventh grade student offered to sell guns to a fellow student. After the fellow student reported this to the principal, the principal took the student out of class and asked him if he had guns at school. The student stated yes and they went to his locker. The principal asked him to open it. When the student complied, two guns were found. The student was found to be a delinquent and transferred to a juvenile training school by the juvenile court. The student appealed this decision to the Supreme Court of Mississippi. The student contended that the search of his locker was unconstitutional under the federal and state constitutions. The court concluded that the search was reasonable and offended no federal standard. Next, the court turned to the Mississippi Constitution and concluded that students have a reasonable expectation of privacy in their school locker. This expectation of privacy, however, is considerably less than that expected in the privacy of the home. Ordinarily, the Mississippi Constitution requires a warrant but since there was a dangerous weapon involved and 900 students at school, the situation suggested an exigency which would nullify the warrant provision. The court affirmed the decision of the juvenile court. *S.C. v. State*, 583 So.2d 188 (Miss.1991).

A team of special police officers set up several metal detector scanning posts in the main lobby of a Manhattan high school. The students had been told searches would take place, but were not told when. All students were subject to search as they entered. If lines became too long, random formulas, such as every third student, could be employed. No particular student could be singled out and searched unless there was reasonable suspicion to do so. Students were told to remove all metal objects after the process had been explained to them. If the student activated the scanning device the student was again asked to remove metal objects. If the student again activated the device, the student was asked to remove metal objects a third time. This was followed by a pat-down search. During this procedure, a student was found to be carrying a switch-blade knife. She was arrested and charged with a misdemeanor. She claimed that the search violated her Fourth Amendment rights. The New York City Criminal Court disagreed. It noted that administrative searches (those aimed at a group or class of people rather than a particular person) are reasonable whenever the intrusion involved in a search is no greater than necessary to satisfy the governmental need for the search. The court stated that the metal detector search was minimally intrusive. Officers were required to terminate the search upon finding the metal which activated the sensor, and they were not permitted to pat-down students until the scanning device had been activated twice. In addition, the officers followed a strict script and they could only search for weapons. The court upheld the search. *People v. Duke*, 580 N.Y.S.2d 850 (N.Y.City Crim.Ct.1992).

4. Other Searches

A New York kindergartner with developmental problems rarely spoke to persons outside her family, having a condition described as "elective autism." She often cried and fell asleep in school. Her teacher believed that the student had tried to communicate that her father was sexually abusing her. She reported this information to her supervisors as required by New York social services law, and a formal report was made to the city Child Welfare Administration (CWA). Upon further investigation and an interview with the family, CWA caseworkers took the child into custody and removed her from school. A physical examination revealed no evidence of sexual abuse, and the case was eventually deemed unfounded. The student's parents filed a lawsuit against the city, school board and CWA, and individual employees in the U.S. District Court for the Eastern District of New York, claiming constitutional violations. The court considered cross motions for summary judgment by the parties.

The court held that each school and social service employee named in the complaint was entitled to qualified immunity and was therefore entitled to summary judgment. The removal of the child from school had been required by an emergency, based on a reasonable belief that sexual abuse had occurred. However, the family's constitutional rights had been violated by the intrusive search of the student without parental permission. Although the school board was not liable for civil conspiracy, a fact question existed concerning whether school employees had conducted a strip search of the student prior to the CWA action. Although the teacher and other school employees were entitled to immunity, the court refused to grant summary judgment on the board's pretrial motions. *Tenenbaum v. Williams*, 862 F.Supp. 962 (E.D.N.Y.1994).

A New Jersey school district policy required parents of students who wished to go on field trips to sign permission slips containing a statement that hand luggage taken on the field trip could be searched. A seventh grader planned to attend a field trip. He was subjected to a search of his gym bag and cooler prior to boarding the bus, and no contraband was discovered. The hand luggage of all other students boarding the bus was also searched. The seventh grader's parents sued the school board, school superintendent, and principal, claiming that the search violated the student's Fourth Amendment rights against unreasonable search and seizure. A New Jersey trial court ruled for the school board and employees, and the parents appealed to the Superior Court of New Jersey, Appellate Division. The appellate division court reviewed the U.S. Supreme Court decision in *New Jersey v. T.L.O.*, above.

According to the U.S. Supreme Court, the Fourth Amendment's probable cause requirement is unsuitable to the school environment. The interest in maintaining school discipline and safety requires only that school officials have individualized suspicion of a violation of school rules and that the search be reasonable. In this case, although there was no individualized suspicion, the school's policy could be justified by the deterrent factor of announcing the hand luggage search. Chaperones on field trips were less able to deal with emergencies, and students had more opportunities to violate school rules while on field trips. Any intrusiveness created by the search was eliminated by the advance notice given and the fact that it was performed in the open. The appellate division court affirmed the trial court's decision for the school board and officials. *Desilets v. Clearview Regional Bd. of Educ.*, 627 A.2d 667 (N.J.Super.A.D.1993).

A West Virginia middle school teacher reported the theft of $100 from her purse. The teacher and a school social worker determined that one student was likely to have been in the room alone; that student was brought to the social worker's office. The student denied taking the money and agreed to a search of his outer clothing. The school's principal then took the student into the boys' lavatory where he conducted a strip search which revealed the missing $100. The teacher filed a criminal complaint resulting in a conviction for theft and a delinquency adjudication. The student appealed the trial court denial of his motion to suppress the evidence revealed in the strip search to the Supreme Court of Appeals of West Virginia, claiming the search was "excessively intrusive." The supreme court of appeals stated that a strip search was the most intrusive search imaginable and could not be equated with the search of a student locker or other personal possessions. The court ruled that the warrantless strip search of a student by school officials was presumed to be excessively intrusive and thus unreasonable in the absence of exigent circumstances requiring an immediate search to ensure the safety of other students. In this case, there was no such exigency and the strip search was held excessively intrusive and in violation of the student's constitutional rights. The trial court's decision was reversed. *State of West Virginia ex rel. Galford v. Mark Anthony B.*, 433 S.E.2d 41 (W.Va.1993).

An Alabama fifth grade public school class accumulated nine dollars to buy an aquarium for a class project. The teacher sealed the money in an envelope and gave it to a student who volunteered to buy fish for the aquarium. After the volunteer student placed the money in a container under her desk, the class and teacher went outside. Two students were left alone in the clasroom for a period of time. When the students returned, the volunteer student found the envelope torn with six dollars missing. The teacher instructed the other students to thoroughly search the classroom. Several students searched the plaintiff's desk. The plaintiff claimed that several other students searched her purse at the teacher's direction, and that she and the other student who had been in the classroom together were ordered to the front of the classroom where they were forced to remove their shoes while the teacher felt their socks. The money was never found. The plaintiff sued her school district claiming that her Fourth Amendment right to be free from unreasonable searches had been violated. An Alabama circuit court held that even if the plaintiff's version of the facts was true, her rights had not been violated. The Alabama Supreme Court upheld this ruling. The teacher "had reasonable grounds for suspecting that a search of the two students who had been alone in the classroom would turn up evidence that one of them had taken the money." *Wynn v. Bd. of Educ.*, 508 So.2d 1170 (Ala.1987).

B. Police Involvement

Most courts have taken the position that where police are involved in a student search, the Fourth Amendment standard of probable cause must exist and students must be advised of their rights.

A police officer was assigned full-time to an Illinois alternative school. His duty there was to investigate criminal activity and disciplinary problems. Two teachers at the school asked the officer to search a student for drugs. The officer performed the requested search, but found no illegal substances. The officer then observed the student and another student laughing. The officer interpreted the laughing as a personal insult, and he grabbed a flashlight from the other student's hand. The flashlight contained drugs, and the student fled. The officer chased him down and obtained a confession of drug possession from him. An Illinois trial court charged the student as an adult, convicting him of unlawful possession of a controlled substance on school property with intent to deliver. The student appealed his four-year sentence to the Appellate Court of Illinois, Third District.

The appellate court considered the case under the principles set forth by the U.S. Supreme Court in the case of *New Jersey v. TLO*, above. Although this standard did not require a warrant or probable cause, it required reasonable suspicion under the circumstances. In this case, the officer's decision to search the flashlight was based only on a hunch. The student with whom the defendant had been associating had been searched and released without any evidence of criminal activity. The student's privacy interests were not diminished so as to permit an intrusion based upon the officer's perception of an affront to his dignity. Because the search was not justified at its inception, it was unreasonable and the trial court had erroneously refused to suppress the evidence. The court reversed the conviction. *People v. Dilworth*, 640 N.E.2d 1009 (Ill.App.3d Dist.1994).

A Texas student was suspected by a school administrator of carrying a pistol. A police officer assigned to the school district confronted the student the following day when she observed the student skipping class. The officer took the student to the administrator's office. The administrator asked the student to empty his pockets. The contents included a pager, cigarette lighter, two small bags of marijuana and over $1,100. The city police department arrived, searched him, and found another bag of marijuana. In criminal proceedings that followed, the student's attorney filed a motion to suppress the evidence obtained in the search, arguing that the U.S. Constitution provided the officer with grounds only to investigate the student for being out of class and not to conduct a search of his pockets. The trial court denied the motion and the student pleaded guilty. On appeal, the Court of Appeals of Texas, El Paso, affirmed the trial court's judgment. The officer had acted appropriately upon receiving information that the student was carrying a weapon and this was her primary reason for detaining the student. The student's truancy developed during the investigation and was reasonably related to the investigation for a weapon. Because the search was reasonably related in scope to the circumstances justifying detention, it did not violate the Constitution. *Wilcher v. State of Texas*, 876 S.W.2d 466 (Tex.App.— El Paso 1994).

C. Anti-Crime Statutes and Ordinances

The City of Phoenix adopted an ordinance making it unlawful for juveniles under the age of 16 to be anywhere in the city except home between the hours of 10 p.m. and 5 a.m., unless accompanied by a supervising adult. The ordinance contained a number of exceptions that permitted juveniles to conduct emergency errands and to undertake reasonable, legitimate and specific activities directed or permitted by a parent or supervising adult. A 15-year-old Phoenix youth went to a friend's house with a group of school-aged youths. Although she had her father's permission to visit the friend's house, she lacked specific permission from her father to go any other place. The youths went to a park near the friend's house and were detained by city police. The 15-year-old was taken into custody by police and cited for violating the curfew ordinance. The juvenile court imposed a $56 fine and the juvenile appealed to the Arizona Court of Appeals.

The court of appeals rejected the juvenile's argument that her presence in the park during curfew hours was protected by the First Amendment to the U.S. Constitution. Although courts have shown increasing recognition of the rights of minors in recent years, state control over the conduct of children exceeds the scope of state authority over adults. Minors were deemed to be vulnerable and subject to parental control. Accordingly, limits on their movement during curfew hours implicated an important state interest. The ordinance was sufficiently narrow in scope to pass strict constitutional scrutiny and was not unconstitutionally overbroad because of the exceptions allowing juveniles to perform legitimate business. The ordinance was constitutional and the juvenile court had based its finding of a violation upon sufficient evidence that the juvenile lacked specific parental permission to be in the park. *Matter of Appeal in Maricopa County*, 887 P.2d 599 (Ariz.App.Div.1 1994).

Appellate courts in Massachusetts and Washington have upheld constitutional challenges by individuals convicted of distributing cocaine in violation of state drug free school zone acts. In the Massachusetts case, the Supreme Judicial Court of Massachusetts found no error in a state trial court's finding that a defendant charged under the statute was guilty of intent to distribute cocaine. It also rejected his claim for unconstitutional selective enforcement of the school zone statute against African-Americans and Hispanics. The court held that the defendant could not demonstrate any discriminatory practice against him. *Epps v. Commonwealth*, 419 Mass. 97, 642 N.E.2d 1026 (1994).

In the Washington case, the defendant claimed that because he was addicted to cocaine and marijuana, he was entitled to a lesser sentence than that called for by state sentencing guidelines. He also claimed that the state first-time offender waiver provision of the sentencing reform act did not constitutionally distinguish between narcotic and non-narcotic drug distribution. Furthermore, the first-time offender waiver was unconstitutionally applied to him, and African-American defendants were disportionatly deprived of liberty interests under the sentencing waiver. The Washington Court of Appeals, Division One, affirmed the trial court's dismissal of the constitutional claims. The first-time offender waiver provisions did not violate federal equal protection because they furthered a substantial state interest. The court reversed and remanded the reduction of the defendant's sentence because it had been inadequate as a matter of law. The school zone enhancement extended the standard sentencing range from between 21 and 27 months to between 45 and 51 months, and the trial court's departure had been inappropriate. *State of Washington v. Clark,* 883 P.2d 333 (Wash.App.Div.1 1994).

A Louisiana statute enhanced the criminal penalties for convictions of distribution or possession of narcotics within 1,000 feet of school property. The statute defines school and school property broadly, incorporating playgrounds, parks and recreational facilities administered by the state parks office, as well as vocational and technical schools, and public and private colleges. Three individuals arrested and charged under the statute filed a motion in a state trial court on grounds that the statute violated their constitutional rights. Although the court rejected most of the arguments advanced by the individuals, it granted the motion, holding that the statutory drug-free zone encompassed too much area. The Supreme Court granted the state's motion for review.

The court rejected the argument of the individuals that the statute was unconstitutionally vague and overbroad. The statute clearly notified individuals of prohibited conduct. It also rejected arguments that the statute violated the equal protection and due process rights of predominantly minority, low income inner-city residents, despite evidence that almost all public housing developments in the city were within drug-free zones. Because of the strong public interest in protecting students, the statute was rationally related to its purpose and did not violate substantive constitutional rights. The statutory minimum mandatory sentence of five years without probation did not subject violators to cruel and unusual punishment. Because the criminal conduct alleged against the individuals fell within the scope of conduct proscribed by the statute, the trial court's decision was reversed. *State of Louisiana v. Brown,* 648 So.2d 872 (La.1995).

The Dallas City Council enacted an ordinance prohibiting juveniles under 17 years of age from remaining in public places and establishments from 11 p.m. until 6 a.m. on weeknights and from 12 a.m. until 6 a.m. on weekends. The ordinance contained numerous exceptions that permitted minors to remain in public areas when under adult supervision. It also permitted juveniles to travel interstate, return from school, civic or religious sponsored functions and to go home from these functions during curfew hours. A group of students and their parents sued city officials in the U.S. District Court for the Northern District of Texas for an order permanently enjoining enforcement of the ordinance. The court ruled that the curfew unconstitutionally restricted the First Amendment rights of the juveniles to associate. The court enjoined enforcement of the curfew and the city appealed to the U.S. Court of Appeals, Fifth Circuit.

The court agreed with the juveniles and their parents that the curfew infringed upon the fundamental right of juveniles to be in public areas. However, the city had a compelling interest in reducing juvenile crime and protecting juveniles from harm. The city presented statistics that juvenile crime in Dallas was increasing, and that many violent crimes were likely to occur during curfew hours. The ordinance was not unconstitutionally broad and was narrowly tailored to meet its stated purpose because of the many exceptions permitting juveniles to carry on legitimate business and respond to emergencies during curfew hours. Because the ordinance infringed only modestly upon the rights of juveniles and their parents, and because the government had a comparatively greater interest in controlling juvenile crime, the ordinance was constitutional. The court reversed the district court's decision. *Qutb v. Strauss*, 8 F.3d 260 (5th Cir.1993).

A faculty member at a Massachusetts high school learned that a student was attempting to sell marijuana to his classmates. The faculty member reported the incident to the principal. According to the faculty member, the student carried three bags of marijuana in a video cassette case in his book bag. Waiting until the student was in class, the principal and a vice-principal opened the student's locker. They found the book bag, the video cassette case, and three bags of marijuana. The principal brought the student to her office and questioned him. He admitted the bags were his and that he had attempted to sell them. The police were summoned and the drugs were turned over to them. After reading the student his rights, the police also questioned him. He gave a written statement to the police concerning the events. The student was tried for possession with intent to distribute and convicted. At trial, he requested that his admissions be suppressed since the principal had not read him his *Miranda* rights before questioning him. He also contended that the search of his locker was illegal. The trial court disagreed. The student appealed his conviction to the Supreme Judicial Court of Massachusetts. The court noted that the student was entitled to Fourth Amendment protections, as well as the protection of the Massachusetts Constitution. However, probable cause existed to search the student's locker and this standard satisfied both state and federal requirements. The additional requirement of a search warrant was not necessary. The court further held that *Miranda* warnings are not necessary for school officials under either the state or federal constitution so long as the official is not acting on behalf of law enforcement officials. *Commonwealth v. Snyder*, 597 N.E.2d 1363 (Mass.1992).

Utah State University experienced numerous incidents of vandalism, damage, and other problems on the second floor of one of its student dormitories. The residents were told that if the problems did not cease, room-to-room inspections would be conducted. Residence hall contracts explicitly stated that university officials retained the right to enter and inspect residence hall rooms at any time. When the incidents continued, the university's director of housing, accompanied by a custodian, a football coach, and a police officer, entered each room on the second floor to conduct an inspection. The director did not obtain a search warrant prior to conducting the search. Upon entering one particular room, the director discovered stolen university property. The items were seized. About an hour later, the resident who occupied the room, and who was not in his room at the time of the search, went to the university police office to complain about the inspection and seizure of items. He was questioned and confessed to the theft. The student was subsequently charged with theft. He filed a motion to suppress evidence of the seized items, as well as his confession, claiming violation of his Fourth Amendment right to be free from unreasonable searches and seizures. The trial court granted the motion and the state appealed. The Court of Appeals of Utah reversed, holding that the warrantless search did not violate the resident's Fourth Amendment rights. It stated that the right of privacy protected by the Fourth Amendment does not include freedom from reasonable inspection of a school-operated dormitory room by school officials. *State v. Hunter*, 831 P.2d 1033 (Utah App.1992).

VI. STUDENT CIVIL RIGHTS

Although many lawsuits are filed each year against school districts and school officials for constitutional rights violations, the legal standard applied by courts limits recovery to those infrequent cases in which the student demonstrates deliberate indifference to well-established constitutional rights. This occurs only where an institutional pattern or practice of civil rights violations is proven to exist that is attributable to policy-making employees.

A Texas grade school teacher was accused of inappropriately touching three students. School administrators nonetheless gave the teacher a good performance evaluation. The school district board of trustees found the evidence insufficient to terminate the teacher's employment and he was transferred to another elementary school in the district. The teacher was then convicted of indecently touching a student at the new school and was fired for committing a felony. The victim's parents sued the school district under 42 U.S.C. § 1983, claiming that the molestation resulted from the district's policies and customs regarding sexual abuse. The U.S. District Court for the Western District of Texas awarded the student $500,000, finding that the district had a formal policy authorizing, tolerating or condoning sexual abuse of students by teachers.

On appeal to the U.S. Court of Appeals, Fifth Circuit, the school district argued that the district court decision was not supported by the evidence. It claimed that the board's actions could not reasonably be found to result from a policy of deliberate indifference to the student's constitutional rights. The court determined that although the district court had failed to instruct the jury according to the deliberate indiffence standard, the case should be reversed because of a lack of evidence that the board had acted with deliberate indifference. Evidence indicated that board members acted with concern in transferring the teacher to another school, and that the teacher's later actions there were unforeseeable. *Gonzalez v. Ysleta Ind. School Dist.*, 996 F.2d 745 (5th Cir.1993).

A group of white Minnesota students called an Asian-American student a "slant-eyed commie," "chink" and "gook" on a repeated basis during the fifth and sixth grades. The Asian-American student claimed that he was called names in the presence of two of his teachers. When a white student at the school was killed in a motor vehicle accident, the other white students accused the Asian-American student of rejoicing in the death. They threatened to "get even" with the Asian-

American student, who then claimed that he was threatened with a knife. He requested permission to stay at home, and was given permission to do so during the last ten days of the school year. The student's father claimed that the student had been excluded from school, and that this constituted a violation of due process and equal protection, because the white classmates were permitted to attend school for the rest of the year. He also asserted that the school's actions violated a state civil rights statute. The U.S. District Court for the District of Minnesota considered the district's summary judgment motions.

The court held that the student's removal from school had been prompted by his own request. There was no violation of his due process rights, because he had received an "informal give-and-take" with school officials prior to the action. The district had taken legitimate action to protect the student's safety and there was no evidence that his treatment was different because of his race or national origin. Accordingly, the court granted the district's motions to dismiss the constitutional claims. However, the court refused to dismiss the student's claim that his exclusion from school constituted a violation of the state civil rights statute. The court also refused to dismiss the student's claim for punitive damages. *Engele v. Indep. School Dist. No. 91*, 846 F.Supp. 760 (D.Minn.1994).

An Illinois high school senior drew a picture of a district high school. He approached school officials with a proposal to sell prints as a joint venture to benefit the school's booster club and himself. The parties could not reach an agreement and the student decided to sell 1,500 copies of the drawing by himself. He began to market prints to local retailers, but the district circulated a letter to the retailers stating that the school had not authorized their sale and that the booster club received no profits. Many retailers then refused to continue selling the prints and the student claimed that the district's action had interfered with his constitutional rights to practice his trade or occupation and had suppressed his freedom of speech. The U.S. District Court for the Central District of Illinois granted the school district's motion to dismiss the lawsuit. The student appealed to the U.S. Court of Appeals, Seventh Circuit. The court observed that the district did not stop the student from selling prints altogether, nor prevent him from otherwise furthering his career and engaging in business. The U.S. Constitution protects individual rights to the pursuit of an occupation against adverse state action but does not protect any interest in a specific job. Because the district had not otherwise restrained the student's business activity, the district court had correctly ruled that the district did not violate the student's constitutional rights. *Bernard v. United Township High School Dist. No. 30*, 5 F.3d 1090 (7th Cir.1993).

Five Chicago high school students filed a lawsuit in the U.S. District Court for the Northern District of Illinois, seeking an order that would require the U.S. Secretary of Labor to regulate work hours for 16 and 17-year-old students under the Fair Labor Standards Act (FLSA). Two teachers from the high school also joined in the case. The labor secretary moved to dismiss the lawsuit on several grounds, including lack of standing by the teachers and students who were over the age of 18. The court agreed that the teachers were without standing. It also dismissed the portion of the lawsuit pertaining to students who were age 18 or over at the time of filing and unprotected by the FLSA. Because one student had turned 18 after the complaint had been filed, her claim was moot. The court then considered the merits of the claim by the student who remained under 18 at the time of the secretary's motion. The court observed that Congress had enacted the FLSA to eliminate oppressive child labor, which was defined as work that was particularly hazardous to children between the ages of 16 and 18 or detrimental to health and well-being. The court stated that any restrictions on hours applicable to younger students did not apply to 16 and 17-year-olds in nonhazardous occupations. It agreed with the secretary that the legislative history of the FLSA indicated no intent to regulate the work hours of students except as expressly stated. The court granted the secretary's summary judgment motion. *Schmidt v. Reich*, 835 F.Supp. 435 (N.D.Ill.1993).

The parents of two Alabama high school students filed a civil rights suit against the school board, the vice principal and the guidance counselor for allegedly coercing a female student to have an abortion and for failing to notify the students' parents of either the pregnancy or the abortion. The parents brought the claim in federal court under 42 U.S.C. § 1985, alleging that racial animosity was the motivation for the coercion of the students. The female student was referred to the school guidance counselor by a teacher because she believed the girl was pregnant. The counselor met with the student and her boyfriend who rejected all options but abortion. The school district moved for summary judgment. The court found that no federal or state law requires school officials to report a student's pregnancy or abortion to her parents. Also, Alabama law allows minors to consent to an abortion. The court found no evidence that the guidance counselor coerced the students into having an abortion, or that she had attempted to dissuade the students from informing their parents. Additionally, there was no evidence whatsoever of any racial animosity on the part of the guidance counselor or the vice principal. Absent a showing of such animosity, a § 1985 claim may be dismissed summarily. Since there were no genuine material facts to be resolved at trial, the court granted summary judgment in favor of the school district. *Arnold v. Bd. of Educ. of Escambia County, Alabama*, 754 F.Supp. 853 (S.D.Ala.1990).

VI. SEX DISCRIMINATION

Sex discrimination is prohibited by Title IX of the Education Amendments of 1972. There has been an increasing amount of litigation under Title IX by students, in addition to claims of discrimination based on violations of the Equal Protection Clause of the U.S. Constitution.

Since 1839, Virginia supported male-only military education at the Virginia Military Institute (VMI). A number of women's organizations and the U.S. government filed a lawsuit against the Commonwealth of Virginia in the U.S. District Court for the Western District of Virginia, claiming that maintenance of the male-only state college violated the equal protection rights of women. The court entered judgment for the Commonwealth, and the U.S. Court of Appeals, Fourth Circuit, vacated and remanded the decision, despite concluding that single-gender education was educationally justifiable and permissible if provided to both sexes. On remand, the district court approved a remedial plan proposed by Virginia that established a women's leadership institute at Mary Baldwin College. The leadership program paralleled some aspects of the VMI program but stressed building self-confidence rather than relying on adversative methods. The U.S. government appealed to the U.S. Court of Appeals, Fourth Circuit.

On appeal, the U.S. argued that the remedial program violated the Equal Protection Clause because the women's leadership institute's program was not identical to VMI's. The court of appeals observed that the proposed program at the women's leadership institute was based upon evidence that its methods were more appropriate for women. The commonwealth's proposed remedy offered the benefits of single-gender education to both sexes. Many other coeducational opportunities were available at other state-supported institutions, including a program in military science. The U.S. government's argument failed to consider the intrinsic benefits of single-sex education, and the court affirmed the remedial program, remanding the case with directions for a continuing court oversight mechanism. *U.S. v. Commonwealth of Virginia*, 44 F.3d 1229 (4th Cir.1995).

The Citadel, South Carolina's all male state supported military college, accepted the application of a South Carolina high school honor student, but promptly rejected it upon learning that she was female. The applicant obtained a preliminary injunction from the U.S. District Court for the District of South Carolina that permitted her to attend classes pending trial. The U.S. Court of Appeals, Fourth Circuit, affirmed the preliminary injunction, finding no evidence that the college would have to alter its program in any material aspect to accommodate a female student. The case returned to the district court, which conducted a trial on the applicant's claim that she was entitled to a permanent injunction against sex discrimination by The Citadel and state officials.

The state officials and college argued that the maintenance of a single-sex military institution for men but not for women could be justified on the basis of supply and demand. Since there was insufficient demand by female applicants to establish a parallel institution for women, they maintained that the student could be excluded from the college. The court stated that lack of demand could never justify denying an individual's right to equal protection of the laws. States are required to observe the equal protection rights of citizens without regard to demand for services. Because the state defendants had failed to propose an appropriate remedy, the court determined that the applicant should become a member of the South Carolina Corps of Cadets as the only available remedy that complied with the Equal Protection Clause of the Fourteenth Amendment. The college was further ordered to propose an adequate remedy for the beginning of the 1995-96 school year. *Faulkner v. Jones*, 858 F.Supp. 552 (D.S.C.1994).

An eighth grade California student complained about harassment by male and female classmates. School officials, including a counselor, met with several of the students in groups to discuss their unacceptable behavior. The student and her parents claimed that the counselor failed to take any action, and the student transferred to a private school. The family filed a lawsuit against the school district and counselor in the U.S. District Court for the Northern District of California, alleging violations of Title IX of the Education Amendments of 1972. The court determined that the school district could be liable for sexual harassment under Title IX, and that, although the counselor could not be sued directly under Title IX, he could be sued for harassment under 42 U.S.C. § 1983. The counselor was not entitled to qualified immunity. The counselor appealed to the U.S. Court of Appeals, Ninth Circuit, which recited the general rule that school officials are entitled to qualified immunity unless the facts show the violation of a clearly established student right. It was not clearly established at the time of the counselor's alleged inaction that he had a duty to prevent sexual harassment of a student by other students. It was therefore unreasonable to hold the counselor responsible for failing to take action to prevent harassment, and he was entitled to qualified immunity. *Doe by and through Doe v. Petaluma City School Dist.*, 54 F.3d 1447 (9th Cir.1995).

Four members of a Utah high school football team tied up the team's backup quarterback in the shower room and displayed him to a female student. The student reported the incident to the school principal and later alleged that the principal disciplined him for reporting the incident. The district superintendent then canceled the rest of the school's season and the student moved to his uncle's home to change schools. The student and his parents filed a lawsuit against the school district and a number of individuals in the U.S. District Court for the District of Utah, alleging that the school and school district's treatment of the hazing incident constituted sexual harassment and violated their constitutional rights. The school district and officials filed a motion to dismiss the lawsuit.

The court found that in order to prove a sexual harassment case under Title IX, the plaintiff must show exclusion or discrimination on the basis of sex. The student's claim failed to make such a showing, and his alternative arguments that district employees violated his constitutional rights also failed. There had been no showing of any intent to discriminate against the student on the basis of sex or that any individual acted to deprive him of his due process rights in causing him to transfer. The individual school defendants were protected by qualified immunity and the student was unable to show a district policy of deliberate indifference to his rights. The court dismissed the student's claims and denied his request for injunctive relief, attorney's fees and damages. *Seamons v. Snow*, 864 F.Supp. 1111 (D.Utah 1994).

A Georgia student alleged that a classmate sexually harassed her on a repeated basis over a period of several months. The incidents of harassing behavior were reported each time to the student's teacher, and eventually to the principal. The student, who was black, claimed that the school took no action against the offending student when she reported his misbehavior, but then disciplined him when he harassed a white girl. The black student filed a lawsuit in the U.S. District Court for the Middle District of Georgia, alleging constitutional violations by the teacher, principal, county board of education and school board members. The court considered motions to dismiss the case advanced by the defendants. The court recited the general principle that the Constitution limits the conduct of state actors, but does not protect citizens from the actions of private parties. Liability extends only to government entities that stand in a special relationship to the complaining party and to government actors who affirmatively place the party in a position of danger. Neither of these conditions applied in the case advanced by the student. The school officials enjoyed qualified immunity from the constitutional complaints and there was no merit to the student's assertion that the board should be liable for failing to enact a policy against sexually harassing behavior. Because she was unable to show that the offensive conduct was the result of the board's policy or custom, the court dismissed the lawsuit. *Aurelia D. v. Monroe County Bd. of Educ.*, 862 F.Supp. 363 (M.D.Ga.1994).

CHAPTER FIVE

EMPLOYMENT PRACTICES

I. PERSONNEL RECORDS

Generally, state law protects the confidentiality of public employee personnel files. Common law rules of defamation may also provide a basis for legal action against a school district or its officers for wrongful disclosure of private facts or erroneous factual statements. Similar cases involving open meetings acts may be found in Chapter 11, Section IV. C., of this volume.

A Connecticut taxpayers association made a written request to a school district for the sick leave records of a school psychologist. The school superintendent notified the psychologist of the request, and when she objected to the disclosure of her leave records, the superintendent denied the request. The association requested a hearing before the state Freedom of Information Commission (FOIC), which noted that the association had requested information limited to the psychologist's sick pay rather than disclosure of the nature of her illness or the state of her health. Finding that the psychologist had no reasonable expectation of confidentiality concerning her sick pay compensation, the FOIC ruled that the records must be disclosed under the state Freedom of Information Act (FOIA). A Connecticut trial court reversed the FOIC order, and the association appealed to the Supreme Court of Connecticut.

The supreme court held that the trial court had applied an unnecessarily technical interpretation of the FOIA, which broadly required disclosure of public records. Individuals seeking to prevent disclosure were required to show that the proposed disclosure would constitute an invasion of personal privacy. Applying the common law standard for invasion of personal privacy, the court stated that the FOIA exempted from disclosure only information not pertaining to legitimate matters of public concern that were highly offensive to a reasonable person. Because the psychologist failed to meet this burden under the statute, the trial court had erroneously reversed the FOIC order requiring disclosure. *Perkins v. Freedom of Information Comm.*, 228 Conn. 158, 635 A.2d 783 (Conn.1993).

A New York statute prohibited employers from inquiring about or acting adversely on information of criminal accusations that were resolved in favor of employees. The statute specified that criminal records "shall be sealed and not made available to any person or public or private agency." A tenured music teacher was arrested on misdemeanor charges for possession of a controlled substance and later acquitted of the charges by a New York court. The court sealed the records as set forth in the human rights law. The teacher's employing board of education brought disciplinary charges against him based upon the misconduct that had been alleged in the criminal matter. The board sought an order from the court unsealing the criminal records, and release of the prosecutor's file and physical evidence. The court granted the board's request, finding that it had inherent discretionary power to unseal the records in extraordinary circumstances. The New York Supreme Court, Appellate Division, affirmed the trial court decision and the teacher appealed to the Court of Appeals of New York.

The court of appeals found that the purpose of the human rights law was to protect exonerated persons from the stigma of dismissed criminal charges. The finding by the court that it possessed inherent authority to unseal records would frustrate the legislative purpose of the statute. The statute contained several exceptions describing when sealed records could be released. Each of these exceptions had a law enforcement purpose which was absent in this case. The court reversed the appellate division order, ruling that the application to unseal the records should be denied. *In the Matter of Joseph M.*, 603 N.Y.S.2d 804 (1993).

Voters in a Vermont school district rejected a local school district budget, which required a reduction in the district's allocation for sports activities. Three faculty members criticized the action and sent district voters a letter printed on official high school stationery. The school board condemned the faculty members in public at a special meeting to consider the budget cuts. The faculty members filed a grievance against the board, which denied the grievance in a closed executive session. The board also denied access by one of the complaining parties to see grievance documents and the board's response. These actions were then formally adopted by the school board at an open session. The complaining faculty members responded by filing a lawsuit against the school district in a Vermont trial court, seeking declaratory relief. The trial court ruled for the school board and the faculty members appealed to the Supreme Court of Vermont.

The supreme court held that the school board had inappropriately conducted the grievance before a closed executive session of the board. The Vermont open meetings law required such action to be open to the public. However, the complaining parties had not raised this issue at the time of the meeting and on remand the trial court was to determine whether they had standing to bring their open meetings violation claim. The supreme court also reversed the trial court's decision concerning access by the complaining parties to the grievance documents. The documents in question did not fall within the exception to the Vermont public records act merely because they were personnel-related documents. In order to invoke the protection of the act on the basis of protecting personal privacy, the information was to be personal in a limited sense, such as intimate details of a person's life. The court had erroneously granted the school district summary judgment and the case was reversed and remanded. *Trombley v. Bellows Falls Union High School Dist. No. 27*, 624 A.2d 857 (Vt.1993).

A Wisconsin high school hired an attorney to investigate sexual harassment complaints at the school, which resulted in the disciplining of a teacher. A broadcasting company asked the district administrator to inspect and copy the attorney's report, and further requested access to grievances filed by the disciplined teacher and another employee, both of which were related to the investigation. When the broadcasting company sued the district administrator in a Wisconsin trial court, the disciplined teacher sought to intervene in the lawsuit, claiming that release of the grievance record and report would violate his right to privacy in his own personnel file, and prejudice his rights in the pending grievance matter. The court denied the teacher's petition and he appealed to the Court of Appeals of Wisconsin. The court of appeals commented that public records custodians, such as the district administrator, were required to balance the public policy favoring disclosure of public records against the competing policy of confidentiality in personnel records. The teacher had failed to show that his due process rights in the grievance would be prejudiced by disclosing records to the broadcasting company. Because the matters were not sufficiently related, the teacher had no legally protected privacy right and his intervention in the matter was properly denied. *Armada Broadcasting, Inc. v. Stirn*, 501 N.W.2d 889 (Wis.App.1993).

A former school administrator sued a Pennsylvania school district for allegedly making defamatory statements to prospective employers. A Pennsylvania trial court granted the district and its officials summary judgment on the basis of governmental and official immunity. The administrator appealed to the Commonwealth Court of Pennsylvania, which affirmed the trial court holding of school district immunity. However, the trial court had inappropriately granted summary judgment to the school district officials. On remand, the trial court had to decide whether their statements had been made wilfully and within the scope of their duties. The court reversed that portion of the decision and remanded the case to the trial court. *Petula v. Mellody*, 631 A.2d 762 (Pa.Cmwlth.1993).

Oregon teachers in a public school district went on strike and the school district hired replacements to fill their positions. The district promised the replacements that their names and addresses would not be disclosed during the strike. A publishing company requested the names and addresses of the replacement teachers. The district denied the request due to its promise to the replacements. When the strike was over the publishing company sued the school district in an Oregon trial court asking for a declaration that the company was entitled to the information requested, to order the district not to withhold such information in the future, and seeking attorney's fees. The trial court held that the district could withhold the addresses of the replacements but not their names. The court also denied the attorney's fees. Appeal reached the Oregon Supreme Court.

The supreme court held that the district initially had to show that exemption from public disclosure was legally and factually justified. Oregon statutes exempt information of a personal nature from disclosure (unreasonable invasion of privacy). However, if the public interest requires disclosure it does not matter if such would constitute an invasion of privacy. The court stated that just because the district promised the replacements that it would not disclose their names and addresses, this did not justify refusing disclosure. It also stated that it was in the public's interest to know the names and addresses of the replacement teachers and that the information was not of a personal nature. *Guard Publishing v. Lane City School Dist. No. 4J*, 791 P.2d 854 (Or.1990).

II. EMPLOYEE QUALIFICATIONS

In determining whether an employee is qualified for a position, schools look to academic records, to past experience and to any certification which is required by state law.

A. Certification and Continuing Education

The leading case in this area is a U.S. Supreme Court case in which the nonrenewal of a tenured teacher's contract because of her failure to earn certain continuing education credits was held to be constitutionally allowable and not a deprivation of her substantive due process and equal protection rights. The teacher persistently refused to comply with her district's continuing education requirements and, in fact, forfeited several salary increases to which she would have been entitled. After several years of this the Oklahoma Legislature mandated certain salary increases for teachers regardless of compliance with the continuing education requirements. Faced with this loss of sanction, the district threatened dismissal unless the requirements were fulfilled. They were not and she was fired. The Supreme Court held in favor of the school board, noting that the desire of the district to provide well-qualified teachers was not arbitrary, especially when it made every effort to give this specific teacher a chance to meet the requirements. There was no deprivation of equal protection since all teachers were equally obligated to obtain the credits, and the sanction of contract nonrenewal was rationally related to the district's objective of enforcing the continuing education obligation of its teachers. *Harrah Indep. School Dist. v. Martin*, 440 U.S. 194, 99 S.Ct. 1062, 59 L.Ed.2d 248 (1979).

The Texas Term Contract Nonrenewal Act confers procedural protections and mandates automatic contract renewal for teachers in the absence of proper notice. The act requires school districts to furnish written notice and an opportunity for a hearing when the district fails to renew a teacher's contract. A Texas school district failed to rehire an experienced school nurse without stating a reason for its decision or providing an opportunity for a hearing. The nurse claimed that she was "certified" within the meaning of the Term Contract Nonrenewal Act because the state board of education's regulations required a school nurse to hold either a provisional school nurse certificate or a current registration with the state board of nurse examiners. The state commissioner of education ruled that the nurse was not protected by the nonrenewal act because she was not a teacher within the definition of the act. The Court of Appeals of Texas affirmed. The nurse appealed to the Supreme Court of Texas.

The supreme court observed that the nonrenewal act protected teachers: defined as superintendents, principals, supervisors, teachers, counselors and other full-time professionals, who were required to hold a valid certificate or teaching permit. Although all school nurses were required to be registered by the state board of nurse examiners, not all school nurses were required to have a provisional school nurse certificate. Although state board regulations made it possible for school nurses to obtain a certificate, the statute did not require certification. Because the nonrenewal act distinguished between employees who were required to hold certificates and those who were not, the commissioner of education had properly ruled that the nurse was not entitled to the act's protections. *Dodd v. Meno*, 870 S.W.2d 4 (Tex.1994).

A New York school district hired a special education teacher under a one-year contract. The teacher advised the school district that she had written to the state education department for renewal of her temporary certificate. During the school year, the teacher alleged that the school's principal made unwanted sexual advances, touched her inappropriately, stared at her outside her classroom for up to 45 minutes and made harassing phone calls to her. She made a complaint to the superintendent of schools, but after a hearing, no action was taken. The school district did not rehire the teacher the following school year, and she filed a lawsuit in the U.S. District Court for the Northern District of New York under Title VII of the Civil Rights Act of 1964. The school district claimed that the teacher had lied about having her teaching certificate. It also argued that the teacher failed to take necessary classes for certification. The court identified the teacher's complaint as a hostile work environment complaint, under which a complaining party must prove that offensive behavior is sufficiently severe to alter conditions of the workplace, in a continuous manner that creates an abusive working environment. In this case, the school district proved that the teacher had lied about several material employment matters. She had failed to produce evidence that she was recertified and able to accept reemployment. Because the school district had proven legitimate nondiscriminatory reasons for refusing to rehire the teacher, the court ruled for the school district. *Locastro v. East Syracuse-Minoa Cent. School Dist.*, 830 F.Supp. 133 (N.D.N.Y.1993).

A temporary teacher in New Jersey did not pass one of the four elements of the National Teachers Examination until her fourth attempt. The administrator of the test, Educational Testing Services (ETS), expressed its concerns about the validity of the teacher's fourth score. The concerns were founded on the unusually high improvement, and because of the statistically improbable similarity to another examinee's answers. The teacher was given a number of options in resolving ETS's concerns. She chose binding arbitration. The arbitrator held that ETS could cancel her score because it had made an adequate showing of a substantial question as to its validity, based solely on statistical evidence. A trial court reversed, holding that actual proof of wrongdoing was needed. The case then came before the Superior Court of New Jersey, Appellate Division.

The contract between the parties granted ETS the right to cancel scores with questionable reliability. The teacher, however, argued that she was forced to take the test because of state regulations and could not negotiate the cancellation term; she contended that it was therefore unenforceable as a contract of adhesion. The court noted that the public has a strong interest in reliance on the scores because of the importance of having qualified teachers. This interest was ruled to justify the contract's enforcement. Applying the cancellation provision to the case at hand, the statistical evidence was held to adequately show the unreliability of the score even without proof of individual wrongdoing. The decision of the arbitrator to cancel the scores was reinstated. *Scott v. Educational Testing Service,* 600 A.2d 500 (N.J.Super.A.D.1991).

The Georgia State Board of Education issued nonrenewable three-year teaching certificates to all new teachers. After the initial three years, teachers were required to pass a performance assessment test to receive renewable teaching certificates. The Supreme Court of Georgia determined in a 1989 case that the board of education had issued its regulations concerning the teaching certificates in violation of the state administrative procedure act. A group of teachers who at one time held nonrenewable teaching certificates were later denied renewable teaching certificates because of their failure to pass the assessment test. They sued the state board and its individual members, claiming a right to receive damages. A Georgia trial court dismissed the complaint against the board members in their individual capacities, but ruled that the teachers were entitled to monetary damages against the board under the theory that it had violated their constitutional property rights to engage in the teaching profession. Appeal reached the Supreme Court of Georgia.

The supreme court ruled that the teachers had no property interest in the nonrenewable teaching certificates, and that the certificates had not been taken from them. The teachers were not entitled to monetary damages based upon the invalidly issued regulations because the teachers had no property interest in certificates that were never issued. The teachers failed to advance a viable complaint under 42 U.S.C. § 1983. The trial court had correctly ruled that the individual board members were not liable for damages and that portion of its decision was affirmed. The state board and its members prevailed on all issues that were appealed. *State Bd. of Educ. v. Drury,* 437 S.E.2d 290 (Ga.1993).

A New York teacher agreed to resign in exchange for the withdrawal of charges by his district that he lacked adequate moral character to teach. However, the state Department of Education conducted an investigation and held a hearing to revoke his teaching certificate based on an alleged incident involving sex between the teacher and a student. The hearing officer recommended revocation of the teacher's certificate, and this decision was affirmed by a New York trial court. The Supreme Court, Appellate Division, Third Department, affirmed the revocation, finding that the teacher had received a fair hearing despite his complaints that a psychiatric report should not have been admitted into evidence and that he should have been entitled to introduce evidence of his own impotence. The teacher had failed to present medical evidence supporting that claim at the original hearing. *Groht v. Sobol*, 604 N.Y.S.2d 279 (A.D.3d Dept.1993).

Several teachers and a teachers' union filed suit against the state of Louisiana seeking declaratory and injunctive relief to have teacher decertification provisions of the Childrens First Act (CFA) declared unconstitutional. The CFA was passed by the Louisiana Legislature in 1988. It provided for the implementation of a teacher evaluation and remediation program. The CFA required the state Board of Elementary and Secondary Education (BESE) to issue three types of regular teaching certificates to state teachers according to their evaluations.

In order to determine whether the teacher meets the requirements for a certificate, each teacher is evaluated every five years by a team of three evaluators. If the teacher receives a superior or satisfactory evaluation, the BESE issues a renewable professional certificate which is valid for five years. A teacher receiving a nonsatisfactory evaluation is directed to undertake a program of remediation of identified deficiencies and reevaluation. At this time the teacher is certified as provisional which is valid for one school year. If at the end of this year the teacher receives a satisfactory evaluation, remediation and reevaluation terminates, and the teacher is not evaluated again for five years. If the teacher does not receive a satisfactory evaluation at the end of the year, the evaluation team may elect to deny certification. Since teachers are required to maintain valid teaching certificates, the plaintiffs contended that by providing for revocation or expiration of teaching certificates, the CFA effectively allows the BESE to discharge a local school employee in violation of the Louisiana Constitution. A district court ruled that the provisions of the act were unconstitutional and the defendants appealed to the Supreme Court of Louisiana. The Louisiana Constitution provides that BESE may exercise supervision and control over the schools. Clearly, the power to certify was at the core of BESE's function of supervision and control. Therefore, the court found that the certification clearly fell within BESE's function and the decertification provisions of the CFA did not violate the constitution. *EICHE v. Bd. of Elementary and Secondary Educ.*, 582 So.2d 186 (La.1991).

Wisconsin public schools formed a contract with Northeastern Wisconsin Technical Institute, a vocational, technical and adult education school (VTAE), to provide some courses to the public schools. Students could obtain credit from the VTAE to apply towards graduation. A local education association sued the Department of Public Instruction because teachers from VTAE did not have department certification. The association claimed that Wisconsin statutes require department certification for every district teacher. The association first petitioned the superintendent, who decided in favor of the policy, after holding a public hearing. The association appealed to a trial court which upheld the superintendent's decision. The association then appealed to the Wisconsin Court of Appeals. The court of appeals stated that Wisconsin statutes authorize the use of a VTAE, even if teachers are not certified by the department. The statutes were enacted by the legislature to authorize contracts with the VTAE with the full knowledge that the teachers were not certified by the department. Further, it stated that the difference in certification requirements for high school and vocationally related courses is obvious and it was unnecessary for the vocational teachers to meet the same requirements as high school teachers. Thus, the court of appeals affirmed the superintendent's decision. *Green Bay Educ. Assn. v. Dept. of Public Instruction*, 453 N.W.2d 915 (Wis.App.1990).

From 1969 until 1983, a Colorado man employed as a teacher decided to undergo sex-reassignment surgery. His teaching certificate expired during the process, but the school district held open a position for the next school year. Following the surgery, she did not report for duty. After unsuccessfully seeking judicial review, the teacher filed a civil action in a Colorado trial court claiming that the district's failure to accord a hearing on her dismissal violated constitutional due process standards. The district court held that a dismissal hearing was necessary, and the hearing officer decided that the teacher should be retained. However, the school board ordered her dismissal. The Colorado Court of Appeals affirmed the school board's order and the teacher appealed to the Colorado Supreme Court. A school board has broad discretion in its authority to define the grounds for dismissal of tenured teachers. In this case, the school board accepted the administrative law judge's findings of evidentiary fact and concluded that such findings supported the conclusion that the teacher should be dismissed. The school board stated that its conclusion was based on the fact that the teacher was advised of the pending expiration of her certificate and that she failed to renew it until after her termination. Had the teacher been on leave of absence at the time she was discharged, or had she been prevented from renewing her certificate because of temporary illness, the order of dismissal might well have been viewed differently. *Snyder v. Jefferson County School Dist.*, 842 P.2d 624 (Colo.1992).

B. Academic Qualifications

A substitute teacher with a masters degree in education administration applied for a full-time teaching position at a West Virginia high school. The school board hired a teacher who had no masters degree but with five years of elementary teaching experience. The substitute teacher filed a grievance with the State Employees Grievance Board, which affirmed the school board's decision. The Supreme Court of Appeals of West Virginia affirmed the trial court's decision, ruling that the board could properly rely upon the greater teaching experience of the selected applicant despite her lack of a masters degree. *Butcher v. Gilmer County Bd. of Educ.* 429 S.E.2d 903 (W.Va.1993).

A Colorado man was employed as a counselor by a school district. Among other qualifications, the school district required that its counselors have a master's degree. He made $36,590 per year. In addition to counselors, the district also employed school social workers who performed many similar duties. The district required that its social workers have a master's or higher degree in social work. Social workers made more money. The counselor sued the school district, contending that it breached his employment contract by paying him less for his work as a counselor than a person with a similar education and the same level of experience would receive for substantially similar work as a school social worker. The Colorado trial court held against the counselor, who appealed to the Colorado Court of Appeals. The court stated that classifications in salary schedule need only be reasonable and result in uniform treatment compared to those performing similar functions and having like training and experience. Differentiations among teachers on a salary schedule need only be based on differences germane to the education function. Here, even if the duties of the counselors and social workers were identical, the different educational requirements provided a reasonable basis under the statute for the salary differential. Moreover, the district's determination that for performance of identical duties as counselor or social worker, a person with a master's degree in social work warranted a higher salary than one with a master's degree in another field was not unreasonable. *Osborn v. Harrison School Dist.*, 844 P.2d 1283 (Colo.App.1992).

A West Virginia county board of education advertised for a teaching position for gifted students in grades five through eight and for learning disabled students in grade six. After the board hired one applicant, another applicant claimed she was better qualified and filed a petition for a writ of mandamus in a West Virginia trial court directing the board to appoint her. The court denied the petition and the applicant appealed to the Supreme Court of Appeals of West Virginia.

Courts have granted boards of education broad discretion in matters relating to the hiring of school personnel. However, this discretion must be exercised in a manner which "best promotes the interest of the schools." The court determined that the interest of the schools would be promoted when the hiring decisions were made on the basis of the qualifications of the persons hired. The court then compared the qualifications of the applicants and noted that the rejected applicant had 14 years teaching experience, a master's degree, was certified to teach grades kindergarten through eight, and was in the process of receiving her certificate to teach gifted children. The applicant who was hired had only a bachelor's degree, was certified to teach grades kindergarten through six, and was not in the process of receiving a certificate to teach gifted children. Since the position in the present case was to teach gifted and learning disabled students grades kindergarten through eight, the court found the rejected applicant clearly had the superior qualifications. Accordingly, the court ordered the board to hire her, and awarded backpay and attorney's fees. *Egan v. Bd. of Educ. of Taylor County,* 406 S.E.2d 733 (W.Va.1991).

C. Residency

The U.S. Supreme Court addressed the issue of citizenship requirements for certification of non-U.S. citizens unless there is a manifested intention to apply for citizenship. Two teachers who consistently refused to seek citizenship despite their eligibility to do so challenged the law under the Fourteenth Amendment to the U.S. Constitution. In upholding the state law, the U.S. Supreme Court held that teaching in the public schools was a state function so bound up with the operation of the state as a governmental entity as to permit exclusion from that function of those who have not become part of the process of self-government. The Constitution requires only that a citizenship requirement applicable to teaching in the public schools bear a rational relationship to a legitimate state interest. Here, the Court said, the rational relationship existed between the educational goals of the state and its desire that citizenship be a qualification to teach the young of the state. *Ambach v. Norwick*, 441 U.S. 68, 99 S.Ct. 1589, 60 L.Ed.2d 49 (1979).

A U.S. district court invalidated a portion of the Illinois school code which required that any candidate for the office of regional superintendent of schools must have at least four years experience in teaching, two of which must have been in the Illinois public schools. Under the Fourteenth Amendment a statute must, at a minimum, bear a rational relationship to a legitimate state purpose. The court struck down the in-state teaching requirement because its supposed purpose, to ensure familiarity with the Illinois school code, could not be attained in many cases by merely having taught in Illinois for two years. For instance, after having taught in a Chicago kindergarten for two years a person would likely know nothing about the state school code. At best the in-state teaching requirement only indirectly served its purpose, and thus the federal court ordered state officers to cease enforcing it. *Hammond v. Illinois State Bd. of Educ.*, 624 F.Supp. 1151 (S.D.Ill.1986).

III. EMPLOYEE EXAMINATIONS

Physical and mental examinations of teachers and other school personnel may be required by school districts as a condition of employment, provided that the examinee's privacy is not unreasonably violated.

A. Psychological Examinations

A personnel official at a Pennsylvania school district became concerned about an employee's fitness to teach. She decided to order a complete medical examination, including a psychiatric evaluation. The teacher missed the first exam and, on the eve of the rescheduled examination, she filed a motion for a restraining order in a federal district court. She contended that a compelled psychiatric examination was an unconstitutional invasion of privacy and that the examination was retaliatory. The teacher was granted a temporary restraining order to allow her time to prepare motions for a preliminary injunction. In her motion for a preliminary injunction, the teacher alleged that the ordering of the examinations was part of a plan of retaliation by the school district's personnel director aimed at driving her out of the school district.

The court acknowledged that although there is generally a high expectation of privacy with regard to medical and psychological records, in positions such as teaching, such information is generally required in the employment application process. Additionally, the court noted that while the gravity of potential harm from disclosure of the information was great, the school district established that the risk of such disclosure was slight. The court also balanced the school district's need for the information against the teacher's privacy interest. It determined that, given the important role teachers play in the lives of children, public policy favored disclosure. The teacher asserted that an administrator must have probable cause in order to compel such an examination. However, the court concluded that the constitution did not require a finding of probable cause. It concluded that the decision to order an examination of the teacher was not made in an arbitrary and capricious manner. There was evidence of frequent absenteeism, confrontations with other school employees, and reports from the teacher's supervisor about her ability to function in the classroom. The court dissolved the temporary restraining order and forfeited the teacher's security bond. *Murray v. Pittsburgh Bd. of Educ.,* 759 F.Supp. 1178 (W.D.Pa.1991).

A Minnesota teacher's mental health became the concern of her school district. In accordance with state law, the district and the teacher assembled a three member panel of mental health professionals to complete an examination. Based on the panel's determination the teacher was suspended. The teacher then received treatment from the physician she had selected from the panel. She was eventually determined by that physician to be fit to return to teaching. The school refused to reinstate her and asserted that she must be reinstated by using the same "panel approach." The teacher refused to be reexamined, and the case was appealed to a state appellate court. The statute which creates the system for suspension provides that a teacher may be reinstated "upon evidence from such a physician" of recovery. The court held that the statute called for evidence of recovery from any physician on the earlier panel. It was held to be irrelevant that the teacher could control the selection of the physician. The teacher had also been fired for insubordination due to her refusal to be examined. Because no such duty existed, her termination was reversed. *In re Mary Silvestri's Teaching Contract,* 480 N.W.2d 117 (Minn.App.1992).

The former assistant principal of a Florida high school sued the county school board and the school's principal, alleging employment discrimination and sexual harassment by the principal. She stated that the principal had prepared incorrect employment evaluations and reprimands and retaliated against her, causing emotional and psychological injury. After commencing the lawsuit, the former assistant principal learned that the principal had undergone psychotherapeutic treatment and had taken prescription drugs. When the assistant principal's attorney attempted to learn more about the principal's psychological history, the attorney for the school district and the principal resisted on the grounds of psychotherapist's privilege and relevance. When the principal refused to answer questions concerning his present use of medication at a deposition, the assistant principal's attorney filed an emergency motion in a Florida trial court, seeking an order to compel the principal to answer the questions. The trial court granted the emergency motion and the school district and principal appealed to the District Court of Appeal of Florida, Fourth District. The court of appeal ruled that the principal had not waived the psychotherapist-patient privilege. The school board had not raised the principal's mental health history as an issue in this case by merely denying the assistant principal's contention that the principal's mental health should be an issue. The assistant principal was not entitled to the emergency order. *Palm Beach County School Bd. v. Morrison*, 621 So.2d 464 (Fla.App.4th Dist.1993).

A Massachusetts school principal was suspended when a parent filed a criminal complaint against him involving the principal's alleged "strangle hold" on a student who swore at him. The suspension followed several parental complaints about the principal. The principal was found not guilty in the criminal matter but the school district ordered a psychiatric examination because the principal admitted that he was under extreme pressure. The principal sued the school district to avoid taking the exam in a federal district court which dismissed the action. On the principal's appeal, the U.S. Court of Appeals, First Circuit, upheld the lower court's decision. The public interest in providing a safe environment to students compelled the examination of the principal as a condition of continued employment. *Daury v. Smith*, 842 F.2d 9 (1st Cir.1988).

B. Physical Examinations

A U.S. district court in New York held that the constitutional right to privacy did not extend to a female teacher who refused to submit to a physical examination by a male physician employed by the school district. The teacher had taken sick leave from her employment. Pursuant to both state law and the collective bargaining agreement she was notified to report to the school district physician for a physical examination. She refused and was subsequently terminated for incompetence and insubordination. In this lawsuit the teacher argued that her constitutional right to privacy was impermissibly violated by school officials. The court rejected her argument saying that the alleged privacy right claimed here was a mere personal predilection against male physicians. *Gargiul v. Tompkins*, 525 F.Supp. 795 (N.D.N.Y.1981).

Two Pennsylvania courts have issued rulings involving physical require-ments for school bus operator licensing. In the first case the Pennsylvania Department of Transportation (DOT) revoked the operator's license of a school bus driver after testing revealed that his hearing had fallen below the minimum standard set by DOT regulations, notwithstanding the fact that the bus driver's doctor had testified that his hearing was sufficient to safely operate a school bus. The school bus driver appealed to the Court of Common Pleas contending that the hearing requirement discriminated against the disabled. The court sustained the decision of the DOT and the school bus driver appealed to the Commonwealth Court which likewise ruled against the driver. The court stated that a minimum hearing requirement does not discriminate against the disabled because such a requirement is rationally related to a legitimate safety interest. Since the bus driver's hearing did not meet the level set by DOT regulations, the revocation of licensing was proper. *Giampa v. Commonwealth*, 492 A.2d 504 (Pa.Cmwlth.1985).

The second case involved a part-time school bus driver who had recently undergone surgery to remove a 95 percent obstruction of a coronary artery. The Pennsylvania DOT withdrew his bus operator's license because of its regulation that mandated such withdrawal on the basis of "coronary insufficiency." A common pleas court reversed the DOT and ordered that the operator's license be reinstated. The DOT appealed to the Commonwealth Court which once again reversed. The Commonwealth Court held that the lower court had erred in finding that since the school bus driver had recovered from the corrective heart surgery he was entitled to reinstatement. At issue was not the driver's present condition but whether he had a history of coronary insufficiency. The DOT's decision to revoke the licensing of the school bus driver was therefore upheld. *Commonwealth v. Miller,* 492 A.2d 121 (Pa.Cmwlth.1985).

C. Drug Testing

A Pennsylvania woman called the transportation services department of her school district and complained that the driver of her son's bus could not stand up and smelled of marijuana. She had never complained before and the administrator of quality services therefore decided that the driver should be tested for drug use. A street supervisor was instructed to meet the bus driver and take him to a health service for a drug test. The bus driver refused to be tested because he felt it was in violation of his rights. The street supervisor reported the refusal to the supervisor who suspended the bus driver. A hearing was held before the personnel administrator and the driver was charged with insubordination. Based on the bus driver's entire work record and the charge of insubordination the personnel administrator recommended that he be discharged. The bus driver then brought a civil rights action in a federal district court claiming that he was discharged for refusing to submit to a urinalysis drug test in violation of his constitutional rights.

A school district may require an employee to submit to a drug test if there is reasonable suspicion of drug use. Factors that may affect the reasonableness of the suspicion are: 1) the nature of the tip or information; 2) the reliability of the informant; 3) the degree of corroboration; 4) other facts contributing to the suspicion. The school district acknowledged that its decision to have the driver tested was based solely on the information taken from the parent's telephone complaint. The court noted that this was not a strong case, but given the nature of the job and the reliability of the parent, there was reasonable suspicion of drug use. Therefore, the school district's motion for summary judgment was granted. *Armington v. School Dist. of Philadelphia,* 767 F.Supp. 661 (E.D.Pa.1991).

A Georgia law required all applicants for state employment to submit to a pre-employment drug screen. The state education association sued the state in a federal district court claiming that the requirement violated its members' right to privacy, due process and equal protection under the Fourth and Fourteenth Amendments. The education association sought a permanent injunction barring enforcement of the act. In reaching its decision the court found that a drug screen constituted a search for purposes of the Fourth Amendment, which protects individuals from unreasonable search and seizure. Generally, before a lawful search can be conducted, the state must have probable cause to believe that the person to be searched has violated the law. However, in recent cases, the Supreme Court has allowed employers to screen employees without probable cause where the employee must "discharge duties fraught with such risks of injury to others that even a momentary lapse of attention can have dangerous consequences." When determining whether a search may be conducted without probable cause, the court must balance the interests of the government with the individual's expectations of privacy. The state attempted to justify the law based upon the government's interest in maintaining a drug free workplace. The court found this justification insufficient to outweigh the individual's Fourth Amendment rights. The court granted the education association's request for a permanent injunction and struck down the law as unconstitutional. *Georgia Assn. of Educators v. Harris*, 749 F.Supp. 1110 (N.D.Ga.1990).

The New York Court of Appeals, the state's highest court, struck down a school district's urine testing plan. Pursuant to the terms of a collective bargaining agreement, the school district in this case imposed a requirement that probationary teachers desiring to be eligible for tenure undergo urine testing as part of a physical examination. The purpose of the testing was to detect drug use by teachers. The local teachers' union sought a court order preventing the urine testing on the ground that the testing infringed upon teachers' Fourth Amendment right to be free of unreasonable searches and seizures. The court agreed that the testing constituted a "search" under the Fourth Amendment. Urine testing therefore could not be undertaken unless a "reasonable suspicion" existed that testing would reflect drug use by the teacher to be tested. The court therefore held that the school district's urine testing plan for probationary teachers was unconstitutional. *Patchogue-Medford Congress of Teachers v. Bd. of Educ.*, 510 N.E.2d 325 (N.Y.1987).

A similar case arising in Washington, D.C., involved mandatory urine testing for school bus attendants. Here a school bus attendant for children with disabilities was forced to give a urine sample as part of a program instituted by the Washington school district to detect drug use by its transportation employees. When the teacher's urine tested positive, she was fired. A U.S. district court agreed with her claim that the urine testing violated the Fourth Amendment and ordered that she be given full backpay and reinstated to her job. The court held that urine testing could not be required of a bus attendant unless "probable cause" existed to suspect the bus attendant of drug use. Unlike bus drivers or mechanics who expect that their privacy rights will be limited by public safety considerations, school bus attendants legitimately expect to retain a zone of personal privacy. Urine testing infringes upon this expectation of privacy, and therefore probable cause was required before such testing could be imposed. *Jones v. McKenzie*, 628 F.Supp. 1500 (D.D.C.1986).

D. Performance Evaluations

A tenured vocational technical school instructor worked for 19 years at a Pennsylvania county school system without ever receiving unsatisfactory performance ratings. The instructor then threatened two school employees on the same day, including a head counselor, after missing a mandatory class. The school terminated the instructor's employment on the basis of immorality, persistent and willful violation of school law, persistent negligence and cruelty. The Commonwealth Court of Pennsylvania reversed the state secretary of education's dismissal of the teacher's appeal. The court held that the two incidents, which occurred about three hours apart, did not indicate a persistent course of conduct, even though an alleged prior incident had occurred in 1985. *Horton v. Jefferson County - Dubois Area Vocational Tech. School*, 630 A.2d 481 (Pa.Cmwlth.1993).

In April 1985, the Superintendent of the St. Louis Public School System informed all teachers that students' achievement as measured by the California Achievement Test (CAT) would be used to evaluate teacher performance. Students' achievement in reading, language and mathematics would be used as part of the evaluations of English language, communications and mathematics teachers. If student performance in all three areas of the CAT was low the teacher would be given a preliminary unsatisfactory evaluation. The superintendent reviewed the evaluations of those teachers who received preliminary unsatisfactory evaluations. If any other deficiencies appeared on a teacher's record, the teacher received a final unsatisfactory evaluation. The teachers' collective bargaining agreement stipulated that teachers who received unsatisfactory evaluation ratings could not receive salary advancement. Several teachers and their union filed a lawsuit against the St. Louis Board of Education in U.S. district court alleging that the evaluation of teachers' performance on the basis of the CAT deprived them of property without due process, because teachers could lose salary advancement without being granted a hearing. On a motion to dismiss, the district court noted that the teachers' collective bargaining agreement did not expressly entitle teachers to salary advancement. If they could establish, however, that they had a "right or legitimate claim of entitlement to salary advancement," they also had a right not to be deprived of that "property" without due process. The court ruled that the teachers could establish such a right or entitlement based upon a common understanding with the board of education or upon some other ground not appearing in the contract. They had therefore stated a valid claim for the denial of property without due process. The court also agreed that the teachers' allegation that the CAT was instituted arbitrarily, capriciously and irrationally for evaluating teachers stated a valid claim against the board of education. The case could proceed to trial. *St. Louis Teachers Union v. St. Louis Bd. of Educ.*, 652 F.Supp. 425 (E.D.Mo.1987).

IV. VOLUNTARY EMPLOYEE LEAVE

This section deals with employee-initiated leaves of absence. For cases concerning involuntary leaves and suspensions, please see Chapter Nine of this volume.

A. Family and Maternity Leave

The federal Pregnancy Discrimination Act 42 U.S.C. § 2000e-(k) prohibits any employer from discriminating against an employee on the basis of pregnancy, and further requires that pregnancy be treated the same as any other disabling illness for purposes of health benefits programs and all other employment-related purposes. The Family and Medical Leave Act of 1993, 29 U.S.C. §§ 2601-2654, allows eligible employees to take up to 12 weeks of unpaid leave per year under specified circumstances relating to family health care and child birth. Many state legislatures have passed parallel statutes protecting the rights of employees to take family leave.

The U.S. Supreme Court has held that rules of school boards requiring that maternity leave be taken at mandatory and fixed time periods violate the Due Process Clause of the Fourteenth Amendment to the U.S. Constitution. Two cases were involved in this appeal to the Supreme Court. In both cases school district rules required mandatory leaves at a fixed time early in pregnancy. The Court said that the rules were unconstitutional. The test in this case and other similar cases is that the maternity policy, in order to be valid, must bear a rational relationship to legitimate school interests. If there is a relationship the rules pass constitutional examination; if not, they are unconstitutional and cannot be enforced. *Cleveland Bd. of Educ. v. LaFleur,* 414 U.S. 632, 94 S.Ct. 791, 39 L.Ed.2d 52 (1974).

Indiana statutes require school districts to grant their employees a leave of absence for the duration of a pregnancy, plus one year following the birth of the child. A teacher who had given birth to a child in March advised her employer that she intended to return to work in August. However, she changed her mind and requested an extension for one year following the birth of her child. The school board voted to reject her request for extension of the maternity leave, and hired another teacher to take her place. The teacher filed a lawsuit in an Indiana trial court, claiming violation of state law. The court granted the teacher's summary judgment motion and the school board appealed to the Court of Appeals of Indiana, Fifth District. The court stated that the school board was required to grant a leave of absence as set forth in the statute, assuming the teacher had complied with statutory notice requirements. Teachers were entitled to take leave for the entire gestational period plus one year following the birth of the child if sufficient notice was given. Here the teacher had given ample notice to the board. The board's contention that it was entitled to hold the teacher to her initial statement was in conflict with the statute, and the trial court's decision had been correct. *Bd. of School Trustees of Salem Comm. Schools v. Robertson,* 637 N.E.2d 181 (Ind.App.5th Dist.1994).

A part-time medical assistance instructor at a Virginia private college suffered from an autoimmune system disorder which caused joint pain and inflammation, fatigue, and urinary and intestinal disorders. She frequently missed work because of her condition and also missed work to take care of her son, who suffered from gastro-esophageal reflux disease. The college permitted the instructor to take sick leave and to take breaks whenever she felt ill. It granted her requests for accommodation and permitted her to keep flexible hours. The instructor was also permitted to take a leave of absence to be with her son while he was undergoing surgery. However, her request for additional time off to take care of his postoperative problems was denied. The instructor resigned, and signed a report prepared by the college stating that her separation was "mutual." She then filed a lawsuit against the college in a U.S. district court, alleging discrimination under the Americans with Disabilities Act (ADA). The ADA proscribes actions taken based on an employer's mere belief that an employee would have to miss work to take care of a disabled person. The court entered summary judgment for the college, and the instructor appealed to the U.S. Court of Appeals, Fourth Circuit.

The court of appeals stated that an employee who cannot meet the attendance requirements of a job is not protected by the ADA. The instructor's absences had rendered her unable to function effectively as a teacher. Consequently, she was not a "qualified individual with a disability" under the ADA and was unable to avail herself of ADA protections. The court also rejected her claim that the discharge constituted discrimination based on her association with her disabled son. The ADA did not require the college to restructure the instructor's work schedule. The instructor was permissibly discharged based on her past absences and her statement that she would miss more work to take care of her son. This, coupled with the college's reasonable accommodations, established that disability was not a motivating factor in the dismissal. The district court decision was affirmed. *Tyndall v. National Education Centers*, 31 F.3d 209 (4th Cir.1994).

A tenured New Jersey English teacher lost her job through a reduction in force. The board of education placed her name on its preferred eligibility list for rehire, but failed to hire her as a long-term substitute for another tenured English teacher who took a one-year maternity leave. The teacher who had been laid off claimed that the maternity leave had created a vacancy within the meaning of a New Jersey tenure statute and brought an administrative proceeding challenging the board's action. The state commissioner of education adopted an administrative law judge's decision, ruling that the board had violated the laid off teacher's tenure rights, but this decision was reversed by the state board of education. Appeal reached the Supreme Court of New Jersey. The supreme court upheld the education board's decision. In doing so, it adopted the reasoning of courts in Michigan, Pennsylvania, and New York which held that where positions are temporarily unoccupied due to extended sick leave, no vacancy is created because the incumbent teacher has a right to return to the position. The term vacancy applies only to unoccupied positions for which the incumbent has no intent to return. Because the teacher who took the maternity leave intended to return to her position in this case, there was no vacancy under the New Jersey tenure statute and, accordingly, the teacher who had been laid off was not entitled to it. *Lammers v. Bd. of Educ. of Borough of Point Pleasant*, 633 A.2d 526 (1993).

A teacher who worked for an Ohio school district decided to become pregnant by artificial insemination. After one miscarriage, the teacher, who was unmarried, gave birth to a child conceived by artificial insemination. While the teacher was on maternity leave, the school board voted not to renew her contract. Previously, the teacher had been given mixed evaluations. She sued the school district, claiming that it had violated Title VII and also violated her due process, privacy and equal protection rights. She also made a claim for intentional infliction of emotional distress. The school district moved for summary judgment, claiming that it was entitled to judgment as a matter of law. The U.S. District Court, Southern District of Ohio, stated that the school district was not entitled to judgment on the teacher's Title VII discrimination claim. There was a genuine factual dispute as to the reasons behind the dismissal. The court also stated that if the school district was shown to have fired the teacher because she chose to have a child through artificial insemination, it violated her substantive due process rights. According to the court, there was a constitutional right to become pregnant by artificial insemination. Therefore, the school district would need to prove at trial that it did not fire her for that reason. The court denied summary judgment to the school district. *Cameron v. Bd. of Educ. of Hillsboro*, 795 F.Supp. 228 (S.D.Ohio 1991).

A Wisconsin teacher was covered by a collective bargaining agreement which provided that certificated employees would be granted ten days of paid leave each year up to a maximum of 120 days. The teacher had accumulated 18 days of reimbursable leave under the collective bargaining agreement when he learned that a child would be placed with his family for adoption. He requested five days leave to be used upon the child's arrival. The school district refused his request to substitute the accumulated reimbursable leave for the unpaid leave which was provided by the Wisconsin Family and Medical Leave Act. The act stated that an employee could substitute, for portions of family or medical leave, "paid or unpaid leave of any other type provided by the employer." However, the school district maintained that although the teacher had accumulated 18 days of reimbursable leave, he had not met any of the conditions for leave under the collective bargaining agreement. He had only met the *statutory* conditions for leave. The Department of Industry, Labor and Human Relations ruled in favor of the teacher, a state trial court affirmed this decision, and the court of appeals also affirmed.

On further appeal to the Supreme Court of Wisconsin, the school district maintained that because the teacher had not met any of the conditions for leave under the collective bargaining agreement, it had no obligation to provide him with a substitution for the unpaid leave to which he was entitled under the act. The court, however, disagreed. It stated that the act was intended to make the employee eligible for paid leave if any was provided by the employer. Accordingly, if an employer already provided other types of paid leave, employees could substitute that leave for unpaid leave available under the act. The supreme court also determined that the teacher was entitled to attorney's fees. The decision of the court of appeals was affirmed. *Richland School District v. Department of Industry, Labor and Human Relations*, 498 N.W.2d 826 (Wis.1993).

B. Sabbatical Leave

During the 1980-81 school year eleven teachers were notified by their Pennsylvania school board that due to declining enrollment they would be suspended for the 1981-82 school year. Aware of this possibility, all eleven of the teachers applied for sabbatical leave for the 1981-82 school year. Although the teachers were qualified for leave, their applications were denied on the grounds that they were to be suspended. The teachers sued their school district in state court. The Supreme Court of Pennsylvania ordered that the sabbatical leave be granted. The school district could not deny the teachers their vested right to take sabbatical leave merely because it planned to suspend them the following year. *Bristol Township School Dist. v. Karafin*, 498 A.2d 824 (Pa.1985).

A Washington teacher received a paid sabbatical leave for the 1979-80 school year. At the end of that leave the teacher requested further unpaid leave but the school district denied her request. She then asked for a nonteaching position because she believed that her emotional problems made it impossible for her to return to work. The teacher's school administrator refused to consider such a reassignment. The teacher's bargaining agreement provided that "an employee who has been granted sabbatical leave will agree to return for at least two years of regular service in the District upon the expiration of her/his leave. If the employee does not return to regular service with the District, all salary paid during the leave will become immediately due and payable to the District at the expiration of such leave ... except in the case that other mutually agreeable arrangements are made between the employee and the board." The school district asked the teacher to repay the money received during her sabbatical as required in the contract; she refused to do so. The school district filed suit against the teacher in a state court. The Court of Appeals of Washington determined that the teacher had the choice of returning to work or returning sabbatical funds. The teacher's offer to be reassigned, found the court, did not satisfy the "regular service" requirement of the collective bargaining agreement. *Bellevue School Dist. No. 405 v. Bentley*, 684 P.2d 793 (Wash.1984).

Suit was brought by a New York school district against an industrial arts teacher seeking to recover salary and other benefits paid to the teacher while he was on sabbatical leave. The contract between the district and the teachers' association provided for sabbatical leaves if a teacher agreed in writing that if he voluntarily resigns within two years after termination of the sabbatical leave he is required to repay to the district gross pay and other benefits received while on sabbatical leave. The teacher took a sabbatical leave for the 1977-1978 school year and tendered his resignation before the next school year started. The New York Supreme Court, Appellate Division, in ruling for the school district, rejected the teacher's contentions that he did not agree in writing to repay the district and that he was replaced by another employee while he was on leave. Since the resignation was voluntary, the teacher was required to repay the district. *Trumansburg Cent. School Dist. v. Chalone*, 449 N.Y.S.2d 92 (A.D.3d Dept.1982).

C. Vacation and Sick Leave

A Louisiana teacher exhausted her accumulated sick leave due to a complicated pregnancy. Her request for extended sick leave was awarded by the school board, subject to a reduction in salary for the amount paid to her substitute, as authorized by Louisiana law. The board then denied the teacher's request for an additional award of sick leave over one month later, and it adopted a policy that no employee would be granted extended sick leave. The teacher sued the school board in a Louisiana trial court, claiming that state law prohibited the board from denying her request for extended sick leave. The court granted the board's summary judgment motion and the teacher appealed to the Court of Appeal of Louisiana, First Circuit. The court rejected the teacher's argument that she was entitled to an unlimited extension of her approved sick leave after her paid leave was exhausted. Louisiana school boards were not obligated to provide extended sick leave, and the statutory requirement that teachers on extended leave were entitled to differential pay representing the difference between their wage and that of their substitute was inapplicable. Louisiana school boards have the right to deny or grant additional sick leave, and are required to pay differential wages only where they first agree to grant additional leave. *Dagenhardt v. Terrebonne Parish School Bd.*, 636 So.2d 1203 (La.App.1st Cir.1994).

A Georgia statute requires that teachers for grades kindergarten through five be provided with a 30-minute lunch break during which they shall not be assigned any responsibilities. A school principal required his teachers to remain on campus during their lunch break. A fifth grade teacher at the school challenged the rule as a violation of the statute. The state superintendent of schools affirmed the rule, and this decision was affirmed by the state board of education. However, a Georgia trial court reversed the state board's decision, finding that the rule violated the statute. The board appealed to the Court of Appeals of Georgia. The court of appeals determined that the intention of the statute was to ensure that teachers had a period during the day when they could be free from instruction and daily planning. The court found no legislative intent to permit unconditional leave from campus during the lunch break. Because the statutory language prohibited only the assignment of instructional, administrative or supervisory responsibilities, the rule restricting teachers from leaving school campus during lunch break was not in conflict with the statute, and the court of appeals reversed the trial court judgment. *Griffin-Spalding County School System v. Daniel*, 451 S.E.2d 480 (Ga.App.1994).

A Colorado school district employed a superintendent of schools under a written contract which stated that he was entitled to take 20 days of vacation each year. The superintendent could accumulate up to 60 days from year to year. The contract did not specify whether the superintendent would be entitled to compensation for unused vacation upon the expiration of the contract. However, if the school board unilaterally terminated the employment contract without cause, the superintendent would not be entitled to compensation. After two contract extensions, the superintendent advised the school district that he would not renew the contract for a third year. The school district refused to pay the superintendent for 33 days of accrued unused vacation time and he sued it in a Colorado trial court for over $9,000, which was the value of the unused vacation time. The court granted the school district's summary judgment motion. The Colorado Court of Appeals reversed the judgment and held that the superintendent was entitled to compensation. The school district appealed to the Supreme Court of Colorado.

The supreme court observed that silence in a contract creates an ambiguity where the matter involved is naturally within the scope of the contract. Because compensation for approved vacation time was naturally within the scope of this contract, an ambiguity existed that required remand of the case to the trial court. The trial court would have to consider on remand whether the parties intended to compensate the superintendent upon expiration of the contract. Because this subject was missing from the contract, the parties were free to introduce additional evidence outside the contract in support of their arguments. The court refused to adopt a ruling by the court of appeals that public employees had an implied right of compensation for unused vacation time. *Cheyenne Mountain School Dist. No. 12 v. Thompson*, 861 P.2d 711 (Colo.1993).

A Nebraska teacher with 20 years of experience was employed by a school district under a contract allowing employees to take a maximum of 70 days of sick leave per year. The contract explicitly permitted employees to use sick leave for deaths in the immediate family, including their parents. Teachers taking leave were required to make detailed lesson plans for their substitutes. The teacher took leave when her mother became seriously ill. She kept in contact with the school superintendent and discussed lesson plans with her substitute. The substitute allegedly advised the teacher that she would be more comfortable preparing her own lessons, which she did. The teacher's mother died, and the teacher did not return to work for over one month, using 21 and a half days of sick time. The school board determined that the teacher had neglected her duties by taking an unreasonable leave. A Nebraska trial court affirmed the termination of the teacher's contract, as did the Nebraska Supreme Court of Appeals.

On the teacher's appeal to the Supreme Court of Nebraska, she alleged that there had been insufficient evidence to support the board's action. The supreme court agreed, observing that she had merely exercised her contractual right to take paid leave upon the death of an immediate family member. The board's argument that the teacher had failed to prepare sufficient lesson plans for her substitute was irrelevant based on the substitute's testimony that she preferred to prepare her own lessons. The court reversed and remanded the case with instructions to reinstate the teacher's contract with backpay and benefits. *Drain v. Bd. of Educ. of Frontier County School Dist. No. 46*, 508 N.W.2d 255 (Neb.1993).

An Iowa driver's education instructor began an indefinite, voluntary sick leave because of a mental impairment which resulted in aberrant behavior (including shouting and cursing at students). The school district notified him that he would have to get a second medical opinion of his fitness to return to teaching before he could return. The instructor then sued the district in federal court, alleging that it had deprived him of his protected property interest in continued employment without due process. The court ruled for the school district, and the U.S. Court of Appeals, Eighth Circuit, affirmed. Requiring the second medical opinion did not violate due process. *Scheideman v. West Des Moines Community School District*, 989 F.2d 286 (8th Cir.1993).

An administrative rule was adopted by an Ohio university dealing with the use of sick leave by university employees. It read in pertinent part: "Sick leave shall be granted to an employee only upon approval of the manager for the following reasons: 1) Illness or injury of the employee, or a member of his or her immediate family who requires the care of the staff member. A physician's certificate is required if sick leave is being requested for a member of the immediate family." A university employee and a union brought an action challenging this rule in an Ohio trial court. The trial court granted summary judgment in favor of the employee and union, and the university appealed to the Court of Appeals of Ohio. The plaintiffs contended that the rule and policies were unreasonable and conflicted with a civil service rule. The court noted that it would be unreasonable to require an employee to obtain a medical certificate if no medical attention was required for the illness involved. To require an employee to obtain a medical certificate for every illness that prevented his coming to work was clearly unreasonable and would add immensely to health insurance costs. Therefore, the court affirmed the decision of the trial court, and granted summary judgment in favor of the employee and union. *Steinhour v. Ohio State Univ.*, 577 N.E.2d 413 (Ohio App.1989).

In 1983, an Alabama school board approved a policy authorizing a payment of $100 to all employees who achieved perfect attendance for the 1983-84 school year. The policy was amended at the next school board meeting to provide that instead of the $100 bonus, a bonus of $20 would be paid for each unused sick leave day up to a maximum of nine unused days per year. When teachers attempted to collect benefits under the policy at the end of the year, however, the school district refused to pay, having decided that the plan was unconstitutional and therefore unenforceable against the school district. The Supreme Court of Alabama ruled that the plan did not violate the Alabama Constitution as additional payment for services already rendered, and that it was enforceable against the school board prospectively from the time of its enactment. *Kohen v. Bd. of School Comm'rs*, 510 So.2d 216 (Ala.1987).

Prior to 1970, Kentucky law provided that up to 20 unused sick leave days could be accumulated by teachers. That number was raised to 60 days in 1970, and was made unlimited in 1974. These limits applied unless a greater number of accumulated days was "authorized" by a district board of education. Despite a lack of such authorization, a superintendent recorded an unlimited number of sick leave days for teachers in his district. In 1984, the district's board of education authorized a new superintendent to correct errors in the accumulated sick leave records by reducing the number of days accumulated by the amount that those records exceeded 20 days at the start of 1970, or 60 days at the start of 1974. This resulted in the reduction of a teacher's sick leave by 69 days. A U.S. district court ruled that this reduction was not unconstitutional because the teacher had no entitlement to the sick leave days that had been erroneously recorded on her record. *Sublette v. Bd. of Educ.*, 664 F.Supp. 265 (W.D.Ky.1987).

CHAPTER SIX

EMPLOYMENT DISCRIMINATION

I. FEDERAL CONSTITUTION AND STATUTES

Employment discrimination on the basis of race, sex, religion or national origin is expressly prohibited by Title VII of the Civil Rights Act. Disparate treatment on the basis of those characteristics violates the Equal Protection Clause of the U.S. Constitution.

A. U.S. Constitution

The constitutional prohibition against employment discrimination is found in the Equal Protection Clause of the Fourteenth Amendment, which commands that no state shall "deny to any person within its jurisdiction the equal protection of the laws." The Equal Protection Clause is an important safeguard against discrimination by states and state agents, such as school boards. Its coverage, however, is limited both to government bodies and to situations involving *intentional* discrimination. The latter requirement was imposed by the U.S. Supreme Court in *Washington v. Davis*, 426 U.S. 229 (1976). This case involved a written verbal skills test which was a requirement for employment as a police officer. The test resulted in a disproportionately high percentage of black applicants being rejected for employment. The Supreme Court held that an adverse impact or effect on racial minorities was insufficient to show a violation of the Equal Protection Clause. Proof of intent to discriminate was required. Because in most cases it is difficult to prove an intent to discriminate (except in affirmative action-"reverse discrimination" cases), federal civil rights statutes provide a much more common basis for claims of employment discrimination in the school context.

B. Federal Statutes

Title VII of the Civil Rights Act of 1964 prohibits discrimination in employment based upon race, color, sex, religion or national origin. It applies to any employer with 15 or more employees. Members of the Communist Party are not protected by Title VII, and discrimination based upon age, disability and alienage is covered by other federal statutes. The prohibition against discrimination in employment extends to all "terms or conditions of employment," including hiring and firing decisions, promotions, salary, seniority, benefits, and work assignments. Reverse discrimination claims are also recognized under Title VII. The U.S. Equal Employment Opportunity Commission (EEOC) is empowered to enforce Title VII. Private individuals alleging discrimination must pursue administrative remedies within the EEOC before they are allowed to file suit against employers under Title VII. Plaintiffs who prevail in employment discrimination lawsuits are entitled, where appropriate, to backpay, front pay, accumulated seniority and other benefits, and attorney's fees. Punitive and compensatory damages are now available in Title VII cases where the discrimination has been shown to be intentional.

Title VII lawsuits may be divided into two categories: disparate treatment and disparate impact. In a disparate treatment lawsuit an individual usually claims that he or she was not hired, was fired, or was denied a promotion simply because of his or her race, color, sex, religion or national origin. Such lawsuits proceed in three stages. First, the plaintiff must show: a) that he or she belongs to a protected class (male, female, black, white, Jew, Catholic, etc.); b) that he or she was qualified for the position; c) that despite the plaintiff's qualifications, he or she was rejected; and d) that after rejection the position remained open. Second, the burden then shifts to the defendant to "articulate" a legitimate, nondiscriminatory reason (such as incompetence or lack of qualifications) for rejecting the plaintiff. Third, the plaintiff must show that the reason given by the employer in step two is a pretext for unlawful discrimination. As illustrated by the U.S. Supreme Court case *Board of Trustees of Keene State College v. Sweeney*, 439 U.S. 24, 99 S.Ct. 295, 58 L.Ed.2d 216 (1978), Title VII disparate treatment lawsuits often become credibility disputes in which a court must decide whether it believes the employer or the employee.

Title VII's bona fide occupational qualification (BFOQ) exception allows employers (especially religiously-affiliated private schools) to use sex, religion or national origin as a hiring criteria if one of those three characteristics is a "bona fide occupational qualification necessary to the normal operation of that particular business or enterprise." However, the BFOQ exception is narrowly construed by the courts. While being female can be a BFOQ for counseling high school girls, numerous cases have indicated that BFOQ defenses will fail unless the qualification at issue is a matter of "necessity," not merely employer convenience. In any case, successful assertion of a BFOQ defense will result in dismissal of a disparate treatment claim. It is important to note that race can never be a BFOQ. Disparate impact lawsuits differ from disparate treatment in that claims of the former type do not allege overt discriminatory actions. Instead, disparate impact lawsuits claim that a facially neutral employer policy (e.g., high school diplomas or I.Q. testing as a condition of employment) has an adverse or disparate impact on minorities. If such a policy does have an adverse impact, it will constitute a violation of Title VII unless the policy is "necessary" to the operation of the employer's business. Simply put, the policy must be related to job performance.

A separate issue under Title VII is affirmative action. Generally, an affirmative action in employment plan voluntarily adopted by a school district will not result in unlawful reverse discrimination under Title VII if the institution was guilty of discrimination in the past. See *United Steelworkers of America v. Weber*, 443 U.S. 193 (1979), and *Johnson v. Transportation Agency*, 480 U.S. 616 (1987). However, as indicated in § I.A. above, school districts need to comply with the Equal Protection Clause as well as Title VII when devising affirmative action programs. To that end the U.S. Supreme Court struck down a no-minority-layoff (or "affirmative retention") clause in a teacher collective bargaining agreement in *Wygant v. Jackson Bd. of Educ.,* below.

The Age Discrimination in Employment Act of 1967, 29 U.S.C. § 621 *et seq.*, (ADEA) is part of the Fair Labor Standards Act. It prohibits discrimination against persons ages 40 and above.

A Utah school district terminated the employment of one of its teachers. He filed a lawsuit against the district under 42 U.S.C. § 1983, alleging constitutional rights violations. The U.S. District Court for the District of Utah granted the school board's summary judgment motion, ruling that the Eleventh Amendment to the U.S. Constitution prohibits federal courts from issuing money judgments against the states. The teacher appealed to the U.S. Court of Appeals, Tenth Circuit. The court of appeals noted that although the Eleventh Amendment forbids suits for damages against states in federal courts, immunity extends only to those governmental entities which are "arms of the state." Utah school districts may be characterized as political subdivisions created by state law, which exercise a great deal of responsibility without state control. Local school boards are not so controlled by the state that they can be characterized as arms of the state. In this case, the potential money judgment would not be paid directly from the state treasury, but rather from the state risk management fund, for which local school boards paid premiums from their own receipts. The risk management fund was primarily composed of revenue from local property tax and state grants. Because the school district was a political subdivision under Utah law, which exercised significant local authority and obtained local funding, it was not an arm of the state entitled to immunity. *Ambus v. Granite Bd. of Educ.*, 995 F.2d 992 (10th Cir.1993).

The U.S. Court of Appeals, Tenth Circuit, refused to recognize a cause of action for sexual orientation discrimination in a case which arose in Kansas. A teacher worked continuously since 1987 in various capacities for a Kansas school district. He was rejected twice, however, for full-time high school teaching positions. The teacher filed suit in federal court under 42 U.S.C. § 1983 alleging that he was not hired because of the principal's belief that he was a homosexual. In denying the principal's motion for summary judgment, the district court held that material issues of fact existed regarding whether the principal had violated the teacher's equal protection rights by denying employment based on a perceived homosexual classification. It noted that, as of 1991, homosexuals and those perceived as homosexuals were a suspect class deserving of heightened scrutiny in the equal protection context. The principal appealed to the U.S. Court of Appeals, Tenth Circuit. The court of appeals held that the principal was entitled to qualified immunity from the teacher's civil rights claim. There was no clearly established line of cases proscribing adverse action against civilian job applicants based on homosexual or perceived homosexual orientation. The court also held that the school district could not be held liable for damages resulting from the teacher's civil rights action based on the principal's official capacity. Section 1983 liability for the single act of an employee may not be imposed on a local government entity under a *respondeat superior* theory. Rather, such liability may be imposed only if the employee possesses "final authority" under state law to establish policy with respect to the challenged action. Since the principal had no such final authority, the school district could not be held liable for the principal's actions. *Jantz v. Muci*, 976 F.2d 623 (10th Cir.1992).

C. Sex Discrimination

An Ohio university graduate student enrolled in a two-year master's degree program in psychology. She received a full scholarship and a graduate student assistant stipend under three separate contracts. The university advised her in writing that her current grade average was lower than was permissible for the doctoral program and that her practicum performance was only average. She advised her supervisor that she was expecting a child and requested leave from her clinical practicum cases for one semester. She also asked to forgo her employment as a graduate assistant for the entire school year. Her supervisor admonished her, stating his belief that she would neglect her duties. The following semester, the student received an incomplete grade for one class and poor evaluations for her practicum. Although the student's grades later improved and she was able to successfully defend her master's thesis, the incomplete grade caused her to lose her graduate assistant position. She filed a lawsuit against the university in the U.S. District Court for the Northern District of Ohio, alleging violations of Title VII and Title IX.

The court held that the student was an employee for purposes of federal antidiscrimination laws, despite her status as a student. The fact that she received a stipend under contract bolstered the reasoning for considering her an employee.

Although her advisor's comments were blatantly discriminatory, the university had articulated a legitimate nondiscriminatory reason for assigning the student an incomplete grade. The student had been unable to show that this reason was a pretext for discrimination. The evidence indicated that the grading was caused by her poor performance. Accordingly, the court granted the university's summary judgment motion. *Ivan v. Kent State Univ.*, 863 F.Supp. 581 (N.D.Ohio 1994).

A Virginia school board eliminated 299 full-time administrative positions due to declining revenues. A female employee who lost her job sued the school board in the U.S. District Court for the Eastern District of Virginia, alleging sex discrimination and retaliatory and constructive discharge under Title VII, and denial of her constitutional due process and equal protection rights. The court granted the board's summary judgment motion, observing that the board had presented overwhelming evidence that the decision was not based on sex discrimination. The board had eliminated an equal number of men and women from positions in the employee's division, indicating a neutral decisionmaking process. The board had also presented evidence that the employee had poor communication skills. *Green v. Fairfax County School Bd.*, 832 F.Supp. 1032 (E.D.Va.1993).

A Michigan school district employed a female substitute custodian. She applied for a full-time position upon the retirement of another employee. The hiring supervisor failed to interview any of the applicants for the full-time position, and requested a reference only from a male applicant who was eventually hired. The female applicant sued the school district in a Michigan trial court, claiming that the hiring supervisor had made a derogatory statement and was predisposed against hiring women. The court granted the district's summary disposition motion. The Court of Appeals of Michigan reversed and remanded the case, stating that the female applicant had presented sufficient evidence of sex discrimination to make summary disposition inappropriate. *Ginther v. Ovid-Elsie Area Schools*, 506 N.W.2d 523 (Mich.App.1993).

A Louisiana woman served as a public relations officer for a community college for three years and was then discharged. The college hired a male to fill her position at a higher salary and the woman sued the college in a federal district court. The district court stated that the college had violated Title VII and awarded the woman backpay. However, the court did not award the woman full pay for the whole time she was unemployed because she had been employed in several positions which she voluntarily resigned. The woman then appealed to the U.S. Court of Appeals, Fifth Circuit, which remanded the case to the district court to determine if equivalent jobs were available at the time the woman was unemployed and if she pursued these jobs with diligence. The district court held that the woman did not mitigate her damages because she did not act with diligence in seeking employment. The court awarded backpay for the period in which the woman did diligently seek employment. The woman appealed again to the U.S. Court of Appeals, Fifth Circuit.

The court of appeals stated that the woman had a duty to act with reasonable diligence to obtain substantially equivalent employment. The woman did not exercise reasonable diligence for the full time she was unemployed because the first year of unemployment she only submitted one job application and she did not register with any employment agencies. Further, there were many advertisements for comparable jobs for which the woman did not apply. The court of appeals affirmed the district court's decision that the woman should not be awarded full backpay because she did not act with reasonable diligence in pursuing comparable employment. *Sollars v. Delgotto College*, 902 F.2d 1189 (5th Cir.1990).

1. Pregnancy

The Pregnancy Discrimination Act of 1979 [42 U.S.C. § 2000e(k)], an amendment to Title VII, prohibits employers from discriminating on the basis of pregnancy. The courts have held that the Act requires employers to treat pregnancy the same as any other disabling illness for purposes of health benefits programs and all other employment-related purposes. For example, if an employer's policy is to allow two months unpaid leave to employees with disabling illnesses, a pregnant employee must be granted two months unpaid leave. The Act requires only that pregnancy be treated the same as other disabilities. Some states grant more protection to pregnant employees. For other cases involving employee maternity and family leave, please see Chapter Five, Section III. A.

An Illinois high school teachers' association entered into a collective bargaining agreement with the board of education. The agreement prohibited pregnant teachers from taking sick leave for pregnancy-related disability and then taking maternity leave at the expiration of the sick leave. The collective bargaining agreement excluded maternity benefits from the sick leave bank. The government brought suit in a federal district court against the board of education and the teachers' association for violation of the Pregnancy Discrimination Act, which amended Title VII. The court determined that the collective bargaining agreement allowing teachers to take sick leave in conjunction with any other leave exclusive of maternity leave did not violate Title VII as maternity leave was a gratuitous extra option. However, it did determine that the sick leave bank provisions which automatically excluded maternity benefits discriminated against pregnant teachers who elected to utilize accumulated sick leave for a pregnancy-related disability. This clearly violated the Pregnancy Discrimination Act of Title VII. *U.S. v. Bd. of Educ. of Consol. High School Dist. 230,* 761 F.Supp. 519 (N.D.Ill.1990).

After an Illinois teacher became pregnant, she requested to use the sick leave she had accumulated during her employment for a period of disability caused by her pregnancy, followed by a maternity leave that would last for the remainder of the school year. The superintendent responded by informing the teacher that the collective bargaining agreement between the union and the school district barred teachers from taking maternity leave immediately following a period of disability for which they used sick leave. Therefore, the teacher had to choose between using sick leave or maternity leave. After obtaining a right to sue letter from the EEOC, the teacher brought this action in a federal district court. The district court found in favor of the school district and the teacher appealed to the U.S. Court of Appeals, Seventh Circuit.

The teacher alleged that the school district's leave policy violated the Pregnancy Discrimination Act by preventing women from using their sick leave for pregnancy-related disability, leading them to forego the use of accumulated sick days for what was likely to be the longest period of disability they would experience during their careers. The teacher pointed out that when a teacher retired, the school district compensated the teacher for unused sick days at a lower rate than the teacher's per diem pay. This, she argued, resulted in teachers accumulating sick days that were worth less at retirement than if they were used during the teacher's career. She claimed that the school district's leave policy resulted in women who choose to have children accumulating a greater number of sick days than men or women who choose to forego childbirth. A statistical basis for this argument might have been established by showing that women who have been disabled due to pregnancy accumulated sick days at a higher rate per year of service than their male coworkers or women who have not experienced a pregnancy-related disability. However, the teacher offered evidence only on the absolute number of sick days women accumulated over their teaching careers. This evidence failed to establish that the school district's leave policy had a disproportionate and adverse impact on women teachers who experience a pregnancy-related disability. The court found in favor of the school district and determined that the policy did not have a disparate impact on women. *Maganuco v. Leyden Cmty. High School Dist. 212,* 939 F.2d 440 (7th Cir.1991).

After a Massachusetts university professor became pregnant and took eight months maternity leave, she requested to return part-time for another three months. Her request was denied in a letter which also stated that the university looked forward to having her rejoin the staff full-time. She did not return to work for failure to find suitable childcare. She then filed a complaint, alleging gender discrimination in a Massachusetts trial court which granted summary judgment to the university. The professor appealed to the Supreme Court of Massachusetts. The court agreed that pregnant women were a protected group, but found, based upon the letter, that the teacher was not terminated; rather, she had failed to show up for work. Therefore, she could not establish a *prima facie* case of gender discrimination. *White v. Univ. of Massachusetts at Boston,* 574 N.E.2d 356 (Mass.1991).

The Equal Employment Opportunity Commission (EEOC) sued the Elgin, Illinois, Teachers Association (ETA) for violating Title VII. The EEOC complained that the ETA violated § 703 of Title VII by entering into and maintaining collective bargaining agreements which treat employees who are disabled as a result of pregnancy less favorably than those who are disabled for other reasons. The EEOC moved for summary judgment, arguing that the leave positions contained in the collective bargaining agreements at issue constituted either *per se* discrimination, disparate treatment, or disparate impact in violation of the Pregnancy Discrimination Act, 42 U.S.C. § 2000e(k).

The U.S. District Court for the Northern District of Illinois stated that a facially discriminatory policy may constitute *per se,* or explicit, sex discrimination. Explicit sex discrimination obligates a defendant to meet a higher evidentiary burden in justifying the discrimination than either disparate treatment or disparate impact. If a policy is explicitly discriminatory, the employer must establish it as a bona fide occupational qualification. This is different than a disparate treatment case which requires the employer to first articulate a legitimate nondiscriminatory reason for its action. However, the court held that the ETA provisions were not facially discriminatory. Therefore, the court denied the motion for summary judgment, and allowed the disparate treatment claim to proceed to trial. *EEOC v. Elgin Teachers Assoc.,* 780 F.Supp. 1195 (N.D.Ill.1991).

2. Equal Pay Act

Enacted by Congress in 1963, the Equal Pay Act requires that employers pay males and females the same wages for equal work. The Act applies only to sex discrimination in pay, and thus racially-based equal pay claims must be litigated under the more general provisions of Title VII. Because the Equal Pay Act is part of the Fair Labor Standards Act, employees are protected by the Act as long as the employer is engaged in an enterprise affecting interstate commerce. The employee's burden of proof under the Act has been interpreted by the courts to require only that the jobs under comparison be "substantially" equal. Strict equality of the jobs under comparison is not required. The Act requires equal pay for jobs involving "equal skill, effort, and responsibility, and which are performed under similar working conditions, except where such payment is made pursuant to (i) a seniority system; (ii) a merit system; (iii) a system which measures earnings by quantity or quality of production; or (iv) a differential based on any other factor other than sex."

A Michigan woman was employed by a school district as a substitute custodian at $5.75 per hour. In June 1988, she was promoted to temporary custodian. During the period of her employment the school paid male temporary custodians between $7.18 and $7.48 per hour. In her first paycheck for her work as a temporary custodian the school district paid her more than a dollar an hour less than it paid her male counterparts. She filed a charge with the EEOC which commenced an action in a U.S. district court. The district court granted summary judgment for the school district. The EEOC appealed to the U.S. Court of Appeals, Sixth Circuit.

The court stated that in order to prevail in an Equal Pay Act lawsuit, the EEOC must show that an employer paid different wages to employees of opposite sexes for equal work on jobs that require equal skill, effort, and responsibility. Since it was undisputed that her paycheck compensated her at a rate that was more than a dollar per hour less than that paid to male employees, a pay disparity existed. Although the school district temporarily increased her wages in response to the complaint, it ultimately dealt with the disparity by reducing the wage it paid to all substitute custodians in temporary assignments. The Equal Pay Act expressly prohibits an employer who violates the act from curing the violation by lowering the wages of male employees. Because the school district had done this, a *prima facie* case had been established. The claim was to be addressed at a trial on the merits. *EEOC v. Romeo Community Schools,* 976 F.2d 985 (6th Cir.1992).

Under New York law, high school principals' salaries were $10,000 higher than those of elementary school principals. A group of male elementary school principals brought suit against the New York City school system to equalize the salaries. They argued in a federal district court that the difference constituted gender discrimination in violation of Title VII of the Civil Rights Act of 1964.

The principals reasoned that they were being paid less not because they were male, but because they were supervising female teachers. The group also argued that the salary difference devalued the elementary principals' position because of the historical perception that elementary schools traditionally have female faculty. The court rejected the principals' claims, first noting that the fact that lower paying jobs were traditionally held by females was not enough to establish a Title VII violation. The court ruled that evidence of past discrimination against females was insufficient to prove present discrimination. It held that the legislation establishing principals' salaries reflected a judgment that high school principals had greater responsibilities and should therefore be compensated more than elementary school principals. The court further ruled that the board had a valid defense under the Bennett Amendment to Title VII, which permits disparate wages if the discrepancy is based on factors other than gender. The elementary school principals' claim was dismissed. *Siegel v. Bd. of Educ. of City of New York*, 713 F.Supp. 54 (E.D.N.Y.1989).

An Alabama woman was employed by a board of education at the textbook and resource center. Throughout her years of employment, the board of education adopted various salary schedules. In 1987, she learned that a male employee was seven steps above her on the pay scale. The woman's primary duties were as a printer. The male worker operated a different printer but had similar job duties. The woman filed suit in a federal district court alleging violations of the Equal Pay Act (EPA) and Title VII. The district court concluded that the disparity in wages resulted from a bona fide seniority system and the woman appealed to the U.S. Court of Appeals, Eleventh Circuit.

A seniority system "allots to employees ever improving employment rights and benefits as their relative lengths of pertinent employment increase." The evidence presented at trial indicated that none of the salary schedules adopted by the board reflected length of employment but rather were based solely on the job description that the board had placed upon the employee's duties at an earlier time. Length of employment is the key element for bona fide seniority systems. The court concluded that the salary schedule here did not constitute a seniority system. However, as the woman failed to prove intentional gender discrimination, the appellate court agreed with the trial court's ruling for the board on the Title VII claim. Next, the court noted that the EPA requires the employer not to discriminate between employees on the basis of sex for "equal work the performance of which requires equal skill, effort and responsibility." The trial court had dismissed the EPA claim on the basis of its conclusion that the difference in wages resulted from the operation of a bona fide seniority system. The two employees had basically the same job. The appellate court remanded the case to fully determine if the employees performed equal work as defined in the EPA. *Mitchell v. Jefferson County Bd. of Educ.*, 936 F.2d 539 (11th Cir.1991).

3. Sexual Harassment

A New Jersey teacher who was a tenured music supervisor claimed that she was fired because she refused unwanted sexual advances from her supervisor. She also claimed that the supervisor and another lesbian teacher conspired to embarrass, discredit and punish her for rejecting the sexual advances. The teacher lost her tenure when the school district initiated and prosecuted state revocation proceedings against her. The teacher filed an unsuccessful challenge to the termination action in the New Jersey state court system. She then filed a Title VII discrimination complaint against school administrators and the school board in the U.S. District Court for the District of New Jersey. The court granted the board's summary judgment motion on several grounds, including the fact that the board was not the teacher's employer at the time of the alleged discrimination. The teacher appealed to the U.S. Court of Appeals, Third Circuit. The court of appeals determined that although Title VII is generally inapplicable after the cessation of the employment relationship, the act was written broadly enough to cover discriminatory actions following the termination of an employment relationship. Because post-employment blacklisting could be more damaging than on-the-job discrimination, the district court had improperly granted the summary judgment motion. It was conceivable that the school board's continued inquiries into the revocation action were retaliatory and violated Title VII. *Charlton v. Paramus Bd. of Educ.*, 25 F.3d 194 (3d Cir.1994).

A male school bus driver attempted to form a relationship with a female driver, sending her a valentine, cookies and candy, attempting to give her a surprise birthday party and playing minor pranks on her. A district superintendent determined that the male driver had sexually harassed the female driver by creating a hostile work environment. He sent a reprimand letter to the male driver, warning that future such actions could lead to employment termination. The New York Supreme Court, Monroe County, determined that the superintendent had inappropriately judged the conduct from the perspective of the female driver's subjective experience. The focus of hostile work environment sexual harassment should have been the male's conduct, not the female driver's reaction. It was unclear whether the male driver's actions were unwelcome and gender-based. The district was ordered to remove the reprimand letter from his file. *Becker v. Churchville-Chili Cent. School Dist.*, 602 N.Y.S.2d 497 (Sup.Ct.-Monroe County 1993).

D. Race Discrimination

Section 1983 of the federal Civil Rights Act prohibits any "person" (including school districts) from depriving any other person of rights protected by the U.S. Constitution or federal statutes. Thus, for example, it is a violation of § 1983 for a school district to deprive a person of his or her Fourteenth Amendment right to equal protection of the laws, or any other federally protected right. Accordingly, the vast majority of lawsuits claiming constitutional violations are litigated under § 1983. The remedies available to a § 1983 plaintiff are broader than those available under many other statutes; Title VII is one such statute. While Title VII allows chiefly for backpay, reinstatement and attorney's fees, § 1983 allows compensatory and punitive damages to be awarded in appropriate cases.

Section 1981 of the federal Civil Rights Act provides, among other things, that all persons will enjoy the same right to make and enforce contracts as "white citizens." A post-Civil War measure, § 1981 has been held by the U.S. Supreme Court to apply in the employment context. It applies to claims of discrimination on the basis of race or ethnic origin where a contract is involved. Unlike § 1983, § 1981 does not require that the discriminatory action be attributed to the state or a state actor; it applies equally to claims against public or private persons or entities.

A white male was employed by the Dallas Independent School District (DISD) as a teacher, athletic director and head football coach at a predominantly black high school. After numerous problems, the principal recommended that the teacher be relieved of his duties as athletic director and coach. The district's superintendent reassigned the teacher to a teaching position in another school where he had no coaching duties. The teacher sued the school district and the principal, claiming that they had discriminated against him on the basis of race in violation of 42 U.S.C. § § 1981 and 1983. A federal district court held in the teacher's favor. The U.S. Court of Appeals, Fifth Circuit, reversed in part and remanded, finding that the district's § 1981 liability for the principal's actions could not be predicated on a vicarious liability theory and that municipalities could not be liable for their employees' acts. The court noted that Congress did not intend that municipalities be subject to vicarious liability under § 1983. The teacher appealed to the U.S. Supreme Court.

The Supreme Court stated that a municipality may not be held liable for its employees' violations of § 1981 under a vicarious liability theory. The express "action at law" provided by § 1983 for the deprivation of rights secured by the Constitution and laws of the United States is the exclusive federal remedy for the violation of rights guaranteed by § 1981 when the claim is pressed against a state actor. The Supreme Court affirmed part of the court of appeals' decision and remanded the case in order to determine if the superintendent possessed policy-making authority in the area of employee transfer, and if so, whether a new trial was required to determine the DISD's responsibility for the principal's actions in light of this determination. *Jett v. Dallas Indep. School Dist.*, 491 U.S. 701, 109 S.Ct. 2702, 105 L.Ed.2d 598 (1989).

On remand, the court of appeals observed that there was no evidence in the record that the principal or the superintendent had policymaking authority that would create liability. Because it was inappropriate for a court to base liability upon the actions of officials who lacked final policymaking authority, there could be no liability placed upon the school district. The court reversed the judgment and remanded the case to the district court. *Jett v. Dallas Indep. School Dist.*, 7 F.3d 1241 (5th Cir.1993).

The U.S. Supreme Court unanimously ruled that persons of Arab descent are protected from racial discrimination under § 1981 of the federal Civil Rights Act of 1866. This Pennsylvania case involved a college professor, born in Iraq, who was a U.S. citizen and a member of the Muslim faith. The professor sued St. Francis College in U.S. district court under Title VII and § 1981 of the Civil Rights Act after St. Francis denied his tenure request. The district court ruled that § 1981, which forbids racial discrimination in the making and enforcement of any contract, did not reach claims of discrimination based on Arab ancestry. The professor appealed. The U.S. Court of Appeals, Third Circuit, reversed. St. Francis appealed to the U.S. Supreme Court.

Section 1981 states that "[a]ll persons ... shall have the same right to make and enforce contracts ... as is enjoyed by white citizens. . . ." In affirming the court of appeals' decision, the Supreme Court noted that although § 1981 does not use the word "race," the Court has construed the statute to forbid all racial discrimination in the making of private as well as public contracts. The Court cited several dictionary and encyclopedic sources to support its decision that for the purposes of § 1981, Arabs, Englishmen, Germans and certain other ethnic groups are not to be considered a single race. Based on the history of § 1981 it concluded that Congress "intended to protect from discrimination identifiable classes of persons who are subjected to intentional discrimination solely because of their ancestry or ethnic characteristics." If the professor could prove that he was subjected to intentional discrimination because he was an Arab, rather than solely because of his place of origin or religion the lawsuit could proceed under § 1981. The court of appeals' decision in favor of the professor was affirmed. *St. Francis College v. Al-Khazraji*, 481 U.S. 604, 107 S.Ct. 2022, 97 L.Ed.2d 749 (1987).

A Florida school board employed a substitute food service worker of East Indian descent who was born in Guyana. When the worker was passed over for promotion to a full-time job, she confronted her supervisor and got into an argument with her. She later alleged that the supervisor called her a "Cuban refugee," which the supervisor denied. The worker filed a national origin discrimination complaint with the EEOC. The EEOC issued a right-to-sue letter to the worker and she sued the school board in the U.S. District Court for the Middle District of Florida. The court held a trial and determined that the board had refused to hire the worker for discriminatory reasons in violation of Title VII. Despite this finding, the court limited the worker's damage award to $1 for failure to prove her claim for back or front pay. Both parties appealed.

The U.S. Court of Appeals, Eleventh Circuit, held that the worker had failed to prove a *prima facie* case of national origin discrimination. Proof of this would require that, among other things, the school board hired a member of a nonprotected class for a position for which the worker was qualified. In this case, there was no evidence produced at trial that the school board had hired a Caucasian, American-born employee instead of the worker. Because the district court had not made this necessary finding of fact, the worker failed to establish a *prima facie* case and the court should have dismissed the case. The court ruled for the school board. *Green v. School Bd. of Hillsborough County, Florida*, 25 F.3d 974 (11th Cir.1994).

An African-American math teacher employed by an Indiana public school district was criticized by the math department head for inability to maintain control of her classroom. She received unfavorable reviews by two different evaluators. She filed several grievances, alleging that the lack of support from the district and large class sizes caused disciplinary problems. The district twice renewed the teacher's contract subject to her compliance with a performance improvement plan. After her performance failed to improve, the department head recommended that her contract not be renewed. The school board discharged her three weeks later. The teacher filed suit against the school board in a U.S. district court, alleging race, sex and age discrimination as well as First Amendment violations. The district court granted summary judgment to the board, and the teacher appealed to the U.S. Court of Appeals, Seventh Circuit.

The court of appeals held that the teacher's complaints about the size of her math class and general disorder in the district did not address a matter of public concern. Further, she had never attempted to call public attention to these matters. Because the teacher's speech involved only her individual employment dispute, the court dismissed her First Amendment retaliation claims. The conclusory nature of the teacher's allegations also precluded her discrimination claims under the Equal Protection Clause of the Fourteenth Amendment and 42 U.S.C. § 1981. The district court decision was affirmed. *Cliff v. Bd. of School Comm'rs of City of Indianapolis*, 42 F.3d 403 (7th Cir.1994).

A California teacher taught Native American students enrolled in an independent studies program. He alleged that another teacher in the program failed to instruct students assigned to her and forged student records. The teacher claimed that when he reported the illegal activities to the school's principal and district superintendent, they helped perpetuate the fraud in order to collect state and federal funds under false pretenses. A grand jury considered the teacher's evidence, but did not issue any indictments. The teacher was then fired. He sued the school district in the U.S. District Court for the Northern District of California, seeking reinstatement of his employment, damages and injunctive relief. The court considered dismissal motions filed by the school district and by several school district employees named as parties by the teacher.

The court granted dismissal motions for claims based upon 42 U.S.C. §§ 1981, 1982 and 1985 because the teacher was a white male who had no standing to advance a discrimination complaint under these federal civil rights statutes. It also dismissed the teacher's civil rights complaint under 42 U.S.C. § 1983 as barred by the Eleventh Amendment. The court refused to grant the teacher a writ of mandamus and refused to grant supplemental jurisdiction to his state law claims because they sought a state remedy. However, it ruled that the teacher had standing to advance complaints against the school district under Title VI and Title IX because these federal education statutes broadly prohibited discrimination against any person. The court also refused to dismiss the teacher's cause of action under the federal False Claims Act, which prohibits retaliation against whistle-blowing employees. *Clemes v. Del Norte County Unif. School Dist.*, 843 F.Supp. 583 (N.D.Cal.1994).

In 1989, the Illinois legislature created local councils in all school districts, giving them the power to hire and fire school principals. Under the legislation, principals served four-year renewable contracts requiring a majority vote of the local council for contract renewal. A white Chicago high school principal who had served for six years claimed that black local council members had discriminated against him on the basis of race by failing to vote for renewal of his contract. He sued the Chicago Board of Education and the council members who had failed to vote for him in the U.S. District Court for the Northern District of Illinois, which awarded him over $62,000 in wages and over $92,000 in forfeited pension benefits. The court dismissed the board of education from the lawsuit. The council members appealed to the U.S. Court of Appeals, Seventh Circuit. The court of appeals stated that in order to prevail in a civil rights discrimination case, the complaining party must first present evidence of racial discrimination. The employer may then articulate legitimate reasons for the personnel action. The complaining party must then demonstrate that the stated reasons are pretextual in order to recover. In this case, the evidence did not show that the council members voted against the principal for discriminatory reasons. There was evidence that the principal was not meeting expectations. Because there was no proof of discrimination, the court reversed the district court's decision. *Pilditch v. Bd. of Educ. of City of Chicago*, 3 F.3d 1113 (7th Cir.1993).

A white male associate professor alleged that he was discriminated against in the repeated denial of his promotion to full professor. The persons in charge of the promotion were black, and the professor alleged that the promotion criteria were faulty and purposefully skewed each year in order to further the promotion of minority faculty members. Specifically, the ranking of the weight given to each category of the criteria was changed annually—after the candidates and their backgrounds had become known. A lawsuit was brought by the professor in a federal district court. The court found that the promotion procedure was "ripe for manipulation" and that the annual and skewed revamping of the criteria evidenced an intent to discriminate. Since the professor had been promoted by the time of the trial, his damages were held to be equal to backpay from the date when he should have been promoted. *Bachman v. Board of Trustees of University of District of Columbia,* 777 F.Supp. 990 (D.D.C.1991).

A black college senior filed an application with a Virginia school district for a teaching position. When she became certified to teach she notified the school district to update her application accordingly. However, the district failed to notify her of job openings on three separate occasions. For one position, the district hired a less qualified white applicant who was the spouse of a teacher already employed in the district. The unsuccessful applicant sued the school district in a federal district court, claiming that she had been discriminated against on the basis of her race in violation of Title VII. She requested monetary damages and an injunction to prevent the district from continuing its discriminatory hiring practices. At trial, the school district explained that it had overlooked the black applicant's application due to a clerical error. The trial court found in favor of the school board. The applicant appealed to the U.S. Court of Appeals, Fourth Circuit.

The appeals court was bound by the trial court's finding of fact that the school district had not intentionally discriminated against the applicant. However, the court did examine the district's hiring practices. The evidence at trial disclosed that at the time the district was desegregated in 1963 there were six black teachers. Up until 1988 when the action was filed, only one additional black had been hired. Notices of vacancies were not advertised publicly, only by word of mouth. As a result, 46 relatives of school district employees had been hired in the past seven years. Although nepotism is not a *per se* violation of Title VII, where the workforce is predominantly white, such practices tend to exclude minorities. The court remanded the case and instructed the trial court to issue an injunction requiring the district to advertise future job openings and fill them in a nondiscriminatory manner. *Thomas v. Washington County School Bd.*, 915 F.2d 922 (4th Cir.1990).

E. Affirmative Action

Generally, an affirmative action in employment plan voluntarily adopted by a school district will not result in unlawful reverse discrimination under Title VII if: 1) there exists a statistical disparity between the races or sexes in a given job category, or if the institution was guilty of discrimination in the past; 2) the affirmative action plan does not "unnecessarily trammel" the rights of nonminority employees; 3) the plan does not stigmatize nonminority employees; and 4) the plan is temporary in nature and is scheduled to terminate upon the achievement of a racially or sexually integrated work force. See *United Steelworkers of America v. Weber*, 443 U.S. 193 (1979), and *Johnson v. Transportation Agency*, 480 U.S. 616 (1987). However, school districts need to comply with the Equal Protection Clause as well as Title VII when devising affirmative action programs. To that end the U.S. Supreme Court struck down a no-minority-layoff (or "affirmative retention") clause in a teacher collective bargaining agreement in *Wygant v. Jackson Bd. of Educ.*, below. While such clauses generally are acceptable under Title VII, the Court held that the clause ran afoul of the Constitution.

An affirmative action (or "affirmative retention") plan implemented by the Jackson, Michigan, board of education, called for the layoff of nonminority teachers with greater seniority than some minority teachers. The district court ruled that the importance of providing minority teachers as "role models" for minority students as a remedy for past "societal discrimination" justified the layoff provision. The U.S. Court of Appeals, Sixth Circuit, affirmed the district court's decision and the nonminority teachers appealed to the Supreme Court. The Supreme Court reversed the lower courts' decisions and held that the nonminority teachers had been unfairly discriminated against in violation of the Equal Protection Clause.

The Court held that clear and convincing evidence must be presented that the government entity in question had engaged in past racial discrimination. Similarly, the Supreme Court rejected the "role model" justification for retaining minority teachers (i.e., minority children benefit from having minority teachers) on the ground that such a theory would allow racially-based layoffs long after they were needed to cure the ills of past discrimination. The majority held that even if the Jackson school board had sufficient justification for engaging in remedial or "benign" racial discrimination, layoff of white teachers was too drastic and intrusive a remedy. While hiring goals and promotion policies favorable to minorities are acceptable under the Equal Protection Clause, the actual laying off of a certain race of employees was held to be unconstitutional. "Denial of future employment is not as intrusive as loss of an existing job," observed the Court. The lower court rulings were reversed. *Wygant v. Jackson Bd. of Educ.,* 476 U.S. 267, 106 S.Ct. 1842, 90 L.Ed.2d 260 (1986).

Four non-Indian tenured teachers were placed on unrequested leave of absence by a Minnesota school district which was located entirely on an Indian reservation and whose student population was almost entirely American Indian. They were employed under a collective bargaining agreement which was executed after the passage of a Minnesota statute that permitted some school districts to create Indian teacher retention policies irrespective of the state tenure act. The act provided for Indian teacher recruitment and retention for districts in which at least ten American Indian students attended. The non-Indian teachers requested an administrative hearing which resulted in a decision in their favor. However, the school district rejected some of the findings, determining that the complaining teachers should remain on unrequested leave of absence, while less senior Indian teachers should be retained. The teachers appealed to the Court of Appeals of Minnesota.

The court of appeals distinguished the Indian teacher retention statute from the affirmative action statute considered by the U.S. Supreme Court in *Wygant v. Jackson Bd. of Educ.*, above. The statute in that case concerned a layoff preference policy permitting the retention of less senior minority teachers over nonminority teachers. Whereas the Court in that case was bound to apply strict scrutiny because of a government-created racial classification, the statute under consideration in this case employed the less exacting rational basis test. This was because American Indians constituted a political classification rather than a racial classification. The court determined that the school district could give preference to American Indian teachers with less seniority than non-Indian teachers. *Krueth v. Indep. School Dist. No. 38*, 496 N.W.2d 829 (Minn.App.1993).

A white Massachusetts woman applied for the position of general counsel for a school. The school had two positions open. The woman applied for both positions but was not hired for either. The school to which the woman applied had a plan to give preference to minorities until minorities made up at least 25 percent of the staff. The woman sued the school alleging that she was discriminated against on the basis of her race. A Massachusetts trial court granted summary judgment in favor of the school and the applicant appealed to the Supreme Court of Massachusetts. On appeal, the court stated that affirmative action programs are not unlawful but that programs can be implemented in an illegal way. The court stated that this affirmative action plan was unlawful because the black applicant who was hired did not meet the minimum requirements for the job. The court decided that the affirmative action order did not require the blind appointment of members of minorities to administrative positions, but only required a racial preference with regard to otherwise qualified candidates. The Supreme Court of Massachusetts reversed the summary judgment order. *Drinkwater v. School Comm. of Boston*, 550 N.E.2d 385 (Mass.1990).

A white social worker was laid off by a Colorado school district along with all but its two most senior social workers. The sole black social worker employed by the district was also laid off. The white social worker had the third most seniority. All of the terminated social workers requested hearings. After the hearings, the officer found that the board should give special consideration to the black social worker since he was the only black administrator in the district. The board rescinded his termination. A few months later the board rehired a Hispanic social worker who was also lower in seniority than the white social worker. After having exhausted her administrative appeals, the social worker filed a discrimination suit in a federal district court. The court found that the school district's actions constituted intentional racial discrimination and were not justified by legitimate, nondiscriminatory reasons. The court awarded the social worker backpay and attorney's fees. The school district appealed to the U.S. Court of Appeals, Tenth Circuit. On appeal, the district did not challenge the court's finding that its actions were discriminatory. It claimed that its actions were appropriate because of the district's affirmative action plan. The court, however, noted that the purpose of an affirmative action program must be to remedy the effects of past discrimination against a particular group. Because there was no evidence of any past discrimination in hiring within the district, the court found that its affirmative action plan unnecessarily discriminated against the white social worker. The court affirmed the trial court's decision. *Cunico v. Pueblo School Dist. No. 60*, 917 F.2d 431 (10th Cir.1990).

F. Religion

Discrimination on the basis of religion is also forbidden by Title VII. However, § 702 of Title VII (42 U.S.C. § 2000e-1) exempts religious organizations from this command. The U.S. Supreme Court has held that an employer's duty under Title VII is discharged by making a reasonable accommodation of an employee's religious needs, but no duty to accommodate arises where it would work an undue hardship upon the employer.

In a U.S. Supreme Court case, a Connecticut high school teacher sued his school district under Title VII. He belonged to a church which required members to refrain from secular employment during designated holy days. This required the teacher to miss approximately six school days each year for religious purposes. The district's collective bargaining agreement allowed only three days of paid leave for religious observation. The agreement also allowed three days paid leave for "necessary personal business" which, the district said, could not be used for religious purposes. The teacher repeatedly asked to be granted permission to use three days of his "necessary personal business" leave for his religious purposes. He also offered to pay for a substitute teacher if the school board would pay him for the extra days that he missed. These alternatives were turned down by the school board. When all administrative alternatives were exhausted, he filed a lawsuit alleging that the school board's policy regarding "necessary personal business" leave was discriminatory on the basis of religion. A U.S. district court dismissed the teacher's lawsuit and he appealed. The U.S. Court of Appeals, Second Circuit, said that the school board was bound to accept one of the teacher's proposed solutions unless "that accommodation causes undue hardship on the employer's conduct of his business."

On appeal, the U.S. Supreme Court modified the appellate court's decision. It decided that the school district was not required to accept the teacher's proposals even if acceptance would not result in "undue hardship." The school board was only bound to offer a fair and reasonable accommodation of the teacher's religious needs. The bargaining agreement policy of allowing three days paid leave for religious purposes, but excluding additional days of "necessary personal business" leave if needed for religious purposes, would *not* be reasonable, explained the Court, if paid leave was provided "for all purposes *except* religious ones." Because none of the lower courts had decided whether the "necessary personal business" leave policy had been administered fairly in the past, the case was remanded for a determination of that question. *Ansonia Bd. of Educ. v. Philbrook,* 479 U.S. 60, 107 S.Ct 367, 93 L.Ed.2d 305 (1986). On remand, it was determined that the accommodation was reasonable. *Philbrook v. Ansonia Bd. of Educ.,* 925 F.2d 47 (2d Cir.1991).

A graduate student in physics sued his doctoral committee chairman claiming that his termination from the doctoral program was a result of religious discrimination. The student was a Shi'ite Muslim and the chairman was a Sunni Muslim. The student claimed that the chairman tried to get him to sign a petition asserting the correctness of Sunni beliefs and to have other Muslim students sign the petition. The student claimed that when he refused to do so, the chairman of his doctoral committee convinced the other committee members to recommend that the student's studies be terminated. The committee chairman claimed that regardless of his discriminatory actions, the student would have been terminated anyway because his laboratory work was inadequate. Following a trial in federal court in which the jury awarded the student $450,000, the chairman moved for judgment notwithstanding the verdict. The trial judge granted the motion, finding that the evidence overwhelmingly proved that the student would have been terminated regardless of the chairman's actions toward him. The student then appealed to the U.S. Court of Appeals, Fourth Circuit.

The appeals court affirmed the lower court's decision. In order for the student to have prevailed he needed to show that but for the chairman's conduct, he would not have been terminated from the program. The court noted that the student had received numerous negative assessments prior to his termination. His original committee chairman resigned because the student took too much of his time and was poorly qualified for experimental research. Although the evidence strongly suggested that the chairman attempted to discredit the student because he refused to sign a petition, the court did not find this evidence sufficient to overturn the lower court's decision. *Al-Zubaidi v. Ijaz,* 917 F.2d 1347 (4th Cir.1990).

G. Age

The use of age as a criterion for employment is forbidden by federal law with respect to persons ages 40 and above. Like the Equal Pay Act, the Age Discrimination in Employment Act of 1967 (ADEA) (29 U.S.C. § 621 *et seq.*) is part of the Fair Labor Standards Act. It applies to institutions which have 20 or more employees and which "affect interstate commerce." Also, the ADEA contains an exception allowing the use of age as an employment criterion "where age is a bona fide occupational qualification reasonably necessary to the normal operation of the particular business."

An Indiana high school teacher/football coach filed an age discrimination complaint against his local education agency. The parties settled, but the coach later claimed that the agency retaliated against him for filing the complaint by giving him poor employment performance reviews. He asserted that the agency's conduct created a hostile work environment in violation of the Age Discrimination in Employment Act (ADEA). He filed a lawsuit against the agency and several other employees in the U.S. District Court for the Northern District of Indiana, which considered dismissal motions filed by the defendants. The court refused to dismiss the teacher's hostile work environment lawsuit. Such a lawsuit was permissible under the ADEA because the conditions alleged by the teacher suggested that a hostile environment existed. EEOC regulations require employers to maintain a work environment that is free of harassment. The court then granted summary judgment motions filed by two administrative employees who could not be found liable for the harassment. The court allowed the teacher to seek compensatory damages, but held that the ADEA did not permit an award of punitive damages. The court also dismissed the teacher's state law complaint for intentional infliction of emotional distress. *Eggleston v. South Bend Comm. School Corp.*, 858 F.Supp. 841 (N.D.Ind.1994).

A Kentucky teacher worked as an English instructor from 1959 to 1972. From 1972 to 1982, he worked at a private business interest. In 1983, he interviewed with the school district for several positions for which younger people were hired. He was then hired as a permanent part-time librarian at a school. He filed suit in 1988 alleging that he was discriminated against because of his age in violation of the Age Discrimination in Employment Act (ADEA) when the school district hired those younger and less experienced. Additionally, he claimed that the board's salary policy, which limited the credit a teacher received for experience that was more than ten years in the past, violated the ADEA because it adversely affected those over 40 years of age. The trial court entered summary judgment in favor of the board and the teacher appealed to the U.S. Court of Appeals, Sixth Circuit. The teacher had proved a *prima facie* case of age discrimination. The board then produced a legitimate nondiscriminatory reason for failure to hire the teacher. The board's policy limiting credit for teachers' experience to less than ten years suggested common sense in that the policy treated teachers whose experience was greater than ten years old differently from those whose experience was more recent. The teacher argued that each year of experience, whether the first year or twenty-first year, should be treated alike. However, the appellate court upheld the decision of the trial court and granted summary judgment to the board. *Wooden v. Bd. of Educ. of Jefferson County,* 931 F.2d 376 (6th Cir.1991).

In 1985, the faculty at an Illinois university entered into a collective bargaining agreement whereby each faculty member's salary would be determined at the time he or she was hired, but thereafter a faculty member could only obtain an individual raise by presenting a bona fide offer of employment from another employer. Seventeen months after the agreement was signed a 58-year-old professor filed a complaint with the EEOC claiming that the compensation system discriminated on the basis of age. The professor then filed suit in a federal district court, which found that the statute of limitations had started to run when the collective bargaining agreement was signed. Therefore, the professor's claim was barred by the Illinois statute of limitations which required a claim to be filed with the EEOC within 300 days of the alleged act of discrimination. The professor appealed the dismissal to the U.S. Court of Appeals, Seventh Circuit. The court of appeals held that the statute of limitations did not start running until the professor obtained the minimum evidence necessary to determine whether he had a claim under the age discrimination law. The university argued that even if the professor's claim was not time-barred, it was still not a valid claim of age discrimination. The appeals court agreed. It noted that although the law forbids discrimination on the basis of age, it does not require employers to pay older employees higher salaries than younger employees. Since the university's salary increase policy depended on outside offers of employment, each professor's salary was determined by his value in the employment market. The court of appeals affirmed the trial court's dismissal of the case. *Davidson v. Bd. of Governors of State Colleges and Universities for Western Illinois Univ.*, 920 F.2d 441 (7th Cir.1990).

In 1980, Illinois enacted a statute raising the mandatory retirement age for university instructors from 65 to 70. In 1982, the federal government enacted the Age Discrimination in Employment Act (ADEA), which raised the mandatory retirement age for university instructors from 65 to 70 and eliminated all mandatory retirements for academic employees after 1993. An Illinois college adopted an early retirement program (ERP) in 1982 in response to the pressures of declining enrollment and budget decreases. The ERP was implemented to replace highly paid senior faculty members with lower paid younger faculty members. It was available to faculty members between the ages of 55 and 69, but gave greater benefits to those who retired before 65. Three professors sued the college in a federal district court, claiming that the ERP violated the ADEA. The district court ruled in favor of the college and the professors appealed to the U.S. Court of Appeals, Seventh Circuit. The court of appeals reversed the district court decision. It noted that early retirement programs do not necessarily constitute discrimination against employees. However, in this case discrimination was discernible against persons between the ages of 65 and 69 relative to those between 55 and 64. The sharp drop in benefits to employees under the college's ERP in effect created two separate early retirement programs, one for workers age 55 to 64 and another for workers between 65 and 69. The college had failed to correlate evidence of higher costs for the older group as a reason for the drastic reduction in benefits at age 65. The ERP was merely a subterfuge by the college designed to eliminate faculty members over 65. The case was remanded to the district court for further proceedings. *Karlen v. City Colleges of Chicago*, 837 F.2d 314 (7th Cir.1988).

H. Disability

Section 504 of the Rehabilitation Act of 1973 and the Americans with Disabilities Act (ADA) prohibit employment discrimination on the basis of disability. The acts require that an "otherwise qualified individual with a disability" shall not be denied employment based upon his or her disability. An otherwise qualified person with a disability is one who can perform the "essential functions" of the job "with reasonable accommodation" of the person's disability by the employer. Employers are relieved of the duty to reasonably accommodate if to do so would create undue hardship.

The U.S. Supreme Court ruled that tuberculosis and other contagious diseases are to be considered disabilities under § 504 of the Rehabilitation Act. The law defines an individual with a disability as "any person who (i) has a physical or mental impairment which substantially limits one or more of such person's major life activities, (ii) has a record of such impairment or (iii) is regarded as having such an impairment." It defines "physical impairment" as disorders affecting, among other things, the respiratory system and defines "major life activities" as "functions such as caring for one's self ... and working." The case involved a Florida elementary school teacher who was discharged because of the continued recurrence of tuberculosis. The teacher sued the school board under § 504 but a U.S. district court dismissed her claims. The U.S. Court of Appeals, Eleventh Circuit, reversed the district court's decision and held that persons with contagious diseases fall within § 504's coverage. The school board appealed to the U.S. Supreme Court.

The Supreme Court ruled that tuberculosis was a disability under § 504 because it affected the respiratory system and affected ability to work (a major life activity). The school board contended that in defining an individual with a disability under § 504, the contagious effects of a disease can be distinguished from the disease's physical effects. However, the Court reasoned that the teacher's contagion and her physical impairment both resulted from the same condition: tuberculosis. It would be unfair to allow an employer to distinguish between a disease's potential effect on others and its effect on the employee in order to justify discriminatory treatment. Allowing discrimination based on the contagious effects of a physical impairment would be inconsistent with the underlying purpose of § 504. The Supreme Court remanded the case to the district court to determine whether the teacher was "otherwise qualified" for her job and whether the school board could reasonably accommodate her as an employee. *School Board of Nassau County v. Arline*, 480 U.S. 273, 107 S.Ct. 1123, 94 L.Ed.2d 307 (1987).

On remand, the Florida federal district court held that the teacher was "otherwise qualified" to teach. The teacher posed no threat of tuberculosis to her students. The court ordered her reinstatement or a front-pay award of $768,724 representing her earnings until retirement. *Arline v. School Bd. of Nassau County*, 692 F.Supp. 1286 (M.D.Fla.1988).

The Omaha School District employed two diabetic school van drivers. The state Department of Motor Vehicles and state Department of Education modified their licensing procedures requiring school van drivers to undergo examinations and be certified to work by doctors under federal Department of Transportation regulations. The Department of Motor Vehicles then refused to issue licenses to either of the drivers. The school district demoted the drivers to van aide positions, at lower pay rates. The drivers sued the school district, Department of Motor Vehicles and Department of Education in the U.S. District Court for the District of Nebraska, claiming violations of § 504 of the Rehabilitation Act of 1973 (29 U.S.C. § 794). The court granted motions to dismiss the lawsuit, and the drivers appealed to the U.S. Court of Appeals, Eighth Circuit. The court of appeals held that the drivers had shown that their disabilities could be reasonably accommodated and that they were at low risk for hypoglycemic episodes. Because they had demonstrated a material fact issue under the Rehabilitation Act, summary judgment was inappropriate.

On remand, the district court determined that the drivers were Type II Insulin-using diabetics who had an appreciable risk of developing hypoglycemic symptoms without warning. Because this constituted a danger to students and others using public roads, there was no reasonable accommodation that could be offered by the school district. Accordingly, the Rehabilitation Act afforded no protection to the drivers. The drivers appealed again to the U.S. Court of Appeals, Eighth Circuit, which found that the district court's factual findings were not clearly erroneous. Because hypoglycemia created an increased risk of sudden and unexpected vision loss and loss of consciousness, the district court's decision that the van drivers presented a danger to themselves and others was supported by the evidence. The court of appeals affirmed the district court's judgment. *Wood v. Omaha School Dist.*, 25 F.3d 667 (8th Cir.1994).

An Arkansas science teacher was injured in a traffic accident which caused memory loss, concentration difficulties and anxiety. His condition was chronic and it deteriorated over time. He also suffered from chronic high blood pressure. About 18 years after the accident, the teacher experienced a personality conflict with a principal and requested a transfer. The school district created a position for the teacher in which he had no teaching duties. He then requested a return to teaching, and was assigned six periods of life science. The assignment caused the teacher nervousness, high bood pressure and sleeplessness. His blood pressure increased and he required additional medication. He began sending students to the principal's office for relatively minor disciplinary problems and again sought reassignment. The teacher made alternate plans for retirement, and his request for disability retirement benefits was approved by the state retirement system. He then decided to retire, but alleged that the school district had violated the Rehabilitation Act by refusing to allow him to take a one-year sick leave. He sued the district in the U.S. District Court for the Western District of Arkansas.

The court determined that the teacher's alleged disability, anxiety panic disorder, apparently rendered him unable to complete his teaching assignments. He could no longer perform essential functions of his job. The teacher had no protection under the Rehabilitation Act because he was not an otherwise qualified individual with a disability. The school district had accommodated his requests for help by creating a job for him and transferring him. *Cadelli v. Fort Smith*

School Dist., 852 F.Supp. 789 (W.D.Ark.1993). The U.S. Court of Appeals, Eighth Circuit, affirmed the district court's decision in favor of the school district. 23 F.3d 1295.

An Arkansas teacher exhibiting symptoms of bipolar manic illness was let go by two school districts. She sued the two school districts in the U.S. District Court for the Eastern District of Arkansas, which granted summary judgment to the school districts. The court stated that the teacher's claim sought only monetary damages, which were unavailable under § 504 of the Rehabilitation Act. The teacher appealed to the U.S. Court of Appeals, Eighth Circuit. The court of appeals noted the general federal law principle that traditional legal and equitable remedies are available unless a statute expressly indicates otherwise. Because § 504 incorporated remedies and procedures available under Title VI of the Civil Rights Act of 1964, the court analyzed Title VI to determine the teacher's right to monetary damages. Title VI had in turn been construed by the courts as permitting monetary damage awards. Therefore, the teacher's right to monetary damages under § 504 should not be restricted. The court reversed the order for summary judgment and remanded the case for further proceedings including a determination of whether the teacher had a disability and was otherwise qualified to perform her job. *Rodgers v. Magnet Cove Pub. Schools*, 34 F.3d 642 (8th Cir.1994).

A recent college graduate with a learning disability obtained employment with a Virginia school district. She was conditionally employed to teach emotionally disturbed middle school students, with renewal of her contract dependent upon achieving passing scores on the National Teacher Examination (NTE). After failing the NTE six times under regular conditions, the teacher obtained the opinion of a clinical psychologist who proposed accommodations for the teacher's learning disability, including untimed examinations. The school board rejected the psychologist's proposal, but permitted the teacher to take the test in a separate room with 50 percent more time and access to a tape-recorded script played at a slow rate. The teacher failed the test twice despite these accommodations. She filed a Rehabilitation Act complaint against the board in the U.S. District Court for the Eastern District of Virginia. The court ruled for the school board. This decision was reversed and remanded by the U.S. Court of Appeals, Fourth Circuit. On remand, the teacher requested a jury trial. The district court refused to acknowledge any right of the teacher to this under the Rehabilitation Act. It conducted a court trial after which it again entered judgment for the school board. The teacher appealed again to the U.S. Court of Appeals. According to the court of appeals, the Rehabilitation Act provided a full range of legal remedies for disabled persons, including monetary damages. Accordingly, even though the act did not specify the right to a jury trial, this right was constitutionally mandated for complaining parties who requested legal (monetary) damages. Because the teacher had requested legal damages in the form of backpay, she was entitled to a jury trial. The court reversed and remanded the district court's decision and ordered a jury trial. *Pandazides v. Virginia Bd. of Educ.*, 13 F.3d 823 (4th Cir.1994).

A University of Wisconsin-Madison employee worked for over four years at the university's small business development center. The university advised him that it would not renew his employment contract for the upcoming year because of the conflict between his "personal needs," resulting from a disability and the school's objectives. The employee elected not to file an Equal Employment Opportunity Commission (EEOC) complaint, instead filing a lawsuit in the U.S. District Court for the District of Wisconsin for violation of the Americans with Disabilities Act (ADA). The university filed a motion to dismiss the lawsuit, claiming that the employee had failed to exhaust his administrative remedies as set forth under Department of Justice regulations arising under ADA Title I. The employee argued that by filing the lawsuit under ADA Title II, he was under no obligation to exhaust administrative remedies by filing an EEOC complaint.

The court compared Titles I and II of the ADA and found that only Title I contained the requirement to exhaust administrative remedies. ADA Title I applies broadly to employers with 15 or more employees, while Title II applies only to public entities and broadly prohibits discrimination, only incidentally referring to employment discrimination. The court held that even though Title I was the ADA's primary means of combating employment discrimination, a complaint under Title II was expressly permitted and carried no requirement for exhausting administrative remedies. Title II of the ADA was modeled after § 504 of the Rehabilitation Act, while Title I was patterned after Title VII of the Civil Rights Act of 1964, accounting for the different procedural requirements. The court denied the university's motion to dismiss the lawsuit. *Petersen v. Univ. of Wisconsin Bd. of Regents,* 818 F.Supp. 1276 (W.D.Wis.1993).

Three Pennsylvania school bus drivers suffered from epileptic conditions. The Pennsylvania Department of Transportation recalled or suspended the license of each driver. In separate proceedings in Pennsylvania trial courts, the license suspensions were held to violate the drivers' procedural due process rights. The Commonwealth Court of Pennsylvania consolidated the cases and asked the parties to submit supplemental briefs on the issue of potential affirmative defenses arising under § 504 of the Rehabilitation Act, 29 U.S.C. § 794. The commonwealth court determined that the Rehabilitation Act applied to these cases and remanded them to the trial court for further proceedings. The Department of Transportation appealed to the Supreme Court of Pennsylvania.

The supreme court ruled that the commonwealth court had exceeded its authority in introducing the Rehabilitation Act affirmative defenses issue. The proper scope of inquiry for the appeal was whether the trial court had made a correct ruling on the issue of alleged procedural due process rights violations by the department. The court vacated the commonwealth court's order and remanded the case to it for a determination of the issues which had been originally raised by the parties. *Commonwealth v. Boros,* 620 A.2d 1139 (Pa.1993).

A teacher in a suburban Milwaukee school district was diagnosed as having a fungus allergy. She was on medical leave from the school for two and a half years when the school board terminated her employment. She sued the school board in federal court claiming that it had violated her rights, first by failing to accommodate her disability in the workplace and then by firing her because of her disability. The federal district court denied her motion for summary judgment, and a trial was held. The jury found for the school board. The teacher appealed to the U.S. Court of Appeals, Seventh Circuit. The court stated that the teacher's sensitivity to fungus was a physical impairment. However, an inability to perform a particular job for a particular employer is not sufficient to establish a disability. The impairment must substantially limit employment generally. During the time the teacher was on medical absences, she earned a master's degree and handled two part-time jobs. Because there was plausible evidence that her impairment did not substantially limit her ability to work, it was proper for the court to submit the issue to a jury. The court affirmed the holding for the school board. *Byrne v. Bd. of Educ.*, 979 F.2d 560 (7th Cir.1992).

I.   Retaliation

A New Jersey administrator applied for a vice principalship in her school system, but was not appointed. She successfully pursued a claim of racial discrimination and the director ordered her appointed to the position. The school subsequently implemented a position as assistant superintendent for which three people applied, including the administrator. The superintendent of schools spoke privately with the administrator, informing her that she would not be recommended for the position and intimating that it was because of her ongoing litigation with the school system. The administrator sought an order from the Director of the Division on Civil Rights preventing the board from hiring anyone but herself for the position. Following a hearing, an administrative law judge (ALJ) found that the administrator had met the minimum requirements needed to show discrimination. The director adopted the ALJ's findings and ruled that the administrator had proven her claim. The board of education appealed.

On appeal, the New Jersey Superior Court held that an employee must first prove that she engaged in a protected activity known to the employer, that the promotion she sought was denied and that engaging in the protected activity resulted in the promotion denial. The employer must then show that there was a legitimate, nonretaliatory reason for the denial. If so, then the employee is given an opportunity to show that the employer was motivated by discriminatory intent. If the employee succeeds in meeting this burden, then the employer must prove, by focusing on the qualifications of the other candidates, that the employee would not have been promoted regardless of retaliatory intent. The court held that the administrator had met the burden placed on her to prove retaliatory discrimination. However, the school district had only been allowed to present evidence as to the qualifications of the successful candidate and not the other unsuccessful candidate. The court found this to be in error and remanded the case for a limited hearing to determine whether the administrator was more qualified than the other unsuccessful candidate. *Jamison v. Rockaway Twp. Bd. of Educ.*, 577 A.2d 177 (N.J.Super.A.D.1990).

II. STATE STATUTES

A. Sex Discrimination

A Massachusetts vocational school selected a male candidate for its superintendent. A female applicant filed an administrative complaint against the school claiming sex discrimination. A hearing officer ruled for the applicant and awarded her $48,507. The damages were based upon the difference between her starting salary at the job she eventually accepted, and the amount paid to the vocational school's superintendent until the hearing date. The Massachusetts Commission Against Discrimination affirmed the hearing officer's decision, but a state trial court vacated and remanded the case based on the school's motion for leave to present additional evidence concerning the complaining party's interim salary. The motion had been based upon information that the complaining party earned more at her present job than she would have earned at the vocational school. The commission then appealed to the Appeals Court of Massachusetts, which reinstated the commission's award.

The vocational school filed a motion in the trial court to rule on its previously filed motion to consider the evidence of damages. The court ruled that it had no authority to allow the motion and the school appealed to the Appeals Court of Massachusetts. The appeals court ruled that the trial court had the discretion to consider the motion and that there was a strong state interest in preserving state education funds by disallowing compensation of a discrimination victim who did not suffer any financial loss. The court vacated the denial of the school's motion. *Northeast Metropolitan Regional Voc. School Dist. School Comm. v. Mass. Comm. Against Discrimination*, 626 N.E.2d 884 (Mass.App.Ct.1994).

A woman served as coach for a school's co-ed tennis team for four years. The district then decided to split the team into two, with the girls playing in the fall and the boys playing in the spring. The woman applied for both positions and was chosen to coach the girls. Before the spring, the woman was denied a position coaching the boys' team. The district stated that she was not hired because of her excessive absenteeism. The district hired a man, and the woman alleged discrimination. The New York State Division of Human Rights (Division) found that the absenteeism justification was a mere pretext for discriminatory intent. The school appealed to the New York Supreme Court, Appellate Division. The Division had found that the woman's attendance record had no effect on her ability to coach. The appellate court, however, noted that there was no evidence presented that the district's concern over attendance was pretext. The school had denied a male a coaching position on the same grounds. The Division's decision was annulled as unsupported by the evidence. *New Paltz Central School Dist. v. State Division of Human Rights,* 577 N.Y.S.2d 510 (A.D.3d Dept.1991).

B. Race Discrimination

An African-American student complained that a substitute teacher, who was also African-American, called him a disparaging racial name. The school's assistant principal talked to the complaining student and other students who confirmed the report, but failed to talk to the substitute. On the basis of the assistant principal's report, the district superintendent immediately removed the substitute's name from the district's substitute teacher list. The substitute filed a race discrimination lawsuit against the school district in the U.S. District Court for the Eastern District of Missouri. The court granted summary judgment to the school district and the substitute appealed to the U.S. Court of Appeals, Eighth Circuit. The court of appeals agreed with the district court's finding that the substitute had successfully made out a *prima facie* case of racial discrimination. However, the only evidence of discriminatory intent advanced by the substitute was that the superintendent had failed to meet with her before removing her name from the substitute list. Because the record indicated a factual basis for the assistant principal's report of the name-calling incident, the superintendent's decision was appropriate and nondiscriminatory. The court of appeals affirmed the district court's judgment. *Gill v. Reorganized School Dist. R-6, Festus, Missouri*, 32 F.3d 376 (8th Cir.1994).

A Minnesota school district hired a black elementary school principal who became embroiled in controversy. The parents of a white student attending the school wrote a letter to the district superintendent and school board and the principal sued them for defamation. The U.S. District Court for the District of Minnesota considered whether the principal was a public official for purposes of applying the higher standard of "actual malice" that must be met for any public official to make a recovery for alleged defamation. The court held that the principal should be considered a public official due to the importance of education, the need to avoid stifling public debate about important local issues, and the significant authority wielded by the principal. *Johnson v. Robbinsdale Ind. School Dist. No. 281*, 827 F.Supp. 1439 (D.Minn.1993).

A Florida school board chose not to hire an experienced African-American teacher who was certified to teach social studies and held a Ph.D. The Florida Commission on Human Relations (FCHR) held that the board had violated the state human rights act, ordered it to offer the teacher the next available fulltime position for which he was qualified and ordered backpay. The District Court of Appeal of Florida, First District, affirmed the FCHR order in part, but refused to affirm the backpay award because the teacher had presented no evidence of economic damages. On remand to the FCHR, the teacher unsuccessfully sought to reopen administrative proceedings to present evidence of economic damages. On appeal for a second time, the court of appeals ruled that the FCHR had properly refused to consider the economic damages claim and had appropriately applied a contingency risk multiplier to the attorney's fees award. *Weaver v. School Bd. of Leon County*, 624 So.2d 761 (Fla.App.1st Dist.1993).

After having taught at an Alabama school during the 1987-88 school year under a one-year contract, a black nontenured teacher's employment contract was not renewed for the 1988-89 school year. The principal of the school, who was black, had the responsibility to evaluate her performance as a teacher and make recommendations. He rated her performance as unacceptable and recommended that she not be reemployed for the 1989 school year. She filed a complaint alleging race discrimination in the hiring practices of the board of education. An Alabama trial court awarded summary judgment to the board of education and the teacher appealed to the Court of Civil Appeals of Alabama. The appellate court noted that the teacher offered no evidence establishing that the nonrenewal was pretextual or that a discriminatory reason motivated the nonrenewal. Therefore, the court granted summary judgment to the board of education. *Summerville v. Tuskaloosa City Bd. of Educ.,* 579 So.2d 628 (Ala.Civ.App.1991).

C.   Age Discrimination

An Arkansas university employee was hired for a nontenured position. Two years later he celebrated his seventieth birthday. At that time, the university had in effect a policy which stated that: "All employees of the university, except tenured employees, are automatically retired at the age of seventy years." The employee was terminated at the end of the school year. He sued the university in the U.S. District Court, E.D. Arkansas, for age discrimination under federal and state law. The district court noted that in order for the employee to sue on his age discrimination suit, he must have a property interest in his continued employment. As a result, the district court looked to Ark. Code Ann. § § 21-3-201 to 21-3-205, to determine whether the statutes conferred a property interest in the continued employment of the employee. The district court held that the statutes only prohibited discharge of employees who had not yet reached their seventieth birthday. Since the employee had reached his seventieth birthday, he was not covered under the statutes and therefore had no property interest in continued employment. *Evans v. U of A Bd. of Trustees,* 715 F.Supp. 249 (E.D.Ark.1989).

D.   Disability Discrimination

A 51-year-old New Mexico resident applied for a security officer job with a public school board. He had high blood pressure, diabetes, a thyroid condition, an injured leg and was overweight. The job screening process included a physical agility test. During a timed 1.5 mile run, the applicant collapsed from cardiovascular failure and died. The medical examiner performed an autopsy that included alcohol and drug tests. The applicant's estate filed a lawsuit against the school district and medical examiner in a state trial court for various claims of discrimination, including violation of state human rights law, the Americans with Disabilities Act (ADA), the Rehabilitation Act and 42 U.S.C. §§ 1981 and 1983. The district removed the action to the U.S. District Court for the District of New Mexico, which considered motions by the defendants to dismiss.

The court noted that because the estate had failed to exhaust its administrative remedies under the state human rights act, that part of the complaint was dismissed for failure to exhaust administrative remedies. The ADA provided no relief to the estate because the applicant was not an employee for purposes of the ADA and the ADA was not in effect at the time of the applicant's death. The ADA has no retroactive application. The estate's claim for compensatory damages under the Rehabilitation Act was dismissed because such damages are only available in cases of intentional discrimination. In this case, the complaint did not allege intentional discrimination by any of the defendants. For the same reasons, the §§ 1981 and 1983 claims were properly dismissed. The performance of the drug and alcohol tests on the applicant's body did not violate any constitutional rights, and the court granted dismissal on each of the claims advanced by the estate. *Tafoya v. Bobroff,* 865 F.Supp. 742 (D.N.M.1994).

A Washington school counselor suffered from asthma, which was aggravated by secondary smoke from cigarettes. In the fall of 1983, the faculty smoking lounge was moved into the same building in which the counseling offices were located. The counselor advised the principal that she was bothered by smoke coming from the lounge, even though it was located 35 feet from her door. The school installed hydraulic door closers and posted signs. The counselor placed an air purifier in her office, but these measures did not eliminate the secondary smoke and in 1985, the counselor had to take a medical leave. The counselor was later reassigned to a district middle school and the following year, she filed a workers' compensation claim in which she prevailed and received benefits. In 1987, the counselor filed a handicap discrimination complaint against the district for failing to provide a safe and healthful workplace under Washington law. The court granted the school district's summary judgment motion, ruling that the three-year statute of limitations barred the teacher's handicap discrimination complaint and that the cause of action for failure to provide a safe and healthful workplace should be dismissed because of her prior workers' compensation award. The teacher appealed the dismissal of the handicap discrimination complaint to the Court of Appeals of Washington, Division Three.

The court of appeals ruled that the statute of limitations did not begin to run until 1985, because the school administration had failed to keep its promises to move the smoking lounge. The statute of limitations did not begin to run in 1983 when the counselor first advised the school district of the second-hand smoke problem. There was also a genuine fact issue concerning the counselor's emotional distress complaint. The case was reversed and remanded for a trial. *Hinman v. Yakima School Dist. No. 7,* 850 P.2d 536 (Wash.App.Div.3 1993).

A New Hampshire high school Spanish teacher suffered from chronic asthma. Over a six-year period, he missed an average of 22 school days because of his condition. He was the only full-time Spanish teacher in the district. He was informed by letter that his contract would not be renewed. After receiving the letter, he contacted a specialist in respiratory disorders who prescribed a new course of treatment. The specialist asserted that this new treatment would effectively control the teacher's respiratory problems. The school district, however, went through with the teacher's planned nonrenewal. The teacher appealed, claiming that the nonrenewal violated federal and state disability discrimination laws. The State Board of Education affirmed the nonrenewal, and the teacher sought review from the New Hampshire Supreme Court.

The supreme court noted that the teacher fell within the protection of the state handicap discrimination law. Because the statute does not protect present performance-related impairments, however, the teacher needed to prove that he had only a past record of substantial impairment. In order to make this showing under New Hampshire law, the teacher need only show that nothing other than his handicap precluded a finding of job competence; the burden then shifted to the employer to prove that the handicap affected the teacher's ability to perform.

Since the school district conceded that he was a competent Spanish teacher, and presented no medical evidence that the attacks would continue, the teacher satisfied the requirements of New Hampshire law. The teacher was ordered reinstated. *Petition of Dunlap*, 604 A.2d 945 (N.H.1991), *rehearing denied* (N.H.1992).

An Ohio University purchasing agent suffered from a respiratory problem characterized by shortness of breath and difficulty in breathing. When these attacks occurred at work, she would step outside or to another part of the building for a few minutes until the symptoms dissipated, and then return to work. Although these incidents were somewhat disturbing to her coworkers, they did not detract from the quality of her work. There was a dispute among her doctors as to the cause of the spasms. However, the general consensus among the physicians was that she must be separated from the environment where the irritants were present. The university made several attempts to improve her situation. After the university decided that it could not provide her with a suitable working environment, it placed her on a medical disability leave. She was suspended for physical incapacitation for a period of three years and was then reinstated to her former position two years after her suspension. Following her suspension she filed a charge of unlawful handicap discrimination with the Ohio Civil Rights Commission. The commission determined that the university had unlawfully discriminated against her due to her respiratory disability. The university appealed to a trial court which reversed the commission's decision. The purchasing agent appealed to the Court of Appeals of Ohio.

The court of appeals held for the agent. The university had claimed that it accommodated the agent to the best of its ability. The appellate court determined that this was not supported by the evidence. At the very least, it could have accommodated her by maintaining the status quo and allowing her to leave the office to briefly obtain fresh air when necessary. This method had worked before as evidenced by the fact that her work was being performed at a satisfactory level. Therefore, she had established a *prima facie* case of handicap discrimination. The appellate court reversed the decision of the trial court and awarded backpay to the agent. *Kent State Univ. v. Ohio Civil Rights Commission*, 581 N.E.2d 1135 (Ohio App.1991).

After a Missouri instructional coordinator was struck by a school van, sustaining a concussion, she began exhibiting convulsive seizures. Several of these attacks occurred while at school. As her job required her to cross concrete steps, medical experts believed that she could not work safely in this position. She was therefore suspended and reassigned to a comparable nonteaching position at a nonschool site at which she was paid $3,000 more per year. After a Missouri trial court upheld the board's action, she appealed to the Missouri Court of Appeals. The appellate court determined that in Missouri a person is not handicapped for purposes of unlawful discrimination if the physical impairment interferes with the performance of her job. Clearly, her physical impairment interfered with the performance of her job. The court determined that the teacher was not handicapped and thus her transfer was not an unlawful employment practice. *Umphries v. Jones*, 804 S.W.2d 38 (Mo.App.1991).

A Wisconsin school board met and created a policy requiring all employees with AIDS or AIDS related complex (ARC) to be placed on sick leave or leave of absence. One board member voted for the policy because he felt that homosexuals should not be allowed to teach. The local newspaper published the policy, and the district published the policy in its employment guidelines. Before choosing to implement the policy, the district sought an advisory ruling on its legality from the Wisconsin Attorney General. A teachers' union brought suit against the district challenging the policy. The attorney general then refused to rule on the policy because it was being currently litigated. The union alleged that the policy discriminated against homosexual and bisexual men as well as persons with handicaps, and that the publication of the policy was in violation of Wisconsin law. The union's claim was successful, and the district's appeal came before the Wisconsin Court of Appeals.

Wisconsin law prohibits the publication or circulation of an employment policy with an intent to discriminate. The first issue considered the publication requirement. The district successfully argued that it was obligated to allow the press to attend the meetings, and could not be held liable for that publication. It then contended that, since the policy was never implemented, its publication in district guidelines was harmless. The law, however, imposes liability for publication—not adoption. The issue then became whether the policy discriminated. The union first asserted that the policy would have a disparate impact on homosexual and bisexual men. A disparate impact theory focuses on the effect of the policy and thus requires no showing of intent. The record was insufficient to show such discrimination. The union next contended that the policy discriminated against persons with disabilities. AIDS and ARC constitute a disability. The district argued that its policy was justified by job-related concerns. An employer may consider the safety of a worker and the public while evaluating the employment opportunities for individuals with disabilities. However, it may not do so through the use of a "blanket rule" which precludes individual case-by-case consideration. The policy was discriminatory, and the trial court judgment was affirmed. *Racine Unif. School Dist. v. Labor and Industry Review Commission*, 476 N.W.2d 707 (Wis.App.1991).

E. Other Discrimination

Colorado voters approved an initiative for a constitutional amendment that prohibited the state and its departments and political subdivisions, including school districts, from enacting statutes, regulations, ordinances or policies that would protect homosexuals or bisexuals from claims of discrimination and other protections. A number of individuals and cities and a Colorado school district filed a lawsuit in a state trial court, seeking a permanent order enjoining the governor and attorney general from enforcing the amendment. The trial court granted an order for a preliminary injunction and the governor and attorney general appealed to the Supreme Court of Colorado. The supreme court found no compelling state interest behind the constitutional amendment and found that it was not narrowly tailored to meet its intended purposes. The supreme court affirmed the temporary and permanent injunctions against enforcing the amendment. *Evans v. Romer*, 882 P.2d 1335 (Colo.1994).

A Wisconsin school district obtained health insurance coverage for its employees by the purchase of a nonduplication policy. Married employees had to choose between the district's policy and their spouse's policy. However, single employees with health insurance from another source were not forced to choose between coverages. The Supreme Court of Wisconsin found that the policy discriminated on the basis of marital status because it did not account for an employee's death or divorce, which could terminate the former spouse's coverage through the district and leave him or her unable to obtain insurance elsewhere. The policy violated the Wisconsin Fair Employment Act. *Braatz v. LIRC,* 496 N.W.2d 597 (Wis.1993).

An Illinois woman was employed by a school district as a fifth grade teacher since 1966. Her husband was also employed by the district as an elementary school principal. In 1983, the husband was assigned to act as principal for the school in which his wife taught. The board of education had a policy which forbade the placement of a spouse under the direct supervision of his or her spouse. As a result, the teacher was transferred to another school. The teacher filed a complaint with the Illinois Department of Human Rights, alleging that she had been discriminated against on the basis of her sex and marital status. An administrative law judge held against the teacher, but the marital status discrimination portion of that decision was overturned by a three-member panel of the Human Rights Commission. The school district then appealed to the Appellate Court of Illinois.

On appeal, the school district argued that discrimination based on marital status only refers to the condition of being married or single, but does not include decisions based on the identity of the spouse. The appellate court disagreed. It stated that the district's spousal supervision policy was clearly triggered by a party's marital status and imposed a direct burden upon marriage. A person who remained single would not be affected by the rule. The commission's finding, that discrimination based on the identity of one's spouse fell within the conduct proscribed by the Human Rights Act, was not unreasonable. In addition, the district could not show that the rule qualified as a bona fide occupational qualification, since it had introduced no evidence showing that one spouse is unable to effectively supervise another. The court affirmed the decision of the commission. *River Bend Comm. Unit School Dist. No. 2 v. Illinois Human Rights Commission,* 597 N.E.2d 842 (Ill.App.3d Dist.1992).

CHAPTER SEVEN

TERMINATION, RESIGNATION AND RETIREMENT

I. DECLINING ENROLLMENT AND BUDGET REDUCTION

In cases of layoffs and employment termination due to economic factors, school districts are bound to observe seniority rights and teacher qualifications when selecting employees who will be retained. For more cases involving employee tenure rights, see Chapter Eight of this volume.

A. Declining Enrollment Dismissals

A Massachusetts high school's committee, voted to dismiss a tenured teacher because of falling enrollment. She was certified to teach grades K-8 as well as children with disabilities. At the time of the committee vote, a nontenured teacher was in his first year at the high school. He taught three classes of eighth grade English and one ninth grade English class. The committee retained him. The tenured teacher turned down an offer to teach at a school for $30,000 and instead took another job at a private school for $25,000. She then sued the school committee in a Massachusetts trial court. The trial court found that the school committee had failed to justify its action, and ordered the teacher reinstated and compensated. The school committee appealed unsuccessfully to the Massachusetts Court of Appeals, and further appealed to the Supreme Judicial Court of Massachusetts. The supreme judicial court held that the "critical date" for assessing a tenured teacher's qualifications for a position filled by a nontenured teacher is the date when the school committee voted to dismiss. At that time, even though the tenured teacher was not certified to teach ninth grade English, the Massachusetts Department of Education allowed certified teachers to work up to 20 percent of their time in levels for which they were not certified. Thus, the tenured teacher had been qualified to fill the position the nontenured teacher held. Further, the court held that the tenured teacher's refusal of the higher paying job was not unreasonable so as to prevent compensation being paid. Accordingly, the court affirmed the lower court's decision. *Assad v. Berlin-Boylston Regional School Committee*, 550 N.E.2d 357 (Mass.1990).

Several teachers in Pennsylvania were laid off due to declining enrollment while other less senior teachers were retained. The discharged teachers brought an action challenging their lay-offs due to realignment. Teachers with more seniority were fired and a teacher with less seniority was retained to be the coordinator of a program for gifted students. The superintendent chose the less senior employee because she had been involved with the program from the start and had a greater breadth of experience with arts and humanities. Further, the less senior employee had a greater ability to interact with the students and with the talented people within the community. A state trial court ruled in favor of the school district, stating that retaining a less senior employee did not violate the statute. The teachers appealed to the Supreme Court of Pennsylvania which stated that in a realignment school districts have no choice but to replace less senior employees with more senior ones who carry proper certification. The benefit of giving school districts discretion to make appointments on the basis of a person's qualifications is still limited by a requirement that retentions be based on seniority and certification. This method protects higher salaried long tenured employees from removal simply to save the district money and it also provides an incentive for employees to broaden their professional abilities. The supreme court decided that since the teachers in this case were dismissed seven years earlier, an order for reinstatement would not be appropriate. A monetary award would be appropriate for lost wages. The court of appeals reversed the trial court's decision. *Dallap v. Sharon City Sch. Dist.*, 571 A.2d 368 (Pa.1990).

A Minnesota school district sought to place a full-time social studies teacher on unrequested leave of absence due to declining enrollment. The teacher requested and received a hearing, but she was still placed on unrequested leave. She sought judicial review of that decision, and the case came before the Court of Appeals of Minnesota. The district, while acknowledging that realignment of teaching positions would be reasonable and practical, stated that under the provisions of the collective bargaining agreement, it did not have a duty to realign to save the teacher's position. The court of appeals held that Minnesota law required the district to realign. Further, the district had conceded that realignment was practical and reasonable. The court thus ordered the district to reinstate the teacher and realign teaching positions to preserve the teacher's continuing contract rights. *Matter of Bristol*, 451 N.W.2d 883 (Minn.App.1990).

An Ohio teacher's union sued a school district for violations of the collective bargaining agreement. The school district had implemented a reduction-in-force policy due to declining student enrollment, and the union contended that the school district had not made a sufficient showing of a decline. The trial court found that the policy was an abuse of discretion and ordered the district to rehire the laid-off teachers. The district appealed to the Court of Appeals of Ohio, which noted that the agreement provided that teachers could be discharged if there was a decrease in the number of students. Here, student enrollment went from 6,564 in 1983 to 6,087 in 1988. The union contended that the most recent years showed almost no decline, but the court determined that the agreement did not state that the decline had to be a continuing decline. Thus, it reversed the trial court's decision and found for the school district. *Cuyahoga Falls Educ. Assn. v. Cuyahoga Falls School Bd.*, 574 N.E.2d 442 (Ohio 1991).

B. Termination for Budgetary Reasons

A Wyoming school district employed a welding teacher from 1974 until 1988. His contract with the school district included a reduction in force (RIF) policy which allowed the school district to reduce the number of teachers when it became necessary due to reduced enrollment or other events beyond its control. Nonrenewal of contracts was to be accomplished on the basis of seniority. When the teacher was notified that his contract was not being renewed under the RIF policy, he sued the school district in federal court, seeking to recover damages for his lost wages and fringe benefits, both past and future. A jury found that the school district had violated its RIF policy by renewing the contracts of other teachers who had less seniority. The jury awarded him $90,000. The school district then sought a declaration in a state trial court to determine whether the RIF policy obligated it to give a preference to the welding teacher when it rehired. The trial court granted summary judgment to the school district and the welding teacher appealed to the Supreme Court of Wyoming.

On appeal, the welding teacher argued that despite the fact that he had already recovered damages for all potential future employment with the school district, he was still entitled to receive preferential treatment under the RIF policy's rehire provisions. He asserted that the jury's future damage award was relatively small because it was under the impression that he would be quickly rehired pursuant to the rehire provisions. However, the court noted that the teacher's recovery was for all potential future employment and that a preference on rehiring would amount to a double recovery of damages. Since the federal court had instructed the jury to award wages and benefits for the reasonable length of time the jury thought the teacher's employment would have continued, the supreme court affirmed the trial court's grant of summary judgment to the school district. *Hansen v. Sheridan County School Dist.*, 847 P.2d 1026 (Wyo.1993).

The Chicago school board reduced its subdistricts from 23 to eleven by combining some of them. Thirteen subdistrict superintendents lost their jobs because of the change, and they sued the board in an Illinois trial court, seeking injunctive relief and damages. They claimed that the Illinois School Reform Act established a contract of employment with them. They alleged that the reduction in force had deprived them of property without due process of law. The Appellate Court of Illinois, First District, Fifth Division, reversed the trial court's decision to grant the school board summary judgment. Although the board had the power to change its subdistricts, the statute created a contract with the superintendents by operation of law which bound the school board. *Kaszubowski v. Bd. of Educ. of City of Chicago*, 618 N.E.2d 609 (Ill.App.1st Dist.1993).

A North Dakota school district decided to eliminate the position of one elementary teacher in an effort to reduce expenses. The district had a written policy for force reductions. The policy stated that retained teachers would be those who gave the district the greatest adaptability to meet the district's staffing needs, giving preference to teachers with superior academic and professional preparation. The district also placed terminated employees on a "notification of openings" list for one year following termination. A teaching position was chosen to be eliminated, and after a hearing, the teacher's employment was terminated. Before the next school year, a position became vacant. However, the district advertised for a teacher with coaching experience, so the terminated teacher was not considered. The teacher sued the district in a state court, claiming that it failed to properly apply the reduction-in-force policy, and discriminated against her by combining the coaching position. The trial court held for the district and the teacher appealed to the North Dakota Supreme Court. The supreme court stated that the staffing policy did not restrict what criteria the district could use to determine teacher adaptability. As long as the information used had some reasonable relevance to the teacher's qualities and qualifications, the decision would stand. In addition, combining the teaching position with the coaching position was not sex discrimination, since the district had no history of using coaching positions to discriminate against women. *Kent v. Sawyer Pub. School Dist.*, 484 N.W.2d 287 (N.D.1992).

A West Virginia woman worked with a university-affiliated organization for 13 years under a series of one-year contracts. In 1986 she entered into a one-year contract which appointed her to a position with the University-Affiliated Center for Developmental Disabilities. The program was funded solely through grants and contracts from the federal and state governments and was staffed solely by temporary employees who, according to the university, were hired on one-year contracts with no expectation of continued employment. The West Virginia Department of Human Services indicated that the funding for the employee's position would be eliminated. She filed a grievance and the hearing examiner determined that she should be reinstated and given backpay. After a West Virginia trial court affirmed the hearing examiner's decision, the university appealed to the Supreme Court of Appeals of West Virginia.

On appeal, the court noted that, with respect to nontenured faculty members, for a protected property interest to arise there must be rules, understandings, and a relationship between the employee and the institution. The record indicated that although the employee was hired under a contract which provided for one year of employment only, she had been hired under such contracts for many years. She had always been offered a new contract, even though at times grants had been terminated. Thus, the court determined that she had a reasonable expectation that her employment would continue. However, due to the unavailability of grant money, she was not entitled to an award of backpay. *West Virginia Univ. v. Sauvageot,* 408 S.E.2d 286 (W.Va.1991).

In anticipation of a shortfall in funding for the upcoming year, an Oklahoma board of education implemented a reduction in force and voted unanimously not to renew a probationary teacher's contract. The teacher sued the school district in a state court, and the district asserted that its decision was final and nonappealable by virtue of state law. The teacher claimed that the shortfall never came to pass. The Court of Appeals of Oklahoma stated that Oklahoma law grants broad nondelegable discretion in matters of probationary teachers' contracts. A teacher who merely seeks review of a school district's nonrenewal decision is not entitled to court review. The statute providing for the decision's finality did not violate equal protection standards. *Childers v. Ind. School Dist. No. 1,* 842 P.2d 355 (Okl.App.1992).

On April 3, 1987, a continuing contract teacher was notified that she would be terminated for the 1987-1988 school year due to a reduction in force. Virginia law allowed teacher reductions "whether or not such teachers have reached continuing contract status" if there has been a decrease in enrollment. Because the school board kept probationary teachers who performed extra duties, the teacher sued the school board in a Virginia trial court, alleging that the RIF policy violated state law and was a breach of her contract with the board. The trial court ruled in favor of the school board, and the Supreme Court of Virginia affirmed. The court stated that Virginia law clearly supported the board's action in applying its policy concerning reductions in force. Also, since the notice came before April 15 (another statutory requirement), the notice of termination was timely given. The school board was not required to give continuing contract teachers priority over probationary teachers during a general reduction in force. *Underwood v. Henry County School Board,* 427 S.E.2d 330 (Va.1993).

C. Reinstatement and Recall

A Minnesota social studies teacher was placed on unrequested leave of absence (ULA). Twice he was denied reinstatement when the school district reestablished positions and recalled two less senior teachers to fill them. The teacher brought a declaratory judgment action seeking to force the district to realign teachers with less seniority to make his reinstatement possible. The trial court held for the district and the teacher successfully appealed. The district then appealed to the Supreme Court of Minnesota. Holding that protection of teachers' seniority rights was paramount, the supreme court held that the most senior teacher on ULA was to be recalled first, either for his former position if open, or after reasonable realignment to another position for which he was licensed. The court ordered the district to realign positions and reinstate the teacher, and affirmed the appellate court's decision. *Harms v. Indep. School Dist. No. 300*, 450 N.W.2d 571 (Minn.1990).

A Pennsylvania teacher was hired in October 1972. He worked from this date until the end of 1983 when he was suspended because he had less seniority than another teacher who was retained as a guidance counselor. The counselor was hired in September 1972. During the 1973-74 school year, funding was delayed and the counselor worked half-time for a month. The teacher sued the school district in a Pennsylvania trial court asking to be reinstated since the counselor's part-time service constituted a leave of absence which reduced the counselor's seniority. The trial court ordered the teacher to be reinstated. The school district appealed to the Commonwealth Court of Pennsylvania. On appeal, the court held that the counselor's part-time service did not constitute a leave of absence which would reduce seniority. *School Dist. of Duquesne v. Sturm*, 547 A.2d 891 (Pa.Cmwlth.1988).

II. EXCESSIVE ABSENCE AND TARDINESS

Excessive absence or tardiness is a valid ground for discipline, but written warnings should be given to the employee in advance of any disciplinary action.

An Oregon man worked in maintenance for a local school district and was habitually late for work. In 1983 and 1984 the school district followed the proper procedure and notified the worker of its concern of his habitual tardiness. Later in that year the school district orally reprimanded the man for not coming to work. The maintenance worker continued to be late and his tardiness was reflected on his time cards. However, the maintenance worker received no written warnings during this time. In June of 1985 the maintenance worker was discharged upon arriving at work. He filed a grievance claim with the Employment Relations Board (ERB) alleging an unfair labor practice by the school district. The school district's procedure stated that any infraction for which an employee would be disciplined had to be made in writing and dated and a copy had to be placed in the employee's personnel file. The ERB dismissed the maintenance worker's claim because the school district had given him a warning notice three years earlier. The maintenance worker then sought review of ERB's ruling from an Oregon trial court. The trial court remanded the case to the ERB, which ruled in favor of the district. The worker further appealed to the Oregon Court of Appeals. The court of appeals noted that the maintenance worker did not receive any written notices other than the two dismissal letters. Thus, he did not receive timely notice because the district did not follow procedure after each incident of tardiness on which it relied when discharging the employee. The court of appeals reversed the ERB's ruling, and decided that the district had violated the bargaining agreement. *Osea v. Ranier School Dist. No. 13*, 786 P.2d 1311 (Or.App.1990).

A woman was employed by a New Jersey board of education on January 13, 1986. She worked actively until November 17, 1988, when a work-connected injury forced her to take involuntary sick leave. She continued to receive full salary. On April 11, 1989, prior to her return to service, but after the expiration of three academic years (30 months) within four consecutive academic years, the school board terminated her employment. Under New Jersey law, tenure is achieved after employment for the equivalent of more than 3 academic years within a period of any four consecutive academic years. The commissioner of education responded favorably to her administrative challenge, holding that in sick leave situations a case by case subjective approach to statutory tenure requirements was appropriate. The commissioner stated that the district had ample opportunity to evaluate her during the 28 months of active service prior to her injury. The state board of education affirmed. The local school board then appealed to the Superior Court of New Jersey, Appellate Division. The appellate court stated that the school board was required to give timely notice of dismissal or nonrenewal before expiration of the tenure period. The court stated that were it to adopt the school board's interpretation of New Jersey law, a teacher injured on the job during a third year of satisfactory performance, and unable to perform service during the consecutive year because of that injury, would necessarily lose all credit to tenure for prior service. The state board had reasonably interpreted the law to provide the teacher with continued appointment while she was receiving full salary. *Kletzkin v. Bd. of Educ.*, 619 A.2d 621 (N.J.Super.A.D.1993).

III. IMMORALITY AND OTHER MISCONDUCT

Teacher immorality is a ground for discharge from employment.

A. Sexual Misconduct

A Missouri middle school teacher hugged and kissed an eighth grade student in the school hallway. The student was undergoing counseling for behavior problems. The following day, he asked the school principal if he could go to in-school suspension rather than to class. He then described the incident, stating that the teacher's actions had shocked him and that he interpreted the hugging and kissing as a pass. The principal and superintendent of schools met with the teacher and decided to recommend termination of the teacher's employment contract. Although the teacher explained that he had no sexual motive and that he came from a physically demonstrative family, the board determined that his actions were inappropriate and could have been perceived by the student as sexual harassment. The board found the teacher guilty of immoral conduct and fired him as unsuitable to teach in district schools. A Missouri trial court affirmed the dismissal action, and the teacher appealed to the Missouri Court of Appeals, Eastern District. The court determined that the district had no policy on sexual harassment, and it failed to show intentional conduct and knowledge by the teacher that his conduct was wrongful. The board had not succeeded in showing improper motive and the teacher had no prior notice that his physical demonstrativeness was impermissible. Subjective reactions by a student could not transform a well-intended act into an immoral one, and because the evidence did not support a finding of immoral conduct, the court reversed and remanded the case with orders to reinstate the teacher. *Youngman v. Doerhoff*, 890 S.W.2d 330 (Mo.App.E.D.1994).

A tenured music teacher at a California middle school was accused of repeatedly sexually harassing female students. The school district suspended the teacher and began dismissal proceedings against him on the basis of immoral conduct. The state education commission conducted a hearing and determined that the teacher had not engaged in immoral conduct. It ordered reinstatement of the teacher with backpay. The district appealed the decision to a California superior court, which reversed the commission's decision, finding that evidence supported dismissal of the teacher. The teacher appealed to the California Court of Appeal, Second District. The court reviewed the evidence, finding a number of incidents of inappropriate touching, hugging, sexual comments and other unwanted behavior by the teacher. Contrary to the commission's finding that the alleged conduct was not immoral, the court determined that sexually harassing behavior could be construed as immoral under the statute. Proof of immoral conduct could demonstrate unfitness to teach upon consideration of the likelihood of adverse effect on students or other teachers. In this case, the repeated and pervasive nature of the conduct supported dismissal. The court affirmed the judgment for the school district. *Governing Board of ABC Unified School Dist. v. Haar*, 33 Cal.Rptr.2d 744 (Cal.App.2d Dist.1994).

A Maine teacher engaged in a sexual relationship with a 15-year-old high school student. The student had psychological problems which worsened after this relationship. The school district notified the teacher of her termination, stating that she was unfit to teach because of her poor exercise of judgment. It asserted that she would be unable to effectively deal with child abuse cases, that she damaged the school's reputation and that the public would lose respect and trust in the public school system. After the board held a hearing, it decided to discharge the teacher. She appealed to the Supreme Court of Maine, which stated that the findings of the board were supported by substantial evidence. The board rationally concluded that the teacher was unfit to teach after engaging in a sexual relationship of long duration with a high school student whom the teacher knew had previous psychological problems. The teacher had been afforded all fundamental fairness and due process. The supreme court affirmed the trial court's decision. *Elvin v. City of Waterville*, 573 A.2d 381 (Me.1990).

A Tennessee band teacher slept with one of his students on several occasions. After the student quit going to the teacher's house, the teacher became critical of his performance. The student then became a disciplinary problem. The school's principal advised the teacher "to conduct school business at school and not at home," but took no other action until he made formal charges to the county school board recommending dismissal for conduct unbecoming a member of the teaching profession. The board resolved to dismiss the teacher based on these charges. The teacher appealed to a Tennessee trial court, which conducted a hearing consisting only of the teacher's testimony. The court disregarded the administrative record, a deposition, and the recorded testimony from the teacher's criminal proceedings. The court also refused to permit the school board to produce the student as a witness. Nonetheless, the court ruled that the dismissal was justified. The teacher appealed to the Court of Appeals of Tennessee.

The court of appeals observed that because the principal's advice to the teacher did not amount to an order, there could be no finding of insubordination. The pertinent Tennessee statute governing dismissal of tenured teachers permitted dismissal or suspension for unprofessional conduct, among other things. "Conduct unbecoming a member of a profession in good standing" was part of the definition of "unprofessional conduct" in several legal authorities. Because the teacher's conduct compromised his ability to teach, his dismissal was affirmed. *Morris v. Clarksville-Montgomery County Cons. Bd. of Educ.*, 867 S.W.2d 324 (Tenn.App.1993).

A Washington math teacher engaged in an extensive and intimate friendship with a female student which included conversations about his troubled marriage and her personal problems. The teacher wrote the student a note alluding to his fantasies about her. The student took the note to school authorities who subsequently sent the teacher notice that he was suspended without pay. School administrators then notified the teacher that he was discharged. The teacher requested an administrative hearing and the hearing officer concluded that there was sufficient evidence to discharge him. The teacher then appealed to a Washington trial court which affirmed the dismissal and the teacher appealed to the Washington Court of Appeals.

The court of appeals stated that the hearing officer's findings of fact were supported by substantial evidence. The teacher took the initiative by engaging in improper conversations with a student. The court also stated that to discharge a teacher there must be sufficient cause such as irremediable behavior and behavior which materially affects performance or the teacher's conduct. The court stated that there was sufficient cause because the conduct in which the teacher engaged affected his fitness to teach by altering his relationships with students, teachers, parents and the community. The Washington Court of Appeals affirmed the trial court's decision and upheld the discharge. *Sauter v. Mount Vernon School Dist. 320*, 791 P.2d 549 (Wash.App.1990).

A New York school district transportation supervisor was charged with 17 counts of alleged misconduct. The charges against him included touching women daily on the buttocks and in other inappropriate places. A two-day hearing was conducted and upon finding the supervisor guilty, the hearing officer recommended that he be suspended for three months and that he should seek therapy for sexual harassment in the workplace. The board of education elected to adopt the findings of fact and the conclusions of law made, but elected not to adopt the hearing officer's penalty. Instead, the board decided to discharge the employee. The employee instituted a claim in a New York trial court and the case was transferred to the Supreme Court, Appellate Division, by motion of the trial court. The appellate court found that ample evidence warranted affirming the board of education's decision to discharge the employee. *Comeau v. Bd. of Educ. of Ballston Spa*, 554 N.Y.S.2d 359 (A.D.3d Dept.1990).

A nontenured Minnesota high school teacher allegedly had a sexual relationship with a student. The school district received a letter from the former student and then began proceedings to fire the teacher. The teacher requested a hearing after which the independent hearing officer recommended that he be suspended without pay for one year. The school board passed a resolution rejecting the hearing officer's findings and discharged the teacher immediately. He appealed to the Minnesota Court of Appeals alleging that his due process rights were violated. The court found that the termination proceedings provided by state law did not violate due process, since the hearings were conducted by an independent hearing officer and the teacher was entitled to be represented by counsel. The court also held that the findings made by the hearing officer were not binding on the school board. The court affirmed the school board's decision. *In Re Etienne*, 460 N.W.2d 109 (Minn.App.1990).

A Chicago teacher was discharged for conduct unbecoming a teacher. The school board alleged that she had had an inappropriate relationship with two female students which allegedly included sexual contact. Deeming her conduct to be irremediable, the board served notice on the teacher and suspended her pending the outcome of a hearing. The hearing officer determined that the allegations of sexual misconduct were largely fabricated. However, the teacher was held to have an inappropriately close personal relationship with the two students. The hearing officer concluded that even though the charges of sexual impropriety were not proven, the teacher's conduct was irremediable and a sufficient cause for termination. The teacher appealed to an Illinois trial court which affirmed the hearing officer's findings. The teacher then appealed to the Appellate Court of Illinois, First District.

On appeal, the school board abandoned all charges of sexual impropriety and asserted only those charges upheld by the hearing officer. The Illinois School code provides for the removal of tenured teachers only for cause. Although the appeals court found sufficient evidence in the record to support the hearing officer's conclusion that the teacher had engaged in an inappropriate personal relationship with the students, it rejected the hearing officer's finding that the teacher's conduct was irremediable. Under the Illinois School Code, a school board must provide written warning prior to termination to any teacher charged with remediable misconduct. Since the school board did not give the teacher proper notice, the court reversed the decision of the trial court. *Hegener v. Bd. of Educ. of City of Chicago,* 567 N.E.2d 566 (Ill.App.1st Dist.1991).

B. Other Misconduct

1. Immoral Conduct

An Idaho teacher impregnated a 15-year-old student. Prior to the birth of the child, the teacher and the student's father signed a confidential agreement under which the teacher was required to resign his position prior to the beginning of the following school semester. Meanwhile, he applied for employment with an Alaska school district, and accepted a job there. Ten years later, the district received notice from the student of the prior relationship and conducted an investigation. The Alaska district then terminated the teacher's employment on grounds that his prior conduct constituted immorality and substantial noncompliance with school law. The teacher appealed to an Alaska trial court, which granted the school district's summary judgment motion. The teacher appealed to the Supreme Court of Alaska. On appeal, the teacher argued that conduct prior to being hired by the Alaska district could not constitute grounds for dismissal. The supreme court disagreed, stating that such a policy would immunize from punishment a teacher who had engaged in prior illegal or immoral conduct and successfully concealed it. The teacher's prior immoral conduct and failure to disclose his criminal behavior provided ample evidence that the teacher's employment had been properly terminated. *Toney v. Fairbanks North Star Borough School Dist., Bd. of Educ.*, 881 P.2d 1112 (Alaska 1994).

A New York physical education instructor married a former member of his volleyball team shortly after she graduated from high school. The school board then investigated his prior relationships with members of the team and removed him from his position as coach, refused to appoint him coach of the boys' team, and denied him tenure at the end of his probationary period. The former coach filed a lawsuit against the school board and several of its officials in the U.S. District Court for the Northern District of New York, asserting a violation of his constitutional right to marry and claiming damage to his reputation. The court awarded summary judgment to the school board and the former coach appealed to the U.S. Court of Appeals, Second Circuit. The court of appeals held that public employees claiming constitutional violations by their employers must demonstrate evidence of unfavorable employment action that is substantially motivated by the employee's constitutionally protected conduct. The former coach had presented only conclusory allegations of the board's decision and there was insufficient evidence that the board sought to penalize him because of the marriage. The court affirmed the judgment for the board. *Finnegan v. Bd. of Educ. of City School Dist. of Troy*, 30 F.3d 273 (2d Cir.1994).

A Kansas high school teacher permitted several students to make a videotape as part of a social time for a student who was transferring. The school board learned of the tape and claimed that the incident demonstrated lack of classroom control and that material in the video constituted sexual harassment. The board terminated the teacher's employment, but its decision was vacated by a due process hearing committee, which found no substantial evidence of good cause for termination. The Court of Appeals of Kansas affirmed the committee's decision, finding that substantial evidence supported its decision. No female student had complained of sexual harassment and the videotape incident was apparently isolated. The teacher was reinstated with backpay. *Unif. School Dist. No. 434, Osage County v. Hubbard*, 868 P.2d 1240 (Kan.App.1994).

A tenured vocational technical school instructor worked for 19 years at a Pennsylvania county school system without ever receiving unsatisfactory performance ratings. The instructor then threatened two school employees on the same day, including a head counselor, after missing a mandatory class. The school terminated the instructor's employment on the basis of immorality, persistent and willful violation of school law, persistent negligence and cruelty. The Commonwealth Court of Pennsylvania reversed the state secretary of education's dismissal of the teacher's appeal. The court held that the two incidents, which occurred about three hours apart, did not indicate a persistent course of conduct, even though an alleged prior incident had occurred in 1985. *Horton v. Jefferson County - Dubois Area Vocational Tech. School*, 630 A.2d 481 (Pa.Cmwlth.1993).

A Washington physical education teacher was fired by his school district for unprofessional conduct, using his position of authority for personal reasons, and assaulting or engaging in nonconsensual touching of students as an improper means of discipline. The decision was upheld by a hearing officer and a Washington trial court. The Court of Appeals of Washington, Division Three, affirmed the termination. It rejected the teacher's argument that the school district had impermissibly relied upon similar prior incidents which no longer appeared in his permanent record pursuant to the collective bargaining agreement between the school district and teachers. There was also no merit to the teacher's argument that he had a right to rely upon favorable employment evaluations. *McCorkle v. Sunnyside School Dist. No. 201*, 848 P.2d 1308 (Wash.App.Div.3 1993).

On the last day of class, two Pennsylvania high school teachers engaged in a good natured water fight with their students. School authorities had warned the staff that while such horseplay was traditional, it would result in severe disciplinary action. During the water fight, one of the teachers reached for the nearest bottle of liquid, which happened to be a bottle of cleansing solution. Several students suffered minor skin and eye irritations. The school board suspended both teachers for a period of 15 days for "immoral behavior" under Pennsylvania law. On appeal, the Commonwealth Court of Pennsylvania noted that previous cases dealing with immorality had involved sexual improprieties, stealing, and operating an illegal gambling establishment. The court stated that while the teachers' conduct may have been outrageous and uncalled for it was not immoral. The court overturned the school board's decision and reinstated the teachers. *Everett Area School Dist. v. Ault*, 548 A.2d 1341 (Pa.Cmwlth.1988).

An instructor at a North Carolina technical institute was notified by her employer that it believed she was in violation of North Carolina law regarding repayment of her state-funded student loans. At a hearing, she testified that there was a clerical error on the part of the lender. Shortly thereafter her employer determined that there was no clerical error, nor any voluntary attempt to pay the state. She was fired. The instructor alleged wrongful termination and brought suit against the college in a state court. After two adverse rulings, the instructor appealed to the Court of Appeals of North Carolina. North Carolina law provides that "employees of the state who owe money to the state must make full restitution of the full amount as a condition for continued employment." Without deciding whether the repeated garnishment of income tax amounted to "repayment," the court agreed that the lack of a voluntary attempt at repayment justified the termination. *Battle v. Nash Technical College,* 404 S.E.2d 703 (N.C.App.1991).

A Florida school board leveled two charges against one of its teachers: misconduct in office and gross insubordination. The hearing examiner found the evidence sufficient to support the first charge, but found that the second charge was not proved by a preponderance of the evidence. While accepting all the hearing examiner's findings of fact, the school board's attorney took exception to the conclusion that the facts did not support a finding of gross insubordination. Further, the school board increased the penalty from suspension to dismissal. The teacher appealed this ruling to the District Court of Appeal of Florida. The court of appeal examined the record and found that there was substantial evidence that the teacher had been instructed to refrain from touching or publicly demeaning students as a disciplinary measure. Therefore, the court determined that the board's decision was supported by the record. *Johnson v. School Bd. of Dade County,* 578 So.2d 387 (Fla.App.1991).

2. Criminal Conduct

The wife of the director of maintenance for a Texas school district advised authorities that she believed her husband was stealing school property. The sheriff's department executed a search warrant and school property was found in the employee's home. Although a grand jury indicted the employee on theft charges, the wife became unwilling to testify and the indictments were dismissed. The school board held a hearing and voted to fire the employee for misconduct. The state commissioner of education upheld the board's decision. The local school board then formulated a policy prohibiting its contractors from employing former school district employees at school worksites. The former employee alleged that this rule caused him to lose his job with a contractor. He filed a lawsuit against the district, school officials and law officers in a Texas trial court for malicious prosecution, invasion of privacy, tortious interference with contract and civil conspiracy. He also claimed that the board's termination action and vendor exclusion policy violated his constitutional rights. The court dismissed the lawsuit and the former employee appealed to the Court of Appeals of Texas, Texarkana.

The court of appeals found no error in the trial court's decision. The former employee's case relied on conclusory statements, speculative arguments and insufficient evidence. The facts indicated that school officials and law enforcement officers were merely carrying out their duties and were not guilty of malicious prosecution, civil conspiracy, invasion of privacy or interference with contract rights. The board had provided adequate due process protections concerning the termination and the vendor policy. The court affirmed the dismissal of the lawsuit. *Closs v. Goose Creek Cons. Indep. School Dist.*, 874 S.W.2d 859 (Tex.App.—Texarkana 1994).

An Oregon teacher was fired after a police search of her home revealed that her husband had used their home to grow, use, and sell marijuana. The grounds for dismissal were cited as neglect of duty. The state Fair Dismissal Appeals Board (FDAB) reversed the termination action. The Oregon Court of Appeals held that the FDAB had misinterpreted the teacher's statutory duty, and remanded the case. The teacher appealed to the Supreme Court of Oregon. The court first reviewed the interpretation of the teacher's duty. It held that a school district may lawfully consider off-the-job conduct. The FDAB ruling required the school district to consider individual circumstances such as concern for the teacher's family and children, or fear of violence. The supreme court held that a district is not required to grant consideration of such "limitless variables"; personal considerations were ruled to be irrelevant. Another issue concerned whether the teacher had sufficient notice of the extent of her duty. Because of the school's anti-drug program, the notice was held to be sufficient. Finally, the court noted that appropriateness of termination as a sanction was viewed by the FDAB in light of its misinterpreted view of the teacher's duty, and needed to be reconsidered on remand. *Jefferson County Sch. Dist. 509J v. Fair Dismissal Appeals Bd.,* 812 P.2d 1384 (Or.1991).

In a similar case, an Iowa woman was employed as a psychology teacher at a Des Moines area community college. Her psychology classes were taken by students interested in becoming drug counselors. While she was teaching, the instructor allowed a student and a cocaine user to live at her house. An undercover police operation eventually led to a search of the instructor's home which yielded 29 grams of cocaine, packaged in bundles for sale. In the instructor's own room marijuana, hashish, and a pipe were found. There were also several loaded firearms in the house. She was convicted of possession, given a suspended sentence, and placed on probation. While the criminal charges were pending, the instructor was suspended from her teaching position. Shortly after the conviction, she was fired. She appealed her employment termination to an independent adjudicator claiming that she was unaware that illegal activities were occurring at her house. The adjudicator stated that there was no just cause for termination, and the college board appealed to an Iowa trial court, which reinstated the board's termination decision. The instructor then appealed to the Court of Appeals of Iowa.

The court of appeals stated that the board, and not the adjudicator, was in the best position to pass judgment on the credibility of witnesses. The factual findings of the board are normally conclusive. The evidence clearly showed that drug sales were taking place at the instructor's house, and that the neighbors were aware of that fact. The board had chosen not to believe the teacher's testimony that she only suspected drug sales were occurring, and that she was unaware of any illegal activity. The teacher would be unable to perform her professional duties because of the impact of her conduct and her conviction. A teacher, especially one involved in the training of drug counselors, must be a good role model. The court concluded that there was just cause for the termination of the instructor. *Bd. of Dir. of Des Moines Area Com. Col. v. Simons*, 493 N.W.2d 879 (Iowa App.1992).

A North Carolina teacher was arrested at his home and charged with feloniously maintaining a dwelling to keep and store marijuana and with manufacture of a controlled substance. The assistant superintendent of the county schools suspended the teacher with pay the next day. The school board agreed to delay any action on termination until after the criminal charges were resolved. The criminal charges were dismissed. The school board, however, brought dismissal proceedings. The board fired the teacher, stating that the superior court's reason for dismissing the criminal charges was unknown, and sufficient evidence of the teacher's use of marijuana justified the decision. The teacher appealed the board's decision to a North Carolina superior court which affirmed the dismissal. The teacher then appealed to the Court of Appeals of North Carolina. On appeal, the teacher argued that the board could not have relied on the evidence since it was obtained in violation of the Fourth Amendment. The court of appeals stated, however, that the superior court had not given any reason for its dismissal of the criminal proceedings. The teacher had not given specific reasons or stated on what basis the search violated the Fourth Amendment. The mere dismissal of the criminal case did not render the evidence obtained in violation of the Fourth Amendment. The court of appeals affirmed the termination order. *Matter of Freeman*, 426 S.E.2d 100 (N.C.App.1993).

An Illinois teacher failed to file federal income tax returns for two years. The IRS investigated him and filed felony tax evasion charges against him. The teacher failed to appear at his arraignment and sent notice to the court that it did not have jurisdiction over him. The teacher was arrested and the court ordered a psychiatric evaluation. He was found competent to stand trial. The teacher refused to cooperate during the trial and was put in jail. While in jail he began a hunger strike. He was released from jail and was admitted to a psychiatric hospital. After four months in the hospital, he wrote to the court apologizing for his behavior and agreed to plead guilty. The school district dismissed the teacher for incompetency, negligence and immorality. After a hearing which the teacher requested, the hearing officer found that the termination action was justified. The teacher appealed the hearing officer's findings to an Illinois trial court, which affirmed the teacher's dismissal. He then appealed to the Appellate Court of Illinois, Fifth District. On appeal, the court noted that Illinois courts have held that criminal conduct by a teacher diminishes his effectiveness and warrants dismissal. The court held that the teacher's conduct justified dismissal and that his personality disorder did not constitute a mental incapacity. Accordingly, the court affirmed the judgment of the trial court. *McCullough v. Illinois State Bd. of Educ.*, 562 N.E.2d 1233 (Ill.App.5th Dist.1990).

A teacher employed by an Iowa school district was arrested for shoplifting at a Sioux City department store. It was later revealed that she had shoplifted extensively. The teacher also had a history of behavioral incidents including statements to her fifth grade class that she carried a handgun. Her school district's board of directors convened a termination hearing at which the teacher claimed that her unlawful activity was the result of medically induced mania. This mental state was supposedly induced by a chemical imbalance from taking Lithium and Marplan. Despite that, the teacher's employment was terminated. The teacher appealed to an adjudicator who disagreed with the board and ordered further consideration. The board appealed to the Iowa district court, which affirmed the adjudicator's decision, and then to the Iowa Supreme Court. The supreme court noted that the teacher's contract could be terminated for "just cause." It further noted that just cause for termination could be found as a result of mental or physical disability. Since a teacher must be a good role model for her students, and that status had been permanently damaged by her actions, just cause for termination was established. *Bd. of Dir. of Lawton-Bronson v. Davies*, 489 N.W.2d 19 (Iowa 1992).

A school district employee pleaded guilty in federal court to charges of conspiracy to extort money. The employee solicited a political contribution from a business person who supplied material to the school board. The federal judge in the criminal case found that the employee had been asked to collect political contributions by the superintendent of schools and that he was under the impression that his continued employment depended on his participation. The board subsequently discharged the employee. He then filed a grievance and the hearing examiner concluded that he had been dismissed without cause. The board appealed unsuccessfully to a West Virginia trial court, and further appealed to the Supreme Court of Appeals of West Virginia. That court concluded that the employee's criminal conduct was directly related to his work, since he was in charge of purchasing materials for the board. Consequently, it reversed the trial court's decision and upheld the dismissal of the employee. *Bledsoe v. Wyoming County Bd. of Educ.*, 394 S.E.2d 885 (W.Va.1990).

In Tennessee, the superintendent of a school system prepares an annual budget along with the estimate of the average daily attendance for the upcoming year. A Claiborne County superintendent had estimated daily attendance at 4,933 students, but the actual attendance was 341 fewer students. To cope with the lack of funds, the superintendent transferred certain designated funds to the general purpose fund. The state then began ouster proceedings in a state trial court. The trial court entered judgment ousting the superintendent and he appealed to the Supreme Court of Tennessee. The superintendent contended that his activities did not rise to the level of misconduct because he did not benefit personally from the transfer of funds. The court disagreed stating that the diversions violated state and federal law making the actions misconduct for purposes of the ouster statute. *State, Ex Rel. Estep v. Peters*, 815 S.W.2d 161 (Tenn.1991).

3. Neglect of Duty

A Colorado fourth grade teacher encouraged boys to come to his home for help with homework and to play games. The teacher developed a close relationship with a ten-year-old student, who gradually began to spend most of his time at the teacher's house with the permission of his mother. Within one year, the student and teacher had developed a father-son relationship, and the teacher engaged in a custody battle with the student's illiterate, Spanish-speaking mother. The custody battle became widely publicized in local newspapers, and after dependency and neglect charges were filed against both the teacher and mother, six sets of parents requested that their children be assigned to a different teacher. The school superintendent recommended dismissal of the teacher, and the school board affirmed this decision. A hearing officer determined that there were adequate grounds for termination. The Colorado Court of Appeals, affirmed the judgment of a Colorado trial court upholding the hearing officer's order. The court observed that the student had been without significant academic or behavioral problems prior to becoming close to the teacher and that the teacher had taken advantage of his position to foster the relationship. Good cause for dismissal existed under a Colorado statute because the teacher's actions were reasonably related to his fitness to discharge his duties and had affected his performance. The record supported termination. *Kerin v. Bd. of Educ., Lamar School Dist. No. Re-2, Prowers County*, 860 P.2d 574 (Colo.App.1993).

A Louisiana bus driver failed to notice that a five-year-old special education student had been left behind on the bus. The student was to get off at the bus driver's last stop but instead fell asleep under a seat and awoke when the bus driver had returned to her home. The child was found wandering around the bus driver's neighborhood. The principal recommended to the superintendent that the bus driver be suspended without pay for 30 days and the superintendent adopted this recommendation. After 30 days, the assistant superintendent recommended that the bus driver's employment be terminated and the superintendent adopted this recommendation. Following a full hearing, the termination was upheld. The bus driver appealed to the school board, which affirmed the superintendent's decision and, subsequently, the bus driver appealed the board's decision to a Louisiana trial court. The trial court ruled in favor of the school board and the bus driver then appealed to the Louisiana Court of Appeal.

The court of appeal stated that sufficient evidence existed to find that the bus driver had neglected her duty. Further, it found that the bus driver had been afforded due process because she was informed of the charges against her, and received a full hearing where she confronted adverse witnesses. The court also stated that the driver was not prejudiced in any way by first being suspended without pay and then being discharged. The court of appeal affirmed the trial court's decision and upheld her discharge. *McLaughlin v. Jefferson Parish Sch. Bd.*, 560 So.2d 585 (La.App.5th Cir.1990).

A tenured Colorado teacher served as an advisor to a high school cheerleading squad. The high school competed in a basketball tournament at which the squad and advisors were lodged in motel rooms. The teacher allegedly drank beer with the cheerleaders in their room. The school board charged the teacher with neglecting her duty to supervise students under her care. A hearing was held, at which the hearing officer made no determination on whether the teacher's conduct constituted neglect of duty. He recommended that the teacher be retained with a five-day suspension. The school board adopted the hearing officer's fact-findings but rejected his recommendations for retention and ordered her dismissal. The teacher appealed to the Colorado Court of Appeals which affirmed her dismissal. The Colorado Supreme Court agreed to hear the teacher's appeal. It noted that tenured teachers may be dismissed only for proven misconduct or incompetence after a fair hearing. The Colorado Teacher Tenure Act permits school boards to review the evidence to determine whether the hearing officer's findings are justified. School boards have ultimate authority to dismiss or retain tenured teachers. They are bound by the fact-finder's evidence but are not bound by its final recommendations. The evidence was sufficient to find the teacher guilty of neglecting her duties and her dismissal was justified. *Blaine v. Moffet County School Dist.*, 748 P.2d 1280 (Colo.1988).

A Florida bus driver, who had been driving for 15 years, volunteered to complete the route of another driver whose riders were acting "completely out of control." When the most disruptive student failed to get off the bus at his stop, the driver ordered him to leave at the next stop. He did so only after striking her head and verbally abusing her. He then "mooned" her from the other side of the road. The driver swerved the bus across the center line to yell out the window that she intended to press charges against him. As a result, she was suspended and put in a nondriving position by the school board. The District Court of Appeal of Florida affirmed this decision despite the hearing officer's finding that the driver's actions had not been misconduct. The court upheld the board's conclusion that her behavior was misconduct under the circumstances. *Goss v. District School Board of St. Johns County*, 601 So.2d 1232 (Fla.App.5th Dist.1992).

C.   Homosexuality, Bisexuality and Transsexuality

Homosexuality among teachers has been the subject of a number of lawsuits dealing with dismissal. Generally the courts agree that homosexuality *per se*, absent a flaunting of sexual preference, is not grounds for dismissal or for not hiring a teacher. Additionally, however, in *Bowers v. Hardwick*, 106 S.Ct. 2841 (1986), the U.S. Supreme Court held that homosexual sodomy is not conduct protected by the privacy rights found in the U.S. Constitution.

A teacher was dismissed for immorality by his Oregon school district after a police officer observed him engaging in homosexual intercourse in a booth at an adult bookstore. The Fair Dismissal Appeals Board (FDAB), a review board composed of teachers, administrators and school board members, found that sexual intercourse in a public place offended the moral standards of the school community and the people of the state of Oregon. The board ruled that the teacher was guilty of immorality under Oregon law and upheld his dismissal. Following a series of appeals, the supreme court issued its decision holding that teacher "immorality" should not be defined by reference to community standards. The court proposed two possible immorality definitions but left to the FDAB the ultimate decision as to which of the two definitions to adopt. The FDAB was ordered to decide on a definition and then hear the teacher's case. *Ross v. Springfield School Dist. No. 19*, 716 P.2d 724 (Or.1986).

Teachers in Oklahoma brought a First Amendment challenge to a state statute that prevented teachers from advocating, soliciting, encouraging or promoting public or private homosexual activity in a manner that created a substantial risk that such conduct would come to the attention of school children. While recognizing that the state has an interest in regulating the speech of teachers that differs from its interest in regulating the speech of its general citizens, the U.S. Court of Appeals, Tenth Circuit, held that the statute was overbroad and that it had a deterrent effect on legitimate expression. Under the statute, any public statement that could come to the attention of school children, their parents, or school employees could result in a teacher's dismissal. Accordingly, the court held that those portions of the statute referring to the advocacy of public or private homosexual activity were unconstitutional. However, the portion of the statute which provided for the dismissal of any teacher for "public homosexual activity" was upheld. *Nat'l Gay Task Force v. Bd. of Educ.*, 729 F.2d 1270 (10th Cir.1984).

In 1968, a North Carolina principal sexually assaulted a male junior high school student. The principal was confronted by the school superintendent about the incident and he decided to resign. The principal did not admit or deny the assault to the superintendent. The next year, the principal decided to apply for a teaching position in another North Carolina school district. The new school district checked with two of the principal's references and was told he had left his previous position for health reasons. He was hired to teach and, at the end of the school year, he became principal of a high school in the district. Before he assumed this new position, the district's associate superintendent investigated a rumor that the principal was a homosexual. In doing so, the associate superintendent interviewed the principal's previous superintendent. The assault was not mentioned in this interview. In 1984, the principal resigned his position following a complaint that he had twice assaulted a fourth grade student. The student's parents sued the principal and numerous school officials, claiming that the officials were negligent in their hiring and investigation of the principal. The trial court dismissed the claims against the school officials and the parents appealed to the North Carolina Court of Appeals.

The court held that the dismissal was proper. It stated that there was no evidence that the school officials knew about the previous incident of abuse or that they could have discovered it through conducting a more thorough investigation. It also stated that yearly evaluations of the principal revealed no evidence that school officials had knowledge of the assaults. The school district could not be held liable for the assaults since they were committed outside the scope of the principal's employment. *Medlin v. Bass*, 286 S.E.2d 80 (N.C.App.1989).

D. Inappropriate Language

Several cases have occurred where objectionable language has been used in the classroom resulting in attempted dismissals of teachers. The courts generally look at the surrounding circumstances and consider the culpability of the teachers involved in making their decisions. If the language had a definite educational purpose and was not used merely for its own sake or if the teacher could not have prevented the language from being used, dismissal will usually not be upheld.

A Colorado middle school industrial arts teacher who also coached athletic teams was accused of making inappropriate comments to several students. The school board suspended the teacher with a warning that future such acts warranted dismissal. Within two years of the teacher's reinstatement, he became involved in several other incidents, including allegedly snapping a student's bra strap. The Colorado Court of Appeals affirmed the decision of a hearing officer upholding the dismissal of the instructor. The hearing officer had made no error in excluding some character evidence offered by the instructor. The instructor was not entitled to the defense of good faith under the state disciplinary code, because it was never alleged that any of the incidents involved student discipline. *Knowles v. Bd. of Educ.*, 857 P.2d 553 (Colo.App.1993).

A nonteaching assistant, employed by a school in Pennsylvania, was alleged to have made sexual advances toward a female high school student, which included physical contact. The principal filed a report concerning the allegation, and, after an investigation, the district recommended that the employee be discharged for violating school district regulations, for immorality and for other improper conduct. The employee was discharged. He then appealed pursuant to the grievance procedures set forth in the collective bargaining agreement. An arbitrator found that the employee had made verbal sexual advances, but concluded that the district had failed to prove that physical sexual harassment had occurred. The arbitrator converted the discharge into a disciplinary suspension. A state trial court reversed the arbitrator, upholding the discharge. Appeal was taken to the Commonwealth Court of Pennsylvania, where the court noted that the School Code gave the school district the right to remove an employee for violation of any school laws or for "other improper conduct." The employee's actions clearly fell within this area. Even though the physical harassment had not been proven, the repeated verbal harassment was sufficient to support the district's decision to discharge the employee. The court thus upheld the decision of the trial court against the employee. *Bd. of Educ. of School District of Philadelphia v. Philadelphia Federation of Teachers*, 610 A.2d 506 (Pa.Cmwlth.1992).

E.   Drug or Alcohol Abuse

Dismissal for drug or alcohol abuse has been at the center of a number of cases. Usually the seriousness of the offense as well as the continuation of abuse are factors weighed by courts in making their decisions.

A Kansas gym teacher was suspended for two days with pay after reports that he was intoxicated during class. Although cleared in a formal hearing, the school board did not renew the teacher's contract. The teacher received notice of the board's decision as well as an outline of his procedural rights. The teacher waived his right to a hearing and sued the school district in a federal court claiming that his suspension and eventual termination deprived him of property without due process. The district court held for the school district and the teacher appealed to the U.S. Court of Appeals, Tenth Circuit. The court held that by waiving his procedural rights, the teacher had destroyed his own due process claim. The court of appeals affirmed the district court's ruling. *Pitts v. Bd. of Educ. of U.S.D. 305*, 869 F.2d 555 (10th Cir.1989).

A continuing contract elementary school teacher engaged in an alcohol-related binge for three days after the end of a school year. The school board initiated an investigation of the teacher, and a hearing officer determined that since the events concerned were all privately conducted, there should be no sanctions. Nevertheless, the board dismissed the teacher for incompetence and misconduct. The teacher appealed to the Florida District Court of Appeal which reversed the dismissal. Here, a tenured teacher had "exhibited a human weakness to a few persons for a few days during a troubled time in her life." This was not enough to warrant a dismissal. The teacher was ordered reinstated. *Clark v. School Bd. of Lake County,* 596 So.2d 735 (Fla.App.5th Dist.1992).

Two 15-year-old girls testified at a grand jury hearing that they had smoked marijuana at the apartment of two brothers who were also teachers. The teachers both pleaded guilty to the misdemeanor of unlawful transactions with a minor. The board of education took statements from the girls and discharged the teachers. The issue before the Kentucky Supreme Court was whether the teachers could be dismissed for acts committed during off-duty hours, in the summer, and in the privacy of their own apartment. The court noted that "[a] teacher is held to a standard of personal conduct which does not permit the commission of immoral or criminal acts because of the harmful impression made on the students." The court decided that the brothers' misconduct was serious and of an immoral and criminal nature. It said that there was "a direct connection between the misconduct and the teachers' work," and held that the teachers' dismissals were proper because their actions constituted "conduct unbecoming a teacher." *Bd. of Educ. v. Wood,* 717 S.W.2d 837 (Ky.1986).

A Michigan high school teacher was charged with furnishing pills to students, encouraging a student to use marijuana, helping the student obtain marijuana, and failing to report the student's use of marijuana. A school board hearing was held at which the teacher stated that he was opposed to drug use and that he had never used marijuana. He also testified that he had previously enforced school drug and alcohol policies during a ski club trip that he chaperoned. The school board offered four student witnesses who testified that students used alcohol on the ski trip and that the teacher used marijuana. The teacher's employment was terminated. The teacher then received a hearing before a State Tenure Commission hearing officer. The commission affirmed the school board's actions. The teacher then filed a lawsuit charging that the student testimony should have been disregarded as prejudicial. The Michigan Court of Appeals held that the testimony was properly considered. The teacher's termination was upheld. *Nolte v. Port Huron Area School Dist. Bd. of Educ.,* 394 N.W.2d 54 (Mich.App.1986).

The Missouri Court of Appeals upheld the dismissal of a tenured teacher due to problems stemming from his habitual abuse of alcohol. At the dismissal hearing conducted by the school board, the evidence established that the teacher had a serious alcoholism condition dating back several years. On many occasions he had been in the presence of students while intoxicated, and at least once he was discovered by other school personnel on school grounds in a state of intoxication. Although he had spent 25 days at an alcohol treatment program, a substitute teacher later discovered a half-full bottle of vodka in his desk drawer, which he admitted to having consumed on school grounds. He was also involved in two alcohol-related automobile accidents, one of which occurred only 36 minutes after he left school in the afternoon and which found him with a blood alcohol content of .25 percent. The court held that this evidence justified the school board's conclusion that the teacher had a "physical or mental condition unfitting him to instruct or associate with children," as set forth by Missouri law, and upheld the dismissal. *Christy v. Bd. of Educ.*, 694 S.W.2d 280 (Mo.App.1985).

IV. INCOMPETENCE

Incompetence usually suffices as a reason for dismissal provided the proper procedures are followed.

A. Teaching Deficiencies

A Louisiana reading teacher showed his junior high school classes part of *Child's Play*, an R-rated movie about a doll possessed by the spirit of a maniacal killer. The superintendent of schools recommended dismissing the teacher, and sent the school board a letter listing alleged violations committed by the teacher up to five years before he showed the movie. The board voted for dismissal and the teacher appealed to a Louisiana trial court. The court held that the teacher had not received adequate notice of the charges against him and that the board had failed to sufficiently prove grounds for dismissal. The court ordered the teacher reinstated with backpay, and the board appealed to the Court of Appeal of Louisiana, Third Circuit. The court of appeal agreed with the trial court that the teacher had been substantially prejudiced by having to defend against the old charges. The board had no current policy concerning the showing of movies, and a colleague of the teacher had been suspended, rather than fired, for showing the same movie. The court of appeal affirmed the trial court's decision for the teacher. On rehearing, the court determined that a two-semester suspension was reasonably justified under the circumstances. It remanded the case for the imposition of a maximum two-semester suspension. *Jones v. Rapides Parish School Bd.*, 634 So.2d 1197 (La.App.3d Cir.1993).

A tenured teacher at a Louisiana junior high school showed a portion of the movie *Child's Play* to her second hour reading class of seventh graders. The school principal recommended to the school superintendent that the teacher be dismissed. The school board viewed the movie, and decided to suspend the teacher without pay for the first semester of the following school year, and to place her on probation for the remainder of the school year. She appealed unsuccessfully the school board's decision to a state trial court, and further appealed to the Court of Appeal of Louisiana. On appeal, the court noted that students had testified that there was no class discussion either before or after the movie. Also, the teacher admitted that she did not preview the movie before watching it in class. The court determined that the foul language and violent scenes documented in the record provided a rational basis for the conclusion that the teacher had wilfully neglected her duty, and that she had demonstrated incompetence by showing the movie to seventh graders. The court could perceive no educational value in the showing of the movie to a reading class. Accordingly, the court affirmed the trial court's decision against the teacher. *Roberts v. Rapides Parish School Board,* 617 So.2d 187 (La.App.3d Cir.1993).

A Missouri physical education teacher was fired by his school board. In support of its decision, the board noted that the teacher's style was too remedial for the students he was teaching; he used militaristic commands, he made frequent errors in grading, he used a pay phone outside his classroom after being instructed not to, he inappropriately referred to the school secretary as the principal's "lap dog," and he told a seventh grade student "we are going to make love" when asked what the day's class plan was. The teacher had been warned about his behavior on previous occasions. The teacher appealed, arguing that the findings did not rise to the level of incompetency, but rather reflected only a few errors and minor differences in teaching style. A circuit court upheld the termination, and the teacher appealed to the Missouri Court of Appeals. The court of appeals stated that the school board's findings were supported by the facts. It also stated that when viewed in their totality, the shortcomings of the teacher did rise to the level of incompetency and insubordination necessary for termination. Finally, the court held that the teacher had failed to remedy the complaints during a curative period between written warnings and the formal charge. The court affirmed the termination. *Nevels v. Bd. of Educ.,* 822 S.W.2d 898 (Mo.App.1991).

During a meeting with school officials, a Florida teacher was advised that deficiencies in her teaching must be remedied by the end of the school year or she would not be recommended for continued employment. After several additional meetings regarding deficiencies in her teaching, she was informed that the principal would not recommend renewal of her employment contract. The State Division of Administrative Hearings and the school board upheld the teacher's dismissal. She appealed to the District Court of Appeal of Florida, Third District, claiming that the order terminating her employment must be reversed because the school board did not comply with the notice requirements of Florida law. The appellate court held that, although the school board did not technically comply with the notice requirements, this was a harmless error and did not require reversal. *Krischer v. School Bd.,* 555 So.2d 436 (Fla.App.3d Dist.1990).

A North Dakota man was employed as superintendent of a school district for one academic year. After a negative evaluation of his performance, the school board voted unanimously not to renew his contract "for good cause." The superintendent sued the school district for reinstatement of his contract for the next academic year or for monetary damages. He claimed that he was discharged and not nonrenewed and thus the district did not follow the proper statutory procedures. A North Dakota trial court disagreed with the superintendent and dismissed the lawsuit. He then appealed to the North Dakota Supreme Court. The superintendent alleged that he was discharged because the school district used the words "for good cause." The supreme court stated that the superintendent asserted no legal authority for his argument. Thus, it affirmed the trial court's decision and held that the superintendent's contract had merely been nonrenewed. *Sailer v. Rhame Pub. School Dist. No. 17*, 455 N.W.2d 588 (N.D.1990).

A teacher in New York was responsible for grading his students' regents examinations. Regents examinations are achievement tests used to evaluate the quality of instruction and learning on state courses of study in New York secondary schools. After the examinations were graded, school officials noticed that the teacher's students' scores were significantly higher than those of other classes on the objective part of the examination. A large number of answers on the students' examinations were changed, some in ink different from that used by the students. The school district brought charges against the teacher for failing to guard the examinations and for altering the answers. A hearing panel found the teacher guilty of failing to guard the examinations only and recommended a six-month suspension period, but the state commissioner of education ruled that the teacher had changed the answers and ordered his dismissal. The teacher appealed. The New York Supreme Court, Appellate Division, noted that the teacher admitted that he realized the answers had been tampered with but that he did nothing about it. The court held that "[a]ltering the answers given on an examination, or even ignoring alterations obviously not made by the student, amounts to a serious breach of the teacher's obligations." The dismissal was affirmed. *Carangelo v. Ambach*, 515 N.Y.S.2d 665 (A.D.3d Dept.1987).

B. Procedural Problems

Two Baltimore school system teachers were dismissed for incompetence. In both cases, the teachers received "needs improvement" evaluations in consecutive years and received separate two-day hearings before the local education board. Both teachers were excessively late and absent, and both had classroom problems including poor lesson plan preparation and high failure rates. An administrative law judge determined that the teachers had received defective hearings because they had not been allowed to present arguments before the local board. The administrative law judge's decision was overturned by the state board of education, which reasoned that its *de novo* hearing had afforded the teachers an opportunity to present evidence in their favor. A Maryland trial court reversed this action, finding that the teachers had been denied important procedural benefits. The school board appealed to the Court of Special Appeals of Maryland. The Court of Special Appeals found that there was adequate evidence supporting the board's findings. The purpose of city public school procedures for evaluating teaching staff was to improve the instructional ability of the teachers, not to confer procedural benefits upon them. The teachers had been provided sufficient oral and written notice of the incompetence charges and the court reversed the trial court's decision, reinstating the board's action. *Bd. of School Commissioners of Baltimore City v. James*, 625 A.2d 361 (Md.App.1993).

A West Virginia school board fired a teacher for incompetency, cruelty, insubordination and neglect of duty. It sent him a termination letter, advising him that he had two days to request a hearing. The board then sent the teacher a letter advising him of his termination as of the end of the school year and giving him five days to request a hearing, without instructions about how to appeal. Four days later, the teacher presented a written request for a hearing to the board's assistant superintendent, who accepted it. However, no hearing was granted. Nearly two months later the teacher's attorney filed a petition in a West Virginia trial court. The court denied the teacher's petition for a writ of mandamus. The teacher then requested a hearing with the state education employee grievance board, which ruled that he was still entitled to a hearing. On the school board's appeal to a West Virginia trial court, the court ruled that the teacher had improperly filed the grievance and the teacher appealed to the West Virginia Supreme Court of Appeals. The court ruled that due process required school districts to properly notify and provide hearings to their employees prior to dismissal. The statute did not specify where to file grievances and it was reasonable for the teacher to give his request to the board. Notice to the teacher should have included instructions on where to file a grievance. Ruling that the teacher was still entitled to a hearing, the court reversed the trial court's decision. *Duruttya v. Bd. of Educ.*, 382 S.E.2d 40 (W.Va.1989).

An Illinois school district's collective bargaining agreement provided that during a necessary reduction in force the district could discharge a tenured teacher for "'discernible differences' in his teaching abilities, such that the teacher is not 'the best qualified candidate' for a position." Dismissals for "discernible differences" could be made regardless of a teacher's seniority in the school district, and could be made without notice or hearing. The Appellate Court of Illinois ruled that a teacher's dismissal for "discernible differences" was actually a dismissal for incompetence, and that a teacher dismissed under the provision has a right to due process. The court ordered the teacher reinstated. *Schafer v. Bd. of Educ.*, 510 N.E.2d 1186 (Ill.App.1st Dist.1987).

V. INSUBORDINATION

Courts will generally uphold the discharge of school employees if insubordination can be proven. However, where a charge of insubordination is based upon an employee's spoken words or writings, a school district must be careful to avoid disciplining the employee for speaking on matters of "public concern," which are matters protected by the First Amendment's free speech guarantees.

An Alabama school board reorganized its district, combining its high schools and a vocational school into a single facility. It notified affected teachers of their upcoming employment transfers prior to the commencement of the school year. The new facility was not completed at the start of the school year and teachers and students continued to report to old facilities until instructed otherwise. After several months, the board ordered an auto mechanics teacher to report to the new facility. He claimed that the new facility was not secure enough to protect his tools and equipment, and refused to report there. Administrators scheduled a meeting at which the teacher voiced his concerns. The teacher then stated that he would report to the new facility. However, when he failed to do so, the school board voted to terminate his contract. The state tenure commission affirmed the dismissal and appeal reached the Court of Civil Appeals of Alabama. The court of appeals found that the teacher's termination for insubordination and neglect of duty was justifiable under state law. Insubordination was defined as "the wilful refusal of a teacher to obey an order that a superior officer is entitled to have obeyed so long as such order is reasonably related to the duties of the teacher." Because the order to report to the new school was reasonable, the teacher's refusal to report there after receiving two reprimands constituted insubordination, and the court affirmed his dismissal. *Stephens v. Alabama State Tenure Comm.*, 634 So.2d 549 (Ala.Civ.App.1993).

A North Carolina teacher included a doll-making project in her seventh grade social studies class which the school's principal felt had no educational value. The principal instructed the teacher to quit the project but she refused, and also refused to participate in a professional development plan. The principal recommended dismissal on the grounds of inadequate performance, insubordination, and neglect of duty. The school board terminated the teacher's employment following a hearing before the board. The teacher claimed that the board violated her due process rights because the attorney who advised the board was from the same law firm as the attorney who presented the superintendent's case against her. The Court of Appeals of North Carolina affirmed a trial court decision for the school board, ruling that there was no evidence of bias or unfair prejudice and that there was substantial evidence supporting the trial court's decision. *Hope v. Charlotte-Mecklenburg Bd. of Educ.*, 430 S.E.2d 472 (N.C.App.1993).

A Kansas teacher scheduled a job interview in a Texas district and requested leave for that day. The principal denied the request because it was during the last week of the school year. The teacher went to the interview anyway and had his wife call in sick for him. Later that day, the principal of the district where he had interviewed called the principal of the school where the teacher worked asking for a recommendation. The principal, upon learning that the teacher had interviewed in Texas on the day he called in sick, called the teacher to his office and told him to leave school property. He was later fired for insubordination. After a hearing, the board approved the termination. The teacher appealed to a trial court for review of the board's decision. The court affirmed the board's termination of the teacher. The teacher then appealed to the Court of Appeals of Kansas. Insubordination is defined as a wilful or intentional disregard of reasonable instructions. The court held that a single incident of insubordination can be sufficient to justify termination. It stated that the teacher's act of calling in sick in order to attend a job interview was insubordination and justified his termination. *Gaylord v. Bd. of Educ., School Dist. 218*, 794 P.2d 307 (Kan.App.1990).

A Missouri school district terminated the employment of a teacher for inefficiency, misconduct, and insubordination. In support of its decision, the board of education noted that the teacher used profanity in front of students, physically accosted students, engaged in a physical confrontation with the parents of a student, and refused to accept duty schedules. The teacher sued the school board in a state trial court, which affirmed the board's decision. The teacher appealed to the Missouri Court of Appeals. On appeal, the teacher argued that his acts were insufficient to justify termination. The court, however, did not agree. It stated that even though the board's regulations on misconduct did not specifically mention use of profanity, the teacher's use of profanity could still be used to justify termination. In any case, the board had the discretion and authority to dismiss for a proven, one-time violation of board regulations. Since that was the case here, the court upheld the termination. *Catherine v. Bd. of Educ.*, 822 S.W.2d 881 (Mo.App.1991).

A South Dakota teacher requested leave of absence for personal reasons. While on leave, he took a teaching position in Alaska. In April, he filed a written notice of his intent to return to the South Dakota school. Although positions were open for which he was qualified, the school board refused to hire him. He then contacted his union representative and attempted to file a grievance with the board. The board informed him that he could not file a grievance because he was no longer considered an employee of the district. He then appealed to the state Department of Labor, Labor and Management Division, where the board maintained that he deceived it as to his reasons for his leave of absence. He was never told there were conditions or limits on the leave nor that he was prohibited from teaching while on leave. His leave of absence was never rescinded by the board and he was never advised that he had violated the terms of the leave until he was refused employment upon returning to the district. After rehearing, the department concluded that he did not deceive the superintendent or the board and was therefore entitled to personal leave and employment upon returning to the district. The decision was appealed to a South Dakota trial court which affirmed the department's decision that he was entitled to reinstatement. The board appealed to the Supreme Court of South Dakota. On appeal, the court determined that the leave of absence was valid on its face. It was authorized by the school board, his request was presented to and approved by the board, he was never informed he had violated the terms of his leave, and the board took no action to rescind or otherwise invalidate it. Therefore, the district did not carry its burden of proving deceit. The court upheld the decision of the trial court. *Rininger v. Bennett County School Dist.*, 468 N.W.2d (S.D.1991).

A teacher at a Colorado middle school received a letter of reprimand and a warning never to use physical measures to discipline a student. The warning came after two incidents in which she had touched or shaken students, although she never had struck a student. Thereafter, the teacher stopped two students from passing notes. When she did this, the student slapped her hand and struck her in the back. In response, the teacher pushed one student and lightly struck another student. As a result of the incident, her employment was terminated. An administrative law judge upheld the termination, and the teacher appealed to the Colorado Court of Appeals, claiming that the facts did not support a termination for good cause. The court noted that the termination was clearly based on the teacher's failure to comply with the letter of reprimand's prohibition against physical discipline. Such a directive, however, conflicted with the district's own written policy of allowing physical force when reasonably prudent. The principal's order was unreasonable since it divested the teacher of expressly granted authority. The court ordered reinstatement with full backpay and benefits. *Fredrickson v. Denver Public School Dist.*, 819 P.2d 1068 (Colo.App.1991).

A Florida school principal disagreed with the school's head custodian about whether to renew another custodian's contract. The principal considered the head custodian's conduct concerning this disagreement to be impolite and disrespectful, so he terminated his employment. The school board upheld the termination, but the District Court of Appeal of Florida reversed. The head custodian was supposedly fired for gross insubordination in accordance with Florida law. However, the court stated that while the head custodian's behavior may have been disrespectful, there was no competent substantial evidence that the custodian refused to obey a direct order of the principal. If the principal had given the custodian a letter of warning directly instructing him to cease his disruptive actions the result would have been different. The head custodian was reinstated for the remainder of the term of his annual contract. *Rosario v. Burke*, 605 So.2d 523 (Fla.App.2d Dist.1992).

VI. RESIGNATION AND RETIREMENT

Generally, once a resignation is tendered by an employee to the superintendent or school board, it may not be withdrawn unless the board approves of the reinstatement.

A.   Resignation

A Connecticut high school male teacher wrote flirtatious notes and a birthday card to a 16-year-old female student. The student showed the notes to her parents and they complained to the school's principal. He advised the teacher to refrain from any contact with the student pending an investigation, but the teacher instead approached the student to ask why she had reported him. He was then suspended with pay, and the school board voted to consider termination of his contract. The teacher agreed to resign in exchange for a severance pay package under which his resignation took effect after one year. During the year, the teacher sought to revoke his resignation, claiming that he had been forced to quit while suffering from depression and stress. The revocation was not accepted, so the teacher filed a lawsuit against the school board in a Connecticut trial court. The court awarded judgment to the board and the teacher appealed to the Appellate Court of Connecticut. The court of appeals determined that the trial court's ruling should be affirmed. *Geren v. Bd. of Educ. of the Town of Brookfield*, 36 Conn.App. 282, 650 A.2d 616 (1994).

A New York elementary school teacher, who had acquired tenure, obtained a probationary appointment to a special education position. During the term of this position, she was notified that the superintendent of schools would recommend her appointment be terminated. She tendered her resignation so that the adverse recommendation would not appear in her file. She later sought to withdraw her resignation because she had already acquired tenure by estoppel according to state education law. A trial court held in the teacher's favor, but the New York Supreme Court, Appellate Division, reversed. The resignation was not involuntary, and there had been no wrongdoing on the part of the school board, so the resignation was allowed to stand. *Gould v. Board of Education*, 584 N.Y.S.2d 910 (A.D.2d Dept.1992).

An Alabama woman was the secretary of a school for twelve years. After she was notified that she would be going from the position of secretary to that of a teacher's aide, she delivered a letter of resignation to the principal which was accepted. A replacement secretary was hired and began working. Two weeks later, the secretary attempted to rescind her resignation. However, one week later the board formally accepted her resignation. She filed a complaint in an Alabama trial court requesting that the board reinstate her. The court found for the school board. The secretary appealed to the Court of Civil Appeals of Alabama. She contended that her resignation was improperly accepted by the board because it had been previously withdrawn. However, the appellate court disagreed and determined that because the board had relied on her letter by hiring a replacement, it had accepted her resignation despite the informality. *Mitchell v. Jackson County Bd. of Educ.*, 582 So.2d 1128 (Ala.Civ.App.1991).

An Ohio geography teacher wished to resign his position so that he could begin work with a private employer. The superintendent indicated that the teacher would be allowed to resign if a certified teacher could be hired to replace him. After a replacement was found, the teacher immediately tendered his resignation. However, after only one day of work, the teacher called the superintendent and requested a withdrawal of his resignation. The superintendent declined. The teacher then unsuccessfully filed a complaint in an Ohio trial court asking the superintendent to reinstate him to his teaching position. The teacher appealed to the Court of Appeals of Ohio. The court of appeals held that the teacher's withdrawal of his resignation was ineffective where the board impliedly accepted the resignation by hiring a replacement. The court affirmed the trial court's decision. *Mullen v. Fayetteville-Perry Local School Dist.*, 557 N.E.2d 1235 (Ohio App.1988).

A Massachusetts school teacher submitted her resignation to the district superintendent. The district found a replacement and the teacher went to work at another school district. After two days of work, she decided that the position was not what she had expected. She requested her old district to take no action on her letter of resignation. She stated that she was ready to resume her teaching duties. The district refused to withdraw the resignation and the teacher sued seeking reinstatement. The trial court entered judgment in favor of the teacher and the district appealed. The Supreme Judicial Court of Massachusetts held that the teacher's attempt to withdraw her letter of resignation had no legal effect since the board did not actually need to take any action on a resignation. The court vacated the trial court's decision and entered judgment for the school committee. *Sinkevich v. School Comm. of Raynham*, 530 N.E.2d 173 (Mass.1988).

In 1980, parents began complaining to their West Virginia school board about a female kindergarten teacher's style of dress, which they considered too masculine. Rumors circulated that the teacher was involved in a homosexual relationship. In 1983, a public outcry arose after the state Attorney General issued an opinion stating that a school board could use public reputation in the community to establish a teacher's homosexuality and that it could dismiss a reputed homosexual teacher for immorality. Four hundred people appeared at a school board meeting to protest the teacher's continued presence in the classroom. The board postponed action on the matter until the next school board meeting. Prior to that meeting the teacher signed an agreement in which she agreed to resign her classroom teaching position. She later changed her mind and filed a lawsuit against the board of education seeking reinstatement and backpay. She alleged that she had signed the resignation under duress. The Supreme Court of Appeals of West Virginia ruled that even though the teacher's resignation was made in the face of allegations of homosexuality and improper dress, evidence supported the decision that it was not the product of duress. Reinstatement was denied. *Conway v. Hampshire County Bd. of Educ.*, 352 S.E.2d 739 (W.Va.1986).

B. Retirement

The Age Discrimination in Employment Act of 1967 (ADEA) and the Fourteenth Amendment's Equal Protection Clause provide evaluation standards for public school employee retirement. Please see Chapter Six, Section I. G. of this volume for cases brought under the ADEA. Where the ADEA is inapplicable (for example, where the employer maintains fewer than 20 employees), state law takes effect.

The Pennsylvania Public School Employees' Retirement System permits public school teachers to purchase service credit for work performed in public schools. Three public school teachers who had formerly worked for private schools sought to purchase service credit for their work at approved private schools. The state Public School Employees' Retirement Board denied the request, and the teachers appealed to the Commonwealth Court of Pennsylvania. On appeal, the teachers argued that they should be entitled to purchase credit in the system because the private schools were subject to regulation by the state education department. They also argued that they were entitled to purchase credit because the private schools were reimbursed by the education department for teaching exceptional students placed in private schools by public school districts. The commonwealth court determined that state regulation was insufficient to confer public school status upon private schools. The legislative intent of the retirement code provision was to benefit public school employees, and the teachers' private school employment did not relate to public employment. Accordingly, the court affirmed the retirement board's order denying the purchase of service credit. *Cain v. Pub. School Employees' Ret. System*, 651 A.2d 660 (Pa.Cmwlth.1994).

A Michigan school superintendent was accused of making unauthorized expenditures and the board of education unanimously voted not to renew his contract. The superintendent sued the board in a Michigan trial court claiming that an employment handbook published by the board created a valid entitlement to a one-year assistance program prior to termination for unsatisfactory performance. The court awarded the superintendent over $1.1 million, which included his salary for six years and an early retirement benefit. The Court of Appeals of Michigan held that the employment handbook entitled the superintendent to only one year's salary, which was the duration of the assistance program. Accordingly, the court reduced the damages to $118,000, an amount equal to one year's salary plus the early retirement benefit. *Thorin v. Bloomfield Hills Bd. of Educ.*, 513 N.W.2d 230 (Mich.App.1994).

A West Virginia teacher worked for a county school board from 1960 to 1971, when she resigned. She was tenured from 1963 to 1971. Beginning in 1979, she contracted with the school board, on an annual basis, to be a substitute teacher. In 1987, she sought a full-time teaching position with the board. She applied for roughly 29 posted vacancies. She maintained that she should have been hired because her qualifications were superior to the successful applicant in at least three cases. She filed a grievance. The teacher was found to be entitled to employment, but a state hearing examiner reversed that decision. A state circuit court upheld the examiner's decision and the teacher appealed to the Supreme Court of Appeals of West Virginia. On appeal, the teacher argued that she had seniority in matters of employment because her reemployment as a substitute teacher resurrected her seniority of eleven years. Because of this, she argued that she was entitled to a written statement of the reasons why she was not selected. The supreme court disagreed. It held that seniority is not resurrected upon reemployment with the same board of education. Resurrection of seniority would be inconsistent with West Virginia law dealing with seniority and the usual meaning of the term. In addition, the teacher could produce no evidence that she was decidedly superior to the other candidates aside from longer length of service. Since seniority is a tie-breaker only among equally qualified candidates, the decision not to hire the teacher was upheld. *Triggs v. Berkeley County Bd. of Educ.*, 420 S.E.2d 260 (W.Va.1992).

A tenured secretary gave early notice of her intent to return to a school district so that she could gain additional benefits under a collective bargaining agreement. The district accepted. After her husband died and her child fell ill, she requested a two-year extension of her intended retirement date. The school board conditioned its acceptance of the request on a satisfactory job performance evaluation. A problem later developed which eventually led to a denial of the requested extension. The secretary appealed, arguing that none of the other 17 recent extensions had been subject to such conditions. The issue reached the Supreme Court of New Jersey. The court held that the dispute must be resolved in light of the parties' mutual intent. The collective bargaining agreement addressed notification of intent to retire, but did not address whether it could be modified. Therefore, the court ruled that the board's past practices evidenced the parties' intent. Specifically, the board's almost rubber stamp acceptances of other extension requests was held to have had the legal effect of notice to employees that the notices could be rescinded. The court noted, however, that the limited scope of this decision did not extend to cases of a board's reliance and estoppel, nor did it apply where an alteration in past practices was adequately distinguished. The cause was remanded for a determination of damages. *Hall v. Bd. of Educ.*, 593 A.2d 304 (N.J.1991).

New Jersey law allowed institutions of higher education within the state the discretion to retire tenured faculty at age 70. A group of previously and currently tenured faculty members at various New Jersey state colleges sued, claiming that the statute which granted that discretion was unconstitutional because it amounted to discrimination on the basis of age. They claimed that such discrimination violated the Equal Protection and Due Process Clauses of the Fourteenth Amendment and similar provisions of the New Jersey state constitution. The state claimed that the statute violated neither constitution and moved for summary judgment. The U.S. District Court, District of New Jersey, stated that in order to withstand constitutional scrutiny, statutes which make classifications based on age must be rationally related to a legitimate governmental interest. Making way for the young, planning for the future, creating greater diversity, injecting new energy, reducing costs, and similar interests all supported the statute. Even though these same bases are often used to support acts of age discrimination, they were sufficient to support the statute against constitutional challenge. *Freund v. Florio,* 795 F.Supp. 702 (D.N.J.1992).

An Oklahoma teacher, who was 69, received a notice that her teaching contract would not be renewed for the next year. The letter stated that the sole reason for nonrenewal was the mandatory retirement policy, and that she was otherwise a competent teacher. She requested an administrative hearing at which the hearing officer determined that the school board had the authority to set a mandatory age requirement. She then filed this action in an Oklahoma trial court seeking reinstatement. The trial court affirmed the hearing officer's decision stating that the school board had the authority to set a mandatory retirement age so long as it was not discriminatory. The woman then appealed to the Court of Appeals of Oklahoma. The court noted that "the school board has and can exercise those powers that are granted in express words." The teacher asserted that there was no express statutory authority and power in the local school board to establish a mandatory retirement age. The appellate court noted that the state legislature excluded a mandatory retirement age for teachers in its education laws. In fact, the education statutes clearly contemplated teachers remaining active beyond age 70. Therefore, in the absence of statutory authority the school board was not empowered to adopt a mandatory retirement policy based solely on age. The appellate court reversed the decision of the trial court. *Carlyle v. Indep. School Dist. I-71,* 811 P.2d 618 (Okl.App.1991).

An Oklahoma certified teacher with 33 years of experience taught for eight of those years as a substitute teacher—working more than 120 days in each of those years. She was told that she could purchase those years for retirement purposes, but eventually the board of trustees of the retirement system denied her credit for the eight years in question. She sued in state court, and won. On appeal to the Court of Appeals of Oklahoma, the court agreed that the board's decision to deny retirement credit was arbitrary and capricious. The decision for the teacher was affirmed. *State Ex Rel. Board of Trustees of Teachers' Retirement System v. Garrett,* 848 P.2d 1182 (Okl.App.1993).

A Massachusetts public school tutor worked part-time for five years during which she was ineligible to participate in the state teachers' retirement system. The system withheld five percent of compensation from each employee who was a "member in service of the system." After becoming a full-time teacher and serving for ten years, the former tutor petitioned the retirement board to purchase creditable service for her part-time work. The county retirement board accepted liability for only part of the tutor's part-time service. Contrary to the teacher's assertion that she should only pay five percent of her compensation for that time period, the board required the former tutor to contribute seven percent of her compensation in order to receive creditable service. The Supreme Judicial Court of Massachusetts affirmed a state level hearing officer's decision, ruling that the former tutor should contribute seven percent of all her past, present and future contributions. This was because the effective date of her entry into the retirement system determined her rate of contribution, rather than the date of her commencement of employment. *McIntire v. Contributory Retirement Appeal Bd.*, 417 Mass. 35, 627 N.E.2d 910 (1994).

C. Retirement Benefits

A retired Washington school superintendent challenged a Department of Retirement Systems ruling regarding the computation of his retirement pay. The superintendent's retirement pay was to be calculated using his "average earnable compensation" for his two highest compensated consecutive years of service. In each of the years used in calculating his retirement pay the superintendent submitted travel expense vouchers in the amount of $2,400. The Department of Retirement Systems did not include the travel expense reimbursement in calculating his earnable compensation. The superintendent appealed. The Court of Appeals of Washington affirmed the Department's ruling, holding that reimbursement of travel expenses was not earnable compensation. *Coble v. Hollister*, 788 P.2d 3 (Wash.Ct.App.1990).

A grade school teacher obtained health insurance coverage under a policy issued to the Mississippi Association of Educators. After undergoing extensive medical treatment, she found that the insurer would not pay her claims. She hired an attorney, and eventually the insurer provided coverage. She then sued the insurer for bad faith in a state court. The insurer removed the case to federal court, asserting that the suit was preempted by the Employee Retirement Income Security Act (ERISA). The teacher asserted that ERISA did not preempt her suit, and the court granted her summary judgment on the issue because the policy fell within the "safe-harbor" provisions of the Department of Labor regulations. That is, the plan was completely voluntary; no contributions were made by the association; the association did not endorse the plan; and it received no compensation from the insurer. *Cooley v. Protective Life Ins. Co.,* 815 F.Supp. 189 (S.D.Miss.1993).

A New Jersey school psychologist retired after almost 23 years of service at a monthly pension of $1,465. The psychologist was later charged with and convicted of criminal sexual contact with a former student which occurred during the psychologist's school employment. The school board determined that any services by the psychologist after the abuse incident should not be included for retirement benefit purposes. It reduced the psychologist's monthly pension benefit to $655 and claimed an overpayment of over $46,000, for which it demanded repayment. An administrative law judge affirmed the school board's action and the psychologist appealed to the Superior Court of New Jersey, Appellate Division. On appeal, the psychologist claimed that the board's action was arbitrary and capricious and violated his constitutional guarantee against double jeopardy as an additional punishment for the same offense. The school board argued that its action was a remedial civil sanction that did not involve punishment. The court stated that forfeiture of pension rights may be based on the violation of an implied condition that public employees will render honorable service. It likened the forfeiture to damages for breach of contract. Although the forfeiture did not violate the psychologist's guarantee against double jeopardy, the case was remanded for a determination of whether repayment of the $46,000 in excess payments to the pension fund at $270 per month constituted a hardship to the psychologist. *Leprince v. Bd. of Trustees, Teachers' Pension and Annuity Fund*, 631 A.2d 545 (N.J.Super.A.D.1993).

An employee of a Florida county school board filed an application for regular and in-line-of-duty disability retirement benefits, stating that she had experienced "on the job" accidents on two previous occasions. After being denied benefits, she asked for an administrative hearing. She was notified that all documents, including depositions, had to be received by the state retirement commission at least 10 days before the hearing. She failed to make the deadline, was granted a continuance, and again failed to make the deadline. The commission refused to accept the "late" depositions, and the District Court of Appeal of Florida affirmed the denial of benefits. There was no abuse of discretion in refusing the depositions. *Alsobrook v. State, Division of Retirement*, 600 So.2d 1173 (Fla.App.1st Dist.1992).

A Washington school teacher announced her retirement, and elected to receive a lump sum of her accumulated retirement contributions, together with a reduced monthly retirement allowance. She designated her husband as her beneficiary upon death. The teacher died before the end of the month in which she announced her retirement. The state retirement system stated that because the teacher did not survive until her first retirement payment became due, the husband was limited to receiving either the lump sum or an unreduced monthly allowance, but not both. The husband sued the retirement system in a Washington trial court, which granted summary judgment to the system. He then appealed to the Washington Court of Appeals. The court of appeals initially reversed the trial court's decision, but granted the system's motion for reconsideration. On reconsideration, the court noted that because the teacher had not survived until the end of the month, when pension payments became due, the survivorship requirement governed the husband's benefits. He was therefore to receive either the full monthly allowance or a lump sum, but not both. The court affirmed the trial court decision. *Knack v. Dept. of Retirement Systems*, 776 P.2d 687 (Wash.App.1989).

A California physical education teacher had taught only physical education during her 25-year teaching career. In the fall of 1984, the teacher fell and twisted her right knee while performing her duties as a physical education teacher. After she returned to work, the condition of her knee deteriorated. She underwent arthroscopic surgery and the doctor concluded that she was legitimately disabled from her normal activities as a physical education teacher. She then filed an application with the teachers' retirement board for a disability allowance. The board determined that the teacher had obtained sufficient educational units 30 years earlier to obtain teaching credentials in subjects other than physical education. It thus denied her application. A California trial court ordered the board to provide the allowance and the board appealed to the Court of Appeal of California. The appellate court held that benefits could not be denied to the teacher because the board had not sufficiently shown that the teacher could become a classroom teacher. The award of benefits was affirmed. *Abshear v. Teachers' Retirement Bd.*, 282 Cal.Rptr. 833 (Cal.App.1991).

A retired Montana school administrator applied for benefits under the voluntary career option plan which offered retirement benefits identical to those offered to teachers. His contract provided that he receive fringe benefits in the same amounts as all the other employees of the school district. The school district denied his application because he was specifically excluded under the plan. After the state superintendent affirmed, the administrator appealed to a Montana trial court. The trial court affirmed and the administrator appealed to the Supreme Court of Montana. Although the supreme court affirmed the decision of the superintendent and denied benefits, it determined that he was eligible to later receive benefits under the plan. However, he had not attained the required 13 years in district service and did not yet qualify. *Throssell v. Bd. of Trustees,* 812 P.2d 767 (Mont.1991).

VII. UNEMPLOYMENT BENEFITS

Generally, where a school employee has worked a specified minimum amount of time, unemployment benefits will be available. However, if the employee has committed misconduct resulting in dismissal for cause, benefits are properly denied or lowered.

A Rhode Island school committee voted not to renew the employment contracts of eight teachers because of the anticipated return from leave of several more senior teachers. The committee also voted not to renew the contract of the least senior of three speech pathologists employed by the district. The district's deputy superintendent advised the teachers that he expected at least 20 vacancies the following school year. The superintendent of schools sent a letter to each teacher advising them that they could expect reemployment the following year. The teachers and the speech pathologist filed claims for unemployment compensation that were denied on the basis of reasonable assurances of being reemployed the following year. The employees appealed to a Rhode Island district court, which held that the unemployment compensation board's decisions were clearly erroneous. The state board appealed to the Supreme Court of Rhode Island.

The court observed that the state unemployment compensation statute distinguished between school employees who were unemployed, and those who were temporarily out of work because of holidays or summer break. Teachers who were currently under contract or who received reasonable assurances of employment for the upcoming school year were ineligible for unemployment benefits. There was sufficient evidence in the record that the teachers had received reasonable assurances of reemployment. The speech pathologist's claim was distinguishable because her certification was limited to speech pathology and she had not received assurances from the district that she would be reemployed. She was entitled to receive unemployment compensation benefits. *Baker v. Dept. of Employment and Training Bd. of Review*, 637 A.2d 360 (R.I.1994).

A custodial supervisor with 21 years of experience was fired for misconduct by a Texas school district. This was done on the basis of his relationship with a coworker. The employee claimed that the district had never given him a written warning not to have relations with the coworker and that his supervisor had told him that whatever he did after hours was his own business. The Texas Employment Commission denied the employee's claim for unemployment benefits, but its decision was overruled by a Texas trial court. The Court of Appeals of Texas, Amarillo, affirmed the trial court's decision, finding strong evidence that the employee was never told not to engage in the behavior for which he had been fired. *Levelland Indep. School Dist. v. Contreras*, 865 S.W.2d 474 (Tex.App.— Amarillo 1993).

A New York school district hired a probationary teacher to teach business education for a three-year probationary term. The district informed her that her continued employment with the district was contingent upon her taking and passing the National Teacher's Examination (NTE). Although the NTE consists of three separate parts, the teacher chose to take only one part, which she failed. She was again told that she had to take and pass the NTE to continue working in the district. However, the next time the test was offered, she registered for only two of the three parts. She was then discharged. When she sought unemployment insurance benefits, the New York Supreme Court, Appellate Division, found that she had voluntarily engaged in conduct which eliminated any possibility that she could keep her employment. Accordingly, she was disqualified from receiving unemployment insurance benefits. *Matter of Ambrose* 595 N.Y.S.2d 126 (A.D.3d Dept.1993).

A Minnesota woman worked for a school district as a full-time educational assistant in an adult student program. She worked continuously, twelve months per year. On June 7, 1991, the district discharged her for economic reasons. She applied for unemployment benefits and was found to be eligible. However, the school district informed her that it would rehire her beginning in July 1991. She signed a contract to that effect and resumed working July 1. The state Department of Jobs & Training held that the assistant was ineligible for unemployment from the time she was informed she would be rehired to the time she began working (a period of two weeks). The assistant appealed, but the department commissioner affirmed the denial. She then appealed to the Minnesota Court of Appeals. The court noted that Minnesota law prohibited the payment of unemployment compensation to a public school employee whose unemployment commences between academic years if there are assurances that the employee will be employed again at the beginning of the next academic year. The court stated that this was true even if the employee normally worked year round, as was the case here. The employee was denied the benefits. *Swanson v. Indep. School District. No. 625*, 484 N.W.2d 432 (Minn.App.1992).

A woman worked for a Vermont school as a secretary in the housekeeping and maintenance departments. During the course of her employment, the head of maintenance (her supervisor) made sexual advances toward her on at least three occasions. Although the employee objected to and fended off the supervisor's harassment, she never told anyone else of the offending behavior. She quit, but when she sought unemployment compensation the Vermont Employment Security Board denied her benefits. The board stated that the school's business manager had no knowledge of the harassment. Therefore, he had no opportunity to remedy the problem. The employee then appealed to the Vermont Supreme Court. The supreme court stated that a person is disqualified from receiving unemployment benefits if she voluntarily terminates employment without good cause attributable to the employer. An employee who is harassed on a job by a coworker may have good cause to quit. The crucial determination is whether the actions can be attributable to the employer. The court held that knowledge may be imputed to the employer in situations where the harassment took place at the office, during working hours, and was carried out by someone with the authority to hire, fire, promote and discipline. This conclusion was also bolstered by the fact that the school had an inadequate procedure for dealing with acts of sexual harassment. The court reversed the board's conclusion that sexual harassment could not be attributable to the school because of lack of notice. It remanded for a determination on whether the employee quit for good cause given the circumstances. *Allen v. Dept. of Employment Training*, 618 A.2d 1317 (Vt.1992).

The superintendent of an Iowa community school district was rated unsatisfactory by his school board. At a public meeting evaluating his performance, the superintendent refused to answer any of the board's questions. The board terminated the superintendent's contract. The superintendent immediately applied for unemployment benefits which were ultimately denied on the basis of misconduct. The superintendent appealed that decision to the Iowa Supreme Court. The supreme court stated that there must be a direct causal relationship between the misconduct and the discharge in order for an employee to be ineligible for unemployment benefits. The record did not indicate that the superintendent was discharged for refusing to answer the questions. Rather, he was discharged for poor performance. As a result he was eligible for benefits. *West v. Employment Appeal Bd.*, 489 N.W.2d 731 (Iowa 1992).

A physical education instructor had an altercation with another instructor. No threats were made by him and there was no physical contact between the two. Nevertheless, he was discharged. He filed for unemployment benefits, and the Unemployment Insurance Appeal Board found that he was entitled to receive benefits. The school appealed to the New York Supreme Court, Appellate Division. The court stated that while the teacher may have displayed bad judgment in the altercation, this did not automatically render him ineligible to receive benefits. The teacher's actions were not misconduct so as to disqualify him from receiving benefits. *Matter of Warnock*, 583 N.Y.S.2d 614 (A.D.3d Dept.1992).

A teacher distributed a joke sheet to another faculty member, and it was further distributed throughout the faculty and the community. The joke sheet contained racial jokes and was described as a "hate sheet." The school terminated the teacher, and he was subsequently denied unemployment compensation benefits. The teacher appealed the denial of benefits by claiming that he read only the first two jokes and that he did not realize their racial nature. He further contended that the conduct was unintentional, and not sufficiently related to his work. The teacher's appeal came before the Commonwealth Court of Pennsylvania. The nature of the jokes was held to be evident from the first joke. The teacher's conduct was found to be "a horrible example" for students. Because the conduct took place during the school term, and involved a fellow worker, it was held to be sufficiently related to work so as to justify the denial of benefits. *Reitmeyer v. Unemployment Compensation Board of Review*, 602 A.2d 505 (Pa.Cmwlth.1992).

VIII. WRONGFUL DISCHARGE

The chair of the reading department at an Illinois high school learned that a male teacher in her department was accused of sexual misconduct by two students. Although the teacher was reprimanded, school administrators did not file a report in his personnel file or file a report with the state children and family services department. The chair reported the incident to the family services department and gave the teacher a harsh evaluation. Before the end of the month, school officials merged the English department with the reading department and eliminated the chair's position. The chair believed that this action was taken in retaliation for her report to the state agency. She sued the school board in the U.S. District Court for the Northern District of Illinois, alleging constitutional violations. After two years of pretrial activity, the chair's attorney accepted a job with the law firm that represented the school board. She filed a motion for disqualification of the school board's firm. The court denied the motion, and also granted the school board's summary judgment motion. The chair appealed to the U.S. Court of Appeals, Seventh Circuit.

The court of appeals ruled that the trial court had properly dismissed the motion to disqualify the school board's law firm. The evidence indicated that the board had taken adequate precautions to screen the chair's former attorney from involvement in the lawsuit. There was also no evidence that the chair's former attorney divulged any client confidences to the law firm. The district court had properly granted summary judgment to the school board as there was uncontradicted evidence that the department had been reorganized for legitimate reasons. *Cromley v. Bd. of Educ. of Lockport Township High School Dist. 205*, 17 F.3d 1059 (7th Cir.1994).

A New Jersey shop teacher who had not acquired tenure complained to the school principal about safety and air quality conditions in his metal shop. After submitting numerous complaints and being transferred to teach plastic shop, he complained to the superintendent of schools. The principal obtained an air quality test which determined that the teacher's classroom was safe. He then recommended that the teacher not be rehired, thus depriving him of tenure. The teacher filed a lawsuit against the board of education, alleging retaliatory discharge in violation of the state Conscientious Employee Protection Act (CEPA), and seeking punitive damages. A trial court awarded the teacher compensatory damages of $60,000 as well as punitive damages. The court granted the board of education's posttrial dismissal motion, but the jury's verdict was reinstated by the New Jersey Superior Court, Appellate Division. The school board appealed to the Supreme Court of New Jersey.

The supreme court considered whether the board of education could be held vicariously liable for the principal's actions under CEPA for refusing to rehire the teacher because of his concern for school safety conditions. The court found that traditional principles of *respondeat superior* (vicarious employer liability) applied in CEPA actions, and that punitive damages should be allowed under the act regardless of whether the employer is a public entity. The record supported a finding that the board's action constituted retaliatory discharge. The teacher had reasonably believed that his workplace was unsafe and his complaints were protected by public policy. The court affirmed the judgment for the teacher. *Abbamont v. Piscataway Bd. of Educ.*, 138 N.J. 405, 650 A.2d 958 (1994).

A Tennessee school board employed a personnel secretary under two successive one-year employment contracts. She underwent cosmetic surgery, which her supervisor felt was unnecessary. He advised the school's insurance carrier against paying for the surgery, but it eventually paid the claims when the secretary threatened legal action. When the school superintendent failed to recommend reemployment of the secretary for a third year, she filed a lawsuit against the superintendent, education board and supervisor in a Tennessee trial court, alleging retaliatory discharge, interference with employment relationships and interference with contractual rights under the insurance plan. The court granted summary judgment to the board and school officials and the secretary appealed to the Court of Appeals of Tennessee.

The court of appeals held that sovereign immunity was a complete defense to the secretary's retaliatory discharge claim. The complaint failed to state a valid claim against any individual school officers for retaliatory discharge or intentional interference with employment relationships. However, the trial court had improperly granted summary judgment on the insurance contract interference claim. The supervisor had failed to contravene evidence that he had tried to prevent payment of the claim and there was evidence of malice in his action. Because a showing had been made that the supervisor had openly opposed payment of the medical bills, the secretary's claim for interference with her insurance contract was remanded to the trial court. The Supreme Court of Tennessee refused to consider further appeal of the case. *Williams v. Williamson County Bd. of Educ.*, 890 S.W.2d 788 (Tenn.App.1994).

A North Carolina teacher was employed to teach health and physical education. However, her principal reassigned her to a coordinator position and allegedly placed her in a small office in the girls' locker room, where the temperature was 90 to 100 degrees. The teacher complained that these and other conditions were so intolerable that she was forced to resign. She sued the board of education, principal and several others in a North Carolina trial court for intentional infliction of emotional distress, constructive wrongful discharge, malicious interference with contract and punitive damages. The court granted summary judgment motions by the school board and individuals, and refused to compel discovery concerning the successor teacher's relationship with the student. The teacher appealed to the Court of Appeals of North Carolina. The court of appeals agreed that it was within the trial court's discretion to hold that the conduct in this case did not amount to extreme and outrageous behavior. Insults and indignities did not support a claim for intentional infliction of emotional distress. There was no evidence of malicious interference with contract and no legitimate claim for constructive wrongful discharge. Because all the other claims were dismissed, there was no basis for the punitive damages claim. The court affirmed the summary judgment order of the trial court. *Wagoner v. Elkin City Schools' Bd. of Educ.*, 440 S.E.2d 119 (N.C.App.1994).

A Kentucky woman worked in her local high school as the principal's secretary. The principal was also her husband. The secretary worked under a year-to-year contract. Her husband and the superintendent subsequently had a disagreement over personnel policy. The decision to rehire the secretary each year rested with the superintendent. Following his dispute with her husband, he recommended that she not be rehired. She sued in a Kentucky federal court, which held against her, finding that there was no constitutional right implicated. The secretary then appealed to the U.S. Court of Appeals, Sixth Circuit. The court of appeals stated that the evidence was clearly sufficient to support a jury determination that the superintendent refused to recommend the secretary for continued employment because of her marriage to the principal. If this were indeed the case, this would infringe on her constitutional right of privacy in association. While the secretary had no contractual right to a job, she could not be deprived of her public employment for exercising a constitutional right. The court remanded the case for a second trial, stating that the superintendent would still be given the opportunity to prove that the secretary's marriage relationship was not a substantial or motivating factor in the decision not to continue her employment. *Adkins v. Bd. of Educ. of Magoffin County,* 982 F.2d 952 (6th Cir.1993).

A Texas man worked as a substitute teacher for the Houston school district. He signed a substitute teaching form, not a standard teaching contract. The form stated that there might not be an assignment available each day. He agreed to study the substitute teacher guidelines, and refrain from administering corporal punishment, touching students, or using inappropriate language. After teaching for some time, the school district received complaints from two different schools that the substitute teacher yelled at students, often used profanity, and pinched students. As a result, the substitute's name was removed from the district's available teacher list. The teacher sued, claiming that the district violated his right to due process when it removed him from the substitute teacher list. He also claimed he was denied equal protection of the laws and that he was entitled to damages under 42 U.S.C. § 1983. The U.S. District Court, Southern District of Texas, held for the school district. It stated that the substitute had failed to prove that he had a property interest in continued employment with the school district as required by *Bd. of*

Regents v. Roth, 408 U.S. 464, 92 S.Ct. 2701, 33 L.Ed.2d 548 (1972). Employment for an indefinite term may be terminated at will and without cause under Texas law unless a teacher is entitled to continued employment due to tenure or some other statutory protection. No such protection applied here. The substitute also failed to show a violation of a protected liberty interest, since the school district did not publicize the reason for his discharge. The court also stated that the class of substitute teachers is not a protected class for equal protection analysis. Since the teacher was unable to prove a constitutional violation, he was not entitled to damages under 42 U.S.C. § 1983. *Jones v. Houston Ind. School Dist.*, 805 F.Supp. 476 (S.D.Tex.1991).

A member of a Colorado board of education applied for a position as a teacher of educationally disabled students at a school with her school district. She was offered a half-time position subject to the approval of the board of education. The board voted not to hire her, reasoning that as long as she was a member of the board, her employment within the district would constitute a conflict of interest. She sued, claiming that the board's conflict of interest policy created an impermissible classification in violation of her right to equal protection of the laws. Specifically, she claimed that spouses of board members may teach without creating a conflict of interest and there was no logical distinction between the two. A trial court held for the board, but the court of appeals reversed. The board appealed to the Colorado Supreme Court. The supreme court stated that the board had a legitimate interest in establishing and enforcing a conflict of interest policy for its members. It also stated that the current policy was rationally related to that goal because there was a difference between board member employment and spousal employment. Board member employment effects are more direct. In addition, husband and wife cannot be viewed as a single entity, so including close relations within the conflict policy creates line drawing problems. The supreme court reversed the court of appeals. *Montrose County School Dist. v. Lambert*, 826 P.2d 349 (Colo.1992).

A teacher consultant was employed by the New Hampshire State Board of Education from 1974 until 1979 under a series of year-to-year contracts, and by the school board of a school administrative unit (SAU) from 1980 until 1983. The SAU was comprised of six school districts. In 1982, the SAU informed him that his contract would not be renewed. It also informed him that it would not provide him with either a statement of reasons or a hearing. The consultant sought the commissioner of education's review, but after a hearing, the commissioner upheld the termination decision. Bypassing his right to a full evidentiary hearing before the state board of education, the consultant sued in New Hampshire state court, claiming that he had been fired in violation of public policy for refusing to criticize the superintendent in public. He also claimed a due process violation. The trial court found for the consultant and the SAU appealed to the New Hampshire Supreme Court. The supreme court reversed the trial court's decision. First, the court stated that the consultant's due process claim must fail because he did not have a protected property interest in continued employment with the SAU. There was nothing binding the SAU to renew his contract. Even if he had a protected property interest, he had been afforded all the process that was due, since he bypassed the state evidentiary hearing on his own. Second, his wrongful termination claim also failed. While loyalty to the superintendent may be an admirable quality, it is not the type of public policy sufficient to maintain a wrongful termination claim. *Short v. School Administrative Unit No. 16*, 612 A.2d 364 (N.H.1992).

CHAPTER EIGHT

TENURE AND DUE PROCESS

I.   TENURE AND DUE PROCESS

State tenure laws create property rights in public employment that vest school employees with certain procedural rights. These rights vary from state to state according to the type of personnel action. In cases of employment termination, tenured school employees are generally entitled to notice and an opportunity to respond to the charges, a hearing with the right to confront and cross-examine witnesses, and the right to be represented by counsel. These and other related procedural protections are referred to as due process rights.

Two U.S. Supreme Court decisions, *Board of Regents v. Roth*, 408 U.S. 564, 92 S.Ct. 2701, 33 L.Ed.2d 548 (1972) and *Perry v. Sindermann*, 408 U.S. 593, 92 S.Ct. 2694, 33 L.Ed.2d 570 (1972), help define the due process rights of teachers. The *Roth* case explained that in order for a teacher to be entitled to due process, the teacher must have a "liberty" or "property" interest at stake. The teacher in *Roth* was hired at a Wisconsin university for a fixed contract term of one year. At the end of the year, he was informed that he would not be rehired. No hearing was provided and no reason was given for the decision not to rehire. In dismissing the teacher's due process claims, the Supreme Court stated that no liberty interest was implicated because in declining to rehire the teacher, the university had not made any charge against him such as incompetence or immorality. Such a charge would have made it difficult for the teacher to gain employment elsewhere and thus would have deprived him of liberty. As no reason was given for the nonrenewal of his contract, the teacher's liberty interest in future employment was not impaired and he was not entitled to a hearing on these grounds. The Court declared that because the teacher had not acquired tenure he possessed no property interest in continued employment at the university. To be sure, the teacher had a property interest in employment during the term of his one-year contract, but upon its expiration the teacher's property interest ceased to exist. The Court stated: "To have a property interest in a benefit, a person clearly must have more than an abstract need or desire for it. He must have more than a unilateral expectation of it. He must, instead, have a legitimate claim of entitlement to it."

The *Sindermann* case involved a teacher employed at a Texas university for four years under a series of one-year contracts. When he was not rehired for a fifth year he brought suit contending that due process required a dismissal hearing. The Supreme Court held that "a person's interest in a benefit is a 'property' interest for due process purposes if there are such rules and mutually explicit understandings that support his claim of entitlement to the benefit that he may invoke at a hearing." Because the teacher had been employed at the university for four years, the Court felt that he may have acquired a protectible property interest in continued employment. The case was remanded to the trial court to determine whether there was an unwritten "common law" of tenure at the university. If so, the teacher would be entitled to a dismissal hearing.

Roth and *Sindermann* emphasize, first, that there must be an independent source for a liberty or property interest to exist. Such interests are not created by the Constitution, but arise by employment contract or by operation of state tenure laws. Second, if a liberty or property interest is not established, no requirement of due process exists under the Fourteenth Amendment. Third, if a teacher possesses a liberty or property interest in employment, then due process is required and the teacher may not be dismissed without a hearing. A tenured teacher, or an untenured teacher during the term of his or her contract, possesses a property interest in continued employment. An untenured teacher who is not rehired after expiration of his or her contract is entitled to a due process hearing if the decision not to rehire is accompanied by a finding of incompetence or immorality, because the teacher's liberty of employment would be impaired by such a finding.

A Texas teacher who was head football coach for his school suffered a losing season and was notified that his contract would not be renewed the following year. The school district denied the teacher's request for a hearing and a statement of the reasons for nonrenewal. The state commissioner of education ordered the district to reinstate the teacher. The district reassigned the teacher to a job without coaching duties. The teacher filed a lawsuit in a Texas district court seeking declaratory relief. The parties eventually settled the breach of contract issue. A trial was held on the due process issue, and the court found no evidence of damages. The teacher had been successfully reemployed as an insurance salesman and now earned far more money than he had as a teacher. The Court of Appeals of Texas affirmed the trial court's decision and held that the state Term Contract Nonrenewal Act did not grant the teacher a constitutional property interest in his employment. The Supreme Court of Texas reversed and remanded the case, holding that the tenure act granted the teacher a property interest. *Grounds v. Tolar Indep. School Dist.*, 856 S.W. 2d 417 (Tex.1993).

On remand, the court of appeals again affirmed the trial court's decision, finding no evidence of damages arising from the due process violation. The teacher's annual salary had increased from $18,000 as a teacher to $45,000 in his new career, and he had never again applied for a coaching position. Since the U.S. Supreme Court has ruled that a procedural due process violation requires the award of nominal damages, the court awarded $1 to the teacher but otherwise affirmed the trial court's decision. *Grounds v. Tolar Indep. School Dist.*, 872 S.W.2d 823 (Tex.App.—Fort Worth 1994).

The Texas Term Contract Nonrenewal Act confers procedural protections and mandates automatic contract renewal for teachers in the absence of proper notice. The act requires school districts to furnish written notice and an opportunity for a hearing when the district fails to renew a teacher's contract. A Texas school district failed to rehire an experienced school nurse without stating a reason for its decision or providing an opportunity for a hearing. The nurse claimed that she was "certified" within the meaning of the Term Contract Nonrenewal Act because the state board of education's regulations required a school nurse to hold either a provisional school nurse certificate or a current registration with the state board of nurse examiners. The state commissioner of education ruled that the nurse was not protected by the nonrenewal act because she was not a teacher within the definition of the act. The Court of Appeals of Texas affirmed. The nurse appealed to the Supreme Court of Texas.

The supreme court observed that the nonrenewal act protected teachers, a term that was defined as superintendents, principals, supervisors, teachers, counselors and other full-time professionals, who were required to hold a valid certificate or teaching permit. Although all school nurses were required to be registered by the state board of nurse examiners, not all school nurses were required to have a provisional school nurse certificate. Although state board regulations made it possible for school nurses to obtain a certificate, the statute did not require certification. Because the nonrenewal act distinguished between employees who were required to hold certificates and those who were not, the commissioner of education had properly ruled that the nurse was not entitled to the act's protections. *Dodd v. Meno*, 870 S.W.2d 4 (Tex.1994).

A New Jersey school district hired a learning disabilities teacher consultant, and later reclassified her as a school psychologist. She worked in that capacity for over two years, until a work-related injury forced her to take an involuntary leave of absence. Six months later, the school district terminated her employment. The psychologist claimed that although she had worked for only 28 months at the time of her injury, she had accumulated the necessary 30 months to obtain tenure prior to the board's termination action. She filed an appeal with the state board of education, which agreed that the termination violated her tenure rights. The New Jersey Superior Court, Appellate Division, affirmed the board's decision and the school district appealed to the Supreme Court of New Jersey. The supreme court stated that employees who took sick leave remained school district employees for the duration of their leave. The psychologist was not prohibited from completing her probationary period while on leave, as the district had argued. The use of leave did not prevent the psychologist from attaining tenure and the appellate division court's decision was affirmed. *Kletzkin v. Bd. of Educ. of the Borough of Spotswood*, 136 N.J. 275, 642 A.2d 993 (1994).

A tenured administrator worked for an Alaska school district for over 14 years, but then received a poor written evaluation threatening a demotion. A dispute emerged concerning the procedural process to which the administrator was entitled. The administrator claimed that he was entitled to binding arbitration under both an Alaska statute and his employment contract, while the school district maintained that the school board had final authority under a collective bargaining agreement. The administrator filed a lawsuit in an Alaska trial court prior to the school board's meeting and he eventually signed an employment contract for about $10,000 less than his prior salary under a reservation of rights. The school board moved to strike the administrator's summary judgment motion and convert the matter to an administrative appeal. It asserted that the administrator had failed to exhaust his administrative remedies because he had failed to present his grievance at the school board meeting. The administrator then resigned to accept a position with another school district.

The trial court judge denied the administrator's summary judgment motion as moot. The administrator then filed a second lawsuit in which he sought to have 48 grievances remedied. The trial court judge ruled that the administrator lacked standing to pursue his grievances and granted the school district summary judgment with substantial attorney's fees. The Supreme Court of Alaska consolidated the administrator's appeals and determined that the trial court had properly dismissed the second action. However, the trial court had incorrectly ruled that the first lawsuit was moot. The administrator had been reassigned to a job paying almost $10,000 less and there was no merit to the school district's argument that he had failed to exhaust his administrative remedies. This was because "when the form of the administrative procedure is itself contested, no further exhaustion of remedies is required." The court remanded the first case to the trial court and vacated the award of attorney's fees. *Kleven v. Yukon-Koyukuk School Dist.*, 853 P.2d 518 (Alaska 1993).

A probationary professor at the university of Oklahoma was denied tenure despite the unanimous recommendation of the members of her department. The tenure committee had denied tenure because it felt her research was deficient. Claiming that the tenure committee breached university procedures by performing an independent evaluation of her scholarship, the professor sued the university in a state court, arguing that she had a property interest in being granted tenure. The Court of Appeals of Oklahoma disagreed. The court stated that there was no evidence to suggest that tenure was meant to be granted routinely or that it could be withheld only "for cause." Once tenure was granted, a property interest would arise, but not until then. In addition, it was within the power of the committee to perform an independent evaluation of the teacher's scholarship. *Stern v. Univ. of Oklahoma Bd. of Regents*, 841 P.2d 1168 (Okl.App.1992).

After five years of employment, an assistant German professor at a Texas university was notified that his contract would not be renewed for financial reasons. The professor asked that he be allowed to undergo the tenure approval process so he could tell potential employers he was being considered for tenure. According to the faculty handbook, he was eligible for tenure consideration. He was not, however, granted tenure. He sued the university in a federal district court, claiming he was denied due process of law in being refused tenure and in being fired. A jury agreed, but the judge overturned the jury's decision. The professor appealed to the U.S. Court of Appeals, Fifth Circuit. The court of appeals stated that the handbook was a guide for the faculty and not a self-contained policy document. It did not create a constitutionally protected property right in continued employment or an assurance of tenure. The handbook was not a contract. The only process due to the professor was the exercise of professional judgment in a nonarbitrary fashion. Since there was evidence to support the termination, it was not arbitrary. *Spuler v. Pickar*, 958 F.2d 103 (5th Cir.1992).

A principal at a North Carolina elementary school was on probationary employment status for three years. At the end of the third year his board of education denied him tenure. He sued the board in state court, claiming that he had not received a written evaluation for his second year of duty. He argued that the failure of the school board to comply with statutory evaluation procedures established a cause of action and meant that his dismissal was arbitrary and capricious. The Court of Appeals of North Carolina disagreed. The state law providing for evaluation procedures did not establish an independent right. Rather, the failure of school boards to comply with these procedures could be submitted as evidence in an action to establish that a dismissal was arbitrary or capricious. However, the failure could not itself be the basis of an action. *Clinton v. Wake County Bd. of Educ.*, 424 S.E.2d 691 (N.C.App.1993).

An Alabama university employee was dismissed from his job as director of the library. He contested his removal and requested a written statement of reasons for the dismissal. He received the writing and then filed a written request with the university president, seeking review of the dismissal. An interview committee consisting of three deans and two faculty members concluded unanimously that his dismissal was appropriate. He then filed a complaint in an Alabama trial court alleging that he had been denied due process. The trial court granted the university summary judgment and the teacher appealed to the Court of Civil Appeals of Alabama. The court upheld the decision of the trial court because the employee had been afforded ample opportunity to present his side of the case, which met with due process. *Warren v. Univ. of Alabama*, 579 So.2d 1375 (Ala.Civ.App.1991).

A teacher's contract specified that she must agree to accept reassignment to any area in which she held a valid certificate. The district asked the teacher to sign a contract accepting reassignment to supervise mathematics. The teacher responded in writing that she would accept, but felt that she could better serve the district in another capacity, and that she held reservations about her qualifications to supervise math. The district later "withdrew" its offer and claimed that the teacher had no right to employment. A state court reversed, and the district appealed to the Supreme Court of Mississippi. The teacher was held to be employed upon the school's receipt of the acceptance letter, and the "withdrawal" by the district amounted to a termination in violation of due process. The termination was thus ineffective, and the judgment for the teacher was affirmed. *Dean v. Pringle*, 592 So.2d 49 (Miss.1991).

An Alaska university hired an employee to work as a mail clerk. Because other employees had applied for the same position, the employee's selection caused tension in the mail room. During the first six months of her employment, the employee was to be on probationary status. Less than a month after being hired, her supervisor informed her that her job performance was unacceptable. A week later, he fired her. A university grievance council found that the supervisor's reasons for terminating the employee were not accurate. It found that she had not been judged objectively, and the supervisor had negligently supervised, trained, and evaluated her. However, it let the termination stand, stating that the supervisor could fire probationary employees without just cause. A university chancellor and the university president affirmed that decision, but an Alaska trial court ordered the employee reinstated. The university appealed to the Alaska Supreme Court. The supreme court stated that according to university regulations, probationary employees were to be evaluated before the end of their probationary period. If found unsatisfactory, they would be discharged. The court stated that the use of the words "evaluated" and "found" suggested a process involving objective standards rather than mere personal beliefs. Accordingly, university regulations required an objective, "just cause" termination of probationary employees. The court remanded the case to the university chancellor for further proceedings. *Univ. of Alaska v. Tovsen*, 835 P.2d 445 (Alaska 1992).

II. COMPLIANCE WITH STATE LAW

Failure to respect the procedural formalities of state law may result in reversal of a school board action if a court determines that the procedural error constitutes a denial of due process in violation of state law.

A Missouri teacher worked part-time for 18 years and enjoyed annual salary increases. The state general assembly amended the Teacher Tenure Act by allowing part-time teachers to accrue prorated credit toward tenure. The following year, the teacher's school district offered her a full-time contract, but indicated that it was probationary rather than permanent, and decreased the teacher's compensation to an amount equivalent to a first year teacher's salary. The teacher signed the contract and submitted a letter protesting her salary decrease and demotion to probationary status. She then sued the district in a Missouri trial court, which ruled that she was entitled to a permanent contract, but not a salary increase. Both parties appealed, and after the Court of Appeals of Missouri affirmed the trial court decision, the matter was transferred to the Supreme Court of Missouri.

The court agreed with the teacher that she should be given retroactive credit toward permanent status for the years she had worked part-time. Because the teacher had worked approximately 18 years part-time prior to the amendments to the tenure act, she had accrued more than five years toward permanent status. The court affirmed this part of the trial court's decision. It then reversed the trial court's determination that the teacher was not entitled to a salary increase. The contract did not indicate the teacher's salary level, but the custom of the parties was to grant a step increase for each year worked. Because fixed practices existing for a sufficient duration to become custom may be implied as contractual terms, the teacher was entitled to a salary increase. *Dial v. Lathrop R-II School Dist.*, 871 S.W.2d 444 (Mo.banc 1994).

A tenured Louisiana school board employee was promoted to principal of a high school under a two year contract. During the contract term, the state legislature amended the Teacher Tenure Law by requiring school boards to offer new contracts to employees with satisfactory performance ratings at the expiration of each existing contract. The school superintendent rated the principal's performance satisfactory and recommended reappointment. However, the school board voted not to renew his contract. The principal petitioned a Louisiana trial court for a writ of mandamus that would require the board to negotiate a new contract. The court granted the petition, but the Louisiana Court of Appeal, Fourth Circuit, reversed. The principal appealed to the Supreme Court of Louisiana. On appeal, the school board argued that because the legislative amendment was passed during the contract term, application in this case would be retroactive and therefore impermissible. The supreme court disagreed, ruling that the amendment pertained to all contracts existing at the time of the legislation. Because the principal's contract existed at the time of the amendment, there was no issue of retroactive application in this case. The board was required to offer a new contract to the principal based upon the superintendent's satisfactory recommendation. *Rousselle v. Plaquemines Parish School Bd.*, 633 So.2d 1235 (La.1994).

A New York local education board abolished the position of school nurse teacher and refused to allow the incumbent to displace any less senior health teacher. The board claimed that the nurse teacher was neither tenured under New York law nor certified to teach health. The teacher, who had taught health and health-related topics at the district's schools for 15 years, filed a lawsuit in a New York trial court, seeking reinstatement. The court ordered the board to reinstate the teacher and the board appealed to the New York Supreme Court, Appellate Division, Second Department. The court found error in the trial court's order to reinstate the teacher. The law did not require placement of a teacher having seniority rights unless a vacancy was presently available in a similar position. The nurse teacher had not successfully alleged that a vacancy existed for which she was qualified. However, the teacher had gained tenure by operation of law by teaching health classes in excess of the two-year probationary period under state law. The case was reversed and remanded to the trial court for a hearing and further determination of whether a vacancy existed in health instruction. If the teacher could show that a vacancy existed, she would be entitled to placement. *Freeman v. Bd. of Educ. of Hempstead School Dist.*, 616 N.Y.S.2d 911 (A.D.2d Dept.1994).

Missouri elementary school administrators determined that a teacher had many communication problems. After giving her warnings, the administrators imposed a professional development plan upon her, requiring her to attend teaching workshops and to read materials on communication and instruction. Later assessments determined that the teacher's performance was still deficient and that she had difficulty maintaining classroom discipline. After further meetings and warnings, the administrators issued the teacher a warning letter in compliance with the state tenure act advising her that formal charges would be brought unless improvement was made within 120 days. The administrators then videotaped class sessions instructed by the teacher and met to discuss them with her. Although the teacher's deadline was extended, the administrators ultimately recommended termination. The school board approved the dismissal, and a Missouri circuit court affirmed its decision. The teacher appealed to the Missouri Court of Appeals, Eastern District.

The court of appeals observed that the state tenure act mandated the procedure for removing teachers for incompetency, inefficiency or insubordination. The teacher must receive a written warning specifying the grounds for action, which may result in charges if the grounds are not removed within a probationary period of at least 30 days. Teachers are then entitled to confer with the superintendent. The court rejected the teacher's argument that the board had not acted in good faith under the tenure act. Administrators had made many efforts to help improve her performance and gave her more than the minimum time required by statute to comply with the development plan. The court affirmed the board's decision. *Johnson v. Francis Howell R-3 Bd. of Educ.*, 868 S.W.2d 191 (Mo.App.E.D.1994).

A Kansas school board decided not to renew the contract of a tenured teacher. He requested a due process hearing at which the hearing committee ruled that the school board had failed to show good cause not to renew the contract. The committee instructed the board to rescind the resolution and reinstate the teacher with backpay. As required by Kansas law, the board adopted the hearing committee's opinion. It then appealed the decision to a Kansas district court, which held that the statute requiring automatic adoption of committee decisions was unconstitutional. The Kansas Supreme Court reversed and remanded the district court's decision. The teacher then petitioned the district court for an order to compel the school board to continue paying his salary while the due process matter was pending. The district court denied the petition and the teacher appealed to the Kansas Supreme Court.

The supreme court determined that the teacher had a protected property interest in continued employment because of his tenured status and therefore had certain due process rights. Although the teacher was not entitled to salary continuation throughout the statutory appeals process, he was entitled to his salary until the time of the pretermination hearing. In this case, the actual time of the contract termination and entitlement to salary rights was when the school board rejected the hearing committee's opinion and filed its district court appeal. The court reversed and remanded the district court's decision. *McMillen v. U.S.D. No. 380, Marshall County, Kansas*, 855 P.2d 896 (Kan.1993).

Four Alabama teachers filed a complaint in a Alabama trial court alleging that they were entitled to a past due ten percent pay raise pursuant to the Teacher Pay Raise Act. Three of the teachers took maternity leave and one took an emergency leave during their first three years as school teachers. Due to the leaves of absence, the teachers' tenure dates were delayed. Further, because each one's tenure date was delayed until sometime in the fourth year their pay raise was delayed until the following school year. The trial court entered judgment in favor of the teachers and the school board appealed to the court of civil appeals of Alabama. The appellate court determined that it would be unjust to deny the teachers their pay raise when, through no fault of their own, they met the criteria during the school year rather than at the beginning of the next school year. The appellate court affirmed the decision of the trial court and stated that it would be unjust to use the leaves of absence to postpone tenure. *Bd. of School Comm'rs v. ARDIS*, 575 So.2d 1125 (Ala.App.1990).

A New York teacher was tenured in the area of physical education/health. The school district then split the departments and assigned her to the physical education department. She was later cut from that department as the least senior teacher, but accepted a position in the health department. Twelve years later she was cut as the least senior teacher in the health area. The teacher argued that her seniority established as a physical education teacher must be considered, and that with this additional seniority she would not be the least senior teacher in the health area. A trial court ordered her reinstated, and the school district appealed to the Supreme Court, Appellate Division, of New York. The reinstatement was affirmed. Although the school was free to restructure its tenure departments, it could do so only prospectively—it could not be done so as to deprive a teacher of earned seniority or tenure rights. *Kulick v. Bd. of Educ. of Middale Country Central School Dist.*, 577 N.Y.S.2d 666 (A.D.2d Dept.1991).

An Illinois school board operated a vocational center which conducted a cooperative vocational educational program. The board implemented a reduction in force which resulted in the dismissal of two tenured cooperative vocational education program teachers. The teachers (who were not special education teachers) claimed they had rights to bump less experienced teachers within the school district who participated in the joint education program. They claimed that an Illinois statute which created "super-tenure" rights for special education teachers also applied in their case because of a reference in the statute to cooperative educational programs and joint educational programs. The school board rejected requests by the teachers to place them in any position for which they were legally qualified within the district, claiming that they were not legally entitled to do so under the special education tenure statute. The teachers sued the board in an Illinois circuit court, which dismissed their complaint. They then appealed to the Appellate Court of Illinois, Second District.

On appeal, the teachers renewed their argument that the special education tenure statute applied to them, and that differential tenure protection to special education teachers would result in a violation of their equal protection rights. The appellate court ruled that the teachers had strained the meaning of the special education tenure statute, which clearly did not protect teachers in the vocational educational program. The legislature intended to treat special education teachers differently. Tenure rights under the statute were to be strictly construed and the legislature could properly "offer special protection to this unique class of teachers." Because the statute rationally advanced reasonable and identifiable governmental objectives, and did not involve a suspect classification, it had a rational basis and did not violate the teachers' equal protection rights. The court affirmed the circuit court's decision. *Aken v. Bd. of Control of Lake County Area Vocational Center*, 604 N.E.2d 524 (Ill.App.2d Dist.1992).

From 1974 to 1990, a South Dakota school district offered separate contracts for teaching and extracurricular duties assigned by the district. In 1991, the district offered a single contract which required a signature for each set of duties. Several teachers alleged that this contractual change violated the tenure law: first by not allowing teachers the chance to reject an extracurricular duty without losing their teaching contract, and second by allowing nonrenewal based on the inefficient performance of an extracurricular duty. The teachers' lawsuit eventually reached the Supreme Court of South Dakota. The earlier contracts were held to require that the teachers accept the assigned extracurricular duties. Similarly, teaching duties and extracurricular responsibilities were grouped together for review purposes. Therefore, the revised contract did not vary from the earlier contracts. The judgment in favor of the school was affirmed. *Lemmon Education Association v. Lemmon School District #52-2,* 478 N.W.2d 821 (S.D.1991).

A Montana principal was notified by the school board that his position was being eliminated due to budget cuts. The school board decided to combine the position of principal with that of district superintendent. However, the school board told the principal that he could bump a nontenured teacher and resume teaching since he was tenured and had over 14 years of experience. The principal filled out the proper paperwork and obtained his official teaching certificate. The school board met again and decided not to let the principal bump a nontenured teacher, but the board did not notify the principal prior to this decision of its intent. After several administrative appeals, the principal appealed to a Montana trial court which ordered his reinstatement as a teacher. The board appealed to the Supreme Court of Montana. The supreme court emphasized the importance of the rights of tenured teachers notwithstanding the board's assertion that the principal was not protected because he did not obtain an official certificate while principal. The supreme court stated that paperwork does not deny a tenured teacher his or her rights. It further stated that a tenured teacher's rights cannot be taken away except for good cause. The court also stated that the board violated the principal's due process rights when it did not notify him that it was firing him. The supreme court affirmed the trial court's decision. *Holmes v. Bd. of Trustees of School Dist. 4,* 792 P.2d 10 (Mont.1990).

A New York teacher acquired tenure under the state Education Law in 1965 as a New York City elementary school teacher. She was hired years later as a special education teacher by another school district for a three-year probationary term. At the time, the parties were unaware that New York Education Law § 3012(1)(a) reduces probationary periods to only two years where teachers have achieved tenure in other New York school districts. Six months prior to the end of the three-year probationary term, the superintendent of schools recommended termination of the teacher's appointment and met with her for a review. He stated that there would be nothing negative in her file if she voluntarily resigned. The teacher submitted her resignation effective in two months. Prior to the effective date of the resignation, the teacher's attorney notified the board that the teacher had acquired tenure in New York City, and thus qualified for the two-year probationary period. The school board refused to reinstate the teacher, and she sued it in a New York trial court, which reinstated her with backpay and benefits.

The New York Supreme Court, Appellate Division, Second Department, reversed, and the teacher appealed to the New York Court of Appeals.

The court of appeals reasoned that the teacher would not have voluntarily relinquished her tenure rights had she known of the two-year limitation on probationary positions for tenured teachers. Because the parties were apparently unaware of the statute, the acceptance of the teacher's resignation was based on a mutual mistake of fact. Under principles of contract law, the formation of the contract was defective and could be rescinded. The teacher had also acquired tenure in the new district under the legal doctrine of estoppel, because the district had permitted her to teach beyond the expiration of her probationary term. The court reversed the decision of the appellate division court. *Gould v. Bd. of Educ. of Sewanhaka Cent. High School Dist.*, 616 N.E.2d 142 (N.Y.1993).

Three public school teachers received unfavorable classroom observation reports from a Maryland board of education. The teachers filed grievances pursuant to their collective bargaining agreement, seeking final and binding arbitration. However, the county education board obtained a Maryland trial court order staying arbitration and requiring the teachers to exhaust their remedies before the state education board. Although the hearing officer ruled that the observation report dispute was a subject which constituted a controversy or dispute under § 4-205(c) of the Maryland Education Article, the state education board ultimately ruled that classroom observation disputes were purely local matters which were appealable only to local superintendents. This result was affirmed by the Maryland trial court and the teachers appealed to the Court of Special Appeals of Maryland.

The court of special appeals determined that the state board's position was inconsistent with the legislative purpose of Maryland Education Article §§ 2-205 and 4-205, the latter of which provided for rights of appeal in Maryland courts from unfavorable local decisions. The unfavorable classroom observation reports were appealable controversies or disputes, and the case was remanded to the trial court with directions to reverse the decision of the state education board and for a consideration of the merits of each case. *Strother v. Bd. of Educ. of Howard County*, 623 A.2d 717 (Md.App.1993).

A Wisconsin high school hired an attorney to investigate sexual harassment complaints, which resulted in the disciplining of one teacher. A broadcasting company requested the district's custodian of records to inspect and copy the attorney's report, and further requested access to grievances filed by the disciplined teacher and another employee which were related to the investigation. When the broadcasting company sued the district administrator in a Wisconsin trial court, the disciplined teacher sought to intervene in the lawsuit, claiming that release of the grievance record and report would violate his right to privacy in his personnel file, and that it would prejudice his rights in a pending grievance matter. The court denied the disciplined teacher's petition and he appealed to the Court of Appeals of Wisconsin. The court of appeals commented that public records custodians needed to balance a public policy favoring disclosure of public records against the competing policy of confidentiality in personnel records. The disciplined teacher had failed to show that his due process rights in the pending grievance would be prejudiced by disclosing the records to the broadcasting company. Because the matters were not sufficiently related, the teacher had no legally protected privacy right and his intervention in the matter was properly denied. *Armada Broadcasting Inc. v. Stirn,* 501 N.W.2d 889 (Wis.App.1993).

III. NOTICE REQUIREMENTS

In most cases, adequate notice includes a statement of the reasons for the action and time to respond. This affords the employee an opportunity to take remedial action or to prepare a defense.

An instructive case in this area is a U.S. Supreme Court case from Virginia which applied three factors in determining that reasons for dismissal must be given to a teacher. First, the interest of a teacher with renewable contract rights is substantial; second, the administrative cost of providing a statement of reasons would be minimal; and third, the benefits of such a requirement are evident. Consideration of these factors dispenses with the appearance of arbitrariness which attends a discharge without explanation; encourages the board to come to grips with and articulate its reasoning process; encourages fairness by holding the decision up for public and judicial scrutiny; enhances the visibility of the decision-making process; provides for a more meaningful judicial inquiry should the case subsequently be litigated in the courts; and prevents a reviewing court from impermissibly substituting its judgment for that of a board. *Mathews v. Eldridge,* 424 U.S. 319, 96 S.Ct. 893, 47 L.Ed.2d 18 (1976).

Ohio law required school boards to give notification to school administrators on or before the last day of March of the year in which the contract expired if the district did not intend to rehire the administrator. One section of the statute stated that nothing prevented a board of education from making a final decision to employ or fail to renew an administrator's contract. An Ohio school district failed to give the required written notice to an assistant principal, and eliminated her position along with those of ten others. The assistant principal accepted a high school teaching assignment, but petitioned an Ohio court for an order requiring the school board to issue her a two-year contract as an assistant principal with backpay and fringe benefits. The court granted summary judgment to the school board and the administrator appealed to the Supreme Court of Ohio.

The court determined that the conflict between statutory sections should be resolved in favor of the school board. Even though the board had failed to comply with the notice statute, its ability to nonrenew the contract was not undermined. The language of the statute vesting the board with final authority was distinct from a similar statute governing teacher contracts, which the assistant principal had relied upon in her argument. The legislature would have used the same language from the teacher statute if it had intended the same result. The administrator failed to demonstrate her right to reappointment and the court affirmed the decision in favor of the school board. *State ex rel. Cassels v. Dayton City School Dist. Bd. of Educ.,* 69 Ohio St.3d 217, 631 N.E.2d 150 (1994).

An Arkansas school district hired a teacher/basketball coach under a nonprobationary teaching contract. During the contract period, the district asked the teacher/coach to give up coaching two girls' basketball teams and to take a pay cut. He refused, but the district hired another coach to take over the teams. The district then proposed that the teacher accept a pay cut of $6,000 for the following school year and the elimination of all his coaching duties. The teacher filed a petition for a writ of mandamus to compel the district to reinstate him to a contract under the same terms and salary as the prior school year under the state Teacher Fair Dismissal Act. The court granted the writ and the district appealed to the Supreme Court of Arkansas. On appeal, the district argued that the case should be dismissed because the fair dismissal act was inapplicable and because the teacher had failed to appeal to the school board, instead filing the matter directly in state court. The supreme court disagreed, finding that the dismissal act applied because of the district's failure to renew the contract under substantially the same terms as the prior year. The district had failed to comply with the statute's strict notice requirements, which required superintendents to give teachers prior notice of nonrenewal. The school district's action was void because of its failure to give proper statutory notice, and the teacher was therefore not limited to a direct appeal to the board. *Western Grove School Dist. v. Terry*, 885 S.W.2d 300 (Ark.1994).

A Mississippi school board voted to reemploy a number of teachers and counselors for the following school year despite acknowledging that a reduction in staff would be necessary over the next three years due to budget shortfalls. At the end of the school year, the board learned of a $400,000 budget shortfall and sent notice to a guidance counselor that he would not be rehired the following year because of a staff reduction. A hearing officer determined that the school district's financial crisis constituted good cause for contract termination. A Mississippi trial court reversed this decision and awarded damages to the counselor. The district appealed to the Supreme Court of Mississippi.

The supreme court observed that in states such as Iowa and Massachusetts, budgetary restraints could serve as just cause for termination of employee contracts because their tenure statutes did not differentiate between contract termination and nonrenewal. Mississippi's termination, suspension, and contract renewal statutes made a clear distinction between discharges and contract nonrenewals. Because the school board did not provide written notice to the guidance counselor of its intention not to renew his contract as required by the state employment procedures law, it was liable for the employment contract. Its budgetary problems could not constitute good cause for suspension or removal under the statute. The court affirmed the trial court's damage award. *Byrd v. Greene County School Dist.*, 633 So.2d 1018 (Miss.1994).

An Ohio school district employed a transportation supervisor under a contract calling for 260 days of work per year plus 15 vacation days. The following year, the contract called for 245 days, and in subsequent years, the schedule was reduced to 219 days with no vacation. Although an Ohio statute permitted contributions to the state retirement system, the board paid no retirement contribution on the supervisor's behalf. Despite the declining work schedule, the board increased the salary for the position each year. In 1993, the transportation supervisor refused to sign a one-year contract, claiming that her prior contract had been automatically renewed under Ohio law because the board had failed to timely notify her of nonrenewal. She filed a lawsuit against the board in an Ohio trial court, which granted the board's summary judgment motion. The supervisor appealed to the Court of Appeals of Ohio.

On appeal, the supervisor contended that the board's failure to advise her that it was not renewing her contract resulted in automatic contract renewal. The court of appeals determined that the Ohio statute did not require the board to "nonrenew" her contract in writing prior to issuing a one-year contract. There was also no requirement that the board contribute to her retirement account. Because the supervisor had never contested the reduction in work and vacation days during a period of over eight years prior to the lawsuit, she could not now complain of the reduction. The board did not owe her any backpay or vacation pay. The court affirmed summary judgment for the school board. *State ex rel. Willbond v. Oberlin School Dist., Oberlin Bd. of Educ.*, 94 Ohio App.3d 419, 640 N.E.2d 1179 (1994).

Students, faculty and staff members of a Tennessee community college complained to a speech department chairperson that a tenured faculty member was acting inappropriately. The chairperson attempted to mediate the complaints, but the problems continued and she met with the faculty member to discuss eight areas in which improvement was required. The chairperson sent the faculty member a follow-up memo stating that she was at risk for employment termination. When complaints continued, the college sent the faculty member a letter documenting the complaints, and identifying the complaining parties. The board of regents held an informal hearing and recommended employment termination on the grounds of capricious disregard of accepted standards of professional conduct. The professional conduct standard was based on language in the regents' policy. The termination action was affirmed by a formal hearing committee and sustained by the chancellor of the board of regents. A Tennessee trial court affirmed the chancellor's decision and the faculty member appealed to the Supreme Court of Tennessee.

On appeal, the faculty member argued that the college had violated her due process rights because the regents' policy was unconstitutionally vague and because she had received inadequate notice of the charges. The supreme court stated that while the regents' policy was broad and general, it was not unconstitutionally vague. The chairperson had advised the faculty member several times about specific conduct that could result in dismissal. The faculty member also had received a new hearing in the trial court to correct any deficiencies in the college's termination procedures. The supreme court affirmed the college's actions, also ruling that there was no merit to the faculty member's First Amendment complaint. *Phillips v. State Bd. of Regents*, 863 S.W.2d 45 (Tenn.1993).

A tenured Missouri teacher with over 20 years of experience received satisfactory performance ratings from a succession of principals. However, during the 1988 school year, the school superintendent urged her to retire. The school's principal began to scrutinize the teacher's performance and then sent her a warning letter. The school followed up with a statement of charges for termination, and the teacher requested a hearing. The board ordered termination, and the decision was affirmed by a Missouri trial court. On appeal to the Missouri Court of Appeals, the court agreed with the teacher's assertion that the notice was insufficient under Missouri law because it failed to specify the charges against her with particularity. The state statute required detailed and specific charges, whereas the district had only given generalized summaries. The court reversed the decision, reinstating the teacher with backpay. *Jefferson Cons. School Dist. v. Carden*, 772 S.W.2d 753 (Mo.App.1989).

An Illinois school district hired a teacher to teach agriculture classes. Both the teacher and the principal mistakenly believed the teacher was qualified for the position. After nine years, the principal of the school district discovered the mistake and dismissed the teacher without notice. The teacher sued in an Illinois trial court, seeking to be reinstated. The trial court found for the teacher and the district appealed. The Appellate Court of Illinois noted that the question of whether the teacher could be dismissed without notice could be answered by determining whether the cause for dismissal was remediable. In this case the cause was remediable, and the teacher was required to have received notice before dismissal. The school district was thus without authority to discharge the teacher. *Morris v. Illinois State Bd. of Educ.*, 555 N.E.2d 725 (Ill.App.3d Dist.1990).

IV. HEARING REQUIREMENTS

Tenured employees must be given a fair and impartial hearing, conducted in accordance with statutory procedural safeguards, if there is a property or a liberty interest involved or if the dismissal involves a stigma upon the character of the teacher.

A. Minimum Requirements

Hearings are always required before dismissal of tenured teachers. This is because tenured teachers are considered to have a property interest in their employment and this interest cannot be taken away without due process of law. However, there are a number of cases regarding adequacy of hearings and there are many situations where the type of employment involved raises the question of whether a hearing is required.

In two consolidated cases, the U.S. Supreme Court was asked to consider what pretermination process must be afforded a public employee who can be discharged only for cause. In the first case, a security guard hired by a school board stated on his job application that he had never been convicted of a felony. Upon discovering that he had in fact been convicted of grand larceny, the school board summarily dismissed him for dishonesty in filling out the job application. He was not afforded an opportunity to respond to the dishonesty charge or to challenge the dismissal until nine months later. In the second case, a school bus mechanic was fired because he had failed an eye examination. The mechanic appealed his dismissal after the fact because he had not been afforded a pretermination hearing. The Supreme Court held that because the employees possessed a property right in their employment, they were entitled to a pretermination opportunity to at least respond to the charges against them. The pretermination hearing need not fully resolve the propriety of the discharge, but should be a check against mistaken decisions. The Court held that in this case the employees were entitled to a pretermination opportunity to respond, coupled with a full-blown administrative hearing at a later time. *Cleveland Bd. of Educ. v. Loudermill*, 470 U.S. 532, 105 S.Ct. 1487, 84 L.Ed.2d 494 (1985).

An Ohio school board decided not to reemploy a ninth grade teacher who had three years of experience. Although the board held an executive session upon the teacher's request, it prohibited her from calling witnesses to testify on her behalf. It later issued an order affirming its decision denying her reemployment. The teacher filed a lawsuit in an Ohio trial court claiming that the board had failed to comply with statutory evaluation and hearing procedures. The trial court denied her request for backpay and reemployment, finding that although the board had not adopted statutory evaluation procedures, the procedures it had used were not unlawful. The Ohio Court of Appeals affirmed the trial court's decision, and the teacher appealed to the Supreme Court of Ohio.

The supreme court observed that the collective bargaining agreement in effect between the district and teacher's association had been entered into prior to the effective date of the statute and did not specifically exclude rights contained in the statute. Because the board of education was required to adopt statutory evaluation procedures for teachers and was also bound by the collective bargaining agreement, it had improperly decided not to reemploy the teacher without giving her specific recommendations for improvement. The board's notice to the teacher failed to inform her of the reasons for the decision not to rehire her. The teacher was entitled to a hearing to present evidence, confront witnesses and make arguments. The court reversed and remanded the judgments of the lower courts, with orders to reinstate the teacher for one year with benefits and backpay. *Naylor v. Cardinal Local School Dist. Bd. of Educ.*, 69 Ohio St.3d 162, 630 N.E.2d 725 (1994).

A Louisiana principal was demoted to classroom teacher by a school board which found him guilty of wilful neglect of duty. He was notified of a hearing by a letter which indicated his offenses but did not include specific names or dates. After his demotion, the former principal then filed suit against the school board in a Louisiana trial court which affirmed the disciplinary action and he appealed to the Court of Appeal of Louisiana. The former principal contended that the disciplinary action did not comply with procedural requirements and, therefore, he should be reinstated as principal. Procedural requirements indicated that the statement had to include charges and a complete list of the specific reasons (including the date and place of each alleged offense, names of the individuals involved in each offense, and names of the witnesses). The court determined the letter to be legally sufficient even though it did not state specific names and dates because the information given the former principal was sufficient to enable him to prepare a defense. Therefore, the court affirmed the decision of the trial court. *Baker v. St. James Parish School Bd.*, 584 So.2d 369 (La.App.5th Cir.1991).

A nontenured teacher, under a one-year contract, was arrested for possession of crack cocaine. The superintendent of the Alabama school system where the teacher worked recommended that the employee's contract be canceled. During a hearing on the issue, conflicting testimony on the possession charge was presented. The board of education voted to cancel the contract. The teacher sued the school board, claiming his due process rights had been violated. A trial court ruled for the board, and the Court of Civil Appeals of Alabama affirmed. It found that the one-year contract gave the teacher a property right in continued employment, but that the hearing had satisfied due process. *Stovall v. Huntsville City Bd. of Educ.*, 602 So.2d 407 (Ala.Civ.App.1992).

B. Hearing Procedures

Usually when a hearing has been inadequate or unfair or where there has been evidence of bias the courts will require that procedural problems be corrected prior to dismissal or demotion. On occasion reinstatement will be ordered. Again, the courts insist that hearings be held in strict accordance with statutory law.

An Ohio school district fired a high school custodian for suspected drug dealing and sexually suggestive behavior with students. The custodian filed a grievance under the collective bargaining agreement between his union and the district. A former student at the school was called to give evidence concerning drug dealing at the arbitration hearing. She claimed to be afraid of the custodian. Accordingly, the arbitrator permitted her to testify from a separate room via closed-circuit video screen by which she was subjected to direct and cross-examination. The cross-examination yielded evidence that the custodian had not actually threatened her. The arbitrator determined that the sexual misconduct charge was insufficient to warrant employment termination, but that the former student's testimony established the custodian's involvement in a drug deal. The grievance was denied, and appeal reached the Supreme Court of Ohio.

The supreme court determined that while deprivation of a property right such as public employment mandated due process, there was no explicit right to confrontation and cross-examination in a public employee's pretermination or posttermination hearing. The purpose of due process was to protect substantial rights, but the same procedures were not mandated in every case. The custodian's right to present evidence and to conduct cross-examination was outweighed by the state's interest in securing necessary testimony. The student had a reasonable fear of reprisal and the arbitrator's action had been appropriate. The court declined to rule that a face-to-face confrontation was an absolute requirement of due process and it reinstated the arbitrator's decision. *Ohio Assn. of Pub. School Employees v. Lakewood City School Dist. Bd. of Educ.*, 68 Ohio St.3d 175, 624 N.E.2d 1043 (1994).

A Pennsylvania school maintenance employee was questioned by police for displaying pornography and for possible sexual misconduct. He was immediately suspended by the school district and two days later charged with assault and corruption of a minor. Within a month the school notified the employee that there would be a termination hearing. The employee appeared at the hearing with counsel and asked for postponement until resolution of his criminal charges. He claimed that because of the pending criminal trial he was privileged against self-incrimination. The school hearing would force him to give evidence which could be used against him at the criminal trial. The school board refused to delay the hearing. The board unanimously voted to discharge him. The employee sued the school district in a federal district court. He claimed his Fifth and Fourteenth Amendment rights had been violated and demanded reinstatement with damages. He claimed the school board forced him into a choice between protecting his job or remaining silent in the face of criminal charges. The court ruled for the school board, noting that the employee was given the opportunity to participate in the hearing. There was no due process right to stay the hearing until after the criminal trial. The employee appealed to the U.S. Court of Appeals, Third Circuit, which also rejected his arguments. He was not privileged to withhold testimony from the board and suffered no constitutional violations. *Peiffer v. Lebanon School Dist.*, 848 F.2d 44 (3d Cir.1988).

A nonprobationary school teacher in Arkansas acted as one of several chaperones on a field trip to Hot Springs. Two elementary school girls claimed that the teacher molested them on the trip. At the beginning of the teacher's dismissal hearing, the school district indicated that the girls and their parents would not be present at the hearing. The teacher did not object. Later, he contended that he had been denied his right to due process because he did not have the opportunity to cross-examine these witnesses. The Court of Appeals of Arkansas stated that due process had been satisfied. The teacher's failure to object to the absence of the witnesses resulted in a waiver of that right. *Helena-West Helena School Dist. v. Davis*, 843 S.W.2d 873 (Ark.App.1992).

A former Tennessee teacher employed by a school district since 1965 was appointed principal of a high school in 1984. The board soon dismissed the principal for unsatisfactory performance following a discharge hearing. The principal then filed a petition in a Tennessee county court. The county court limited review of the board decision to the record generated at the discharge hearing. The principal's suit was dismissed. The Tennessee Supreme Court held that the county court decision was contrary to the Teacher Tenure Act. The act expressly provides for a new county court hearing whenever a tenured teacher is dissatisfied with the school board's decision. Protection of teachers from arbitrary dismissal is one of the fundamental purposes of the act. The supreme court reversed and remanded the case for a new hearing. The principal would be allowed to supplement the record with evidence which was previously excluded. *Cooper v. Williamson County Bd. of Educ.*, 746 S.W.2d 176 (Tenn.1987).

After a New York principal brought charges against a teacher, the teacher requested a hearing. She was not suspended. After the teacher took a day off of work to attend the hearing, the state commissioner of education denied her request that she be paid one day's salary for the day she was absent from work. The teacher sought a court order directing that she be paid for the day in question. A New York appellate court noted that New York law provided that a teacher suspended pending a hearing must be paid for the day spent at the hearing. The court ruled that the commissioner's decision that a nonsuspended teacher need not be paid was irrational because such a decision would provide harsher treatment for a teacher who has not been suspended than for one who has. *Kubisa v. Ambach*, 521 N.Y.S.2d 187 (A.D.3d Dept.1987).

C. Impartiality

In 1985, a New York board of education initiated disciplinary charges against a teacher with more than 25 years of experience in the district. The charges alleged both incompetence and insubordination. Consistent with New York law, the teacher chose a hearing panel member, the board of education chose a hearing panel member, and those two designees in turn chose a third person to serve as panel chairperson. At the conclusion of the proceedings, the panel unanimously found the teacher not guilty of incompetence but, by a two to one vote, determined that she was guilty of insubordination and recommended termination. The board of education dismissed the teacher. Three days later, the teacher learned that the board of education had violated New York law by paying the panel member it had nominated an additional $100 per day to serve on the panel. The teacher claimed that the compensation scheme violated her right to have an impartial decisionmaker under the Due Process Clause of the U.S. Constitution. A New York appellate court concluded that the board of education's actions violated the teacher's rights. The school board appealed to the Court of Appeals of New York.

The court of appeals stated that it was not necessary to address the constitutional issues involved because the case could be resolved on other grounds. The board of education's material departure from the mandatory provision of New York law constituted error entitling the teacher to relief. While not all deviations from statutory procedures justify the reversal of an administrative determination, when the procedure provided is mandatory and the rule is intended to prevent bias and financial influence, the failure to follow those procedures results in at least the appearance of an unfair hearing. Accordingly, the determination had to be vacated. The court of appeals ordered a new hearing. *Syquia v. Bd. of Educ. of the Harpursville Central School Dist.*, 591 N.Y.S.2d 996 (Ct.App.1992).

A fifth grade teacher at a Florida elementary school was suspended for ten days without pay for misconduct. The misconduct was based upon several incidents of misconduct including using the word "bitch" in class. The teacher appealed her suspension, claiming that not only was the evidence insufficient to support her suspension, but also that the school's attorney had inappropriately played a dual role during the misconduct hearing before the school board. According to the teacher's argument, the attorney acted as both the prosecutor and as the school board's legal advisor. The Florida Court of Appeal vacated the suspension and ordered a new hearing. It agreed with the teacher, stating that due process requires an administrative board, such as a school board, conducting disciplinary proceedings to designate one person to act as its legal advisor and a different person to fulfill the role of prosecutor. Since a new hearing was to be held, the evidence would be reheard. However, the court stated that the teacher's use of the word "bitch," used by the teacher in the sense of "to complain," could not legally constitute conduct so serious as to impair the individual's effectiveness in the school system. *Forehand v. School Board of Gulf County*, 600 So.2d 1187 (Fla.App.1st Dist.1992).

A Connecticut teacher was arrested and charged with electronic eavesdropping. He was suspended with pay. Following a trial, he was acquitted of the charges against him. Thereafter, the school board voted to consider terminating him. The teacher requested a hearing and an impartial panel was chosen. The panel concluded that the evidence was sufficient to support a termination. However, the majority of the panel believed that the evidence of criminal wrongdoing was inadmissible because of Connecticut's Erasure Act, which erases the court and police records of criminal proceedings when the accused is acquitted. Prior to the meeting of the board to vote on the panel's recommendation, the teacher filed a motion to disqualify four members of the board for personal bias or conflict of interest. The board denied the motion and voted to terminate the teacher. The board issued a written opinion in which it stated that the nondisputed evidence was sufficient to justify termination for moral misconduct. The teacher unsuccessfully appealed to a Connecticut trial court and further appealed to the Connecticut Supreme Court. On appeal, the court held that the erasure act was limited to court documents and police reports. Since the disputed testimony did not fall into either of these categories, it was admissible and provided a sufficient basis for termination. The teacher's remaining argument that four members of the board were biased against him was also rejected. The court held that the teacher needed to show actual bias, not merely a presumption of bias based on past altercations. The court upheld the lower court's decision affirming the termination of the teacher. *Rado v. Bd. of Educ. of the Borough of Naugatuck*, 583 A.2d 102 (Conn.1990).

D.   Whether a Hearing Is Required

An Oregon elementary school principal was employed under a probationary employment contract. The district school board voted to dismiss him. It gave him a letter stating the reasons for dismissal, but did not publicly disclose them. The principal was formally notified of his dismissal and his right to have a posttermination hearing upon request. He never requested a hearing, but sued the district in an Oregon federal district court, claiming his dismissal was in violation of 42 U.S.C. § 1983 and the Due Process Clause. The district court entered summary judgment for the school district, and the principal appealed to the U.S. Court of Appeals, Ninth Circuit. The appellate court noted that procedural due process only applies where a person has been deprived of a liberty interest. The principal's dismissal implicated no liberty interest and the court affirmed the district court's decision. *Hayes v. Phoenix-Talent School Dist.*, 893 F.2d 235 (9th Cir.1990).

A teacher's aide was employed by a Mississippi school board. The aide had a son who was a student in the school district. The son was suspended for five days as a result of a fighting incident. Two other students at the same school had been involved in a separate fighting incident, but were only given reprimands. A teacher at the school told her of the discrepancy in discipline, and gave her confidential information about the students who had received the reprimand. This unauthorized release of information was against school rules and federal regulations. The aide attended a meeting of the school board in order to object to her son's suspension and to protest what she claimed was an inconsistency in the school's discipline policy. The aide was then suspended from her job. A pretermination hearing was held and the aide was unanimously terminated. The aide appealed the board's decision to the Chancery Court of Harrison County, which reversed the school board's decision. The school board then appealed to the Supreme Court of Mississippi. The supreme court held that the aide could not have been deprived of her constitutional rights at the hearing, since she was not entitled to a hearing at all. An employee hired for an indefinite period may be discharged at will. The court also held that even if the aide was entitled to a hearing, she was not deprived of due process because the board had conducted a hearing. The court also held that the teacher's aide was not entitled to appeal the school board's decision. The supreme court reversed the chancery court and reinstated the school board's decision. *Harrison County School Bd. v. Morreale*, 538 So.2d 1196 (Miss.1989).

A Kentucky board of education suspended two tenured teachers, citing declining enrollment. The teachers sued the board in a Kentucky trial court stating that the decision deprived them of a constitutionally protected right without due process of law. The teachers argued that they were entitled to presuspension hearings. The trial court dismissed the case and the teachers appealed to the Court of Appeals of Kentucky. The court of appeals stated that the teachers had insufficient property rights in continued employment to entitle them to presuspension hearings. The court of appeals affirmed the trial court's dismissal. *Downs v. Henry County Bd. of Educ.*, 769 S.W.2d 49 (Ky.App.1989).

A nontenured research scientist working for the University of Florida on an overseas project was notified by the university that his annual contract would not be renewed. He petitioned for a hearing which the university denied. He further appealed to the District Court of Appeal of Florida, challenging the factual accuracy of the reasons advanced by the university. The appellate court stated that even though the scientist had no right to continued employment at the university, he was entitled to a hearing regarding the allegations in the letter he had received. They could have a stigmatizing effect on his opportunity for new employment. The court remanded the case for a hearing. *Yunker v. University of Florida*, 602 So.2d 557 (Fla.App.1st Dist.1992).

A full-time college professor at an Oklahoma community college was fired following a contract dispute with college administrators. Although the community college did not have a formal tenure process, each year professors entered into individual contracts with the college. Following acceptance of the contract, a period of time was left open for the college to modify the contract. According to the professor, in the year in question the college had not modified the contract and his salary and compensation details had been completed and communicated to him in writing. A month after the modification deadline had passed, the college attempted to make the professor sign a revised contract with numerous new obligations. When the professor refused to sign the new contract, he was discharged. He was not given a hearing. He sued under 42 U.S.C. § 1983 claiming that he was deprived of a property interest in his employment without due process of law. A federal district court, however, granted summary judgment to the community college, stating that the professor had received adequate post-termination due process. The professor then appealed to the U.S. Court of Appeals, Tenth Circuit.

The court of appeals stated that the professor had a constitutionally protected property interest in continued employment because he had been offered and had accepted employment for the upcoming college year, and the terms of his contract and elements of compensation had been fixed in writing. Given the professor's version of the situation, the college's attempt to add performance objectives to his contract after all deadlines established by the community college had passed violated his procedural due process rights. A reasonable public official would have known that a protected property interest had accrued and that the process afforded to the professor in this case was not constitutionally adequate. The court reversed the summary judgment for the college and remanded the case to the district court. *Calhoun v. Gaines*, 982 F.2d 1470 (10th Cir.1992).

A tenured teacher signed a supplemental contract to coach baseball. The contract did not specify a duration. Later that year, the school board informed him that it was terminating the coaching contract. The coach contended that he was entitled to a list of reasons and a hearing, which he was denied. He unsuccessfully sought judicial review, and appealed to the Commonwealth Court of Pennsylvania. Pennsylvania law provides that professional school employees may be removed only after a notice of reasons and a hearing upon request. The court construed the term "removed" to apply only to a teacher's professional duties — not extracurricular activities. Further, it stated that in this case the coach was not "removed," because his contract had in fact expired; it was terminable at will. The court noted in closing that school boards are generally given wide latitude in the selection and firing of coaches. *Moriarta v. State College Area School Districts*, 601 A.2d 872 (Pa.Cmwlth.1991).

CHAPTER NINE

EMPLOYEE REASSIGNMENTS, SUSPENSIONS AND DEMOTIONS

I. ECONOMY MEASURES

Declining enrollment or revenue problems within school districts often force employee reassignments or demotions. Personnel transfers, if done with proper procedures and for legitimate reasons, will be upheld.

A West Virginia school board responded to declining student enrollment by eliminating 57 employment contracts for school services personnel. It then issued new contracts for service workers that reflected shorter employment terms and proportionate decreases in salary. Most of the employment terms for these employees were reduced from 261 days to 240 days per year. The employees filed a grievance that resulted in a decision for the school board. A West Virginia trial court reversed this decision and the school board appealed to the Supreme Court of Appeals of West Virginia. The supreme court of appeals observed that the state law under which the contracts had been terminated prohibited adverse action against a service employee who remained in the same job or classification during the same or a subsequent year (the non-relegation clause). In this case, however, the reclassification had changed the positions in a manner that did not violate the statutory non-relegation clause. The hearing officer had properly dismissed the grievance and approved the board's action. The supreme court of appeals reversed and remanded the trial court's decision. *Lucion v. McDowell County Bd. of Educ.*, 446 S.E.2d 487 (W.Va.1994).

A Louisiana school district contracted with its teachers to maintain its existing salary schedule but reserved "the right to make an adjustment within the funds available," in the event of insufficient finances. During the school year in which the contract was applicable, the school board announced that it would close all public schools for three days due to financial problems, and would not

287

pay employees for the period. Teachers in the district filed a lawsuit in a Louisiana trial court, which granted them summary judgment on the issue of their lost earnings. The Court of Appeal of Louisiana, First Circuit, reversed and remanded the decision, finding that the contract language was sufficiently ambiguous to preclude summary judgment. The term "sufficient financial resources" was open to several interpretations which had to be considered by the trial court on remand. *EICHE v. East Baton Rouge Parish School Bd.*, 623 So.2d 167 (La.App.1st Cir.1993).

The Michigan Tenure Act permits discharge or demotion of a tenured teacher only with just cause and after notice and a hearing. Faced with declining enrollment and impending layoffs, a teachers' union and school district negotiated an early retirement incentive (ERI) program. The ERI program permitted qualified teachers to opt for early retirement at half pay with the remainder of their salaries placed in a pool from which laid off teachers could draw salaries for half pay positions in the school district. Compensation for laid off teachers amounted to approximately one half of their pre-layoff salaries. Forty-three teachers were notified that they would be laid off and 23 applied for the ERI program. These applicants were placed in positions generally held by lower seniority teachers. Non-ERI teachers filed petitions with the State Tenure Commission, alleging that the school district engaged in a subterfuge to lay off teachers and then rehire them at half pay. The State Tenure Commission ruled for the teachers but a trial court reversed, stating that there was no evidence to show the board knew of available vacancies at the time the layoffs were made. The Michigan Court of Appeals upheld the decision for the school district based on the lack of evidence of subterfuge and a failure by the teachers to show that "demotions" had occurred within the meaning of the Tenure Act. The court found that the board had acted in good faith at a time when layoffs were inevitable, pursuant to an agreement which the teachers' union had helped to negotiate. *Bd. of Educ. for Garden City v . Brisbois,* 417 N.W.2d 84 (Mich.App.1987).

A Michigan school district decided to reorganize its special education services for hearing-impaired students. Prior to the reorganization, two school districts had provided these services. After the reorganization, the services were discontinued and a third school district provided them. Five special education teachers who had lost their jobs in the reorganization were hired by the third district. The teachers were given credit for seniority earned with the other districts. A teachers' union representative challenged the propriety of granting teachers credit for seniority earned in other districts. The trial court held in favor of the school district and the union appealed to the Court of Appeals of Michigan. The appeals court noted that the Michigan State School Aid Act provided that if special education personnel were transferred from one district to another they would be "entitled to the rights, benefits and tenure to which the person would otherwise be entitled had that person been employed by the receiving district originally." The overall statutory scheme did not recognize a transfer procedure different from the arrangement used in this case. Thus the five teachers were "transferred" within the meaning of the statute and they were entitled to benefits including retention of their seniority. The court of appeals affirmed the trial court's decision. *Local 681 v. Dearborn Bd. of Educ.* 431 N.W.2d 253 (Mich.App.1988).

Due to declining enrollment an Alabama school board voted to reduce a lunchroom worker's hours from 35 to 30 hours per week. The worker requested a hearing under the state's Fair Dismissal Act but the school board denied the request stating that its action was neither a "termination" nor a "transfer" within the meaning of the Act. After a trial court upheld the school board decision, the worker appealed to the Alabama Supreme Court which observed that the trial court did not address the principle that a public employee with a "legitimate claim of entitlement to continued employment must be given an opportunity to prove the legitimacy of his claim." The board's reduction of the worker's hours was a partial determination, and the trial court's decision was reversed. *Ledbetter v. Jackson County Bd. of Educ.*, 508 So.2d 244 (Ala.1987).

A Minnesota school district determined that certain administrative positions should be discontinued or realigned. Consequently, a principal was "bumped" from that position and hired as a teacher. He appealed to the Court of Appeals of Minnesota. At issue before the court was whether the school district was wrong in appointing a less senior superintendent to the new position of principal-superintendent instead of the principal. The court reasoned that realignment to protect seniority rights was mandated by the Teacher Tenure Act but that realignment without regard to practicality and the welfare of the students was not. Here, it was most practical to combine the position of principal and superintendent. The decision to hire the less senior superintendent was upheld. The court stated that if the principal wanted to work in the district, he had to work as a teacher. *Matter of Buys*, 398 N.W.2d 622 (Minn.App.1986).

When a Pennsylvania school district was hit by declining enrollment, the superintendent reviewed the teaching staff to determine where staff reductions and realignments should be made. He decided to dismiss the two lowest-rated elementary school teachers while retaining the school's principal, a certified teacher who was only acting as principal on a temporary basis. The lowest-rated teacher brought suit against the school district, claiming that the superintendent had erroneously retained the principal while dismissing teachers who possessed greater seniority. She argued that the school district should have dismissed the temporary principal and elevated a teacher to that position, which would have had the effect of preserving her teaching job. The Commonwealth Court of Pennsylvania ruled against the teacher, holding that administrators and teachers are separate and distinct categories of employees. The school district had respected seniority rights within the teaching staff in making its staff reductions, and that was all that was required under the tenure statutes. The court held that the school district was not required to dismiss the principal in order to retain a senior teacher. *Derry Township School Dist. v. Finnegan*, 498 A.2d 474 (Pa.Cwmlth.1985).

II.   SCHOOL DISTRICT DISCRETION

Personnel transfers and reassignments will be upheld by courts if they conform with applicable law and procedures and are not arbitrary or capricious.

A.   Unsatisfactory Job Performance

A biology teacher with 17 years of experience at a West Virginia high school was assigned to supervise the school cafeteria. He observed a student cutting ahead of other students in a line and ordered him to go to the end of the line. The student responded with profanity and the teacher then escorted him to the principal's office. The student cursed the teacher all the way. When they reached the office, the student shoved the teacher. The teacher then slapped the student with the back of his hand, causing a nosebleed. The board of education imposed a ten-day suspension on the teacher, finding that the action constituted neglect of duty, insubordination and corporal punishment, based on findings that the teacher did not act in self-defense. A state-level employee grievance board upheld the board's actions, and the board's decision was affirmed by a West Virginia trial court. The teacher appealed to the Supreme Court of Appeals of West Virginia.

The court found no lack of evidence in the record that the teacher's actions constituted neglect of duty and insubordination. It was insignificant that the legal notice of his suspension lacked the statutory language of wilfull neglect of duty. The teacher was on notice that his conduct had been wilful and the board's action was not unreasonable, arbitrary or capricious. The finding that the teacher's action was not in self-defense supported the board's action. Accordingly, the court affirmed the board's imposition of the ten-day suspension. *Parham v. Raleigh County Bd. of Educ.*, 453 S.E.2d 374 (W.Va.1994).

The District Court of Appeal of Florida, First District, considered the case of a 48-year-old assistant principal who married a 16-year-old former student. In this case, the state Education Practices Commission (EPC) disciplined the assistant principal by suspending his teaching certificate for two years and prohibiting his employment as an educational administrator. The court of appeal, while affirming the EPC's power to take disciplinary action, disagreed with the findings of the hearing officer. There was no clear and convincing evidence of an inappropriate personal relationship between the teacher and student prior to their marriage. Although the two had been seen together by many individuals, this only gave rise to suspicion, which could not form the basis for disciplinary action. No witness gave competent, credible evidence that the two had engaged in sexual activity prior to marriage or otherwise acted inappropriately while on campus. School administrators had taken no action against the former principal and the EPC's decision apparently rested on conclusory evidence presented without firsthand knowledge of the case. Accordingly, the court reversed the suspension. *Tenbroeck v. Castor*, 640 So.2d 164 (Fla.App.1st Dist.1994).

A Louisiana assistant principal was demoted to classroom teacher after he was late for work on numerous occasions and because he had left the campus without the principal's permission several times. The school board found that these actions constituted incompetence and wilful neglect of duty. A Louisiana trial court upheld that determination and the assistant principal appealed to the Court of Appeal of Louisiana. The court held that being tardy and leaving the campus without permission could be evidence of incompetence and insubordination. In addition, these actions supported the school board's decision to demote. *Hargis v. LaFourche Parish School Bd.*, 593 So.2d 400 (La.App.1st Cir.1991).

A California high school teacher was arrested and charged with possession and use of cocaine. The school suspended the teacher pursuant to the California Education Code, although the suspension was not required. The teacher completed a drug diversion program for first time offenders. As a result, the criminal charges were dropped, as required by California law. The school district allowed the teacher to resume his position. The teacher then sued for $40,000 for the two years he was completing the drug diversion program. California law states that teachers who have been suspended for criminal charges of which they are later acquitted or which are dismissed are entitled to full compensation for the leave of absence. The trial court awarded backpay and the district appealed to the California Court of Appeal. The court of appeal agreed with the trial court that state law compelled it to award backpay. It stated, however, that the amount awarded would be offset by the teacher's earnings during the two-year period. Since he had made $30,000 during that period his award was reduced to $10,000. *Unzueta v. Ocean View School Dist.*, 8 Cal.Rptr.2d 614 (Cal.App.1992).

An assistant professor in a Massachusetts university Russian Department was accused of plagiarizing a book. The accusations were leveled by the chair of the department, with whom the assistant professor had a history of animosity. Following an investigation, the personnel committee recommended that the professor be censured for "seriously negligent scholarship." As a result, the professor was publicly censured and barred from serving as a department chair or voting on degrees. The professor sued university officials under 42 U.S.C. § 1983 for violating her procedural and substantive due process rights. She also sued the department chair for intentional interference with an economic relationship, intentional infliction of emotional distress, and defamation. The officials asked a federal district court to grant them qualified immunity, but the court refused. The officials appealed to the U.S. Court of Appeals, First Circuit. The court of appeals noted that the officials were immune from damages on the due process claim if they reasonably believed that the manner in which the investigation was carried out satisfied the requirements of due process. The professor had been given notice at every step of the process and had had an opportunity to refute allegations made against her. Even though due process may have been denied, the officials would be immune from damages. However, the court refused to grant immunity to the department chair. Since there were genuine questions regarding her motives in this case, it would be inappropriate to grant her the good faith immunity given to public officials acting in the scope of their duties. If, on remand, it was determined that censure was unwarranted, the chair would not be entitled to immunity. *Newman v. Com. of Massachusetts*, 884 F.2d 19 (1st Cir.1989).

A certified Colorado music teacher was employed to teach music to kindergarten through twelfth grade students. As a result of poor performance the school board decided to reassign the teacher as a permanent substitute teacher. With few exceptions, the teacher was assigned to teach a vocational education class. The teacher refused each assignment, stating that she was not qualified to teach that subject. After about three months the teacher tendered her resignation. She then sued the school district in a Colorado trial court seeking recovery based upon constructive discharge, breach of contract, and violation of the Colorado Tenure Act. The court held for the school district and the teacher appealed to the Colorado Court of Appeals. The court of appeals held that there was no constructive discharge because the evidence showed no harassment or coercion by the school board. There also was no breach of the employment contract by reassigning her as a permanent substitute teacher. Finally, the court noted that to show a violation of the Tenure Act, the teacher was required to demonstrate that she was unqualified for her new assignments. This, she could not do. *Christie v. San Miguel County School Dist.*, 759 P.2d 779 (Colo.App.1988).

A black school principal who was "voluntarily reassigned" to a teaching position filed suit in U.S. district court under Title VII of the Civil Rights Act of 1964 claiming that his demotion was racially motivated. He appealed to the U.S. Court of Appeals, Seventh Circuit, which observed that the principal was induced to return to teacher status because the school officials had legitimate doubts about the principal's good judgment, a characteristic absolutely necessary for a principal. The principal had also failed to be diligent in investigating the theft of athletic equipment and in following administrative rules in handling two sexual misconduct incidents among the students. *Morgan v. South Bend Comm. School Corp.*, 797 F.2d 471 (7th Cir.1986).

B. Discretionary Reassignments and Demotions

School districts do not always specify their reasons for taking personnel action. In other cases, reasons unrelated to job performance are the cause of demotion. In these cases, school districts can anticipate employee accusations of arbitrariness.

Full-time guidance counselors and a librarian at a West Virginia school filed a grievance contesting the board of education's practice of requiring them to be substitute teachers. They claimed that this practice was unnecessary and that they were not certified to teach in the areas to which they had been assigned. The board justified the assignments as an "emergency" measure under W.Va.Code 18-4-10(10), which authorized a county superintendent to "[a]ct in case of emergency as the best interest of the school demands." The board stated that at the time of the assignments it had spent the money budgeted for substitute teachers. A hearing examiner ruled in favor of the guidance counselors and the librarian, but a trial court reversed the hearing examiner's decision. The counselors and librarian appealed to the Supreme Court of Appeals, West Virginia. The appellate court held that no emergency existed which would have justified the county superintendent to assign the guidance counselors and librarian to substitute teach. The board of education made no showing of its financial straits forcing it to utilize budget reduction measures, nor did it make a reasonable effort to adequately provide for substitute teacher expense. The appellate court reversed the trial court decision and reinstated the hearing examiner's decision. *Randolph County Bd. of Educ. v. Scalia*, 387 S.E.2d 524 (W.Va.1989).

A New York teacher was assigned to a support skills program because of various health problems, including visual and mobility problems. The teacher was also the grievance coordinator for the teachers' association. He advised his fellow teachers that they were not obligated to attend an after-school meeting called by the principal. Shortly thereafter, the teacher was informed that the support skills program was being discontinued for lack of space. He was then reassigned to a regular classroom. After a hearing, the New York State Public Employment Relations Board (PERB) determined that the school had violated the Public Employees Fair Employment Act when it eliminated the support skills program in retaliation for the teacher's engaging in a protected activity. The PERB ordered the school to reinstate the support skills program and return the teacher to his former position. The school district petitioned the New York Supreme Court, Appellate Division, for review of the PERB decision.

On appeal, the court concluded that there was ample evidence to support the PERB's finding. Most convincing was the fact that the support skills program was terminated almost immediately after the teacher advised his colleagues that they were not obligated to attend the after-school meeting. The district's stated reason for terminating the program, lack of space, was clearly pretextual, according to the court, since the program used only the rear corner of a classroom which was shared with another class. The court upheld the PERB's determination that the school district had retaliated against the teacher in reassigning him and ordered him reinstated to his previous position. *Uniondale Union Free School v. Newman*, 562 N.Y.S.2d 148 (A.D.2d Dept.1990).

A New York board of education hired a teacher to teach business education. The teacher also had certification in driver and safety education. Years later, his position as a high school business teacher was eliminated as part of the district's reduction in force. Driver's education courses were cut and the remaining business classes were assigned to a more senior teacher. New York law, however, allowed the teacher to "bump" a teacher having less seniority within his tenure area, i.e. the general secondary school area. Since there were less-senior teachers within his tenure area (teaching subjects he was not certified to teach) the school district fired a tenured and certified secondary science teacher and moved the business teacher into that position. It then began incompetency proceedings against him for lack of certification, but the teacher sued the district in a state trial court for backpay and continuing pay during the pendency of the incompetency proceedings. A New York trial court concluded that the board of education did not have the authority to suspend the teacher without pay, but an appellate division court reversed. The teacher then appealed to the New York Court of Appeals. The Court of Appeals stated that pay is a substantive right that cannot be taken away except pursuant to explicit statutory or collective bargaining authorization. The court stated that qualified teachers must be paid. It also stated that the board could not equate teacher qualification with certification *in a specific subject area*. Since the teacher was certified on the day he was suspended, he was qualified under New York law and, therefore, had to be paid. *Winter v. Bd. of Educ. for Rhinebeck Central School Dist.*, 588 N.E.2d 32 (N.Y.1992).

A tenured Connecticut teacher filed a grievance against his board of education. He was then transferred to a less desirable position at a different school. The teacher sued the school district in a federal district court, alleging that his First Amendment right to assemble and petition the government for a redress of grievances had been violated. The court agreed, holding that the First Amendment protects the right of public employees to associate in a labor union and seek redress of grievances through collective action. The school district could not retaliate against the teacher for doing so. The teacher's lawsuit continued to trial. *Stellmaker v. DePetrillo*, 710 F.Supp. 891 (D.Conn.1989).

A Pennsylvania substitute industrial arts teacher temporarily filled the vacancy left by another industrial arts teacher who had assumed a temporary administrative position. When the second teacher wished to return to his permanent position, the temporary teacher was suspended. The district contended that the temporary teacher's suspension was proper in order to relocate the permanent teacher who was the more senior employee. The temporary teacher appealed to the Commonwealth Court of Pennsylvania. The court upheld the suspension. The court stated that the senior teacher's acceptance of the administrative position did not terminate his status with the district and the temporary teacher filled the senior teacher's position only as a substitute. *Waslo v. North Allegheny School Dist.*, 549 A.2d 1359 (Pa.Cmwlth.1988).

The superintendent of a South Carolina school district had an employment contract with the school board by which he was to be employed as a superintendent until June 30, 1983. However, on January 11, 1983, he was notified by the board that effective immediately he was being relieved of his duties. The board stated that he would receive full pay and benefits until June 30, the date of the expiration of his contract. No reasons were given by the board for its decision. The superintendent brought suit against the board under the federal civil rights laws, contending that he should have been allowed to perform his duties until June 30. The U.S. Court of Appeals, Fourth Circuit, disagreed. The superintendent did possess the right to full monetary compensation under the terms of his contract, but he possessed no property right in the actual performance of his duties. All that is required when a school district employee is dismissed for reasons outside the contract is that the employee be compensated in full for the duration of his contract. The court held that the superintendent had no right to continue performing his duties. *Royster v. Bd. of Trustees*, 774 F.2d 618 (4th Cir.1985).

A tenured teacher was promoted to principal of her high school for the 1984-85 school year. The superintendent gave her a positive written evaluation showing satisfactory performance. In 1986, the superintendent left the district, and his replacement advised the school board to reassign the principal. The superintendent stated that low employee morale, lack of long-range improvement strategies and lack of effective communication at the school required a dramatic leadership style which the principal did not have. He stated that conditions at the school required a "superstar," and suggested reassignment of the principal as an assistant principal or teacher. The board unanimously voted to reassign the principal to a teaching position and sent her a notice which conformed to the California Education Code. She requested a written statement of the reasons for reassignment and received a response from the board which reiterated the superintendent's explanation that the school required new leadership. The principal unsuccessfully requested an order for reinstatement from a California trial court. She appealed to the California Court of Appeal. The principal tried to show that she had been reassigned due to incompetence. The California Education Code requires an incompetency hearing where incompetency is alleged. The court of appeal upheld the trial court ruling. It noted that incompetency was not a basis for the reassignment. Under the Education Code the board was free to reassign the principal for any reason without cause or evaluation. *Quirk v. Moore Park Unified School Dist.*, 244 Cal.Rptr. 924 (Cal.App.2d Dist.1988).

A former Illinois high school principal brought suit against his school board alleging violation of his property rights after he was demoted without notice, but also without salary reduction, from his position as principal to that of a regular classroom teacher. The plaintiff had only a one-year contract and the demotion came at the end of the contract year. He relied on the Illinois School Code which stated that no principal who, like himself, had two or more years of administrative service in the school district "[could] be reclassified by demotion or reduction in rank from one position to another for which a lower salary [was] paid without written notice from the board." The former principal asserted that this statement meant that all reclassification must be preceded by written notice. The U.S. Court of Appeals, Seventh Circuit, rejected that contention. It noted that the same statute also provided that nothing "prohibits a board from ordering lateral transfers of principals to positions of similar rank and equal salary." The court concluded that the school board's action did not constitute a violation of the plaintiff's property rights. *Lyznicki v. Bd. of Educ.*, 707 F.2d 949 (7th Cir.1983).

III. PROCEDURAL REQUIREMENTS

In many instances, reassigned or demoted personnel bring suit solely on procedural grounds. Courts have upheld the transfers involved where the procedures followed were adequate.

A. In General

An industrial arts teacher with 19 years of experience at an Iowa high school got into a fight with a student. Although the teacher and school administrators attended meetings on the subject, he was not granted a formal hearing before being suspended without pay for four days. Following the suspension, the teacher was transferred to another school. The teacher then sued the district in the U.S. District Court for the Southern District of Iowa, claiming deprivation of his due process rights under the U.S. Constitution and damage to his reputation. The court granted the district's summary judgment motion and the teacher appealed to the U.S. Court of Appeals, Eighth Circuit. The court found that the teacher had a strong interest in continued employment because of his good record and years of service at his former high school. Conversely, the administrative burden of holding a hearing for the teacher at an appropriate time was minimal to the school district. The teacher had never been given an opportunity to cross-examine witnesses and the student had apparently not been disciplined, even though he had started the fight. The court reversed and remanded the case to the district court. *Winegar v. Des Moines Indep. Comm. School Dist.*, 20 F.3d 895 (8th Cir.1994).

An Indiana junior high school teacher removed the glossaries from 146 of his school's science textbooks in order to force his students to learn the material from the text rather than referring to the glossaries. The local education agency (known as a school corporation in Indiana) suspended the teacher without pay for two days and fined him $1 for each damaged textbook. The teacher filed a lawsuit in an Indiana trial court under 42 U.S.C. § 1983 for alleged violations of his rights to academic freedom and due process. The court denied the school corporation's motion for summary judgment and held for the teacher. The Court of Appeals of Indiana, First District, reversed and remanded the case to the trial court, which again entered judgment for the teacher. The court of appeals reversed the trial court's decision a second time, holding that the teacher could not maintain a § 1983 action because Indiana school corporations were not persons for the purposes of the act.

On rehearing, the court of appeals reversed its decision concerning the status of Indiana school corporations under § 1983. Because Indiana school corporations had statutory authority to enter into contracts, sue and be sued, and had the power to levy taxes and issue bonds, they were political subdivisions and not arms of the state. Accordingly, they were not protected by the Eleventh Amendment in § 1983 cases. However, the teacher's acts violated the Indiana criminal code, and his First Amendment argument was insignificant. The school corporation's interest in the protection of its property far outweighed the teacher's asserted right to academic freedom. Because the teacher had no First Amendment right to remove the glossaries, the trial court should have granted the corporation's summary judgment motion. The court of appeals reversed and remanded its prior judgment. *Bd. of Trustees of Hamilton Heights School Corp. v. Landry*, 638 N.E.2d 1261 (Ind.App.1st Dist.1994).

A student at the University of Wisconsin-Oshkosh enrolled in an English class. The class syllabus stated that spot quizzes would account for 20 percent of the grade and an optional book report would account for 10 percent. The student complained to the professor during class that she felt spot quizzes were unfair. She also complained to another student that an "optional" book report that counted for 10 percent of her grade was hardly "optional." The professor apparently overheard the remark. Following a disagreement over whether the student had attended the proper amount of end-of-semester conferences, the professor submitted a grade of "Incomplete" for the student. The professor, in a series of telephone calls and lengthy summertime correspondences with the student, refused to change the student's grade until she "appropriately apologized" both for missing a conference and for criticizing his policies. The professor deemed none of the student's apologies appropriate and submitted an "F" for her final grade.

The student sought the assistance of the university's chancellor, who conducted a hearing. The faculty rights advocate assigned to investigate found the professor's behavior to be inappropriate and his correspondence with the student to be improper. The chancellor ordered the professor to change the grade and issue an apology or else face demotion. The professor refused and was demoted. Several hearings were held, ultimately finding that reduction in rank and salary were appropriate due to the serious nature of the violation. The professor sued, claiming that his free speech and due process rights had been violated. The federal district court rejected the professor's claims and the professor appealed to the U.S. Court of Appeals, Seventh Circuit. The court stated that the unusual number of hearings in the case had afforded the professor all the process that was due, "probably more than was due." The professor's claim that he was being sanctioned for failing to change the student's grade and issue an apology in violation of his free speech rights was ill-founded. The professor was not sanctioned for refusing to change the grade or apologize. Rather, he was subject to disciplinary action because of his unprofessional conduct. The order to change the grade and apologize was merely an alternative punishment for his sanctionable conduct, and not the sanctionable conduct itself. When he refused, he simply chose demotion as the appropriate punishment. The court affirmed the demotion. *Keen v. Penson,* 970 F.2d 252 (7th Cir.1992).

A principal at a Wisconsin school was suspended with pay because he reprimanded a teacher for calling the fire department after smelling smoke. The principal had a policy that all calls to emergency services must first be directed to him. Following the suspension, the principal was reassigned to an elementary school. The principal sued, claiming that the suspension violated his Fourteenth Amendment right to due process. The U.S. District Court, Eastern District of Wisconsin, stated that although the principal had a property interest in the term of his employment, this interest did not entitle him to come to work every day; it merely entitled him to status as a school district employee and to his paycheck. Although the court concluded that a public employee might, in some circumstances, enjoy a protected property interest in coming to work, in this case the principal's contract did not guarantee such a right. *Terry v. Woods,* 803 F.Supp. 1519 (E.D.Wis.1992).

A New York teacher was accused of conduct unbecoming a teacher, neglect of duty and unfitness to properly perform. A hearing was held on the allegations and the hearing panel recommended that the board issue a letter of reprimand, finding the teacher guilty of one charge. The board challenged the leniency of the penalty and the New York Commissioner of Education authorized the board to suspend the teacher without pay for one semester. The teacher appealed that decision to a New York appellate court. The appellate court stated that the board was usually required to follow the hearing panel's penalties. However, here the decision was arbitrary and capricious because the commissioner did not explain his deviance from acceptable conduct. Thus, the appellate court reversed the teacher's suspension. *Engel v. Sobel*, 556 N.Y.S.2d 179 (A.D.3d Dept.1990).

An Indiana teacher held a public school teacher's certificate with elementary and handicapped endorsements. The teacher signed a regular teacher's contract with an Indiana school. The school board assigned the teacher to a special education class. A month later the teacher requested medical leave from the special education position because of stress-related problems. The leave was to last only as long as it took to reassign her to a regular education class. The board denied the teacher's request to be transferred, but approved her request for immediate medical leave. After the board failed to assign her to a regular class which became available in January, she sued the board in an Indiana trial court. The court found for the teacher and the board appealed to the Court of Appeals of Indiana, Third District. The court of appeals held that the teacher was entitled to compensation for the salary she would have received had the board assigned her to the elementary teaching position. The court noted that state law required that where a board had granted a leave of absence, the teacher had the right to return to a teaching position for which she was certified. The teacher was certified, qualified and had a statutory right to return to the elementary teaching position. Because the board did not transfer her to the open position, it had failed to honor her statutory right. The court of appeals affirmed the trial court's decision. *Jay School Corp. v. Cheeseman*, 540 N.E.2d 1248 (Ind.App.3d Dist.1989).

A Tennessee teacher had been having problems getting her third graders to do their assignments. Therefore, in the presence of a teacher's aide and the rest of the students in the class she paddled at least eight of her students for failing to do their assignments. On the following morning, she was barred by school officials from entering her class. She was then informed that she was suspended, pending an investigation of the previous day's events. The investigation revealed that the principal of the school had previously instructed her not to paddle students. Under a proposed settlement the teacher was to remain suspended through the end of the term, forfeit some pay and undergo counseling. However, she refused to sign the conditions without her attorney present, nor did she sign an offer of employment as a librarian. She received a letter which indicated that she was not rehired because she neglected to sign the agreement or comply with any of the provisions of the document. Some five months later, the school board again voted on the question of her dismissal in an attempt to fully comply with the Teacher Tenure Act and the Open Meetings Act. After a public hearing, the board voted to dismiss her. She filed a complaint in a Tennessee trial court which determined that the school board was justified in dismissing her. She then appealed to the Supreme Court of Tennessee.

On appeal, the teacher asserted that the manner in which her case was brought before the school board violated the Open Meetings Act and the Teacher Tenure Act. The court determined that the board's violation of the Open Meetings Act did not entitle her to reinstatement. She could be reinstated only if, after remand, the chancellor found that the evidence presented against her at the public hearing failed to establish any of the causes for dismissal set forth in the statute. The court noted that the actions of the teacher and her attorney contributed to the ultimate violation of the act. Therefore, the court would be hesitant to grant her relief because of this fact alone. The teacher asserted finally that the manner with which her suspension from teaching was handled violated the Teacher Tenure Act, and she sought backpay and reinstatement. The court found that she was in fact offered reinstatement as a librarian. Therefore, the court remanded the case to determine if she was dismissed properly. *Van Hooser v. Warren County Bd. of Educ.*, 807 S.W.2d 230 (Tenn.1991).

A West Virginia high school principal with 25 years experience with his school district overcharged the school board for hotel expenses at a principal's conference. Although he repaid some costs, an audit revealed the overcharge and, after giving notice to him, the superintendent suspended the principal. The school board voted to dismiss the principal, who then appealed to a West Virginia trial court. After the court ruled for the school board, the principal appealed to the West Virginia Supreme Court of Appeals. The supreme court noted evidence that the principal's predecessors had also charged room reservations for their wives and guests at school functions. Although the board had followed correct statutory procedures, it had no formal written policy for travel expenses. Without a written policy, the principal could not have acted wilfully. He could repay the minimal damage to the school system by repaying improperly charged expenses. The court reversed the trial court's decision. *Rovello v. Lewis County Bd. of Educ.*, 381 S.E.2d 237 (W.Va.1989).

An elementary school teacher was charged with unprofessional conduct. A hearing panel found the teacher guilty and recommended a reprimand and suspension without pay for one term. The school board notified the teacher that it intended to follow the recommendations. The teacher appealed the decision to the New York Supreme Court, Appellate Division. The teacher claimed that the finding of guilt was not supported by the evidence. The court noted that its review was limited and that it could not weigh the evidence on the record nor substitute its own judgment for that of the hearing panel. The teacher asserted that the penalties were excessive. The school board argued that the hearing panel should have recommended dismissal. The court held that the sanctions were not disproportionate to the offenses committed. However, it said that imposing two penalties was improper. New York Education Law § 30202-a(4) provided that a penalty should consist "of reprimand, fine, suspension without pay or dismissal." The hearing panel was entitled to impose only one penalty. Because the teacher's suspension had already taken place the court held that the reprimand could not be placed in the teacher's file. *McSweeney v. Bd. of Educ. of Johnsburg Cent. School Dist.*, 525 N.Y.S.2d 956 (A.D.3d Dept.1988).

A Virginia physical education teacher was suspended from her coaching position as the girl's basketball coach pending an investigation by the human relations office concerning complaints that had been made about her coaching conduct and judgment. The coach was paid her full stipend while suspended. She had been hired for the coaching position under a supplemental assignment contract for the 1990-91 coaching season which was separate and distinct from her teaching contract. A supplemental assignment contract must be renewed each year by the principal. Following her suspension, the coach brought this suit against the school district claiming that the school violated her due process rights under the Fourteenth Amendment to the Constitution. The Due Process Clause prohibits arbitrary deprivations of liberty or property interests. The coach claimed that she had been deprived of a property interest in continued employment under her supplemental assignment contract. She contended that she could only be relieved of her coaching duties for good cause. However, the court noted that the Virginia Code governed the suspension of teachers for good cause and did not apply to supplemental employees hired pursuant to supplemental contracts separate from their teaching contracts. Accordingly, the court granted summary judgment to the school district. *Schneeweis v. Jacobs,* 771 F.Supp. 733 (E.D.Va.1991).

B. State Law Requirements

A New York high school science teacher with 18 years of experience was disciplined twice for improper conduct with students. Three months after the second incident, the teacher distributed flyers at a school polling place protesting the fairness of a school election. He encouraged voters to vote against two incumbent board members who were running unopposed. A New York education statute required the placement of markers 100 feet from polling places, within which electioneering was prohibited. The district failed to use any markers. School officials (and eventually the police) directed the teacher to quit distributing flyers within the prohibited area. A disciplinary panel charged the teacher with violating the education statute. The teacher moved to dismiss the matter, claiming a violation of his First Amendment rights. The motion was dismissed and the teacher appealed to the U.S. District Court for the Southern District of New York. The court granted the teacher's request for a permanent injunction against restraining his free speech rights and awarded him attorney's fees of over $19,000. The school district appealed to the U.S. Court of Appeals, Second Circuit. The court held that the district's failure to mark the boundary of the campaign free zone resulted in inadequate notice to the teacher. His conduct did not constitute a criminal violation of the statute. The district's selective enforcement of the statute was arbitrary and discriminatory. There was no justification for the disciplinary proceedings brought by the district, and the court affirmed the district court's decision in favor of the teacher. *Cullen v. Fliegner,* 18 F.3d 96 (2d Cir.1994).

The Florida Constitution describes the governor's suspension authority for county officers, including suspensions resulting from indictment for crimes. A Florida statute specifies the means for suspending officials not described as county officers. A school board member was convicted of one board-related misdemeanor count with no adjudication on twelve other counts. The governor suspended her under the statute, and she filed a lawsuit in a Florida court for a declaration that she was entitled to the constitutional suspension procedure. The Supreme Court of Florida issued an advisory opinion in response to a letter request by the governor, stating that board members were county officers who were entitled to the constitutional suspension procedure. *In re Advisory Opinion to the Governor*, 626 So.2d 684 (Fla.1993).

An Ohio school administrator worked for a school board for 20 years in various capacities, including attendance officer and coordinator of community education. One month after the end of a school year, the school district superintendent advised the employee that the district had abolished his unclassified position effective at the conclusion of the prior school year. The county civil service commission found that it had no jurisdiction to consider the employee's appeal because he did not perform duties within the classified civil service. An Ohio county court affirmed the commission's order and the administrator appealed to the Court of Appeals of Ohio. The court of appeals found that the board of education had a clear duty to retain the employee under an Ohio statute pertaining to school administrators. The school board appealed to the Supreme Court of Ohio.

The board argued that it had the right to suspend the employee's contract under an Ohio statute pertaining to reductions in force due to decreased enrollment. The supreme court disagreed, ruling that the applicable statute was the one relied on by the court of appeals, which deemed any school administrator reemployed unless the contract was terminated in writing on or before the last day of March of the year in which the contract expires. Because the board had not notified the employee of its intention not to reemploy him until after the March deadline, he had already been reemployed by operation of law. The court affirmed the court of appeals' judgment, reinstating the employee's contract with backpay and benefits. *State Ex Rel. Donaldson v. Athens City School Dist. Bd. of Educ.*, 68 Ohio St.3d 145, 624 N.E.2d 709 (1994).

An Illinois high school psychologist received a note written by a student which expressed guilt about his sexual orientation and hinted about suicide. The psychologist met with the student that day. The student denied an allegation that he was sexually involved with a male teacher at the school. The psychologist arranged for a therapist. Nine days later, the psychologist met with the student again. This time, the student admitted having engaged in homosexual activity with the teacher. The psychologist promptly notified school authorities about the teacher's abusive act. The school board suspended the psychologist for five days without pay for his failure to promptly report the potential suicide and sexual abuse. The psychologist sued the school board in a federal district court on constitutional grounds. The school board prevailed and the psychologist appealed to the U.S. Court of Appeals, Seventh Circuit, which upheld the suspension. The court noted language in the Illinois Abused and Neglected Child Reporting Act requiring psychologists to report child abuse immediately to the state family services department. The student's denial of abuse did not absolve the psychologist of his responsibility to report possible abuse. *Pesce v. J. Sterling Morton High School*, 830 F.2d 789 (7th Cir.1987).

Where school board policies contradict state statutes, the statutory provisions prevail. A man began teaching landscape technology at a Minnesota vocational institute in 1971. A second man began teaching the same subject at the vocational institute in 1973. In 1981, the first teacher was granted a five-year extended leave of absence through the 1985-86 school year. In February 1986, the school board proposed placing one of the teachers on "unrequested leave" for financial reasons. The teacher returning from leave was retained on the basis of seniority, and the second teacher requested a judicial review of the decision. The Minnesota Court of Appeals noted that the school district had an unrequested leave of absence plan under the collective bargaining agreement which provided that teachers accrued no seniority while on extended leave. Minnesota statutes, however, provided that teachers returning from such leave would "retain seniority and continue in contract rights" as though they had been teaching during the leave period. The court ruled that where a statute and the provisions of a collective bargaining agreement are in conflict, the statute controls. The teacher returning from extended leave was therefore the more senior teacher. The school board's decision was affirmed. *Urdahl v. Indep. School Dist. No. 181*, 396 N.W.2d 244 (Minn.App.1986).

A tenured Alabama high school principal was transferred by his school board to the position of elementary school principal. This involved a salary reduction of $4,000 per year. The principal contested this transfer on the grounds that it violated the Alabama tenure statutes. The Tenure Commission found that the transfer of a high school principal to elementary school principal involved a "loss of status" which is prohibited by the tenure statutes. The Alabama Court of Civil Appeals reversed the commission, finding that no loss of status had occurred in the transfer. The court's reasoning rested on the fact that the principal would still be tenured as a principal after his transfer to the elementary school. Hence the term "loss of status" was deemed to apply only to tenure, not rank or position. In this case, the principal retained his tenure. As such there was no loss of status and the transfer was approved. *Alabama State Tenure Comm'n v. Shelby County Bd. of Educ.*, 474 So.2d 723 (Ala.Civ.App.1985).

The Supreme Court of Wyoming held that when a tenured teacher accepts a promotion to school principal, the teacher does not forfeit his or her tenure rights. A tenured teacher was appointed to school principal and served in that capacity for nine years. In 1982, the school board declined to renew the principal's contract due to a shouting incident involving the principal and two faculty members. The school board also refused to employ the principal as a teacher, and the principal sued in state district court alleging that his tenure rights had been violated. The court ordered the school board to hold a hearing to determine whether the principal was protected under the tenure laws. The board determined that the principal was not entitled to tenure and the district court affirmed this decision. On appeal, the Wyoming Supreme Court affirmed in part and reversed in part, stating that while a principal serves at the pleasure of the school board, once tenure is acquired the only way a school board may discharge a teacher is for good cause after a hearing. The reasons given by the board for the discharge as a teacher all applied to his position of principal and that was improper, said the court. Accordingly, while the dismissal as principal was affirmed, the court ordered that the man be reinstated as a fully tenured teacher. *Spurlock v. Bd. of Trustees*, 699 P.2d 270 (Wyo.1985).

In May 1985, a secondary school principal was placed on "administrative transfer" because of the impending closure of his school. On administrative transfer his placement in another secondary principalship was "entirely contingent upon the uncertain possibility that another secondary principal would retire or resign." The principal filed a petition in a West Virginia circuit court requesting the issuance of an order placing him in the secondary principalship occupied by the district's least senior secondary principal. After the circuit court issued the order, the board of education sought a prohibition of the order's enforcement from the West Virginia Supreme Court of Appeals. The board argued that the order should not be enforced because that would require the board to violate statutory provisions with respect to the least senior principal's removal. The Supreme Court of Appeals observed that the school closure constituted a reduction in the number of professional personnel employed. The board was therefore bound by state tenure law, which provided that in cases where such a reduction was necessary, the employee with the least amount of seniority had to be released. *State v. Casey*, 349 S.E.2d 436 (W.Va.1986).

CHAPTER TEN

LABOR RELATIONS

I. REPRESENTATION BY PROFESSIONAL ASSOCIATIONS

School employees are entitled to form professional associations to represent their employment interests. Once elected, professional associations become exclusive collective bargaining agents for their members. They are under a legal duty to fairly represent all association members.

The exclusive bargaining representative of the faculty at a state college in Michigan entered into an agency-shop arrangement with the college, requiring nonunion bargaining unit employees to pay a service or agency fee equivalent to a union member's dues. Employees who objected to particular uses by the unions of their service fee brought suit under 42 U.S.C. § 1983, claiming that using the fees for purposes other than negotiating and administering the collective bargaining agreement violated their First and Fourteenth Amendment rights. A federal district court held that certain collective bargaining expenses were chargeable to the dissenting employees, the U.S. Court of Appeals affirmed, and the U.S. Supreme Court granted certiorari. The Court first noted that chargeable activities must be "germane" to collective bargaining activity and be justified by the policy interest of avoiding "free riders" who benefit from union efforts without paying for union services. It then stated that the local union could charge the objecting employees for their pro rata share of costs associated with chargeable activities of its state and national affiliates, even if those activities did not directly benefit the local bargaining unit. The local could even charge the dissenters for expenses incident to preparation for a strike which would be illegal under Michigan law. However, lobbying activities and public relations efforts were not chargeable to the objecting employees. The Court affirmed in part and reversed in part the lower courts' decisions and remanded the case. *Lehnert v. Ferris Faculty Ass'n*, 500 U.S. 507, 111 S.Ct. 1950, 114 L.Ed.2d 572 (1991).

Detroit teachers elected a labor association to become their exclusive collective bargaining representative, and it instituted an agency shop agreement. A group of teachers filed a class action lawsuit in a Michigan trial court, stating that they would not pay dues or agency fees because of their opposition to collective bargaining in the public sector. They specifically disapproved of the union's political and social activities, which they claimed were unrelated to the collective bargaining process. The teachers argued that the agency shop agreement violated state law and the First and Fourteenth Amendments to the U.S. Constitution. The court dismissed the lawsuit for failure to state a claim upon which relief could be granted. While the matter was pending before the Michigan Court of Appeals, the case was consolidated with the complaint of another group of Michigan teachers. At about the same time the Michigan legislature expressly authorized the agency shops by amending the state Public Employment Relations Act. The court of appeals then held that the amendment applied retroactively to the teachers, who argued that retroactive application violated the federal Constitution. When the Michigan Supreme Court refused to review the case, the U.S. Supreme Court accepted jurisdiction on the federal constitutional complaints.

The Supreme Court drew on its earlier private sector decisions concerning labor relations and noted that compelled support of collective bargaining representatives implicated teacher First Amendment rights to free speech and association and religious freedom. However, some constitutional infringement on free speech, association and religious exercise was justified in the interest of peaceful labor relations. As long as the union acted to promote the cause of its membership, individual members were not free to withdraw their financial support. The Court agreed with the teachers that compelled agency fees should not be used to support political views and candidates which were unrelated to collective bargaining issues. Because the state court had dismissed the case without a trial, the teachers had not received the opportunity to make specific allegations that their contributions were being used to support activities with which they disagreed. There was no evidentiary record and the Court remanded the case, vacating the court of appeals' decision. If the teachers could prove a First Amendment violation, they were entitled to relief in the form of an injunction or a pro rata refund of fees being used for such purposes. *Abood v. Detroit Board of Education*, 431 U.S. 209, 97 S.Ct. 1782, 52 L.Ed.2d 261 (1977).

Although the Supreme Court held in *Abood v. Detroit Board of Education*, above, that nonunion teachers could be compelled to pay a service fee to the union to help defray the cost of contract administration and grievance handling, the Court prohibited the use of such funds by the union for political or ideological activities not germane to the union's duties as collective bargaining agent. This prohibition was designed to prevent any infringement of nonmember teachers' free speech rights in being forced to fund political causes with which they might disagree. The Supreme Court found that the Chicago Teachers Union had not adequately protected the free speech rights of nonunion teachers. In 1982, the Chicago school board and the teachers' union agreed to deduct "proportionate share payments" from the paychecks of any nonunion employee. The deduction was fixed at 95 percent of the dues for union members, and no explanation was given as to how that figure was reached. This method of deduction was held to violate First Amendment freedom of speech protections. To guard against the possibility of nonunion teachers' service fee payments being used for political purposes disagreeable to the nonmembers, the Supreme Court ruled that there must be an adequate accounting and explanation of the basis for the deduction. In case of challenge there must be an opportunity for a reasonably prompt decision by an impartial decisionmaker as to whether any part of the service fee deduction has gone to fund political causes. Any amount which was reasonably in dispute must be held in an escrow account during pendency of the challenge. *Chicago Teachers Union v. Hudson*, 475 U.S. 292, 106 S.Ct. 1066, 89 L.Ed.2d 232 (1986).

The Michigan Education Association (MEA) represents approximately 127,000 Michigan school and college employees as their exclusive bargaining representative. A group of nonunion employees who were required to pay the MEA agency for its representational services objected to the MEA's notice of required services. The notice advised nonmember employees of the amount of the agency fee with an explanation of its expenditures. It gave nonunion members 30 days to file a written objection, and provided a form and prepaid business reply envelope in which to return the form. Nonunion members who objected to the amount of the agency fee could request that the entire amount be escrowed until the legality of the fee was determined by an arbitrator. The objecting employees filed a lawsuit against the MEA and the National Education Association in the U.S. District Court for the Western District of Michigan, which granted the MEA's motion to dismiss the lawsuit. The employees appealed to the U.S. Court of Appeals, Sixth Circuit, which remanded the case for reconsideration in view of the U.S. Supreme Court's decision in *Lehnert v. Ferris Faculty Assn.*, above. The district court again granted the union's dismissal motion and the employees appealed to the U.S. Court of Appeals, Sixth Circuit.

The court of appeals found no constitutional violation in the MEA's notification procedures. It provided all nonmember employees with an explanation of their agency fee calculation and provided a clear procedure for objecting parties to appeal. Because the notice accurately informed the nonunion members about the fee, there was no constitutional violation and the court of appeals affirmed the district court's judgment. *Jibson v. Michigan Educ. Assn.—NEA*, 30 F.3d 723 (6th Cir.1994).

Nonunion teachers employed by a California school district were required to pay an agency fee to the district's exclusive collective bargaining agent. Because the collective bargaining agency conducted some activities unrelated to collective bargaining duties, the nonunion employees were entitled to a refund of a portion of the agency fee. The school district placed the agency fee deductions in an interest-bearing escrow account, and nonunion teachers had the opportunity to apply for a prorated refund. The refunded portion represented amounts used by the collective bargaining agency for ideological purposes, including campaign contributions. Although nonunion teachers were forced to make advance contributions to the collective bargaining agency for the first few months of the school year, the refund resulted in a moderate cash advance when it was received in December each year. The nonunion teachers argued that the deduction and escrow procedure violated their free speech rights under the First Amendment. They sued the school district in the U.S. District Court for the Central District of California, which upheld the constitutionality of the agency fee deduction procedure. The teachers appealed to the U.S. Court of Appeals, Ninth Circuit.

The court of appeals originally issued a decision reversing the district court opinion. However, it then issued a superseding opinion affirming the district court's decision. The deduction and escrow process did not interfere with the teachers' First Amendment rights and the escrowed funds were not available to the union for ideological purposes. The procedure was reasonable and the small amount of money involved did not rise to the level of a constitutional violation. An arbitration process was also available for nonunion teachers who objected to the amount prorated for escrow purposes. The procedure properly balanced the collective bargaining organization's right to collect fees and the nonunion teachers' First Amendment rights. The district court decision was affirmed. *Grunwald v. San Bernardino City Unif. School Dist.*, 994 F.2d 1370 (9th Cir.1993).

In 1986, New York appropriated Excellence In Training (EIT) funds to supplement the salaries of teachers employed by local school districts. School districts received EIT funds according to specified aid ratios. A portion of funds received were to be used to increase the salaries of certain teachers. Regulations defined "teachers" for purposes of EIT salary supplements as employees in the same bargaining unit as full-time classroom teachers, employees not represented by a bargaining unit but designated as teachers and full-time classroom instructors. Several administrators who were not engaged in full-time classroom teaching and did not belong to bargaining units sued the New York Commissioner of Education. They claimed the regulations were unconstitutional. A New York trial court held for the administrators and the commissioner appealed to an appellate division court. The administrators argued that they were qualified teachers and taught several classes in addition to their administrative duties. These administrative duties were identical to those performed by administrators in nearby school districts who were eligible for the EIT salary benefits solely because of membership in the same bargaining units as full-time classroom teachers. The appellate division court affirmed the trial court decision in favor of the administrators. There was no valid basis for discriminating between the administrators and other similarly situated administrators who were members of teachers' bargaining units. The regulations violated the Equal Protection Clause of the U.S. and state constitutions. *Schneider v. Ambach,* 526 N.Y.S.2d 857 (A.D.3d Dept.1988).

A Michigan teacher's union filed a petition for a certification election to determine whether substitute teachers could vote on union representation. The Michigan Employment Relations Commission (MERC) ruled that substitutes who worked a specific number of days were entitled to union representation. The school district affected by the MERC's decision appealed the determination to the

Michigan Court of Appeals claiming that the administrative determination was unsupported by evidence and departed from previous decisions. The court affirmed the administrative determination by MERC. It ruled that substitute teachers were public employees within the meaning of Michigan statutes. The MERC had the power to determine the "community of interests" necessary to determining the appropriateness of union representation to the part-time teachers. The objective in designating bargaining units was to create the largest possible unit within a community of interests. There was sufficient evidence to justify the MERC's decision and the MERC gave its reasons for departing from previous decisions. The administrative decision was affirmed by the court. *Taylor Federation of Teachers v. Taylor Bd. of Educ.*, 423 N.W.2d 44 (Mich.App.1988).

II.   NEGOTIATION OF COLLECTIVE BARGAINING AGREEMENTS

Federal labor law imposes an obligation upon employers to bargain with duly-elected collective bargaining representatives over the terms and conditions of employment.

A union collective-bargaining agent who represented the employees of two schools owned and operated by the U.S. Army, submitted proposals asking for mileage reimbursement, paid leave, and salary increases on behalf of the schools' employees. The schools refused to negotiate, stating that under Title VII of the Civil Service Reform Act of 1978 they were not required to negotiate these matters. The union filed a complaint with the Federal Labor Relations Authority (FLRA) which held that the union's proposals were negotiable. The schools appealed to the U.S. Court of Appeals, Eleventh Circuit, which upheld the FLRA's decision. The schools then appealed to the U.S. Supreme Court. Title VII of the Civil Service Reform Act defines conditions of employment as matters "affecting working conditions" but excludes matters relating to prohibited political activities, classification of positions, and those specifically provided for by federal statute. The Court determined that the union's proposals were "conditions of employment." The Supreme Court, affirming the district court's decision, held that the schools were required to negotiate salary increases and fringe benefits. *Fort Stewart Schools v. Federal Labor Relations Authority*, 495 U.S. 641, 110 S.Ct. 2043, 109 L.Ed.2d 659 (1990).

A Kansas school board appointed an evaluation committee to devise a new teacher evaluation form. The board failed to notify the collective bargaining organization representing teachers in the district that it was revising the evaluation form. It then adopted the new form at a board meeting. The collective bargaining organization filed a complaint with the state department of human resources, claiming that the board had engaged in a prohibited practice by unilaterally imposing a change in evaluation procedures. A hearing officer determined that the board had failed to negotiate in good faith in violation of a Kansas labor statute, and this result was affirmed by a Kansas trial court. The board appealed to the Court of Appeals of Kansas. The court of appeals noted that appraisal procedures constituted negotiable terms and conditions of professional employment under a Kansas labor statute. However, evaluation criteria were not negotiable under the statute. The court of appeals then rejected the school board's argument that the new form concerned only evaluation criteria. The form was an evaluation procedure involving the mechanics of employer evaluation. Accordingly, the institution of the new evaluation form was mandatorily negotiable and the court affirmed the trial court decision. *Bd. of Educ., Unif. School Dist. No. 314 v. Kansas Dept. of Human Resources*, 856 P.2d 1343 (Kan.App.1993).

The president of the Vermont Technical College reviewed the faculty schedule and decided that the faculty workload was inequitable. He formed an ad hoc committee which was to propose workload recommendations. The committee's guidelines were then utilized for scheduling purposes. The result was an increase in workloads, often without compensation. The Vermont State College Faculty Federation brought a grievance to the Vermont Labor Relations Board, claiming that the president's unilateral action was an unfair labor practice. The board agreed and the college appealed to the Supreme Court of Vermont. The supreme court upheld the board's decision stating that the board's order that proposed changes in the workload should be negotiated was not overbroad and did not overstep the board's authority. *Faculty Federation v. Vt. State Colleges*, 547 A.2d 1340 (Vt.1988).

The Jersey City school board and the local teachers' union entered into a collective bargaining agreement governing administrative and supervisory positions which stated: "All vacancies and positions shall be filled without regard to race, age, creed, color, religion, nationality, sex or marital status." The school board later implemented an affirmative action plan which gave hiring and other preferences to blacks and Hispanics. The teachers' union sued on the ground that the affirmative action plan was contrary to the collective bargaining agreement. The New Jersey Superior Court, Appellate Division, upheld the board's affirmative action plan, ruling that the implementation of such a plan was a managerial prerogative of the school board. It observed that the teachers' union had been on notice that the board had an affirmative action plan because it referred to itself as "an Equal Opportunity and Affirmative Action Employer." The court also held that the board's affirmative action plan was acceptable under both New Jersey law and the Equal Protection Clause of the U.S. Constitution. The plan was a legitimate effort to further the board's educational goals through the attainment of an integrated work force. *Jersey City Educ. Ass'n v. Bd. of Educ.*, 527 A.2d 84 (N.J.Super.A.D.1987).

III. ENFORCEMENT OF COLLECTIVE BARGAINING AGREEMENTS

School districts and employees become bound by the terms of their agreements. Failure to abide by the terms of a collective bargaining agreement is an unfair labor practice.

In a five-to-four decision, the U.S. Supreme Court upheld a collective bargaining agreement between an Indiana school board and the local teacher union which provided that the teacher union, to the exclusion of a rival union, had access to the school district's internal mail and delivery system. The rival union challenged the denial of access to the mail system on grounds that the restriction violated free speech rights under the First Amendment and the Equal Protection Clause under the Fourteenth Amendment. The Supreme Court held that since the interschool mail system was not a public forum generally available for use by the public, access to it could be reasonably restricted without violating either free speech or equal protection rights. The Court noted the special responsibilities of the exclusive bargaining representative and the fact that other channels of communication remained available to the rival union. *Perry Educ. Ass'n v. Perry Local Educators' Ass'n*, 460 U.S. 37, 103 S.Ct. 948, 74 L.Ed.2d 794 (1983).

In another U.S. Supreme Court case, Minnesota community college faculty members brought suit against the State Board for Community Colleges. The faculty alleged that a state statute requiring public employers to engage in official exchanges of views only with their professional employees' exclusive representatives on certain policy questions violated their First Amendment rights. Under the statute, public employers were required to bargain only with the employees' exclusive bargaining representative. The statute gave professional employees, such as college faculty members, the right to "meet and confer" with the employer on matters outside the scope of the collective bargaining agreement. The faculty members objected to the "meet and confer" provision, saying that rights of professional employees within the bargaining unit who were not members of the exclusive representative were violated. The Supreme Court held that the "meet and confer" provision did not violate the faculty members' constitutional rights. There was no constitutional right to force public employers to listen to the members' views. The fact that an academic setting was involved did not give them any special constitutional right to a voice in the employer's policymaking decisions. Further, the state had a legitimate interest in ensuring that its public employer heard one voice presenting the majority view of its professional employees on employment related policy questions. *Minnesota Comm. College Assn. v. Knight*, 465 U.S. 271, 104 S.Ct. 1058, 79 L.Ed.2d 299 (1984).

A New York school district adopted a policy banning smoking in open areas of its schools and prohibiting smoking in school buses whether or not students were present. The smoking ban was designed to eliminate smoking and prevent second hand smoke. The school district refused to negotiate over the smoking ban with the collective bargaining organization representing the school bus drivers. The organization filed an improper labor practices charge with the state Public Employment Relations Board (PERB). An administrative law judge determined that no state law preempted the school district's obligation to negotiate a ban on smoking, and the judge's decision was confirmed by the PERB. The district obtained annulment of the PERB's decision in a state trial court, but the New York Appellate Division, Third Department, reversed. The school district appealed to the Court of Appeals of New York.

The court of appeals determined that neither the state education law nor the public health law preempted the district's obligation to bargain with the drivers. Because smoking regulations affected a term or condition of employment, the board's refusal to bargain with the drivers was improper. The public health law in its present state prohibited only smoking in vehicles when occupied by passengers. The court observed that after the commencement of the lawsuit, the state assembly had passed an amendment to forbid smoking in any school vehicle. It affirmed the appellate division's decision. *Newark Valley Cent. School Dist. v. PERB*, 83 N.Y.2d 315, 610 N.Y.S.2d 134, 632 N.E.2d 443 (1994).

A number of instructors worked for an Ohio public school board as special education and English as a second language tutors. They held valid teaching certificates and worked on an as-needed basis at hourly rates. Their salary levels were not equivalent to teachers in the district and they were not members of the bargaining unit representing teachers who worked in district schools. After several years, the tutors were brought into the bargaining unit under a separate wage schedule and they became aware of Ohio state court decisions that interpreted teacher wage statutes as also applying to tutors. The tutors filed a petition for an order to compel the school board to pay them back wages for the difference between their actual pay and teachers' salaries prior to joining the collective bargaining association. The court denied the petition and the tutors appealed to the Supreme Court of Ohio.

The supreme court held that tutors were "teachers" under Ohio law and were therefore entitled to the same pay where they were employed by a school board and were providing instruction to students. The court of appeals had properly held that the tutors had no right to back pay under the collective bargaining agreements for the period prior to joining the union. However, an Ohio statute that applied in the absence of a collective bargaining agreement required payment in accordance with applicable teacher wage schedules. Accordingly, the tutors had a right to receive the difference between the amounts they were actually paid and the amount that would have been due under the teachers' salary schedule after joining the teachers' union. The court reversed and remanded the case. *State ex rel. Chavis v. Sycamore City School Dist. Bd. of Educ.*, 71 Ohio St.3d 26, 641 N.E.2d 188 (1994).

A Wisconsin school district and the union representing its teachers negotiated a contract that did not state the minimum usable increment of sick leave. As an unwritten policy, the district allowed employees to use sick leave in one-hour increments. The contract contained a management clause, purporting to reserve the board's right to establish reasonable work rules and a "zipper clause" stating that supplemental amendments and past practices were not binding on either party. When the contract expired, the parties were unable to reach a new agreement. The district then unilaterally changed its leave policy so that sick leave was limited to minimum half-day (four-hour) increments. The union filed a complaint with the Wisconsin Employment Relations Commission (WERC), claiming that the unilateral change in sick leave policy was a prohibited practice. The WERC agreed with the union, and the district appealed to a Wisconsin trial court. The court affirmed the WERC's decision and the district appealed to the Court of Appeals of Wisconsin.

The court of appeals stated that zipper clauses did not authorize unilateral changes in employment practices and that the normal function of the clause was to maintain the status quo, not to facilitate change. Because sick leave was a matter that was mandatorily subject to collective bargaining, the district was not authorized to unilaterally change the sick leave policy between contracts. The district could not rely on the management contract to enforce the sick leave policy change for the same reason. The court affirmed the judgment for the union. *St. Croix Falls School Dist. v. Wisconsin Employment Relations Comm.*, 522 N.W.2d 507 (Wis.App.1994).

The Los Angeles Unified School District and the labor association representing its teachers adopted a collective bargaining agreement granting part-time status to eligible employees on terms dictated by district regulations. The district's regulations limited part-time status to five years, at the district's discretion. However, California statutes required that part-time status be available for a ten-year maximum to qualified employees. It also made such status available upon request by qualified employees, with revocation possible only through the mutual consent of the employer and employee. The school district eventually stopped granting requests for part-time status. The association petitioned a California trial court for an order to compel the school district and board to honor requests for part-time status as required by the statute. Although the court found the district's regulations in violation of the statute, it held that it was without authority to grant relief to the association. The association appealed to the California Court of Appeal, Second District.

The court of appeal found that the statutes in question were mandatory and had been in effect at the time of the collective bargaining agreement. It disagreed with the trial court's decision that it was without authority to rule the regulations void. The statute expressly permitted qualified employees to work part-time. The statute prevailed over the district's conflicting regulations and the collective bargaining agreement. The court of appeal reversed and remanded the trial court's judgment, with directions to grant the association's petition. *United Teachers— Los Angeles v. Los Angeles Unified School Dist.*, 29 Cal.Rptr.2d 897 (Cal.App.2d Dist.1994).

New York Education Law § 1709[22] prevents school districts from operating cafeteria programs that are not completely self-sustaining. One district submitted a budget proposal to voters that included a $60,000 breakfast and lunch program. The proposal was defeated three times. The district then hired an outside food service to comply with the statute causing a district cafeteria employee to lose her job. The employee filed an improper labor practice charge against the district through her collective bargaining organization. The state Public Employment Relations Board (PERB) upheld the improper labor practice charge and ordered the employee reinstated with backpay and full benefits. It also ordered the private contract voided. The district appealed to a New York trial court, which transferred the matter to the New York Supreme Court, Appellate Division, Third Department. On appeal, the court agreed with the district's argument that state education law required it to terminate the school lunch program and hire a private food service because of the school budget defeat and consequent imposition of a contingency budget. The employee was not entitled to reinstatement through collective bargaining because the elimination of her job was the result of operation of law and not school district discretion. The court annulled the PERB action. *Germantown Central School Dist. v. PERB*, 613 N.Y.S.2d 957 (A.D.3d Dept.1994).

An Ohio school district employed a Spanish teacher under a three-year contract. In the final year of the contract, the school's principal recommended that the teacher not be rehired based on classroom evaluations, and the school board did not renew the contract. The teacher requested a written statement of the reasons for the board's failure to rehire him. The board provided a statement that advised the teacher that the contract was terminated according to the terms of the collective bargaining agreement. The teacher was not allowed to make an oral presentation at the termination hearing. He claimed that he was entitled to introduce witnesses and cross-examine evaluators who had performed in-class observations under an Ohio statute. He argued that the statute took precedence over the collective bargaining agreement and sued the board in an Ohio county court. The court held for the board, and the teacher appealed to the Court of Appeals of Ohio, Fourth District.

The court of appeals reasoned that even though the collective bargaining agreement had lapsed prior to the teacher's final year, the school board and collective bargaining association had continued to act according to its terms and were deemed to have acquiesced to them. Under contract law, where parties continue to act as though a contract is valid, the status quo continues, and contract terms prevail as long as neither party expresses an intent not to be bound by the contract. The terms of the lapsed contract took precedence over the provisions of the Ohio statute during the interim period, and the board had fully complied with them. The trial court decision for the school board was affirmed. *Young v. Washington Local School Dist. Bd. of Educ.*, 619 N.E.2d 62 (Ohio App.4th Dist.1993).

A New York school district transferred a kindergarten teacher to a first grade class in contravention of the applicable collective bargaining agreement. A state arbitrator ordered the teacher's return to the kindergarten class, but a New York trial court vacated the arbitrator's decision. The New York Supreme Court, Appellate Division, affirmed the trial court decision. The Court of Appeals of New York reinstated the arbitrator's decision, finding that it was consistent with New York Education Law § 1711, which had been amended while the matter was being litigated. The amendment reversed New York's existing public policy so that teacher transfers could be negotiated under collective bargaining agreements. *Bd. of Educ. of Greenburgh Cent. School Dist. No. 7 v. Greenburgh Teachers Fed.*, 82 N.Y.2d 771, 603 N.Y.S.2d 823, 623 N.E.2d 1173 (1993).

A Connecticut school district and a labor organization representing district employees reached three agreements governing the terms and conditions of employment in the school district. One agreement between the parties established a seniority system and two additional agreements protected tenured teachers in alternative education programs from layoffs and involuntary transfers without regard to seniority. The district laid off a tenured English teacher as part of a workforce reduction. She claimed that the district had taken the action unlawfully and had violated the labor agreements by employing tutors in teaching positions for which she was qualified. She also claimed that the alternative education agreements had been improperly ratified by the labor organization. A Connecticut trial court affirmed a hearing officer's decision for the school board, and appeal reached the Supreme Court of Connecticut.

The supreme court rejected the board's argument that the teacher had no standing under the collective bargaining agreement to bring her lawsuit as a means of enforcing her individual rights. However, the trial court decision for the school board was supported by the evidence. The trial court was justified in its finding that the teacher had no interest in accepting a tutor job and that the school had experienced difficulty finding tutors able to speak Spanish. Finding no merit to the teacher's argument that the labor organization was without authority to ratify the labor agreements, the supreme court affirmed the trial court's decision. *Tomlinson v. Bd. of Educ. of City of Bristol*, 629 A.2d 333 (Conn.1993).

A physical education teacher in Maryland also served as the coach for several athletic teams, including the football team, and received supplemental pay for these positions in accordance with the provisions of the collective bargaining agreement. At the conclusion of the 1983 season, the principal decided not to reappoint the teacher to the position of head football coach. The teacher then filed a grievance and the arbitrator found that there was no just cause for not reappointing him and that the County Board of Education was required to negotiate with him. The teacher was awarded damages. The county board of education sought a court order to vacate the award in a Maryland trial court. The trial court found no error and the county board appealed to the Court of Special Appeals of Maryland. Maryland law provides that local boards of education must engage in collective bargaining. It mandates that a public school employer shall meet and negotiate in all matters that relate to salaries, wages, hours, and working conditions. Clearly, the coaching position dealt with matters of wages. Since the failure to reappoint the coach was a legal topic of collective bargaining, the court affirmed the decision of the trial court and granted damages to the teacher. *Bd. of Educ. v. Regala,* 589 A.2d 993 (Md.App.1991).

A Connecticut teacher filed a grievance when the position of English department head, which he had applied for, was filled by a less senior teacher. The teachers' collective bargaining agreement required that when two candidates for a position were equally qualified, the position should go to the most senior teacher. An arbitrator ordered the school district to promote the teacher to the position. Instead of appealing the arbitrator's decision, the school district eliminated the department head position. The teacher filed an unfair labor practice complaint with the state labor relations board. The board ordered the school district to reinstate the position and appoint the teacher to it. The school district appealed the board's decision to a Connecticut trial court. The trial court held that the elimination of a teaching position was a discretionary act of the school board and that the labor relations board could not order the district to reinstate the position. The labor relations board appealed to the Supreme Court of Connecticut.

On appeal, the board of education admitted that its sole reason for eliminating the position was to prevent the teacher from holding a position for which the board believed he was not qualified. It argued that because the arbitrator's decision concerned only the teacher's entitlement to the position when it did exist, the subsequent elimination of the position, which was a discretionary act, was not an unfair labor practice. The labor board argued that the school board's action constituted a refusal to participate in good faith in mediation and arbitration, and was an unfair labor practice in violation of Connecticut law. The court examined the relevant statutes and concluded that the school board's action was an unfair labor practice. The court reversed the judgment of the trial court and dismissed the board of education's appeal. *Bd. of Educ. of Town of Thomaston v. State Bd. of Labor Relations*, 584 A.2d 1172 (Conn.1991).

An Indiana school board adopted its 1985-86 school calendar without bargaining with the teachers' association. The teachers filed a complaint with the Indiana Education Employment Relations Board, which ordered the school board to bargain with the association on all school calendar items included in their collective bargaining agreement, so long as bargaining did not infringe upon the school board's exclusive managerial power. An Indiana trial court set aside the IEERB's order, stating that all items were subject to mandatory bargaining; but the Court of Appeals of Indiana reversed. The court stated that Indiana law prohibits contracts which delegate the school board's exclusive managerial powers. Only those items set out in the IEERB's order which do not assume any managerial powers are bargainable. *Indiana EERB v. Teachers Ass'n*, 546 N.E.2d 101 (Ind.App.3d Dist.1989).

A Pennsylvania school district suffered a financial crisis. Without consulting the teachers' labor association, the district sent students in grades 7-12 to a neighboring school district. The labor association demanded collective bargaining, but the district concluded a contract with the other district and laid off 13 teachers. The state labor relations board ruled that the action was equivalent to contracting out bargaining unit work and was a proper subject for collective bargaining. A Pennsylvania trial court reversed the board's order and the labor association appealed to the Pennsylvania Commonwealth Court. The commonwealth court ruled that the board had properly held that a transfer of bargaining unit work was an unfair labor practice. It reversed the trial court's decision, reinstating the board's order. *Midland Borough School Dist. v. PLRB*, 560 A.2d 303 (Pa.Cmwlth.1989).

A probationary New York City school teacher was terminated by a letter from the school system's chancellor. The teacher pursued a grievance under the applicable collective bargaining agreement and the chancellor reinstated him six months later. The teacher claimed he was entitled to interim benefits and backpay for the period of his appeal. A New York trial court found in his favor and the school board appealed to the New York Court of Appeals. The court noted that under New York education law, decisions to grant or deny tenure to probationary teachers are final. The grievance procedure followed by the teacher was from the collective bargaining agreement. Nothing in New York education law provided for reinstatement or backpay. State law did not establish an optional grievance procedure like the one this teacher had followed. If teachers were entitled to full benefits during the review process, they would only have to petition for review to receive interim benefits. The chancellor's decision was final and the teacher was not entitled to interim pay or benefits. *Frasier v. Bd. of Educ. of City School Dist.*, 525 N.E.2d 725 (N.Y.1988).

A collective bargaining agreement between an Indiana school corporation and a teachers' union provided that the union could use the school corporation's interschool mail delivery system to communicate with the teachers. The school corporation brought an action seeking to determine whether its carriage of the union's letters violated the U.S. Postal Service's monopoly on mail delivery. The U.S. Court of Appeals, Seventh Circuit, noted that federal law provided an exception to the federal government's monopoly on postal services for "letters of the carrier." The court stated, however, that this exception did not apply to the union's use of the school district's interschool mail delivery system. The collective bargaining provision was invalid. *Fort Wayne Community Schools v. Fort Wayne Education Association, Inc.*, 977 F.2d 358 (7th Cir.1992).

IV. GRIEVANCES AND ARBITRATION

Collective bargaining agreements contain grievance procedures for the resolution of contractual items on which the parties cannot agree. Where the item in contention concerns the interpretation of the agreement, the school board must enter into arbitration with the teachers' union if it is called for in the collective bargaining agreement.

A Pennsylvania bus driver abandoned his vehicle while returning to school with a busload of seventh and eighth graders who had been to a theater. He left the bus to confront a motorist who was shouting obscenities and threatening him. Prior to exiting the bus, the driver turned the engine off and set the parking brake. He returned to the bus within approximately 15 seconds. The school district conducted an investigation and determined that the driver had intentionally abandoned the students. It fired the driver and he filed a grievance through his union. An arbitrator sustained the grievance, finding that the driver's behavior constituted negligence rather than intentional misconduct. He reduced the disciplinary action from employment termination to a 90-day suspension. The school district filed a Pennsylvania county court action to vacate the arbitration award, but the court denied the petition. The district then appealed to the Commonwealth Court of Pennsylvania, where it argued that the trial court had misapplied the law.

The commonwealth court disagreed, stating that the trial court had applied the proper standard of law. Contrary to the district's assertion that its decision was a core responsibility that was entitled to due deference, the decision involved the interpretation of a collective bargaining agreement. Accordingly, the appropriate standard of review was contained in the state arbitration act. The arbitrator had properly decided to refashion a remedy once it was determined that the driver had committed mere negligence and not wilful misconduct. Where an arbitrator determines that no cause for dismissal exists and the collective bargaining agreement does not forbid the modification of a school district penalty, the arbitrator may modify the discipline. The commonwealth court affirmed the denial of the petition. *Upper St. Clair School Dist. v. Upper St. Clair Educ. Support Personnel Assn.*, 649 A.2d 470 (Pa.Cmwlth.1994).

A Pennsylvania school district entered into a collective bargaining agreement with a teachers' association. The district's athletic director position was customarily a nonpaying, voluntary, part-time assignment for a full-time teacher who was a member of the bargaining unit. However, over the years, the district expanded its extracurricular activity program. The district created a full-time athletic director position and published a new job description. An arbitrator sustained the association's grievance challenging the new job description, and the school board approved a supervisory position incorporating the athletic director duties. It then eliminated the athletic director position as a bargaining unit job and promoted the present athletic director to the supervisory position. The teachers' association filed another grievance claiming that this action resulted in the transfer of bargaining unit work to a nonbargaining unit employee. An arbitrator determined that the board's action violated the collective bargaining agreement. The Pennsylvania Commonwealth Court ruled for the school district and the association appealed to the Supreme Court of Pennsylvania.

The supreme court found no contractual provision between the parties concerning the arbitrability of extracurricular activities. It only stated that after-hour assignments performed by teachers were nonteaching duties. Extracurricular work performed by teachers was traditionally considered nonarbitratable and there was no language in the collective bargaining agreement on which the arbitrator could base the decision that the matter was subject to arbitration. It affirmed the commonwealth court's decision for the school district. *Harbor Creek School Dist. v. Harbor Creek Educ. Assn.*, 640 A.2d 899 (Pa.1994).

A tenured New Jersey teacher supervised special education students in a high school resource room. Because the students required special attention and supervision, the teacher's frequent absences created difficulty. She missed 55 days during one four-month period due to surgery and another 27 days because of injuries received in a train accident. The teacher was denied a salary increase for the following school year based on her record of absences. The district asserted that the withholding of the salary raise was for predominantly educational reasons. The state Public Employment Relations Commission (PERC) determined that the withholding was for predominantly disciplinary reasons and was therefore arbitrable under the applicable collective bargaining agreement. An arbitrator then determined that the withholding of the salary increase had been arbitrary and capricious because it was based only on the number of absences without regard for the reasons for absence. Appeal reached the Supreme Court of New Jersey.

The teacher's labor association argued that the arbitrator had properly applied the just cause standard of review because the denial of the salary raise was based on disciplinary reasons. The district argued that the arbitrator had improperly imposed this standard of review because it was not contained within the collective bargaining agreement. The court determined that the weight of labor relations authority held that the just cause standard was properly used even if not specified in the agreement. Because the PERC had determined that the denial of the raise had been based on discipline, the arbitrator was bound by this determination and had applied the correct legal standard. Accordingly, the arbitrator's decision was affirmed. *Scotch Plains-Fanwood Bd. of Educ. v. Scotch Plains-Fanwood Educ. Assn.*, 139 N.J. 141, 651 A.2d 1018 (1995).

A Rhode Island labor organization representing teachers of English as a second language disputed a memorandum from the director of the program requiring them to submit copies of their lesson plans to the director each month. The union argued that this procedure constituted a unilateral change in working conditions that violated the collective bargaining agreement. Its request for arbitration was denied by the local school committee, which stated that the appropriate recourse was appeal to the state education commissioner. A Rhode Island trial court determined that the lesson plan memorandum constituted a management prerogative that was not subject to arbitration. The union appealed to the Supreme Court of Rhode Island. According to the supreme court, the English as a second language program was mandated by state law. It was subject to the state education department's rules and regulations, and the committee had a necessary oversight and evaluation role in day-to-day operations of the program. The school committee did not have the power to bargain away statutory responsibilities and the trial court had properly found that there was no arbitrable grievance. *Pawtucket School Comm. v. Pawtucket Teachers' Alliance, Local No. 930*, 652 A.2d 970 (R.I.1995).

In a second Rhode Island case, the state supreme court affirmed a trial court judgment in favor of a local school committee that had denied the grievance of a nontenured teacher whose contract was not renewed. The court rejected the teacher and union's argument that nontenured teachers could file grievances to challenge unfavorable employment evaluations. The teacher was required to follow the statutory procedure for appealing unfavorable employment decisions of a school committee to the state education department and from there to a state trial court. The supreme court affirmed the denial of the teacher's grievance. *School Comm. of the Town of Johnston v. Johnston Fed. of Teachers*, 652 A.2d 976 (R.I.1995).

A New Mexico school superintendent was employed for 12 years under successive two-year contracts. His relationship with the school board deteriorated until the board suspended him with pay while it investigated charges of abuse of his office and failure to disclose a conflict of interest. The board's decision to fire the superintendent was affirmed by an arbitrator pursuant to a New Mexico statute, and the superintendent appealed to a New Mexico trial court. The trial court confirmed the arbitration award and the superintendent appealed to the Supreme Court of New Mexico.

The supreme court held that by accepting employment with the district, the superintendent had implicitly agreed to the contract cancellation procedures contained in New Mexico law, including the requirement that any dispute would be arbitrated. He had suffered no due process violation in being suspended with pay. The minimal requirements of due process had been met, including adequate notice, a neutral decisionmaker, opportunity to present evidence and confront witnesses, the right to an attorney and a record of the proceedings. However, the statute limited review of an arbitrator's decision to cases of "corruption, fraud, deception or collusion." In order to comply with due process by providing for meaningful judicial review, the appropriate standard of review of an administrative action was to determine whether the decision was arbitrary, unlawful, unreasonable, capricious or not based on substantial evidence. The court reversed the trial court order and remanded it for review under the appropriate standard. *Bd. of Educ. of Carlsbad Mun. Schools v. Harrell*, 882 P.2d 511 (N.M.1994).

A Montana school district hired lay readers to assist high school teachers in reading and grading papers. The employment of teachers in the district was governed by a collective bargaining agreement establishing a grievance procedure for unresolved, grievable matters. When the school district eliminated the lay reader program at the beginning of the school year, the teachers' association filed a grievance with the school board requesting reinstatement of the program. The board determined after a hearing that the program was not grievable under the collective bargaining agreement and that it should be eliminated. The board later refused to arbitrate the matter, claiming that if the matter was not grievable it was also not arbitrable. The teachers' association sued the school board in a Montana trial court, which granted the school board's summary judgment motion. The teachers' association then appealed to the Supreme Court of Montana.

The supreme court held that under Montana law, collective bargaining agreements are to be enforced under their own terms, and if there is no applicable arbitration clause in the agreement, the matters are not required to be submitted to arbitration. Even though the state policy encouraged the resolution of disputes through grievances and arbitration, not all controversies were arbitrable. Since there was no agreement to arbitrate the lay reader program in the collective bargaining agreement, the failure to provide grievance and arbitration proceedings did not violate the agreement. The supreme court upheld the trial court's decision for the school board. *Missoula County High School Educ. Ass'n. v. Bd. of Trustees, Missoula County High Schools,* 857 P.2d 696 (Mont.1993).

Two Virginia elementary school teachers were reassigned to different schools in the district for the following school year. Each of the teachers claimed that the transfers were punishment for availing themselves of the school's "open door" policy, under which they discussed school matters with administrators instead of bringing them to their own immediate supervisors. The school board determined that the transfers were not grievable under Virginia law, but this result was reversed by a Virginia trial court. The school board appealed to the Supreme Court of Virginia. The supreme court observed that under Virginia law, school boards had the exclusive right to manage their own affairs. The hiring, transfer, assignment and retention of teachers within school districts constituted a category of activities which was expressly excluded from matters which were grievable under the statute. The teachers had tried to miscast their reassignment as a layoff and had raised the free speech issue in order to circumvent statutory language. Because the teachers had not stated any facts indicating that the board had violated its own policies, and because the school board was clearly within its powers to transfer the teachers, the trial court reversed and dismissed the lawsuit. *County School Bd. of York County v. Epperson*, 435 S.E.2d 647 (Va.1993).

A Montana school superintendent recommended that a tenured teacher be dismissed. After a hearing, the school district dismissed the teacher. The teacher initiated a statutory appeal which he later dismissed. Subsequently, his union filed suit to compel arbitration under the terms of the collective bargaining agreement. A trial court granted summary judgment to the union, and the school district appealed to the Supreme Court of Montana. Despite the fact that the teacher had two distinct remedial avenues, the doctrine of election of remedies did not preclude the pursuit of a grievance to arbitration. The court affirmed the trial court's decision in favor of the union. *Frazer Education Ass'n v. Board of Trustees, Valley County Elementary School Dist. No. 2*, 846 P.2d 267 (Mont. 1993).

A Minnesota school district employed five cooks under a collective bargaining agreement. The school district notified the cooks that it was considering replacing the current food service with a subcontractor because of rising costs. The district proposed a three-year wage freeze, a waiver of the comparable worth requirements under Minnesota law, and elimination of vacation and holiday benefits. The cooks requested that the issue be submitted to arbitration and the district refused. It entered into a contract with an outside food service company and notified the cooks that they were no longer employees of the district, but could obtain employment with the subcontractor. The cooks filed a grievance asserting that they had been terminated without just cause in violation of the collective bargaining agreement. The cooks filed a motion with the trial court to compel arbitration. The trial court denied the motion, ruling that the decision to subcontract was an inherent managerial right and as such was exempt from arbitration. The cooks appealed to the Minnesota Court of Appeals. The appellate court determined that subcontracting is a mandatory subject of negotiation. The court ordered the parties to submit the issue of the subcontracting to arbitration. *School Service Employees Union Local No. 284 v. Indep. School Dist. No. 88*, 459 N.W.2d 336 (Minn. App. 1990).

A Maine school superintendent hired a department head who was not a member of the teachers' association. Two in-house applicants for the position filed a grievance with the school board. They claimed that the hiring violated the collective bargaining agreement because it did not comply with the board's policy that department heads show successful classroom experience. The board denied the grievance and sought a stay of arbitration which the Superior Court of Maine granted. The teachers' association appealed to the Supreme Judicial Court of Maine. The court held that the superintendent and the school board had a statutory responsibility to fill teaching positions. Arbitration would involve an investigation of the qualifications of the new department head and a review of the board's decision to hire him, and this would impede the board's statutory responsibility. The supreme court affirmed the superior court decision. *Maine School Admin. Dist. v. Teachers Ass'n*, 567 A.2d 77 (Me. 1989).

An Iowa elementary teacher was given poor evaluations by her supervisor. She filed a grievance challenging the evaluations as not supported by the evidence. The school district notified her that termination was being recommended in accordance with Iowa Code § 279.27 based on her negative performance evaluations. She then filed another grievance concerning the termination recommendation. The superintendent denied both grievances and concluded that neither grievance was arbitrable. She then moved to compel arbitration of her performance evaluation in an Iowa trial court. After the trial court denied the motion, she appealed to the Iowa Supreme Court. The supreme court determined that arbitration takes precedence over an ongoing § 279 proceeding only if the decision to terminate a teacher was arbitrable. In the present case, the school's bargaining agreement did not clearly provide for arbitration for grievances concerning performance evaluations. Therefore, the court affirmed the trial court's decision. *Atlantic Educ. Ass'n v. Atlantic School Dist.*, 469 N.W.2d 689 (Iowa 1991).

A group of Indiana special education teachers were assigned to a school corporation that had a 180-day school year. Their previous assignment was to a school corporation that offered a higher salary, but which had a 183-day school year. They received a prorated salary which was incorporated into each individual teacher's contract with the LEA. Desiring the full contract salary from their previous assignment, the teachers filed a grievance. Their grievance was granted by their principal at an interim level. That interim disposition was later rescinded by the superintendent of schools. The teachers sued the school corporation in state court, claiming that the grievance disposition was valid and binding, and that the salary proration violated their rights. An Indiana trial court found for the cooperative and the teachers appealed to the Indiana Court of Appeals.

The court of appeals held that the interim level grievance disposition was not binding. The principal had no actual authority to fix or pay the salaries of the teachers, nor was there any reason for the teachers to believe that he had such authority. The court further held that the salary proration did not violate the teachers' rights. The direct benefits the teachers were seeking to draw was pay for three days not actually worked. The amount the teachers received was in line with what they had been promised in both their own contracts and the cooperative agreement between the districts. The court of appeals affirmed the trial court's decision. *Prairie Heights Educ. v. Bd. of School Trustees*, 585 N.E.2d 289 (Ind.App.1992).

At the recommendation of a citizen's committee, a North Dakota school district decided to increase the class load of its high school teachers from five classes per day to six. At the time the decision was made, high school teachers who taught six classes per day received extra compensation. In fact, five classes per day had been the norm for the prior 15 years. Soon after the district adopted the announced schedule of classes for the next year, the superintendent informed the high school teachers who currently worked six classes per day that there would be no extra compensation for teaching six the following year. These teachers had to either conditionally resign, subject to rehire if they agreed to the new terms, or be fired. When contract negotiations occurred, however, there was no mention of the change in class load and the final contract did not specify what the course load would be. All high school teachers then taught six classes per day. They filed a grievance, claiming that they were entitled to extra compensation. The district denied the grievance and noted that an exclusive management clause in the contract allowed it to specify any terms not covered in the contract. The teachers sued the district and a state trial court held that they were owed extra compensation. The district appealed to the North Dakota Supreme Court.

The supreme court stated that for 15 years "extra class" had meant six, rather than five, classes per day. As such, it had acquired that meaning to the parties. The district could not fail to mention it at negotiations and then utilize the exclusive management clause to unilaterally change the meaning of the contracted teaching day. The term had a specific meaning which it had acquired over time. Since the contract covered compensation for teaching an extra class, and "extra class" meant six, it was covered by the contract, and the exclusive management clause did not apply. The teachers were entitled to extra compensation. *Williston Educ. Assn. v. School Dist. No. 1*, 483 N.W.2d 567 (N.D.1992).

V. STRIKES

The purpose of state legislation to prohibit or limit strikes by public employees is to protect the public and not to circumvent meaningful collective bargaining. Courts have upheld punitive actions taken against unlawfully striking teachers and their unions.

Wisconsin education law prohibited strikes by teachers. Under state law, school boards had sole authority to make hiring and firing decisions and were required to negotiate employment terms and conditions with authorized collective bargaining representatives. When contract negotiations between teachers and their local school board became protracted, the teachers called a strike. The board attempted to end the strike, noting it was in direct violation of state law. When the teachers refused to return to work, the board held disciplinary hearings and fired the striking teachers. The teachers appealed to the Wisconsin courts, arguing that the school board was not an impartial decisionmaker and that their discharges had violated their due process rights. The Wisconsin Supreme Court ruled that due process under the Fourteenth Amendment required that the teachers' conduct and the board's response to that conduct be evaluated by an impartial decisionmaker and that the board itself was not sufficiently impartial to make the decision to discharge the teachers. The board appealed this decision to the Supreme Court of the United States.

The Supreme Court reversed the Wisconsin Supreme Court decision and held that there was no evidence that the board could not make an impartial decision in determining to discharge these teachers. The mere fact that the board was involved in negotiations with the teachers did not support a claim of bias. The board was the only body vested with statutory authority to employ and dismiss teachers and participation in negotiations with the teachers was required by law. This involvement prior to the decision to discharge the teachers was not a sufficient showing of bias to disqualify the board as a decisionmaker under the Due Process Clause of the Fourteenth Amendment. *Hortonville Joint School District No. 1 v. Hortonville Education Association*, 426 U.S. 482, 96 S.Ct. 2308, 49 L.Ed.2d 1 (1976).

Teachers in a Michigan school district went on a strike that resulted in a 14-day school closure that was never made up during the school year. As a consequence, school was open only 166 days of the 180 days required by Michigan law. The district was able to keep its special education program open for the minimum required 230 days. Michigan's state school aid act called for the deduction of a prorated amount of total state aid for each day a district failed to hold school when the district did not meet the 180-day requirement. The state department of education required the district to forfeit over $1.6 million, including in its calculations the district's special education program budget and federal insurance collection act (FICA) payments made by the state to the district. These items accounted for over $408,000 of the total reduction. The district filed a lawsuit in a state court against the department of education to challenge the reduction, but the court held for the department. The district appealed to the Court of Appeals of Michigan.

The court of appeals held that the state legislature had not intended to penalize school districts that met the special education requirement merely because they failed to meet the requirement for general education programs. This would be inconsistent with and beyond the purpose of the statutory scheme, which addressed regular and special education in different sections. It was also improper for the department to withhold FICA reimbursement for unpaid salaries, because this had been taken into account by the district's nonpayment of salaries during the strike. The court of appeals reversed and remanded the trial court's decision. *School Dist. of the City of Pontiac v. Dept. of Educ.*, 516 N.W.2d 516 (Mich.App.1994).

Pennsylvania teachers and professional employees who were represented by a collective bargaining organization called a strike against their school district in 1986. Approximately one month later, a group of students and their parents sued the school district, the collective bargaining organization and the Commonwealth of Pennsylvania, seeking an order declaring the state Public Employee Relations Act (PERA) unconstitutional because it allowed teachers to strike. The Commonwealth Court of Pennsylvania dismissed the lawsuit and determined that the students and their parents had no standing to bring the action. In further proceedings, the commonwealth court reconsidered an appeal of the dismissal, determined that the matter should not have been dismissed, and ruled that the parents had standing to bring the action. It remanded the case to the trial court, which determined that the PERA was unconstitutional insofar as it granted public school teachers the right to strike. The labor organization appealed to the Supreme Court of Pennsylvania.

The supreme court rejected the collective bargaining organization's argument that the case should have been dismissed as moot because the teachers had long since returned to work. The supreme court noted that the constitutional question on appeal had been advanced by a party with a legal right to raise it (standing). The matter was an important question which was capable of repetition yet evading review. The PERA had a reasonable relation to the purpose expressed in the Pennsylvania Constitution's education article. The lower court had exceeded its authority in determining that the PERA was unconstitutional. The state general assembly had presumably found it appropriate to award teachers the right to strike, and only the general assembly had the authority to change this. The supreme court reversed the trial court's decision. *Reichley by Wall v. North Penn School Dist.*, 626 A.2d 123 (Pa.1993).

The collective bargaining agreement between a Pennsylvania school district and its teachers expired, and the teachers' association called selective strikes. The school district deducted pay for each day of the selective strikes. The association sued the school district in a Pennsylvania trial court, arguing that the district had to fully compensate employees under the state wage law. The court granted the injunction and the district appealed to the Commonwealth Court of Pennsylvania. The court ruled that the trial court had erroneously applied the wage law, and should have applied the state Public Employee Relations Act, which requires mandatory arbitration of labor disputes and expressly states that public employees are not entitled to pay for any strike period. The trial court had no jurisdiction in the dispute and the commonwealth court vacated its injunction. *Philipsburg-Osceola Educ. Assn. v. Philipsburg-Osceola Area School Dist.*, 633 A.2d 220 (Pa.Cmwlth.1993).

A group of West Virginia teachers began a strike to protest the failure of the local government to enact a wage and benefit package to their satisfaction. The local board of education filed suit in a West Virginia trial court and the judge granted it injunctive relief. The teachers then appealed to the Supreme Court of Appeals of West Virginia. The court noted that the trial court had ruled correctly on the current law in West Virginia, and looked to see if it was not time to change that law. The current law held that the strike was illegal in the absence of legislation requiring the public employer to recognize the association as a union. Other jurisdictions outside West Virginia had recently changed their laws allowing public employees to form unions. In the jurisdictions allowing unions, contracts were formed by negotiation. In West Virginia contracts are formed solely by the legislative body. When contracts are formed this way, allowing public employees to strike would give them excessive bargaining leverage and threaten the public welfare. These factors would continue to be problems in West Virginia unless a legislative act changed the process. In order to avoid irreparable harm to the public welfare, teachers in West Virginia would not be recognized as a union and therefore would not be allowed to strike. The supreme court upheld the decision of the trial court. *Jefferson Cty. Bd. of Educ. v. Educ. Ass'n*, 393 S.E.2d 653 (W.Va.1990).

An Oregon property owner sued his local school board for misapplication of public funds because the district hired teachers to substitute for striking teachers during a labor conflict. The property owner claimed that the school district had violated an Oregon law which prevents employers from knowingly employing professional strikebreakers to replace employees involved in a strike. An Oregon trial court dismissed the claim for failure to allege sufficient facts to constitute a claim for relief. The property owner appealed to the Court of Appeals of Oregon. The court of appeals held for the school district. It stated that the term "employer" as used in the strikebreaker statute did not include school districts. The term was defined as "any person, partnership, firm, corporation, association or other entity" that employs individuals to perform services for a wage. Although the term "entity" could be given such a broad meaning that it included a school district, the court believed that the legislature would have defined the term more broadly if it had intended to include public employers like school districts. The court stated that the term "entity" referred only to private entities, and not public employers. Therefore, the school district was not subject to the dictates of the statute. *Sullivan v. Kizer*, 839 P.2d 227 (Or.App.1992).

After only four days of instruction, teachers in a Pennsylvania school district went on strike. The Pennsylvania Public Employees Relations Act gave the teachers the right to strike. The school district asked the Court of Common Pleas to order the teachers back to work because the Pennsylvania Public School Code mandates that school districts provide 180 days of instruction. Pennsylvania law allows the court to end a strike only if the strike creates a clear and present danger or threat to the health, safety or welfare of the public. The court ordered the teachers back to work, finding that the school district's impending inability to schedule 180 days of instruction presented a clear and present danger because of a threatened loss of state subsidies. The teachers appealed to the Commonwealth Court of Pennsylvania which affirmed the lower court's decision. They then appealed to the Supreme Court of Pennsylvania. On appeal, the teachers argued that forcing them back to work would effectively destroy their right to strike. The school district argued, though, that there was more at stake than the loss of subsidies, including declining SAT scores, scholarship disadvantages for graduating seniors, grade delays to college admission committees, and loss of funding for remedial programs. Although the supreme court agreed with the teachers that the loss of state educational subsidies for failing to provide 180 days of instruction did not alone constitute a clear and present danger, it held for the school district. The court found the economic and educational disadvantages cited by the district constituted a clear and present danger. The supreme court affirmed the lower court's order. *Jersey Shore Area School Dist. v. Jersey Shore Educ. Ass'n*, 548 A.2d 1202 (Pa.1988).

Parents of elementary school children brought suit in the Oregon District Court seeking to bar the local education association from striking. They also sought to require the association and school district to submit labor disputes to arbitration, and to have the Oregon Public Employees Collective Bargaining Act declared unconstitutional. Because the strike ended before the final judgment was entered, the court dismissed the lawsuit as moot. The parents appealed. The Oregon Court of Appeals upheld the dismissal because all of the parents' allegations related to the strike and therefore the issues were moot when the strike ended. *Reiman v. Eugene Educ. Assoc.*, 759 P.2d 295 (Or.App.1988).

CHAPTER ELEVEN

SCHOOL OPERATIONS

I. BUDGET AND FINANCE

Education is not a fundamental right under the U.S. Constitution. However, state constitutional requirements that public education be pro-

vided to children include the requirement that the state provide financing for public education.

A. Taxation And Equal Educational Opportunity

Many of the cases in this area involve constitutional challenges to school funding disparities within states or regions. The most frequent challenges occur when differing tax bases result in unequal revenues among districts.

A group of New Jersey students filed a lawsuit in the state court system seeking a declaration that the state educational financing system was unconstitutional. The students, who attended school in relatively poor districts, called special needs districts, argued that the New Jersey Constitution required the state to provide a free education that was "thorough and efficient," and that the present financing system created educational disparities. The Supreme Court of New Jersey agreed with the students, ruling that the state constitution required a certain minimum level of educational quality. The court ordered the state legislature to enact legislation that would ensure that each child received a thorough and efficient education. The legislature responded by passing the Quality Education Act, which increased state funding to special needs districts by approximately $700 million. The students then claimed that the act failed to remedy the disparity of expenditures between regular and special needs districts. The trial court agreed, and the state commissioner of education appealed to the Supreme Court of New Jersey.

The supreme court determined that the Quality Education Act failed to guarantee equality of funding among districts in New Jersey. The act's complex funding formula employed a spending calculation that depended upon discretionary action by the executive and legislative branches. Because the act did not mandate adequate funding but instead left state officials with discretion, there was no assurance of substantial equivalence among school districts and the act violated the state constitution. Observing that the Quality Education Act had partially succeeded in closing the gap in funding, the court reaffirmed its prior holding, giving the legislature a clear message that additional funding for the special needs districts was necessary. *Abbott by Abbott v. Burke*, 136 N.J. 444, 643 A.2d 575 (1994).

A group of Arizona school districts and parents of children attending schools in these districts claimed that the state funding system created educational disparities and that the quality of schools varied enormously among state school districts. They claimed that some buildings were unsafe and violated safety codes, that some districts had only dirt lots for playgrounds and that some had no libraries, computers, art programs and other facilities. An Arizona trial court determined that although educational disparities existed among districts, the state should be granted summary judgment. The parents and school districts appealed to the Supreme Court of Arizona.

The supreme court noted that the quality of school facilities in Arizona was directly proportional to the value of real property located in the district. The assessed value of school district property per student in the state ranged from $5.8

million to $749. Demographic factors including income and student population also created disparities. An Arizona statute created educational funding disparities by using an arbitrary funding formula. Although the formula provided for state equalization assistance, property-poor districts were often unable to generate necessary capital funding despite taxing at higher rates than wealthier districts. This was because funding in excess of the equalization level depended on bonded indebtedness, which required voter approval. The court did not award injunctive relief as requested by the school districts and parents, but instead pronounced general principles to guide the legislature in approving a uniform public school system to adequately educate children on substantially equal terms. *Roosevelt Elem. School Dist. No. 66 v. Bishop*, 877 P.2d 806 (Ariz.1994).

The Kansas School District Finance and Quality Performance Act of 1992 substantially changed the financing method of Kansas public schools. The act required all school districts to levy ad valorem taxes on tangible property at a uniform rate. This was deemed the "local effort," and included other tax receipts and funds. Local effort funds which exceeded a district's state financial aid were "recaptured" by the state treasury. A district's state financial aid was determined by a statutory formula that adjusted (weighted) enrollment by factors including the number of students enrolled in bilingual education, vocational education, and the number of at-risk students attending district schools. Districts were allowed to adopt a local option budget which could not exceed 25 percent of state financial aid. The act included a quality performance accreditation system, which specified ten school goals. A group of school districts, taxpayers and students filed a lawsuit in a Kansas trial court, challenging the constitutionality of the act. The court upheld the act and the group appealed to the Supreme Court of Kansas.

The court held that the act did not violate the state constitutional provision requiring local authorities to maintain, develop and operate local public schools. The act did not unreasonably hamper local school board authority to operate schools. Local boards had no inherent powers of taxation and had always been funded through legislation. The act also did not violate the Kansas state constitutional provision requiring suitable school finance. This question could not be resolved in terms of the level of finance. The evidence presented before the trial court indicated that state schools were suitable under the constitution. There was also no equal protection violation as there was no proof of a correlation between educational expenditures and the quality of education. The act did not penalize districts that were subject to the recapture provision, and taxpayers in those districts had not suffered a taking in violation of the constitution. Accordingly, the supreme court affirmed the constitutionality of the act. *Unif. School Dist. No. 229 v. State of Kansas*, 885 P.2d 1170 (Kan.1994).

Virginia's public school aid system consisted of mandated state and local funds, and local funds not mandated by the state. Eleven Virginia students and seven local school boards filed a lawsuit in a Virginia trial court seeking a declaration that the state school financing system violated the Virginia Constitution. They claimed that the system deprived students residing in poorer school districts of equal educational opportunities. The trial court considered evidence that wealthier districts spent more than twice the amount per student than did poor school districts. There was a large disparity in the student-to-instructor ratio between rich and poor districts. Wealthier districts spent up to 12 times more per student on instructional materials, library books and supplies than did poorer districts. The court held that although public education was a fundamental right under the Virginia Constitution, the constitution did not require equalization of funding. The Supreme Court of Virginia agreed to hear the appeal of the students and school boards.

The supreme court agreed that although education was a fundamental right guaranteed by the state constitution, the constitution also delegated to the state general assembly the responsibility for insuring the standards of quality for public schools. The requirement to insure standards of quality did not include any duty to require substantial equality in spending or programs among school districts. Because the general assembly had fulfilled its duty of prescribing minimal standards for quality in schools, the trial court had properly dismissed the lawsuit. *Scott v. Commonwealth of Virginia,* 443 S.E.2d 138 (Va.1994).

A Missouri statute provided for school funding from property taxes and state aid under the state foundation formula. A group of 89 Missouri school districts formed a nonprofit corporation that filed a lawsuit in a state trial court claiming that the statute resulted in financial and educational inequities among state school districts. It asserted that students in the member districts were denied fundamental rights to equal access in education. The court agreed with the corporation, and determined that the statute violated the Missouri Constitution. The judgment did not order any redistribution of funds and required the state General Assembly to provide adequate funding for all public schools. The court retained jurisdiction over the matter and stayed entry of judgment for 90 days after the adjournment of the state legislature's regular session to allow time for the General Assembly to enact a constitutionally sufficient plan for funding public education and to allow time for appellate review of the judgment. The state of Missouri appealed to the Supreme Court of Missouri.

The supreme court observed that the trial court's judgment did not dispose of all claims in the lawsuit and therefore lacked finality. Accordingly, it was not an appealable order and the supreme court lacked jurisdiction to consider it. The court also refused to consider legislative amendments that had been passed in the interim which had unconditionally repealed the statute in issue. Passage of the legislation mooted the original trial court order, and there were no trial court proceedings concerning the amended statute. The court dismissed the appeal. *Committee for Educational Equality v. State of Missouri,* 878 S.W.2d 446 (Mo.1994).

Five New Hampshire school districts with comparatively low property tax bases and a number of resident taxpayers and students filed a petition in a New Hampshire trial court, seeking a declaration that the state educational finance system violated the New Hampshire Constitution. The complaining parties argued that the state failed to equitably distribute educational opportunities among students by inadequately funding the school system and limiting the state assistance rate to eight percent. They also claimed that the school finance system and foundation aid statutes denied students equal protection of the law and that the state's heavy reliance on property taxes to finance public schools violated the education clause of the state constitution. The trial court dismissed the complaint, finding that the state constitution contained no language requiring equity, uniformity, or adequacy in education. It held that the constitution imposed no qualitative educational standards or financial duties. The petitioners appealed to the Supreme Court of New Hampshire.

The supreme court compared the constitutional mandate contained in the education clause with historical papers from the state constitutional convention. It also examined pertinent dictionary definitions to interpret language used in the state's 1784 constitution. The constitution commanded the state to provide an education to all citizens and to support all public schools. A free public education is an important, substantive right enforceable by the public. The court refused to define the parameters of public education, as that duty was delegated to the legislature and governor. The court reversed and remanded the trial court's decision, expressing confidence in the legislature and governor to fulfill their responsibilities. *Claremont School Dist. v. Governor*, 635 A.2d 1375 (N.H.1993).

The city of New York and its education board filed a complaint against the state of New York in a state trial court, seeking a declaration that the state education financing system was unconstitutional and an order for injunctive relief. A companion action was filed by a nonprofit organization, city community school boards and parents of city public school students. The New York Supreme Court, New York County, considered dismissal motions filed by the state. The court agreed with the state that the city, city education board and community school boards had no legal standing to assert constitutional and statutory claims on behalf of students residing in the city. Accordingly, that part of the state's motion was granted. However, the complaint advanced by the nonprofit organization was legally sufficient to withstand dismissal. The complaint alleged a failure of the city's public school system to meet minimum standards established by the state commissioner of education and board of regents, and alleged that this failure created inequality of educational opportunity.

The complaint also sufficiently stated a claim of intentional discrimination because it alleged that students attending New York schools were deprived of a meaningful education on the basis of race, color or national origin in violation of the state constitution and education statutes. The court granted and denied the motions in part. *Campaign for Fiscal Equity, Inc. v. State of New York*, 616 N.Y.S.2d 851 (S.Ct.—New York County 1994). On appeal to the New York Supreme Court, Appellate Division, First Department, the remaining claims were dismissed. The appellate division court further held that those claims which had been dismissed by the trial court on grounds of lack of capacity to sue had been properly dismissed. 619 N.Y.S.2d 699 (A.D.1st Dept.1994).

Thirty-seven Illinois school districts and a number of students and parents filed a lawsuit in an Illinois trial court, seeking a declaration that the state educational financing system violated the Illinois Constitution. They claimed that students residing in districts with lower property values received fewer educational opportunities than students in wealthy districts. They argued that the state constitution's requirement of "an efficient system of high quality public educational institutions and services" required elimination of the disparity among school district revenues. The trial court dismissed the complaint for failure to state a cause of action and the complaining parties appealed to the Appellate Court of Illinois, First District. The appellate court stated that elimination of the disparity among school district revenues was a goal, but not a requirement, of the state constitution. The plaintiffs were unable to persuade the court that they constituted a class for the purposes of an equal protection claim or that they were denied basic, adequate or a minimal quality of education. The complaint also failed to state a connection between the amount of money spent by schools and the quality of education. The state education code furthered a legitimate government interest in allowing local control over school revenues. The appellate court affirmed the dismissal of the lawsuit. *Committee for Educational Rights v. Edgar*, 641 N.E.2d 602 (Ill.App.1st Dist.1994).

Public schools in Idaho are funded by a combination of local, state, and federal funds. The state partially or totally reimburses the school districts for certain expenses, and the State Educational Support Program also provides funds to the districts. Each school district's portion of the money received under the program is reduced by a projected "local contribution" equal to the money which would be collected by a .36 percent property tax levy. School districts with low assessed property values collect less money than those with higher property values, and they thus contribute less money to the program fund. Also, chartered school districts have greater authority to levy money than do nonchartered districts. In this case, a group of taxpayers, as well as certain school districts and superintendents, filed lawsuits alleging that the current system of funding public schools was unconstitutional because it did not provide a "uniform and thorough" education to all students (in violation of the education clause of the Idaho Constitution). After the lawsuits were consolidated, the trial court dismissed the case. Appeal was taken to the Supreme Court of Idaho.

The supreme court noted that a prior case, *Thompson v. Engelking*, 537 P.2d 635 (Idaho 1975), had held that the state's system of school funding did not violate the "uniformity" requirement of the education clause. The court refused to overturn *Thompson*, stating that it continued to believe that the uniformity requirement in the education clause required "only uniformity in curriculum, not uniformity in funding." The supreme court next determined that *Thompson* did not foreclose the present action because that case did not address the issue of whether the funding system violated the "thoroughness" requirement. Finally, the court noted that the taxpayers did not have standing to sue. However, the school districts and the superintendents could continue the lawsuit. The court affirmed in part and reversed in part the lower court's decision, remanding the case for further proceedings. *Idaho Students for Equal Educational Opportunity v. Evans*, 850 P.2d 724 (Idaho 1993).

The Tennessee Constitution contains an equal protection clause similar to that of the U.S. Constitution. It also contains an education clause requiring the state to provide free public schools. The federal government provides only ten percent of Tennessee's educational funding and the balance is obtained from state and local government sources. Although total state expenditures for one year were approximately $2.5 billion, only $60 million was available for equalization. Because many poor school districts lacked the fiscal capacity to generate more funds, a great disparity arose in public school financing. A group representing the poorer districts sued state officials in a Tennessee trial court for a determination that the state educational funding system violated the Tennessee Constitution. The court determined that the system violated the state constitution. The Tennessee Court of Appeals reversed the trial court decision and the school districts appealed to the Tennessee Supreme Court. The supreme court noted that the state funding scheme violated the equal protection clause of the state constitution because it was unjust and without any reasonable basis. The court reversed the court of appeals' decision and held in favor of the poorer school districts. *Tennessee Small School Systems v. McWherter*, 851 S.W.2d 139 (Tenn.1993).

Two separate groups of students in different Massachusetts communities sued the state board of education and several of its officers seeking a declaration that the commonwealth had failed to provide them with an adequate education. They maintained that this was required under the state constitution. The lawsuits, which were begun in 1978, went through a series of procedural delays until late in 1992. The cases were then reserved and reported by a single justice of the Massachusetts Supreme Judicial Court for disposition. A stipulated record was presented to the supreme judicial court, consisting of six volumes and over 500 stipulated factual items, including evidence that many Massachusetts school districts suffered from grossly inadequate financial support resulting in large classes, staff reduction, inadequate teaching of basic subjects, neglected facilities, high turnover of teachers, poor curriculum development and other administrative problems. A review of the Massachusetts Constitution determined that it imputed a duty upon state officials to provide an adequate education and that this duty had been breached by the current financing system. Local school districts were funded primarily by property taxes and commonwealth funding was directed to equalization. However, since 1984, the commonwealth had failed to equalize existing funding imbalances among most school districts. Because the commonwealth was not obeying its mandate to provide an adequate education for all students, the supreme judicial court instructed it to develop a funding plan to meet the constitutional mandate. *McDuffy v. Secretary of Exec. Office of Educ.*, 615 N.E.2d 516 (Mass.1993).

In 1987, the Minnesota legislature reformed the state educational finance system. It eliminated separate funding by category for educational programs, creating a foundation program that increased the basic allowance to individual school districts. Districts could then allocate lump sums as needed. The reformed system substantially equalized revenues received by districts, which received approximately 93 percent of their state funds from the basic revenue formula. The Minnesota Supreme Court upheld the system as constitutional. *Skeen v. State of Minnesota*, 505 N.W.2d 299 (Minn.1993).

Nebraska's school system was funded primarily by local tax revenue, with only 25 percent provided by state foundation and equalization funds. A group of parents and taxpayers sued state officials including the governor in a Nebraska trial court, claiming that the state finance system denied students residing in the poorest districts equal protection of the law, and denied them equal and adequate educational opportunities. The trial court ruled that the petition stated a cause of action, but then granted the state officials' summary judgment motion and the parents and taxpayers appealed to the Supreme Court of Nebraska. The supreme court observed that while the petition of the taxpayers and parents identified a disparity in school district funding within the state, it failed to specifically allege that the disparity in funding resulted in inadequate schooling or funding within various school districts. There was no allegation of how the disparities affected the quality of education and no demonstration that the educational system violated the constitutional rights of students. Because the parents and taxpayers failed to state a cause of action the trial court should have dismissed the lawsuit prior to the filing of the summary judgment motion. The supreme court reversed and remanded the case. *Gould v. Orr*, 506 N.W.2d 349 (Neb.1993).

A group of Alabama students and parents sued state officials in an Alabama trial court, seeking a declaration that the state deprived them of an adequate education. The court entered an order detailing evidence that the state financing system failed to equalize expenditures among school districts. Evidence indicated that wealthier districts spent twice as much on students as poorer districts. The court found that the state had tolerated the disparity by failing to equalize local funding with state funds. The disparity in resources among school districts resulted in unequal educational opportunity for students attending poorer districts. The court held that the state educational system failed to meet state constitutional standards. Many Alabama schools failed to meet state accreditation standards and failed to provide minimally adequate educational opportunities. The system deprived many students of such basics as adequate textbooks, sanitary facilities, adequate student-to-teacher ratios, libraries, healthcare and transportation. Alabama students had an enforceable state constitutional right to an education and had the right to attend schools offering adequate educational opportunities. The system of public schools violated student constitutional rights on equal protection and due process grounds and violated the state constitution's education clause. The court ordered state officers to establish, organize and maintain a constitutionally adequate public school system. The Alabama senate requested the opinion of the state supreme court concerning the trial court's order. The supreme court issued an advisory opinion informing the legislature that it was required to follow the order. *Opinion of the Justices,* 624 So.2d 107 (Ala.1993).

A group of North Dakota high school districts, taxpayers and parents sued the state of North Dakota for a declaration that the state's public school financing system was unconstitutional. They claimed that state revenues failed to equalize local revenues and that the corresponding disparity in resources among school districts created unequal educational opportunities. A North Dakota district court determined that the statutory method for distributing funds to public schools violated both the education and equal protection clauses of the state constitution. The Supreme Court of North Dakota agreed that the system was unconstitutional, but held that it was up to the legislature to enact an appropriate remedy. *Bismarck Pub. School Dist. No. 1 v. State of North Dakota*, 511 N.W.2d 247 (N.D.1994).

B. Property Taxes and Other Local Funding Issues

Connecticut statutes require local and regional boards of education to meet a specific minimum expenditure requirement. Regular education programs must be funded at the minimum level set by the statutory formula in order to ensure that students receive a minimally adequate education. Local education boards submit formal budget requests to their local municipal governments. The New Haven board of education submitted a formal budget request of $116 million for the 1990-91 school year. However, the city appropriated only $96 million. Following a sequence of budget revisions and meetings, the state education board determined that the city must appropriate an additional $2 million. It then held a hearing after which it ordered the city to appropriate the additional funds, and ordered the local board to submit a plan indicating that the additional funds would be spent on permissible expenditures. Appeal reached the Supreme Court of Connecticut. The court disagreed with the city's argument that the state board had no authority to order it to comply with an education statute. The town was obligated to appropriate sufficient funds to the local board to meet the minimum expenditure requirement. The local board maintained discretion to allocate appropriations made by the municipality. There was no evidence in the record that the local board had inaccurately calculated its budget. The supreme court affirmed the decision of the state board. *New Haven v. State Bd. of Educ.*, 228 Conn. 699, 638 A.2d 589 (1994).

The South Carolina Constitution requires voter approval for school district general obligation debt in excess of eight percent of the assessed value of taxable property in the school district. A school board attempted to finance a new middle school by issuing debt in excess of eight percent of assessed taxable property values. However, the bond referendum was defeated by voters. The board then approved a lease-purchase agreement for a new middle school site. Property owners in the district filed a class action suit to prohibit the board from entering into the lease-purchase agreement. They sought a temporary order prohibiting the agreement and a writ of mandamus to compel the board to repair and renovate existing schools. A South Carolina trial court dismissed the lawsuit and the property owners appealed to the Supreme Court of South Carolina.

The court stated that lease-purchase agreements were not designated general obligation debt, and that voter approval was unnecessary. South Carolina courts were permitted to intervene in school board decisions only where there was a clear abuse of discretion. School boards were vested with the discretion to select school sites, order repairs and perform related duties. Courts could not intervene unless there was evidence of corruption, bad faith or a clear abuse of discretion. The property owners could not demonstrate that the proposed site for the new school was unlawful, and they were not entitled to a preliminary order preventing the action. They were also not entitled to a writ of mandamus to require the board to repair existing schools, because this duty was also within the board's discretion. The supreme court affirmed the trial court's decision. *Redmond v. Lexington County School Dist. No. 4*, 445 S.E.2d 441 (S.C.1994).

An Arizona statute required that absentee ballots be mailed to electors, and that only the electors could actually possess ballots. Employees of an Arizona school district personally delivered absentee ballots to 41 voters residing in the district. The election concerned a budget override measure in which the employees had a vested interest. Distribution of the absentee ballots changed the result of the election, resulting in a vote for the override. A group of voters contested the result by filing a lawsuit in an Arizona trial court, which set aside the election. The Arizona Court of Appeals reversed the trial court's decision. It held that actual fraud must be demonstrated in the inappropriate delivery of ballots in order to set aside an election. The district appealed to the Supreme Court of Arizona. The supreme court disagreed with the court of appeals' decision that a showing of fraud was necessary to invalidate the absentee balloting in this case. The distribution of the absentee ballots had changed the election result, constituting a substantive irregularity. There was evidence that district employees went to the homes of electors whom they knew and stood beside them as they voted. Accordingly, the court vacated the court of appeals' decision and reinstated the trial court's judgment. *Miller v. Picacho Elementary School Dist. No. 33*, 877 P.2d 277 (Ariz.1994).

The state of Mississippi held title to all 16th section lands in the state and delegated management of the sections to county education boards. The state constitution limited oil and gas lease terms to 25 years until a 1992 constitutional amendment allowed leases that were coextensive with mineral operations. The state legislature then amended its code to permit the renegotiation of leases that expired due to the former constitutional limitation. Four Mississippi county school boards had entered into oil and gas leases with a refining company for the extraction of minerals from state-owned lands. The leases were executed between 1943 and 1960 and called for terms of six years and for as long thereafter as oil, gas or other minerals continued to be produced. An oil corporation that succeeded to the refinery's interest in the leases filed a lawsuit in the U.S. District Court for the Southern District of Mississippi, seeking a declaration that the leases remained in full effect because of the amendment. The school boards filed motions for summary judgment, arguing that the leases were terminated by operation of law. The court determined that the leases had expired because the state constitutional limit of 25 years applied to each lease. This result was mandated because the leases were executed prior to the 1992 constitutional amendment. However, because of the legislative act, the corporation should have the opportunity to renegotiate the leases subject to accounting for production pending the outcome of the litigation. The court granted the school boards' summary judgment motions. *Exxon Corp. v. Bd. of Educ. of Lamar County, Miss.*, 849 F.Supp. 479 (S.D.Miss.1994).

The California Landscaping and Lighting Act of 1972 permits assessment districts, including special districts, to levy and collect special assessments to fund specified public improvements. Two California school districts operated elementary, middle and high schools whose facilities were used by community members for scout meetings, arts and crafts, sports and many other recreational activities. Because of the heavy community use, school facilities deteriorated, requiring many improvements. However, the districts lacked sufficient funding, so they formed a special assessment district under the Landscaping and Lighting Act to finance the improvements. A taxpayer association challenged the school districts' status as a special district, seeking to prevent the special assessment. A trial court entered summary judgment for the school districts, and the taxpayers appealed to the California Court of Appeal, Second District.

The court of appeal ruled that school districts were nonmunicipal public corporations which operated under the direct authority of the legislature, with powers to maintain, service and improve schools within their geographic areas. Because school buildings were centers of free public assembly, the Landscaping and Lighting Act definition of special district was broad enough to encompass school districts, and the special assessment violated no California statute or constitutional provision. The court of appeal affirmed the trial court's decision for the school districts. *Howard Jarvis Taxpayers Ass'n v. Whittier Union High School Dist.*, 19 Cal.Rptr.2d 109 (Cal.App.2d Dist.1993).

The North Carolina Constitution requires that all proceeds of penalties, forfeitures and fines collected for violation of state laws must be appropriated for the maintenance of public schools. The state Racketeer Influenced and Corrupt Organizations Act (RICO) states that forfeitures for violations of that act are to be paid to the state treasurer. A North Carolina trial court awarded summary judgment to the state of North Carolina against a school district which claimed that property forfeited in a case prosecuted under RICO should be paid to the school district. The Supreme Court of North Carolina reversed the trial court decision, and ruled that funds recovered under RICO must be paid to the state to benefit public schools as set forth in the state constitution. *State of North Carolina, ex rel. Thornburgh v. House and Lot located at 532 B. St., Bridgeton, NC*, 432 S.E.2d 684 (N.C.1993).

A Maryland school district built a fence that was some distance inside its actual property line. A neighboring landowner planted fruit trees on property that belonged to the district, but was located outside the fence. After a number of years had passed, she claimed that the area on which she had planted trees was legally hers because of adverse possession or because of abandonment by the school board. She filed a lawsuit to quiet title in a Maryland trial court, which dismissed the complaint. The landowner appealed to the Court of Special Appeals of Maryland. The court of special appeals observed that under common law, no state or government property could be lost or divested due to adverse possession. Although property rights such as easements could be lost through abandonment, there was no legal authority indicating that a possessory interest in property could be lost through abandonment. Such a rule would lead to absurd results and the impossibility of establishing a chain of ownership in land records. The court of special appeals affirmed the trial court decision for the school board. *Cristofani v. Bd. of Educ. of Prince George's County*, 632 A.2d 447 (Md.App.1993).

A California school district obtained approval from its voters to finance a lease-purchase arrangement for three school sites in 1977. After approval of the ballot measure, the district leased school sites to a nonprofit school corporation that sold tax-exempt bonds to construct the facilities and lease them back to the district. The ballot measure created enough revenue to pay for amounts due on the lease obligations and, in 1984, the district created an irrevocable trust to fund the remaining lease obligations. It then decreased the tax levy to zero. However, the district remained liable for the debt in the event of a default by the trust. Because the district was without funds to build additional required facilities, it placed a new ballot before its voters in 1991 for the lease-purchase of five new facilities and the renovation of 19 existing facilities. It sought approval by voters to use the existing 1977 indebtedness to finance the new obligations. This was done to avoid the restrictions of Proposition 13, a 1978 California constitutional amendment that limits ad valorem taxes on real property. The district filed a lawsuit in a California court to validate its action.

The California Court of Appeal, Second District, affirmed the trial court decision in favor of the school district. California Education Code § 39308.5 expressly permitted state school districts to "piggyback" new school construction financing on existing prior indebtedness by codifying an exception to Proposition 13. Even though the ballot measure had been reduced to zero in 1985, the district retained the power to tax until the indebtedness was paid in full in 2002. The ballot measure did not constitute a new tax in violation of Proposition 13 and the trial court decision for the school district was affirmed. *San Luis Coastal Unif. School Dist. v. Kunkel*, 20 Cal.Rptr.2d 724 (Cal.App.2d Dist.1993).

C. Federal Funding

Virginia permitted students with disabilities to be disciplined in the same manner as non-disabled students where there was no causal connection between the misconduct and the disability, and where the student's placement was appropriate. Under the Individuals with Disabilities Education Act (IDEA), states must submit comprehensive special education plans for three-year periods to the U.S. Department of Education (DOE). The DOE conditionally approved a plan submitted by the Commonwealth of Virginia for fiscal years 1993-95. At the end of 1993, the DOE advised the Virginia Department of Education that its disciplinary policy for students with disabilities violated federal requirements, although the requirement had not been formally published by regulation. The DOE threatened to withhold Virginia's 1994 IDEA fiscal year grant of over $50 million. Virginia sought an administrative hearing to contest the DOE action, but the DOE refused to release funds pending appeal. The Virginia Department of Education requested relief from the U.S. Court of Appeals, Fourth Circuit.

The court of appeals held that the federal government was required to clearly state any conditions attached to the grant of funds to a state. The condition imposed by the DOE was a new and potentially costly policy that justified procedural protections for Virginia. The court noted that these procedural protections were similar to those granted to disabled students under the IDEA. Because the DOE had violated Virginia's right to receive notice and an opportunity to be heard, the DOE could not now withhold the 1994 grant. *Virginia Dept. of Educ. v. Riley*, 23 F.3d 80 (4th Cir.1994).

The U.S. Supreme Court ruled that the Secretary of Education has the authority to demand a refund of misused funds granted to states under Title I of the Elementary and Secondary Education Act of 1965 (ESEA). Title I provides funding for local education agencies to prepare economically underprivileged children for school. Recipient states must provide assurances to the secretary that local educational agencies will spend the funds only on qualifying programs. After federal auditors determined that the states of New Jersey and Pennsylvania had misapplied funds, the secretary ordered those states to refund to the federal government the amount of the misapplied funds. Both states appealed to the U.S. Court of Appeals, Third Circuit, arguing that the secretary exceeded his statutory authority in ordering the refunds. The Supreme Court stated that the ESEA, as originally enacted, gave the federal government a right to demand repayment once liability was established. The 1978 amendments to the ESEA were designed merely to clarify the secretary's legal authority and responsibility to audit recipient states' programs and to specify the procedures to be used in the collection of any debts. *Bell v. New Jersey*, 461 U.S. 773, 103 S.Ct. 2187, 76 L.Ed.2d 312 (1983). The U.S. Supreme Court also held that the 1978 amendments' new, relaxed standards concerning local schools' eligibility to receive Title I funds could not be applied retroactively. *Bennett v. New Jersey*, 470 U.S. 632, 105 S.Ct. 1555, 84 L.Ed.2d 572 (1985). In a companion case, the Court held that the state of Kentucky's lack of bad faith was irrelevant in assessing its liability to repay misused Title I funds. *Bennett v. Kentucky Dept. of Educ.*, 470 U.S. 656, 105 S.Ct. 1544, 84 L.Ed.2d 590 (1985).

Four Illinois school districts sued the state treasurer, comptroller, superintendent of education, and a regional education superintendent for failing to immediately disburse federal funds to which the districts were entitled, including funds received under the Individuals with Disabilities Education Act, Vocational Education Act, National School Lunch Act, and Child Nutrition Act. The school districts sought an order that would require state officials to immediately disburse funds or entitle them to recover interest on the funds during the time they were held by the state. A U.S. magistrate judge was appointed by the U.S. District Court for the Northern District of Illinois to consider issues raised by the parties. The magistrate judge determined that the funding statutes were not intended to benefit school districts, but rather were intended to benefit the students attending the school districts. None of the funding statutes contained any timetable for the state-level disbursement of federal funds to local school districts. Accordingly, the magistrate judge found that the state officials did not have to immediately disburse the funds. The district court adopted the magistrate judge's report and recommendation, dismissing the lawsuit and determining that the school districts could not prevail under 42 U.S.C. § 1983. *Bd. of Educ. of Township High School Dist. No. 205 v. Leininger*, 822 F.Supp. 516 (N.D.Ill.1993).

Title VI of the Civil Rights Act of 1964 prohibits discrimination in federally assisted programs. The Department of Education (DOE)'s current regulations interpreting Title VI have been in force since 1980. The regulations state that even in the absence of prior discrimination, a recipient in administering a program may take affirmative actions to overcome the effects of conditions which result in limiting participating by persons of a particular race, color, or national origin. Several white law and college students sued the DOE, alleging that it violated Title VI by providing federal funds to educational institutions that offer some scholarships only to minority students and encouraging them through its regulations. A federal district court dismissed the suit, holding that the students had no cause of action against the government under the Administrative Procedure Act (APA), the act which authorizes and empowers government agencies, because an adequate alternative remedy existed—a suit directly against the institutions administering the allegedly unlawful scholarships. The students then appealed to the U.S. Court of Appeals, District of Columbia Circuit.

On appeal, the students argued that the APA gave them a cause of action because the DOE had a policy against minority scholarships, but had failed to enforce that prohibition against the specific schools. Second, they argued that they had an APA cause of action because the department had abdicated its responsibility to enforce Title VI. The court stated that the first argument failed because the students had an implied right of action under Title VI against the individual colleges and law schools to address any discrimination they suffered. That alternative remedy precluded a remedy under the APA. The court also stated that the students had not claimed that the DOE had found federally funded institutions to be in violation of Title VI and that it had refused to enforce its anti-discrimination policy with respect to those institutions. Accordingly, the court affirmed the lower court's decision. *Washington Legal Foundation v. Alexander*, 984 F.2d 483 (D.C.Cir.1993).

A group of parents of allegedly economically disadvantaged Chicago public school children brought a lawsuit against the state of Illinois and the board of education of the city of Chicago challenging the method by which Title I funds intended exclusively for economically disadvantaged students were allocated to the Chicago School Board. A trial court dismissed their claim because of lack of standing, but the Appellate Court of Illinois reversed. So long as the parents had suffered an injury in fact to a legally recognized interest, they had standing to maintain the lawsuit. The court remanded the case for further proceedings. *Noyola v. Board of Education*, 592 N.E.2d 165 (Ill.App.1st Dist.1992).

D. State Funding

The governor of West Virginia issued an executive order calling for a 1.5 percent budget cut for public education expenditures based on a projected shortfall in revenue. Due to an unanticipated estate tax receipt, the expected revenue shortfall did not occur and the general revenue fund showed a surplus at the end of the fiscal year. A group of school boards, an education association and a collective bargaining association representing West Virginia teachers filed a petition for a writ of mandamus in a West Virginia trial court, seeking revocation of the executive order. The court granted the writ, ordering the governor to restore the full budget. The governor appealed to the Supreme Court of Appeals of West Virginia. On appeal, the governor stated that he had no authority to restore budget cuts because the appropriation of public money was a duty delegated to the legislature. The plaintiffs argued that the state constitution required the governor to restore funds inasmuch as he had the power to reduce expenditures. The court held that although the governor was uniquely situated to consider all facts and circumstances relating to the state's financial condition, any restoration of funds by him, and any challenge to an appropriations reduction, had to occur before the end of the relevant fiscal year. Because the petition had not been filed prior to the end of the fiscal year, the governor had no authority to restore funds. The court reversed and remanded the trial court's decision. *State of West Virginia ex rel. the Bd. of Educ. of County of Kanawha v. Caperton*, 441 S.E.2d 373 (W.Va.1994).

The Florida Constitution provides in part that counties, "school districts and municipalities shall... be authorized by law to levy Ad valorem taxes...." The 1991-92 general appropriations act substantially reduced the maximum mill rate for nonvoted discretionary millage that could be levied by school districts. One school board estimated a reduction of $7 million in discretionary Ad valorem taxes due to the appropriations act. It filed an action against the county tax collector in a Florida trial court, requesting an order to determine the validity of the appropriations act and another Florida enabling statute. The state department of education attempted to intervene as the real party in interest. The trial court declared the statutes unconstitutional and ordered the tax collector to collect taxes levied by the school board, irrespective of appropriations legislation. The parties stipulated to vacate the trial court order. The department of education was then permitted to intervene and it appealed. The Florida District Court of Appeal, Second District, affirmed the trial court decision and the department of education appealed to the Supreme Court of Florida.

The supreme court agreed with the department of education that the state constitution did not contain self-executing language that would permit school districts to levy Ad valorem taxes without legislative authority. Ad valorem taxes could be authorized only with legislative approval. The trial court should have named the state education department a party when first requested. The court ruled that the appropriations legislation did not violate the Florida Constitution, and reversed and remanded the case. *Florida Dept. of Educ. v. Glasser*, 622 So.2d 944 (Fla.1993).

Arkansas's legislature approved an equalizing formula which guaranteed that the combination of local and state funds received by local districts equaled a minimum amount per student. To achieve this result, the state board of education disbursed funds to local school districts in the form of Minimum Foundation Program Aid (MFPA). MFPA funds were based upon estimates, and a state fund was set aside in the event that a reassessed property value exceeded the original value by more than five percent. A school district was overpaid by more than $600,000 over two years and, according to state law, was required to repay the amount to the state board over a period of five years. When the school district learned that the state would withhold almost $125,000 from it each year to recover the overpayment, it filed a lawsuit in an Arkansas court seeking a preliminary injunction preventing the state board of education from recovering the first year payment. The trial court rejected the application.

The school district appealed to the Supreme Court of Arkansas, which affirmed the trial court's decision for the state board of education, noting that the same school district had recorded a budget surplus of nearly $1,000,000 during the year in question. The overpayment was less than two percent of all MFPA funds which the school district had received during the school year. The school finance act did not violate the Arkansas Constitution and the trial court decision was affirmed. *Fayetteville School Dist. No. 1 v. Arkansas State Bd. of Educ.*, 852 S.W.2d 122 (Ark.1993).

In April 1991, after a period of mounting deficits, a California school district announced that it lacked the funds to complete the final six weeks of its 1990-91 school term. The district proposed to close its doors on May 1, 1991. Parents in the district filed a class action suit for temporary and permanent injunctive relief. A California trial court ordered the state of California to approve an emergency state loan, and also ordered the appointment of an administrator to take temporary charge of the district's operation. The state appealed the decision to the California Supreme Court which granted review but denied a stay of execution of the trial court's order. The supreme court stated that the district's financial inability to complete the final six weeks of its 1990-91 school term threatened to deprive district students of their California constitutional right to basic educational equality with other public school students in the state. Unlike the federal constitution, the California constitution places special obligations on the state to provide education. The state itself, as the entity with full constitutional responsibility for operation of the common school system, had a duty to protect district students against loss of their right to basic educational equality. The trial court had thus properly ordered the state and its officials to protect the students' rights. *Butt v. State*, 15 Cal.Rptr.2d 480, 842 P.2d 1240 (Cal.1992).

E.   Student Fees and Tuition

1.   **Transportation Fees**

North Dakota statutes authorized thinly populated school districts to reorganize into larger districts for efficiency. Reorganized districts had to provide for student transportation to and from their homes. School districts choosing not to reorganize were authorized by statute to charge students a portion of their costs for transportation. Parents of a nine-year-old student refused to sign a transportation contract with the school district. The family was near or at the poverty level. Claiming inability to pay the fee, the family made private transportation arrangements which were more costly than the school's fee. The parents sued the school district in a North Dakota trial court for an order to prevent the school district from collecting the fee on grounds that it violated the state constitution and Equal Protection Clause. After losing at the trial court level, the parents appealed to the North Dakota Supreme Court which upheld the lower court decision on state and federal constitutional grounds. The U.S. Supreme Court upheld the statute's validity. The parents claimed that the user fee for bus service unconstitutionally deprived poor persons of minimum access to education and placed an unconstitutional obstacle to education for poor students. The Court noted that the student continued to attend school during the time she claimed she was denied access to the school bus. The Equal Protection Clause did not require free transportation. Education is not a fundamental right under the U.S. Constitution. The statute bore a reasonable relationship to the state's legitimate objective of encouraging local school districts to provide bus service. Payment of bus fees was not directly imposed by the statute. The statute did not discriminate against any class and did not interfere with any constitutional rights. *Kadrmas v. Dickinson Pub. Schools*, 487 U.S. 450, 108 S.Ct. 2481, 101 L.Ed.2d 399 (1988).

A Kentucky school board furnished bus transportation and allowed students to attend schools that were outside their attendance area but within the same district. However, to limit class sizes, the board instituted a revised transportation policy that permitted students to attend schools within the district but outside their attendance areas only if they utilized private transportation. The parent of a student affected by the change filed a lawsuit in a Kentucky trial court, claiming that the transportation policy was arbitrary, capricious and unreasonable and violated his constitutional rights to due process. The court granted summary judgment to the school board and the parent appealed to the Kentucky Court of Appeals. The court of appeals affirmed the trial court's judgment, finding that the board's decision was not arbitrary, capricious or unreasonable. The due process rights of students and parents had been protected by numerous public meetings held during the policy revision. Its impact on students already availing themselves of the policy was mitigated by the use of a grandfather clause. Any change in school policies might have an adverse impact on some students, but some such impacts could not be avoided. The court affirmed the trial court's decision. *Swift v. Breckinridge County Bd. of Educ.*, 878 S.W.2d 810 (Ky.App.1994).

A New Jersey statute required school districts to furnish free transportation for elementary students to and from school where the distance was beyond two miles. Measurement was to be made using the shortest route by public road or walkway. A New Jersey school district revoked the bus passes of several children after redetermining the distance from their houses to their school. This was done by using a walkway maintained by the local township as part of the shortest route between the homes and the school. Parents of the students claimed that the walkway should not be used for calculating the distance from the school because it was not a public walkway as defined in the statute and was a dangerous route. The school board denied the parents' request for relief, and this order was affirmed by the state commissioner of education. The parents appealed to the Superior Court of New Jersey, Appellate Division. The court determined that the word "public" as used in the statute referred not only to ownership, but to commonality of usage, freedom of access and reasonable expectations of safe passage. Most important was the expectation of safe passage under the auspices of a responsible government entity. Because there was evidence that the walkway was not safely maintained, it was improper to use it for determining the distance between the school and the homes of the children. The court reversed and remanded the case to the state board of education. *Bd. of Educ. of the Township of Wayne v. Kraft*, 274 N.J.Super. 211, 643 A.2d 1029 (1994).

California's Education Code allowed school districts to charge fees for student transportation. It also stated that indigent students would be granted a waiver of the fee. A taxpayer filed suit in state court alleging that the statute violated the Free School Clause of the California Constitution, and the Equal Protection Clause of the federal constitution. The California Court of Appeal agreed with the taxpayer, and the Supreme Court of California granted review. The court stated that the Free School Clause has been construed to forbid any school district from charging a fee for any activity which is a fundamental part or necessary element of education. It then distinguished transportation from book and extracurricular activities. Instead, transportation was held to be a supplemental service. The equal protection claim was based on allegations that the statute discriminated against poor students and would affect their ability to exercise their fundamental right to education. However, the exemption for indigent students was added to the statute so that no child would be denied an educational opportunity based on poverty. The statute was held to be rationally related to legitimate state concerns. The court closed by noting that its decision was in accord with most other jurisdictions which have considered the issue in light of similar free school guarantees. *Arcadia Unified School District v. Dept. of Ed.,* 5 Cal.Rptr.2d 545 (Cal.1992).

The school district for Kelley's Island in Ohio decided that it had become unreasonable to continue to provide transportation to students of a nonpublic school on the mainland. It offered payment in lieu of transportation. The payment alternative was objected to by the parents, who appealed to the State Board of Education. The board confirmed the district's decision. The parents then added the board as a defendant, and appealed to a state court, which granted injunctive relief and ordered the continuation of transportation services. The board disputed the propriety of its addition to the suit as well as the reversal of the district's decision. An Ohio appellate court agreed with the board on both points, and the record was certified to the Supreme Court of Ohio. Ohio law specifies that the issues concerning the reasonableness of transportation are to be decided through the judgment of such district, confirmed by the State Board. The board's authority and role in the decision was held to be that of an adjudicator. Its addition to the suit as a defendant was therefore improper. The declaratory and injunctive relief afforded the parents was also improper because both these remedies are available only when no legal remedy is adequate; if the parents had correctly appealed the board's decision, adequate remedies were potentially available through the statutory laws. The judgments releasing the board and affirming the district's decision were upheld. *Haig v. Ohio State Bd. of Educ.,* 584 N.E.2d 704 (Ohio 1992).

2. Tuition and Other Fees

The University of Virginia collected a mandatory $14 student activity fee from full-time students each semester. The fees supported extracurricular activities that were related to the educational purposes of the university. University-recognized student groups could apply for funding by the activities fund, although not all groups requested funds. University guidelines excluded religious groups from student funding. A university-recognized student group published a Christian newspaper for which it sought $5,862 from the activities fund for printing costs. The student council denied funding because the group's activities were deemed religious under university guidelines. After exhausting appeals within the university, group members filed a lawsuit against the university in the U.S. District Court for the Western District of Virginia, claiming constitutional rights violations. The court granted summary judgment to the university, and its decision was affirmed by the U.S. Court of Appeals, Fourth Circuit. The students appealed to the U.S. Supreme Court.

The Court observed that government entities must abstain from regulating speech on the basis of the speaker's opinion. Upon establishing a limited public forum, state entities must respect the forum by refraining from the exclusion of speech based upon content. Because the university had opened a limited public forum by paying other third-party contractors on behalf of student groups, it could not deny the religious group's claim for funds on the basis of its viewpoint. Allowing the payment of the group's printing costs amounted to a policy of government neutrality for different viewpoints. The Court distinguished the student fee from a general tax and placed emphasis on the indirect nature of the benefit. The Court reversed the lower court decisions, ruling that access to public school facilities on a neutral basis does not violate the Establishment Clause of the First Amendment. *Rosenberger v. Rector and Visitors of Univ. of Virginia*, 115 S.Ct. 2510 (1995).

The California Constitution guarantees a free education to school-aged children. The state education code requires education and training classes for drivers prior to licensing as part of the high school curriculum. Driver training programs are funded by fines imposed under the vehicle code, but fines are deposited into the state general fund and distributed among several funds. A public interest organization and its individual members filed a lawsuit in a California trial court, claiming that the state was required to fund driver training with money collected from driver fines and that fees charged by high schools for such training violated the state constitution. The trial court denied their request for an order compelling the state treasurer to make the funds available for driver training by transferring an amount from the state general fund. The organization appealed to the California Court of Appeal, Sixth District.

The court agreed with the public interest group that the fees charged by high school districts for driver training violated the free school guarantee of the California Constitution. Driver training was an integral component of a public high school education. The legislature intended violation fees to fund driver training. However, the legislative scheme required a specific appropriation by the legislature for driver training expenses and the act did not create a continuing appropriation. The court was unable to order the legislature to make an appropriation of funds. Because an annual appropriation of funds was required before violation fee funds could be used, the court denied the organization's request for an order. *California Assn. For Safety Educ. v. Brown*, 36 Cal.Rptr.2d 404 (Cal.App.6th Dist.1994).

North Carolina statutes permit local education boards to charge tuition to students who do not reside within the school's administrative unit or district. A school district determined that a student who resided in its administrative area was not properly domiciled within the territory and attempted to charge tuition to her parents. The district filed a lawsuit in a North Carolina trial court to recover tuition from her parents. The court held for the parents and the school district appealed to the Court of Appeals of North Carolina, which observed the distinction between residence and domicile. Residence was defined as an actual place of abode while domicile was a permanent, established home. It was possible for a student to reside in a place other than with his or her parents and therefore have different places of domicile and residence. In this case, the student resided within the school's administrative unit and could not be assessed tuition charges. The court remanded the case for the entry of judgment for the parents. *Chapel Hill-Carrboro City Schools System v. Chavioux*, 446 S.E.2d 612 (N.C.App.1994).

Another North Carolina case involving the same statute arose where a school district had imposed exit fees on students. A small, rural North Carolina county with rapidly declining enrollment experienced a significant loss of students because of transfers to schools in other counties. The county board of education passed a student transfer policy that imposed an exit fee of $200 for resident student transfers to different districts. The parent of a student who transferred out of the school unit filed a lawsuit in a North Carolina trial court for an injunction against enforcement of the policy. The court granted the injunction and the school board appealed to the Court of Appeals of North Carolina. The court of appeals found no statutory support for the policy. The statute authorized tuition only for students who did not reside within a particular school district. Because there was no authority for the exit fee, the court affirmed the permanent injunction against enforcing the policy. *Streeter v. Greene County Bd. of Educ.*, 446 S.E.2d 107 (N.C.App.1994).

Part of the student activity fee paid by students at a New York university was allocated to a public interest research group. The public interest group had chapters on 19 New York public university campuses, and payment of the fee resulted in mandatory student membership in the group. Students who objected to the allocation of fees to the group filed a lawsuit against state university officials in the U.S. District Court for the Southern District of New York, which denied their request for an order based on their First Amendment rights. The U.S. Court of Appeals, Second Circuit, affirmed parts of the district court decision, reversed others and remanded the case. The district court entered an order on remand, and the students appealed to the court of appeals a second time.

The court affirmed the district court's decision to allow student activity fees to support activities and projects beyond the geographical limits of the campus. However, the district court had committed error by broadly allowing use of the activity fees for any activities that benefited or involved students. The court modified the district court order by restricting the use of fees to activities that provided hands-on educational experiences for students, extracurricular activities on and off campus, and certain other educational objectives. The court affirmed other aspects of the district court's decision and awarded attorney's fees to the students. *Carroll v. Blinken*, 42 F.3d 122 (2d Cir.1994).

Students at the Berkley campus of the University of California are required to pay an activities fee. Part of the income from that fee is used to support student groups that pursue political and ideological causes. A group of students sued the university challenging the validity of the mandatory student activities fee, claiming that the regents did not have sufficient authority to collect a mandatory student activities fee and that the use of the fee to fund politically or ideologically active groups violated their First Amendment rights. A California trial court entered judgment in favor of the university and the court of appeal affirmed. The students then sought review from the Supreme Court of California. The supreme court stated that the regents had the power to collect the mandatory fee. The California Constitution expressly invested the regents with "full powers of organization and government" over the university. This general grant of power was plainly adequate to permit the regents to levy a student activities fee. The court went on, however, to state that the mandatory fee could not be used to fund groups to which a student might object. The court stated that government may not compel a person to contribute money to support political or ideological causes. The groups could still be funded from student fees of those students who did not object, but a partial refund was due those students who disagreed with the activities of certain funded associations. *Smith v. Regents of the Univ. of California*, 844 P.2d 500 (Cal.1993).

A divorced Pennsylvania woman wished to enroll her daughter in the school district in which the girl's father resided. The district did not allow her to attend tuition-free because it considered her to be a nonresident student. The mother then filed suit in a Pennsylvania trial court seeking injunctive relief. The trial court found for the school district and the mother appealed to the Commonwealth Court of Pennsylvania. The mother argued that the daughter was not limited to being a resident of one school district. The court noted that a person can have only one domicile or principal residence. Upon divorce of the parents, the child's residence is with the parent with whom he or she resides or to whom custody has been given. Therefore, the court upheld the decision of the trial court and determined that the girl was a resident of the school district in which her mother lived. *Mathias v. Richland School Dist.*, 592 A.2d 811 (Pa.Cmwlth.1991).

Faced with a budget shortfall, the University of New Hampshire sent letters to all its in-state students that tuition would possibly be raised $200 to $400 the following semester. The university graduate and undergraduate catalogs specifically reserved the university's right to raise tuition following publication of the tuition rates in those catalogs. However, by the final day of registration when all tuition was due, the university had not yet raised tuition. One month later, the university raised its tuition and told all in-state students, and selected out-state students, that they owed an additional amount for the current semester. A group of students sued the university in a state trial court, claiming that it could not arbitrarily raise tuition at any time. The university defended its action, stating that it specifically reserved the right to raise tuition at any time, even in midsemester. A New Hampshire trial court summarily ruled for the university, and the students appealed to the New Hampshire Supreme Court. The supreme court stated that the university's reservation of rights clause was not nearly so broad as the university claimed. The university did not have the right to arbitrarily raise tuition after the registration tuition deadline. Rather, its reservation of rights clause was rendered ineffective at that time. However, the university had advised all in-state students of a potential increase. The court held that this notification was sufficient to allow the university leeway to raise tuition after the start of the semester. This raise could not be applied against out-state students, who had not been notified by the university of the possible increase. *Gamble v. Univ. System of New Hampshire*, 610 A.2d 357 (N.H.1992).

The parents of four Indiana elementary school students failed to pay textbook rental fees totaling $235.00. Because the parents met the eligibility standards for financial assistance, the state paid roughly one-half of the fee. The district sued the parents in a state trial court seeking to recover the remainder. The trial court found that an Indiana statute concerning book fees allowed the district to compel payment and entered judgment in favor of the school district. The parents appealed to the Court of Appeals of Indiana. The appellate court rejected the trial court's interpretation of the statute. The court held that parents who meet the financial eligibility requirements cannot be required to pay book fees. A school district may request, but it may not compel low income parents to pay the fees through legal action. The trial court's ruling was reversed. *Gohn v. Akron School*, 562 N.E.2d 1291 (Ind.App.3d Dist.1990).

F.   Private Contractors

A Texas school district fired an employee for stealing and later adopted a policy prohibiting its contractors from employing former school district employees at school sites. The former employee filed an unsuccessful lawsuit against the school district that was partially based on interference with contract and civil conspiracy claims. A contractor that employed the former school district employee was not allowed to bid for the construction of portable buildings for the district. The district also canceled the contractor's existing contract for failure to begin performance on time because the contract stated that time was of the essence. A Texas trial court granted summary judgment to the school district and the contractor appealed to the Court of Appeals of Texas, Waco.

The court of appeals held that the school district had appropriately canceled the contract and awarded it to the next lowest bidder when the contractor failed to begin performance by the specified date. When time is of the essence, performance must occur within the specified time, or the nonperforming party is in material breach of the contract. The contractor also had no valid claim against the district for adopting the policy against hiring its former employees. The district's refusal to accept a low bid for the construction of portables by the contractor was also permissible under Texas law. The court of appeals affirmed the trial court's summary judgment order. *Beavers v. Goose Creek Cons. ISD*, 884 S.W.2d 932 (Tex.App.—Waco 1994).

A Pennsylvania public school joint purchasing board awarded an exclusive fuel and gasoline contract to a fuel distributor pursuant to competitive bidding. The distributor performed the contract successfully and was rehired in two subsequent years. The board then determined that the distributor had failed to pledge collateral as acceptable performance security and demanded a letter of credit. The distributor provided the letter of credit and placed $300,000 in a pledged collateral account naming the board as sole payee in the event of default. Despite the distributor's compliance with the board's request, the board unilaterally terminated the contract for failure to provide acceptable performance security. The distributor filed a lawsuit against the board, two schools and certain employees in the U.S. District Court for the Eastern District of Pennsylvania, claiming constitutional violations. The court considered dismissal motions filed by the defendants.

The court determined that the complaint had alleged sufficient grounds for deprivation of the distributor's constitutional liberty interest in the contract. Termination of the agreement may have hampered the distributor's ability to enter into public contracts in the future, and the unilateral action may have deprived the distributor of its due process rights. The board should have provided notice and an opportunity for the distributor to respond before taking unilateral action. While denying some of the other motions requested by the defendants, the court allowed the liberty interest complaint to survive. *Fox Fuel v. Delaware County Schools Joint Purchasing Bd.*, 856 F.Supp. 945 (E.D.Pa.1994).

A New York school district contracted with a private company for support management services in the custodial and maintenance areas. After the three year contract expired, the board and company signed a new agreement that was to be automatically renewed thereafter. When voters of the school district approved a merger with another district, the new consolidated district approved the contract. A group of taxpayers claimed that the contract constituted a gift of public money to a private organization in violation of the New York constitution. The taxpayers sued the consolidated school district in a New York trial court to challenge the validity of the contract. The court granted summary judgment to the taxpayers and the consolidated school district appealed to the New York Supreme Court, Appellate Division, Third Department.

The appellate court observed that if the contract called for the use of specialized skills, expertise and the exercise of judgment and discretion, it was a professional services contract that was outside the state law requirement for competitive bidding. Conversely, if the contract was not for professional services, the competitive bidding statute applied. The trial court had committed error by granting summary judgment, and the appellate division court reversed and remanded the case to the trial court to determine the nature of the services under the contract. *Schulz v. Cobleskill-Richmondville Central School Dist. Bd. of Educ.*, 610 N.Y.S.2d 694 (A.D.3d Dept.1994).

A California school district purchased land that needed decontamination. The cleanup cost was greatly underestimated and the school district sought partial relief by filing an action against two oil companies that held an easement for a pipeline running across the property. The school district sued the oil companies in the U.S. District Court for the Central District of California, claiming violations of the Comprehensive Environmental Response, Compensation and Liability Act (CERCLA), 42 U.S.C. § 9601 *et seq.* The court granted summary judgment to the oil companies, and the school district appealed to the U.S. Court of Appeals, Ninth

Circuit. On appeal, the school district argued that the oil companies were "owners" or "operators" for purposes of CERCLA by virtue of their pipeline easements. The court of appeals noted that the district had failed to allege that the pipeline leaked toxic waste. The mere maintenance of the pipeline did not create liability, and the holding of an easement did not constitute ownership for CERCLA purposes. The court affirmed summary judgment for the oil companies. *Long Beach Unif. School Dist. v. Godwin California Living Trust*, 32 F.3d 1364 (9th Cir.1994).

The Ohio Attorney General's office filed a lawsuit in the U.S. District Court for the Southern District of Ohio against 15 dairies that were alleged to have fixed prices of milk sold to Ohio schools. Prior to trial, the dairies filed a number of motions, including a motion to dismiss the lawsuit for failing to state a claim upon which relief could be granted, lack of standing by the state to advance the claim, and the passing of the statute of limitations. Three dairies alleged that the claims did not arise from the same transactions as the claims against the other dairies and that they should therefore be dismissed from the case.

The court held that the amended complaint adequately alleged the existence of a conspiracy among the dairies to submit prearranged, complimentary losing bids on milk supply contracts in order to conceal a contract allocation scheme that gave the illusion of competition. Contrary to the argument of the dairies, the attorney general had standing to advance a complaint under Ohio's Valentine Act on behalf of the school districts. Although the complaint alleged claims from as early as 1977 through 1989, the filing of the complaint in 1993 did not violate the four year statute of limitations contained in the Clayton Antitrust Act. This was because there was evidence that the defendants had fraudulently concealed the existence of the conspiracy. The statute did not begin running until the school districts gained actual knowledge of the alleged conspiracy. The court refused to dismiss from the lawsuit the dairies that alleged they had not participated in the conspiracy. The motions of the dairies were denied. *State of Ohio ex rel. Fisher v. Louis Trauth Dairy, Inc.*, 856 F.Supp. 1229 (S.D.Ohio 1994).

An Arizona school board ordered a contractor to stop working on a project for over two months because of problems obtaining building permits. The contractor claimed that the board breached its contract. The contractor filed for arbitration under a contractual clause, and an Arizona trial court refused to stay arbitration. The Arizona Court of Appeals held that an Arizona statute preserved the contractor's right to arbitrate delay-related claims, but that all procurement-related claims must be resolved under procedures specified by the board. The Supreme Court of Arizona reinstated the trial court's decision, ruling that the board had exceeded its authority by adopting a contractual remedy procedure in contravention of the statute. The contractor was entitled to arbitrate all of its claims, plus its attorney's fees and costs. *Canon School Dist. No. 50 v. W.E.S. Const. Co., Inc.*, 869 P.2d 500 (Ariz.1994).

The Chicago Board of Education decided to limit the number of HMO plans available to its employees to only four plans for the 1990-91 school year. Previously it had offered eight. It determined to simply retain the four HMOs with the highest employee enrollments. The fifth largest HMO sued the school district in an Illinois trial court, arguing that the district was required by Illinois statutes to award HMO contracts by the competitive bidding process. The trial court ruled for the HMO, and the school district appealed to the Appellate Court of Illinois, First District. The appellate court rejected the board's argument that HMO contracts involved the provision of professional services and therefore were not susceptible to the competitive bidding process. The selection of HMOs for school district employees was one that should be determined through the competitive bidding process. The trial court's decision was affirmed and the board's petition for a rehearing was denied. *Compass Health Care Plans v. Bd. of Educ. of City of Chicago*, 617 N.E.2d 6 (Ill.App.1st Dist.1992).

An Indiana community school solicited bids for its school bus contract. The day after bids were received, the school board adopted an affirmative action form. Two weeks later, the board rejected all bids for the contract, declared an emergency rebidding and changed a specification. A bus company that had served the school for at least 16 years submitted bids both times and alleged that it was the lowest responsible bidder. The school board awarded the contract to another bidder, and the bus company sought review in an Indiana trial court. The court ruled that the board's failure to give any notice of the changed specification violated Indiana's public bidding statute. It enjoined the board from granting any bid based on this faulty procedure and remanded the case to the board. The bus company appealed this decision, claiming that there should be no remand and that it should have been awarded the contract as the lowest responsible bidder.

The Court of Appeals of Indiana, Second District, held that the trial court had properly enjoined the board from awarding the contract because of its irregular bidding procedure. It further held that the trial court could only remand the case to the board for further proceedings. The bus company's argument that it should be automatically awarded the contract due to its prior low bid was without merit. Under Indiana law, only the school board could properly make the decision to award a contract. The court of appeals affirmed the trial court's decision, remanding the case to the school board for solicitation of new bids under the proper procedure. *M & M Bus Co., Inc. v. Muncie Comm. School Corp.*, 627 N.E.2d 862 (Ind.App.2d Dist.1994).

A commercial studio photographer contracted with two Pennsylvania school districts to be their exclusive yearbook photographer. In exchange for the exclusive contract, the studio photographed student events and club activities for inclusion in the yearbooks. It also received the opportunity to sell additional graduation portraits to students. A competing photography studio sued the school districts and the studio in the U.S. District Court for the Western District of Pennsylvania, claiming that the agreement between the studio and school districts violated federal antitrust laws because it was not the product of competitive bidding. The court dismissed the lawsuit as frivolous, ruling that in order to find an antitrust violation, there must be a showing of predatory pricing or similar anticompetitive conduct, a specific intent to monopolize and a dangerous probability of achieving monopoly power. There was no showing of any antitrust violation by the competing studio. *Burns v. Cover Studios, Inc.*, 818 F.Supp. 888 (W.D.Pa.1993).

An Arkansas school district obtained bids for a new school building and selected the lowest of four bids. The selected contractor obtained a surety bond as required by law. It soon determined that it had made an error of almost $86,000 and refused to perform the contract. The next lowest bidder then performed the work, which included additional services and an increased dollar amount over its original bid under a contingency clause for rock removal. Despite the extra work, the school district wound up paying $42,000 less than it would have had it used the originally selected bidder. This was because the second lowest bidder's rock removal rate was only one-third that of the originally selected bidder.

The school district sued the originally selected bidder in an Arkansas trial court, which held that the contract could not be rescinded in equity but that the district should recover nothing because it had suffered no damages. Both parties appealed to the Supreme Court of Arkansas. The supreme court ruled that the surety bond and Arkansas law could be construed together so that the district was entitled to the difference between the amount of the original bid and the amount of the contract it eventually signed with the second lowest bidder. The originally selected bidder was not entitled to rescind the contract even though the school district ultimately wound up paying less than it would have under its original bid. The court reversed and remanded the case and awarded the district prejudgment interest. *Mountain Home School Dist. No. 9 v. T.M.J. Builders, Inc.*, 858 S.W.2d 74 (Ark.1993).

A New Mexico statute concerning competitive sealed bids for public contracts prohibited the modification of bid prices after submission, and permitted the withdrawal of bids only when based upon clear evidence of a mistake. A general contractor submitted a bid to a school district to build a high school. The bid was accepted, and upon signing the contract, the parties agreed to a change order which deducted the cost of paving the parking areas. The parties failed to realize that this item had already been deducted from the contract, resulting in a double deduction. The contractor claimed that it lost more than $73,000 because of the error and it sued the district in a New Mexico trial court, seeking contract reformation. The trial court dismissed the complaint. The Supreme Court of New Mexico reversed the trial court's order, finding that the parties had made a mutual mistake that justified reformation of the contract. *Ballard v. Chavez*, 868 P.2d 646 (N.M.1994).

Several public school districts in New Mexico formed a nonprofit corporation for the primary purpose of obtaining educational services for the member districts at a reduced cost. They also formed an educational cooperative to pool their efforts and resources in order to procure services for the school districts at an affordable cost. The corporation was designated as the administering agency of the cooperative. One of the corporation's primary activities was the delivery of ancillary or special education services to member school districts. The corporation issued a "request for proposal for ancillary services" which an offeror of such services protested against. The offeror's protest was administratively denied. However, rather than seeking judicial review of the decision, it brought suit against the corporation in a state trial court, alleging that the corporation had violated the procurement code, which applies to all expenditures by state agencies and local public bodies for the procurement of items of tangible personal property, services, and construction. The court dismissed the offeror's suit, and it appealed to the Court of Appeals of New Mexico.

On appeal, the court affirmed the dismissal of the lawsuit, finding that even though the corporation was required to comply with the procurement code, there was no private right of action available under the code. Here, the offeror had been given a reasonable opportunity to participate in the administrative protest process which was afforded by the procurement code. Accordingly, the lawsuit was dismissed. *State Ex Rel. Educational Assessments Systems, Inc. v. Cooperative Educational Services of New Mexico, Inc.,* 848 P.2d 1123 (N.M.App.1993).

A Michigan school board hired a general contractor to construct and renovate athletic facilities within its district. State law requires contractors to furnish performance and payment bonds for submission to the school board. Bonds must be issued by licensed companies and filed in the school board office. Several of the general contractor's subcontractors complained that the general contractor was failing to make payments. The school board reassured the subcontractors that the payment bond protected their interests. The school board then learned that the bond was fraudulent, but failed to notify the subcontractors for over two months. A Michigan trial court consolidated several actions filed by subcontractors against the school board with the school board's action against the general contractor. The trial court granted the school district summary disposition on several issues.

Appeal reached the Supreme Court of Michigan, which held that a Michigan statute unambiguously imposed a duty upon government entities to verify the validity of payment bonds upon request by subcontractors. Although the school board had provided a certified copy of the bond to the subcontractors upon request, its failure to inform the subcontractors of facts within its knowledge created an issue which precluded summary judgment. Summary disposition on the subcontractors' claims that the school district was unjustly enriched by receiving services and supplies was also inappropriate. The subcontractors would be allowed to prove on remand that they were entitled to the imposition of a constructive trust on the $1.3 million paid to the general contractor for work performed. The case was affirmed in part and reversed in part. *Kammer Asphalt Paving Co., Inc. v. East China Township Schools,* 504 N.W.2d 635 (Mich.1993).

G. Insurance

An Alaska school district was insured under two all risk insurance policies that covered the replacement cost of property at the time of loss. Both policies excluded coverage for loss or increased costs caused by a civil authority's enforcement of an ordinance or law regulating the construction or repair of the insured property. When fire destroyed a high school in the district, the insurers paid the replacement cost of the building, which was approximately $3.5 million. They refused to pay an additional $206,000 for equipment required by changes in the building code citing the exclusions in their policies. The school district sued the insurers in an Alaska trial court, which granted a motion by the insurers for judgment on the pleadings. The district appealed to the Supreme Court of Alaska, which found that the exclusions relied upon by the insurers were ambiguous and did not defeat the school district's reasonable expectations that it could expect replacement of a building destroyed by fire. The loss was caused by a fire, not by a civil authority's enforcement of an ordinance as the insurers claimed. The court disagreed with the insurers' interpretations of the policies and construed them in favor of the school district. It reversed and remanded the trial court's decision. *Bering Strait School Dist. v. RLI Ins. Co.*, 873 P.2d 1292 (Alaska 1994).

A Missouri school district was a member of a self insurance association that administered a risk management pool which protected its members from property losses. The association provided insurance coverage of up to $250,000. The association in turn purchased excess insurance coverage from a private insurance company for claims over $250,000. When a fire destroyed buildings and property owned by the school district, the district claimed that the association owed it $250,000 and the excess insurer owed it over $3 million. The excess insurer rejected the claim, stating that the district had overvalued the damages and that it was unclear whether the district was a named insured entitled to payment under the excess policy. The district sued the insurer in a Missouri trial court, which granted the insurer's combined motion for dismissal and summary judgment. The school district appealed to the Missouri Court of Appeals, Southern District.

The court of appeals noted that the insurer interpreted its own policy as insuring property located in the various school districts in the association, while also claiming that the policy limited the negotiation and settlement of claims to the insurer and association. The insurer's uncertainty about the meaning of the term "named insured" within the policy created an ambiguity that must be construed against it. Construction of the term "named insured" in order to defeat coverage would be inconsistent with the insurer's duty to negotiate with the association and was repugnant to the limits of liability clause. Although the named insured was typically specified in the policy, sufficient ambiguity existed in this case to make summary judgment inappropriate. The court of appeals reversed and remanded the case to the trial court. *Dent Phelps R-III School Dist. v. Hartford Fire Ins. Co.*, 870 S.W.2d 915 (Mo.App.S.D.1994).

A Minnesota school district purchased a liability protection insurance policy to cover losses and expenses from claims arising from wrongful acts based on errors or omissions, negligence, breach of a duty, misstatements or misleading statements. The district became involved in two lawsuits filed by employees, one of which alleged age discrimination. The district tendered defense of both claims to the insurer, which refused to defend. The district filed a lawsuit against the insurer in a Minnesota trial court, which held for the school district. The Court of Appeals of Minnesota affirmed this decision and the insurer appealed to the Supreme Court of Minnesota. On appeal, the insurer argued that the policy excluded intentional acts from coverage. Alternatively, it argued that no insurance policy should be construed to cover intentional acts, as a matter of public policy. The supreme court disagreed, holding that the policy did not exclude intentional acts from coverage, even though it did exclude coverage for some specific types of intentional conduct. The policy unambiguously covered intentional discrimination because discrimination was a wrongful act based on the breach of a duty. It also covered the district's failure to reinstate the other employee because it was based on a claimed wrongful act. The supreme court affirmed the judgments of the lower courts. *Indep. School Dist. No. 697, Eveleth, Minnesota v. St. Paul Fire and Marine Ins. Co.*, 515 N.W.2d 576 (Minn.1994).

A New York school district granted a swim club permission to use its pool facilities. The club agreed to purchase a comprehensive liability insurance policy naming the school district as an additional insured. The club applied for insurance, but before it received the certificate of insurance, a swim club participant was injured in a diving accident in a district pool. The insurer denied coverage, claiming that it did not intend to insure claims occurring prior to issuance of the certificate. The New York Supreme Court, Appellate Division, Third Department, observed that the policy was a claims-made policy which imposed a duty upon the insurer to provide coverage during the entire policy period. The accident occurred within the policy period and coverage existed regardless of the date of issuance of the certificate. The court ruled for the school district. *Dryden Central School Dist. v. Dryden Aquatic Racing Team*, 600 N.Y.S.2d 388 (A.D.3d Dept.1993).

A hurricane damaged property owned by a South Carolina school district. The property was covered under four insurance policies provided by the State Budget Control Board. When the district submitted proof of loss claims, the board disallowed the costs of repair for preexisting damage allegedly caused by improper building maintenance. It also claimed that the district had submitted claims for noncompensable architectural design fees, inspection fees, asbestos removal charges, excessive and unreasonable items and matters that were not covered by the policies. The district sued the board in a South Carolina trial court for breach of contract and bad faith. After some limited discovery, the board filed a motion for appraisal of the damage under a South Carolina insurance statute, and filed a motion to dismiss the bad faith claim. The trial court granted both motions and the district appealed to the Supreme Court of South Carolina.
On appeal, the school district argued that the board had waived its statutory rights to the appraisal procedure by signing a contract containing an alternative appraisal procedure. The court held that mandatory procedures contained in state insurance law superseded contractual provisions. It also ruled that the board's failure to promptly avail itself of the statutory appraisal procedure did not prevent the school district from obtaining discovery documents. The court ruled that dismissal of the bad faith claim was appropriate because the district's claimed damages greatly exceeded the statutory maximum under the state Tort Claim Act. The same statute barred any punitive damage award against the board. The court affirmed the dismissal of the bad faith claim. *Charleston County School Dist. v. State Budget and Control Bd.*, 437 S.E.2d 6 (S.C.1993).

After certain Wisconsin school districts were named as defendants in federal racial discrimination litigation—which sought declaratory, injunctive and remedial relief—they sought coverage from their liability insurers. The insurers refused to provide a defense and the school districts eventually entered into a settlement agreement, denying that they had violated the law, but agreeing to such remedial measures as minority recruitment programs. They then sued their insurers for the expenses associated with their compliance with the settlement. The supreme court of Wisconsin initially looked at the term "damages" in the liability policies and determined that it would include the costs of complying with injunctive or equitable relief. Accordingly, it held for the school districts. Subsequently, on a motion for reconsideration, the Wisconsin Supreme Court reversed its decision without explanation and without giving the parties notice or opportunity for further written or oral arguments on the merits of the case. On a further motion for reconsideration by the school districts, the supreme court held that the insurers would not be liable for the remedial relief costs. *School District of Shorewood v. Wausau Ins. Co.,* 498 N.W.2d 823 (Wis.1993).

II. DESEGREGATION

The Equal Protection Clause of the Fourteenth Amendment to the U.S. Constitution requires that public schools not be operated by the state on a racially segregated basis. The U.S. Supreme Court has firmly adhered to the view that *de jure* segregation, or a current condition of segregation resulting from intentional state action, is constitutionally impermissible. However, *de facto* segregation, or segregation resulting from housing patterns or other factors beyond government control, does not violate the constitution.

A. Generally

Courts continue to play a major role in implementing the mandate of the U.S. Supreme Court in *Brown v. Board of Education,* 347 U.S. 483, 74 S.Ct. 686, 98 L.Ed.2d 873 (1954). A variety of plans have been designed and implemented in order to eliminate the vestiges of dual, racially segregated school systems and to achieve unitary systems.

In 1977, the Kansas City, Missouri, School District (KCMSD), its school board and a group of resident students sued the State of Missouri and a number of suburban Kansas City school districts in the U.S. District Court for the Western District of Missouri, claiming that the state had caused and perpetuated racial segregation in Kansas City schools. Following realignment of the parties to make the KCMSD a nominal defendant, the district court held that the state and KCMSD were liable for an intradistrict constitutional violation. The defendants were ordered to eliminate all vestiges of state-imposed segregation. Because the district's student population was almost 70 percent African-American, the district court ordered a wide range of quality education plans which converted every high school and middle school, and some elementary schools, into magnet schools to attract white students. This action was based upon the court's finding that KCMSD student achievement levels still lagged behind national averages in some grades. The state contested its court-ordered responsibility to help fund capital improvements for KCMSD schools. It also contested district court orders requiring it to share in the cost of teacher salary increases and quality education plans.

The U.S. Court of Appeals, Eighth Circuit, affirmed the district court orders. The state appealed to the U.S. Supreme Court. The Court observed that the district court's remedial plan had been based on a budget that exceeded KCMSD's authority to tax. There was a lack of evidence in the district court record to substantiate the theory that continuing lack of academic achievement in the district was the result of past segregation. The Court determined that the district court had exceeded its authority by ordering the construction of a superior school system to attract white students from suburban and private schools. Its mandate was to remove the racial identity of KCMSD schools, and the interdistrict remedy went beyond the intradistrict violation. The magnet district concept of KCMSD schools could not be supported by the existence of white flight and the district court orders for state contribution to salary increases, quality education programs and capital improvements were reversed. *Missouri v. Jenkins*, 115 S.Ct. 2038 (1995). See also *Missouri v. Jenkins*, 495 U.S. 33, 110 S.Ct. 1651, 109 L.Ed.2d 31 (1990), where in earlier stages of the litigation, the Court prevented the district court from imposing a property tax increase, ruling that relief should be directed against local authorities who could then impose the tax increase.

Mississippi maintained a dual system of public education at the university level—one set of universities for whites, and another set for blacks. In 1981, the State Board of Trustees issued "Mission Statements" to remedy this, classifying the three flagship historically white institutions (HWI) as "comprehensive" universities, redesignating one of the historically black institutions (HBI) as an "urban" university and characterizing the rest as "regional" institutions. However, the universities remained racially identifiable. A federal district court found that state policies need merely be racially neutral, developed in good faith, and must not contribute to the racial identifiability of each institution. The court held that Mississippi was currently fulfilling its duty to desegregate. The U.S. Court of Appeals, Fifth Circuit, affirmed. The U.S. Supreme Court granted review.

The Supreme Court held that the district court had applied the wrong legal standard in ruling that Mississippi had brought itself into compliance with the Equal Protection Clause. If a state perpetuates policies and practices traceable to its prior dual system that continue to have segregative effects, and such policies are without sound educational justification and can be practicably eliminated, the policies violate the Clause. This is true even if the state has abolished the legal requirement that the races be separated and has established neutral policies. The proper inquiry is whether existing racial identifiability is attributable to the state. Because the district court's standard did not ask the appropriate questions, the court of appeals erred in affirming. Applying the proper standard, several surviving aspects of Mississippi's prior dual system were constitutionally suspect. First, the use of higher minimum ACT composite scores at the HWIs, along with the state's refusal to consider high school grade performance was suspect. Second, the unnecessary duplication of programs at HBIs and HWIs was suspect. Third, the mission statements' reflection of previous policies to perpetuate racial separation was suspect. Finally, the state's operation of eight universities had to be examined to determine if it was educationally justifiable. On remand, the state would have to justify all these decisions as sound. *U.S. v. Fordice*, 505 U.S. —, 112 S.Ct. 2727, 120 L.Ed.2d 575 (1992).

In 1969, a Georgia school system was enjoined by a federal district court from discriminating on the basis of race and was required to close all legally recognized black schools. The system complied and the case remained inactive until the 1970s. In 1983, the plaintiff class returned to court contending that the school system improperly limited minority transfers to a predominantly white school and that the proposed expansion of a white high school would perpetuate segregation. The district court ruled that the school system had achieved unitary status, and did not have a discriminatory intent in deciding to expand the high school. The U.S. Court of Appeals, Eleventh Circuit, reversed, stating that the school system could not be declared unitary without a hearing, and that until it was declared unitary, its intent was immaterial. On remand, the district court held that the school system had not yet achieved unitary status. The school system would achieve unitary status when all schools possessed minority staffs within 15 percent of the system average. However, the court refused to impose additional duties on the school system in the areas of student assignment, transportation, and extracurricular activities. Both parties appealed the ruling.

The court of appeals stated that the system had not discharged its duty in the areas of student assignment, transportation, and extracurricular activities by closing all legally recognized black schools in response to the 1969 order. The court stated that the system would not achieve unitary status until it maintained at least three years of racial equality in the six categories set out in *Green v. New Kent County School Bd.,* 391 U.S. 430, 88 S.Ct. 1689, 20 L.Ed.2d 716 (1968): student assignment, faculty, staff, transportation, extracurricular activities, and facilities. The court of appeals ordered the district court to require the system to file a plan in accordance with its opinion. The U.S. Supreme Court, however, held on appeal that the *Green* framework did not need to be applied as construed by the court of appeals. Through relinquishing control in areas deemed to be unitary, a court and school district may more effectively concentrate on the areas in need of further attention. The Court held that the "incremental" approach was constitutional, and that a court may declare that it will order no further remedy in any area which is found to be unitary. The order of the court of appeals was reversed, and the case was remanded to the district court. *Freeman v. Pitts,* 503 U.S. 467, 112 S.Ct. 1430, 118 L.Ed.2d 108 (1992).

In 1989, the U.S. Court of Appeals, Tenth Circuit, found that the board of education of Topeka had not yet removed the vestiges of illegal segregation in the Topeka schools. *Brown v. Board of Education,* 892 F.2d 851 (10th Cir.1989). The U.S. Supreme Court vacated that opinion and remanded for further consideration in light of *Board of Educ. of Oklahoma City Public Schools v. Dowell,* below, and *Freeman v. Pitts,* above. After consideration of *Dowell* and *Freeman,* the court of appeals reinstated its prior opinion in full. The court stated that one of the reasons it had previously reversed the district court's decision was because it had erred in placing the burden on the plaintiffs to prove intentional discriminatory conduct rather than presuming that current disparities were causally related to past intentional conduct. The court of appeals noted that *Freeman* stated that the school district bears the burden of showing that any current racial imbalance is not traceable, in a proximate way, to the prior violation. It also noted that after an initial finding of liability, the district court may enforce this duty without any new proof of a constitutional violation. Here, the question was whether Topeka had successfully discharged the duty imposed by the Constitution to eliminate the vestiges of illegal segregation. Neither *Dowell* nor *Freeman* required the plaintiffs in the remedial phase of school desegregation litigation to make a new showing of discriminatory intent. Once a school district has achieved unitary status, then, and only then, does an intentional discrimination test apply to school district actions. The court of appeals remanded the case to the district court for determination of an appropriate remedy. *Brown v. Board of Educ.*, 978 F.2d 585 (10th Cir.1992).

In 1972 a federal district court issued an injunction imposing a school desegregation plan on Oklahoma City. In 1977, the court found that the school district had achieved unitary status and issued an order terminating the case. In 1984, because of an increase in young black students, which would result in them being bused farther away, the board adopted the Student Reassignment Plan (SRP). The SRP assigned students who were in grades K-4 to their neighborhood schools, but continued busing for grades 5-12. The parents who had brought the original desegregation case filed a motion to reopen the case, claiming that the SRP was a return to segregation. The federal district court refused to reopen the case and held that its 1977 finding that the school district was unitary could not be relitigated. The parents appealed to the U.S. Court of Appeals, Tenth Circuit. The court held that the trial court's 1977 finding was binding, but this did not mean that the 1972 injunction itself was terminated. The case was remanded to determine if the injunction should be lifted. On remand, the trial court found that the SRP was not designed with discriminatory intent and ordered the injunction lifted. The case was again appealed to the U.S. Court of Appeals which reversed the lower court's decision. The school board then petitioned the U.S. Supreme Court for review and its petition was granted.

The Supreme Court first determined that the 1977 order did not dissolve the desegregation decree and that the district court's finding that the school district was unitary was too ambiguous to bar the parents from challenging later actions by the board. However, the Court stressed that supervision of local school districts by the federal courts was meant as a temporary means to remedy past discrimination. The Court remanded the case and instructed the trial court to determine whether the school district had shown sufficient compliance with constitutional requirements when it adopted the SRP. *Bd. of Educ. of Oklahoma City Public Schools v. Dowell*, 498 U.S. 237, 111 S.Ct. 630, 112 L.Ed.2d 715 (1991).

On remand, the district court reaffirmed its prior findings without allowing additional hearings. It ruled that the parties had already received a full opportunity to present their evidence and adopted the school board's proposed order almost verbatim. The court of appeals affirmed the district court's decision, ruling that it had not violated the Supreme Court's remand instructions by failing to hold a new hearing and by adopting the board's proposed order. The school board had complied with the desegregation decree and maintained a unitary school system. Because the school board met its burden of showing that the current racial imbalance at its schools was not traceable to prior violations, the court affirmed the district court's decision. *Dowell v. Bd. of Educ. of Oklahoma City Pub. Schools*, 8 F.3d 1501 (10th Cir.1993).

An Alabama school district was under federal court supervision from 1967 until 1985 as the result of desegregation litigation. The lawsuit was dismissed and the school system declared unitary by stipulated order in 1985. A group of African-American parents alleged that after dismissal of the original lawsuit, the district entered into actions which had a disparate impact on black students attending district schools. The group alleged that the district closed an all-black school, built a new school located within a white community, tolerated white student transfers to other public school systems, and ignored their concerns at school board meetings. The parents sued the district in an Alabama federal district court, claiming violations of the Fourteenth Amendment to the U.S. Constitution, Title VI of the Civil Rights Act of 1964, state laws such as the open meetings act, and breach of contract of the 1985 stipulation. The court dismissed the case, and the parents appealed.

The U.S. Court of Appeals, Eleventh Circuit, held that the district court had properly dismissed the constitutional and Title VI complaints because of the parents' failure to prove that the board's actions had been motivated by discrimination. The reasons given by the school board for closing and updating its facilities were supported by evidence that the actions met legitimate, necessary educational goals. There was insufficient evidence that the board could have taken action against white students who transferred to schools located outside the district. The district court had properly dismissed the breach of contract and state law claims, but its decision stated no reasons for ruling against the parents on their complaint that the board had prohibited recordings of its public meetings. That portion of the district court's decision was vacated. *Elston v. Talladega County Bd. of Educ.*, 997 F.2d 1394 (11th Cir.1993).

B.   Staff Reductions and School Closings

A Georgia school district was restrained by court order from taking any action that would perpetuate racial segregation of students in its facilities. The case became inactive in 1979. In 1986, the board proposed consolidating its three existing high schools and building a new one. The state allocated $6.5 million for the new school. However, in 1988, a school board consisting of a different membership voted against consolidation. The state threatened to withhold money earmarked for the project, and a group of citizens attempted to reactivate the case. They claimed that the board had failed to comply with the 1973 injunction by permitting white students to transfer among its schools. The court ordered the state to continue withholding funds from the board, and held a trial. The court ordered closure of one high school and halted student transfers. A new board, elected in 1992, voted to adopt the 1986 consolidation plan. A group of citizens claimed that the new board had "caved in" to pressure by the U.S. government. The court denied the group's motion to intervene. The group then appealed to the U.S. Court of Appeals, Eleventh Circuit.

On appeal, the citizens argued that consolidation would result in resegregation because of anticipated transfers of white students to private schools. They argued that this issue was constitutional, rather than political. The court of appeals disagreed, ruling that the district court had properly found that the group had no legally protectable interest in the litigation. The dispute was political in nature and could not be dealt with by a federal court. The court of appeals affirmed the district court's decision. *U.S. v. State of Georgia*, 19 F.3d 1388 (11th Cir.1994).

The Cincinnati Board of Education and a teachers' union adopted a teacher transfer policy designed to assure a balanced racial composition in the school district. When various teachers were told where they had to teach because of this policy, they sued, challenging the policy. The district found that the policy did not violate either equal protection or the collective bargaining agreement, and the U.S. Court of Appeals, Sixth Circuit, agreed. It stated that school authorities have broad discretion to implement educational policy and that an integrated teaching staff is a legitimate concern in achieving a school system free of racial discrimination. The teachers could be required to teach at particular locations under the policy. *Jacobson v. Cincinnati Bd. of Educ.*, 961 F.2d 100 (6th Cir.1992).

C. Busing

Busing has been utilized by many school districts in order to achieve racial balance. Courts have affirmed intradistrict school district desegregation plans which have included busing. See *Columbus Bd. of Educ. v. Penick*, 443 U.S. 449, 99 S.Ct. 2941, 61 L.Ed.2d 666 (1979). However, in the landmark Detroit school busing case, the U.S. Supreme Court rejected a federal court approved plan which would have required multi-district, interdistrict busing. The Court said that there was no evidence that the districts outside Detroit which were included in the plan either themselves operated segregated school systems or by their actions affected segregation in other districts. The Court went on to say that absent some interdistrict constitutional violations with interdistrict effects, racial segregation existing in one district could not be remedied by interdistrict solutions. *Milliken v. Bradley*, 418 U.S. 717, 94 S.Ct. 311, 41 L.Ed.2d 1069 (1974).

In 1961, the Fort Worth, Texas, Independent School District was placed under federal supervision to enforce integration orders. In 1987, a hearing was conducted in federal district court to review the district's busing policy in achieving integration. The district hoped to end the mandatory busing program and presented evidence that the racial composition within its schools was equivalent to the racial composition within the district. The district presented evidence that busing was no longer required to bring about integration within the district. The district court terminated the remaining busing, and the matter was appealed to the U.S. Court of Appeals, Fifth Circuit. The court of appeals noted that the cost of busing outweighed its utility. More viable segregation techniques—gerrymandering boundaries, magnet schools, majority-to-minority transfer policies, and integrated faculties and staff—had been continuing successfully. As a result, the appeals court found that the district court had not abused its discretion in discontinuing the limited busing and it affirmed the decision. *Flax v. Potts*, 864 F.2d 1157 (5th Cir.1989).

D. Government Assistance

A Georgia county education board proposed the consolidation and closure of four schools. A taxpayer filed a lawsuit against the board in a Georgia trial court, seeking an order requiring an evidentiary hearing or referendum on the proposals. The trial court permanently enjoined the board of education from consolidating and closing the schools. The decision was based upon the court's finding that the board had failed to comply with the state Quality Basic Education Act, a 1969 desegregation agreement and the Individuals with Disabilities Education Act (IDEA). The court ordered the county board to renovate the schools, utilize school trustees as set forth under Georgia law and comply with state and federal funding statutes. The board appealed to the Supreme Court of Georgia.

The supreme court observed that the school board's proposed consolidation plan was in compliance with applicable sections of the Quality Basic Education Act, because the board had duly met with opponents of consolidation. It also complied with the 1969 desegregation plan by insuring that the proposals did not create racially-based dual school systems. The trial court should not have issued a permanent injunction against the school board's accumulation of undesignated funds without designating a special account in its budget for the consolidation measures. Georgia statutes permitted local school systems to establish single reserve funds or accounts for spending and future use if the anticipated date of expenditure is clearly identified. The supreme court reversed the trial court's order finding that the board action violated the IDEA. Contrary to the trial court's decision, the transfer of disabled students from one school to another with a comparable program did not constitute a change in placement that would require notification of parents under the IDEA. The trial court had abused its discretion and the supreme court reversed its decision. *Powell v. Studstill*, 441 S.E.2d 52 (Ga.1994).

In 1984, the U.S. Court of Appeals, Eighth Circuit, set forth a comprehensive program to integrate the St. Louis public schools. In one of the lawsuits relating to the desegregation order, the U.S. District Court for the Eastern District of Missouri issued an order which modified the school desegregation plan. The Board of Education of the City of St. Louis appealed the modification order to the Eighth Circuit, challenging the order. The first issue before the court of appeals was whether the state was responsible for its proportionate share of those desegregation-related capital improvement costs which exceeded previously budgeted items. The court of appeals agreed with the district court that there was no basis for altering the state's obligation with respect to construction costs for either magnet or nonmagnet schools. The next issue was whether the district court should have modified, without an evidentiary hearing, the desegregation program's racial balance goal. Again, the court of appeals affirmed the district court's decision, holding that it was within the lower court's discretion to change the goal from 50 percent black/50 percent white to 55 percent black/45 percent white. The final issue was whether the district court could modify student assignment patterns, school closings and school utilizations without giving the school board an opportunity to present its opinion. On this issue, the court held that the board should have been given an opportunity to refute the facts asserted by an amicus group in its report (and upon which the court apparently relied in ordering the modifications). The court remanded that matter to the district court so that the issue could be resolved before September 1993. *Liddell v. Board of Education of St. Louis,* 988 F.2d 844 (8th Cir.1993).

III. SCHOOL DISTRICT OPERATIONS

School districts are responsible for the operation of the district, including staff assignments and redistricting. They are also empowered to make decisions regarding the maintenance and regulation of the district.

A. Generally

A New Jersey superintendent of schools advised the local school board that a nontenured music teacher should not be rehired. The board did not offer to renew her contract, and many of her students and their families protested to the point that the board reversed its decision. It offered the teacher a new contract over the superintendent's objection. A local board member who had not attended the meeting at which the employment decision was reversed filed a petition with the state commissioner of education to set aside the decision as inappropriate under New Jersey education regulations. An administrative law judge determined that the board's decision had been reasonable and that it was not bound to follow the superintendent's recommendation. This decision was reversed by the state education commissioner, and his decision was affirmed by the state education board. The school district appealed to the Superior Court of New Jersey, Appellate Division.

The appellate division court found no justification in New Jersey law for the contention that the superintendent had the exclusive right to recommend teaching candidates. Although certain New Jersey statutes permitted superintendents to exclusively recommend administrators, no statute limited a school board's ability to select a teaching candidate or granted the superintendent the power to veto teacher appointments. To the extent that state education regulations were to the contrary, they were invalid. The court reversed and remanded the state board's decision. *Rotondo v. Carlstadt-East Rutherford Regional High School Dist.*, 276 N.J.Super. 36, 647 A.2d 174 (1994).

A Michigan school district sought voter approval of a $65 million bond issue. The proposal failed and the district cut $7 million from the budget and proposed another $5 million cut for the following year. Soon after the failure of the bond issue, a newspaper editorial columnist published a satirical, fictional interview of a school official who advocated "punishment cuts" from the school budget while retaining $80,000 per year employees. The superintendent of schools believed that the satirical article was patterned after himself and filed a defamation lawsuit against the newspaper and editorial columnist in a Michigan trial court. The newspaper defendants filed a motion for summary disposition, which the court denied, and they appealed to the Court of Appeals of Michigan. The court of appeals observed that the editorial had been placed on the newspaper's editorial page and was clearly a work of satire. The column was written in a humorous fashion, did not concern actual events and could not possibly be construed as stating actual facts attributable to the superintendent. The column was therefore protected speech and not a false statement of fact. The newspaper defendants were entitled to summary disposition. *Garvelink v. The Detroit News,* 522 N.W.2d 883 (Mich.App.1994).

An Arizona student was arrested by a University of Arizona police officer for driving while under the influence of alcohol. He challenged the arrest, claiming that the university did not have the statutory authority to establish a police force. A trial court agreed and dismissed the charges. The state, by special action, was able to get the charges reinstated, and appeal was taken to the Court of Appeals of Arizona. The appellate court found that even though the legislature had not expressly authorized the university to establish a police department, the grant of power to the institution was broad enough to include the authorization to create a police force. The reinstatement of charges was upheld. *Goode v. Alfred*, 828 P.2d 1235 (Ariz.App.1991).

B. School Closings

A Pennsylvania school district considered options for maintaining acceptable student to teacher ratios in its schools. It decided to close one school, reassigning students from the closed school to other schools in the district. Prior to the action, it published a notice referencing § 780 of the state Public School Code, and announcing a public hearing to consider the permanent closing of a public school in the district. However, the notice failed to state the name of the school. The meeting itself was moved to a different location and a final draft of the meeting minutes was not completed until after a group of parents had filed a lawsuit against the district in a Pennsylvania trial court. The district denied that it had passed a resolution permanently closing the school and denied that it was legally required to comply with § 780. Instead, it claimed that § 13-1311 of the state code gave it the unconditional authority to close schools within the district. The trial court ruled for the parents, and the district appealed to the Commonwealth Court of Pennsylvania. The commonwealth court affirmed the trial court decision, noting that § 780 applied because it was passed subsequent to § 13-1311 and carried with it a three-month notice requirement in order to obtain community input before closing public schools. The school district had failed to give adequate notice by omitting the name of the school to be closed. The trial court decision for the parents was affirmed. *Save Our School v. Colonial School Dist.*, 628 A.2d 1210 (Pa.Cmwlth.1993).

In the spring of 1990, a Comprehensive Educational Facilities Plan (consolidation plan) was completed by the board of education of a West Virginia county. The plan was filed with the state board of education. It called for the construction of a new high school and the closing down of two others. The state board of education approved the plan, and a $7.8 million grant was awarded to help meet the expenses of the plan. Subsequently, an election for the county board of education was held, changing the makeup of the board with respect to the consolidation plan. The new county board placed a "cease and desist" order on any action on the consolidation plan. The new board attempted to submit an alternative plan of consolidation to the state, but a lawsuit resulted instead. A state trial court ordered the county board to implement the consolidation plan, and the county board appealed to the Supreme Court of Appeals of West Virginia.

The appellate court noted that the primary issue was not whether consolidation was a good idea, but whether the county board's actions in refusing to implement the consolidation plan were arbitrary and capricious. Even though the county board had the authority to close and consolidate schools, the discretion to exercise that authority was not unfettered. Here, the consolidation plan had been approved and extensive steps had been taken at the time the new board sought to submit an alternative plan. To stop implementation of the plan at this late stage "and further jeopardize the possibility of funding for an alternative plan" would constitute arbitrary and capricious action. Also, the court noted that the new county board had not stated any reasons for not implementing the consolidation plan. Accordingly, it ordered the county board to implement the plan and affirmed the trial court's decision. *Pell v. Board of Education of Monroe County,* 426 S.E.2d 510 (W.Va.1992).

A Kentucky school board operated two high schools in different parts of the same county. The board determined that, because of declining enrollment and older facilities, one of the high schools should be closed. The board held several public hearings to consider its options. When it adopted a plan to close one of the schools, a group of county residents filed a complaint in a Kentucky trial court claiming that the decision was arbitrary and capricious, and that it violated provisions of the Kentucky Constitution. The trial court granted their request for a restraining order prohibiting the school board from taking any action to close the school pending a hearing. It then ordered the school board to reconsider its prior order in an open meeting. The board then considered public comments and voted to close the school immediately. The trial court rejected the residents' motion for a new restraining order, dissolved the previous order and set aside the order prohibiting the board from implementing its prior decision to close the school. On appeal, the Court of Appeals of Kentucky held that the school board had complied with all applicable provisions of Kentucky law in making its decision to close the school. The board had complied with the state Open Meetings Act in publishing notice of the rescheduled hearing, and the constitutional complaint was without merit. The trial court decision was affirmed and the Supreme Court of Kentucky denied review of the case. *Coppage v. Ohio County Bd. of Educ.,* 860 S.W.2d 779 (Ky.App.1992).

A group of Wyoming parents were concerned that the secondary school in their town would be closed. They circulated a petition requesting that the school board not close the school. The board's superintendent scheduled two informational sessions and a special meeting in advance of its regular meeting to consider the district's budgetary problems. The informational sessions were held within five days of each other and did not comply with the requirements of the state administrative procedure act. The board members also excluded an attorney employed by one set of parents. The regular and special meetings complied with the state administrative procedure act, and the parents' attorney was allowed to attend. At its regularly scheduled meeting, the board voted to close the school, and the parents appealed to a Wyoming trial court. The court upheld the board's decision and the parents appealed to the Supreme Court of Wyoming.

On appeal, the parents argued that the informational sessions were "meetings" within the meaning of the administrative procedure act because the board had taken action. The court observed that while notice had not been given for these sessions as required by the act, it agreed with the board that no action had been taken. The parents' argument that the decision had actually been made at these sessions was purely speculative. The court also rejected the parents' argument that the exclusion of their attorney was a due process violation, because no student had any property interest in attending a specific school. The board's decision to close the school was supported by substantial evidence and its decision was affirmed. *Ward v. Bd. of Trustees of Goshen County School Dist. No. 1*, 865 P.2d 618 (Wyo.1993).

C. Redistricting and Zoning

A New York school district provided special education services at private, religious schools to students with disabilities who were members of the Satmar Hasidic group. The group's religious beliefs include segregation of school-aged boys and girls, and separation from mainstream society. A U.S. Supreme Court decision in 1985 prohibited the state from paying public school teachers for teaching on parochial school grounds. See *Aguilar v. Felton*, Chapter Thirteen, Section V.B., below. Hasidic children were then sent to public schools while the group continued to challenge the matter. The state legislature passed a statute establishing a new, separate school district entirely within the Hasidic community. The district provided only special education services, and Hasidic regular education students continued to attend private religious schools. New York taxpayers and an association of state school officials sought and obtained a state trial court declaration that the statute was unconstitutional. The New York Court of Appeals held that the statute conveyed a message of government endorsement of religion in violation of the Establishment Clause of the U.S. Constitution. The U.S. Supreme Court agreed to review the matter.

The Supreme Court held that a state may not delegate authority to a group chosen by religion. Although the statute did not expressly identify the Hasidim as recipients of governmental authority, it had clearly been passed to benefit them. The result was a purposeful and forbidden fusion of governmental and religious functions. The creation of a school district for the religious community violated the Establishment Clause. The legislation extended a special franchise to the Hasidim that violated the constitutional requirement of religious neutrality by the government. The statute crossed "the line from permissible accommodation to impermissible establishment," and the Supreme Court affirmed the judgment of the court of appeals. *Bd. of Educ. of Kiryas Joel Village School Dist. v. Grumet*, 114 S.Ct. 2481, 129 L.Ed.2d 546 (1994).

The New York legislature then promptly repealed the statute and abolished the Kiryas Joel Village School District, and passed two statutes that provided a mechanism for organization of new school districts. The laws authorized school districts consisting of the entire territory of a municipality coterminous with preexisting school districts when the educational interests of the community required such action, and where certain student enrollment and property tax requirements were satisfied. The taxpayers filed a motion in a New York trial court for a temporary restraining order or preliminary injunction, seeking a declaration that the new statutes were unconstitutional. They argued that the statutes unconstitutionally disbursed over $500,000 to the village school district. The court determined that the 1994 statutory amendments were non-specific, religiously neutral general statutes that were justified by reasonable educational concerns. Although Kiryas Joel was currently the only district taking advantage of the statutes, other municipalities might also seek to use the procedures. Any harm alleged by the taxpayers was outweighed by the risk of harm to students attending the village school, which limited its services to disabled students, and the court denied the taxpayers' motion for a temporary order. *Grumet v. Cuomo*, 617 N.Y.S.2d 620 (Sup.Ct.—Albany County 1994).

A group of Illinois parents filed a petition with the Regional Board of School Trustees of Clinton and Washington Counties, seeking to detach the territory in which they resided from their school district and to annex it to neighboring elementary and high school districts. The annexation/detachment action would reduce the bus ride for their elementary students from 45-60 minutes to 15 minutes. However, transportation time to the high schools would be somewhat increased. The parents presented evidence that they had closer social ties with the annexing districts and that they identified more closely with those communities. The regional board denied the petition and the parents appealed to an Illinois trial court. The court reversed the board's decision, and the board appealed to the Appellate Court of Illinois, Fifth District.

The appellate court rejected the board's assertions that the petition should have been denied for technical reasons, including a statutory requirement that each page of the petition include the complete text of the petition and be signed by a circulator. These technical requirements did not deprive the trial court of jurisdiction or disqualify the petition. The court determined that the weight of the evidence supported granting the petition. The petitioning parents' homes were closer to schools in the annexing districts and it was appropriate to give greater weight to the distance that younger students were required to travel. The budget implications of the annexation/detachment were insignificant, involving the loss of only a fraction of a percent of the assessed value of the property in the detaching district. The court affirmed the trial court's judgment. *Seelhoefer v. Regional Bd. of School Trustees of Clinton and Washington Counties, Illinois*, 640 N.E.2d 360 (Ill.App.5th Dist.1994).

An Illinois regional board of school trustees decided to take property from a residential subdivision in the second largest school district in the state and annex it to a relatively small district. The financial aspects of the action were relatively unimportant. The regional board conducted hearings at which conflicting evidence was presented. Ten resident witnesses testified concerning the preferences of themselves and their children. A psychologist testified that children residing in the residential subdivision had a community of interests with schools in the annexing district. Two parents testified that they preferred their children to attend school in the annexing district. Other parents objected on less specific grounds. The regional board decided to go through with the annexation and the objecting parties appealed this decision to an Illinois trial court. The trial court affirmed the regional board's decision and appeal reached the Appellate Court of Illinois, Second District.

The appellate court observed that the detachment of the subdivision had no significant adverse financial impact on either district, that the districts had equivalent educational facilities, and that there was sufficient evidence in the record to support the board's decision. The court did not agree with the objecting parties' primary argument that the trial court had failed to consider generalized evidence of educational benefits to their children. It was permissible for the board to consider specific evidence of the welfare of the children whose parents testified. The court affirmed the trial court's decision. *Bd. of Educ. of St. Charles Comm. Unit School Dist. No. 303 v. Regional Bd. of School Trustees*, 633 N.E.2d 177 (Ill.App.2d Dist.1994).

Two Iowa school districts began a whole-grade sharing program that entitled them to receive supplemental weighted enrollment school aid funding from the state Department of Education. The funding was paid by the department under two state statutes that assigned students attending classes in other school districts (or who were taught by teachers employed jointly or by another school district and in certain other circumstances) a weight of 1.5 per student for a maximum of five years. If school districts reorganized during the five year period, additional weighted funding was to be transferred to the reorganized district until the expiration of the five year period. When the two districts merged pursuant to an election, the department denied additional weighted enrollment funding claimed by the new district under the statutes. The department stated that the predecessor districts had failed to apply for the funding during the five year statutory period. The consolidated district applied to an Iowa trial court for relief, which was granted, and the education department appealed to the Supreme Court of Iowa.

The supreme court held that the intent of the legislature in passing the statutes was to give reorganized school districts additional time to apply for additional funding, and not to deprive them of the funding. Prior to the merger, the two districts had taken action to reorganize within the five year period and they were therefore qualified to receive the additional weighted funding. The new district had acted to initiate reorganization procedures prior to the limitation time set forth in the statutes. The court affirmed the trial court's decision. *Wellsburg-Steamboat Rock Comm. School Dist. v. Iowa Dept. of Educ.*, 523 N.W.2d 749 (Iowa 1994).

A South Dakota family purchased a new home about four miles out of the city in which they had lived for eleven years. In doing so, they moved out of their former school district into a new, consolidated district. The family petitioned their new school district for a boundary change that would transfer their property to their former district. They argued that they had significant economic, social and religious ties to their former community, and that the bus trip was over nine miles shorter for their sixth grade child. The board denied the petition, and the family appealed to the state education secretary. The secretary reversed the denial, and his decision was affirmed by a South Dakota trial court. The education board appealed to the Supreme Court of South Dakota.

The supreme court identified several factors that were important in evaluating minor boundary change petitions. These included the petitioning family's economic, social and religious ties to the community, availability of bus service, arbitrariness of the current boundary line, special needs of the student involved, and relative proximity to the schools. In this case, the board had denied the petition for economic reasons, citing concern over stabilization of its tax base. The family had not previously complained about the length of the bus ride. They had also voluntarily moved into the new school district, knowing that a minor boundary change would have to be obtained in order to prevent a change in schools. Because they had voluntarily moved into the new district, they could not now raise the issue of their ties to their former community. Since there was substantial evidence in the record supporting the denial of the petition, the court reinstated the board's decision. *Colman-Egan School Dist. No. 50-5 v. Jones*, 520 N.W.2d 890 (S.D.1994).

A real estate developer submitted an application to a California city proposing a zoning change to allow him to develop an unincorporated tract of land. He intended to construct single family residential homes. The city planning commission published notice, held public hearings and conducted a study pursuant to the California Environmental Quality Act (CEQA). The city development agency approved the application, finding it in conformity with the city's general land use plan. The city then published notice of a public hearing and the city council approved the zoning change. The school district failed to appear at the hearing and several months later sent letters to the city council requesting the right to demand a certification from the developer that the school district had adequate capacity to handle students who would reside within the development. The city council then held a meeting at which a zoning change was approved, but the school district proposal was rejected.

The school district filed a petition challenging the zoning change in a California trial court, which held for the city. The district appealed to the California Court of Appeal, Fourth District, Division Two. The court of appeal stated that the trial court had appropriately ruled that the school district had failed to show that the zoning change was inconsistent with the city's general plan. It had also failed to exhaust its administrative remedies under CEQA. Although the district argued that its facilities were overcrowded and that the development would impose additional burdens upon its facilities, its objections were only general and failed to show that the city action was arbitrary. The trial court decision was affirmed. *Corona-Norco Unif. School Dist. v. City of Corona*, 21 Cal.Rptr.2d 803 (Cal.App.4th Dist.1993).

IV. SCHOOL BOARDS

States may impose certain requirements for membership on boards of education. In addition, school boards are given state constitutional and statutory authority to operate and maintain school districts.

A. Membership

1. Appointments, Elections, Residency and Recall

An Arkansas statute required school districts having ten percent or more minority populations to elect school board members in compliance with the federal Voting Rights Act of 1965. It further required that local board directors choose from between five or seven single-member zones or five single-member zones and two at-large zones 90 days prior to annual school board elections. The Arkansas Department of Education was required to withhold 20 percent of state funding from any district that failed to comply with the act. An Arkansas school district filed a lawsuit in the U.S. District Court for the Eastern District of Arkansas, seeking a declaratory order that it was in compliance with previous federal court desegregation orders so as to be exempted from the requirements of the Voting Rights Act and therefore did not have to elect board members by single-member zones. The state department of education filed a motion to dismiss the lawsuit, arguing that the board had no standing under the act.

The court determined that the school board was not seeking a declaration on behalf of any aggrieved voters. It had failed to allege that any minority voters would suffer voting rights violations by the proposed change from at-large electoral districts to single-member districts. Because the Voting Rights Act conferred standing only to the U.S. Attorney General and to aggrieved voters, the district had no standing under the act. It was not entitled to an advisory opinion concerning its electoral policies. Accordingly, the court granted the state education director's motion to dismiss the lawsuit. *Conway School Dist. v. Wilhoit*, 854 F.Supp. 1430 (E.D.Ark.1994).

An educator sought election as school superintendent of an Arizona county. He submitted nominating petitions containing several hundred more signatures than the required minimum. A complaint was filed challenging the petition, claiming that many of the signatures and addresses were illegible, and that many signatories were not registered voters or were otherwise unqualified to sign. An Arizona trial court issued a one-sentence order finding at least 568 signatures invalid and nullifying the educator's candidacy. The Supreme Court of Arizona held that although insufficient fact findings by a trial court generally required a remand, the unique nature of an election appeal and the limited time span required dismissal of the case. The trial court order was reversed and the candidate was allowed to stand for election. *Miller v. Bd. of Sup. of Pinal County*, 855 P.2d 1357 (Ariz.1993).

An administrative law judge with the Social Security Administration was elected to serve as a member of the Ohio Board of Education. He received permission from the federal government to serve in this elected, part-time position. He was reelected for a second term in 1988 and subsequently served as vice president of the board. However, Ohio law specified that board members may not hold "any other public position of trust or profit." Another board member questioned the judge's entitlement to serve on the board because of his position. The majority of the board, including the judge, sought an attorney general opinion to clarify the application of Ohio law to a person in the judge's situation. The judge wrote the letter requesting the advisory opinion. Both the outgoing attorney general and the new attorney general concluded that the judge held a position of public trust under the statute and could not serve simultaneously. After a five-month delay, the governor appointed a replacement. The judge then sued under 42 U.S.C. § 1983 in federal district court claiming that his removal from his elected position violated the Due Process Clause by depriving him of a property interest without affording him an adequate opportunity for a hearing. The district court dismissed the case and the board member appealed. The U.S. Court of Appeals, Sixth Circuit, held that the member had received due process. It stated that the essence of due process is that a deprivation of property or liberty must be preceded by notice and an opportunity for a hearing. In this case, the board member clearly had notice of the situation. He had an opportunity to offer any arguments or material relating to the issue in his letter to the attorney general. Further, he had adequate opportunity under Ohio law to review the decision to discharge him after the fact. Since he chose not to do so, the court affirmed the district court's judgment. *Brickner v. Voinovich*, 977 F.2d 235 (6th Cir.1992).

2. Conflict of Interest and Nepotism

A Virginia teacher worked for a county school board for six years. Following a 13-year absence from teaching, she reapplied to the board for employment. However, during her absence, her brother-in-law was elected chairman of the board. Because the Virginia Code prohibited the employment of a person related to a board member, her employment application was denied. The teacher filed a lawsuit against the board in a Virginia trial court, claiming that she was entitled to an exception applicable "to any person within such relationship who has been (i) regularly employed ... by any school board prior to the taking of office of any member of such board." The court held for the school board, and the teacher appealed to the Supreme Court of Virginia. The supreme court noted that the legislature had used the present perfect tense in the statute, indicating action beginning in the past and continuing to the present. This required an interpretation that persons seeking to avail themselves of the exception be employed by the school board at the time the conflict of interest arose. Because the teacher was not employed by the board at the time her brother-in-law was elected chairman, she could not avail herself of the exception, and the trial court had properly held for the school board. *Williams v. Augusta County School Bd.*, 445 S.E.2d 118 (Va.1994).

The Kentucky State Board for Elementary and Secondary Education charged three county board of education members with misconduct for being financially interested in the sale of property to the board and for failing to comply with state statutes regarding the expenditure of school funds. The state board removed the three board members. A state trial court reinstated the board members and the state board appealed to the Supreme Court of Kentucky. The supreme court held that the state board not only had the authority to remove the board members, but also, that there was sufficient evidence of misconduct to support removal from the county board. *State Board For Elementary and Secondary Education v. Ball,* 847 S.W.2d 743 (Ky.1993).

As part of a comprehensive restructuring of its educational system Kentucky passed a series of new laws including a series of laws prohibiting relatives of school district employees from seeking school board membership in that district. Two long time members of a particular school board sued, challenging the constitutionality of the new laws. The members alleged that the new laws not only abridged their First Amendment right to participate in the political process, but also abridged the voters' right to an unfettered choice of candidates. The trial court upheld the constitutionality of the challenged provisions, and the appeal to the Kentucky Court of Appeals was transferred directly to the Kentucky Supreme Court. The supreme court stated that the laws passed constitutional muster. The laws did not significantly impact on the members' ability to seek public office, but only that particular office which they already held. The laws also did not meaningfully limit the choices available to voters at large. Further, the eligibility disability is removed provided the relative is transferred or changes jobs entirely. Therefore, the court upheld the constitutionality of the statutes. *Chapman v. Gorman*, 839 S.W.2d 232 (Ky.1992).

The wife of a board of education member worked for the board as a teacher despite the fact that a Mississippi law did not allow board members to be directly or indirectly interested in any contract with the state or county. The state attorney general sued to obtain restitution or forfeiture of her salary for the period after she and her husband had notice of the violation. The circuit court held for the attorney general, and the couple appealed. They argued that they had acted in good faith and that the contract had been performed. However, the law was clear, despite an earlier decision which did not require restitution or forfeiture, so the Supreme Court of Mississippi affirmed. *Waller v. Moore ex rel. Quitman County School District*, 604 So.2d 265 (Miss.1992).

B. School Board Powers and Duties

In 1989, the Kentucky Supreme Court declared the state school system unconstitutional and directed the General Assembly to design a new system establishing, maintaining and funding schools under the sole responsibility of the general assembly. The legislature was directed to take an oversight role to assure freedom from waste, duplication, mismanagement and political influence. The general assembly responded with the Kentucky Educational Reform Act (KERA), under which it assumed the responsibility for providing for school finances. KERA also decentralized school power by establishing local councils with decisionmaking authority for school curriculums. Local school boards were also responsible for administrative functions such as funding, managing school property and appointing school superintendents.

A county board of education announced a policy that required each council in the county to submit a written proposal for the school year's goals and objectives for approval by the county board. A local council within the school system filed a state court action challenging the board's directive. The court found the policy entirely within the board's authority, but the state court of appeals reversed this decision. The board appealed to the Supreme Court of Kentucky. The supreme court reviewed the KERA and noted the local council's role in determining curriculum, student assignments, scheduling, planning and implementation of local school issues. On the other hand, the role of local school boards under KERA was to allocate funds, manage school property, appoint the school superintendent and determine local compensation levels. Although there was some overlap among duties, the board in this case had overstepped its authority in demanding to oversee the local council's goals, objectives and implementation plan. Because the legislature did not require local education boards to approve of council actions, the court affirmed the court of appeals' judgment. *Bd. of Educ. of Boone County v. Bushee*, 889 S.W.2d 809 (Ky.1994).

A regional school board encompassing seven New Jersey towns retained a demographics expert who projected a local population increase that would require expansion of existing facilities and construction of a new high school. On the basis of the expert's opinion, the regional board authorized a bond referendum which was approved by district voters. However, the regional board failed to comply with the referendum, and a board of education and township committee within the region sued the regional board in a state trial court. This case was dismissed based upon the regional board's assurances of its intention to complete the new school. The regional board then passed a resolution declaring that construction of the new high school would be "decommitted" based on evidence of a substantial change in circumstances within the region. The court granted an order requested by the township boards of education requiring the regional board to approve plans for the new school. The regional board appealed to the Superior Court of New Jersey, Appellate Division.

On appeal, the regional board argued that the trial court had improperly required it to show extraordinary or unexpected events to nullify the referendum. It claimed that because of economic recession, the population estimate from the demographic study had been excessive. The appellate division court ruled that the trial court had properly imposed the burden of proof upon the regional board. The referendum established a legal mandate which the board could not disturb without an extraordinary showing. There was compelling testimony at trial of the need for the new high school and a shift in the board's policy was not an extraordinary showing sufficient to nullify the referendum. *Bd. of Educ. of Township of Colts Neck v. Bd. of Educ. of Freehold Reg. High School Dist.*, 270 N.J.Super. 497, 637 A.2d 566 (1994).

The Los Angeles Unified School District responded to overcrowded conditions in South Central Los Angeles by proposing four new elementary schools, a new junior high school and a new senior high school. Construction of one of the elementary schools required the demolition of 67 affordable dwelling units. A group of area residents opposed the demolition and challenged the board's draft environmental impact report. The parties reached an agreement to prepare a subsequent environmental impact report, but when the report was completed the residents continued to object to the loss of affordable housing. They requested injunctive and declaratory relief from a California trial court, complaining that the reports were legally inadequate under the state Environmental Quality Act and that the board had failed to make adequate written findings. The court denied the residents' petition for a writ of mandate and they appealed to the California Court of Appeal, Second District.

On appeal, the court disagreed with the residents, finding that the board had prepared adequate environmental impact reports that attempted to fully disclose and mitigate the loss of housing in the attendance area. Substantial evidence indicated that alternatives to the board's proposal were less desirable than the project itself. State environmental quality act guidelines permitted approval of environmental impact reports despite inability to fully mitigate undesirable consequences. Because the board had complied with the state environmental and public resources statute, the court affirmed the trial court's decision. *Concerned Citizens of South Central Los Angeles v. LAUSD*, 29 Cal.Rptr.2d 492 (Cal.App.2d Dist.1994).

An Iowa school district employed a superintendent for 17 years under a series of one-year contracts. It then voted to consider contract termination under an Iowa statute governing school administrators. The superintendent requested an administrative hearing, but before it took place, the board called an emergency meeting to consider the superintendent's proposal to extend his contract for one year with a performance review by an outside consultant. Although attorneys for the board and superintendent initialed a proposal prepared at the meeting, many terms were omitted or left open. The administrative law judge granted a joint motion by the parties to continue the hearing pending finalization of the agreement. However, both sides submitted conflicting draft contracts at the next board meeting, and the board unanimously voted to rescind the agreement. The administrative proceeding was then dismissed with prejudice, and the superintendent filed a lawsuit in an Iowa trial court, arguing that the settlement agreement was a valid oral contract subject to written finalization. The court granted the school board's summary judgment motion and the superintendent appealed to the Supreme Court of Iowa. The court ruled that the superintendent had failed to prove that a written contract existed as required by the Iowa statute. No oral contract was enforceable where a statute required a writing. Although a document had been prepared at the settlement meeting, the terms were not fixed and the parties had reached no agreement. The superintendent could have reinstated the administrative proceeding at any time during contract negotiations and failed to do so. There was no merit to the superintendent's complaint and summary judgment for the board was affirmed. *Bradley v. West Sioux Comm. School Bd. of Educ.*, 510 N.W.2d 881 (Iowa 1994).

Since 1988, the Los Angeles Unified School District (LAUSD) regularly televised its board of education meetings on a station operated by LAUSD. A group of voters formed an organization which lobbied for a statewide ballot initiative to create scholarships for all students at qualifying public and private schools. When LAUSD board members publicly opposed the initiative and adopted a resolution against it at a televised board meeting, the organization sued LAUSD in a California trial court. The organization sought an order that board members had improperly used their positions by opposing the initiative in violation of the voters' constitutional free speech and voting rights. The court issued a preliminary injunction preventing LAUSD board members from using public funds and public employee work time to advocate against the initiative. LAUSD appealed to the Court of Appeal, Second District.

The court of appeal observed that the state education code contained no statute expressly dealing with school district authority to adopt positions on statewide initiatives. The LAUSD policy provided full notice of public meetings and provided an opportunity for interested persons to sign up in advance to address the board on specific items. There was no evidence that LAUSD did not comply with state public meeting requirements. There was no merit to the organization's argument that televising the board meetings resulted in a partisan use of funds or improper opposition to the initiative. The trial court had abused its discretion by finding that the organization was likely to prevail at trial and that it had suffered irreparable harm. The case was reversed and remanded. *Choice-In-Education League v. Los Angeles Unif. School Dist.*, 21 Cal.Rptr.2d 303 (Cal.App.2d Dist.1993).

A North Carolina county board of commissioners substantially reduced the proposed budget request of the county board of education. The education board then reduced its request, including the deletion of $9,000 for an increase in salaries for education board members. When additional funds became available during the school year, some items were restored to the budget by resolution. The education board chairman contacted individual board members by telephone to obtain their approval for reinstatement of their raise. The raise was never considered at a public meeting, but was nonetheless reinstated and board members received retroactive paychecks. When the education board closed a regular meeting, allegedly to discuss another matter, members of the press overheard discussion of the raise. A newspaper publisher then filed a lawsuit in a North Carolina trial court for a declaration that the board violated the state open meetings law, and for an order nullifying the raise and prohibiting further violations. The court ruled for the board and awarded it attorney's fees. The publisher appealed to the Court of Appeals of North Carolina.

The court found deliberation of the salary increase to be the type of matter that the legislature intended to be conducted in public. The budget amendment failed to mention the raise and the court rejected the education board's argument that its earlier decision to make the raise contingent upon receipt of additional funds covered the later action. Although the action violated the open meetings law, the court held that there would be no purpose in requiring a refund of the raise. The court reversed and remanded the case for reconsideration of the attorney's fee award. *Jacksonville Daily News Co. v. Onslow County Bd. of Educ.*, 439 S.E.2d 607 (N.C.App.1993).

C. Open Meeting Laws And Open Records

A Kentucky newspaper publisher and reporter requested personnel records from a Kentucky education board. The records included employment histories, grievances and disciplinary actions, including nonfinal documents. Employees who claimed that disclosure would violate their personal privacy filed a motion in a Kentucky circuit court for a restraining order. The motion was granted, but following review of the requested documents by the court, it issued a final order requiring production. The Court of Appeals of Kentucky held that the employees had no standing to challenge the decision under the Kentucky open records act. The employees appealed to the Supreme Court of Kentucky. The supreme court noted that the state open records act provided a right of enforcement "on application of any person." The employees accordingly had standing under the act to seek an order against disclosure. The act contained specific exclusions for information of a personal nature that constituted clearly unwarranted invasions of personal privacy. The act also excluded disclosure of preliminary drafts and correspondence not intended to give notice of a final action. Because the general assembly had demonstrated a clear intent to exclude from public disclosure private and nonfinal decisions of administrative agencies, the court reversed and remanded the case. *Beckham v. Bd. of Educ. of Jefferson County,* 873 S.W.2d 575 (Ky.1994).

A private association of Oregon school administrators formed a "fact-finding team" to investigate operations at an Oregon high school. The team consisted of two retired public school administrators and another administrator who was on leave. A group of parents whose children attended school in the district sought permission to inspect the team's records but was denied access to them. The parents filed a lawsuit against the team in an Oregon trial court, claiming violations of the state open records act. The trial court granted the team's motion to dismiss the lawsuit, but the Oregon Court of Appeals reversed and remanded the case. The fact-finding team appealed to the Supreme Court of Oregon. The supreme court analyzed the team's function in order to determine whether it was a "public body" within the meaning of the open records act. The team had been created for school board purposes but was without authority to do anything but make recommendations. There was no evidence in the record to indicate that the team was financed with public funds, or that the board or district exercised control over its operations. The parents would ultimately have the right to inspect any of the team's records that were submitted to their local school board or district. Because the team was not significantly involved in government operations, it was not a public body within the meaning of the state law and did not have to open its records. The court affirmed the trial court's judgment. *Marks v. McKenzie High School Fact-Finding Team,* 319 Or. 451, 878 P.2d 417 (1994).

A Pennsylvania school board hired a consultant to help select a new superintendent of schools. The consultant screened candidates and reduced the pool of applicants to six. After one candidate removed his name from consideration, the board held executive sessions to interview the remaining five. It then selected three finalists and convened a public meeting to obtain citizen input. After another public meeting, the board held an executive session to interview the three finalists and rank them in their order of preference. Following a fourth executive session, a public meeting was held, at which the board voted for its choice. A newspaper publisher filed a lawsuit in a Pennsylvania trial court for a declaratory ruling that the board had violated the state Sunshine Act by actually voting in an executive session rather than at the public meeting. The court held that the executive sessions were permissible under the Sunshine Act because they were deliberations or discussions rather than "official action." The publisher appealed to the Commonwealth Court of Pennsylvania.

The commonwealth court observed that employment matters constituted an exception to the Sunshine Act. It rejected the publisher's argument that "votes" taken in executive session constituted official action under the act. The actions in the executive sessions were taken to reduce the field of candidates and constituted only deliberations. Accordingly, it was unnecessary for these meetings to be open to the public or for the school board to take recorded votes. The commonwealth court affirmed the judgment of the trial court. *Morning Call, Inc. v. Bd. of School Directors of the Southern Lehigh School Dist.*, 642 A.2d 619 (Pa.Cmwlth.1994).

An Atlanta television station producer requested permission from the city board of education to inspect the personnel records of a number of school bus drivers employed by a private company under contract with the city school system. The board released the few documents in its possession, but claimed that it need not furnish records from the private company's personnel files. The company refused to produce the files, claiming that it was a private entity whose records were not subject to the Georgia Open Records Act. The producer sued the board of education and the company in a Georgia trial court, seeking disclosure under the open records act. The court granted summary judgment to the board and company, and the producer appealed to the Court of Appeals of Georgia.

The court of appeals determined that the delegation of the school board's duty to transport public school students to a private entity did not convert the personnel records of the drivers into private records. Records received or maintained by a private person or entity on behalf of a public agency remained public under the open records act. It was irrelevant that the board had no access or interest in the particular documents requested. The public had a strong, legitimate interest in production of the driving records because of the safety interest of public school students. This outweighed the privacy interests of the drivers and the private company. The court reversed and remanded the trial court judgment. On remand, the trial court was to determine whether some of the records might be protected from disclosure as medical records. *Hackworth v. Bd. of Educ. for the City of Atlanta*, 447 S.E.2d 78 (Ga.App.1994).

The Kansas City School Board experienced difficulties because of poor interpersonal communications among board members. A majority of the board members decided to improve relationships by attending a weekend workshop conducted by a psychologist at a Missouri resort. Prior to attending the workshop, board members sought advice from an attorney to determine if attendance at the workshop without public notice would violate the Missouri Open Meetings Law. The attorney advised the board members that they should discuss only the improvement of interpersonal relations and communication skills. The attorney accompanied the board members to the workshop. Even though the meeting was not publicly announced, newspaper reporters arrived at the workshop and attempted to enter the meeting room. The reporters were excluded and the newspaper filed a petition in a Missouri court, seeking an order that the board had violated the open meetings law. It also sought an order enjoining the board from excluding the press from future meetings. The trial court granted the injunction and fined several board members, who appealed to the Missouri Court of Appeals.

The court of appeals determined that the trial court had improperly characterized the workshop as a public meeting under the open meetings law. The board members had conscientiously avoided discussing public business at the workshop, exempting them from the coverage of the act. By limiting the discussion to issues of social interaction, the board was entitled to close the workshop to the public and did not need to give public notice. The court reversed the trial court's decision. *Kansas City Star Co. v. Fulson*, 859 S.W.2d 934 (Mo.App.W.D.1993).

A representative of the Texas Education Agency met with members of the Dallas Independent School District to present a preliminary report on the district's accreditation. A Dallas newspaper learned about the meeting and made a written demand for an open meeting pursuant to the Texas Open Meetings Act. The board did not respond to the demand and reporters were sent to cover the meeting. When the education agency representative asked the reporters to leave and closed the meeting, the newspaper sued the school district board of trustees in a Texas trial court, seeking a declaration that the board should have opened the accreditation review and seeking an injunction to prohibit further violations of the open meetings act. The court ruled for the school board and the newspaper appealed to the Court of Appeals of Texas, Dallas.

The court of appeals observed that in order to come within the application of the Texas Open Meetings Act, there must be a finding that a quorum of school board members engaged in a verbal exchange among themselves or others about public business. The trial court expressly found that no verbal exchange on public business had occurred during the accreditation review, and properly concluded that the review did not fall within the meaning of the word "meeting" as defined by the act. The court expressly rejected the newspaper's argument that the open meetings act should apply even if no board members spoke on public business. The trial court decision was affirmed. *Dallas Morning News Co. v. Bd. of Trustees of Dallas Indep. School Dist.*, 861 S.W.2d 532 (Tex.App.—Dallas 1993).

An admissions officer for an Ohio university received several anonymous letters containing threats to kill him. He reported the letters to university police, who agreed to preserve his confidentiality during their investigations. Within one month of the receipt of one of the threatening letters, a university custodian was shot and killed. The next month a university student was injured in another shooting. Soon after this action, university police shot and killed a suspect. The individual was later identified as the probable suspect in the two shooting incidents, but was never linked with the threatening letters. When police found a suspect in the matter of the threatening letters, the admissions official refused to press charges and the police ended their investigation. A local newspaper sought disclosure of police records related to the threatening letters and shootings. An Ohio county court of appeals held that most of the documents were confidential law enforcement investigatory records. The newspaper appealed to the Supreme Court of Ohio. The court construed the Ohio Public Records Act to require disclosure of law enforcement investigatory records with only four exceptions. Because witness safety was one of these exceptions, it was appropriate to delete the official's name from any records to be released. However, the text of the threatening letters was not subject to any privacy interest and had to be disclosed. The court reversed and remanded the case to the court of appeals with directions to release the text of the threatening letters and many other investigatory records, after taking confidentiality precautions. *State ex rel. Beacon Journal Pub. Co. v. Kent State Univ.*, 623 N.E.2d 51 (Ohio 1993).

A Minnesota school board began deliberations to discuss dismissal of its superintendent due to alleged financial mismanagement in the district. The board scheduled a closed meeting to investigate charges against the superintendent and to receive advice from legal counsel. A publisher petitioned a state trial court for a writ of mandamus to compel the school board to conduct its future meetings in public. The trial court granted the writ, which stated that the board could meet in closed session to seek legal advice only if a lawsuit was actually commenced. The Minnesota Court of Appeals reversed and vacated the writ, ruling that the attorney-client privilege created an exception to the open meetings act and applied where litigation was imminent. There was no requirement that a lawsuit actually be commenced. *Star Tribune v. Bd. of Educ., Special School Dist. No. 1*, 507 N.W.2d 869 (Minn.App.1993).

V. ACADEMIC PRACTICES

A. Grading and Curriculum

Courts infrequently review school grading policies, and will intervene only where a school has acted arbitrarily or capriciously in assigning grades. Opt-out programs protect school districts from liability for controversial programs such as sex education and condom distribution programs.

New York Department of Education regulations required school boards to maintain AIDS education programs to provide accurate information to students about the disease, its methods of transmission and prevention. The regulations required school districts to stress abstinence as the most appropriate and effective protection against AIDS. State regulations also required local education boards to establish advisory councils that were responsible for recommending the content of AIDS instruction programs, and to implement and evaluate the programs. The City of New York Board of Education embellished on the state regulations by adopting a policy to spend substantially more instruction time on abstinence than on other protection methods and to discuss abstinence whenever students were assembled for instruction on AIDS prevention. The state commissioner of education invalidated the city board's resolution, and the city board filed a lawsuit in a New York trial court seeking to vacate the commissioner's decision. The court observed that the city board had completely ignored the role of the AIDS advisory council in enacting its resolution. The requirement of including abstinence in any classroom AIDS discussion effectively changed the regulations issued by the state. The city education board had robbed the advisory council of its essential role and gone far beyond the state policy governing AIDS prevention instruction. The court affirmed the commissioner's decision and the case was dismissed. *Bd. of Educ. of City of New York v. Sobol*, 613 N.Y.S.2d 792 (Sup.Ct.—Albany County 1993).

The New York City Board of Education expanded its HIV/AIDS Education Program in response to a state directive to include HIV information as part of its health education programs. It enacted a two-part classroom instruction program. The first part was mandatory, but included a parental opt-out provision in which parents could keep their children out of the classroom upon assurances that they received the information at home. The second part of the program required high schools to make condoms available for students upon request along with personal health guidance counseling. Unlike the first part of the program, there was no provision for parental consent or opt-out. A group of New York City parents challenged the distribution of condoms in high schools, claiming that it violated their due process rights to raise their children, violated their rights to free exercise of religion, and violated the New York Public Health Law. A state trial court dismissed the lawsuit. The parents appealed to the New York Supreme Court, Appellate Division, Second Department.

The parents argued that distribution of condoms was a health service under the public health law, rather than health education. The court agreed, holding that the lack of a parental consent or opt-out provision violated the public health law, which required parental consent for provision of health services to minors. The furnishing of condoms was a separate service that was not part of the educational phase of the program. The program did not violate the parents' free exercise rights, but was a violation of their substantive due process right to raise their children. Even though the state had a compelling interest in controlling the spread of disease, condoms were readily available from other sources. The court reversed the trial court's decision. *Alfonso v. Fernandez*, 606 N.Y.S.2d 259 (A.D.2d Dept.1993).

A Michigan student forged excuse notes more than six times in her senior year. The high school refused to award her course credit for several classes and did not award her a diploma. The student sued the school district in a Michigan trial court on constitutional, contractual and equitable claims. The trial court determined that the school's attendance policy was unreasonable and that the student was entitled to a diploma under equitable principles. It granted the student's summary disposition motion and the school district appealed to the Court of Appeals of Michigan. The court of appeals observed that under equitable principles, the party seeking equity must "come into court with clean hands." Because the student had forged the notes she was barred from receiving equitable relief. The court of appeals reversed the trial court's decision. *Isbell v. Brighton Area Schools*, 500 N.W.2d 748 (Mich.App.1993).

A Washington community college maintained a written policy whereby one-third of a student's grade was based on attendance. One student allegedly missed a significant portion of his computer class and received a failing grade. The student sought to have his grade changed through the college's appeal process, but to no avail. He presented evidence that the teacher was sometimes an hour late in getting to class and that many students left out of frustration. The student brought an action in a Washington trial court alleging breach of the contract to educate. After the trial court granted summary judgment to the college, the student appealed to the Court of Appeals of Washington. On appeal, the student contended that there were triable issues of fact in dispute. The appellate court agreed and remanded the case to the trial court to determine if the college's actions were arbitrary or capricious. *Ochsner v. Bd. of Trustees of Wash. Comm. Col.,* 811 P.2d 985 (Wash.App.1991).

B. Student Records

The Family Educational Rights and Privacy Act of 1974 (FERPA) (20 U.S.C. § 1232g) establishes student and parent rights with regard to student records. FERPA applies only to records pertaining to individuals who have been admitted as students at private or public educational institutions. Like Title VI, Title IX, § 504 and other federal civil rights statutes, FERPA applies only to schools receiving federal funding. Unlike the other statutes, however, the Act applies to the entire institution and not only to the "program or activity" receiving federal funding. Educators should be familiar with FERPA and its very detailed implementing regulations, which are found at 34 CFR Part 99. FERPA's major requirements are that student records be kept confidential, that parents be allowed access to their children's educational records, and that parents be allowed to challenge information kept in their children's records. Students who are 18 years of age or older have all the rights granted to parents.

The Ohio General Assembly enacted legislation creating the state Educational Management Information System (EMIS), a statewide computer information network for the state public school system. EMIS required the state education board to collect information on student participation, performance, enrollment and demographics for its computer network. The board developed guidelines concerning specific methods and information to report, and the forms to use for reporting. Four local school boards filed a lawsuit in a state trial court against the state education board, department of education and state school superintendent, claiming that the guidelines violated the state administrative procedure act as an improper delegation of legislative authority. They also claimed that the disclosure of certain information under EMIS would violate the federal Family Educational Rights and Privacy Act (FERPA), 20 U.S.C. § 1232g. The court held for the state board and the local districts appealed to the Court of Appeals of Ohio.

The court of appeals found the statute, administrative rule and guidelines valid and constitutional. The school districts were unable to demonstrate that violation of the guidelines would result in a penalty. The legislature had not improperly delegated authority to the state board, but merely left it with flexibility to determine effective data collection procedures. The districts were also unable to demonstrate that complying with EMIS would result in a violation of FERPA. FERPA contained specific exemptions that allowed the release of the information collected under EMIS. Both statutes expressly prohibited the reporting of personally identifiable information relating to any student. Because EMIS did not require Ohio schools to release any information that violated FERPA, the two statutes were not in conflict, and the trial court had properly held for the state board. *Princeton City School Dist., Bd. of Educ. v. Ohio State Bd. of Educ.,* 96 Ohio App.3d 558, 645 N.E.2d 773 (1994).

A New Hampshire student with disabilities was placed in a residential education facility in Massachusetts under a juvenile court order following his prosecution under the state juvenile delinquency statute. The school district in which the student resided was joined as a party to the juvenile court proceedings so that it could take part in placement and education services decisions. The school district's attorney obtained copies of the juvenile court proceedings and was a member of the student's IEP team. The student's mother requested the student's education records from the district because she was concerned about the appropriateness of the placement. The district gave her a copy of the student's cumulative folder but refused to supply records related to the juvenile court proceeding. Asserting that access to the juvenile court records was critical for pursuit of her claim for reimbursement, the student's mother filed a lawsuit in the U.S. District Court for the District of New Hampshire, seeking access to the records. The school district asserted that the juvenile court records were not "education records"as defined by the Family Educational Rights and Privacy Act (FERPA), 20 U.S.C. § 1232g and the IDEA. The court considered cross motions for summary judgment filed by the parties.

The court determined that the student's parent was entitled to advance a claim against the district under 42 U.S.C. § 1983 despite failing to exhaust her administrative remedies. This was because FERPA imposed no exhaustion requirement and did not provide an explicit cause of action for relief. Education records were broadly defined under FERPA as records, files, documents and other materials containing information directly related to a student and maintained by an educational agency, institution or employee acting for an agency or institution. The court held that the source of the documents was irrelevant, and that they had a direct bearing on the student's educational and residential placement. Accordingly, the juvenile records were part of the student's education records under FERPA. The student and his parent should have access to the juvenile court records and the court granted their summary judgment motion. *Belanger v. Nashua, New Hampshire, School Dist.*, 856 F.Supp. 40 (D.N.H.1994).

A Georgia university's student newspaper was denied access to the records and disciplinary proceedings of the student judiciary—specifically, the Organization Court (OC). The OC adjudicated cases involving university rule and regulation violations on the part of fraternities and sororities. Hearings of the OC were closed to the public at the request of the defendant organization. The school newspaper filed this action in a Georgia trial court for injunctive relief against the board of regents seeking access to the records and disciplinary proceedings of the OC. The trial court granted access to the records under the Open Records Act, but denied access to the proceedings under the Open Meetings Act. Both parties appealed to the Supreme Court of Georgia.

The board conceded that the records of the OC were public records. However, the defendants contended that they were exempted by the federal Family Educational Rights and Privacy Act (FERPA). The court noted that the OC's documents were not education records within the meaning of the FERPA. The records were similar to those maintained for law enforcement purposes, which were expressly excluded from the FERPA. Thus, the court concluded that the records were subject to the Georgia Open Records Act and granted access to the student newspaper. The Open Meetings Act provides that all meetings of agencies' governing bodies be open to the public. The board contended that the OC was not a governing body of an agency. The court noted that the OC did not fit within the literal language of the act. However, the OC did stand in the place of the board of regents under the Open Meetings Act. The OC was a vehicle by which the university carried out its responsibility to regulate student organizations. The supreme court reversed the decision of the trial court and concluded that the hearings of the OC were subject to the Open Meetings Act and could not be held in secret. *Red and Black Publishing v. Board of Regents*, 427 S.E.2d 257 (Ga.1993).

A Michigan mother submitted a written request to the school district to obtain a copy of her son's school file. She executed an authorization for the release of the information and offered to pay copying charges as calculated in the Freedom of Information Act (FOIA). The school refused to disclose the information, claiming that it fell within the privacy exemption of the FOIA. The mother subsequently filed suit in a Michigan trial court which awarded summary judgment to the school district. She then appealed to the Court of Appeals of Michigan. The purpose of the FOIA is to provide access to public records. The FOIA presumes that all records are subject to disclosure unless the public body can show that the requested information falls within one of the statutory exemptions. The privacy exemption excludes from disclosure information of a personal nature where public disclosure would constitute an unwarranted invasion of the individual's privacy. In the case at hand, the mother requested the disclosure in her capacity as mother of her minor son. As a minor, the boy was unable to make the request himself. Therefore, the court ruled that disclosure to the mother would be disclosure to the son and thus would not run afoul of the privacy exemption. The court of appeals reversed the decision of the trial court and ordered the school to release the file as requested. *Lepp v. Cheboygan Area School,* 476 N.W.2d 506 (Mich.App.1991).

A number of students were emotionally and physically abused by their fourth grade teacher. In an attempt to determine the extent of the abuse and the resulting need for treatment, a group of parents and administrators agreed to have the children examined by a psychologist who could turn over "all information gathered" to the parents. A dispute later arose concerning the disclosure of the personal notes made by the psychologist. A trial court ordered the notes to be disclosed, and the psychologist appealed to the Commonwealth Court of Pennsylvania. Parental access to student records is regulated by the Family Educational Rights and Privacy Act and by Department of Education regulations. The psychologist contended that his notes were outside the purview of those student record laws, and were properly within another law which "in some instances" precludes disclosure of a counselor's notes when made for personal use in treatment. This preclusion, however, is subject to the terms of any special agreements or employment contracts. Moreover, the notes could not have been made for the psychologist's own use because he would not be later treating the students. The parents' rights were thus not solely contractual in nature—they had also a clear statutory right to the notes. The decision of the trial court was affirmed. *Parents Against Abuse v. Williamsport*, 594 A.2d 796 (Pa.Cmwlth.1991).

C.   Achievement Tests

Placement testing, ability groupings, and achievement tests may be used to assist in determination of classroom assignments, provided that the test results are not merely a reflection of past racial segregation policies, the testing is "validated" (that is, the test must accurately measure what it is intended to measure), and the results of the tests are open to public scrutiny.

Louisiana required all public school graduating seniors to pass a graduate exit examination (GEE) in order to get their diplomas. Private school students were not required to take the test. Five public school students who had completed their required coursework but failed the GEE prior to the end of their senior year sued the state Board of Elementary and Secondary Education (BESE) in a Louisiana trial court, seeking a declaration that the policy was invalid and an order requiring the awarding of their diplomas. The court issued a preliminary order prohibiting BESE from withholding the diplomas. BESE appealed to the Court of Appeal of Louisiana, First Circuit. The court found that the GEE requirement was permissible under BESE's broad discretionary power to supervise public education. The policy did not violate the U.S. Constitution's Equal Protection Clause, even though the test was not administered to private school students in Louisiana. BESE had no authority to control private school curriculums or to set examination requirements without violating the rights of parents who sent their children to private schools. Although public and private school students were treated differently as a result of the BESE's inability to administer the GEE test to private school students, the court of appeal upheld the testing requirement because it was rationally related to the goal of insuring minimum competency in public school graduates. *Rankins v. Louisiana State Bd. of Elementary and Secondary Educ.*, 637 So.2d 548 (La.App.1st Cir.1994).

A Texas high school senior had completed all the classes required for graduation, but had not passed the Texas Assessment of Academic Skills test. She sued her school district in a Texas trial court, seeking an order which would permit her to participate in graduation ceremonies, but she did not seek the right to be awarded a diploma. The trial court ordered that she be allowed to participate. The Court of Appeals of Texas vacated the trial court's temporary injunction, ruling that it had been improperly granted. The trial court order had the effect of awarding the student the complete relief she had sought and it deprived the school district of any means of contesting the matter until it was moot. The injunction also failed to set forth the reasons for its issuance and failed to set a bond amount. *Edgewood Indep. School Dist. v. Paiz*, 856 S.W.2d 269 (Tex.App.-San Antonio 1993).

In response to the public outcry concerning the qualifications of the state's teachers, the Alabama State Board of Education instituted a "cut-off" score—the minimum score that students would have to attain on the ACT exam in order to be eligible for teacher-training courses. After a 30-minute meeting, the state board adopted a minimum score of 16. A class action was brought on behalf of minority students under Title IV in a federal district court on the claim that the "cut-off score" had an adverse impact on minority students. To succeed on a claim of racial discrimination under Title IV the class must show that the practice has a sufficiently adverse racial impact (that it falls significantly more harshly on a minority racial group than on the majority) and that the practice is not adequately justified. The court found that the "cut-off" requirement had an adverse impact on minority students as a larger percentage of minority students fell below the minimum ACT score. Next, the court noted that since most students take the ACT exam in their junior year in high school, there was no rational basis from which to infer that otherwise qualified students scoring at or above the "cut off" level would be competent to teach several years in the future. Thus, the court enjoined the state board from using the "cut-off" score. *Groves v. Alabama State Board of Education,* 776 F.Supp. 1518 (M.D.Ala.1991).

A group of female high school students sued the New York state education department claiming that the state's exclusive reliance on the SAT test to award scholarships discriminated against female students in violation of the Fourteenth Amendment's Equal Protection Clause, Title IX of the 1972 Education Amendments, and Title IX regulations. The students argued that the state's reliance upon the SAT disproportionately burdened female students, who consistently scored lower on the test, without advancing the legislature's purpose of recognizing and rewarding superior high school achievement. Prior to a trial on the merits of the case, the students asked the court to prohibit the state from relying exclusively on the tests in the interim period. The court noted that while the SAT had been statistically validated in order to predict academic performance in college the SAT had never been validated as a measure of past high school performance. The court noted that in order for the state to maintain its goals of recognizing and rewarding high school achievement the state must show a manifest relationship between use of the SAT and recognition and reward of academic achievement. Since the preliminary arguments that the state raised were without merit, the court temporarily prohibited the exclusive use of the SAT test. *Sharif v. New York State Education Dept.,* 709 F.Supp. 345 (S.D.N.Y.1989).

D. Educational Malpractice

A second-grade Michigan student hanged himself the night after viewing a film at school featuring the attempted suicide of a young disabled character who eventually learns to overcome his disability. The student's estate filed a lawsuit in a Michigan trial court against the school district, school superintendent, members of the board of education, principal, teacher, staff members and the distributor and producer of the film *Nobody's Useless.* The court held that the distributor and producer had no duty to state the age-appropriateness of the film, and that the school principal, teachers, and other school staff had no duty to refrain from showing the film to second graders. However, the court denied a motion by the district, school board and superintendent for summary disposition on the grounds of absolute governmental immunity. Appeal reached the Court of Appeals of Michigan.

The court of appeals held that Michigan's governmental immunity statute applied to the board members, the superintendent and the district. The school district was a governmental entity performing duties contemplated in the immunity statute. Likewise, school board members and the superintendent were entitled to absolute governmental immunity. The court affirmed the finding of the lack of a duty to refrain from showing the film to a second grader. This theory was rooted in educational malpractice, a claim which the court refused to recognize. Any lawsuit based upon educational malpractice was impossible to prove and unreasonably burdensome to the educational system. The court also affirmed the lack of liability by the film's producer and distributor. *Nalepa v. Plymouth-Canton Comm. School Dist.*, 525 N.W.2d 897 (Mich.App.1994).

A Kansas high school basketball star was recruited by a private university in Nebraska to play on its team. The student came from an academically disadvantaged background and was unprepared for a university education. The university allegedly assured the student that he would receive sufficient tutoring so that he would receive a meaningful education. During the student's four years at the university, his language and reading skills never rose to even a high school level. The university then made arrangements with an Illinois preparatory school for a year of remedial education. After that, the student attended another university in Chicago, but had to withdraw for lack of funds. Following a depressive and destructive episode, the student sued the Nebraska university for educational malpractice and breach of contract. A federal district court granted the university's motion to dismiss the complaint. The student then appealed to the U.S. Court of Appeals, Seventh Circuit. The appellate court first looked at the educational malpractice claim. It noted that courts in at least eleven states have considered and rejected such claims. On the breach of contract claim, the court found that a student would have to show more than that the education was not good enough. This would be nothing more than a repackaging of an educational malpractice claim. Instead, the student "must point to an identifiable contractual promise that the [university] failed to honor." Here, the student had alleged a breach of promise with respect to certain services, which effectively cut him off from *any* participation in and benefit from the university's academic program. The court thus affirmed in part the dismissal of the student's complaint, but allowed the breach of contract claim to proceed. *Ross v. Creighton University*, 957 F.2d 410 (7th Cir.1992).

E.   Scholarships, Grants, and Financial Aid

The University of Maryland maintained a merit scholarship program open only to African-American students. It alleged that the program redressed prior constitutional violations against African-American students by the university, which had formerly been segregated by law. A student of Hispanic descent attempted to obtain a scholarship under the program, but was denied on the basis of his race. He filed a lawsuit against the university and a number of its officials in the U.S. District Court for the District of Maryland. The court granted summary judgment to the university and the student won reversal from the U.S. Court of Appeals, Fourth Circuit. On remand, the parties again filed cross motions for summary judgment, and the district court again awarded summary judgment to the university.

The case was again appealed to the court of appeals. It determined that the district court had improperly found a basis in the evidence for its conclusion that a remedial plan of action was necessary. It had also erroneously determined that the scholarship program was narrowly tailored to meet the goal of remedying past discrimination. The court had misconstrued statistical evidence presented by the parties and had erroneously found a connection between past discrimination and present conditions at the university. The reasons stated by the university for maintaining the race-based scholarship—underrepresentation of African-American students, low retention and graduation rates and a negative perception among African-American students—were legally insufficient. The court reversed the summary judgment order for the university and awarded summary judgment to the student. *Podberesky v. Kirwan*, 38 F.3d 147 (4th Cir.1994), *cert. den.*, 115 S.Ct. 2001 (1995).

Two honorably discharged veterans who were recovering alcoholics sought an extension of the ten-year Veterans' Administration (VA) limitation for receipt of educational assistance under the G.I. Bill. The ten-year limitation on educational benefits can be extended by the VA if the veteran can show that a disability prevented the earlier use of the benefits. VA regulations state that the deliberate drinking of alcohol is considered willful misconduct and disallows eligibility.

Both veterans requested extension of benefits after expiration of their respective ten-year limitation periods. These requests were based on grounds that they were disabled by alcoholism. The VA denied their requests stating that their alcoholism had been willful misconduct. One veteran sued the VA in a New York district court. The other veteran sought review in the District Court for the District of Columbia. The New York district court held for the VA, but its decision was reversed by the U.S. Court of Appeals, Second Circuit. The District of Columbia district court ruled that the VA regulation was contrary to the Rehabilitation Act, but the District of Columbia Court of Appeals reversed that decision.

Noting the disagreement between two federal courts of appeal the U.S. Supreme Court granted review and heard the cases together. The Court held that the Rehabilitation Act does not preclude an action against the VA. The Court noted that Congress had changed the time limit for benefits several times, most recently in 1977. The Rehabilitation Act of 1978 did not repeal the "willful misconduct" provision of the 1977 regulations. According to the Court, Congress had the right to establish the allocation priorities for veterans' benefits. The District of Columbia Court of Appeals decision was affirmed and the Second Circuit Court of Appeals decision was reversed. The VA prevailed in both matters. *Traynor v. Turnage*, 485 U.S. 535, 108 S.Ct. 1372, 99 L.Ed.2d 618 (1988).

A Bureau of Indian Affairs (BIA) regulation authorized funds for higher education grants and loans to students of one quarter or more degree of Native American blood who enrolled at accredited institutions of higher education.

However, this regulation was struck down as invalid in a 1986 decision by the U.S. Court of Appeals, Ninth Circuit. The BIA then adopted a rule requiring students to be members of a federally recognized tribe to be eligible for funds. Two students, who were both five-sixteenths Wintun Indian, were denied higher education grants because the tribe they belonged to was not federally recognized. The BIA's decision was affirmed by the U.S. District Court for the Eastern District of California, and the students appealed to the Ninth Circuit.

The court found that the BIA had violated federal administrative law requirements to publish proposed rules in the Federal Register when announcing new criteria for student loans and grants. Accordingly, it could not use the eligibility criteria it had relied on since the 1986 Ninth Circuit decision. Although the students prevailed on this question, the court determined that without a properly published regulation, there could be no basis for an order directing the BIA to award higher education grants to the students as they had requested. The court encouraged the BIA to adopt criteria consistent with federal law tending to exempt the California Indian population from federal recognition requirements. The court reversed the district court decision concerning the validity of the BIA's current criteria and affirmed the denial of injunctive relief. *Malone v. Bureau of Indian Affairs*, 38 F.3d 433 (9th Cir.1994).

A student borrowed $3,000 as a student loan in 1971. His repayment obligation was guaranteed by the New York Higher Education Assistance Corporation. Claiming that the student never made any payments on the loan, the guarantor paid off the entire loan balance in 1975. The guarantor sued the student in 1984 to recover the amount paid. The student claimed that this action was barred by New York's six-year statute of limitations for contractual disputes. The trial court denied the motion and the student appealed to the New York Supreme Court, Appellate Division. On appeal, the guarantor conceded that the six-year statute of limitations expired prior to commencement of its lawsuit. However, while this appeal was pending, Congress amended 20 U.S.C. § 1091(a) to provide that no limitation period applies to guaranty agencies trying to collect reimbursement. The guarantor argued that it was no longer barred. The appellate court agreed. It stated that the new law unquestionably governed in this case. Since federal law overrides conflicting state law, the guarantor's action was not time-barred. This was true even though the new law had the effect of reviving a claim which was already time-barred. *State of New York Higher Education Services Corp. v. Starr*, 579 N.Y.S.2d 210 (A.D.2d Dept. 1992).

CHAPTER TWELVE

DISABLED STUDENTS' RIGHTS

I. STATE AND LOCAL RESPONSIBILITIES UNDER THE IDEA

The major federal legislation governing the education of children with disabilities is the Individuals with Disabilities Education Act (IDEA), which provides federal funds to state and local agencies for the education of children with disabilities. The IDEA has remedied situations in which local school districts, prior to the act, often excluded children with disabilities from participating in any school programs. To qualify for federal assistance, a state must demonstrate that it has in effect a policy that assures all children with disabilities the right to a free appropriate public education. Each student's education program must be tailored to the unique needs of the disabled child by means of an individualized education program (IEP). The IEP must be prepared (and reviewed at least annually) by school officials with participation by the child's parents or guardian and at least one of the teachers presently instructing the student. Students with disabilities must be educated with regular students, to the greatest extent possible. The IDEA term for this is "mainstreaming." The act also requires that a participating state provide specified administrative procedures under which the child's parent or guardian may challenge any IEP or proposed change in placement, evaluation and education of the child.

The IDEA defines children with disabilities as those having mental retardation, hearing impairments including deafness, speech or language impairments, visual impairments including blindness, serious emotional disturbance, orthopedic impairments, autism, traumatic brain injury, other health impairments, and specific learning disabilities, who, by reason of their disabilities, are in need of special education and related services. See 20 U.S.C. § 1401(a). For further definitions, see Federal regulations under the IDEA located at 34 CFR Part 300.7. The IDEA imposes an affirmative duty on the states, through local education agencies, to provide eligible students with a free appropriate public education, defined at 20 U.S.C. § 1401(a)(18) as special education and related services provided at public expense that meet the standards of the state educational agency in conformity with an individualized education program (IEP).

Local educational agencies receiving IDEA funds must meet the requirements of 20 U.S.C. § 1414(a), which include satisfactory assurances that they are identifying and providing special education services to all students with disabilities residing within the local jurisdiction, regardless of the severity of the disability. Local educational agencies (LEAs) must identify, locate and evaluate students in need of special education and related services and establish a goal of providing full educational opportunities to all their students with a disability with the participation and consultation of the parents of each student. The method of ensuring that each student with a disability receives a free appropriate public education is the provision of an individual education program (IEP) to be reviewed at least once a year. IDEA regulations require the inclusion of transition services in the IEP of each student with a disability no later than the age of 16, and earlier if appropriate, as in the case of students at risk of dropping out. See 34 CFR Part 300.346, Note 3.

Related services are defined as "transportation, and such developmental, corrective, and other supportive services (including speech pathology and audiology, psychological services, physical and occupational therapy, recreation, including therapeutic recreation, social work services, counseling services, including rehabilitation counseling, and medical services, except that such medical services shall be for diagnostic and evaluation purposes only) as may be required to assist a child with a disability to benefit from special education, and includes the early identification and assessment of disabling conditions in children" [20 U.S.C.§ 1401(a)(17)]. While medical services are excluded from the definition of related services, they are not excluded insofar as they may be needed by a child for diagnostic and evaluative purposes. Chapter 20, U.S.C. § 1401(a)(17) states that psychological services are related services and thus are to be provided free of charge by school districts to students with disabilities who require such services.

Chapter 20, U.S.C. § 1415, contains mandatory procedures designed to safeguard the rights of students with disabilities. The safeguards emphasize, among other things, notice to parents and an opportunity for parental participation in the development of a child's special education program. Each LEA must provide students with disabilities all available procedures and methods by which any grievances may be resolved. Written notice must be given to parents if a school proposes to change or refuses to initiate a change in a child's educational program, or if the school refuses to perform an initial evaluation and placement of the child [20 U.S.C. § 1415(b)(1)(C)]. In case of any dispute over their child's placement, the IDEA states that parents have the right to an impartial hearing before a hearing officer who is neither an employee of the school district nor of the state education department [20 U.S.C. § 1415(b)(2)]. If either the parents or the school are unhappy with the hearing officer's decision, appeal may be taken to the state education department [20 U.S.C. § 1415(c)]. During the pendency of a dispute over any aspect of a special education program, the child must remain in his or her "then current" education program [20 U.S.C. § 1415(e)(3)]. The U.S. Supreme Court has held that indefinite suspensions of children with disabilities violate this provision. See *Honig v. Doe*, below. A lawsuit may be commenced in either state or federal court after a decision has been reached by the state education department [20 U.S.C. § 1415(e)(2)]. Attorney's fees may be awarded to parents who prevail in IDEA lawsuits [20 U.S.C. § 1415(e)(4)(B)].

Because the IDEA's only qualitative standard for the provision of special education and related services is that they "meet the standards of the state educational agency," the courts have refrained from extensive review of contested IEPs, focusing instead on the protection of IDEA procedural rights. In the following case, the U.S. Supreme Court ruled that the IDEA establishes a basic floor of opportunity for students with disabilities, and imposes no requirement on LEAs to maximize their potential.

A New York student with hearing impairments sought the provision of a sign language interpreter from her school district. She had residual hearing and was an excellent lipreader, which allowed her to attain above average grades and to advance through school easily. The student's parents requested the services of a sign language interpreter at school district expense, arguing that the IDEA required the district to maximize her potential. The U.S. District Court for the Southern District of New York held that the disparity between the student's achievement and her potential to perform as she would if not for her disability deprived her of a free appropriate public education. This decision was affirmed by the U.S. Court of Appeals, Second Circuit, and the U.S. Supreme Court agreed to review the case.

The court reviewed the IDEA's legislative history and found no requirement that public schools maximize the potential of each student with a disability. The opportunities provided to each student by their school varied from student to student. The IDEA was primarily designed to guarantee access to students with disabilities to allow them to meaningfully benefit from public education. The IDEA protected the right to access by means of its procedural protections, including the annual IEP meeting and review process. The Court was unwilling to recognize the substantive requirement urged by the parents in this case. In IDEA cases, courts were to limit their inquiry to whether the school had complied with IDEA procedural protections, and whether the IEP was reasonably calculated to enable the student to receive educational benefits. *Bd. of Educ. v. Rowley*, 458 U.S. 176, 102 S.Ct. 3034, 73 L.Ed.2d 690 (1982).

For two consecutive years, the mother of a South Dakota student with autism participated in the development of her child's IEP. She attached a typed statement to IEP documents stating that each of the student's classroom teachers would receive a five-day training course in the TEACCH method of instructing students with autism. However, when the student's IEP was reviewed during the course of the second year, the district stated that while it would continue to instruct the student in the TEACCH method, it would no longer include in the IEP a specific requirement for teachers to take the five-day teacher course. The mother requested an IDEA due process hearing, believing that the lack of the five-day course requirement would cause her son to regress. A hearing officer determined that the teacher training requirement had been improperly removed. A South Dakota trial court reversed the hearing officer's decision. The mother appealed to the Supreme Court of South Dakota.

The supreme court observed that the school district had complied with the IDEA by proposing an IEP that was reasonably calculated to confer educational benefits to the student. It rejected the mother's argument that teacher training was a related service under the IDEA and disagreed with her assertion that there was no other way to objectively measure teacher competence. The teacher training requirement could not be included in an IEP as a related service, and the fact that the district had bound itself to the training requirement in two prior years was now irrelevant. The IDEA required annual review of each IEP so that each could be revised, if appropriate, but did not allow parents to dictate teacher training and competency standards. The court affirmed the decision in favor of the school district. *Sioux Falls School Dist. v. Koupal*, 526 N.W.2d 248 (S.D.1994).

A Maryland school district did not notify parents of students with disabilities of the right of eligible students to receive extended school year (ESY) services as required by Maryland law and the IDEA. The district openly resisted making ESY placements over a ten-year period. Two students filed due process appeals against the district for failing to consider ESY placements and refusing to acknowledge its duty to provide such services. The U.S. District Court for the District of Maryland certified a class action in view of evidence that the district had failed to provide ESY services to a large number of students with disabilities residing in the district. The court conducted a bench trial at which it considered evidence that the district had been hostile to the provision of ESY services and had devised guidelines directing its personnel to improperly steer potentially eligible students with disabilities into a summer enrichment program that required paying tuition, instead of providing ESY services without charge when required. The district had also established a two-step appeal process which caused delay and inconvenience for parents seeking to obtain ESY services for their children.

The court determined that the district had improperly discouraged many parents from considering ESY placements and had deprived many others of the opportunity to learn about ESY by failing to advise them of the right to ESY placement. It directed the district to comply with state and federal law requiring the provision of ESY services to eligible students. It also directed the district to dismantle the two-level appeal procedure, finding that it had been devised to delay and minimize the availability of ESY services. The district had violated the IDEA by failing to provide adequate ESY notice, improperly delaying ESY decisions by making them late in the school year, and failing to address ESY at IEP meetings. The court ordered the district to bring itself into compliance with IDEA requirements, to cease and desist from its present violations and to pay the students' attorney's fees. *Reusch v. Fountain*, 872 F.Supp. 1421 (D.Md.1994).

A New Jersey student displayed autistic-like behavior. He was enrolled in a public preschool education program which included occupational therapy. The student's parents provided him with supplemental speech and occupational therapy. The student made minimal progress in his first public school year and suffered from serious behavioral problems as he entered first grade. He then began to respond quickly to behavioral therapy provided at home at the parents' expense. They sought placement in a full day behavioral program for the summer; however, the school district refused, stating that the program was available only to students with irrevocable regression problems. The parents then enrolled the student in a private school where he made dramatic progress. The school district's IEP for the next year recommended placement in a new program offered by the district. The parents claimed that the school district had violated the student's procedural rights under the IDEA by failing to place him appropriately. A federal court found that the school district had complied fully with the IDEA, and the parents appealed to the U.S. Court of Appeals, Third Circuit.

The court of appeals adopted the district court's opinion in its entirety, finding that the school district had complied with the IDEA in its procedural and substantive requirements. The parents had clearly participated in the IEP formulation in a meaningful manner, and the IEP complied with the U.S. Supreme Court's leading IDEA case, *Bd. of Educ. v. Rowley*, above, which required only that IEPs be reasonably calculated to enable the child to receive educational benefits at the time of the proposed IEP. The child's subsequent progress at the private school was not relevant to the reasonableness of the proposed IEP. The court of appeals affirmed the district court's judgment for the school district. *Fuhrmann v. East Hanover Bd. of Educ.*, 993 F.2d 1031 (3d Cir.1993).

II. PLACEMENT OF STUDENTS WITH DISABILITIES

The IDEA requires each local education agency (LEA) to identify and evaluate students with disabilities in its jurisdiction. After a school district identifies a student as disabled, it must develop an appropriate educational placement. The district must develop and implement an individualized education program (IEP) for each student with a disability in the district. The IEP must be calculated to provide an educational benefit and where possible, to mainstream the student with nondisabled students.

A. Identification and Evaluation

In 1969, California education officials implemented standardized IQ testing for determining the appropriate placements of educable mentally retarded (EMR) students. Within two years of the commencement of standardized testing, a class representing African-American students filed a lawsuit in the U.S. District Court for the Northern District of California, claiming that the overrepresentation of

African-American students in EMR classrooms and the standardized testing violated the IDEA and Title VI of the Civil Rights Act of 1964. In 1979, the district court issued an injunction banning the use of IQ tests for evaluating EMR students and for students who attended classes that were the substantial equivalent of EMR classes. The parties reached a settlement agreement that abolished the EMR category and banned the use of standardized tests to evaluate African-American students for any special education assessment. Based on the settlement, the court entered an order in 1986 modifying the 1979 injunction.

Years later, another group of African-American students petitioned the district court for an order to vacate the injunction modification because they wanted to take IQ tests. The district court consolidated the case with the original action and vacated the 1986 modification, awarding summary judgment to the students seeking to be tested. Members of the original plaintiff class and the state superintendent of public instruction appealed the summary judgment order to the U.S. Court of Appeals, Ninth Circuit. The court of appeals affirmed the district court's decision to vacate the 1986 modification and reinstate the original order. It also affirmed the district court order for further proceedings to determine whether all special education classes were substantially equivalent to the EMR designation and whether IQ tests were effective in placing African-American students. The new class of plaintiffs should not be bound by the prior judgment because its members had not been adequately represented by the original class. The 1986 ban on all IQ tests expanded the scope of the original injunction and was unsupported by the original factual findings. These findings pertained only in the context of EMR placements. *Crawford v. Honig*, 37 F.3d 485 (9th Cir.1994).

A Texas student with a learning disability, a speech impairment and an emotional impairment received special education services from his public school district. He suffered severe emotional shock and distress and was hospitalized after being hazed by fellow students. Following the hospitalization, a child psychologist determined that the student suffered from Gerstmann Syndrome, a condition causing tremendous anxiety and presenting a risk of psychopathology. The psychologist determined that the hazing incident had aggravated the student's condition and made it unwise for him to return to school. The school district began to provide homebound academic instruction and sought to impose a comprehensive educational reevaluation. The student's parents refused to permit testing on the advice of the psychologist. The parents obtained five private evaluations in an attempt to establish the student's eligibility for public special education services. However, the school district insisted upon its own comprehensive reevaluation. The parents rejected each evaluator from the school district's list and requested a due process hearing to determine the student's special educational services eligibility. The hearing officer determined that the student must undergo a district reevaluation in order to qualify for special education services. The parents appealed to the U.S. District Court for the Eastern District of Texas. The school district filed a motion for summary judgment. The court ruled that no student should be forced to choose between an appropriate education and emotional well-being. The risk of harm to the child in being reevaluated violated his constitutional right to privacy. The court determined that an exception existed to the district's right to evaluate the child because of the high risk to his health. A material issue of fact existed precluding summary judgment on this cause of action. *Andress v. Cleveland ISD*, 832 F.Supp. 1086 (E.D.Tex.1993).

An eight-year-old District of Columbia student was diagnosed with attention deficit and hyperactivity disorder. A multidisciplinary evaluation determined that the student was ineligible for special education services under both the IDEA and § 504 of the Rehabilitation Act. The student's test scores were from average to superior in all areas, but social maladjustment adversely affected his behavior. A hearing officer determined that the student was ineligible for special education under the IDEA but that he was a qualified child with a disability under § 504 and ordered the school district to develop an IEP. The district completed an IEP calling for a public school placement. However, the student's parents requested a second due process hearing to argue for a private school placement. A second hearing was held, and the hearing officer affirmed the initial determination that the student was not qualified for special education services under the IDEA. He also determined that he had no authority to order the district to provide special education services under § 504. The student's parents appealed to the U.S. District Court for the District of Columbia.

The court agreed with the hearing officer's finding that the student was not "other health impaired" under the IDEA. His academic performance was superior and his behavior problems were limited to social interaction. However, the hearing officer in the second hearing had erroneously determined that he had no authority under § 504 of the Rehabilitation Act to order a special education placement. Section 504 does not impose affirmative duties upon entities to serve children with disabilities, but rather prohibits discrimination on the basis of disability. The case was remanded to the hearing officer for a determination of whether the student was an otherwise qualified child with a disability under § 504 and whether failing to provide special education services to him amounted to discrimination. *Lyons by Alexander v. Smith*, 829 F.Supp. 414 (D.D.C.1993).

An Ohio high school student had difficulty learning and also experienced behavioral problems. As a result, he was disciplined by school authorities. He also underwent psychological testing at the request of the school. The testing did not reveal any disability. The student withdrew from the school and was later diagnosed as having epilepsy. The student's parents sued the school district, claiming that as an epileptic their son was considered a child with a disability under state law. The parents claimed that the school district negligently failed to identify the student as disabled as it was required to do under state law. They also claimed that the actions violated the student's constitutional rights. The school district and its employees moved to dismiss the negligence charges, claiming sovereign immunity. The trial court granted the request, and the parents appealed to the Court of Appeals of Ohio. The court noted that political subdivisions in Ohio are immune from liability for damages incurred as a result of an act or omission of the subdivision or one of its employees. The employee is also immune, with certain exceptions. An exception exists where another portion of Ohio law expressly provides for liability for an action. Although the parents argued that this exception applied, the court held that it did not. Imposing responsibility for an action is not the same as imposing liability for that action. *Zellman v. Kenston Bd. of Educ.*, 593 N.E.2d 392 (Ohio App.1991).

B. Placement

An Ohio student with autism attended a public school multi-handicapped class but displayed increasingly inappropriate and aggressive behavior. His symptoms became so severe that he was suspended and removed from the school for home instruction. His parents obtained an independent evaluation recommending a 24-hour per day behavior management program. The school district proposed continuing home instruction, and the parents requested an IDEA due process hearing. The hearing officer determined that the district failed to provide the student a free appropriate public education and ordered it to enroll him in a residential behavior management program in West Virginia. An Ohio county court also held that a full-time residential program was required. The parents were not entitled to home aide reimbursement and were not entitled to an additional two years of compensatory education, but were awarded $23,000 in attorney's fees, which the district did not contest. However, both parties appealed unfavorable parts of the decision to the Court of Appeals of Ohio.

The court of appeals found adequate support in the record for the trial court's determination that the proposed IEP was inappropriate and that the student's goals could only be met with a 24-hour residential behavior management program. It rejected an argument by the school district that the placement was inappropriate because it would expend approximately $94,000 of the district's $572,000 budget for all 208 of its students with disabilities. While cost was a consideration in placement issues, it was only relevant when choosing from among a number of appropriate placements. In this case, the residential placement was the only appropriate proposal. Therefore, the high cost of the residential placement did not make it inappropriate. The court affirmed the trial court's decision concerning placement, and determined that compensatory education should also be available. The parents were not entitled to reimbursement for their home aide costs, and the trial court's decision was otherwise affirmed. *Cremeans v. Fairland Local School Dist. Bd. of Educ.*, 91 Ohio App.3d 668, 633 N.E.2d 570 (4th Dist.1993).

An eleven-year-old California student with an IQ of 44 attended special education classes in her public school district. Her parents requested full-time placement in regular classes. The school district rejected this request and proposed special education instruction in academic classes and regular classes in nonacademic subjects and activities. The parents enrolled the student in regular classes at a private school and requested a hearing before a state hearing officer. The hearing officer found that the district had failed to comply with the IDEA's mainstreaming requirement, that the student had benefited from her placement in regular classes at the private school and that she was not too disruptive to attend regular classes in public school. The hearing officer ruled that the district had overstated the cost of placing the student in regular classes and ordered the district to place her in a regular classroom with support services. The U.S. District Court for the Eastern District of California affirmed the hearing officer's decision, and the district appealed to the U.S. Court of Appeals, Ninth Circuit.

On appeal, the district argued that the student was too severely disabled to benefit from full-time regular education placement. The parents argued that the student was learning social and academic skills in regular classes and would not benefit from special education. The court determined that the hearing officer and district court had properly considered the applicable factors in their decisions to mainstream the student. These included the educational benefits of full-time placement in a regular class, nonacademic benefits, the effect of placement on other students in the regular class, and the cost. The evidence indicated that the student could benefit educationally from regular classes without being too disruptive and that the district had exaggerated the cost of such a placement. The court of appeals affirmed the district court's judgment in favor of the parents. *Sacramento City Unif. School Dist. v. Rachel H.*, 14 F.3d 1398 (9th Cir.1994).

Two Michigan students with hearing impairments attended the Michigan School for the Deaf for three years. When their IEPs were reviewed, their IEP meetings were held without the presence of the students' present teachers and speech therapists. The IEP committee decided to transfer the students to a public school located in their home school district. The students' parents filed an administrative appeal of the new placements, resulting in a decision for the school district. The parents appealed to the U.S. District Court for the Western District of Michigan. They argued that the hearing officer had not been selected with their approval under Michigan law, that the IEPs were flawed in substance and that they were also invalid because of procedural errors.

The court agreed with the parents' argument that the IEP committee had improperly lacked the participation of the students' present teachers. The failure of the school district to ensure the participation of present teachers deprived the committee of input from any professionals with actual knowledge about the students and required a remand for reformation. The district also failed to comply with IDEA regulations requiring the evaluation of students at least every three years. The district would be required to reevaluate the students in reformulating the IEPs. The court reversed and remanded the hearing officer's decision with instructions to more closely scrutinize the proposed IEPs under Michigan's special education law which required the delivery of special education programs and services at a higher level than the minimum requirements of federal law. The hearing officer was directed to closely consider whether a public school placement constituted the least restrictive appropriate environment for the students. Notwithstanding the IDEA preference for mainstreaming, a segregated environment can be the least restrictive. *Brimmer v. Traverse City Area Pub. Schools*, 872 F.Supp. 447 (W.D.Mich.1994).

A New York student with mental disabilities attended the same kindergarten class for three consecutive years. The student was eventually classified mentally retarded and was placed in a restrictive classroom environment. The placement continued the student's speech therapy program, but mainstreaming was limited to music and gym classes. The school district permitted the student to advance from grade to grade until sixth grade, when she was 13. The parents expressed dissatisfaction with the placements devised by the school district over the years, whereas the district claimed that its placement decisions had been motivated by the desire to compromise and comply with the IDEA's stay-put provision. An impartial hearing officer determined that the student had been appropriately classified but remanded the matter to the trial study team to prepare a new IEP. The hearing officer later affirmed the modified IEP, even though mainstreaming was only provided in art, music and gym. The decision was affirmed by the state Commissioner of Education, and the parents appealed to the U.S. District Court for the Northern District of New York. The parents filed a motion for summary judgment, and the school district and commissioner of education brought cross-motions for summary judgment.

The court determined that the appropriate analysis to apply in mainstreaming cases was set forth in the case of *Daniel R.R. v. State Bd. of Educ.*, 874 F.2d 1036 (5th Cir.1989). According to that case, it must be determined whether satisfactory instruction of the disabled student may take place in a regular classroom with the use of supplemental aids and services. Next, it must be determined whether the school has mainstreamed the child to the maximum extent that is appropriate. The school district bore the burden of showing that its proposed placement complied with the IDEA's presumption in favor of mainstreaming. In this case, the student had not received an opportunity to show that she could be mainstreamed because the district had never provided sufficient supplemental aids and services. The relevant inquiry was whether the disabled student could achieve IEP goals in a regular education program with the assistance of appropriate aids and services. The case was remanded to the special education committee to develop an IEP in compliance with the mainstreaming requirement. The court also awarded attorney's fees to the parents. *Mavis v. Sobol*, 839 F.Supp. 968 (N.D.N.Y.1993).

The parents of a Kansas student with pervasive developmental disorder and mild cerebral palsy disputed a sequence of IEPs prepared by their school district. The student's physical difficulties and behavior problems disrupted classrooms and kept him out of mainstream education classes. After attending an intermediate level classroom for behaviorally disordered students, the student was mainstreamed in several regular classrooms. His behavior and educational performance greatly improved. However, his behavior problems at home worsened. The parents unilaterally removed the student from school and placed him in a private residential education facility where an evaluation determined that the student was performing at or near his grade level. The parents filed a due process hearing for a determination of the appropriateness of the placement and tuition reimbursement from the school district. The hearing officer ruled that the district's proposed IEP was appropriate and that the district was only obligated to reimburse the parents for an independent evaluation. A review officer affirmed the decision and the parents filed an IDEA lawsuit in the U.S. District Court for the District of Kansas.

The court stated that the evidence contained in the record showed that the student was performing academically at his grade level and that his behavior problems at school were very minor. The student's poor home behavior was not to be remedied by placement in a residential facility at school district expense. There was no evidence in the record that a residential placement was required for educational purposes. The court found a precedent in the case of *Swift v. Rapides Parish Pub. School System,* below. In that case, a federal district court determined that a student's home behavior problems were not the legal responsibility of the school board. Because a residential placement was not required under the IDEA and would probably violate the IDEA's mainstreaming requirement, the court granted judgment to the school district.*Hall v. Shawnee Mission School Dist.*, 856 F.Supp. 1521 (D.Kan.1994).

A California child suffered from rubella syndrome as well as deafness, blindness and a developmental disability. The child attended a public school for seven years. When school district officials decided to close the school, they reassigned disabled students who had attended classes there to another public school in the county. The child's parents refused to send the child to the other school and requested a private school placement. A hearing officer determined that the public school placement proposed by the school district was inappropriate under the IDEA. The district was unable to locate an appropriate private residential program. Because the private school located by the parents had no vacancies in its residential program, the hearing officer determined that the child should be placed in the school's daytime program until a vacancy in the residential program was available. He also ordered the school district to pay costs for tuition, transportation, caretaker fees, and room and board at the child's grandparents' home, which was close to the school. A federal district court heard the case and granted the school district's summary judgment motion, rejecting all the hearing officer's conclusions. The parents appealed to the U.S. Court of Appeals, Ninth Circuit. The court of appeals determined that the child had not benefited from public education over the course of seven years and the school district's proposed placement was inappropriate. The placement proposed by the parents was an appropriate, certified private school that could meet the child's educational needs. The relief designed by the hearing officer was appropriate under the unique circumstances of the case and was supported by IDEA regulations. The court of appeals upheld the hearing officer's decision and remanded the case to the district court for a determination of attorney's fees. *Ojai Unif. School Dist. v. Jackson*, 4 F.3d 1467 (9th Cir.1993).

An Ohio local school district operated a developmental center which provided residential care for mentally disabled adults and children. The center did not provide educational services. Residents needing educational services participated in community-based programs at other facilities. Four residents of the center were placed in a school operated by the county board pursuant to IEPs which were all adopted with the consent of the residents' parents. The county board superintendent advised the local school superintendent that none of the residents would be accepted at the school because of a lack of funds. The county superintendent claimed that they were nonresidents in the district even though the center was located in the county (because their parents lived in other counties). A state trial court held that the children were residents of the school district and must be placed in the school under Ohio law. The Ohio Court of Appeals reversed the trial court's decision and an appeal was brought to the Ohio Supreme Court.

The supreme court reviewed state statutory provisions that required students to be admitted to schools where they resided or were institutionalized in a residential facility. Because the residents were institutionalized in the local district, the local school board had the authority to place them appropriately. The county-run school was the least restrictive environment and therefore the appropriate placement for the residents. The supreme court reinstated the trial court's decision. *Bd. of Educ. of Austintown Local School Dist. v. Mahoning County Bd. of Mental Retardation and Developmental Disabilities*, 613 N.E.2d 167 (Ohio 1993).

A Texas high school student suffered from behavior, learning and speech disorders and an inability to tolerate frustration. The student's behavioral problems led to prosecution by the state juvenile justice system. The student's school district developed an IEP emphasizing one-on-one instruction in specially equipped classrooms with two-hour days as an accommodation of his inability to tolerate a full school day without becoming frustrated. The student made behavioral and academic progress at the public school, but when he was placed on probation for his prior juvenile offense, his parents unilaterally removed him from public school and placed him in a highly restrictive psychiatric hospital. The residential placement limited educational programming to two hours per day and the student was confined to a locked ward. The school district refused to pay for the residential placement, stating that it was far too restrictive. A special education hearing officer determined that the parents should be reimbursed for the placement, a decision that was reversed by the U.S. District Court for the Western District of Texas.

On appeal to the U.S. Court of Appeals, Fifth Circuit, the court observed that there was ample evidence in the record that the student received significant benefits from the public school placement. While in public school, he advanced educationally and was able to focus for increasingly longer periods of time without debilitating frustration. He also had an opportunity to interact with nondisabled peers. The private psychiatric hospital program focused on behavior management and was the most restrictive placement available. The district court decision for the school district was affirmed. *Teague Indep. School Dist. v. Todd L.*, 999 F.2d 127 (5th Cir.1993).

A disabled student attended special education classes in Maine public schools through eighth grade. His educational progress then stopped because of a severe nonverbal disability. The student was hospitalized for one month during eighth grade after which his parents selected a private school placement in Massachusetts. The parents obtained a number of educational and psychological examinations for the student and rejected the school district's IEP for ninth grade. The IEP called for mainstreaming in regular classes, with small class instruction and private programming in compensatory skills. After rejecting the IEP, the parents unilaterally enrolled the student in a full-time residential facility and requested a due process hearing. The hearing officer determined that the public school's IEP was reasonably calculated to educationally benefit the student in a much less restrictive environment than the residential school. The U.S. District Court for the District of Maine affirmed the hearing officer's decision, and the parents appealed to the U.S. Court of Appeals, First Circuit. The court of appeals emphasized the "modest goals" of the IDEA, stating that it required school districts to provide only an appropriate (rather than an ideal) education, and therefore an adequate rather than optimal IEP. The IDEA also contained a preference for mainstreaming. In this case, the district court had applied appropriate standards of review to the hearing officer's decision. Accordingly, the district court's decision was affirmed. *Lenn v. Portland School Comm.*, 998 F.2d 1083 (1st Cir.1993).

A child with Down's Syndrome was placed in segregated special education classes by a New Jersey school district. The child's parents disagreed with the placement and requested an IDEA hearing. As the result of a mediated settlement with the child's parents, the school district agreed to consider future mainstreaming possibilities, but placed the child in another special education class in which he demonstrated behavior problems. A second due process hearing resulted in a decision favorable to the school district, based upon a finding by the hearing officer that the student's disruptive behavior prevented him from obtaining any meaningful educational benefit in regular classes. The student's parents appealed the hearing officer's decision to the U.S. District Court for the District of New Jersey, which reversed the hearing officer's decision. The school board appealed to the U.S. Court of Appeals, Third Circuit. The court of appeals observed that the district court had not reached a clearly erroneous decision in determining that the student could be educated in a regular classroom with the use of appropriate supplementary aids and services. The district court had also made no error in determining that integrating the student into regular classes would enable him to improve his social skills by interacting with nondisabled students. The school district had taken no meaningful steps to integrate the student into regular classrooms and the student's alleged behavior problems may have been exacerbated by the school district's failure to provide appropriate aids and services. The district court's decision was affirmed. *Oberti v. Bd. of Educ. of Borough of Clementon School Dist.*, 995 F.2d 1204 (3d Cir.1993).

A Texas preschooler had profound hearing loss in both ears. Her parents enrolled her in the total communication methodology program of their local school district. The program included sign language instruction in which the parents participated. The student received a cochlear implant and made significant progress in speech development. The student was then placed in a self-contained classroom with four other preschool students, where she received instruction from a teacher certified in speech methodology and therapy as well as deaf education. The student also received weekly individual speech therapy. Despite the progress made by the student, she began to prefer sign language over speech. The student's father determined that he did not want her using sign language, fearing that she would become part of "the deaf subculture." He requested that she be placed in an aural/oral program without use of sign language, plus one hour per day of individual speech therapy and auditory training. He then placed his daughter in a private school. A hearing officer determined that the school district had provided a free appropriate public education and the parents appealed to the U.S. District Court for the Southern District of Texas. The court determined that overwhelming evidence indicated that the student had received a free appropriate public education from the school district. The IEP developed by the school district had been reasonably calculated to enable the student to receive educational benefits and the father's fears were unjustified. Parents who made private placements on their own initiative did so at their own risk, and the school district was not required to reimburse the student's parents for tuition. *Bonnie Ann F. by John R.F. v. Calallen Indep. School Dist.*, 835 F.Supp. 340 (S.D.Tex.1993).

A Maine student suffered from a profound hearing impairment as a result of having meningitis at the age of 18 months. He was placed in public school, where he demonstrated slow but steady progress in classes in which he had individual instruction and classroom instruction with cued speech interpreters. When he reached grade six, the student's language and vocabulary development were a primary concern and his skills were estimated to be four or five years behind his peers. The student's parent rejected the school district's proposed IEP, and a hearing officer modified it, dividing the student's time between mainstream classes for which the student was proficient, and part-time instruction at a school for the deaf for subjects in which he experienced difficulty. The parent then unilaterally placed the student in a full-time program at another school for the deaf. She sought reimbursement for the student's tuition and expenses by filing a lawsuit in the U.S. District Court for the District of Maine. The student's parent argued that the only appropriate placement for the student was a full-time oral program for hearing impaired students. The school district argued that the IDEA's mainstreaming policy required the dual placement in public school with part-time instruction at the school for the deaf. The court agreed with the school district, stating that parental preference alone could not compel the school district to provide a particular placement. *Brougham by Brougham v. Town of Yarmouth*, 823 F.Supp. 9 (D.Me.1993).

A twelve-year-old Louisiana student was diagnosed as behavior disordered and emotionally disturbed. He was of average intelligence, but evidence indicated that, due to attention deficit disorder with hyperactivity, his behavior was worsening. When a dispute arose as to the student's placement, a hearing officer ruled that because the student's medical and educational needs were so "intertwined," residential placement was necessary in order for the student to receive a free appropriate public education. This decision was reversed by a state-level review panel, and the student's grandparents filed an appeal in the U.S. District Court for the Western District of Louisiana, Alexandria Division. The court cited U.S. Supreme Court and Fifth Circuit authority for the proposition that the IDEA does not require provision of optimal services for each child with a disability. Specialized instruction was designed only to confer some meaningful educational benefit to students with disabilities. Although most of the psychologists and professionals who had evaluated the student believed that a residential placement was necessary, there was evidence in the record that the student was progressing in his current IEP. The fact that the student was becoming more rebellious at home did not affect the legal responsibility of the school board. The court affirmed the state-level hearing panel decision. *Swift v. Rapides Parish Pub. School System*, 812 F.Supp. 666 (W.D.La.1993).

A 20-year-old New Jersey student was entitled to special educational services under the IDEA because of autism and severe behavioral problems. The state Division of Developmental Disabilities (DDD) placed her in a Delaware school which was not an approved special education facility. The student's mother sought a transfer to a residential facility located in the family's home town. When the DDD refused to transfer the student, her mother filed a due process hearing under 20 U.S.C. § 1415(e)(2). An administrative law judge granted the mother's summary judgment motion, ordering the DDD to place the student at the residential facility in the family's home town. The DDD failed to transfer the student, and the mother filed a petition for enforcement of the administrative order in the U.S. District Court for the District of New Jersey. The DDD responded with a complaint for review of the administrative decision, and the district court consolidated the matters.

Before the district court, the DDD changed its position, arguing that the Delaware school retained a "conditional approval," for special education. The student's mother argued that the programs were comparable and that the IDEA's requirement of placement in the least restrictive environment included placing the student as close as possible to the family's home. The district court agreed, citing 34 C.F.R. § 300.552(a)(3), a regulation published under authority of the IDEA which requires school districts to take into account the location of the placement, "particularly in a residential program." Because the educational program available to the student in her home town was comparable to the Delaware placement, it was the student's appropriate placement under the IDEA. The court affirmed the administrative law judge's decision for the student and awarded attorney's fees and costs. *Remis v. New Jersey Dept. of Human Serv.,* 815 F.Supp. 1410 (D.N.J.1993).

C. Change in Placement

The IDEA requires school districts to provide parents of students with disabilities prior written notice of any proposed change in placement. If the parents wish to contest the change in placement, a hearing must be granted. The IDEA further requires that during the pendency of such review proceedings, the child is to remain in the then current educational placement. Whether suspension or expulsion of students with disabilities from school constitutes a "change in placement" for purposes of the IDEA is an issue which has been presented before the courts. The U.S. Supreme Court has clarified the issue in *Honig v. Doe,* below. Indefinite suspensions violate the "stay put" provisions of the IDEA. Suspensions of up to ten days do not constitute a change in placement.

Honig v. Doe involved two emotionally disturbed children in California who were each suspended for five days for misbehavior which included destroying school property and assaulting and making sexual comments to other students. Pursuant to state law, the suspensions were continued indefinitely during the pendency of expulsion proceedings. The students sued the school district in U.S. district court contesting the extended suspensions on the ground that they violated the "stay put" provision of the IDEA which provides that a student must be kept in his or her "then current" educational placement during the pendency of proceedings which contemplate a change in placement. The district court issued an injunction preventing the expulsion and the school district appealed.

The U.S. Court of Appeals, Ninth Circuit, determined that the indefinite suspensions constituted a prohibited "change in placement" without notice under the IDEA and that there was no "dangerousness" exception to the IDEA's "stay put" provision. It ruled that indefinite suspensions or expulsions of disabled children for misconduct arising out of their disabilities violated the IDEA. The court of appeals also ruled, however, that fixed suspensions of up to 30 school days did not constitute a "change in placement." It determined that a state must provide services directly to a disabled child when a local school district fails to do so. The California Superintendent of Public Instruction filed for a review by the U.S. Supreme Court on the issues of whether there was a dangerousness exception to the "stay put" provision and whether the state had to provide services directly when a local school district failed to do so.

The Supreme Court declared that the intended purpose of the "stay put" provision was to prevent schools from changing a child's educational placement over his or her parents' objection until all review proceedings were completed. While the IDEA provided for interim placements where parents and school officials were able to agree on one, no emergency exception for dangerous students was included. Where a disabled student poses an immediate threat to the safety of others, school officials may temporarily suspend him or her for up to ten school days. The Court affirmed the court of appeals' decision that indefinite suspensions violated the "stay put" provision of the IDEA. It modified that court's decision on fixed suspensions by holding that suspensions up to ten rather than up to 30 days did not constitute a change in placement. The Court also upheld the court of appeals' decision that states could be required to provide services directly to disabled students where a local school district fails to do so. *Honig v. Doe*, 484 U.S. 305, 108 S.Ct. 592, 98 L.Ed.2d 686 (1988).

A California high school senior attended regular education classes and generally received above-average grades. The student was subjected to 16 disciplinary referrals for reasons including fighting, insubordination and disruptive behavior. A school employee spotted a gun in the back seat of the student's car and took the student to the vice-principal's office. The student admitted bringing the gun to school and the school suspended him under a California statute that required the immediate suspension of any student found in possession of a firearm at school. Pursuant to the statute, an expulsion hearing was scheduled within ten days. Although the student had never received special education services, the student then requested an evaluation under the Individuals with Disabilities Education Act (IDEA). The school tested and evaluated the student and held an individualized education program (IEP) meeting, at which it determined that the student was ineligible for special education services. The student nonetheless requested an IDEA due process hearing to review the IEP meeting findings, and claimed that he could not be suspended from school under the IDEA stay-put provision. He filed a motion for a temporary restraining order against suspension or expulsion in the U.S. District Court for the Southern District of California, and the district filed a counterclaim for a restraining order preventing the student from returning to school.

The court agreed with the student's argument that he was entitled to IDEA procedural safeguards regardless of whether he had been previously diagnosed as a student with disabilities. The IDEA broadly extended protection to all students with disabilities, and necessarily applied to students with undetected disabilities. The court, while recognizing the potential for abuse under the statute by a false claim of disability, nonetheless held that it was without jurisdiction to permit a change in placement, including suspension or expulsion. It denied the school district's motion to exclude the student from school on the basis of dangerousness, finding evidence that the student's parents had taken away his access to the gun and that the school's psychologist failed to testify that he was dangerous. The student's motion was granted and the school district's motion was denied. *M.P. by D.P. v. Governing Bd. of Grossmont Union High School Dist.*, 858 F.Supp. 1044 (S.D.Cal.1994).

A Missouri student with multiple mental disabilities exhibited aggressive behavior toward students and teachers. She was placed in a public school's self-contained classroom. She was also enrolled in several regular classrooms. Despite this placement, her aggressive behavior continued to the point that daily lesson plans were not completed and the parents of other students complained of the negative effect on their children. The student's IEP team reevaluated the placement. The parents objected to any change in placement and requested the imposition of the IDEA's stay put provision during the course of administrative proceedings. Shortly thereafter, the student hit another student on the head three times during art class. The school imposed a ten-day suspension, and the parents filed a lawsuit seeking to set it aside in the U.S. District Court for the Eastern District of Missouri. The school district filed a counterclaim to remove the student from school during the revision of the IEP, based on the substantial risk of injury she presented to herself and others. The court granted the district's motion for an order allowing it to remove the student from school. The parents appealed to the U.S. Court of Appeals, Eighth Circuit.

On appeal, the parents argued that the district court should have inquired into whether the student was "truly dangerous," based upon her capacity to inflict injury. The court disagreed, determining that it was only necessary to determine whether a student with a disability posed a substantial risk of injury to herself or others. There was substantial evidence in the record of a likelihood of injury based on almost daily episodes of aggressive behavior by the student. Accordingly, removal of the student had been proper and temporary placement at a segregated facility for students with disabilities was appropriate. The court affirmed the lower court's decision for the school district. *Light v. Parkway C-2 School Dist.*, 41 F.3d 1223 (8th Cir.1994).

A 15-year-old Washington student with Tourette's Syndrome and attention deficit hyperactivity disorder became increasingly uncontrollable and frequently disrupted classes with name-calling, profanity, explicit sexual comments, kicking and hitting. The school ultimately expelled him under an emergency order after he assaulted a staff member. The student's parents agreed with the school's determination that he should be placed in a self-contained program off the school campus for individualized attention and a structured environment. The parents soon changed their minds and requested a due process hearing to contest the interim placement and demand a new IEP. The parties were unable to agree upon a new IEP, and the parents insisted that the student return to regular classes for the rest of the school year. A 10-day due process hearing was held during the summer break, resulting in a determination that the school had complied with the IDEA. The parents appealed to the U.S. District Court for the Western District of Washington, which affirmed the administrative decision. The parents appealed to the U.S. Court of Appeals, Ninth Circuit.

The court held that because the parents had initially agreed with the interim placement, it could be implemented without a current IEP and could be considered the student's "stay-put" placement for IDEA purposes. The school district had complied with substantive requirements of the IDEA by placing the student in the interim placement that constituted the least restrictive environment in which he could receive educational benefits. Accordingly, the court of appeals affirmed the district court judgment. *Clyde K. v. Puyallup School Dist. No. 3*, 35 F.3d 1396 (9th Cir.1994).

A Georgia county education board proposed the consolidation and closure of four schools. A taxpayer filed a lawsuit against the board in a Georgia trial court, seeking an order requiring an evidentiary hearing or referendum on the proposals. The trial court permanently enjoined the board of education from consolidating and closing the schools. The decision was partially based upon the court's finding that the board had failed to comply with the Individuals with Disabilities Education Act (IDEA). The court ordered the county board to renovate the schools, utilize school trustees as set forth under Georgia law and comply with state and federal funding statutes. The board appealed to the Supreme Court of Georgia. The supreme court reversed the trial court's order finding that the board action violated the IDEA. Contrary to the trial court's decision, the transfer of disabled students from one school to another with a comparable program did not constitute a change in placement that would require notification of parents under the IDEA. The trial court had abused its discretion and the supreme court reversed its decision. *Powell v. Studstill*, 441 S.E.2d 52 (Ga.1994).

A New York high school student with a learning disability threatened other students and a teacher, and was apprehended while waving an iron bar and threatening to kill someone. The school suspended the student and placed him in homebound instruction pending a psychiatric evaluation by the school district's special education committee. The district petitioned a New York trial court for a temporary order that would permit the district to extend the suspension beyond ten days until an appropriate evaluation and placement could be made. The student failed to oppose the motion and the court entered an order in favor of the school district, based on its showing of a substantial likelihood of injury to the student or others without the suspension and the continuation of home-bound instruction. In making the order, the court discussed the standard established by the U.S. Supreme Court in student expulsion and suspension cases in *Honig v. Doe*, above. The case interprets the Individuals with Disabilities Education Act (IDEA) stay-put provision as preventing unilateral suspensions of over ten days without application to a court for approval of longer terms on the basis of the threat of injury to self or others. Finding the school district's actions appropriate, the court granted the requested order pending the district's evaluation and placement proceedings. *East Islip Union Free School Dist. v. Andersen*, 615 N.Y.S.2d 852 (Sup.Ct.Suffolk County 1994).

III. RELATED SERVICES

Related services include sign language interpreters, transportation, speech pathology, psychological and counseling services, and physical and occupational therapy. The IDEA requires school districts to provide services that are necessary for students with disabilities to receive educational benefits.

A California student was diagnosed with autism. His school district proposed an IEP consisting of weekly classes in the communicatively handicapped class of a public school with one-on-one behavior modification counseling. The parents argued that the student required a much more restrictive, full-time, one-on-one instructional program because he was unable to benefit from group instruction. They unilaterally placed the student in a counseling program at a clinic far from the school district. He progressed significantly in language skills, cooperation and interaction. The parents sued the school district in the U.S. District Court for the Northern District of California, seeking reimbursement for their expenses, including the cost of maintaining a temporary residence near the clinic. The court granted summary judgment to the parents and the district appealed to the U.S. Court of Appeals, Ninth Circuit. The court stated that the board's failure to make a formal, written, appropriate placement offer violated the IDEA. Even though the placement selected by the parents was for counseling only and not a program of special education, counseling qualified as a related service under the IDEA. Under California law, students with disabilities could be placed in related service programs without receiving simultaneous special education. This state law result did not violate the IDEA. The parents were entitled to reimbursement for tuition, daily transportation costs to the clinic, the cost of commuting between their temporary and permanent residences, and the cost of maintaining the temporary residence. The court affirmed the district court's summary judgment ruling for the parents and remanded the case. *Union School Dist. v. Smith*, 15 F.3d 1519 (9th Cir.1994).

A seven-year-old Tennessee student had congenital central hypoventilation syndrome, a rare condition affecting her breathing. She underwent a tracheostomy procedure and required frequent suctioning and a well-trained person to perform the procedure and respond to emergencies. The student's parents requested the school district, and later the Tennessee Department of Education, to provide a full-time nurse or respiratory care professional to provide tracheostomy services. The district agreed to hire a nursing assistant to provide these services, but the parents insisted that the district provide a licensed practical nurse, which would cost at least $2 more per hour than a nursing assistant. The parents removed their daughter from the school and the district provided home instruction pending their appeal to an administrative law judge. The judge ruled that the district did not have to furnish a full-time nurse, and the parents appealed to the U.S. District Court for the Middle District of Tennessee. The court determined that the requested service was a "medical service" under the IDEA. School districts are generally not required to pay for medical services, unless they are for diagnostic or evaluative purposes. Most courts have focused on the nature of services requested, and the burden imposed on the school district, in determining liability. In this case, the annual cost of a licensed practical nurse was only about $3,000 more than a nursing assistant. Accordingly, tracheostomy service was a related supportive service that was not within the IDEA medical services exclusion. The district was required to pay for a licensed nurse. *Neely v. Rutherford County Schools*, 851 F.Supp. 888 (M.D.Tenn.1994).

A West Virginia high school student with hearing impairments received sign language interpretation services for her basic academic courses, but not for vocational classes or extracurricular activities. She played on the girls' basketball team. At the beginning of her junior year, the student's father requested the services of a signer because of communication problems between the student and her coach. The request was denied. The student filed a petition for a writ of mandamus in the Supreme Court of Appeals of West Virginia, seeking an order that would require the state board of education and the state Secondary School Activities Commission (SSAC) to provide a signer under the IDEA. The court held that the student was entitled to sign language interpretation services. *State of West Virginia ex rel. Lambert v. West Virginia State Bd. of Educ.*, 447 S.E.2d 901 (W.Va.1994).

An Arizona student attended a school for the deaf from grades one through five and a public school from grades six through eight. During his public school attendance, a sign language interpreter was provided by the school district. The student's parents enrolled him in a parochial high school for ninth grade, and requested the school district to continue providing a sign language interpreter. The school district refused, and the student's parents then sued it in the U.S. District Court for the District of Arizona under the IDEA. The court granted the school district's summary judgment motion. On appeal, the U.S. Court of Appeals, Ninth Circuit, affirmed the district court decision. The court of appeals stated that the placement of a public school employee in a parochial school would create the appearance that the government was a joint sponsor of the private school's activities. The U.S. Supreme Court granted the parents' petition for a writ of certiorari. On appeal, the school district cited 34 CFR § 76.532(a)(1), an IDEA regulation, as authority for the prohibition against using federal funds for private school sign language interpreters.

The Supreme Court stated that the Establishment Clause did not completely prohibit religious institutions from participating in publicly-sponsored benefits. If this were the case, religious groups would not even enjoy police and fire protection or have use of public roads and sidewalks. Government programs which neutrally provide benefits to broad classes of citizens are not subject to Establishment Clause prohibition simply because some religiously affiliated institutions receive "an attenuated financial benefit." Providing a sign language interpreter under the IDEA was part of a general program for distribution of benefits in a neutral manner to qualified students. A sign language interpreter, unlike an instructor or counselor, was ethically bound to transmit everything said in exactly the same way as it was intended. The Supreme Court reversed the court of appeals' decision. *Zobrest v. Catalina Foothills School Dist.*, 113 S.Ct. 2462, 125 L.Ed.2d 1 (1993).

The U.S. Supreme Court ruled that clean intermittent catheterization (CIC) is a related service not subject to the "medical service" exclusion of the IDEA. The parents of an eight-year-old girl born with spina bifida brought suit against their local Texas school district after the district refused to provide CIC for the child while she attended school. The parents pursued administrative and judicial avenues to force the district to train staff to perform the simple procedure. After a U.S. district court held against the parents, they appealed to the U.S. Court of Appeals, Fifth Circuit, which reversed the district court ruling. The school district then appealed to the U.S. Supreme Court. The Supreme Court affirmed the court of appeals' ruling that clean intermittent catheterization is a supportive related service, not a medical service excluded from the IDEA. *Irving Indep. School Dist. v. Tatro*, 468 U.S. 883, 104 S. Ct. 3371, 82 L.Ed.2d 664 (1984).

A New York student was paralyzed in a car accident and could not breathe without a respirator. The student had to be assisted at all times by a specially trained nurse to perform tracheostomy suctioning and catheterization, at an estimated cost of $25,000 to $40,000 per year. The student's parents sought an administrative ruling that the school district was required to provide the specially trained nurse as a "related service" under the IDEA. A state review officer ruled for the school district and the parents appealed to a New York trial court. The trial court dismissed the parents' appeal and they sought review by the Supreme Court, Appellate Division, Third Department.

According to the court, medical services qualified as "related services" under the IDEA only if the services were provided for diagnostic and evaluation purposes. Diagnostic and evaluation purposes which assisted a student with a disability to benefit from special education included early identification and assessment. In this case, the trial court had properly determined that the provision of a specially trained nurse did not qualify as a simple school nursing service which constituted a related service under the IDEA. The appellate division court also affirmed the trial court decision that there was no basis for providing a special nurse under New York State social services law. The appellate division court affirmed the trial court's decision for the school board. *Ellison v. Bd. of Educ. of Three Village Central School Dist.*, 597 N.Y.S.2d 483 (A.D.3d Dept.1993).

A Michigan student with muscular dystrophy used a wheelchair and required frequent tracheal suctioning. He completed his graduation requirements, but rejected his high school's recommendation for graduation in three consecutive years. The school continued to allow the student to attend school past his twenty-first birthday. The student requested a due process hearing under the IDEA and the Michigan Mandatory Special Education Act (MMSEA), challenging the school's recommendation to graduate. He also requested an administrative hearing under § 504 of the Rehabilitation Act. A local hearing officer affirmed the recommendation for graduation and found no violation of § 504. This result was affirmed by a state-level hearing officer, and the student appealed to the U.S. District Court for the Eastern District of Michigan.

The student argued that he had been deprived of a free appropriate public education because of the district's failure to incorporate transition services into his IEP. He also claimed that he was entitled to receive physical therapy and transportation services (which the district continued to provide through the hearing date, even though he was now 24 years old). The court observed that the student had completed his graduation requirements and had excelled in mainstream classes. Although the district had failed to document its provision of transition services in the IEP documents, it had provided the student with career counseling and guidance services that were adequate under the IDEA. The student could be properly graduated under both the IDEA and the more stringent MMSEA, which required the state to maximize the potential of every disabled person up to the age of 26. The court dismissed the student's claims under the IDEA and MMSEA. It also dismissed the student's claims under § 504. The court granted the school district's summary judgment motion. *Chuhran v. Walled Lake Cons. Schools*, 839 F.Supp. 465 (E.D.Mich.1993).

IV. HEARINGS TO CONTEST PLACEMENT

Among the most important IDEA protections for students with disabilities are its procedural requirements, including the right to an impartial due process hearing under 20 U.S.C. § 1415(b)(2). State and local educational agencies are obligated to provide "fair and impartial" hearings to attempt to resolve disputes over the placement of children with disabilities. Appeals of local hearings may be heard by state level entities. After administrative remedies have been exhausted, the parties may appeal to state or federal court.

A Massachusetts student with a disability attended public schools for ten years before her parents enrolled her in a private residential high school in Connecticut. The parents did not complain of the special education services provided by the school district while the student attended school there. Two years after removing the student from public school, the parents initiated an administrative appeal of the school's proposed IEP because it did not provide for attendance at the Connecticut private school. The parents then abandoned the appeal prior to a hearing before the bureau of special education appeals. Over a year later, the parents filed a lawsuit against the town and its public schools in a Massachusetts trial court. They claimed that the school system had failed to perform adequate or sufficient evaluations of the student from the time she entered the system until the time of her private school attendance. The court granted summary judgment to the town and schools and the parents appealed to the Appeals Court of Massachusetts, Middlesex.

The appeals court held that the parents had failed to exhaust their administrative remedies under state and federal law. None of the recognized exceptions to the exhaustion doctrine applied in this case, because the student was not threatened with immediate harm, there was no futility in resort to an administrative hearing, and no allegation that the administrative process was inadequate.

The IDEA in Massachusetts special education laws did not provide for any damages for pain and suffering and there was no legal theory justifying an award of damages for the claims advanced by the student. The court affirmed the trial court's award of summary judgment to the town and school system. *Kelly K. v. Town of Framingham*, 36 Mass.App.Ct. 483, 633 N.E.2d 414 (1994).

A Missouri student with moderate to severe retardation and significant behavioral disturbance attended a state school for students with disabilities until the school was closed for budgetary reasons. The parents then received a letter stating that the student would be reassigned to a state school located approximately 50 miles away. The parents expressed concern about lengthy daily bus trips and attempted to raise the issue at an IEP meeting. However, state officials preempted this discussion, stating that the student was too severely disabled to be educated locally. The parents applied for a due process hearing against the school district and state education department, arguing that the proposed placement was predetermined and that they received no opportunity to complain of the possibly harmful long bus rides. A hearing panel agreed with the parents. The school district appealed to the state education board and a state level review officer affirmed this decision. Appeal was brought to the U.S. District Court for the Western District of Missouri. The court found that Missouri's state school referral procedure violated the IDEA in several respects. The procedure prevented consideration of the least restrictive environment until after an actual placement was made and deprived parents of any significant input at a relevant time. In the student's case, state school officials had predetermined the student's placement and deprived the family of a meaningful hearing. The state also failed to comply with IDEA regulations requiring public education agencies to make placements as close as possible to the student's home. *Hunt v. Bartman*, 873 F.Supp. 229 (W.D.Mo.1994).

A Connecticut student with language-based disabilities attended a private school at which he made substantial progress. The public school district in which the student resided agreed to pay for an independent educational evaluation in order to develop an appropriate IEP for the following school year. The evaluation recommended continued placement at the private school. Only two members of the placement team received copies of the evaluation prior to the IEP meeting, and the remaining four members' only exposure to the evaluation occurred when its results were read or summarized during the meeting by the school district's psychologist. The parents failed to invite the psychologist who prepared the evaluation to attend the IEP meeting. After the team failed to incorporate the recommendations of the evaluation into the IEP, the parents complained that they had been deprived of their due process rights under the IDEA. They argued that the placement team had failed to "consider" the evaluation within the meaning of the act and that the team had "orchestrated" the outcome of the IEP by deciding its outcome in advance. They also alleged that team members had "censored" the meeting by limiting the topics of discussion at the meeting. A hearing officer determined that the district had no obligation to pay the student's private school tuition. This result was affirmed by the U.S. District Court for the District of Connecticut. The parents appealed to the U.S. Court of Appeals, Second Circuit.

The court determined that distribution of the evaluation to two team members prior to the meeting and the reading of a summarized portion of the report to the IEP team at its meeting constituted consideration of the evaluation under the IDEA. The parents' procedural rights had not been violated because they had received an opportunity to participate in the IEP process and had attended the meeting. There was no evidence that board employees had "orchestrated" or "censored" the meeting to reach a predetermined result. The court of appeals affirmed the order granting summary judgment to the school board. *T.S. v. Bd. of Educ. of Town of Ridgefield*, 10 F.3d 87 (2d Cir.1993).

V. TUITION REIMBURSEMENT

If a public school district is unable to provide special education services to a student with a disability in its own facilities, it must locate an appropriate program in another school district, hospital or institution. When no public facility is adequate and a private placement is required, the school district becomes responsible for tuition and other costs.

An Illinois student with multiple disabilities including speech and language impairments attended a public facility for students with disabilities. The school district conducted multidisciplinary conferences and an IEP meeting each year. However, the parents and district eventually disagreed on the appropriate educational placement. The district suggested a program that emphasized mainstreaming, while the parents expressed concern that the student's language skills were in regression. The parents then rejected the district's triennial reevaluation of the student, because it called for continued placement in a setting with nondisabled students. The parents requested placement in a private Wisconsin residential school for 24-hour learning. The district rejected the request and the parents withdrew their daughter from her summer placement in public schools. They enrolled her in a private preschool language program for an independent evaluation. They also requested a hearing under the IDEA. The hearing officer determined that the IEP proposed by the school district failed to meet IDEA requirements. A review officer ordered the district to pay for the private placement. The U.S. District Court for the Southern District of Illinois affirmed the administrative decisions. It concluded that because the district had failed to propose an appropriate placement, it had no alternative but to order tuition reimbursement. The district appealed to the U.S. Court of Appeals, Seventh Circuit.

On appeal, the school district argued that the hearing officers had failed to give deference to the decisions of the school employees and had made decisions that were unsupported by the evidence. The court of appeals disagreed, finding substantial evidence in support of the administrative decisions. Because the district had failed to propose an alternate placement that was educationally appropriate, the hearing officers and district court had been left with no choice but to approve the appropriate placement selected by the parents. Although IDEA regulations supported the award of reimbursement for tuition and for a single private evaluation, the regulations limited reimbursement to a single evaluation. The court therefore remanded the question of liability for payment of the second evaluation. It otherwise affirmed the district court's decision. *Bd. of Educ. of Murphysboro Comm. Unit School Dist. No. 186 v. Illinois State Bd. of Educ.*, 41 F.3d 1162 (7th Cir.1994).

The parents of an Arizona student with profound hearing impairments felt that learning sign language would cause her to become dependent upon it and she might never learn to speak. The school district evaluated the student and refused to place her in a program that excluded sign language. Her program called for oral methods with augmentative communication including sign language, lip reading and oral training. The parents filed an administrative appeal that resulted in affirmation of the recommended program. The parents then enrolled the student in a private school in Missouri where no sign language was used. The parents requested tuition reimbursement for speech therapy at the private school. The school district refused the request and the parents filed an administrative complaint with the state department of education. The department issued a letter denying tuition reimbursement and refusing to provide the parents a hearing. The parents filed a lawsuit in the U.S. District Court for the District of Arizona, which granted summary judgment motions by the school district, education department and an education department official. The parents appealed to the U.S. Court of Appeals, Ninth Circuit.

The court of appeals rejected the district's argument that the parents had failed to exhaust their administrative remedies. The refusal to provide a due process hearing left the parents with no recourse but to file suit. However, the school district had no obligation to pay for the student's private school services. Two review officers had expressly determined that the school district had offered the student a free appropriate public education, and the district was not required to provide related services that did not comply with the IEP. Because the special education program at the private school was inconsistent with the appropriate IEP proposed by the school district, the court affirmed the district court's decision. *Dreher v. Amphitheater Unified School Dist.*, 22 F.3d 228 (9th Cir.1994)

A second-grade Pennsylvania student was identified as a gifted student following complaints about her classroom behavior. She began attending a Catholic school and her mother filled out applications for other private schools. She was accepted for a private school program in Delaware, which granted her a scholarship for over 90 percent of her tuition. The student's mother requested reimbursement of the remaining $695 for tuition and transportation to the private school. The district refused the request, based on both her failure to obtain a multidisciplinary evaluation and the location of the school, which was outside Pennsylvania. The district then prepared a multidisciplinary evaluation which determined that the student would benefit from a gifted program. A gifted IEP was prepared for the student which included public school placement, but the mother disapproved it and requested a due process hearing. At the due process hearing, the hearing officer determined that the district had appropriately followed procedural safeguards and that the proposed public school placement was appropriate. The hearing officer also denied the mother's request for tuition reimbursement and the costs of transportation. The mother appealed that decision to a state review panel, which agreed that the student was not entitled to tuition reimbursement or transportation costs. The student appealed to the Commonwealth Court of Pennsylvania. The commonwealth court ruled that because Pennsylvania law did not entitle a gifted student to private school or out-of-state placement, the student was not entitled to tuition reimbursement or transportation expenses. *Ellis v. Chester Upland School Dist.*, 651 A.2d 616 (Pa.Cmwlth.1994).

The parents of a Connecticut student with disabilities rejected the placement proposed by his school district and placed him in a school at their own expense for more than two years. The placement included the summer months. The parents and their attorney communicated with the school district during this time, and rejected the IEPs proposed by the school district for the two years. Shortly thereafter, the parents requested an IDEA hearing, seeking tuition reimbursement for both years. An administrative hearing officer found that the IEP proposed by the school district for the first year placement had been inappropriate, but that the proposed second year placement was appropriate. However, because the parents had not requested a hearing until May of the first school year, the parents were only entitled to tuition reimbursement through the end of summer session of the first year. The parents sought judicial review in the U.S. District Court for the District of Connecticut.

The parents challenged the constitutionality of the Connecticut statute that limited a hearing officer's power to award tuition reimbursement. The court held that nothing in the statute prohibited a hearing officer from awarding more reimbursement than the minimum amount prescribed by law. To the extent that the statute exceeded IDEA minimal standards, it was permissible as not in conflict with the IDEA. Where state law standards are higher than those of federal law, the state law is not subject to federal preemption. It was also permissible for the state law to mandate partial reimbursement, allow for possible total reimbursement and prohibit a hearing officer from denying reimbursement. However, the district court had power to exercise its equitable discretion. It determined that because the parents had fully alerted the school district of their dissatisfaction with the proposed placement, they were entitled to tuition reimbursement from the time of placement through the end of summer term of the first year. *Ivan P. v. Westport Bd. of Educ.*, 865 F.Supp. 74 (D.Conn.1994).

A South Carolina ninth-grader with a learning disability attended special education classes. Her parents disagreed with the individualized education program (IEP) established by their public school district. The IEP called for mainstreaming in regular education classes for most subjects. The student's parents requested a due process hearing under the IDEA. Meanwhile, they unilaterally placed the student in a private school. The hearing officer held that the IEP was adequate. After the student raised her reading comprehension three full grades in one year at the private school, the parents sued the school district for tuition reimbursement. The U.S. District Court for the District of South Carolina held that the educational program and achievement goals of the proposed IEP were "wholly inadequate" under the IDEA and that even though the private school did not comply with all IDEA requirements, it provided the student with an excellent education that complied with IDEA substantive requirements. It held that the parents were entitled to tuition reimbursement, a result that was upheld by the U.S. Court of Appeals, Fourth Circuit. The school district appealed to the U.S. Supreme Court.

The Supreme Court held that the failure of the school district to provide an appropriate placement entitled the parents to tuition reimbursement by the school district, even though the private school was not on any state list of approved schools. This was because the education provided to the student was determined by the district court to be appropriate. Moreover, South Carolina did not release a list of approved schools to the public. Under the IDEA, parents had a right to unilaterally place children in private schools. To recover private school tuition costs, parents must show that the placement proposed by the school district violates the IDEA, and that the private school placement is appropriate. The Supreme Court upheld the lower court decisions in favor of the parents. *Florence County School Dist. Four v. Carter*, 114 S.Ct. 361, 126 L.Ed.2d 284 (1993).

The U.S. Supreme Court ruled that the parents of a child with a disability did not waive their claim for reimbursement of the expenses involved in unilaterally placing their child in a private school during the pendency of proceedings to review the child's IEP. This case involved a learning disabled child who was placed in a public school special education program against the wishes of his parents. The parents requested a due process hearing and, prior to the resolution of their complaint, placed their child in a private residential school recommended by specialists. The parents then sought reimbursement for their expenses. The U.S. Court of Appeals, First Circuit, found the IDEA provision against changing a child's placement during administrative proceedings to be "directory" rather than "mandatory." It decided that the "status quo" provision did not bar claims for reimbursement. The Supreme Court subsequently held that to bar reimbursement claims in cases of unilateral parent placement was contrary to the IDEA, which favors proper interim placements for disabled children. The Court declared, however, that parents who unilaterally change a child's placement during the pendency of proceedings do so at their own financial risk. If the courts ultimately determine that a child's IEP is appropriate, the parents are barred from obtaining reimbursement for any interim period in which their child's placement violated the IDEA provision. The Supreme Court affirmed the appellate court ruling. *Burlington School Comm. v. Dept. of Educ.*, 471 U.S. 359, 105 S.Ct. 1996, 85 L.Ed.2d 385 (1985).

A Tennessee student who attended regular education classes underwent a series of tests to determine whether he suffered from any disability. The tests revealed that he suffered from a neurological impairment that disrupted his ability to process auditory information and to engage in normal thinking and language skills. Although the student had an IQ of 130, he was disabled within the meaning of the IDEA. The student's school district conducted a multidisciplinary team meeting and agreed to develop an IEP after the student selected his classes for the next term. However, the student's parents unilaterally enrolled him in a private school in Illinois and advised his public school representatives that the private school was the only appropriate placement for his needs. The parents also requested private school tuition reimbursement. The parents then commenced an administrative hearing at which the administrative law judge approved the public school placement and denied the parents' request for tuition reimbursement. The U.S. District Court for the Eastern District of Tennessee affirmed the administrative decision and the parents appealed to the U.S. Court of Appeals, Sixth Circuit. The court of appeals rejected the parents' argument that the Tennessee Special Education Statute mandated a higher level of services than that required by the IDEA. The state law predated the IDEA and there was no evidence of a legislative intent beyond remedying the state's past inadequacies in special education. The proposed IEP did not violate the parents' procedural rights and was reasonably calculated to enable the student to receive educational benefits. The proposed public school placement was therefore the least restrictive appropriate placement. Accordingly, the parents were not entitled to tuition reimbursement for the private school placement. *Doe v. Bd. of Educ. of Tullahoma City Schools*, 9 F.3d 455 (6th Cir.1993).

VI. COMPENSATORY EDUCATION

Compensatory education is the belated provision of necessary educational or related services to a student with a disability to which the student was entitled, but which the education agency failed to provide. Compensatory education is awarded to some students who are over the statutory age of entitlement (usually this is 18) to prohibit education agencies from indefinitely delaying the provision of necessary services until the student is beyond school age.

A New Hampshire special education regulation requires school districts to either propose an IEP that is acceptable to the parents of the student or initiate administrative proceedings in order to resolve an impasse in the IEP process. Parents of a special education student newly placed in a New Hampshire school district complained that he was regressing academically. After he suffered a seizure at home, the parents removed him from school. Except for two brief evaluation placements, the student did not receive educational services for the next two years. During this time, the district and parents failed to resolve the placement issue. The parties finally reached agreement on a public school placement, where the student remained until he reached the age of 21. The parents contended that the student was entitled to two years of compensatory education under both the IDEA and the state regulation because the district had allegedly deprived him of an education during the two-year gap in his school attendance. They claimed that the district's failure to initiate administrative proceedings violated the New Hampshire regulation and the IDEA. An administrative hearing officer determined that the parents had unnecessarily delayed filing a complaint and that their claim for compensatory education was barred under the legal doctrine of laches, a doctrine that bars recovery if the other party is unduly prejudiced by the delaying party's inaction. The U.S. District Court for the District of New Hampshire agreed, but on appeal, the U.S. Court of Appeals, First Circuit, reversed. On remand, the district court ruled for the parents. The school district appealed for a second time to the First Circuit Court of Appeals.

The court of appeals determined that IDEA claims for compensatory education were similar to civil rights actions such as 42 U.S.C. § 1983. In such cases, the U.S. Supreme Court has expressed a preference for borrowing state limitations on personal injury actions as the most appropriate limitations periods. Because the parents' claim was within the New Hampshire statute of limitations for personal injury, the claim was not barred. The court also rejected the district's argument that the claim should be barred under the doctrine of laches. This was because the district failed to show that it had been prejudiced by the delay in bringing suit. The district had clearly violated the New Hampshire regulation and IDEA by failing to file an administrative complaint. The court affirmed the district court's judgment for the parents. *Murphy v. Timberlane Regional School Dist.*, 22 F.3d 1186 (1st Cir.1994).

On remand to the district court, the parents requested a contempt citation against the school district for failing to provide compensatory education services in violation of the court's prior order. The court determined that the school district had failed to present an appropriate alternative compensatory education program to the IEP proposed by the student's parents. The school district had intentionally and in bad faith prevented the IEP team from agreeing on an appropriate placement. It had failed to present or approve an appropriate education program and had deprived the student of compensatory education services to which he was entitled for over one year prior to the present order. Accordingly, the student was entitled to an equivalent additional period of education services. The court threatened the school district with criminal contempt sanctions for failure to comply with its order. *Murphy v. Timberlane Regional School Dist.*, 855 F.Supp. 498 (D.N.H.1994).

A Washington student experienced behavior problems and was evaluated for special education services as he entered the seventh grade. The student's school district identified him as having a learning disability in mathematics and enrolled him in a special math class. The student's behavior problems continued as his family moved in and out of the district several times. As a result, his placement had to be changed, his behavior problems persisted, and the district suspended him a number of times. Although the student's mother had actually turned down special education services offered by the school district, the family obtained an attorney to appeal a long-term suspension of the student and subsequently argued that he was entitled to an appropriate IEP. The district agreed to lift the long-term suspension and conducted a multidisciplinary evaluation. An IEP meeting was held at which the parties agreed upon half-day placement of the student in regular junior high classes with the balance of the day spent in special programs. Although the student successfully completed the school year, his parents contested the following year's IEP. An administrative hearing officer dismissed the parents' appeal and ordered the district to hold a new IEP meeting. The parents filed a lawsuit against the district in the U.S. District Court for the Western District of Washington, which entered summary judgment for the school district. The parents appealed to the U.S. Court of Appeals, Ninth Circuit.

On appeal, the parents noted that the district should be required to provide compensatory education to remedy the gaps in the student's educational experience. They claimed that the district's suspension guidelines violated federal law by allowing up to 15 days of suspension during a school year. The court observed that the student had since graduated and compensatory education was no longer a remedy. It was unnecessary at this point. The district guidelines were appropriate because they required a multidisciplinary meeting pursuant to each individual suspension action. Because the guidelines were lawful, the parents were not entitled to an injunction against enforcement. The court also denied an award of attorney fees to the parents because they could not be considered prevailing parties under the IDEA. *Parents of Student W. v. Puyallup School Dist. No. 3*, 31 F.3d 1489 (9th Cir.1994).

An emotionally disturbed Massachusetts student with profound hearing loss and speech deficiencies participated in a residential and educational program for multiply disabled students at a school for the blind. However, his placement was terminated due to his aggressive behavior. His parents became dissatisfied with his later placement in a private facility and unilaterally removed him from school for care at home by two 24-hour attendants. When the student was 19 years old, his mother requested a due process hearing before the state special education appeals board to review her claim that the school district had failed to make an appropriate placement. The hearing officer ordered the district to create a home-based program for the student but deferred making any decision on the student's right to receive compensatory education. The appeals board then granted a motion for reconsideration by the school during which it proposed placement in a residential facility in Texas. It ordered the school district to prepare an IEP calling for placement in the residential facility. The parents filed a lawsuit against the district, state education department and other defendants in the U.S. District Court for the District of Massachusetts, which granted a motion by the state education department to dismiss the lawsuit. The parents appealed to the U.S. Court of Appeals, First Circuit.

On appeal, the state and other defendants argued that the case was moot because the IEP at issue had expired more than five years previously, and because the student was now 27 years old and beyond the age of his entitlement for IDEA services. The parents argued that if the student could show that the state and school district had failed to provide him with a free appropriate education during the relevant time period, he was still entitled to compensatory services even though he was older than the statutory age limit. The court agreed with the parents, stating that a student who failed to receive appropriate services was entitled to compensatory education at a later time to remedy past deprivations. Compensatory education could be awarded to students over the age of 21 and the student should receive an opportunity to show that he had been denied his right to a free appropriate education. The case was reversed and remanded to the district court for consideration of this issue and to consider whether there should be any requirement to exhaust administrative remedies. *Pihl v. Mass. Dept. of Educ.*, 9 F.3d 184 (1st Cir.1993).

VII. DISCRIMINATION

The **Americans with Disabilities Act (ADA), 42 U.S.C. § 12101, *et seq.*, and § 504 of the Rehabilitation Act of 1973, 29 U.S.C. § 794, are federal statutes that prohibit educational institutions from discriminating against persons with disabilities. Both statutes require schools and their employees** to make reasonable accommodations for qualified individuals with disabilities, but no institution is required to lower its academic standards in order to do so. The Rehabilitation Act was the statute construed by the courts as prohibiting the exclusion of students with contagious diseases from public school attendance if they were otherwise qualified to attend and did not present a risk of harm to themselves or others. A line of federal courts applied this rule to students with HIV. See *Martinez v. School Bd. of Hillsboro County*, 861 F.2d 1502 (11th Cir.1988), 711 F.Supp. 1066 (M.D.Fla.1989). For employment cases involving § 504 and the ADA, please see Chapter Six, Section I.H., above.

A Tennessee student attended a private school from first grade through the first semester of her senior year in high school. She maintained a high grade point average and was a member of three school athletic teams. The student developed a blood disorder during her senior year. The disease put the student at risk of spontaneous hemorrhaging and presented a risk of infection, anemia and life-threatening bleeding. The student was hospitalized and underwent surgery. The school was aware of her condition and awarded her course credit even though she missed more than 15 days of the semester. After returning to school, the student cut herself in an art class. According to later accounts by school staff members, the student became hysterical and used profanity. The principal asked the student to withdraw from the school, citing her lack of remorse for her behavior. The following day, he proposed alternatives to expulsion. The student sought a preliminary injunction against the school in the U.S. District Court for the Middle District of Tennessee.

The student claimed that she was a qualified individual with a disability under the Americans with Disabilities Act (ADA) 42 U.S.C. § 12101 *et seq.*, and § 504 of the Rehabilitation Act, 29 U.S.C. § 794. She stated that the school had discriminated against her on the basis of her disability in violation of both acts. The court agreed that the student had a disability and that she was academically qualified to continue at the school. An expert witness for the student submitted evidence that an individual with her condition could be expected to react to an accident in an exaggerated manner. The school's failure to recognize and accommodate this reaction by "blind adherence" to its disciplinary standards resulted in violations of the ADA and § 504. According to the court, discrimination could be found in the form of the rigid application of rules and policies which unreasonably excluded an otherwise qualified individual from receiving the benefits of an educational institution. The student was entitled to a preliminary injunction prohibiting her expulsion. The court retained jurisdiction of the case for the remainder of the school year. *Thomas by and through Thomas v. Davidson Academy*, 846 F.Supp. 611 (M.D.Tenn.1994).

Three students with hearing impairments required the use of sign-language interpreters in their classrooms. The Nebraska school district which they attended provided a modified SEE-II system. However, the students used strict SEE-II signing systems at home, and their parents made numerous requests to use strict SEE-II systems at school. After the district refused to comply with their requests, the parents filed an administrative complaint with the Nebraska Department of

Education, where they alleged that the modified signing system did not provide their children with an adequate individualized special education program. The hearing officer held for the school district, but imposed on it the requirement to develop IEPs for each student that called for interpreters during both academic and nonacademic activities. The parents appealed to the U.S. District Court for the District of Nebraska, which affirmed the administrative decision. The parents appealed to the U.S. Court of Appeals, Eighth Circuit.

On appeal, the parents renewed their argument that the IDEA and ADA required the district to provide their signing system of choice, rather than the one selected by the school district. They argued that the use of the modified SEE-II system amounted to failure to develop an appropriate IEP. They also claimed that the district violated the Americans with Disabilities Act (ADA) by depriving them of access to educational programs and discriminating against them. The court of appeals disagreed. There was no requirement under the IDEA for a school district to maximize the educational potential of each student. Parents and students were not entitled to compel a school district to provide a specific signing system of choice as a related service. Although ADA regulations required a public entity to provide an auxiliary aid or service of choice to an individual with disabilities, the public entity was allowed to demonstrate that another effective means of communication existed. The school district had complied with the ADA by providing the modified SEE-II system as an effective means of communication. The court affirmed the district court's decision. *Petersen v. Hastings Pub. Schools*, 31 F.3d 705 (8th Cir.1994).

A New York student was identified as a gifted child with dyslexia. He had excellent test scores in mathematics but had problems reading. He attended private schools for two years, but returned to the public school system through the tenth grade. During that year, his parents obtained a private testing center evaluation containing a number of instructional recommendations including tutorial support, the use of tape recorded lectures and the provision of other written and recorded materials. The school district agreed to incorporate some of the recommendations into the student's IEP, but deleted many of them. The parents initiated an IDEA hearing, but stated that they were not ready to proceed on two occasions, resulting in dismissal. One day prior to a rescheduled hearing date, the parents filed a lawsuit in the U.S. District Court for the Eastern District of New York, seeking relief under the IDEA and also alleging violations of the Americans with Disabilities Act (ADA), 42 U.S.C. § 1983 and Title VII of the Civil Rights Act of 1964. The court granted a temporary restraining order in favor of the parents, then considered the district's argument that the parents had failed to exhaust their administrative remedies under the IDEA.

The parents argued that the IDEA's exhaustion requirement did not apply to their ADA and Title VII complaints. The ADA expressly allowed the filing of a lawsuit without resorting to any administrative remedies. The court stated that the IDEA administrative exhaustion requirement extended to the ADA, § 1983 and Title VII complaints in this case because the parents were actually seeking relief that was completely obtainable under the IDEA. The parents had merely restated their claims for an insufficient IEP as civil rights violations to avoid application of the IDEA exhaustion requirement. The court held that this contravened the intent of the IDEA by depriving the educational agency of the opportunity to correct its own alleged errors before resort to the courts. The court also rejected the parents' argument that because the student was "gifted," he was not disabled. Dyslexia was specifically listed as a learning disability in the IDEA. The court dismissed the lawsuit for lack of jurisdiction. *Hope v. Cortines*, 872 F.Supp. 14 (E.D.N.Y.1995).

CHAPTER THIRTEEN

PRIVATE SCHOOLS

I.   PRIVATE SCHOOL EMPLOYMENT

State laws governing public school tenure are inapplicable to private schools and colleges. Private schools typically grant tenure according to their own employment policies. State and federal antidiscrimination laws apply to private schools employing at least 15 employees, unless the school has a bona fide reason for using discriminatory practices on the grounds of religion.

A.   Employment Discrimination

In a decision affecting private religious educational institutions, the U.S. Supreme Court ruled that such institutions may discriminate on the basis of religion in hiring for nonreligious jobs involving nonprofit activities. The case involved a man who worked at a Mormon church-operated gymnasium for 16 years. After being discharged for failing to meet several church-related requirements for employment, he sued the church in a U.S. district court alleging religious discrimination in violation of Title VII. The church moved for dismissal claiming that § 702 of Title VII exempted it from liability. The man claimed that if § 702 allowed religious employers to discriminate on religious grounds in hiring for nonreligious jobs, then Title VII would be in violation of the Establishment Clause of the First Amendment. The district court ruled for the man and the church appealed directly to the U.S. Supreme Court.

The question before the Court was whether applying § 702 to the secular nonprofit activities of religious organizations violated the Establishment Clause. Section 702 provides that Title VII "shall not apply ... to a religious corporation, association [or] educational institution ... with respect to the employment of individuals of a particular religion to perform work connected with the carrying on by such [an organization] of its activities." In ruling for the church the Supreme Court applied the three-part test set out in *Lemon v. Kurtzman*, (see § VI of this chapter). The Supreme Court reversed the district court's decision and upheld the right of nonprofit religious employers to impose religious conditions for employment in nonreligious positions involving nonprofit activities. *Corp. of the Presiding Bishop of the Church of Jesus Christ of Latter-Day Saints v. Amos*, 483 U.S. 327, 107 S.Ct. 2862, 97 L.Ed.2d 273 (1987).

An Illinois private school used a 22-step system linking teachers' salaries to work experience. It also used the system to credit new teachers for prior teaching experience. The drama teacher resigned and the school sought a replacement. However, fiscal constraints dictated that the school pay an annual salary not greater than $28,000. After the school had narrowed the field to three candidates, one of its teachers recommended that it consider the resume of a 63-year-old candidate with 30 years of experience. However, the school informed him that he qualified for a salary higher than it could afford and that his resume had been received after the final candidates had been chosen. The school interviewed three different candidates and ultimately hired a teacher with one year of experience and paid her $22,000 per year. The 63-year-old applicant filed suit against the school alleging that its hiring policy resulted in disparate impact age discrimination in violation of the Age Discrimination in Employment Act (ADEA). The district court granted summary judgment in favor of the school, and the applicant appealed to the U.S. Court of Appeals, Seventh Circuit.

The school contended that decisions made for reasons independent of age but which happen to correlate with age are not actionable under the ADEA. The court of appeals agreed, ruling that although the ADEA prevents employers from using age as a criterion for employment decisions, decisions based on criteria which merely tend to affect workers over the age of 40 more adversely than workers under 40 are not prohibited. The ADEA's "safe harbor" provision permits an employer to "observe the terms of a bona fide seniority system ... which is not a subterfuge to evade the purposes of [the ADEA's prohibitions]." Because the decision not to hire the applicant was not based on impermissible misperceptions about the competence of older workers, the school did not violate the ADEA. The holding of the district court was affirmed. *EEOC v. Francis W. Parker School*, 41 F.3d 1073 (7th Cir.1994).

A theology teacher taught exclusively religious subjects at a Colorado Roman Catholic high school associated with the Archdiocese of Denver. Although the teacher's contract had been renewed annually for 13 years, he was not offered a teaching contract for the 1993-1994 school year. The school alleged that it had declined to renew his contract because it needed fewer teachers and because his qualifications and abilities were less desirable than those of other faculty members. The teacher filed suit against the archbishop in the U.S. District Court for the District of Colorado, alleging that the school's failure to renew his contract violated the Age Discrimination in Employment Act (ADEA). The archbishop moved for summary judgment.

The archbishop contended that application of the ADEA would violate the Free Exercise and Establishment Clauses of the First Amendment to the U.S. Constitution. The district court noted that, generally, "the more pervasively religious the institution, the less religious the employee's role need be to risk First Amendment infringement." Here, not only was the school indisputably sectarian, the theology teacher's duties were exclusively religious. Consequently, the school's free exercise rights would be substantially burdened by application of the ADEA. The court also noted that the Religious Freedom Restoration Act requires that the government establish a compelling justification for burdens on religious institutions' free exercise rights. Here, the government's interest in eradicating age discrimination was not compelling in light of the church's right to hire those teaching its ecclesiastical doctrine. Finally, the court held that the Establishment Clause precluded federal court involvement in this matter. The court granted summary judgment to the Archbishop. *Powell v. Stafford*, 859 F.Supp. 1343 (D.Colo.1994).

A married female associate professor of biology was denied tenure by a New York private college, allegedly because she did not demonstrate the "outstanding quality" required by the college promotion guidelines. The biology department, the dean, the Faculty Appointments and Salary Committee and the president all refused to discuss the decision with the professor. She filed suit in the U.S. District Court for the Southern District of New York, alleging retaliation, Title VII sex discrimination, age discrimination, and violations of the Equal Pay Act. At trial, the court found that the professor was more qualified in many respects than the other candidates. The court held that the professor was in a protected class (a married woman), she was qualified for the position and she had demonstrated that the circumstances of her rejection gave rise to an inference of unlawful discrimination. Specifically, the court observed that all the other tenure candidates had less impressive qualifications and that the department had never tenured a married woman. Further, the department's use of unwritten standards which were applied to place importance on the professor's weaknesses and discount those factors in which she was strong established sex discrimination. Second, the professor established age discrimination based on the college's tenure of much younger and less qualified candidates. Third, since married women received smaller salaries than less qualified men and single women, the college had violated the Equal Pay Act. Finally, the professor's retaliation claim, based on the college's post-employment blacklisting, was beyond the scope of Title VII and was therefore dismissed. *Fisher v. Vassar College* , 852 F.Supp. 1193 (S.D.N.Y.1994).

B. Employment Practices

A private Florida school hired an art teacher under a one-year contract. The contract contained a liquidated damages clause which required the teacher to pay two months' wages if she left without the school's consent. A public school system offered the teacher a position. She then tendered her resignation to the private school. However, the private school headmaster refused to release her from the contract. The headmaster telephoned the public schools' authorities and informed them that the teacher was under contract with the private school. Pursuant to the public school system's policy not to hire teachers already under contract with another school, the offer of employment was withdrawn. Subsequently, the headmaster hired a replacement and refused to meet with the teacher. The headmaster then fired the teacher, allegedly because her tender of resignation had breached their employment contract. The private school filed suit in a Florida circuit court seeking liquidated damages for breach of contract. The teacher counterclaimed for breach of contract and intentional interference with a contractual relationship. The circuit court held for the school and the teacher appealed to the District Court of Appeal of Florida, Third District.

The teacher contended that the private school had breached its contract and had intentionally interfered with her contractual relationship with the public school. First, the court determined that the private school breached the contract by firing the teacher following its action to force withdrawal of the public school offer. The headmaster was within his rights not to release the teacher from the contract but was then obliged to comply with its terms. Second, the court found that the headmaster decided to fire the teacher only after his consultation with the public school. Thus, he was not acting out of spite and the teacher was only entitled to contract damages. The court affirmed the trial court's decision in part and reversed it in part. *Weisfeld v. Peterseil School Corp.*, 623 So.2d 515 (Fla.App.3d Dist.1993).

A Missouri Christian school employee was killed in an accident while he was at work. The school had failed to obtain liability insurance and was not approved by the state as a self-insured employer. It did not file a report with the state workers' compensation division, but instead gratuitously paid the funeral parlor used by the worker's family for their burial expenses. The school made payments to the funeral home over a period of years. Almost five years after the employee's death, but within eight months of the final payment by the school to the funeral parlor, the employee's widow and son filed a workers' compensation claim. An administrative law judge of the state workers' compensation division awarded a past due benefits amount to both the widow and the son, and a lump sum for future compensation to the employee's widow. The school appealed to the Missouri Court of Appeals.

On appeal, the Christian school argued that the workers' compensation claim was barred by the state's three-year limitation on actions. It also argued that the school's president had made the payments to the funeral home gratuitously and had done so on other occasions for deceased employees, students and parishioners. The court of appeals ruled that the statute of limitations began to run three years from the date of the last payment made under the workers' compensation act. Because the law provided for the payment of $2,000 in funeral expenses, the payments by the school had been payments under the workers' compensation act, despite the contrary intent of the school's president. The three-year limitation period applied to situations such as this one, where the employer had failed to report the death or injury as required. Otherwise, a two-year limitation period applied. The court of appeals affirmed the decision of the administrative law judge awarding past due and future compensation benefits to the son and widow. *Brown v. Ozark Christian Schools of Neosho*, 847 S.W.2d 888 (Mo.App.S.D.1993).

An elderly West Virginia woman was a Head Start teacher. The director of the Head Start program received reports indicating that the teacher had left children unattended on the playground and had spanked a child in violation of Head Start rules. During an investigation it was discovered that the teacher kept a paddle in her classroom, also in violation of school rules. The teacher was suspended on the last day of the school year. She requested a hearing to contest her suspension. A policy council meeting was held and the council voted to uphold the suspension. The teacher then appealed to the Human Rights Commission, alleging that the school and the state Equal Opportunity Council (EOC) had discriminated against her on the basis of age and handicap. The Commission ordered the teacher reinstated and ordered the EOC to cease and desist any discriminatory practices. The EOC then appealed to the Supreme Court of Appeals of West Virginia. The supreme court noted that evidence of the teacher's violations of Head Start policies was enough to convince the court that the suspension was nondiscriminatory. The court reversed the decision of the Human Rights Commission and upheld the teacher's suspension. *Mingo County EOC v. Human Rights Comm.*, 376 S.E.2d 134 (W.Va.1988).

C. Labor Relations

The courts have ruled that "pervasively religious" schools may be able to avoid any obligation to bargain with employees under the National Labor

Relations Act (NLRA). This exception to the NLRA's coverage is based upon First Amendment religious freedom considerations. Managerial employees are not protected by the NLRA.

The right of employees of a Catholic school system to form a collective bargaining unit was successfully challenged in a case decided by the U.S. Supreme Court. In this case, the unions were certified by the NLRB as bargaining units but the diocese refused to bargain with them. The Court said that the religion clauses of the U.S. Constitution, which require religious organizations to finance their educational systems without governmental aid, also free the religious organizations of the inhibiting effect and impact of unionization of their teachers. The Court agreed with the employers' contention that the threshold act of certification of the union would necessarily alter and infringe upon the religious character of parochial schools, since this would mean that the bishop would no longer be the sole repository of authority as required by church law. Instead he would have to share some decisionmaking with the union. This, said the Court, violated the religion clauses of the U.S. Constitution. *NLRB v. Catholic Bishop of Chicago*, 440 U.S. 490, 99 S.Ct. 1313, 59 L.Ed.2d 533 (1979).

In *NLRB v. Yeshiva University,* the U.S. Supreme Court held that in certain circumstances, faculty members at private educational institutions could be considered managerial employees. Yeshiva's faculty association had petitioned the NLRB seeking certification as bargaining agent for all faculty members. The NLRB granted certification to the association but the university refused to bargain with it. After a U.S. circuit court declined to enforce the NLRB's order that the university bargain with the association, the NLRB appealed to the U.S. Supreme Court, which upheld the appeals court. The Supreme Court's ruling was based on its conclusion that Yeshiva's faculty decided school curriculum, standards, tuition rates and admissions. The Court noted that its decision applied only to schools that were "like Yeshiva" and not to schools where the faculty exercised less control. Schools where faculty members do not exercise binding managerial discretion do not fall within the scope of the managerial employee exclusion. *NLRB v. Yeshiva Univ.*, 444 U.S. 672, 100 S.Ct. 856, 63 L.Ed.2d 115 (1980).

An assistant teacher worked for the Connecticut Institute for the Blind under a collective bargaining agreement governed by the federal Labor Management Relations Act (LMRA), 29 U.S.C. § 185. The institute fired the assistant teacher during her six-month probationary period after a student sprayed himself with Mace from the assistant teacher's purse. The assistant teacher appealed the dismissal and was reinstated. However, the director of personnel at the institute suspected that the assistant teacher had written an anonymous letter reporting child abuse. He conducted an investigation. Although he did not consult a professional handwriting analyst, the director determined that the assistant teacher had written the letter and again terminated her employment. The assistant teacher contacted her collective bargaining organization. At a grievance meeting, the assistant teacher agreed to allow an independent handwriting expert to evaluate the subject letter and agreed that if the letter was proven to be hers, dismissal would become permanent. When a court-qualified handwriting expert reported that the assistant teacher had written the letter, the collective bargaining organization grievance committee denied the grievance. The assistant teacher filed a lawsuit in the U.S. District Court for the District of Connecticut, alleging ten claims arising from her employment termination.

The district court observed that LMRA § 301 preempted state law complaints which were "substantially dependent upon analysis of the terms of an agreement made between the parties in a labor contract." Section 301 did not preempt the assistant teacher's wrongful discharge claim because the claim alleged an important violation of public policy: in this case, the reporting of possible child abuse. Because the labor agreement was governed by the LMRA, it preempted state law complaints for breach of contract and promissory estoppel. The institute and director were entitled to summary judgment against the assistant teacher's intentional infliction of emotional distress claim because she had not alleged extreme and outrageous conduct. However, summary judgment was inappropriate concerning her negligent infliction of emotional distress claim. The institute and director were also entitled to summary judgment on the assistant teacher's libel and slander complaints. *Ziobro v. Connecticut Inst. for the Blind*, 818 F.Supp. 497 (D.Conn.1993).

A Minnesota Catholic high school was created to "provide a well rounded quality education in a Christian context." A majority of the students were Catholic but only teachers of religion were required to be Catholic. The students were required to take one religion course every trimester, and had to attend the monthly mass. The school was college preparatory and taught a wide variety of secular subjects. It fulfilled all accreditation requirements of the State Board of Education and received public subsidies on behalf of its students. The school was run by a nonprofit corporation composed of parents of the children attending the school. The corporation was governed by a 15 member board of education which was appointed by various groups interested in the school. Generally, the board had responsibility to address staff grievances but also set school policy, budgets, and established guidelines for teachers' salaries. However, the teachers were actually under contract with the school administration. The administration was not bound to collectively bargain nor was it bound by the board's determination as to salary disputes. In 1989, the high school teachers federation petitioned the state Bureau of Mediation Services to determine an appropriate labor organization to represent certain lay employees at the school in collective bargaining procedures. The bureau conducted an election and a majority of the staff voted in favor of representation by the Minnesota Federation of Teachers. The bureau certified the federation as the school's exclusive bargaining unit. The court of appeals reversed the bureau's decision to certify the federation on constitutional grounds. The bureau and the federation appealed to the Minnesota Supreme Court which held that the unionization of private school teachers under the MLRA was constitutional even under the more stringent requirements of the freedom of conscience clause in the Minnesota Constitution. The supreme court reversed the court of appeals' decision. *Hill-Murray Federation v. Hill Murray H.S.*, 487 N.W.2d 857 (Minn.1992).

II. STATE AND FEDERAL REGULATION

Mandatory reporting statutes, laws requiring minimum curriculum requirements and teacher qualifications, and compulsory attendance laws have been upheld by courts as a legitimate exercise of the strong public interest in education.

A. Licensing, Certification and Compulsory Attendance Statutes

A private Washington university with a branch campus in Oregon was accredited by the Northwest Association of Schools and Colleges (NASC). Following NASC accreditation, the Oregon Office of Educational Policy and Planning (OEPP) continued to review non-Oregon schools every three years. The statute provided that "no school ... shall confer ... any degree ... without first having submitted the requirements for such degree to the [OEPP] and having obtained the approval of the director." However, pursuant to § 2(c) of the 1979 amendment to the statute, Oregon schools that are in good standing with the NASC are exempt from OEPP review. The private Washington university filed suit in an Oregon circuit court, seeking a declaration that this statute, which exempted only Oregon schools from OEPP review, violated the Commerce Clause. The circuit court held for the university and severed a portion of the amendment but upheld the remaining parts. On appeal, the court of appeals affirmed, but invalidated the exemption in its entirety. The Oregon Supreme Court allowed the university's petition for review solely on the issue of remedy.

The university contended that the entire 1979 amendment had been improperly invalidated. The supreme court disagreed, ruling that the statute as severed was not capable of being executed in accordance with legislative intent. The legislature had intended both to continue the exemption from OEPP authority for Oregon schools that were members of the NASC and to remove the exemption from OEPP authority for out-of-state schools, even if those schools were NASC members. However, the dominant intent of the amendment was to insure that Oregon branch campuses of the out-of-state schools had the same level of faculty and facilities as their main campuses. Because a partial severance would subject these out-of-state schools to lesser scrutiny, the court ordered the 1979 amendment severed in its entirety. The court of appeals' ruling was affirmed. *City University v. Office of Educ. Policy*, 885 P.2d 701 (Or.1994).

A Michigan couple became dissatisfied with their public school system and subsequently began to home school their four children. The parents taught the required classes for five hours each day during the school year. Individualized curricula were submitted to the superintendent and standardized tests showed that three of the four children performed at or above their grade level. The children allegedly had "frequent contact" with certified area teachers through personal visits and conference telephone calls. The state filed suit in a Michigan trial court alleging that the home schooling violated Michigan's compulsory attendance laws. The court found numerous violations, most notably the children's insufficient contact with certified teachers. On appeal, the Michigan Court of Appeals affirmed, holding that the parents did not have a fundamental right to direct their children's education and that the parents were not entitled to a hearing before being prosecuted under the compulsory attendance law. The parents appealed to the Supreme Court of Michigan.

The parents first argued that they had a fundamental right to direct their children's education. Therefore, they argued, the compulsory attendance law had to be "necessary to a compelling state interest." The supreme court disagreed, noting that parents had a fundamental right only to determine their children's religious future. Only those types of First Amendment concerns required that laws conform to the above standard. Here, the parents merely voiced disapproval with the education of their children, and their removal from the public schools was expressly for nonreligious reasons. Consequently, the compulsory attendance law requiring that the children be educated by certified teachers only had to be "rationally related to a legitimate state end." The court noted that many other states had similar requirements and had concluded that certification bore a sufficient relationship to ensuring that all teachers, including parents, had minimum qualifications. However, the court concluded that given that the parents were required to comply with the Private and Parochial Schools Act, they were also entitled to a hearing as to whether they had complied with private school requirements. *People v. Bennett,* 501 N.W.2d 106 (Mich.1993).

North Dakota has upheld the state education law's requirement that home-schooled children be taught by certified teachers. In the case, Christian parents believed that God had given them responsibility for the education of their children. Their religious convictions required that they teach their three children at home. The state education law required that nonpublic schools employ only state certified teachers. It also provided that nonpublic schools be approved by local school boards. The parents were not certified teachers and their home school was not approved by the local school board. The parents were convicted of violating the compulsory school attendance law and they appealed to the North Dakota Supreme Court. The supreme court upheld the convictions. The North Dakota Constitution authorized the state to regulate both public and private schools. Although the parents had a sincerely held religious belief which was burdened by the law, the state had a compelling interest in the regulation of nonpublic schools which justified the burden. This overcame the parents' free exercise claim. The certification requirement was the least restrictive means of ensuring that the state's interest in the education of its children was satisfied. The convictions were affirmed. *State v. Anderson,* 427 N.W.2d 316 (N.D.1988).

Two fundamentalist Baptist church schools challenged Iowa's compulsory attendance laws. A federal district court upheld the laws and the church schools appealed. The U.S. Court of Appeals, Eighth Circuit, substantially upheld the ruling against the church schools but remanded the case to the district court. On remand, the district court was to rule on the effect of Iowa's newly adopted regulations concerning the term "equivalent instruction." At the time of the district court trial the Iowa Education Code required school attendance for children over seven and under 16 years of age. It provided that "[i]n lieu of such attendance such child may attend upon equivalent instruction by a certified teacher elsewhere." Because "equivalent instruction" was not defined, the church schools had successfully argued that the statute was unconstitutionally vague.

The district court noted that the new state regulations specified that the children must be taught the minimum curriculum as listed by a certified teacher, and must fulfill specified minimum attendance requirements. The regulations further provided that the teacher had to allocate institutional time as appropriate to the needs of the pupil. The local school board had the annual duty of determining whether these children were in fact receiving equivalent instruction by reviewing coursework, test results or by any other reasonable method. In view of the regulations the district court ruled that "equivalent instruction" was no longer unconstitutionally vague. The new regulations struck a correct balance between freedom of religion and the need for state regulation of education. They gave private schools fair warning of what was prohibited. They also provided explicit standards for enforcement. *Fellowship Baptist Church v. Benton*, 678 F.Supp. 213 (S.D.Iowa 1988).

B. Federal Income Taxation

Section 501(c)(3) of the Internal Revenue Code provides that "corporations... organized and operated exclusively for religious, charitable ... or educational purposes" are entitled to tax exempt status. The Internal Revenue Service routinely granted tax exemptions under § 501(c)(3) to private schools regardless of whether they had racially discriminatory admissions policies. In 1970, however, the IRS concluded that it could no longer grant tax exempt status to racially discriminatory private schools because such schools were not "charitable" within the meaning of § 501(c)(3). Two private colleges whose racial admissions policies were rooted in their interpretations of the Bible sued to prevent the IRS from interpreting the federal tax laws in this manner. The Supreme Court rejected the colleges' challenge and upheld the IRS's interpretation. The Court's ruling was based on what it perceived as the strong public policy against racial discrimination in education. Because the colleges were operating in violation of that public policy, the colleges could not be considered to be "charitable" under § 501(c)(3). Thus they were ineligible for tax exemptions.The court held that the denial of an exemption did not impermissibly burden the colleges' alleged religious freedom interest in practicing racial discrimination. *Bob Jones Univ. v. United States*, 461 U.S. 574, 103 S.Ct. 2017, 76 L.Ed.2d 157 (1983).

Parents of black public school children sought a federal court order requiring the IRS to adopt more stringent standards for determining whether private schools had racially discriminatory admissions policies. The black parents claimed that the IRS standards were too lax, and that certain private schools were practicing racial discrimination and were nevertheless obtaining tax exemptions. The Supreme Court dismissed the parents' claims, ruling that the parents and children had shown no injury to themselves as a result of the allegedly lax IRS standards. None of the children had sought enrollment at the private schools involved, and the abstract stigma attached to living in a community with racially discriminatory private schools was also insufficient to show actual injury. Further, the parents' theory that denial of exempt status to such schools would result in greater white student enrollment in area public schools, and hence result in a greater degree of public school integration, was only speculation. *Allen v. Wright*, 468 U.S. 737, 104 S.Ct. 3315, 82 L.Ed.2d 556 (1984).

C. State and Local Taxation

A New Hampshire camp school program offered courses in reading, writing, vocabulary, Latin, French, Spanish, English, mathematics, and the sciences for seven weeks each summer. The students were required to take three academic subjects from over 30 faculty members drawn from recognized independent schools. They were tested regularly, given weekly and final academic reports, and some earned credit toward their high school degrees. The program also included a variety of recreational activities such as sporting events and camping. The majority of faculty members resided on school grounds. Seventeen acres of the school's property contained buildings, 28.5 acres were vacant and 4.4 acres were in the process of being developed for future faculty housing. The camp school sought abatement of real property taxes paid to the town in which it was located. A New Hampshire trial court granted a limited abatement, and the town appealed to the Supreme Court of New Hampshire.

A New Hampshire statute exempts from taxation land and structures of schools organized to carry on their principal activities of educating. However, land and buildings not used directly for expressed educational purposes are not exempt. Here, the camp school's purposes were educational. Specifically, it offered an intensive academic program, standard textbooks were used, and the instructors were qualified teachers. Further, the statute requires that the land be directly (not exclusively) used for educational purposes. However, the court held that the 28.5 acres of vacant land and the 4.4 acres designated as the future site of faculty housing were neither occupied by the school nor used directly for educational purposes. Thus, only the 17 acres of land used for educational purposes were exempt from taxation. The holding of the trial court was affirmed in part and reversed in part. *Wolfeboro Camp School v. Wolfeboro*, 642 A.2d 928 (N.H.1994).

A Pennsylvania nonprofit college owned a large house designed for entertaining. The college's vice-president for alumni development lived in the house rent free and was not charged for utilities. The house was used for meetings, special events, receptions and to entertain potential donors from whom one-third of the college's yearly income was derived. These events were allegedly an important part of building trust with major donors. The Delaware County Board of Assessment Appeals determined that the house was not exempt from state real estate tax. On appeal by the college, a Pennsylvania trial court reversed, finding the house exempt from taxation. A local public school district appealed the finding to the Commonwealth Court of Pennsylvania. The commonwealth court stated that the college was not required to prove that the property was absolutely necessary to its needs for the exemption to apply. Rather, it was required to show only that it had a reasonable necessity for the property. Here, the vice-president was required to live in the house, to use it to cultivate personal relationships with donors, and to utilize it for numerous college functions. These uses were directly related to the proper functions of the college. Consequently, the trial court did not err in concluding that the vice-president's house was tax exempt. *In re Swarthmore College,* 643 A.2d 1152 (Pa.Cmwlth.1994).

An Ohio woman was hired as a secretary by a rabbinical seminary. Her position did not entail any religious duties. The seminary ordained rabbis and offered other religious graduate programs. It was affiliated with the Union of American Hebrew Congregations. This organization facilitated the ordination process and the rabbis' subsequent movement among congregations. Less than a year after the secretary was hired, her position was eliminated and she was discharged. The secretary's application for unemployment compensation benefits was denied. The unemployment compensation board and an Ohio trial court affirmed the decision. The secretary then appealed to the Court of Appeals of Ohio. The issue on appeal was whether the rabbinical seminary was operated primarily for religious purposes and was therefore exempt from state unemployment compensation laws. The secretary contended that since the seminary's employees were subject to income and social security tax and some students received federal financial aid, the school was predominately a nonreligious institution. The court of appeals disagreed. It held that the school was a pervasively religious institution. Therefore, the secretary's position was not covered employment under state law and she was not entitled to collect unemployment compensation. The court also noted that the school was not obligated to notify a potential employee of the school's exempt status. The trial court decision was affirmed. *Bach v. Steinbacher,* 609 N.E.2d 607 (Ohio App.1st Dist.1992).

III. PRIVATE SCHOOL STUDENT RIGHTS

Private school students do not enjoy the same level of constitutional protection as the courts have granted to public school students. Courts have demonstrated little interest in interfering with private school academic and disciplinary policies.

A. Admissions, Attendance and School Policies

A New York Jewish theological seminary changed its admission policies after a vote by a quorum of the faculty assembly. The new admission policy allowed the seminary to admit female rabbinical candidates. A tenured professor found this new policy unconscionable to his personal religious beliefs. The professor took a leave of absence and ultimately resigned. He then sued the seminary claiming that this change in policy constituted religious discrimination against him in breach of his employment contract with the seminary. The trial court dismissed the complaint and the professor appealed to the New York Supreme Court, Appellate Division. The appellate division court held that the professor failed to state a claim for breach of his employment agreement and did not prove the existence of any contractual duty on the part of the seminary to refrain from changing its admissions policies or from doing anything which might offend the professor's religious beliefs. The court also held that considering the seminary's change in policy would be an impermissible interference in religious matters by the court. The appellate court affirmed the trial court's decision and dismissed the case. *Faur v. Jewish Theological Seminary of America*, 536 N.Y.S.2d 516 (A.D.2d Dept.1989).

B. Breach of Contract

Two New York residents registered for a Pascal computer programming course at an area private university. The university catalogue and the class schedule noted that there were no prerequisites for the course and their advisor assured them that it did not require an advanced math background. The professor assigned readings from a course textbook designed for computer science majors, scientists and engineers. He also assigned problems requiring an extensive math background. The students' advisor instructed them to keep working on the admittedly difficult problems. The professor attempted unsuccessfully to explain the problems during the first five class periods. However, the students withdrew from the class in frustration. They were unable to contact their advisor for nearly three weeks, at which time they were no longer eligible for any type of tuition refund. The students filed suit against the school in a New York city court, seeking relief for breach of contract, rescission, breach of fiduciary duty, educational malpractice and unfair and deceptive business practices.

The court held that the professor's use of an unsuitable textbook coupled with his inappropriate classroom examples intentionally drawn from math and science constituted breach of the college's educational contract with the students. Rescission of the contract was justified because it was unconscionable and because the students were induced to enter into the contract in reliance upon the college's gross misrepresentations. Further, the college assumed the obligations of a fiduciary when it assigned the students an advisor who made misrepresentations on which the students relied to their detriment. The court also held that the college was liable for educational malpractice, ruling that use of the improper textbook was a *per se* example of negligence, incompetence and malpractice. The school's actions also violated a New York law prohibiting deceptive business practices. The court ordered the school to reimburse the students and imposed punitive damages against it. *Andre v. Pace University*, 618 N.Y.S.2d 975 (City Ct.1994).

A Connecticut father sought admission of his daughter to a private Catholic school. She was accepted and her father and the school signed an enrollment contract. The contract provided that the father would pay two installments of $2,000 along with a nonrefundable $500 deposit. It further stated that if the contract was canceled after August 1, the full amount would become due as liquidated damages. The father subsequently informed the school, after the agreed-upon deadline, that his daughter would not attend. The school filed suit in a Connecticut trial court seeking the contract amount as liquidated damages and attorney's fees. The trial court awarded the school a reduced damage award and also reduced the amount of claimed attorney's fees. The school appealed to the Appellate Court of Connecticut. The school contended that the trial court had incorrectly refused to award the liquidated damages specified in the contract. The appellate court agreed. Since the actual damages were difficult to prove and the amount agreed upon in the liquidated damages clause was reasonable, the school was entitled to the full $4,000. The agreement was not so high that it was void as a penalty. The court also determined that the arbitrary reduction of attorney's fees was not warranted. Neither the court nor the father stated that the fees claimed by the school were excessively high. Thus, the court reversed the damages issue and remanded the case to determine reasonable attorney's fees. *St. Margaret's McTernan v. Thompson*, 627 A.2d 449 (Conn.App.1993).

An Ohio attorney enrolled his son at a private elementary school. He signed a contract with the school, agreeing to pay over $6,000 in tuition unless he notified the school by August 1 that his son was not going to attend. He sent the school a letter postmarked August 7 canceling the contract. After the attorney refused to pay, the school brought a breach of contract claim in an Ohio trial court. The trial court found for the attorney, but the Court of Appeals of Ohio reversed. The attorney then appealed to the Supreme Court of Ohio. He argued that the tuition forfeiture constituted a penalty which was against public policy. The school argued that the payment constituted valid liquidated damages. The supreme court had previously announced the test to determine the validity of contract damages. Where the parties have agreed on the amount of damages, the amount should be treated as liquidated damages and not as a penalty, if the damages would be uncertain, conscionable, and if the contract is consistent with the parties' intent. Using this test, the court concluded that the damages were not a penalty. The damages that the school would suffer were uncertain because it would be impossible to calculate the precise damages caused by the loss of one student's tuition. The contract was not unconscionable as the father was an attorney with 20 years of experience, nor was there evidence of coercion. Finally, the language of the contract fairly represented the intentions of the parties. The supreme court upheld the decision of the appellate court and held for the school. *Lake Ridge Academy v. Carney*, 613 N.E.2d 183 (Ohio 1993).

A Missouri nursing school graduated its first class of students in 1984. The school was accredited by the Missouri State Board of Nursing. It was also a "candidate for accreditation" with the North Central Association for Colleges and Schools (NCA). However, the school's brochure actually stated that the school "has ... been granted [NCA] candidacy for review status" and that "accreditation for [the school] is expected in 1983." In 1981, a letter from the student services coordinator restated the above-quoted information to the class of 1984. The students were not appraised of the NCA accreditation status prior to their graduation and the school was not formally accredited until 1987. This accreditation status did not apply retroactively to the class of 1984. Several members of the class of 1984 filed suit in a Missouri trial court, alleging that the school intentionally misrepresented its accreditation status which limited their job prospects, advanced education and future earning power. The trial court granted the school's motion for summary judgment, and the students appealed to the Missouri Court of Appeals.

The students contended that the school's affirmative statement regarding the likelihood of achieving accreditation legally bound it to disclose all material facts related to its receipt of NCA accreditation. Consequently, they argued, the school's silence on this issue was intentional misrepresentation. The court of appeals rejected the students' appeal. Although misrepresentation of a material fact by silence may amount to actionable fraud, the students failed to show that they relied on the school's allegedly fraudulent statements in enrolling or remaining enrolled in the program. Because the students failed to establish the reliance element of fraud, the court refused to address the issue of whether the school had a duty to disclose all material facts related to the anticipated accreditation. The holding of the trial court was affirmed. *Nigro v. Research College of Nursing*, 876 S.W.2d 681 (Mo.App.W.D.1994).

C. Discipline, Suspension and Expulsion

A New York medical school expelled a student based on his misrepresentations regarding the grades he previously received at another school. The student sought a formal hearing pursuant to a provision in the student handbook, but the college denied his request on the ground that the handbook was inapplicable to his situation. The student appealed to a New York trial court. The trial court directed the college to conduct a hearing concerning the student's alleged misrepresentations, and the college appealed to the New York Supreme Court, Appellate Division. The appellate division reversed, ruling that the college's decision was neither arbitrary nor capricious so as to warrant judicial intervention. The handbook was aimed at misconduct committed by an individual while a student at the medical school, not to fraudulent acts committed prior to admission to the school. Because the settled policy and practice of the school was to summarily dismiss any student who engaged in such misrepresentations, the school properly denied the student a formal hearing. The holding of the trial court was reversed. *Mitchell v. New York Medical College*, 617 N.Y.S.2d 894 (A.D.2d Dept.1994).

A female student at a Vermont private college accused a male student of rape. After conducting an investigation, the county declined to prosecute but the college pursued disciplinary steps prescribed in the college handbook for rape and for inappropriate sexual activity. The handbook provided that the student be given notice of the charges with "sufficient particularity to permit [him] to prepare to meet the charges." When the student asked the dean to clarify the charges against him, the dean allegedly told him to "concentrate on the issue of rape." The student was found not guilty of rape but guilty of engaging in inappropriate sexual activity with the female student. The college's Judicial Review Board upheld the ruling, and the student appealed to the U.S. District Court for the District of Vermont.

The court held that colleges are contractually bound to provide students with promised procedural safeguards. However, the unique relationship between college and student with respect to disciplinary proceedings precluded rigid application of contract law. Here, the college improperly deviated from its procedural obligations when it failed to notify the student prior to the hearing that there were two charges pending against him. He was never told that if he was able to rebut the rape charge, he could still be found guilty of another charge. Because the college did not state the nature of the charges with sufficient particularity to permit the student to meet them, the hearing was fundamentally unfair. However, since the inadequate notice provided the student was the only breach of the student-college contract, his case could be reheard after proper notice was given. *Fellheimer v. Middlebury College*, 869 F.Supp. 238 (D.Vt.1994).

An Ohio couple enrolled their children at a Baptist elementary school. The parents agreed to follow the school's policies. Specifically, the parents agreed to follow the prescribed grievance procedure. The procedure required the parents to consult with the teacher first, then the administrator, and finally, with the school board. While in school, the daughter was chased by two male kindergarten children. One child held her hands behind her back while the other pulled her dress up and ran his hand across her panties. Her mother complained to the administrator, and the students were given a warning. One of the boys allegedly repeated the behavior and the mother demanded that the boy be physically punished. The administrator contacted the boy's parents and, with their consent, "paddled" the boy. Another student allegedly spit on her daughter and the mother again confronted the administrator. The administrator asked the parents to withdraw their children from the school. The parents filed suit in an Ohio court, alleging that they had been unlawfully dismissed. The court granted summary judgment to the school and the parents appealed to the Court of Appeals of Ohio.

The parents contended that the students' dismissal was arbitrary, capricious, and unlawful. The court of appeals disagreed, ruling that private school boards have broad discretion to meet their educational goals. Here, the administrator fairly and promptly addressed the parents' concerns. Conversely, the parents failed to observe the grievance procedures or the student handbook. The mother had also verbally abused the administrator. Thus, the students had been removed legally from the school for failing to comply with the admissions policies and the handbook. The school did not abuse its discretion in enforcing these policies nor did it violate a contractual agreement with the parents. The judgment of the trial court was affirmed. *Allen v. Casper,* 622 N.E.2d 367 (Ohio App.8th Dist.1993).

D.   Constitutional Liability

In order to impute liability to a private entity under a constitutional theory or under state or federal antidiscrimination legislation, such as 42 U.S.C. § 1983, the court must find that the institution is a state actor. This is possible where the private school performs duties normally associated with government entities, and where government and private school cooperation is so close that it is appropriate to attribute government action to the school. Section One of the Civil Rights Act of 1871, which is codified at 42 U.S.C. § 1983, is a frequently used civil rights provision in civil rights cases. Section 1983 provides the basis for a federal court lawsuit to any individual whose constitutional or federal statutory rights have been violated by the government or its officials. Compensatory damages, punitive damages, injunctions and attorney's fees may be awarded under § 1983. Two elements are required for a successful § 1983 lawsuit: 1) action by the state or by a person or institution acting "under color of" state law, which 2) deprives an individual of rights guaranteed by the U.S. Constitution or federal statutes. In 1982, the U.S. Supreme Court sharply limited the circumstances in which an ostensibly private institution can be found to be acting "under the color of state law."

The U.S. Supreme Court applied 42 U.S.C. § 1981 in the private school context, holding that it outlawed racially discriminatory private schools. The case arose in Virginia when parents of black students sought to enter into contractual relationships with private nonreligious schools for educational services advertised and offered to members of the general public. The students were denied admission because of their race. The Supreme Court recognized that while parents have a First Amendment right to send their children to educational institutions which promote the belief that racial segregation is desirable, it does not follow that the practice of excluding racial minorities from such institutions is also protected by the same principle. The Court rejected the school's argument that § 1981 does not govern private acts of racial discrimination. *Runyon v. McCrary*, 427 U.S. 160, 96 S.Ct. 2586, 49 L.Ed.2d 415 (1976).

Private college students held a sit-in in their college president's building to protest the college's refusal to divest itself of South African investments. The college suspended the students when they refused to halt their sit-in. The students sued the college president under § 1983 for violating their constitutional due process rights. They argued that their suspension violated state-prescribed rules of conduct by state officers. The district court dismissed the lawsuit and the students appealed to the U.S. Court of Appeals, Second Circuit. The circuit court ruled that because the college's disciplinary code was based on New York Education Law § 6450 it might be proven that the president had acted "under color of state law," satisfying the § 1983 requirement of state action. The circuit court remanded the case to the district court for further consideration.

Nearly one year after the circuit court issued its opinion, the circuit court vacated its decision in a proceeding in which all members of the circuit court participated. The court found that the private college's adoption of its disciplinary rules pursuant to the New York code did not qualify as "state action." There was no basis for suing the college or any of its officials under the federal civil rights statute. The full court noted that nothing in the state law or the college rules required suspension. The state of New York never actually compelled schools to enforce its rules and did not even inquire about enforcement. The New York statute was not mandatory. The students could show no evidence that the college had adopted the New York statute in the belief that it was enforcing state law. The court vacated its previous panel decision. *Albert v. Carovano*, 851 F.2d 561 (2d Cir.1988).

E. Student Common Law and Statutory Rights

A military college sophomore experienced emotional difficulties. The student consulted the school physician about his problems and informed him that he was contemplating suicide. The physician continued to treat the student throughout the school year but the student eventually hanged himself in his dormitory room. The school conducted an investigation, determined that the physician "periodically exceeded the scope of his assigned duties and his professional competence" and placed him on probation. However, the school found no evidence linking the physician with the suicide. The student's parents filed suit against the school and physician in a South Carolina trial court alleging that they were negligent in caring for the student. A jury determined that the student had assumed the risk that caused his death, and returned a verdict for the school and the physician. The parents appealed to the Supreme Court of South Carolina.

The main issue on appeal was whether the suicide could constitute an assumption of risk. The supreme court noted that the assumption of risk defense applied only where the plaintiff "assumes a risk of harm arising from the defendant's negligent or reckless conduct rather than his own." Here, the physician had a legal duty to prevent the suicide; the suicide arguably resulted from a breach of that duty. The court noted that "it would be anomalous to hold that a breach of duty results in no liability for the very injury the duty was meant to protect against." The court held that the trial court judge erred in instructing the jurors that the assumption of risk defense was available to the school and the physician. Accordingly, the holding of the trial court was reversed and the case was remanded for a new trial. *Hoeffner v. The Citadel*, 429 S.E.2d 190 (S.C.1993).

IV. USE OF PUBLIC SCHOOL PROPERTY AND TRANSPORTATION

The U.S. Supreme Court has determined that the provision of textbooks and bus transportation by states through local school districts to private school students does not violate the Constitution.

A. Textbook Loans

The provision of textbooks by the state to private and parochial school students is permissible under the First Amendment. In *Cochran v. Louisiana State Bd. of Educ.*, 281 U.S. 370, 50 S.Ct. 335, 74 L.Ed.2d 1929 (1930), the U.S. Supreme Court upheld a state law which authorized the purchasing and supplying of textbooks to all school children, including parochial school children, on the basis of what is now called the "child benefit" doctrine. The Court held that the textbook loan statute was constitutional because the legislature's purpose in enacting the statute was to benefit children and their parents, not religious schools.

Nearly 40 years later, the Supreme Court reaffirmed the validity of the child benefit doctrine in a case involving a New York textbook loan statute. This statute required local school districts to lend textbooks free of charge to all children in grades seven through twelve. Parochial school students were included. The Court observed that the textbooks loaned to parochial school children were the same nonreligious textbooks used in the public schools. The loaning of textbooks was permissible here because the parochial school students used them for secular study. Thus, there was no state involvement in religious training. The state of New York was merely providing a secular benefit to all school children. *Bd. of Educ. v. Allen*, 392 U.S. 236, 88 S.Ct. 1923, 20 L.Ed.2d 1060 (1968).

In 1973, the U.S. Supreme Court ruled that private schools with racially discriminatory admissions policies may not benefit from textbook loan programs. This ruling was based on the principle that the state may not give assistance to acts of racial discrimination. Textbooks were "a basic educational tool," said the Court, and to permit racially discriminatory private schools to benefit from state textbook loans would be to allow the state to accomplish indirectly what it could not accomplish directly: a state-funded racially segregated school system. *Norwood v. Harrison*, 413 U.S. 455, 93 S.Ct. 2804, 37 L.Ed.2d 723 (1973).

A Nebraska private school student's father sought a loan of fourth grade textbooks from a public school district. A Nebraska statute required public school boards of education to loan textbooks to private school students upon request if the students were enrolled in kindergarten through grade twelve in state approved private schools. After a request by the school district, the education commissioner refused to fund the textbook purchase without a court ruling on the statute's constitutionality. The student and her father then filed a lawsuit in a Nebraska county court, which found the statute constitutional. The commissioner appealed to the Nebraska Supreme Court.

On appeal, the commissioner argued that the statute violated the Nebraska Constitution and the Establishment Clause of the U.S. Constitution. He also claimed that the statute was unconstitutionally vague. The supreme court first considered a 1972 Nebraska constitutional amendment which prohibited appropriation of public funds for nonpublic schools. The court determined that the constitutional amendment did not prohibit public expenditures on behalf of private school students. The statute in question also did not permit public expenditures on behalf of nonpublic schools but merely permitted private school students to receive loans of public school textbooks at no cost. The statute also satisfied the requirements of the U.S. Constitution's Establishment Clause under the tests developed by the U.S. Supreme Court. Finally, the court ruled that the statute was not unconstitutionally vague. The supreme court affirmed the trial court's decision for the student and her father. *Cunningham v. Lutjeharms*, 437 N.W.2d 806 (Neb.1989).

B. Transportation

The principle that transportation may be provided to parochial school students without violating the First Amendment was established in a 1947 U.S. Supreme Court case. This case involved a New Jersey law which allowed reimbursement to parents of children attending nonprofit religious schools for costs incurred by the children in using public transportation to travel to and from school. The law's purpose was to provide transportation expenses for all school children regardless of where they attended school, as long as the school was nonprofit. The Supreme Court analogized free transportation to other state benefits such as police and fire protection, connections for sewage disposal, and public roads and sidewalks, which also benefited parochial school children. It was not the purpose of the First Amendment to cut off religious institutions from all government benefits. Rather, the state was only required to be neutral toward religion. *Everson v. Bd. of Educ.*, 330 U.S. 1, 67 S.Ct. 504, 91 L.Ed.2d 711 (1947).

However, use of state funds to reimburse private schools for transportation for field trips was declared unconstitutional by the U.S. Supreme Court in *Wolman v. Walter*, 433 U.S. 229, 97 S.Ct. 2593, 53 L.Ed.2d 714 (1977). There was no way public officials could monitor the field trips to assure that the trips had a secular purpose, said the Court. Even if monitoring by the state *was* feasible, the monitoring would be so extensive that the state would become entangled in religion to an impermissible degree.

A Massachusetts school district provided transportation to students who attended private schools located in a neighboring district. However, the district voted to discontinue this service during the 1991-1992 school year. The school district also declined to provide transportation to any student attending a public school outside the district. Although the private schools were located within a regional vocational school district, that district refused the students' parents' request to transport the students. The parents filed suit in a Massachusetts superior court seeking to compel one of the districts to provide transportation to the private school. The superior court granted summary judgment to the school districts, and the parents appealed to the Appeals Court of Massachusetts, Worcester.

The parents contended that the school committees were obligated to provide transportation to all students who attended private schools outside school district boundaries located no further than the public school they were entitled to attend. The appeals court disagreed. School committees were generally obligated to provide such transportation to students attending an approved private school within the boundaries of the school district. A school committee must also provide transportation to private school students outside the school district if it provides such transportation to public school students. Here, since the committee did not provide transportation to students attending public schools outside the district, it was not required to provide transportation to the private school children. Further, none of the children were enrolled in a private school with a comparable vocational curriculum. Consequently, the regional vocational school committee was not obligated to provide the students with transportation. *Garon v. Dudley-Charlton Reg. School Com.*, 633 N.E.2d 1051 (Mass.App.Ct.1994).

V. COOPERATIVE EFFORTS BETWEEN PUBLIC AND PRIVATE SCHOOLS

Any cooperation between public school systems and parochial schools must pass stringent constitutional examination. Cooperative efforts, such as leasing of public or private school classrooms, must avoid the appearance of government approval of religion and must not constitute government aid to, or excessive government entanglement with, religious organizations.

A. Release Time Programs

The courts generally will uphold release time programs only where the religious education takes place off public school grounds.

The first type of release time program to be declared unconstitutional by the U.S. Supreme Court was a Champaign, Illinois, program in which public school students were given religious instruction in public schools. Three religious groups each taught their own classes. The classes were conducted in public school classrooms and were composed of pupils whose parents had given permission for them to attend. Each religious group offered one class per week. Although the groups supplied the religious education teachers at no cost to the school district, the superintendent of schools exercised supervisory powers over them. Only students whose parents released them for religious study attended the religion classes. Attendance was monitored by the religion teachers and absences were reported to the public school authorities. Students in the religious education program were released from regular class study while they attended religion classes. However, the students not released for religious study were not released from regular class study.

A taxpayer in the Champaign school district sued the school board claiming that the release time program violated the Establishment Clause of the First Amendment. The U.S. Supreme Court agreed. Public school authorities engaged in close cooperation with the religious council and its religious education program. Further, taxpayer-supported public school buildings were made available for various religions to propagate their faiths. Also, the Illinois compulsory attendance law helped provide a captive audience of pupils for the religious education classes. "This is beyond all question a utilization of the tax-established and tax-supported public school system to aid religious groups," said the Court. "[T]he First Amendment has erected a wall between Church and State which must be kept high and impregnable." *McCollum v. Bd. of Educ.*, 333 U.S. 203, 68 S.Ct. 461, 92 L.Ed.2d 649 (1948).

However, four years later the U.S. Supreme Court upheld a different kind of release time program. In this New York program, students could be released from public school classes during the school day for a few hours in order to attend religious education classes. However, unlike the program in the *McCollum* case, students in the New York release time program received their religious instruction off the public school grounds. Church officials made out weekly attendance reports and sent the reports to public school officials, who then checked to assure that the released students had actually reported for their off-school-grounds religious instruction. The Supreme Court approved the New York program largely because the religious instruction took place off school grounds. There was no religious indoctrination taking place in the public school buildings nor was there any expenditure of public funds on behalf of religious training. Also, there was no evidence of any subtle or overt coercion exerted by any public school officials to induce students to attend the religious classes. The public schools were merely accommodating religion, not aiding it. The Court declined to invalidate the New York release time program, saying, "We cannot read into the Bill of Rights such a philosophy of hostility to religion." *Zorach v. Clauson*, 343 U.S. 306, 72 S.Ct. 679, 96 L.Ed.2d 954 (1952).

B. Public School Personnel on Parochial School Grounds

The following Supreme Court decisions indicate that programs in which public school personnel offer instruction on the grounds of religious schools are unconstitutional.

In 1985, the U.S. Supreme Court invalidated programs in Michigan and New York aimed at providing supplementary educational services to children attending private religious schools. In the first case, a Michigan public school district adopted a shared time program in which full-time public school teachers offered instruction in remedial courses during the regular school day at various parochial schools. A significant number of these teachers were former parochial school employees. The district also operated a community education program where remedial courses were offered at the close of the day at parochial schools. Unlike their counterparts in the shared time program, community education teachers were full-time employees of private schools who were considered part-time public school employees. In both programs, the instruction was offered on the premises of the parochial schools and the classes were attended only by parochial school students. All religious symbols were removed from any classroom where shared time or community education programs took place. The Supreme Court held that the programs violated the Establishment Clause of the U.S. Constitution by impermissibly aiding religion. *Grand Rapids School Dist. v. Ball*, 473 U.S. 373, 105 S.Ct. 3216, 87 L.Ed.2d 267 (1985).

In the New York case, a group of taxpayers brought suit in federal court challenging a city program in which federal funds received under Title I were used to send public school teachers into parochial schools. The teachers provided remedial educational services to underprivileged children. In this case the city had established a comprehensive supervision program to ensure that no state endorsement of religion could occur. Although the Supreme Court found that the city had succeeded in establishing a program that did not impermissibly aid religion, the very monitoring system that prevented Title I funds from aiding religion created excessive entanglement between church and state. This pervasive monitoring by public authorities created a constitutionally unacceptable level of entanglement between church and state. *Aguilar v. Felton*, 473 U.S. 402, 105 S.Ct. 3232, 87 L.Ed.2d 290 (1985).

An Arizona student attended a school for the deaf from grades one through five and a public school from grades six through eight. During his public school attendance, a sign language interpreter was provided by the school district. The student's parents enrolled him for ninth grade in a parochial high school, and requested the school district to continue providing a sign language interpreter. The school district refused, and the student's parents then sued the school district in the U.S. District Court for the District of Arizona under the Individuals with Disabilities Education Act (IDEA), 20 U.S.C. § 1400 *et seq.* The court granted the school district's summary judgment motion, finding that "the interpreter would act as a conduit for the religious inculcation" of the student—thereby promoting his religious development at government expense. On appeal, the U.S. Court of Appeals, Ninth Circuit, affirmed the district court decision. The U.S. Supreme Court granted the parents' petition for a writ of certiorari.

The Supreme Court stated that the Establishment Clause did not completely prohibit religious institutions from participating in publicly-sponsored benefits. If this were the case, religious groups would not even enjoy police and fire protection or have use of public roads and sidewalks. Government programs which neutrally provide benefits to broad classes of citizens are not subject to Establishment Clause prohibition simply because some religiously affiliated institutions receive "an attenuated financial benefit." Providing a sign language interpreter under the IDEA was part of a general program for distribution of benefits in a neutral manner to qualified students. The provision of the interpreter provided only an indirect economic benefit to the parochial school and was a neutral service which was part of a general program that was not "skewed" toward religion. A sign language interpreter, unlike an instructor or counselor, was ethically bound to transmit everything said in exactly the same way as it was intended. Because the Establishment Clause did not prevent the school district from providing the student with a sign language interpreter under the IDEA, the Supreme Court reversed the court of appeals' decision. *Zobrest v. Catalina Foothills School Dist.*, 509 U.S.—, 113 S.Ct. 2462, 125 L.Ed.2d 1 (1993).

A number of parents and taxpayers challenged the validity of several Louisiana education statutes and programs by filing a lawsuit against state agencies and officials, and the U.S. Department of Education in the U.S. District Court for the Eastern District of Louisiana. The lawsuit challenged special education programs operating under state laws that permitted public school employees to go on the premises of sectarian schools; statutory provisions authorizing special education funds for pervasively sectarian schools; and legislation reimbursing nonpublic schools for transportation costs and capital expenses. The court conducted a trial and filed an extensive opinion.

The court first determined that direct state subsidies to religious schools violated the Establishment Clause, while benefits paid to students and their parents did not violate the Constitution. In this case, a local school district had entered into a series of contracts with an association of Catholic schools to provide public school teachers for special education programs conducted at the private school. The court expressly found that the administration of this system resulted in entanglement between the state and private schools that could violate the Constitution. The second part of the court's decision upheld the constitutionality of a state statute authorizing reimbursement to nonpublic schools for maintaining and completing state reports of their administrative costs associated with state required recordkeeping. However, because the state superintendent of education had failed to conduct an audit of nonpublic schools within the past five years, the department's present application of the statute violated the Establishment Clause.

The court determined that an amended statute that required local school boards to provide free transportation to eligible students did not violate the Constitution despite establishing separate bus routes in certain cases for public and nonpublic school students. This was because students, not nonpublic schools, were the primary beneficiaries of the state funding. However, the direct payment of state transportation funds to two private academies by a local school board was an unconstitutional direct subsidy. With the exception of these two cases, the school board's implementation of the transportation statute did not result in excessive government entanglement with religion. Another Louisiana statute authorized partial reimbursement for transporting private school students to school. The statute limited reimbursement to $125 per student or $375 per family, but because of pending litigation, the state legislature had not appropriated funds since 1985. The court held that the statute was not an impermissible direct subsidy of parochial schools because parents were the direct beneficiaries.

The court considered the taxpayers' argument that Chapter One of the federal Education Consolidation and Improvement Act of 1981 was unconstitutional on its face. The program provided for increased funding for educationally deprived children, including some private school students. The court found that public school students were the primary beneficiaries of Chapter One funding. The U.S. Supreme Court has held that the maintenance of Chapter One services at neutral sites does not violate the Constitution. Because the funding for capital expenses under Chapter One did not impermissibly advance religion, it did not violate the Constitution. The court issued an order requesting the parties to submit proposed judgments in accordance with its findings of fact and conclusions of law. *Helms v. Cody*, 856 F.Supp. 1102 (E.D.La.1994).

C.   Instruction Offered on Public School Grounds

Religious instruction must be strictly neutral toward religion, and there must be no excessive state entanglement with religion from such instruction.

An Ohio school district's practice of leasing public school classrooms to a religious association was declared unconstitutional by a U.S. district court. The school district had a policy authorizing community use of school facilities. Acting under this policy, the school board approved the rental of elementary school buildings for one dollar per year to a private association sponsoring religious education. Religious education classes were conducted weekly by the association on public school premises both before and after regular school hours. The religious education classes were taught by nonpublic school personnel. Attendance by students was voluntary and parental permission was required. Several taxpayers in the school district alleged that the school district's program violated the Establishment Clause of the First Amendment. The district court held that the leasing of public school classroom facilities to the religious education association created an appearance of state endorsement of religion. The court observed that since the religion classes were held immediately preceding or following public school classes, the religious education association directly benefited from the operation of Ohio's compulsory education law. Such a benefit rendered the school board's policy unconstitutional. The court noted that its decision was based primarily on the time and location of the religion classes, as well as the "tender and impressionable ages of the children, whether or not participants, in contact with the program." The court ordered the school board to discontinue its practice of allowing public school buildings to be used for religion classes at times closely related to the opening or closing of the regular school day. *Ford v. Manuel*, 629 F.Supp. 771 (N.D.Ohio 1985).

The city of New York adopted a plan designed to allow it to offer remedial educational services to low income private school students under Chapter One of the Education Consolidation and Improvement Act of 1981, a successor to Title I. One aspect of the plan called for the city to conduct remedial education classes for girls from a Hasidic Jewish school on public school grounds. A section of the public school was to be completely closed off for use by the Hasidic girls through the construction of a wall in a previously open corridor. The plan also provided for the girls to be taught only by women who spoke Yiddish (in accordance with Hasidic tradition). The Hasidic girls were to be segregated from the rest of the public school students in order to accommodate Jewish leaders' concerns that contact with public school students would be harmful to the girls. The U.S. Court of Appeals, Second Circuit, invalidated the New York plan on the ground that it seemed "to create a symbolic link between the state and the Hasidic sect...." *Parents' Ass'n of P.S. 16 v. Quinones*, 803 F.2d 1235 (2d Cir.1986).

D. Leasing of Public or Private School Facilities

Lease agreements between public and private schools must avoid the appearance of state sponsorship of religion.

For 20 years, a New York school district transported students from an elementary school to released time religious classes at a local church. The district also leased buses to the church at a fair market rate for transportation of the students to church. The board then adopted guidelines for released time religious education under which it discontinued the leasing of buses for students being transported from public schools to the church. The church filed a declaratory judgment action in a New York trial court, seeking an order that the change in policy violated state law, the New York Constitution and the U.S. Constitution. The New York Supreme Court, Madison County, considered the church's summary judgment motion.

The district argued that it could not lease its buses to an entirely religious entity. The church maintained that it was entitled to lease buses under a state statute allowing districts in rural counties to lease buses to nonprofit organizations for educational purposes. Accordingly, the failure to continue leasing buses constituted discrimination on the basis of religion. The court agreed with the church, finding that it was a nonprofit organization engaged in education. No state funds were provided to the church, and the arrangement did not advance religion in any way. Refusal to rent buses to the church would violate the Establishment Clause by treating the church differently from nonreligious entities. *In the Matter of the Claim of St. James Church v. Bd. of Educ. of the Cazenovia Central School Dist.*, 621 N.Y.S.2d, 486 (Sup.Ct.—Madison County 1994).

The Los Angeles Community College District sought to generate additional revenue by sale or lease of its surplus real property. Notice of a surplus land sale was given with a listed minimum price, but no offers were received and the property was not sold. The district then mailed notices to people on its real property mailing list of its intention to lease the property. During the bidding process, only one bid was received by the district, which it accepted. A religious organization agreed to pay over $3 million for 75 years and planned to develop a temple, meeting rooms and housing during the term of the lease. A homeowner's organization sought to invalidate the lease and sued in a California trial court, asserting that the lease would involve the district in the unconstitutional establishment of a religious enterprise. The trial court upheld the lease, and the homeowners appealed to the California Court of Appeal, Second District.

The court of appeal noted that the primary purpose of the district's lease was secular. Also, there was no evidence that the lease resulted in government sponsorship or promotion of the organization's religious objectives. Both religious and secular groups had received an equal opportunity to obtain the government benefit of the long-term lease. The court held that the administrative power of the district over the religious organization did not create an impermissible entanglement in the organization's religious affairs. The court affirmed the trial court's decision. *Woodland Hills Homeowners Organization v. Los Angeles Community College District*, 266 Cal.Rptr. 767 (Cal.App.2d Dist.1990).

VI. PRIVATE SCHOOL FINANCE

Lemon v. Kurtzman, Meek v. Pittenger and Wolman v. Walter are the three major U.S. Supreme Court cases which address direct government payments to private schools. The rules which have emerged from these cases appear to be as follows: 1) state-provided salary supplements for teachers of parochial school students are forbidden, 2) state funding may be provided to parochial schools to defray the costs of preparing and administering state-required student testing and the like if such funds are monitored to ensure that none are diverted to religious uses, 3) state-prepared standardized student testing may be paid for by the state without any monitoring, 4) textbooks may be supplied by the state to students at racially nondiscriminatory parochial schools, 5) maps, charts and the like may not be provided by the state to parochial school students, 6) teaching and counseling services may only be provided by the state to parochial school students off the premises of the parochial schools, and 7) diagnostic and therapeutic services may be provided by the state to parochial school students at any location.

A. State and Local Funding

In *Lemon v. Kurtzman*, the U.S. Supreme Court invalidated Rhode Island and Pennsylvania statutes which provided state money to finance the operation of parochial schools. The Rhode Island statute provided a 15 percent salary supplement to parochial school teachers who taught nonreligious subjects also offered in the public schools using only public school teaching materials. The Pennsylvania statute authorized payment of state funds to parochial schools to help defray the cost of teachers' salaries, textbooks and other instructional materials. Reimbursement was limited, however, to the costs of secular subjects which were also taught in the public schools. Applying a three-part test to the two state programs in question, the Supreme Court held that the legislative purpose of the programs was a legitimate, secular concern with maintaining high educational standards in both public and private schools. "First, the statute must have a secular legislative purpose; second, its principal or primary effect must be one that neither advances nor inhibits religion, ... finally, the statute must not foster 'an excessive government entanglement with religion." The Court did not reach the second inquiry under the three-part test because it concluded that the state programs failed to pass muster under the third inquiry.

The Rhode Island salary supplement program excessively entangled the state with religion because of the highly religious nature of the Roman Catholic parochial schools which were the primary beneficiaries of the program. The teachers who received the salary supplements provided instruction in classrooms and buildings containing religious symbols such as crucifixes. Similar defects were found in the Pennsylvania program. The Court also observed that in order to ensure that the state-funded parochial school teachers did not inject religious dogma into their instruction, the state would be forced to extensively monitor the parochial school classrooms. This would result in excessive state entanglement with religion. Consequently, the salary supplement programs were held to violate the First Amendment. *Lemon v. Kurtzman*, 403 U.S. 602, 91 S.Ct. 2105, 29 L.Ed.2d 745 (1971).

One year later the U.S. Supreme Court struck down another form of state funding of instructional services. The case involved a NewYork program which granted annual lump-sum disbursements to parochial schools to help pay the costs of administering state-required student testing and recordkeeping activities. The tests, which were prepared by parochial school personnel, were characterized by the U.S. Supreme Court as "an integral part of the teaching process." The Court concluded that it was likely that the tests would, "unconsciously or otherwise, ... inculcate students in the religious precepts of the sponsoring church." *Levitt v. Comm. for Pub. Educ. & Religious Liberty*, 413 U.S. 472, 93 S.Ct. 2814, 37 L.Ed.2d 736 (1973).

However, the New York legislature responded to the *Levitt* decision by reenacting the reimbursements for teacher-prepared tests but adding a requirement that the funds be audited to ensure that no state subsidizing of religion would occur. The Supreme Court upheld the plan and found that the state audits did not excessively entangle the state in the affairs of parochial schools. *Comm. for Pub. Educ. & Religious Liberty v. Regan*, 444 U.S. 646, 100 S.Ct. 840, 63 L.Ed.2d 94 (1980).

In *Meek v. Pittenger*, the U.S. Supreme Court ruled unconstitutional most of a Pennsylvania program providing various types of state aid to parochial schools. This was a new program enacted by the state legislature after the Supreme Court in *Lemon v. Kurtzman* (above) invalidated Pennsylvania's direct funding of parochial school operations. The state's new program provided that 1) textbooks would be loaned to private school students in grades K-12; 2) classroom equipment such as periodicals, photographs, maps, charts, tapes, records, films, projectors and lab equipment would be "loaned" to private schools; and 3) "auxiliary services" such as counseling, testing, and speech and hearing therapy would be provided on the private school premises by public school personnel.

The Supreme Court upheld the textbook loans but the remainder of the program was invalidated. The loaning of classroom equipment was found to present a danger that public funds would advance religion since there was no guarantee that the maps, projectors and the like would not be used for religious lessons. The Supreme Court also struck down the "auxiliary services" on the ground of excessive entanglement. Because the auxiliary services were to be provided by public school employees on the grounds of parochial schools, there was a danger that public employees might transmit or advance religious doctrines in the course of their employment. *Meek v. Pittenger*, 421 U.S. 349, 95 S.Ct. 1753, 44 L.Ed.2d 217 (1975).

The state of Ohio attempted to circumvent the Supreme Court's ruling in *Meek v. Pittenger* by enacting a program which loaned classroom equipment to parochial school students, who would then place the equipment at the disposal of the school. The Supreme Court rejected this ploy. However one part of the Ohio statute authorized the provision of diagnostic and therapeutic services. The diagnostic services were to consist of speech, hearing and psychological evaluations performed on the parochial school premises by public employees and physicians. Any treatment rendered as a result of the diagnostic evaluations would take place off the parochial school premises. The U.S. Supreme Court upheld this plan and distinguished diagnostic services from teaching or counseling. Accordingly, it made no difference whether the diagnostic services were provided on or off the parochial school grounds.

The provision of therapeutic services, such as guidance counseling and remedial services, was also upheld because these services were provided to parochial school students off the parochial school premises. As long as the services were rendered at a "religiously neutral" site, said the Court, there was no danger of public employees transmitting religious views to the students. Although the Court conceded that some minimal level of monitoring would be necessary to ensure that religious views were not transmitted by the counselors to the students, this monitoring would not result in excessive entanglement. *Wolman v. Walter*, 433 U.S. 229, 97 S.Ct. 2593, 53 L.Ed.2d 714 (1977).

Minnesota's Postsecondary Enrollment Options Act (PSEOA) permits eleventh and twelfth grade students in state public schools to apply for and attend eligible colleges and universities for secondary or postsecondary credit. Participating colleges and universities receive state reimbursement based upon the lesser of actual tuition costs or a formula based upon school district basic revenue where students take courses for secondary credit. Although students are free to enroll in participating private colleges, reimbursement is limited to nonsectarian courses. A collective bargaining organization representing Minnesota teachers filed a federal district court action against the state and a participating college, claiming that the PSEOA violated the Establishment Clause of the Minnesota Constitution. A state trial court judge ruled that the previous decision in a district court action legally prevented the collective bargaining organization from relitigating whether certain colleges were sectarian and how they used PSEOA funds. The Minnesota Court of Appeals affirmed the trial court's decision in part but reversed and remanded the case for a determination on the nature of Bethel College and Seminary, and for a determination of its use of PSEOA funds. Bethel College and the state of Minnesota moved for summary judgment, which was granted. The collective bargaining organization appealed to the Court of Appeals of Minnesota.

The court of appeals applied a two-step inquiry into the constitutionality of the PSEOA, to determine whether the public benefit or support to the school was direct or incidental, and whether the school was pervasively sectarian. If the public benefit or support to the school was merely incidental or indirect, it would be irrelevant whether the school was basically sectarian. Because the PSEOA benefits were designed to benefit high school students and to permit them to take nonsectarian courses at participating colleges, with the opportunity to attend either public or private schools, the benefit to the colleges was incidental. Bethel received only 42 percent of its actual tuition, textbook and material expenses under the PSEOA program. It also segregated its PSEOA reimbursement from its general funds to ensure use for only nonsectarian purposes. The court upheld the constitutionality of the PSEOA and ruled for Bethel College and the state of Minnesota. *Minnesota Fed. of Teachers v. Mammenga*, 500 N.W.2d 136 (Minn.App.1993).

California taxpayers filed a declaratory relief action in a federal district court against the San Francisco Unified School District alleging that remedial educational services were provided to students attending sectarian schools in the district in a manner that violated the Establishment Clause of the U.S. Constitution. The school in question was formed for charitable purposes. The religious activities that occurred at the school were optional. The school district moved for summary judgment stating that the school was nonsectarian. The court noted that the U.S. Supreme Court has relied on an eight step analysis to determine if an institution is sectarian: a sectarian institution is one that 1) imposes religious restriction on admissions, 2) requires attendance of pupils at religious activities, 3) requires obedience by students to the doctrines of a particular faith, 4) requires pupils to attend instruction in the theology of a particular faith, 5) is an integral part of a religious mission of a sponsoring church, 6) has an integral substantial purpose in the inculcation of religious values, 7) imposes religious restrictions on faculty appointments, and 8) imposes religious restrictions on what or how the faculty may teach. The school in question did not have any of these characteristics. The school was best characterized as a nonsectarian school that received both private and public funds. The taxpayers' alleged violations of the Establishment Clause rested solely on the fact that the school was affiliated with the Daughters of Charity, a religious organization affiliated with the Roman Catholic church. The court determined that religious institutions may sponsor social welfare programs and are not disabled by the First Amendment. The court granted summary judgment to the school district and determined that neither the Establishment Clause nor the California Constitution had been violated. *Walker v. San Francisco Unif. School Dist.*, 741 F.Supp. 1386 (N.D.Cal.1990).

The Lynchburg, Virginia, city council and Industrial Development Authority (IDA) approved the issuance of up to $60 million of Educational Facilities Revenue Bonds in order to assist a private university affiliated with a Virginia Baptist church in building and developing academic and administrative facilities in Lynchburg. The university required its students and faculty to comply with clearly spelled out religious requirements. The validity of the bond issue with respect to both the U.S. and Virginia Constitutions came under question. The Supreme Court of Virginia found the bond issuance to be unconstitutional. The court found the university to be "a religious mission" with a "pervasive aim [of] equipping of young people for evangelistic ministry." Because of this pervasive-ness, the bond issue could only have the effect of establishing religion. The judgment of the trial court was reversed. *Habel v. Industrial Dev. Authority*, 400 S.E.2d 516 (Va.1991).

B.   Federal Funding

Private and public school programs or activities receiving federal financial assistance are bound by federal civil rights laws: Title VI, Title IX, the Rehabili-tation Act and the Age Discrimination in Employment Act, among others. These laws proscribe discrimination based upon race, sex, disability or age. Schools where students pay their tuition with Basic Educational Opportunity Grants, National Direct Student Loans and other federal grants will be deemed as receiving assistance for federal law purposes.

The U.S. Supreme Court has ruled on the issue of whether a private college whose students were receiving BEOGs (Basic Educational Opportunity Grants) was "receiving federal assistance" for purposes of compliance with Title IX prohibitions against discrimination on the basis of sex. A private college which had an "unbending policy" of refusing all forms of government assistance in order to remain independent of governmental restrictions was asked by the Department of Education (DOE) to supply "assurance of compliance" with Title IX, which the college refused to do on the ground that it was receiving no federal funding. The DOE disagreed, saying that because the school enrolled large numbers of students receiving federal BEOGs, it was receiving financial assistance for purposes of Title IX. The DOE then cut off students' financial assistance based on the college's failure to execute the assurance of compliance. Four students and the college brought suit challenging the termination of financial assistance. The Supreme Court held that the college was a recipient of federal financial assistance and thus subject to the statute prohibiting sex discrimination. This was so despite the fact that only some of the college's students received BEOG grants and even though the college did not receive any direct federal financial assistance. Thus, the college was obliged to submit assurance of compliance, but only with regard to the administration of its financial aid program, in order for students to continue to receive federal aid. The majority of the Court refused to adopt the dissenting justices' view that the entire college should be subjected to Title IX. *Grove City College v. Bell*, 465 U.S. 555, 104 S.Ct. 1211, 79 L.Ed.2d 516 (1984).

Several Missouri taxpayers challenged the allocation of federal Chapter 1 funds between public and parochial schools, and also challenged the way in which remedial services were provided. Chapter 1 of Title I of the Education Consoli-dation and Improvement Act provides federal funding for remedial education which is provided to low income students, and applies to both public and parochial schools. The taxpayers objected to the "off the top" allocation. This method took the administrative and delivery costs arising because of the location of the parochial students from the entire budget, and then allocated the remainder of the funds between public and parochial students. Additionally, the taxpayers argued that delivering services in mobile classrooms parked outside a sectarian parochial school violated the Establishment Clause. The federal district court agreed with the taxpayers on the allocation issue, and held that parking the classrooms off school grounds was not unconstitutional, but parking them on parochial school property was unconstitutional. The case was then appealed to the U.S. Court of Appeals, Eighth Circuit.

The court noted that mobile classrooms which are parked off school grounds will not be perceived as "annexes" of a parochial school. The issue then became whether mobile classrooms were unconstitutional when parked on school grounds. The appellate court held that the classrooms did not violate the Establishment Clause whether parked on or off school grounds. It noted that the classrooms were separate from the school, taught secular subjects, were controlled by the public school, and were driven away when class ended. Therefore, they could not be perceived as advancing religion or causing excessive entanglement. The court then turned to the question of allocation of funding and held that the "off the top" allocation was constitutional. *Pulido v. Cavazos,* 934 F.2d 912 (8th Cir.1991).

In a similar case, a county board of education determined that private schools could receive proportionately more remedial financial assistance than public schools under Chapter One of the Elementary and Secondary Education Act. The act covered children from low income families attending either public or private schools. In compliance with *Aguilar v. Felton,* which held that public employees teaching in parochial schools violated the Establishment Clause, the district provided services in vans outside parochial school grounds. The cost of the vans was deducted from the entire Chapter One allocation prior to apportionment of the educational funds between the public and private schools. This "off the top" cost allocation method resulted in the public school students paying $17 per student towards the parochial school van services. A taxpayer filed suit alleging that the "off the top" method violated the Establishment Clause. A federal district court agreed. The school district appealed to the U.S. Court of Appeals, Sixth Circuit.

First, the court stated that the cost of services provided to the parochial students was not grossly disproportionate to the cost of providing services to public students. The off the top funding method, which resulted in a $17 gap between public and parochial spending, did not confer a meaningful direct benefit on a church-affiliated private school. Second, the Constitution did not require that expenditures be absolutely equal but rather that they be "roughly proportional" resulting in comparable services. The court did not deem two percent of the total Chapter One funds and $17 per person to be constitutionally significant. Finally, the requirement that the services be comparable mandated this method of funding. If the private school students alone funded the van leasing program, there would be very little left to fund actual programs. This would result in an excessive disparity between public and private schools. Thus, the court found that the off the top method of funding did not violate the Establishment Clause of the Constitution, and it reversed the decision of the district court. *Barnes v. Cavazos,* 966 F.2d 1056 (6th Cir.1992).

C. Private Donations

An alumnus of Yale medical school executed a will codicil which left $225,000 in trust to his wife and gave the remainder to the university. The will gave explicit instructions that the bequest be used to build a wing to the medical school for treatment of the "sick poor." The wife died in 1987 and the trustees paid $312,068 to the university. However, the medical school no longer maintained a separate wing for the "sick poor." Also, the funds were insufficient to construct a comparable addition. The university and the state attorney general were unable to agree to a utilization of the funds which would comply with the testator's intent. The university filed suit in a Connecticut superior court seeking release of the will's restrictions. The trial court held that the bequest was not an institutional fund, refused to release the restrictions, and dismissed the suit. The university appealed to the Supreme Court of Connecticut.

The university contended that the bequest proceeds qualified as an institutional fund which entitled the university to seek relief from the will's restrictions. The supreme court agreed and set out the requirements necessary for the bequest to qualify as an institutional fund. First, an institutional fund must be held for the "exclusive use, benefit or purposes" of the university. Here, since the medical school regularly and lawfully treated the "sick poor" this requirement was satisfied. Second, a noninstitutional beneficiary must not have an interest in the funds. The court did not deem the funds bequeathed for an inchoate group to be held for a noninstitutional beneficiary. Although the fund benefited indigent patients generally, a single patient was not a beneficiary distinct from the university. Therefore, the university was not precluded from seeking relief of the will's "obsolete, inappropriate or impractical" restrictions. The supreme court reversed the trial court's decision. *Yale University v. Blumenthal,* 621 A.2d 1304 (Conn.1993).

An individual proposed the creation of an endowment scholarship fund. The president of a private Georgia university confirmed the arrangement by letter. Scholarships would be limited to graduates of a particular high school and would be based on financial need. The agreement also noted that music majors had first priority, followed by medical students. Following the agreement, the individual made a donation of over $65,000. Within six years, ten awards were made from the fund to four different students. All of them were graduates of the designated high school, but none were music majors or medical students. The donor demanded return of the fund's principal and interest. The university refused and the donor sued the university in a Georgia trial court. The trial court granted the university's motion for summary judgment. The donor appealed to the Georgia Court of Appeals. The appeals court ruled that the donor had made a complete gift. Although the donor and university president had discussed the uses for the endowment fund there was no evidence that the donation was given for a binding promise to use it in the designated manner. Because the donation was given, accepted and delivered, it satisfied the legal requirement for a gift and the donor could not revoke it. The appeals court affirmed the trial court's decision for the university. *Hawes v. Emory Univ.,* 374 S.E.2d 328 (Ga.App.1988).

A Missouri woman served on the board of trustees for a private college. In 1990, the college began a campaign to solicit funds for a new sports complex. The board member signed a pledge card indicating her pledge of $50,000 over five years to the campaign. On the back of the pledge card appeared the statement, "It is understood that this pledge may be changed at the donor's request." The board member paid $10,000 of her pledge in 1990. Prospective pledgers and officials at a bank from which the college was attempting to secure a loan were told the total amount of money which had been pledged during the campaign; this amount included the board member's pledge. In addition the college made a commitment to an architectural firm and a construction firm and began constructing the sports complex. The board member died in April 1991. Her personal representative canceled the rest of her pledge. There was no evidence that any damages occurred as a result of this cancellation. The college sued the estate in a Missouri trial court, which denied the college's claim for the rest of the pledge. The college then appealed to the Missouri Court of Appeals, Eastern District.

On appeal, the college claimed that the pledge was irrevocable because the college changed its position by incurring obligations in reliance on the pledge. It argued that a subscription to a charitable organization is an offer to contract which becomes irrevocable and enforceable if the promisee performs some act or incurs enforceable liabilities in reliance on the promise. The college also claimed that a subscription for a specific purpose, unlike a subscription for a general purpose, is not revocable despite language to that effect on a pledge card. The court of appeals disagreed with both arguments. It stated that it was unreasonable for the college to have changed its position because the language on the pledge card allowed the pledge to be changed at any time. By retaining a right to cancel her promise, the board member promised nothing. Therefore, her promise was illusory. The court also stated that it did not matter that the pledge was for a specific purpose. It remained revocable, and there was no legal authority to support the college's position. *Estate of Buchanan,* 840 S.W.2d 888 (Mo.App.E.D.1992).

VII. SCHOLARSHIPS, GRANTS AND FINANCIAL AID

Grants, loans and tax credits or deductions are the most common forms of state financial assistance to private school students. Such financial assistance programs are constitutionally permissible as long as the state purpose underlying the program is to primarily benefit the students, not their schools. Receipt of federal funding may impose additional obligations on institutions by bringing them under the coverage of certain federal statutes.

The U.S. Supreme Court unanimously ruled that the First Amendment to the U.S. Constitution did not prevent the state of Washington from providing financial assistance directly to a disabled individual attending a Christian college. The plaintiff in this case, a blind person, sought vocational rehabilitative services from the Washington Commission for the Blind pursuant to state law. The law provided that visually impaired persons were eligible for educational assistance. However, because the plaintiff was a student at a Christian college intending to pursue a career of service in the church, the Commission for the Blind denied him assistance. The Washington Supreme Court upheld this decision on the ground that the First Amendment to the U.S. Constitution prohibited state funding of a student's education at a religious college. The U.S. Supreme Court took a less restrictive view of the First Amendment and reversed the Washington court. The operation of Washington's program was such that the Commission for the Blind paid money directly to students, who could then attend the schools of their choice. The fact that the student in this case chose to attend a religious college did not constitute state support of religion because "the decision to support religious education is made by the individual, not the state." The First Amendment was therefore not offended. *Witters v. Washington Dep't of Servs. for the Blind*, 474 U.S. 481, 106 S.Ct. 748, 88 L.Ed.2d 846 (1986).

On remand, the Washington Supreme Court reconsidered the matter under the Washington State Constitution, which is far stricter in its prohibition on the expenditure of public funds for religious instruction than is the U.S. Constitution. Vocational assistance funds for the student's religious education violated the state constitution because public money would be used for religious instruction. The commission's action was constitutional under the free exercise clause because there was no infringement of the student's constitutional rights. The court reaffirmed its denial of state funding for the student's tuition. *Witters v. State Comm'n for the Blind*, 771 P.2d 1119 (Wash.1989).

A private college, which had its main campus in Missouri, provided postsecondary educational courses for profit. The college also offered drafting technology and paralegal courses off campus for incarcerated students at nine correctional facilities in Missouri. As a participant in the Pell Grant financial assistance program, the college awarded federal grants administered by the U.S. Department of Education. It was then reimbursed for these awards by the government. Three variables determined the size of a student's Pell Grant award for an academic year: the maximum grant for that year, the student's cost of attendance for that year, and the amount of funds appropriated to carry out the Pell Grant Program for that year. The amount of a Pell Grant for any academic year could not exceed 50 percent of the actual cost of attendance for that year.

The college determined that 50 percent of the amount of fees and tuition for each of its fulltime incarcerated students exceeded the ceiling on grant awards for certain years. Accordingly, it decided that each student was entitled to the maximum award. However, because the programs for incarcerated students were designed to be completed in four quarters (while the rest of the school operated on three quarters) the department determined that the college had awarded $143,000 too much. This was because the college did not prorate tuition costs. Thus, the college was being reimbursed for the incarcerated students one and one-third times the amounts for regular students. The Secretary of Education required the college to refund the overpaid grant funds, and the college appealed to a federal district court. The district court granted summary judgment to the Secretary of Education. The college's interpretation would have allowed Pell Grants in excess of the amount provided for each academic year. *Platt College of Commerce, Inc. v. Cavazos*, 796 F.Supp. 22 (D.D.C.1992).

While in medical school, a physician received tuition funds from the National Health Service Corps (NHSC) Scholarship Loan Program. Under the program, participating students must serve in designated health manpower shortage areas for each year they received a scholarship, or a minimum of two years, whichever is greater. The final decision on where the student will be placed is left to the discretion of the Secretary of Health and Human Services. After graduation, the physician informed the government that he would not perform his obligation under the NHSC by working at his designated health manpower shortage area. By failing to begin service at the designated area, the government concluded that the physician was in default of his loan. The government sued the physician for payment in a federal district court. The district court noted that the NHSC was intended to ensure an adequate supply of doctors to shortage areas, not to subsidize medical education. The court held that the physician was in default of his loan after he failed to begin service at the designated shortage area and he thus had to repay the loan. *United States v. Gross,* 725 F.Supp. 892 (W.D.La.1989).

In 1973 the U.S. Supreme Court invalidated a New York program which 1) provided $50-$100 in direct money grants to low-income parents with children in private schools and 2) authorized income tax credits of up to $1,000 for parents with children in private schools. The program had the primary effect of advancing religion and thus was constitutionally invalid. The Court characterized the tax credits as akin to tuition grants and observed that they were really cash giveaways by the state on behalf of religious schools. *Committee for Public Educ. & Religious Liberty v. Nyquist,* 413 U.S. 756, 93 S.Ct. 2955, 37 L.Ed.2d 948 (1973).

However, the U.S. Supreme Court upheld a Minnesota program which involved tax deductions (as opposed to tax credits) that were available to parents of public and private school children alike. The Minnesota program allowed state income tax deductions for tuition, nonreligious textbooks and transportation. In upholding the program the Court observed that the state had a legitimate interest in assuring that all its citizens were well educated. Also, the tax deductions in question were only a few among many other deductions such as those for medical expenses or charitable contributions. Unlike the program in the *Nyquist* case, the Minnesota program was part of a bona fide income tax deduction system available to parents of all school children. The Court held that the First Amendment was not offended by the Minnesota tax deduction program. *Mueller v. Allen,* 463 U.S. 388, 103 S.Ct. 3062, 77 L.Ed.2d 721 (1983).

In *Hunt v. McNair*, the Supreme Court upheld a South Carolina plan which allowed both private and public colleges to use the state's authority to borrow money at low interest rates. The case involved a Baptist college which used this money to finance the construction of a dining hall. The college had no religious test for either its faculty or students and the student body was only about 60 percent Baptist, the same percentage found in the surrounding community. The Supreme Court found that the college was not "pervaded by religion." Unlike the situation commonly found in K-12 parochial schools, religiously-affiliated colleges and universities are often not dominated by a religious atmosphere. The Court concluded that both the purpose and effect of the state's borrowing program was secular and thus constitutional. The argument that aid to one (secular) portion of a religious institution makes it free to spend more money on religious pursuits was rejected as unpersuasive and irrelevant. If that were the case, the Court noted that police and fire protection for religious schools would have to be cut off as well. *Hunt v. McNair*, 413 U.S. 734, 93 S.Ct. 2868, 37 L.Ed.2d 923 (1973).

A 1971 case involved the federal Higher Education Facilities Act of 1963. This federal funding program offered assistance to both public and private colleges in constructing academic facilities. Although the program mandated that any building constructed with federal assistance be used by private colleges only for nonreligious purposes, it stated that after 20 years the buildings could be put to religious uses if the private college so desired. The U.S. Supreme Court upheld most of this program against constitutional challenges. The Court, however, invalidated the portion of the program that would have lifted the religious uses provision after 20 years. *Tilton v. Richardson,* 403 U.S. 672, 91 S.Ct. 2091, 29 L.Ed.2d 790 (1971).

The state of Maryland enacted a program which authorized annual, noncategorical grants to religiously affiliated colleges. The program was challenged by taxpayers who alleged that state money was being put to religious uses by the schools, which had wide discretion in spending the funds. The Supreme Court began its analysis of the Maryland program with the following observation:

> *Hunt v. McNair* requires (1) that no state aid at all go to institutions that are so "pervasively sectarian" that secular activities cannot be separated from sectarian ones, and (2) that if secular activities *can* be separated out, they alone may be funded.

The colleges involved in this case were not found to be pervasively sectarian even though they were affiliated with the Roman Catholic Church. The Court held that the "secular side" of the colleges could be separated from the sectarian, and found that state aid had only gone to the colleges' secular side. It was admittedly somewhat difficult to ensure that the colleges and the Maryland Council for Higher Education would take care to avoid spending state funds on religious activities, but the Court expressed its belief that those entities would spend the money in good faith and avoid violating the First Amendment. *Roemer v. Bd. of Pub. Works,* 426 U.S. 736, 96 S.Ct. 2337, 49 L.Ed.2d 179 (1976).

CHAPTER FOURTEEN

INTERSCHOLASTIC ATHLETICS

I. HIGH SCHOOL ATHLETICS

Interscholastic high school athletics are regulated by state athletic associations which impose eligibility, transfer and academic rules and standards upon participating schools and students. Schools and school districts typically have behavior and academic rules for student athletes that are stricter than those regulating the conduct of general student populations. Courts have upheld even-handed rules holding athletes to a higher standard of conduct due to the representative role played by student athletes, and their diminished expectations of privacy.

A. Eligibility rules

1. Drug Testing

Drug testing by urinalysis constitutes a search under the Fourth Amendment to the U.S. Constitution. Courts have frequently found drug testing of general student populations in conflict with constitutional requirements of individualized suspicion. Some of those cases appear in Chapter Four of this volume. This section considers testing of students who wish to participate in interscholastic athletics. Testing limited to potential interscholastic sports participants has met with court approval where the tests are limited in scope, provide for student privacy and clearly state the consequences of positive tests.

An Oregon school district responded to increased student drug use by instituting a random drug testing policy for all students wishing to participate in varsity athletics. Each student athlete was to submit a consent form authorizing a test at the beginning of the season and weekly random testing thereafter. The policy provided for progressive discipline leading to suspension for the current and following athletic seasons. Students who refused to give urine samples were suspended from sports for the rest of the season. A seventh grader who wanted to play football refused to sign the drug testing consent form and was suspended from sports for the season. His parents filed a lawsuit against the school district in the U.S. District Court for the District of Oregon, arguing that the testing policy violated their son's rights under the Fourth Amendment to the U.S. and Oregon constitutions. The court upheld the policy.

The parents appealed to the U.S. Court of Appeals, Ninth Circuit. The court balanced the interest of the school district in improved discipline and educational efficiency with the interest of the student in personal privacy. It held that participation in interscholastic sports did not diminish a high school athlete's reasonable expectation to be free from compelled, suspicionless urinalysis. The government interest in maintaining school discipline was not as strong as in other federal cases upholding random drug tests in high security or high risk areas. The policy violated both the U.S. and Oregon constitutions, and the court of appeals reversed and remanded the district court's decision. The district appealed to the U.S. Supreme Court.

The Court stated that under its prior cases the reasonableness of a search under the Fourth Amendment required balancing the interests between the government and individual. Prior decisions of the Court indicated that students had a lesser expectation of privacy than the general populace, and that student-athletes had an even lower expectation of privacy in the locker room. The invasion of privacy in this case was no worse than what was typically encountered in public restrooms. Positive test results were disclosed to only a limited number of school employees. The insignificant invasion of student privacy was outweighed by the school district's important interest in addressing drug use by students who risked physical harm while playing sports. The Court vacated and remanded the decision of the court of appeals. *Vernonia School Dist. 47J v. Acton*, 115 S.Ct. 2386 (1995).

An Arizona school district experienced success in dealing with a perceived drug problem among its students through the use of a self-esteem program. Despite the program's success, the school board unanimously voted to implement random drug testing for student athletes. Under the testing program, random tests were performed in a lavatory within the school office without direct observation. Students wishing to participate in interscholastic sports were required to consent to the program. In the event of a positive test, parents were notified and students could become temporarily ineligible for sports. A student who twice tested negative under the program objected to continued drug testing because he claimed that it illegally invaded his privacy in violation of the state and federal constitutions. He filed a lawsuit against the school district in the U.S. District Court for the District of Arizona. The court observed that while the school district was authorized to conduct random searches (drug tests) of students, there was a question as to whether the searches were reasonable. Here, there were no emergency circumstances that justified invading student privacy. Because participation depended upon the willingness of students and parents to sign consent forms, the program was not truly voluntary and participation in the program was coercive. Accordingly, the student was entitled to an injunction precluding the district from enforcing the random testing program. *Moule v. Paradise Valley Unif. School Dist. No. 69*, 863 F.Supp. 1098 (D.Ariz.1994).

2. Age and Time Limits

A school district or a state high school athletic association may impose a rule which limits athletic competition to eight consecutive semesters and which begins to toll either upon the completion of the eighth grade or upon the commencement of the ninth grade.

An Illinois student attended a south side Chicago high school for the ninth and tenth grades, with poor academic performance. He was absent 80 days in his eleventh grade year, and was withdrawn from enrollment. He did not participate in interscholastic athletics. At the invitation of his cousin, he moved to Indiana and enrolled as an eleventh grade student. His attendance and grades improved substantially. He was a member of the basketball team that year and earned recognition as an all-conference player. He wished to play on the basketball team his senior year. However, the Indiana High School Athletic Association (IHSAA) determined that he was ineligible because he had attended high school for eight semesters at the end of his eleventh grade year in Indiana. The student sought an injunction in a federal district court against the IHSAA.
The court determined that the IHSAA rule did not violate the Equal Protection Clause of the United States Constitution as it was rationally related to the legitimate state interest of preventing red-shirting. Here, the student did not red-shirt and did not move to Indiana in order to play sports. Therefore, the court found that the IHSAA's rule was overbroad as applied to the student and others who might be similarly situated. The court enjoined the IHSAA from enforcing its decision. *Jordan by and through Jones v. IHSAA*, 813 F.Supp. 1372 (N.D.Ind.1993).

An Arizona high school student was a member of his school basketball team. However, he became dependent on alcohol, cocaine and marijuana during his sophomore year. He dropped out of high school and fled to California to escape drug-related debt. He later returned to Arizona and committed burglary to satisfy the debts. He then confessed to the burglary and was incarcerated at a school where he became rehabilitated. He returned to the high school, achieved good grades and did not return to drug use. He sought an exception to the state interscholastic association's eight-consecutive-semester eligibility rule in order to participate on the basketball team. He hoped to qualify under an exception to the rule which allowed participation where the student was unable to attend school because of disabling illness or injury, met academic requirements and had a doctor's statement. The association denied the student's petition for an exception, determining that the student was incarcerated and not disabled and that his reform school medical reports were not statements from an attending physician under its rules. The student filed a complaint in an Arizona trial court which granted his application for a temporary injunction, permitting him to participate on the basketball team. The court ruled that the decision of the athletic association had been arbitrary. The association appealed to the Arizona Court of Appeals, which vacated the trial court's decision. The student appealed to the Arizona Supreme Court. The supreme court agreed to hear the case even though the student had completed participation on the basketball team for the season. It agreed with the trial court that the student's drug and alcohol dependency had caused his absence from school. The association had arbitrarily refused to consider the student's medical reports as they had clearly shown that he suffered from a disabling illness. The supreme court affirmed the trial court's preliminary order. *Clay v. Arizona Interscholastic Ass'n,* 779 P.2d 349 (Ariz.1989).

A student at an Indiana high school played on his school's basketball team during both the fall 1990 and spring 1991 semesters. During the spring 1991 semester, the student withdrew from school because of a serious sinus infection. He had, at that point, reached the end of the regular basketball season. When he returned to school the following year, the high school allowed him to repeat his entire year, due to poor academic performance in the fall 1990 semester. The student wrote to the Indiana High School Athletic Association (IHSAA) and requested that his 1990-91 year not count against his total years of eligibility for interscholastic athletics. The IHSAA responded that not only would the student's previous year count against his total eligibility, but also that he was ineligible for the coming year for not taking at least five new courses (even though the student had ultimately not received any credit for the courses he had taken the previous year). The student sued the IHSAA in an Indiana trial court and was granted an injunction allowing eligibility in the current year. The IHSAA appealed to the Indiana Court of Appeals. The court of appeals stated that while the IHSAA ineligibility rules were reasonably related to the legitimate purpose of maintaining good academic standards in school athletics, they were arbitrary and capricious when applied to the student in question. Therefore, the lower court's injunction was upheld. *IHSAA v. Shafer,* 598 N.E.2d 540 (Ind.App.5th Dist.1992).

A maximum age rule of 19 years of age has been held to be reasonable in light of the objective of fostering safety and fairness in competition.

An Arkansas student filed suit against the Arkansas Activities Association (AAA), challenging the AAA's rule which disqualified 19-year-olds from participating in sports, but contained a grandfather clause which allowed those over 19 to participate provided they entered school prior to 1980 and made normal educational progress. The student had not made normal progress, because he repeated the fifth grade at his mother's request. The student sought an injunction to allow him to participate. An Arkansas trial court issued the injunction. The

AAA appealed to the Supreme Court of Arkansas. The court held that the clause had a rational basis since it allowed students who started school prior to the rule's enactment to participate, while preventing students from intentionally repeating a grade to participate in sports at an older age. The court vacated the injunction and dismissed the case. *Arkansas Activities Ass'n v. Meyer*, 805 S.W.2d 58 (Ark.1991).

3. Transfer Students

Eligibility rules requiring a sit-out period for athletes transferring into a district, either from a neighboring school district or from out of state, may be enforced if it can be shown that the rules are reasonably related to the prevention of recruiting student athletes.

A 16-year-old Missouri high school student transferred from a public high school to a local private school. The student was in his junior year and was a member of the junior varsity basketball team. Participation in interscholastic athletics was not the primary reason for the move and neither he nor his parents were recruited by the private school. Both schools were members of the Missouri State High School Activities Association (MSHSAA). An MSHSAA bylaw restricted the student's eligibility to participate in interscholastic athletic activities for 365 days following the student's transfer from public to private school. An exception allowed students doing the opposite (transferring from a private to a public school) to be eligible after only five days. Faced with having to sit out a year, the student brought suit against the MSHSAA in federal district court challenging the restriction as violating his due process and equal protection rights under the Fourteenth Amendment as well as his First Amendment freedom of association rights. The court found that although the provision did not violate the student's freedom of association rights, it did violate his equal protection rights.

The court first determined that there had been no violation of the student's right of freedom of association. There was no allegation of a "grave interference with important religious tenets." The student's ability to practice his religion was not affected by the restrictions imposed by the bylaws. The court did, however, find that the existence of an exception to the transfer rule violated the Equal Protection Clause. In arguing for validation of the exception, the MSHSAA correctly claimed that there need be only a legitimate state purpose and a rational basis for the restriction and that its purpose was to remedy an unfair advantage which private schools enjoyed. The court determined that there were no allegations that the student was "school hopping," or was improperly recruited or that he had been unduly influenced, the reason for having the rule in the first place. Despite all this, the student did not prevail in his quest to participate in athletics at the private school as the court determined that it was the exception which was improper. Therefore, all transferring students would henceforth be subject to the one-year restriction on participation. *Beck v. Missouri State High School Activities Assn.*, 837 F.Supp. 998 (E.D.Mo.1993).

A New York student attended public schools until eleventh grade, when he transferred to a parochial school. When he returned to the public school for financial reasons, he was denied eligibility as a transfer athlete by the public school principal and was denied permission to play basketball. The school board had no formal transfer policy and the student alleged that the decision by the superintendent had been arbitrary. He filed a petition for a writ of mandamus in a New York trial court, seeking to reverse the eligibility denial. The court stated that the student had failed to exhaust his administrative remedies by applying to the court rather than the school board. It denied the student's petition, but instructed the school board to promptly consider the application. *Sutterby v. Zimar*, 594 N.Y.S.2d 607 (Sup.Ct.—Yates County 1993).

An Indiana high school student transferred school districts when his custody was changed from his mother to his father. His parents, who were divorced, decided that the student's poor grades and disciplinary problems required him to move in with his father. The student was a golfer who wished to play varsity golf for his new high school. However, the Indiana High School Athletic Association (IHSAA) had a regulation which prohibited a student who transferred to a new school district, without a corresponding change of residence by his parent or guardian, from playing on the varsity team in his new school district unless he presented "reliable, credible, and probative evidence" that the transfer was due to an event outside the control of the student or a change in the student's home status not within the student's control. An assistant commissioner of the association ruled that the student, having failed to present such evidence, could not play varsity golf for his new school. The association's executive committee affirmed that ruling. The student filed suit against the IHSAA alleging that the eligibility rules violated the his protection and due process rights. A federal district court entered a permanent injunction prohibiting the association from declaring the student ineligible. The association appealed to the U.S. Court of Appeals, Seventh Circuit. The court stated that the association's action was arbitrary and capricious and its rule was poorly drafted. Also, the association did not seem to uniformly apply the rule. The court went on to state that the association did not publish any type of written opinion or reasoning for its eligibility decisions. The court of appeals affirmed the district court's grant of a permanent injunction. *Crane v. Indiana High School Athletic Ass'n*, 975 F.2d 1315 (7th Cir.1992).

A Tennessee learning disabled tenth grade student transferred from a Christian school to a metropolitan public school. The executive director of the Tennessee Secondary Schools Athletic Association (TSSAA) ruled that the student was ineligible to participate in interscholastic sports for a period of twelve months. The student submitted an appeal asking that the TSSAA grant a hardship request, which was denied. The student appealed to a number of authorities, but all his appeals were denied. After the first four games, the student's parents filed suit in a federal district court claiming that the student's ineligibility for participation in athletics deprived him of his rights under the Individuals with Disabilities Education Act (IDEA). The court concluded that a student who transfers from one school to another for the purpose of receiving special education could not be prohibited from participating in extracurricular activities since such a prohibition would amount to discrimination based on disability. *Crocker v. Tennessee Secondary School Athletic Ass'n*, 735 F.Supp. 753 (N.D.Tenn.1990).

An Alabama student sought an injunction that would require the state athletic association to allow him to participate in high school athletics. The student had transferred from a private school to a public school after the school district lines were redrawn. The high school athletic association determined that those students who were required to change schools because of the rezoning would not lose their athletic eligibility. The ineligible student argued that the athletic association's decision was arbitrary, since it allowed students who were transferred as a result of rezoning to be eligible, but not students who switched from a private to a public school. The Supreme Court of Alabama rejected the student's argument and held that the athletic association's decision was not arbitrary because the transfer was voluntary. *Alabama High School Athletic Ass'n v. Scaffidi*, 564 So.2d 910 (Ala.1990).

The South Dakota High School Activities Association (SDHSAA) governs activities for South Dakota high schools. A student participated in interscholastic athletics during his freshman year. The following year, the student transferred to a private school in order to study the Bible. The SDHSAA informed the student that he was ineligible to participate in interscholastic athletics for one year under the SDHSAA's transfer rule. The private school filed a request for a waiver because of the student's desire to attend the school for its Bible curriculum. The request was denied and the student sued the SDHSAA for violating his due process and equal protection rights. The trial court held for the student and the SDHSAA appealed to the Supreme Court of South Dakota. The supreme court noted that in order for the student to prove a due process violation, he had to assert a protected life, liberty or property interest in participation in high school athletics. The court held that participation in interscholastic athletics was a mere expectancy, rather than a protected entitlement. The court also held that the transfer rule did not violate the student's equal protection rights since it had a rational relationship to a legitimate purpose. The transfer rule prevented school-switching by athletes and recruiting of athletes by member schools. The supreme court reversed the trial court's decision. *Simkins v. South Dakota High School Activities Ass'n*, 434 N.W.2d 367 (S.D.1989).

4. Academic Standards

A California school district required student athletes to maintain a cumulative 2.0 grade point average. The district's requirement for pep squad was a 2.5 cumulative grade point average. A cheerleader who failed a chemistry class which dropped her grade point average below 2.5 sought an exception to the eligibility standards. When the district refused to make this exception, she sued it in a California trial court. The court held for the district and the student appealed to the Court of Appeal of California, Fourth District. The court found no rational basis for the district's policy, finding instead that interscholastic sports and cheerleading were both nonacademic extracurricular activities that required year-round participation. Both activities shared the necessity to maintain high academic performance, and the distinction drawn by the school district was artificial. The court of appeal reversed the trial court's decision. However, it left to the district the decision of whether to lower the requirements for cheerleaders or raise the requirements for athletics. *Fontes v. Irvine Unif. School Dist.*, 30 Cal.Rptr.2d 521 (Cal.App.4th Dist.1994).

A Kentucky high school student sued his school for not allowing him to compete in interscholastic wrestling. The school had a grade point requirement of 2.0 in order to participate in interscholastic sports, which the student had been unable to achieve. The trial court dismissed the case and the student appealed. The Court of Appeals of Kentucky stated that the student's interest in wrestling was not a property right and therefore the grade point requirement was not unconstitutional. The student did not have a fundamental right to participate in extracurricular activities. The school board's policy of excluding students from activities based on grades did not exceed the reasonable and legitimate interest of the school system. *Thompson v. Fayette County Public Sch.*, 786 S.W.2d 879 (Ky.App.1990).

B. Athletic Suspensions

A New York high school student was a member of his school's varsity wrestling team. While a spectator at a junior varsity wrestling match, he broke into the school cafeteria and stole approximately eight packages of muffins, which he brought to the locker room and gave to the members of the junior varsity wrestling team. When the incident was discovered, he admitted that he had stolen the muffins. As a result of this misconduct, the high school principal imposed an academic suspension of two days. The school's athletic director, however, orally suspended the student from further participation in the wrestling program for the sports season. Claiming that he was of Olympic caliber, the student sued the district, contending that the athletic suspension was disproportionate to the offense and seriously hampered his ability to gain an athletic scholarship. The New York Supreme Court, Albany County, agreed. The court stated that in order for the suspensions to be valid they must contain a legal basis, a legal designation of a person or body authorized to impose the proposed discipline, and a fair and reasonable opportunity for the student to be heard. The court stated that the athletic director's action could not stand because the only source of regulations over the behavior of athletics were contained in a publication entitled "Interscholastic Athletic Guide" which had no actual legal authority since it had never been adopted by the school district. The court stated that even if the interscholastic guide had been adopted, the needs and mandates of due process were not satisfied by the informal procedures and lack of adequate standards provided by the guide. *Manico v. South Colonie Cent. School Dist.*, 584 N.Y.S.2d 519 (Sup.1992).

An Arkansas high school senior was an outstanding athlete in basketball and track. Officials at her high school banned her from participating on the girls' basketball team, and she sued the school district in federal court claiming that the decision had violated her constitutional rights. While the case was pending, the student graduated from high school. The U.S. Court of Appeals, Eighth Circuit, stated that the case was moot. The court was unable to grant any effective relief to the student. It could not place her back on the basketball team, nor was the student representative of a class. Also, this was not a situation "capable of repetition, yet evading review." The activity complained of was not continuous and affected only one student. *McFarlin v. Newport Special School Dist.*, 980 F.2d 1208 (8th Cir.1992).

II. INTERCOLLEGIATE ATHLETICS

Major colleges and universities participate in the National Collegiate Athletic Association (NCAA), which regulates competition and eligibility. Individual colleges and universities typically institute their own rules and regulations, which must be administered in a reasonable manner.

A group of student athletes at a west coast university sued the NCAA, contending that its drug testing program violated their rights to privacy under the California Constitution. Student athletes seeking to participate in NCAA-sponsored competition are required to sign a consent form agreeing to allow the association to test them for banned drugs. Failure to sign the form renders the student ineligible to participate in NCAA-sponsored competition. Drug testing is conducted at NCAA athletic events by urinalysis. All student athletes in championship events for postseason bowl games are potentially subject to testing. Particular athletes are chosen for testing according to plans that may include random selection or other selection criteria such as playing time, team position, place of finish or suspicion of drug use. Upon a written notice following his or her participation in an athletic event, the selected athlete is required to report promptly to a collection station. The sample is then given in the presence of an NCAA official monitor.

The trial court concluded that the NCAA's drug testing program violated the state constitutional privacy rights of the student athletes. The court permanently enjoined any testing of student athletes whether inside or outside the state of California. The NCAA appealed to the Court of Appeal of California which affirmed the trial court's judgment, including the permanent injunction. The NCAA appealed this decision to the Supreme Court of California.

The supreme court reversed the decisions of the lower courts. Although the court rejected the NCAA's assertions that the "Privacy Initiative," by which the right of privacy was added to the constitution, did not govern the conduct of private nongovernmental entities, it found nonetheless that student athletes had a lower expectation of privacy than the general student population. Observation of urination obviously implicated privacy interests. However, by its nature, participation in highly competitive postseason championship events involves close regulation and scrutiny of the physical fitness and bodily condition of student athletes. Required physical examinations (including urinalysis) and the special regulation of sleep habits, diet, fitness and other activities that intrude significantly on privacy interests are routine aspects of a college athlete's life not shared by other students or the population at large. Athletes frequently disrobe in the presence of one another as well as their athletic mentors and assistants in locker room settings where private bodily parts are readily observable by others of the same sex. They also exchange information about their physical condition and medical treatment with coaches, trainers, and others who have a need to know.

The court noted that drug testing programs involving student athletes have routinely survived Fourth Amendment privacy challenges. Finally, the court concluded that the NCAA had an interest in protecting the health and safety of student athletes involved in NCAA-regulated competition. *Hill v. National Collegiate Athletic Assn.*, 26 Cal.Rptr.2d 834 (Cal.1994).

The University of Colorado conducted a drug-testing program for intercollegiate athletes that entailed a urine test at each annual physical with random tests thereafter. The program was amended a number of times, and one amendment substituted random rapid eye examinations for urinalysis. The university prohibited any athlete refusing to consent to the testing from participating in intercollegiate athletics. The program called for progressive sanctions ranging from required participation in rehabilitation programs to permanent suspension from athletics. A group of athletes filed a class action suit against the university in a Colorado trial court seeking declaratory and injunctive relief. The court ruled for the athletes. The Colorado Court of Appeals affirmed this decision, and the university appealed to the Supreme Court of Colorado.

The supreme court observed that the program did not ensure confidentiality and was mandatory inasmuch as refusal to participate disqualified students from participating in university athletic programs. The university was unable to articulate an important governmental interest for the program. Unlike cases involving high school athletes, college students did not have a diminished expectation of privacy under the Fourth Amendment that justified government searches in the absence of an important governmental interest. Random, suspicionless urinalysis was unconstitutional. University student athletes did not consent to participation in the program because there could be no voluntary consent where the failure to give it resulted in denial of a governmental benefit. *Univ. of Colorado v. Derdeyn*, 863 P.2d 929 (Colo.1993).

Following a lengthy investigation of allegedly improper recruiting practices by the University of Nevada, Las Vegas (UNLV), the NCAA found 38 violations, including ten by the school's head basketball coach. The NCAA proposed a number of sanctions and threatened to impose more if the coach was not suspended. Facing an enormous pay cut, the coach sued the NCAA under 42 U.S.C. § 1983 for violating his due process rights. The Nevada Supreme Court held that the NCAA's conduct constituted state action for constitutional purposes. It upheld a Nevada trial court's dismissal of the suspension and award of attorney's fees. The NCAA appealed to the U.S. Supreme Court, which held that the NCAA's participation in the events that led to the suspension did not constitute state action within the meaning of § 1983. The NCAA was not a state actor on the theory that it misused the power it possessed under state law. UNLV's decision to suspend the coach in compliance with the NCAA's rules and recommendations did not turn the NCAA's conduct into state action. This was because UNLV retained the power to withdraw from the NCAA and establish its own standards. The NCAA could not directly discipline the coach, but could threaten to impose additional sanctions against the school. It was the school's decision and not the NCAA's to suspend the coach. *NCAA v. Tarkanian*, 488 U.S. 179, 109 S.Ct. 454, 102 L.Ed.2d 469 (1988).

The NCAA received notice of possible rule violations at a Nevada university. It sent an official inquiry to the university describing the possible violations. The NCAA then investigated the basketball program. Witnesses were interviewed, information was exchanged, and documents were secured in preparation for the official hearing before the NCAA's committee on infractions. Meanwhile, the Nevada state legislature passed a law that required NCAA infraction proceedings to meet certain standards. These mandated standards were not a part of the NCAA's substantive and procedural rules for all member schools. The school involved demanded that the NCAA follow the new rules. The NCAA refused and filed an action in federal court for declaratory and injunctive relief. The case was heard before the U.S. District Court for the District of Nevada. The district court held that the new law violated the Commerce Clause of the U.S. Constitution by imposing a burden on interstate commerce which was nationwide in reach. The practical effect of the legislation would be to compel the NCAA to adopt the procedural rules enacted by the Nevada legislature, thereby allowing the Nevada legislature to effectively dictate enforcement proceedings in states other than Nevada. *NCAA v. Miller,* 795 F.Supp. 1476 (D.Nev.1992).

A student at Brown University spent his first two semesters of college at the University of Nebraska. The student, a talented wrestler, failed a course during his first semester at Nebraska. He had not subsequently repeated the course. The National Collegiate Athletic Association notified him that he would be prohibited from wrestling during the following academic year because he had not successfully repeated the course. The student sued in federal court seeking an injunction to restrain the NCAA from preventing him from wrestling. The federal district court denied the injunction since the student was not likely to succeed on the merits of his case. NCAA regulations prevent athletic participation for one year after transfer. There is an exception to the one-year abstinence rule for students in good academic standing who would have been eligible to participate had they remained at their previous institution. Since he had failed the course, he would have been ineligible at Nebraska, so he was ineligible at Brown. In addition, the student could not bring constitutional claims since the NCAA is a private actor, not a state agent. *Collier v. NCAA,* 783 F.Supp. 1576 (D.R.I.1992).

III. DISCRIMINATION AND EQUITY IN ATHLETICS

Federal civil rights laws forbid discrimination based on sex, race or disability in federally funded school athletic programs. All public school districts must also comply with the Equal Protection Clause.

A. Gender Equity

Title IX of the Education Amendments of 1972 prohibits sex discrimination in any "program or activity" receiving federal financial assistance. The U.S. Department of Education's Title IX regulations (34 CFR Part 106) provide more explicit guidance than the words of Title IX itself. Under the regulations, a school may operate separate teams for male and female athletes if selection for the team is based on competitive skill or the sport is a contact sport (defined as "boxing, wrestling, rugby, ice hockey, football, basketball and other sports the purpose or major activity of which involves bodily contact"). For noncontact sports, female athletes must be allowed to try out for traditionally male teams if there is no such team for females. Further, funding levels and other resource allocations must provide members of both sexes with "equal athletic opportunity."

Although Title IX allows schools to maintain single sex teams for contact sports, several court decisions have questioned whether this practice is constitutional. These courts have reasoned that the Equal Protection Clause of the Fourteenth Amendment, and sometimes state law, go beyond Title IX and require schools to allow physically qualified females to try out for contact sport teams. Differing interpretations of the constitutional and statutory requirements in this area continue to exist.

The University of Illinois eliminated four varsity athletic programs, including men's swimming, in response to a $600,000 budget shortfall. The decision was in part motivated by the need to comply with Title IX, which prohibits discrimination on the basis of sex by recipients of federal financial assistance. Participation in women's intercollegiate athletics at the university was disproportionate to female undergraduate enrollment, and the university therefore did not eliminate the women's swimming program. Members of the men's swim team sued the university and its board of trustees in the U.S. District Court for the Central District of Illinois, alleging violations of Title IX and their equal protection rights. The court granted summary judgment to the university and board and the complaining parties appealed to the U.S. Court of Appeals, Seventh Circuit. The court of appeals observed that elimination of the women's swimming program could have exposed the university to further Title IX violations because of the great disparity between female enrollment and women's sports participation. The university's response to budget constraints had been reasonable and Title IX did not require parallel teams to ensure compliance. There was also no merit to the team members' claim that the university action violated their equal protection rights. The action was justifiable because it furthered the important governmental objective of removing sex discrimination. *Kelley v. Bd. of Trustees, Univ. of Illinois*, 35 F.3d 265 (7th Cir.1994).

Twelve female Kentucky high school student-athletes participated in interscholastic slow-pitch softball, but sought to play fast-pitch softball, which was not sanctioned by the state high school athletic association. The association sanctioned only eight sports for girls, while it sanctioned ten for boys. The students filed a lawsuit against the state education board and athletic association in the U.S. District Court for the Western District of Kentucky, alleging that the board and association violated Title IX of the Education Amendments of 1972 (20 U.S.C. § 1681 *et seq.*) and the Equal Protection Clause of the U.S. Constitution. The court granted summary judgment to the board and association, and the students appealed to the U.S. Court of Appeals, Sixth Circuit.

On appeal, the students argued that since fast-pitch softball was sanctioned by most college sports programs, and slow-pitch softball was not, the lack of an officially sanctioned program in Kentucky hurt their chances to participate at the college level and left them unable to obtain scholarships. The association argued that since it did not receive direct federal funding, it could not be sued under Title IX. The court agreed with the students, ruling that the district court had improperly granted summary judgment. The athletic association's indirect receipt of federal funds opened it up to liability under Title IX. A number of fact issues existed that made pretrial dismissal inappropriate, and the court remanded the case to the district court for further consideration of the Title IX claim. However, the district court had properly dismissed the Equal Protection Clause claim. *Horner v. Kentucky High School Athletic Assn.*, 43 F.3d 265 (6th Cir.1994).

A Colorado university terminated its women's varsity softball team. Former members of the team then sued the university, seeking reinstatement of the team and money damages. They asserted that the university had violated Title IX. Alternatively, they claimed that the termination was the perpetuation of an already existing violation of Title IX by the university. Title IX requires recipients of federal financial assistance who operate or sponsor interscholastic, intercollegiate, club or intramural athletics to provide equal athletic opportunity for members of both sexes. In determining whether equal opportunities are available, one of the considerations is whether the selection of sports and the levels of competition effectively accommodate the interests and abilities of members of both sexes. The U.S. District Court for the District of Colorado ruled that the decision to terminate the women's softball team violated Title IX. In the last twelve years, women's participation opportunities declined by approximately 34 percent while men's participation opportunities declined by only 20 percent. Finally, the court noted that the university had not demonstrated that the interests and abilities of women were being fully and effectively accommodated by the university's present athletic program. It had eliminated varsity athletic opportunities for women in a sport where there was significant interest and talent. The court issued a permanent injunction against the university requiring it to reinstate the women's softball team. *Roberts v. Colorado State University*, 814 F.Supp. 1507 (D.Colo.1993).

A Pennsylvania university with an undergraduate population that was 56 percent female fielded an equal number of male and female varsity athletic teams. However, male teams had more athletes and were better funded. The university cut men's tennis and soccer and women's gymnastics and field hockey teams because of budget problems. Three female athletes sued the university in the U.S. District Court for the Western District of Pennsylvania under Title IX of the 1972 Education Amendments, seeking an order to force the university to reduce the disparity between men's and women's varsity athletics, and to reinstate women's gymnastics and field hockey. The court granted a preliminary injunction and certified a class. It then held that the university was not in compliance with Title IX regulations and ordered reinstatement of the gymnastics and field hockey programs. The university filed a motion to modify the injunction to allow replacement of the gymnastics team with a women's soccer team. The court refused to modify the injunction and the university appealed to the U.S. Court of Appeals, Third Circuit. The court observed that modification of an injunction is appropriate only when there has been a change of circumstances making the original order inequitable. There was no such change in circumstances in this case. The district court had not abused its discretion in ordering the temporary preservation of athletic programs. The university's proposal for a women's soccer program as a replacement for the women's gymnastic team would result in a net reduction in funding for women's athletics that was in contravention of Title IX goals. *Favia v. Indiana Univ. of Pennsylvania*, 7 F.3d 332 (3d Cir.1993).

The protections of Title IX apply equally to males and females. However, due to the "contact sports" limitation in Title IX and the fact that the Equal Protection Clause does not require that the schools be "sex blind," this does not mean that males will automatically be allowed to play on female teams.

A male Rhode Island high school student desired to compete as a member of his school's girls' field-hockey team. However, the regulations of the Rhode Island Interscholastic League forbade boys from participating on girls' athletic teams. A federal district court refused the student's request for an injunction based on the Fourteenth Amendment's Equal Protection Clause. *Kleczek v. Rhode Island Interscholastic League*, 768 F.Supp. 951 (D.R.I.1991). The student then sued the league in Rhode Island state court seeking an injunction based on the state constitution's equal protection provisions. The trial court granted the request, noting that the state constitution required stricter scrutiny of gender classifications than the U.S. Constitution. It granted the injunction and the league appealed to the Rhode Island Supreme Court. The supreme court stated that the trial court had applied the wrong standard. Gender classifications under the state constitution must serve important governmental objectives and be substantially related to the achievement of those objectives. They need not serve "compelling interests" and be "necessary to the objective," as the trial court held. Safety concerns and physical differences between the sexes justified the rule. The injunction was vacated and the action remanded. *Kleczek v. Rhode Island Interschol. League, Inc.*, 612 A.2d 734 (R.I.1992). See also *Williams v. School Dist. of Bethlehem*, 998 F.2d 168 (3d Cir.1993), where the U.S. Court of Appeals, Third Circuit, overturned a district court decision allowing a Pennsylvania boy to compete on a girls' field hockey team.

B.   Students with Disabilities

Section 504 of the Rehabilitation Act of 1973 provides that an otherwise qualified individual with a disability may not, by reason of his or her disability, be excluded from participation in, be denied the benefits of, or be subjected to discrimination under any program or activity receiving federal financial assistance. The key phrase is "otherwise qualified." A person is otherwise qualified only if he or she is qualified to participate in spite of the disability.

Two Michigan students were required to repeat kindergarten because of their disabilities and were placed in special education or ungraded classrooms. As a result, both students became seniors after their nineteenth birthdays. They sought to participate on cross-country and track teams during their senior years, even though their participation in interscholastic sports was prohibited by the state athletic association's rule that required a student to be under the age of 19 as of the first day of September of the current school year. The association denied the students' request for a waiver from enforcement of the rule, and they filed a lawsuit against the association in the U.S. District Court for the Eastern District of Michigan, alleging violations of the Americans with Disabilities Act (ADA), § 504 of the Rehabilitation Act and state law. They sought a preliminary order from the court that would allow them to participate in interscholastic cross-country and track.

The court found that the ADA and § 504 were applicable to the athletic association because it was a private entity operating a public accommodation that was the indirect recipient of federal funding. Because both students alleged that their athletic participation had improved their educational performance, they could be reasonably accommodated by waiver of the age eligibility requirement. There was no countervailing public policy reason to exclude them from interscholastic sports, inasmuch as they were only average performers in noncontact sports who presented no risk of harm to other students. The students were otherwise qualified to participate in interscholastic sports for the purposes of the federal acts and the athletic association was required to allow their participation. The court granted the students' motion for a preliminary order allowing them to compete in interscholastic cross-country and track. *Sandison v. Michigan High School Athletic Assn., Inc.*, 863 F.Supp. 483 (E.D.Mich.1994).

A Montana student played football during the first semester of his ninth grade year, but was reassigned to eighth grade later in the year because of poor academic performance. He began the next year in ninth grade, and later advanced to tenth and eleventh grades, playing football each year. He sought an exception to eligibility rules published by the Montana High School Association (MHSA) prior to his senior year. The rules limited interscholastic sports participation to eight semesters, or four seasons in any one sport. Because the student would enter his ninth semester of high school during his senior year, and had played four years of football, his participation in football would violate both rules. The MHSA refused to make an exception, and the student's parents filed a lawsuit in a Montana court for a temporary restraining order to prohibit the MHSA from enforcing its rules. The court awarded the student an injunction, basing its order on the Individuals with Disabilities Education Act (IDEA). The MHSA appealed to the Supreme Court of Montana.

The supreme court observed that the student and his parents had never requested special education services from the school district. Federal regulations issued under the IDEA did not allow students to receive special education services without placement under an individualized education program. Although the parents argued that the student would have qualified for special education services had they requested them, the court refused to allow the student relief under the IDEA when his parents had failed to follow its procedures. The MHSA was not a state or local education agency as defined by the IDEA, and was not subject to its procedures. Because the student had no right to participate in high school athletics under the IDEA, the court reversed and remanded the case with orders to dissolve the injunction. *J.M., Jr. v. Montana High School Assn.*, 875 P.2d 1026 (Mont.1994).

The multidisciplinary evaluation team and individualized education planning committee of a Michigan high school independently determined that a student with poor grades was not emotionally impaired or learning disabled under state special education regulations. The committee declared the student ineligible for special education services. He became disruptive during his junior year of high school and was suspended for 21 days. At the end of the year, the school expelled the student because of his low grade average and insufficient credits. It also excluded him from varsity sports participation. The school superintendent permitted the student to enroll for his senior year, but denied his request for sports eligibility. The decision was based on state high school athletic association rules requiring a minimum number of credits per semester.

During the summer before his senior year, a clinical psychologist diagnosed the student as having attention deficit hyperactivity disorder. On that basis, the school superintendent requested a waiver of the eligibility requirement for the student. When the association refused to grant the waiver, the student's parents filed a lawsuit in the U.S. District Court for the Eastern District of Michigan, alleging that the association violated the student's rights under the Americans with Disabilities Act (ADA), 42 U.S.C. § 12101 *et seq.*, and § 504 of the Rehabilitation Act (29 U.S.C. § 794). The student's parents also added claims under a Michigan civil rights statute and the Equal Protection Clause of the Fourteenth Amendment. The association filed a motion for summary judgment. The court found questions of fact that precluded summary judgment under the ADA, the Equal Protection Clause, the Michigan civil rights statute and § 504. The athletic association could be considered a public entity under the ADA. The court denied the association's summary judgment motion. *Hoot by Hoot v. Milan Area Schools,* 853 F.Supp. 243 (E.D.Mich.1994).

A Missouri student was held back in grades one and three. After an evaluation, he was identified as having a learning disability, behavior disorder and language impairment in auditory comprehension. Because he had been held back two years, he entered his senior year of high school at age 19. Missouri State High School Activities Association (MSHSAA) regulations prohibited interscholastic sports participation by students over 19 years old. The student filed a petition seeking an exemption from MSHSAA rules. The MSHSAA denied the petition and the student filed a lawsuit in the U.S. District Court for the Eastern District of Missouri under the Americans with Disabilities Act (ADA), § 504 of the Rehabilitation Act and 42 U.S.C. § 1983. The student filed a motion for a preliminary injunction which would allow him to participate in sports. The MSHSAA filed a motion to dismiss the lawsuit, and the court considered the parties' motions.

The court held that the MSHSAA's regulations were designed to prevent older, larger students from harming smaller students, and to prevent schools from holding back students to take advantage of their physical maturity. In this case, the student was slightly below average size and strength, and was a good but not superior player. The MSHSAA was unable to show that his participation would harm other students. On the contrary, taking away the student's final year of high school eligibility would harm his chances for receiving a junior college scholarship. There was also evidence that participation in sports had improved his grades and attitude toward school. The court determined on a preliminary basis that the student was a qualified individual with a disability under the ADA and § 504, and would probably succeed in a § 1983 case. The court granted the student's motion for a preliminary injunction allowing him to participate in interscholastic sports. *Pottgen v. Missouri State High School Activities Assn.*, 857 F.Supp. 654 (E.D.Mo.1994).

In a case in New York, a boy who was always active in school athletics received internal injuries when he was thrown from an unenclosed motor vehicle and struck a tree. The accident resulted in the removal of one of his kidneys. He completely recovered and continued to lead an otherwise normal life. However, following a required physical examination on behalf of the school district, the doctor made a written recommendation to the school that he be prohibited from participating in contact sports because of the potential damage to his remaining kidney. The parents filed this petition in a New York trial court seeking to enjoin the school from prohibiting their son from playing sports. In 1986, the legislature added a new law to create a remedy whereby a student may have recourse through the courts to enjoin a school district from prohibiting participation in an athletic program by reason of a physical impairment. The statute requires that the petition of the student's consenting parent be accompanied by two independent medical opinions attesting to the physical capacity of the student to participate in the desired activity, that such participation would be reasonably safe, and designating any safety or preventive measures or devices needed to protect the student. The ultimate determination whether such participation would serve the student's best interests is then to be made by the court. The court noted that the student's parents and the student fully understood the risks and legal consequences of the decision they made. They had also provided the requisite medical opinions. Therefore, the court enjoined the school district from prohibiting the student's participation in athletics. *Pace v. Dryden Central School Dist.*, 574 N.Y.S.2d 142 (Sup.1991).

IV. ISSUES IN COACHING

A coach is generally free from liability for injuries received from faulty athletic equipment absent a showing of wilful or wanton misconduct. A coach may not use physical coercion. Also, a coach's position may be reassigned or terminated with less restrictions than for regular teaching assignments. (See Chapter Three for employment discrimination and equal pay cases involving coaches.)

A. Employment

Coaching contracts are frequently severable from teaching contracts and the school district typically pays the coach a salary supplement. The courts have not held that coaches have a property interest in their jobs and because coaching duties are severable from teaching, a coach does not attain tenure as a coach. Therefore, coaches can generally be relieved of their coaching duties without formal procedures.

A Georgia high school teacher received a salary supplement of $7,400 for serving as the school's head football coach. The school district was a member of the Georgia High School Association (GHSA), a voluntary association of public and private high schools that enforces eligibility rules for interscholastic sports. A student who wanted to play on the football team was found ineligible. The coach arranged for testing of the student and a determination was made that he had a learning disability. When this information was communicated to some of the student's teachers, four of the student's grades were changed and the school declared the student eligible to play football. The Professional Practices Commission (PPC), a state agency authorized to investigate alleged violations of state education rules and regulations, recommended suspension of the coach's teaching certificate, and within one week, the county school board, without holding a hearing, terminated his coaching duties. The coach submitted a resignation letter. He sued the school district, GSHA, PPC, and various school officials in the U.S. District Court for the Middle District of Georgia.

The district court granted summary judgment motions by the school superintendent on the teacher's equal protection and libel claims. The PPC and its officials argued that the Eleventh Amendment barred any suit against them in federal court. The district court rejected their summary judgment motion and remanded the head coach's claims against the PPC and its officials to a Georgia trial court. The court determined that while Georgia tenure laws extended to written teaching contracts, there was no evidence that the tenure law should protect unwritten coaching contracts. Accordingly, the head coach had no property interest in the coaching position and was not entitled to a pretermination hearing. *Brewer v. Purvis*, 816 F.Supp. 1560 (M.D.Ga.1993).

A Texas newspaper reported on a brawl occurring among players after a football game. It published an article which was sharply critical of the head football coach of one school, who was also the school's athletic director and a classroom teacher. The article faulted the coach for "turning his back on the situation" and implied that his team played "dirty football." The coach and his wife sued the newspaper and one of its sportswriters in a Texas trial court, which granted the newspaper's summary judgment motion. The coach and his wife appealed to the Court of Appeals of Texas, Amarillo. The coach argued that he was not a public official and that he only needed to show negligence by the newspaper to prevail in his libel suit. The newspaper argued that the coach was a public official, whose greater recognition required a showing of actual malice in order for there to be any liability. The court of appeals noted that the coach was by his own admission a very well known individual in the area, and therefore a public official. Because there was no evidence that the newspaper had made a false and defamatory statement with reckless disregard for the truth, the coach failed to show actual malice. Accordingly, the trial court's summary judgment ruling was correct and its decision to dismiss the lawsuit was affirmed. *Johnson v. Southwestern Newspapers Corp.*, 855 S.W.2d 182 (Tex.App.-Amarillo 1993).

Two tenured Kansas junior high school teachers taught full-time and had supplemental coaching assignments. Practices were conducted during school hours in "athletics classes." The teachers resigned their coaching duties. They were offered a reduced primary employment contract for the next school year by their school board. The teachers sued the board in a state court. They alleged that reducing their primary contracts was a violation of their right to resign from supplemental duties without being penalized. The court held for the board and the Kansas Court of Appeals affirmed the decision. The teachers appealed to the Kansas Supreme Court. The supreme court held for the teachers, reversing the lower court decisions. The school board took affirmative steps to reduce the primary contracts in treating the coaching duties as subject to the teachers' primary contracts. The Kansas school code provided that coaching was covered under supplemental contracts. Whether the school board could afford to conduct after school practices was irrelevant. The teachers could resign their supplemental coaching duties without affecting their primary contracts as teachers. They were entitled to reinstatement with backpay. *Hachiya v. Bd. of Educ., Unified School Dist. No. 370, Saline County*, 750 P.2d 383 (Kan.1988).

B. Liability

A 110-pound eighth grade Louisiana student played for his elementary school football team. In a game played against another elementary school team, a 270-pound eighth grade player from the opposing team tackled the student, causing a fracture of the student's leg. There was no penalty called on the play. The student and his parents sued the coaches of both football teams and the insurer of one of the coaches, claiming that they should be held liable for the injury. It was claimed that the accident was caused by allowing smaller elementary school students to scrimmage and play against larger students. The coaches and insurer filed a motion for summary judgment in a Louisiana trial court, claiming that there was no duty by the coaches to prevent players from being injured in supervised, refereed interschool football games and that the tackling was neither unexpected nor unsportsmanlike. The court granted the summary judgment motion and the student and his parents appealed to the Court of Appeal of Louisiana, First Circuit. The court of appeal found that there was no duty imposed upon coaches to protect players against the potential risk of injury from playing football games with players of different weights. Even though the Louisiana Supreme Court had abolished the doctrine of assumption of risk several years previously, the absence of any duty to protect players precluded a finding of liability. The summary judgment decision of the trial court was affirmed. *Laiche v. Kohen*, 621 So.2d 1162 (La.App.1st Cir.1993).

A New Jersey college mailed a letter to an Illinois student advising him that he was being recruited for a basketball scholarship. It mailed the letter in care of the student's high school basketball coach, and the letter was not given to the student for seven months. The student sued the school district in an Illinois trial court, which dismissed the case for failure to state a cause of action. The Appellate Court of Illinois, Fifth District, reversed and remanded the case, holding that the student had a property interest in the information contained in the letter. On remand, the trial court would have to consider whether the student would have received a scholarship except for the late delivery. *Liddle v. Salem School Dist. No. 600*, 619 N.E.2d 530 (Ill.App.5th Dist.1993).

APPENDIX A

UNITED STATES CONSTITUTION

Provisions of Interest to Educators

ARTICLE I

Section 1. All legislative Powers herein granted shall be vested in a Congress of the United States, which shall consist of a Senate and House of Representatives.

* * *

Section 8. The Congress shall have Power To lay and collect Taxes, Duties, Imposts and Excises, to pay the Debts and provide for the common Defence and general Welfare of the United States; but all Duties, Imposts and Excises shall be uniform throughout the United States:

To borrow money on the credit of the United States;

To regulate Commerce with foreign Nations, and among the several States, and with the Indian Tribes;

To establish an uniform Rule of Naturalization, and uniform Laws on the subject of Bankruptcies throughout the United States;

* * *

To promote the Progress of Science and useful Arts, by securing for limited Times to Authors and Inventors the exclusive Right to their respective Writings and Discoveries;

* * *

To make all Laws which shall be necessary and proper for carrying into Execution for the foregoing Powers, and all other Powers vested by this Constitution in the Government of the United States, or in any Department or Office thereof.

* * *

Section 9. * * * No Bill of Attainder or ex post facto Law shall be passed.

Section 10. No State shall * * * pass any Bill of Attainder, ex post facto Law, or Law impairing the Obligation of Contracts, or grant any Title of Nobility.

* * *

ARTICLE II

Section 1. The executive Power shall be vested in a President of the United States of America.

* * *

ARTICLE III

Section 1. The judicial Power of the United States, shall be vested in one Supreme Court, and in such inferior Courts as the Congress may from time to time ordain and establish. The Judges, both of the supreme and inferior courts, shall hold their Offices during good Behaviour, and shall, at stated Times, receive for their Services a Compensation, which shall not be diminished during their Continuance in Office.

Section 2. The judicial Power shall extend to all Cases, in Law and Equity, arising under this Constitution, the Laws of the United States, and Treaties made, or which shall be made; under their Authority; to all Cases affecting Ambassadors, other public Ministers and Consuls; to all Cases of admiralty and maritime Jurisdiction, to Controversies to which the United States shall be a party to Controversies between two or more States; between a State and Citizens of another State; between Citizens of different States; between Citizens of the same State claiming Lands under the Grants of different States, and between a State, or the Citizens thereof, and foreign States, Citizens or Subjects.

* * *

ARTICLE IV

Section 1. Full Faith and Credit shall be given in each State to the public Acts, Records and judicial Proceedings of every other State.* * *

Section 2. The Citizens of each State shall be entitled to all Privileges and Immunities of Citizens in the several States.

* * *

Section 4. The United States shall guarantee to every State in this Union a Republican Form of Government, and shall protect each of them against Invasion; and on Application of the Legislature, or of the Executive (when the Legislature cannot be convened) against domestic Violence.

ARTICLE V

The Congress, whenever two thirds of both Houses shall deem it necessary, shall propose Amendments to this Constitution, or, on the Application of the Legislatures of two thirds of the several States, shall call a Convention for proposing Amendments, which, in either Case, shall be valid to all Intents and Purposes, as part of this Constitution, when ratified by the Legislatures of three fourths of the several States, or by Conventions in three fourths thereof, as the one or the other Mode of Ratification may be proposed by the Congress; Provided that no Amendment which may be made prior to the Year One thousand eight hundred and eight shall in any Manner affect the first and fourth Clauses in the Ninth Section of the first Article; and that no State, without its Consent, shall be deprived of its equal Suffrage in the Senate.

ARTICLE VI

* * *

This Constitution, and the Laws of the United States which shall be made in Pursuance thereof; and all Treaties made, or which shall be made, under the Authority of the United States, shall be the Supreme Law of the Land; and the Judges in every State shall be bound thereby, any Thing in the Constitution or Laws of any State to the Contrary notwithstanding.

The Senators and Representatives before mentioned, and the Members of the several State Legislatures, and all executive and judicial Officers, both of the United States and of the several States, shall be bound by Oath or Affirmation, to support this Constitution; but no religious Test shall ever be required as a Qualification to any Office or public Trust under the United States.

* * *

AMENDMENT I

Congress shall make no law respecting an establishment of religion, or prohibiting the free exercise thereof; or abridging the freedom of speech, or of the press; or the right of the people peaceably to assemble, and to petition the Government for a redress of grievances.

* * *

AMENDMENT IV

The right of the people to be secure in their persons, houses, papers, and effects, against unreasonable searches and seizures, shall not be violated, and no Warrants shall issue, but upon probable cause, supported by Oath or affirmation, and particularly describing the place to be searched, and the persons or things to be seized.

AMENDMENT V

No person shall be held to answer for a capital, or otherwise infamous crime, unless on a presentment or indictment of a Grand Jury, except in cases arising in the land or naval forces, or in the Militia, when in actual service in time of War or public danger; nor shall any person be subject for the same offence to be twice put in jeopardy of life or limb; nor shall be compelled in any criminal case to be a witness against himself, nor be deprived of life, liberty, or property, without due process of law; nor shall private property be taken for public use, without just compensation.

AMENDMENT VI

In all criminal prosecutions, the accused shall enjoy the right to a speedy and public trial, by an impartial jury of the State and district wherein the crime shall have been committed, which district shall have been previously ascertained by law, and to be informed of the nature and cause of the accusation; to be confronted with the witnesses against him; to have compulsory process for obtaining witnesses in his favor, and to have the Assistance of Counsel for his defense.

AMENDMENT VII

In Suits at common law, where the value in controversy shall exceed twenty dollars, the right of trial by jury shall be preserved, and no fact tried by jury, shall be otherwise re-examined in any Court of the United States, than according to the rules of the common law.

AMENDMENT VIII

Excessive bail shall not be required, nor excessive fines imposed, nor cruel and unusual punishments inflicted.

AMENDMENT IX

The enumeration in the Constitution, of certain rights, shall not be construed to deny or disparage others retained by the people.

AMENDMENT X

The powers not delegated to the United States by the Constitution, nor prohibited by it to the States, are reserved to the States respectively, or to the people.

AMENDMENT XI

The Judicial power of the United States shall not be construed to extend to any suit in law or equity, commenced or prosecuted against one of the United States by Citizens of another State, or by Citizens or Subjects of any Foreign State.

* * *

AMENDMENT XIII

Section 1. Neither slavery nor involuntary servitude, except as a punishment for crime whereof the party shall have been duly convicted, shall exist within the United States, or any place subject to their jurisdiction.

Section 2. Congress shall have power to enforce this article by appropriate legislation.

AMENDMENT XIV

Section 1. All persons born or naturalized in the United States, and subject to the jurisdiction thereof, are citizens of the United States and of the State wherein they reside. No State shall make or enforce any law which shall abridge the privileges or immunities of citizens of the United States; nor shall any State deprive any person of life, liberty, or property, without due process of law; nor deny to any person within its jurisdicton the equal protection of the laws.

* * *

Section 5. The Congress shall have power to enforce, by appropriate legislation, the provisions of this article.

APPENDIX B

SUBJECT MATTER TABLE
OF RECENT LAW REVIEW ARTICLES

ACADEMIC FREEDOM

Daughtrey, William H., Jr. *The legal nature of academic freedom in United States colleges and universities.* 25 U.Rich.L.Rev. 233 (1991).

Demma, Anthony D., Jr. Comment. *Educational accountability in Florida: meaningful reform or marginal tinkering?* 19 Fla.St.U.L.Rev. 1145 (1992).

The denial of an academic freedom privilege. [Univ. of Pennsylvania v. Equal Employment Opportunity Comm'n, 110 S.Ct. 577 (1990)]. 18 Pepperdine L.Rev. 213 (1990).

DiMatteo, Larry A. and Don Wiesner. *Academic honor codes: a legal and ethical analysis.* 19 S.Ill.U.L.J. 49 (1994).

Focus on Academic Freedom. Articles by Walter P. Metzger, Douglas Laycock and John T. Noonan, Jr. 20 J.C.& U.L. 1 (1993).

Harrington, Michele L. Note. *Allowing local school boards to turn on "Channel One."* [State v. Whittle Communications, 328 N.C. 456, 402 S.E.2d 556 (1991)]. 70 N.C.L.Rev. 1929 (1992).

Hiers, Richard H. *Academic freedom in public colleges and universities: o say does that star-spangled First Amendment banner yet wave?* 40 Wayne L.Rev. 1 (1993).

Lovely, Linda S. *Comment. Beyond "the freedom to do good and not to teach evil": professors' academic freedom rights in classrooms of public higher education.* 26 Wake Forest L.Rev. 711 (1991).

Pacholski, Susan L. Comment. *Title VII in the university: the difference academic freedom makes.* 59 U.Chi.L.Rev. 1317 (1992).

Russo, Charles J. *School-based decision making in Kentucky: dawn of a new era or nothing new under the sun?* 83 Ky.L.J. 123 (1994-95).

Schweitzer, Thomas A. *"Academic challenge" cases: should judicial review extend to academic evaluations of students?* 41 Am.U.L.Rev. 267 (1992).

Shifting meanings of academic freedom; an analysis of ... Univ. of Pennsylvania v. EEOC, 110 S.Ct. 577 (1990). 17 J.C. & U.L. 329 (1991).

Two Supreme Courts speak on the academic freedom privilege. [Univ. of Pennsylvania v. EEOC, 110 S.Ct. 577 (1990); and Dixon v. Rutgers, 110 N.J. 432, 541 A.2d 1046 (1988)]. 42 Rutgers L.Rev. 1089 (1990).

ATHLETICS

Barkowsky, Lesa A. Student article. *The illiteracy problem and college athletes: an argument for educational malpractice*: 16 Colum.-VLA J.L. & Arts 537 (1992).

Champion, Walter T., Jr. *The NCAA's drug testing policies: walking a constitutional tightrope?* 67 N.D.L.Rev. 269 (1991).

Connolly, Walter B., Jr. and Jeffrey D. Adelman. *A university's defense to a Title IX gender equity in athletics lawsuit: Congress never intended gender equity based on student body ratios.* 71 U.Det.Mercy L.Rev. 845 (1994).

Davis, Timothy. *Absence of good faith: defining a university's educational obligation to student-athletes.* 28 Hous.L.Rev. 743 (1991).

Davis, Timothy. *Examining educational malpractice jurisprudence: should a cause of action be created for student-athletes?* 69 Denv.U.L.Rev. 57 (1992).

Davis, Timothy. Ross v. Creighton University:*Seventh Circuit recognition of limited judicial regulations of intercollegiate athletics?* 17 S.Ill.U.L.J. 85 (1992).

Davis, Timothy. *Student-athlete prospective economic interests: contractual dimensions.* 19 T.Marshall L.Rev. 585 (1994).

Hall, Russell D. Casenote. *Fifth Circuit hands down hard-line intent requirement in schoolyard statute.* [United States v. Wake, 948 F.2d 1422 (5th Cir.1991), cert.denied, 112 S.Ct. 2944, (1992)]. 10 T.M.Cooley L.Rev. 443 (1993).

Harris, Cynthia J. Comment. *The reform of women's intercollegiate athletics: Title IX, equal protection, and supplemental method.* 20 Cap.U.L.Rev. 691 (1991).

Heckman, Diane. *Women & athletics: a twenty year retrospective on Title IX.* 9 U.Miami Ent. & Sports L.Rev. 1 (1992).

Hilborn, Harold B. Comment. *Student-athletes and judicial inconsistency: establishing a duty to educate as a means of fostering meaningful reform of intercollegiate athletics.* 89 Nw.U.L.Rev. 741 (1995).

Hollingsworth, Kerry L. Comment. Kleinknecht v. Gettysburg College: *what duty does a university owe its recruited athletes?* 19 T.Marshall L.Rev. 711 (1994).

Jones, Cathy J. *College athletes: illness or injury and the decision to return to play.* 40 Buff.L.Rev. 113 (1992).

Lufrano, Michael R. *The NCAA's involvement in setting academic standards: legality and desirability.* 4 Seton Hall J.Sport L. 97 (1994).

Mitchell, Scott A. Note. *Hit, sacked and dunked by the courts: the need for due process protection of the student-athlete in intercollegiate athletics.* [National Collegiate Athletic Ass'n v. Miller, 10 F.3d 633 (9th Cir.1993)]. 19 T.Marshall L.Rev. 733 (1994).

Ostdiek, Thomas R. Comment. *Need-based financial aid for college athletes.* 25 Creighton L.Rev. 729 (1992).

Schaller, William Lynch. *Drug testing and the evolution of federal and state regulation of intercollegiate athletics: a chill wind blows.* 18 J.C. & U.L. 131 (1991).

Wilde, T. Jesse. *Gender equity in athletics: coming of age in the 90's.* 4 Marq.Sports L.J. 217 (1994).

CONSTITUTIONAL RIGHTS (see also DISCRIMINATION, EMPLOYMENT, FREEDOM OF RELIGION, FREEDOM OF SPEECH AND SEARCH & SEIZURE)

Barr, Christopher. Recent decision. *Constitutional law — the duty of public schools to protect students from other students under* 42 U.S.C. § 1983. [D.R. v. Middle Bucks Area Vocational Technical School, 972 F.2d 1364 (3d Cir.1992), en banc, cert. denied, 113 S.Ct. 1045 (1993)]. 66 Temp.L.Rev. 1063 (1993).

Bartlett, Larry and James McCullagh. *Exclusion from the educational process in the public schools: what process is now due.* 1993 B.Y.U.Educ.& L.J. 1.

Berestka, Ronald F., Jr. Case comment. *Constitutional law — equal protection in public education: the effect of unitary status on desegregation decrees.* [Board of Education v. Dowell, 111 S.Ct. 630 (1991)]. 25 Suffolk U.L.Rev. 1215 (1991).

Bitensky, Susan H. *Of originalism, reality, and a constitutional right to education.* 86 Nw.U.L.Rev. 1056 (1992).

Egle, James B. Comment. *The constitutional implications of school choice.* 1992 Wis.L.Rev. 459.

Fadeley, Justice Edward N. *Determining the scope of state constitutional education guarantees: a preliminary methodology.* 28 Willamette L.Rev. 333 (1992).

Greenfield, Adam Michael. Note. *Annie get your gun 'cause help ain't comin': the need for constitutional protection from peer abuse in public schools.* 43 Duke L.J. 588 (1993).

Gries, Alan R. Note. *A commendable attempt to apply confusing Establishment Clause standards.* [New York State School Boards Ass'n v. Sobol, 591 N.E.2d 1146 (N.Y.1992), *cert. denied,* 113 S.Ct. 305 (1992)]. 38 Vill.L.Rev. 759 (1993).

Hawk, Morris L. Comment. *"As perfect as can be devised":* DeRolph v. State of Ohio *and the right to education in Ohio.* [DeRolph v. State of Ohio, No. 22043 (*Perry County, July 1, 1994*)]. 45 Case W.Res.L.Rev. 679 (1995).

Hernandez, Wendy. Student note. *The constitutionality of racially restrictive organizations within the university setting.* 21 J.C.& U.L. 429 (1994).

Hevly, Amy C. Note. *Nothing simple or certain: establishment clause barriers to choice systems in American education.* 35 Ariz.L.Rev. 467 (1993).

Hilton, Matthew. *Recognizing constitutional freedoms in the public schools: reasserting state and local educational policy and practice through non-judicial law.* 1994 B.Y.U.Educ.& L.J. 1

Jasperson, Jill. Student article. *Renaissance in education: the constitutionality and viability of an educational choice or voucher system.* 1993 B.Y.U.Educ.& L.J. 126.

Jones, John Paul. *Pennsylvania's choice: "school choice" and the Pennsylvania Constitution.* 66 Temp.L.Rev. 1289 (1993).

Kissam, Philip C. *Constitutional thought and public schools: an essay on* Mock v. State of Kansas. 31 Washburn L.J. 474 (1992).

Leviton, Susan P. and Matthew H. Joseph. *An adequate education for all Maryland's children: morally right, economically necessary and constitutionally required.* 52 Md.L.Rev. 1137 (1993).

Maggs, Gregory E. *Innovation in constitutional law: the right to education and the tricks of the trade.* 86 Nw.U.L.Rev. 1038 (1992).

Maloney, James A. Comment. *Constitutional problems surrounding the implementation of "anti-gang" regulations in the public schools.* 75 Marq.L.Rev. 179 (1991).

McNally, Laura K. *Recent development.* [Doe v. Taylor Independent School District, 15 F.3d 443, 5th Cir., cert. denied, 115 S.Ct. 70 (1994)]. 69 Tul.L.Rev. 273 (1994).

O'Grady, Noreen. Comment. *Toward a thorough and efficient education: resurrecting the Pennsylvania education clause.* 67 Temp.L.Rev. 613 (1994).

Oldaker, Lawrence Lee. *Privacy rights, school choice, and the Ninth Amendment.* 1993 B.Y.U.Educ.& L.J. 58.

Sieminski, Marya. Note. *Michigan's constitutional protection for public education: legal rights or empty promises?* 40 Wayne L.Rev. 1309 (1994).

Symposium: Civil Rights on Campus. Articles by Ann H. Franke, Helen Leskovac, Laura F. Rothstein, Kenneth S. Tollett, Sr., Diane M. Henson, Boyce C. Cabaniss, Thomas M. Melsheimer, Steven H. Stodghill, Diana L. Faust and Kathryn R. Swedlow. 13 Rev.Litig. 383 (1994).

Vallarelli, Julie Huston. Note. *State constitutional restraints on the privatization of education.* 72 B.U.L.Rev. 381 (1992).

Walsh, Thomas J. *Education as a fundamental right under the United States Constitution.* 29 Willamette L.Rev. 279 (1993).

Walters, John W. Note. *The constitutional duty of teachers to protect students: employing the "sufficient custody" test.* 83 Ky.L.J. 229 (1994-95).

DESEGREGATION

The American Association of Law Schools' Law and Education Section Workshop on "Diversity, Desegregation & Affirmative Action." Articles by Leland Ware, Robert L. Carter, Kevin Brown and Wendy R. Brown. 37 St.Louis U.L.J. 883 (1993).

Arnston, Phillip Scott. Commentary. *Thirty years later, is the schoolhouse door still closed? Segregation in the higher education system of Alabama.* 45 Ala.L.Rev. 585 (1994).

Brown-Scott, Wendy. *Race consciousness in higher education: does "sound educational policy" support the continued existence of historically black colleges?* 43 Emory L.J. 1 (1994).

Colloquium: Racial Ceilings and School Choice. 24 Seton Hall L.Rev. (1993). *An empirical and constitutional analysis of racial ceilings and public schools...Micheal Heise; 921 Public school choice and racial integration...Stephen Eisdorfer 937.*

Crump, David. *From* Freeman *to* Brown *and back again: principle, pragmatism, and proximate cause in the school desegregation decisions.* 68 Wash.L.Rev. 753 (1993).

Davis, Robert N. *Diversity: the emerging modern separate but equal doctrine.* 1 Wm.& Mary J. Women & L. 11 (1994).

Dolich, Michael N. Casenote. *Constitutional law—facially race-neutral policies governing public colleges and universities are not sufficient to meet a state's affirmative constitutional obligation to disestablish a prior de jure segregated school system.* [United States v. Fordice, 112 S.Ct. 2727 (1992)]. 43 Drake L.Rev. 457 (1994).

Dugan, Kelli A. Case comment. *Constitutional law — standard established for the desegregation of public institutions of higher education.* [United States v. Fordice, 112 S.Ct. 2727 (1992)]. 27 Suffolk U.L.Rev. 165 (1993).

Finch, Michael. *Fairness and finality in institutional litigation: the lessons of school desegregation.* 4 Geo.Mason U.C.R.L.J. 109 (1994).

Garrow, David J. *Hopelessly hollow history: revisionist devaluing of* Brown v. Board of Education. 80 Va.L.Rev. 151 (1994).

Gastwirth, Joseph L. and Tapan K. Nayak. *Statistical measures of racially identified school systems.* 34 Jurimetrics J. 173 (1994).

Green, Patricia D. Note. *School desegregation: progress or regression.* [Freeman v. Pitts, 112 S.Ct. 1430 (1992)]. 13 Miss.C.L.Rev. 439 (1993).

Johnson, Alex M., Jr. *Bid Whist, Tonk and* United States v. Fordice: *why integrationism fails African-Americans again.* 81 Cal.L.Rev. 1401 (1993).

Jones, Chip. Comment. *Congress can (and should?) limit federal court jurisdiction in school desegregation cases.* [Freeman v. Pitts, 112 S.Ct. 1430 (1991)]. 47 SMU L.Rev. 1889 (1994).

Jones, Darryll K. *An education of their own: the precarious position of publicly supported black colleges after* United States v. Fordice. 22 J.L.& Educ. 485 (1993).

Joondeph, Brandley W. Note. *Killing* Brown *softly: the subtle undermining of effective desegregation in ...* [Freeman v. Pitts, 112 S.Ct. 1430 (1992)]. 46 Stan.L.Rev. 147 (1993).

Kelly, Jane Chambers. Casenote. *Desegregation becomes a mandate for integration in the context of higher education.* [United States v. Fordice, 112 S.Ct. 2727 (1992)]. 39 Loy.L.Rev. 231 (1993).

Klarman, Michael J. Brown v. Board of Education: *facts and political correctness.* 80 Va.L.Rev. 185 (1994).

Klarman, Michael J. Brown, *racial change, and the Civil Rights Movement.* 80 Va.L.Rev. 7 (1994).

Lockwood, Robert W., Jr. Note. *The unfortunate extension of* Green v. New Kent County School Board *to the university level.* [United States v. Fordice, 112 S.Ct. 2727 (1992)]. 37 St.Louis U.L.J. 1067 (1993).

McMullen, Daniel J. and Irene Hirata McMullen. *Stubborn facts of history — the vestiges of past discrimination in school desegregation cases.* 44 Case W.Res.L.Rev. 75 (1993).

Panton, Shelly Ann. Student Article. *Getting around Brown: the resegregation of America's schools through ...* [Freeman v. Pitts, 112 S.Ct. 1430 (1992)]. 1 How.Scroll: Soc.Jus.Rev. 92 (1993).

Scott, Sean M. *Justice redefined: minority-targeted scholarships and the struggle against racial oppression.* 62 UMKC L.Rev. 651 (1994).

Stewart, Lisa A. Recent development. *Another skirmish in the equal education battle.* [Freeman v. Pitts, 112 S.Ct. 1430 (1992)]. 28 Harv.C.R.-C.L.L.Rev. 217 (1993).

Stubbs, Frank H., III. Casenote. *A rethinking of public school desegregation.* [Freeman v. Pitts, 112 S.Ct. 1430 (1992)]. 27 U.Rich.L.Rev. 399 (1993).

Symposium: Brown v. Board of Education *after Forty Years: Confronting the Promise. Articles by Davison M. Douglas, John E. Nowak, Mark V. Tushnet, Richard Delgado, Jean Stefancic, Juan F. Perea, Christine H. Rossell, Jerome M. Culp, Jr., Marilyn V. Yarbrough, Nathan Glazer, J. Clay Smith, Jr. and Lisa C. Wilson.* 36 Wm.& Mary L.Rev. 337 (1995).

Symposium: Race, Education and the Constitution: The Legacy of Brown v. Board of Education. Articles by Bernard James, Julie M. Hoffman, David I. Levine, Donald E. Lively, Drake D. Hill and Richard Cummings. 20 Hastings Const.L.Q. 521 (1993).

Terry, Kelly S. Casenote. *Reviving the presumption of remedies under implied rights of action.* [Franklin v. Gwinnett County Public Schools, 112 S.Ct. 1028 (1992)]. 46 Ark.L.Rev. 715 (1993).

Ware, Leland. *The most visible vestige: black colleges after* Fordice. 35 B.C.L.Rev. 633 (1994).

Washburn, James A. Note. *Beyond* Brown: *evaluating equality in higher education.* 43 Duke L.J. 1115 (1994).

West, Kimberly C. Note. *A desegregation tool that backfired: magnet schools and classroom segregation.* 103 Yale L.J. 2567 (1994).

Wilson, Cory Todd. Note. *Mississippi learning: curriculum for the post-*Brown *era of higher education desegregation.* 104 Yale L.J. 243 (1994).

DISCRIMINATION

Bainbridge, Stephen M. *Student religious organizations and university policies against discrimination on the basis of sexual orientation: implications of the Religious Freedom Restoration Act.* 21 J.C.& U.L. 369 (1994).

Baker, Carrie N. Comment. *Proposed Title IX guidelines on sex-based harassment of students.* 43 Emory L.J. 271 (1994).

Brown, Kevin. *Do African-Americans need immersion schools?: The paradoxes created by legal conceptualization of race and public education.* 78 Iowa L.Rev. 813 (1993).

Caplice, Kristin S. *The case for public single-sex education.* 18 Harv.J.L.& Pub.Pol'y 227 (1994).

Celano, Patricia A. Comment. *A cry for help to the United States Supreme Court: what is the constitutional status of affirmative action in higher education.* 3 Const.L.J. 161 (1993).

Davis, Karen Mellencamp. Note. *Reading, writing, and sexual harassment: finding a constitutional remedy when schools fail to address peer abuse.* 69 Ind.L.J. 1123 (1994).

Devins, Neal. *Interest balancing and other limits to judicially managed equal educational opportunity.* 45 Mercer L.Rev. 1017 (1994).

Frost, Lynda E. *"At-risk" statutes: defining deviance and suppressing difference in the public schools.* 23 J.L.& Educ. 123 (1994).

Gallardo, Elia V. Comment. *Hierarchy and discrimination: tracking in public schools.* 15 Chicano-Latino L.Rev. 74 (1994).

Gant, Elizabeth J. Comment. *Applying Title VII "hostile work environment" analysis to Title IX of the Education Amendments of 1972 — an avenue of relief for victims of student-to-student sexual harassment in the schools.* 98 Dick.L.Rev. 489 (1994).

Horwitz, Barbara L. Casenote. *The duty of schools to protect students from sexual harassment: how much recovery will the law allow?* [Doe v. Taylor Independent School District, 975 F.2d 137 (5th Cir.1992), cert. denied *sub nom.* Caplinger v. Doe, 113 S.Ct. 1066 (1993) *reh'g granted en banc*, 987 F.2d 231 (5th Cir.1993)]. 62 U.Cin.L.Rev. 1165 (1994).

Kaplan, Patricia A. Note. *When states' American Indian teacher preferences in public schools violate equal protection under the Fourteenth Amendment.* [Krueth v. Independent Sch. Dist. No. 38, Red Lake, Minn., 496 N.W.2d 829 (Minn.App.1993), review denied (April 20, 1993)]. 17 Hamline L.Rev. 477 (1994).

Parsons, Laura and Theresa Jordan. *When educational reform results in education discrimination: a case in point.* 23 J.L.& Educ. 211 (1994).

Pate, Kara. Student article. *The legality of race exclusive scholarships.* 2 Kan.J.L.& Pub.Pol. 91 (1993).

Ruhland, Kathleen Smith. Comment. *Equal opportunity education for Minnesota's school children: a missed opportunity by the court.* [Skeen v. State, 505 N.W.2d 299 (Minn.1993)]. 20 Wm.Mitchell L.Rev. 559 (1994).

Sherer, Monica L. Comment. *No longer just child's play: school liability under Title IX for peer sexual harassment.* 141 U.Pa.L.Rev. 2119 (1993).

Torotora, John. Note. *Compensatory damages are available in intentional sexual discrimination cases.* [Franklin v. Gwinnett County Public Schools, 112 S.Ct. 1028 (1992)]. 3 Seton Hall J.Sport L. 197 (1993).

Tribeck, Robert J. Casenote. *Bursting the bubble of sexual discrimination in education.* [Franklin v. Gwinnett County Public Schools, 112 S.Ct. 1028 (1992)]. 19 Ohio N.U.L.Rev. 817 (1993).

Whitis, Norma G. Note. *The Title VII shifting burden stays put.* [St. Mary's Honor Center v. Hicks, 113 S.Ct. 2742 (1993)]. 25 Loy.U.Chi.L.J. 269 (1994).

Wrona, James S. *Eradicating sex discrimination in education: extending disparate — impact analysis to Title IX litigation.* 21 Pepperdine L.Rev. 1 (1993).

EDUCATION, GENERALLY

A survey of cases affecting public education. 4 B.U.Pub.Interest L.J. 171 (1994).

Andrews, Hon. Robert E. *The Middle Income Educational Opportunity Act of 1991.* 16 Seton Hall Legis.J. 341 (1992).

Bartlett, Larry D. and Lelia B. Helms. *Report of the Committee on Public Education.* 26 Urb.Law. 877 (1994).

Brown, Alison McKinney. Student article. *Native American education: a system in need of reform.* 2 Kan.J.L.& Pub.Pol. 105 (1993).

Chemerinsky, Erwin. *Lost opportunity: the Burger Court and the failure to achieve equal educational opportunity.* 45 Mercer L.Rev. 999 (1994).

Culhane, John G. *Reinvigorating educational malpractice claims: a representational focus.* 67 Wash.L.Rev. 349 (1992).

Daniel, Philip T.K. *A comprehensive analysis of educational choice: can the polemic of legal problems be overcome?* 43 DePaul L.Rev. 1 (1993).

Eynon, Gail A. *Education.* 1993 Det.C.L.Rev. 607.

Fairfax, Sally K., Jon A. Souder and Gretta Goldenman. *School trust lands: a fresh look at conventional wisdom.* 22 Envtl.L. 797 (1992).

Foster, Holly J. Student article. *School fees in public education.* 1993 B.Y.U.Educ.& L.J. 149.

Fuller, Ned. *The alienation of Americans from their public schools.* 1994 B.Y.U.Educ.& L.J. 87.

Gardenswartz, Daniel E. Comment. *Public education: an inner-city crisis! Single sex schools: an inner-city answer?* 42 Emory L.J. 591 (1993).

Heise, Michael. *Goals 2000: Education America Act: the federalization and legalization of education policy.* 63 Fordham L.Rev. 345 (1994).

Meyen, Edward L. Symposium Keynote Address: *Education reform: the intent and the risks.* 2 Kan.J.L. & Pub.Pol'y 5 (1992).

Recent developments in the law. 23 J.L.& Educ. 61 (1994).

Robinson, John H. and Mary Elizabeth Huber. *The law of higher education and the courts: 1993 in review.* 21 J.C.& U.L. 157 (1994).

Sanders, Karl J. Comment. *Kids and condoms: constitutional challenges to the distribution of condoms in public schools.* 61 U.Cin.L.Rev. 1479 (1993).

Solomon, Lewis D. *The role of for-profit corporations in revitalizing public education: a legal and policy analysis.* 24 U.Tol.L.Rev. 883 (1993).

Stockdale, Susan R. *School consolidation & Minnesota's fire safety inspection law: a step too far.* 11 Law & Ineq. 117 (1992).

Symposium on Education Law. Articles by Thomas Fischer, Robert Berkley Harper, Stephen R. Ripps, Martin H. Ritchie, Mary Kathryn Chaffee and Pamela W. Dill. 13 Miss.C.L.Rev. 287 (1993).

Unnatural selection: a legal analysis of the impact of standardized test use on higher education resource allocation. 23 Loy.L.A.L.Rev. 1433 (1990).

EMPLOYMENT

Bates, Douglas F. Book review. *(Reviewing Gloria Jean Thomas, David J. Sperry and F. Del Wasden, The Law and Teacher Employment).* 1993 B.Y.U.Educ.& L.J. 183-186.

Buss, William G. *Human immunodeficiency virus, the legal meaning of "handicap," and implications for public education under federal law at the dawn of the age of the ADA.* 77 Iowa L.Rev. 1389 (1992).

Hunter, Jerry M. *Potential conflicts between obligations imposed on employers and unions by the National Labor Relations Act and the Americans with Disabilities Act.* 13 N.Ill.U.L.Rev. 207 (1993).

Kidwell, Brent Edward. *The Americans with Disabilities Act of 1990: overview and analysis.* 26 Ind.L.Rev. 707 (1993).

Loh, David Y. Note. *A critical analysis of academic tenure decisions: the disparate treatment model under Title VII examined.* 12 B.C. Third World L.J. 389 (1992).

McGraw, Edward J. Note. *Compliance costs of the Americans with Disabilities Act.* 18 Del.J.Corp.L. 521 (1993).

Myrick, Amber R. Note. *Implied monetary damages for gender discrimination under Title IX.* [Franklin v. Gwinnett County Public Schools, 112 S.Ct. 1028 (1992]. 28 Gonz.L.Rev. 317 (1992/93).

Payne, Christopher. *Employment law and the Civil Rights Act of 1991.* 69 Denv.U.L.Rev. 939 (1992).

Phillips, S.E. *Extending teacher licensure testing: have the courts applied the wrong validity standard?* 8 Thomas M. Cooley L.Rev. 513 (1991).

Tepker, Harry F., Jr. *Good cause and just expectations: academic tenure in Oklahoma's public colleges and universities.* 46 Okla.L.Rev. 205 (1993).

Thurston, Paul W. *Dismissal of tenured teachers in Illinois; evolution of a viable system.* 1990 U.Ill.L.Rev. 1.

FINANCE

Baida, Andrew H. *Not all minority scholarships are created equal, part II: how to develop a record that passes constitutional scrutiny.* 21 J.C.& U.L. 307 (1994).

Ball, Joe. Comment. *Efficient and suitable provision for the Texas Public School Finance System: an impossible dream?* 46 SMU L.Rev. 763 (1992).

Banks, Jonathan. Note. *State constitutional analysis of public school finance reform cases: myth or methodology?* 45 Vand.L.Rev. 129 (1992).

Bowlin, Tracy. Note. *Rethinking the ABCs of Utah's school trust lands.* [National Parks and Conservation Association v. Board of State Lands, 869 P.2d 909 (Utah 1993)]. 1994 Utah.L.Rev. 923.

Browning, Stephen D. Note. *The misguided application of the Sherman Act to colleges and universities in the context of sharing financial aid information.* 33 B.C.L.Rev. 763 (1992).

Burson, Charles W. and Jane W. Young. *School finance litigation: the state's perspective.* 61 Tenn.L.Rev. 445 (1994).

Cuellar, Henry. *Considerations in drafting a constitutional school finance plan: a legislator's perspective.* 19 T.Marshall L.Rev. 83 (1993).

Czech, Paul. *Education and the school financing problems: has New Jersey found the answer?* 1 Temp.Pol.& Civ.Rts.L.Rev. 149 (1992).

DiGiovanni, Louis. Note. *New York City's school asbestos debacle: an administrative approach to the problem of faulty school inspections and a possible new round of asbestos litigation.* 6 Fordham Envtl.L.J. 79 (1994).

Donelson, Lewis R. *School finance litigation: a rural perspective: the Magna Carta of public education in Tennessee.* 61 Tenn.L.Rev. 445 (1994).

Dormont, David. *Separate and unequal: school district financing.* 11 Law & Ineq. 261 (1992).

Edelson, Jodi L. Note. *Higher education to higher default: a re-examination of the Guaranteed Student Loan Program.* 11 Ann.Rev.Banking L. 475 (1992).

Enrich, Peter. *Leaving equality behind: new direction in school finance reform.* 48 Vand.L.Rev. 101 (1995).

Hackney, James R., Jr. *The philosophical underpinnings of public school funding jurisprudence.* 22 J.L.& Edu. 423 (1993).

Hall, Michael A. Comment. *The constitutionality of property tax based school financing schemes: is Illinois' system next to fall?* 16 S.Ill.U.L.J. 157 (1991).

Kelly, Ernest G., Jr. *School finance litigation: an urban perspective.* 61 Tenn.L.Rev. 471 (1994).

Koski, William S. Note. *Equity in public education: school finance reform in Michigan.* 26 U.Mich.J.L.Ref. 195 (1992).

Martin, Karen V. Case comment. *Constitutional law: opening the door for education reform.* [Tennessee Small Sch. Sys. v. McWherter, 851 S.W.2d 139 (Tenn. 1993)]. 24 Mem.St.U.L.Rev. 393 (1994).

Reitz, John C. *Public school financing in the United States: more on the dark side of intermediate structures.* 1993 B.Y.U.L.Rev. 623.

Sanchez, Juan Carlos. Note. *Texas' public school financing: share and share alike — not!* 19 T.Marshall L.Rev. 475 (1994).

Sarbak, Janine M. Comment. *New York's educational finance scheme: should it be declared unconstitutional?* 10 Touro L.Rev. 775 (1994).

Schmitz, Amy J. Note. *Providing an escape for inner-city children: creating a federal remedy for educational ills of poor urban schools.* 78 Minn.L.Rev. 1639 (1994).

Scinto, Blaise A. Student article. *Talents which nature has liberally sown: promoting fiscal equity in Virginia's public education system.* 9 J.L.& Pol. 749 (1993).

Sheikh, David J. *Comment. Public school finance reform: is Illinois "playing hooky"?* 41 DePaul L.Rev. 195 (1991).

Staros, Barbara J. *School finance litigation in Florida: a historical analysis.* 23 Stetson L.Rev. 497 (1994).

Symposium: Equitable Financing of Our Public Schools. 24 Conn.L.Rev. 675 (1992).

Walston, John F. Note. *The cause, effect and constitutional consequences of unequal funding: public education in Illinois.* 26 S.Marshall L.Rev. 399 (1993).

FREEDOM OF RELIGION

Anderson, William D., Jr. Note. *Religious groups in the educational marketplace: applying the Establishment Clause to school privatization programs.* 82 Geo.L.J. 1869 (1994).

Baker, Michael D. Comment. *Protecting religious speakers' access to public school facilities.* [Lamb's Chapel v. Center Moriches School District, 113 S.Ct. 2141 (1993)]. 44 Case W.Res.L.Rev. 315 (1993).

Brilliant, Marsha C. Note. *The Establishment Clause: a consideration of its protection against allowing prayer in public schools.* [Lee v. Weisman, 112 S.Ct. 2649 (1992)]. 15 Whittier L.Rev. 1193 (1994).

Brown, Deborah M. Note. *The states, the schools and the Bible: the Equal Access Act and state constitutional law.* 43 Case W.Res.L.Rev. 1021 (1993).

Burgess, John E. *Recent development. A critical analysis of the Supreme Court's First Amendment jurisprudence in the context of public schools.* [Lamb's Chapel v. Center Moriches Union Free School District, 113 S.Ct. 2141 (1993)]. 47 Vand.L.Rev. 1939 (1994).

Clemente, Joseph P. Note. *Constitutional law—First Amendment—Establishment Clause prohibits state-sponsored invocations at public school graduation ceremonies.* [Lee v. Weisman, 112 S.Ct. 2649 (1992)]. 23 Seton Hall L.Rev. 1096 (1993).

Cohen, Paula Savage. Case comment. *Psycho-coercion, a new Establishment Clause test: Lee v. Weisman and its initial effect.* [Lee v. Weisman, 112 S.Ct. 2649 (1992)]. 73 B.U.L.Rev. 501 (1993).

Constitutional law—the establishment clause—statute requiring the teaching of creation-science in conjunction with evolution violates the First Amendment. 19 Seton Hall L.Rev. 120 (1989).

Dancing around the establishment clause — religion in the public schools. [Clayton v. Place, 884 F.2d 376 (8th Cir. 1989), cert. denied, 110 S.Ct. 1811 (1990)]. 11 N.Ill.U.L.Rev. 119 (1990).

Duncan, Richard F. *Religious civil rights in public high schools: the Supreme Court speaks on equal access.* 24 Ind.L.Rev. 111 (1990).

Ehrmann, Susan. Note. *Creating greater protection for religious speech through illusion of public forum analysis.* [Lamb's Chapel v. Center Moriches Union Free School District, 113 S.Ct. 2141 (1993)]. 1994 Wis.L.Rev. 965 (1994).

El-Sayd, Dina F. Comment. *What is the Court trying to establish?: An analysis of...*[Lee v. Weisman, 112 S.Ct. 2649 (1992)]. 21 Hastings Const.L.Q. 441 (1994).

The Equal Access Act and Mergens: balancing the religion clauses in public schools. [Bd. of Educ. v. Mergens, 110 S.Ct. 2356 (1990)]. 24 Ga.L.Rev. 1141 (1990).

Freijomil, Derrick R. Comment. *Has the Court soured on* Lemon?: *A look into the future of Establishment Clause jurisprudence.* 5 Const.L.J. 141 (1994).

Futterman, David. Note. *School choice and the Religion Clauses: the law and politics of public aid to private parochial schools.* 81 Geo.L.J. 711 (1993).

Gordus, Allan. Case note. *The Establishment Clause and prayers in public high school graduations.* [Jones v. Clear Creek Independent School District, 977 F.2d 963 (5th Cir. 1992), cert. denied, 113 S.Ct. 2950 (1993)]. 47 Ark.L.Rev. 653 (1994).

Hartenstein, John M. *A Christmas issue: Christian holiday celebration in the public elementary schools is an establishment of religion.* 80 Cal.L.Rev. 981 (1992).

Kennedy, Kirk A. Note. *Opportunity declined: the Supreme Court refuses to jettison the* Lemon *test in...* [Zobrest v. Catalina Foothills School District, 113 S.Ct. 2462 (1993)]. 73 Neb.L.Rev. 408 (1994).

Mangrum, R. Collin. *Shall we pray? Graduation prayers and establishment paradigms.* 26 Creighton L.Rev. 1027 (1993).

Martin, Christina Engstrom. Comment. *Student-initiated religious expression after Mergens and Weisman.* [Board of Education v. Mergens, 496 U.S. 226 (1990); and Lee v. Weisman, 112 S.Ct. 2649 (1992)]. 61 U.Chi.L.Rev. 1565 (1994).

McAndrew, Gregory M. Note. *Invocations at graduation.* 101 Yale L.J. 663 (1991).

Nord, Warren A. *Religion, the First Amendment, and public education.* 8 B.Y.U.J.Pub.L. 439 (1994).

Olivo, Craig L. Note. *When neutrality masks hostility—the exclusion of religious communities from an entitlement to public schools.* [Grumet v. Board of Education of the Kiryas Joel Village School Dist., 592 N.Y.S.2d 123 (A.D.3d Dept.1992)]. 68 Notre Dame L.Rev. 775 (1993).

O'Neill, Michael R. Comment. *Government's denigration of religion: is God the victim of discrimination in our public schools?* 21 Pepperdine L.Rev. 477 (1994).

Perrin, Marilyn. Note. *Unanswered prayers.* [Lee v. Weisman, 112 S.Ct. 2649 (1992)]. 21 Pepperdine L.Rev. 207 (1993).

Phillips, Robert. Note. *The constitutionality of high school graduation prayers under* ... [Harris v. Joint Sch. Dist. No. 241, 821 F.Supp. 638 (D.Idaho 1993)]. 8 B.Y.U.J.Pub.L. 491 (1994).

Raimond, Johanna Josie. Note. *The constitutionality of student-led prayer at public school graduation ceremonies.* 48 Vand.L.Rev. 257 (1995).

Salomone, Rosemary C. *Public forum doctrine and the perils of thinking categorically: lessons from Lamb's Chapel.* 24 N.M.L.Rev. 1 (1994).

Sekulow, Jay Alan, Keith A. Fournier and John D. Etheriedge. Lamb's Chapel v. Center Moriches Union Free School District: *an end to religious apartheid.* 14 Miss.C.L.Rev. 27 (1993).

Symposium: Religion and the Public Schools After Lee v. Weisman. Articles by Jonathan L. Entin, George W. Dent, Jr., Joanne C. Brant, John H. Garvey, Stanley Ingber, Michael Stokes Paulsen, Daniel O. Conkle, Ira C. Lupu, Richard S. Myers, Rodney K. Smith, Edward B. Foley and Ronald C. Kahn. 43 Case W.Rcs.L.Rev. 699 (1993).

Taylor, Kimberly A. Recent decision. *Constitutional law—First Amendment—free exercise of religion.* [Church of Lukumi Babalu Aye, Inc. v. City of Hialeah, 113 S.Ct. 2217 (1993)]. 32 Duq.L.Rev. 915 (1994).

Thomas, Scott S. Note. *Beyond a sour lemon: a look at ...* [Grumet v. Board of Education of the Kiryas Joel Village School District, 618 N.E.2d 94 (N.Y.1993) cert. granted, 114 S.Ct. 544 (1993)]. 8 B.Y.U.J.Pub.L. 531 (1994).

Viar, Robert Paul, Jr. Comment. *A modest home for God in the public schools.* [Lamb's Chapel v. Center Moriches Union Free School District, 113 S.Ct. 214 (1993)]. 71 U.Det.Mercy L.Rev. 965 (1994).

Weinhaus, Amy Louise. Recent development. *The fate of graduation prayers in public schools after...*[Lee v. Weisman, 112 S.Ct. 2649 (1992)]. 71 Wash.U.L.Q. 957 (1993).

Weishaar, Peter J. Comment. *School choice vouchers and the Establishment Clause.* 58 Alb.L.Rev. 543 (1994).

FREEDOM OF SPEECH

Boswell-Odum, Beth C. Note. *The fighting words doctrine and racial speech on campus.* 33 S.Tex.L.Rev. 261 (1992).

Brownstein, Alan E. *Hate speech and harassment: the constitutionality of campus codes that prohibit racial insults.* 2 Wm.& Mary Bill Rts.J 179 (1994).

Dunn, Brendan C. Note. *Status and Oregon's freedom of expression law.* [Merrick v. Board of Higher Education, 116 Or.App. 258, 841 P.2d 646 (1992)]. 72 Or.L.Rev. 729 (1993).

Eco, Umberto. *The university and the mass media.* 6 Yale J.L.& Humanities 81 (1994).

Heiser, Gregory M. and Lawrence F. Rossow. *Hate speech or free speech: can broad campus speech regulations survive current judicial reasoning.* 22 J.L.& Educ. 139 (1993).

Herron, Vince. Note. *Increasing the speech: diversity, campus speech codes, and the pursuit of truth.* 67 S.Cal.L.Rev. 407 (1994).

Horner, Jeff. *Student free speech rights: "the closing of the schoolhouse gate" and its public policy implications.* 33 S.Tex.L.Rev. 601 (1992).

Kaplin, William A. *"Hate speech" on the college campus: freedom of speech and equality at the crossroads.* 27 Land & Water L.Rev. 243 (1992).

Leonard, James. *Killing with kindness: speech codes in the American university.* 19 Ohio N.U.L.Rev. 759 (1993).

Levine, Lana E. and Catherine A. Reardon. Note. *The resurgence of censorship in the twentieth century?: The Ninth Circuit's response in...*Planned Parenthood v. Clark County School District, 941 F.2d 817 (9th Cir.1991). 7 St.John's J.Legal Comment. 681 (1992).

Madved, Lory. Comment. *Protecting the freedom of speech rights of students: the special status of the high school library.* 21 Cap.U.L.Rev. 1183 (1992).

Masler, Ross Paine. *Tolling the final bell: will public school doors remain open to the First Amendment?* 14 Miss.C.L.Rev. 55 (1993).

McAllister, Thomas L. Comment. *Rules and rights colliding: speech codes and the First Amendment on college campuses.* 59 Tenn.L.Rev. 409 (1992).

Moore, Malanie A. Note. *Free speech on college campuses: protecting the First Amendment in the marketplace of ideas.* 96 W.Va.L.Rev. 511 (1993-94).

Prokop, Donna. Note. *Controversial teacher speech: striking a balance between First Amendment rights and educational interests.* 66 S.Cal.L.Rev. 883 (1993).

Renshaw, Edward E. Casenote. *Equal access — the new life of the First Amendment in secondary education.* [Board of Education of Westside Community Schools v. Mergens, 110 S.Ct. 2356 (1990)]. 16 S.Ill.U.L.J. 531 (1992).

Restricting gang clothing in public schools: does a dress code violate a student's right of free expression? 64 S.Cal.L.Rev. 1321 (1991).

Rychlak, Ronald J. *Civil rights, Confederate Flags, and political correctness: free speech and race relations on campus.* 66 Tul.L.Rev. 1411 (1992).

Sacken, Donal M. *Public school administrators and free speech protection.* 23 J.L.& Educ. 167 (1994).

Salomone, Rosemary C. *Free speech and school governance in the wake of Hazelwood.* 26 Ga.L.Rev. 253 (1992).

Sedler, Robert A. *The unconstitutionality of campus bans on "racist speech": the view from without and within.* 53 U.Pitt.L.Rev. 631 (1992).

Steger, Michael. Student article. *A cautious approach: racist speech and the First Amendment at the University of Texas.* 8 J.L.& Pol. 608 (1992).

Symposium: Campus Hate Speech and the Constitution in the Aftermath of Doe v. University of Michigan, 721 F.Supp. 852, (E.D.Mich. 1989). 37 Wayne L.Rev. 1309 (1991).

Syring, Tina Anne. Student article. *Overcoming racism on college campuses by restricting speech: is this effective?* 14 Hamline J.Pub.L.& Pol'y 97 (1993).

Trager, Robert and Joseph A. Russomanno. *Free speech for public school students: a "basic educational mission".* 17 Hamline L.Rev. 275 (1993).

Veltri, Stephen C. *Free speech in free universities.* 19 Ohio N.U.L.Rev. 783 (1993).

HOME INSTRUCTION

Can the Cleavers teach Beaver at home? Without prior state approval "see you back in woodshop, Beaver." [State v. Schmidt, 505 N.E.2d 627 (Ohio 1987)]. 14 Ohio N.U.L.Rev. 443 (1987).

Henderson, Alma C. Student article. *The home schooling movement: parents take control of educating their children.* 1991 Ann.Surv.Am.L. 985.

Lachman, Branton G. Comment. *Home education and fundamental rights: can Johnny's parents teach Johnny?* 18 W.St. U.L. Rev. 731 (1991).

Mangrum, R. Collin. *Family rights and compulsory school laws.* 21 Creighton L.Rev. 1019 (1987-88).

Michigan's teacher certification requirement as applied to religiously motivated home schools. 23 U.Mich.J.L.Ref. 733 (1990).

"Parent v. State": the challenge to compulsory school attendance laws. 11 Hamline J.Pub.L. & Pol'y 83 (1990).

Smith, J. Michael and Christopher J. Klicka. *Review of Ohio law regarding home schooling.* 14 N.U.L.Rev. 301 (1987).

INJURIES

Mahathey, Ryland F. Comment. *Tort law.* [Finstad v. Washburn University, 845 P.2d 685 (Kan.1993)]. 34 Washburn L.J. 147 (1994).

McEvoy, Sharlene M. *Campus insecurity: duty, foreseeability and third party liability.* 21 J.L.& Educ. 137 (1992).

Oshagan, Georgi-Ann. Comment. *Obscuring the issue: the inappropriate application of in loco parentis to the campus crime victim duty question.* 39 Wayne L.Rev. 1335 (1993).

Rinestine, Stacey R. Comment. *Terrorism on the playground: what can be done?* 32 Duq.L.Rev. 799 (1994).

Slim, Robert C. Comment. *The special relationship doctrine and a school official's duty to protect students from harm.* 46 Baylor L.Rev. 215 (1994).

University liability for student alcohol-related injuries: a reconsideration and assessment under Oregon law. 27 Willamette L.Rev. 829 (1991).

INSTRUCTIONAL METHODS

Brennan, Cynthia L. Comment. *Mandatory community service as a high school graduation requirement: inculcating values or unconstitutional?* 11 T.M.Cooley L.Rev. 253 (1994).

Gordon, Lee. Note. *Achieving a student-teacher dialectic in public secondary schools: state legislatures must promote value-positive education.* 36 N.Y.L.Sch.L.Rev. 397 (1991).

Harper, Brian L. Comment. *Peer mediation programs: teaching students alternatives to violence.* 1993 J.Dispute Resol. 323.

Martin, Jeffrey C. *Recent developments concerning accrediting agencies in postsecondary education.* 57 Law & Contemp.Probs. 121 (1994).

Merrill, Marsha Lynn. *No more sacrifice on the altar of educational excellence: ADR & at-risk students.* 9 Ohio St.J.on Disp.Resol. 275 (1994).

Rome, Bruce J. Note. *Mandatory community service in public high schools: constitutional problems in ...* [Steirer v. Bethlehem Area School District, 987 F.2d 989 (3d Cir.1993)]. 28 U.S.F.L.Rev. 517 (1994).

Wyner, Joshua S. Note. *Toward a common law theory of minimal adequacy in public education.* 1992/1993 Ann.Surv.Am.L. 389.

LABOR RELATIONS

Bingham, Lisa B. *Teacher bargaining in Indiana: the courts and the Board on the road less traveled.* 27 Ind.L.Rev. 989 (1994).

Doty, David S. *Forging new partnerships: teacher unions and educational reform in the 90s.* 1994 B.Y.U.Educ.& L.J. 117.

Herbert, Kathleen S. *Balancing teachers' collective bargaining rights with the interests of school districts, students and taxpayers: current legislation strikes out.* 99 Dick.L.Rev. 57 (1994).

O'Reilly, James T. *Education reform or labor peace? Ohio's schools in the 1990's.* 22 U.Tol.L.Rev. 11 (1990).

Speiser, Karen M. Note. *Labor arbitration in public agencies: an unconstitutional delegation of power or the "waking of a sleeping giant?"* [United Transportation Union v. Southern California Rapid Transit, 9 Cal.Rptr.2d 702, Cal.Ct.App. (1992)]. 1993 J.Dispute Resol. 333.

Strauss, Mark. Note. *Public employees' right of association: should Connick v. Myers' speech-based public-concern rule apply?* [Connick v. Myers, 461 U.S. 138 (1983)]. 61 Fordham L.Rev. 473 (1992).

Wagner, Danielle M. Recent decision. *Constitutional law—public education—teacher strikes—the Supreme Court of Pennsylvania held that the provision of the Public Employees Relations Act permitting public school teachers to strike does not violate article III, section 14 of the Pennsylvania Constitution which requires the General Assembly to provide for a thorough and efficient system of public education.* [Reichley v. North Penn School District, 626 A.2d 123 (Pa.1993)]. 32 Duq.L.Rev. 611 (1994).

PRIVATE SCHOOLS

Abolishing "separate but (un)equal" status for religious universities. 77 Va.L.Rev. 1231 (1991).

Adams, T. Jonathan. Note. *Interpreting state aid to religious schools under the Establishment Clause.* [Zobrest v. Catalina Foothills School District, 113 S.Ct. 2462 (1993)]. 72 N.C.L.Rev. 1039 (1994).

Blissard, Mardi L. Note. *Constitutional law: an unanswered prayer to students with disabilities in religious schools.* [Zobrest v. Catalina Foothills School District, 113 S.Ct. 2462 (1993)]. 16 U.Ark.Little Rock L.J. 449 (1994).

Dietrich, James J. Note. *Equal protection, neutrality, and the Establishment clause.* [Zobrest v. Catalina Foothills School District, 113 S.Ct. 2462 (1993)]. 43 Cath.U.L.Rev. 1209 (1994).

Gliedman, John A.   *The choice between educational privatization and parental governance.* 20 J.L. & Educ. 395 (1991).

Grabiel, Ann Marlow. Comment. *Minnesota public money and religious schools: clearing the federal and state constitutional hurdles.* 17 Hamline L.Rev. 203 (1993).

Pokora, Leigh. Casenote. *Opening private schoolhouse doors to government aid.* [Zobrest v. Catalina Foothills School District, 113 S.Ct. 2462 (1993)]. 21 Ohio N.U.L.Rev. 331 (1994).

Randall, E. Vance. *Pluralism, private schools and public policy.* 1994 B.Y.U.Educ.& L.J. 35.

Randall, E. Vance. *Private schools and state regulation.* 24 Urb.Law. 341 (1992).

Reynolds, Osborne M., Jr. *Zoning private and parochial schools — could local governments restrict Socrates and Aquinas?* 24 Urb.Law. 305 (1992).

Segall, Eric J. *Parochial school aid revisited: the* Lemon *test, the endorsement test and religious liberty.* 28 San Diego L.Rev. 263 (1991).

Swygert, Jacob C., Jr. Casenote. *Constitutional law—Establishment Clause—state funding of sign language interpreter for deaf student attending parochial secondary school does not violate First Amendment.* [Zobrest v. Catalina Foothills School District, 113 S.Ct. 2462 (1993)]. 24 Cumb.L.Rev. 587 (1993-1994).

SEARCH & SEIZURE

Blickenstaff, David C. *Strip searches of public school students: can* New Jersey v. T.L.O. *solve the problem?* 99 Dick.L.Rev. 1 (1994).

D'Alesandro, Nicole M. Comment. *Students caught in the crossfire of the war on drugs.* 3 Md.J.Contemp.Legal Issues 233 (1992).

Davis, Charles N. *Scaling the ivory tower: state public records laws and university Presidential searches.* 21 J.C.& U.L. 353 (1994).

Fischer, Thomas C. *From* Tinker *to* TLO; *are civil rights for students "flunking" in school?* 22 J.L.& Educ. 409 (1993).

Fourth Amendment protection in the school environment: the Colorado Supreme Court's application of the reasonable suspicion standard in ... [State v. P.E.A., 754 P.2d 382 (Colo.1988)]. 61 U.Colo.L.Rev. 153 (1990).

Public school drug searches: toward redefining Fourth Amendment "reasonableness" to include individualized suspicion. 14 Fordham Urb.L.J. 629.

Ringel, Susannah Z. *Fourth Amendment protection of public school students: legal and psychological inconsistencies.* 3 Md.J.Contemp.Legal Issues 289 (1992).

Schreck, Myron. *The Fourth Amendment in the public school: issues for the 1990s and beyond.* 25 Urb.Law. 117 (1993).

STUDENT RIGHTS

Biegel, Stuart. *The parameters of the bilingual education debate in California twenty years after* Lau v. Nichol. 14 Chicano-Latino L.Rev. 48 (1994).

Blake, Helen Holt, Note. *The duty to protect school children: the effect of the Third Circuit's* Middle Bucks *decision.* [D.R. v. Middle Bucks Area Vocational Technical School, 972 F.2d 1364 (3d Cir.1992), cert. denied, 113 S.Ct. 1045 (1993)]. 28 Tulsa L.J. 911 (1993).

Brody, Evelyn. *Paying back your country through income-contingent student loans.* 31 San Diego L.Rev. 449 (1994).

Daniel, Philip T.K. and Karen Bond Coriell. *Suspension and expulsion in America's public schools: has unfairness resulted from a narrowing of due process?* 13 Hamline J.Pub.L.& Pol'y 1 (1992).

Educational neglect as a proper harm to warrant child neglect finding. [In re B.B., 440 N.W.2d 594 (Iowa 1989)] 76 Iowa L.Rev. 167 (1990).

Griffaton, Michael C. Note. *Forewarned is forearmed: the Crime Awareness and Campus Security Act of 1990 and the future of institutional liability for student victimization.* 43 Case W.Res.L.Rev. 525 (1993).

Kim, Susanna M. Comment. *Section 1983 liability in the public schools after DeShaney: the "special relationship" between school and student.* 41 UCLA L.Rev. 1101 (1994).

Lallo, Dina. Student note. *Student challenges to grades and academic dismissals: are they losing battles?* 18 J.C.& U.L. 577 (1992).

Lewis, Darryll M. Halcomb. *The criminalization of fraternity, non-fraternity and non-collegiate hazing.* 61 Miss. L.J. (1991).

Mediation: new process for high school disciplinary expulsions. 84 Nw.U.L.Rev. 736 (1990).

Papakirk, James. Comment. *Michigan's new Corporal Punishment Amendment: where the good Act giveth, did the Amendment taketh away?* 10 T.M.Cooley L.Rev. 383 (1993).

Papandreou, Alexander C. Student case comment. *The potential for disclosure of highly confidential personal information renders questionable the use of social security numbers as student identification numbers.* [Krebs v. Rutgers, 797 F.Supp. 1246 (D.N.J.1992)]. 20 J.C.& U.L. 79 (1993).

Pettys, Todd Edward. Note. *Punishing offensive conduct on university campuses.* [Iota Xi Chapter of Sigma Chi Fraternity v. George Mason University, 993 F.2d 386 (4th Cir.1993)]. 72 N.C.L.Rev. 789 (1994).

Rosien, Jane, Lelia Helms and Carolyn Wanat. *Intent v. practice: incentives and disincentives for child abuse reporting by school personnel.* 1993 B.Y.U.Educ.& L.J. 102.

Saferstein, Bennett L. Note. *Revisiting* Plessy *at the Virginia Military Institute: reconciling single-sex education with equal protection.* 54 U.Pitt.L.Rev. 637 (1993).

Sanchez, J. M. *Expelling the Fourth Amendment from American schools: students' rights six years after* T.L.O. 21 J.L.& Educ. 381 (1992).

Stone, Donald H. *Crime & punishment in public schools: an empirical study of disciplinary proceedings.* 17 Am.J.Trial Advoc. 351 (1993).

Zahniser, Timothy S. Note. *The right of Native American public school students to wear long hair.* [Alabama & Coushatta Tribes v. Big Sandy School District, 817 F.Supp. 1319 (E.D.Tex.1993)]. 19 Am.Indian L.Rev. 217 (1994).

Ziegler, Carol L. and Nancy M. Lederman. *School vouchers: are urban students surrendering rights for choice?* 19 Fordham Urb.L.J. 813 (1992).

STUDENTS WITH DISABILITIES

Adams, T. Jonathan. Note. *Interpreting state aid to religious schools under the Establishment Clause.* [Zobrest v. Catalina Foothills School District, 113 S.Ct. 2462 (1993)]. 72 N.C.L.Rev. 1039 (1994).

Blissard, Mardi L. Note. *Constitutional law: an unanswered prayer to students with disabilities in religious schools.* [Zobrest v. Catalina Foothills School District, 113 S.Ct. 2462 (1993)]. 16 U.Ark.Little Rock L.J. 449 (1994).

Dietrich, James J. Note. *Equal protection, neutrality, and the Establishment clause.* [Zobrest v. Catalina Foothills School District, 113 S.Ct. 2462 (1993)]. 43 Cath.U.L.Rev. 1209 (1994).

DiScala, Jeanette, Steven G. Olswang and Carol S. Niccolls. *College and university responses to the emotionally or mentally impaired student.* 19 J.C.& U.L. 17 (1992).

Donohue, David C. Note. *Restricting related services under the Individuals with Disabilities Education Act.* [Clovis Unified School District v. California Office of Administrative Hearings, 903 F.2d 635 (9th Cir.1990)]. 8 J.Contemp.Health L.& Pol'y 407 (1992).

Edmunds, Kara W. Note. *Implying damages under the Individuals with Disabilities Education Act:* [Franklin v. Gwinnett County Public Schools, 112 S.Ct. 1028 (1992)]. 27 Ga.L.Rev. 789 (1993).

Edwards, Robert W. Note. *The rights of students with learning disabilities and the responsibilities of institutions of higher education under the Americans with Disabilities Act.* 2 J.L.& Pol'y 213 (1994).

Engel, David M. *Law, culture, and children with disabilities: educational rights and the construction of difference.* 1991 Duke L.J. 166.

Flitter, Abigail L. *Recent decision. Civil rights—a progressive construction of the least restrictive environment requirement of the Individuals with Disabilities Education Act.* [Oberti ex rel. Oberti v. Bd. of Education, 995 F.2d 1204 (3d Cir.1993)]. 67 Temp.L.Rev. 371 (1994).

Fossey, Richard H. and Perry A. Zirkel. *Educational malpractice and students with disabilities: "special" cases of liability.* 23 J.L.& Educ. 25 (1994).

Glennon, Theresa. *Disabling ambiguities: confronting barriers to the education of students with emotional disabilities.* 60 Tenn.L.Rev.295 (1993).

Goldman, Rebecca Weber. Comment. *A free appropriate education in the least restrictive environment: promises made, promises broken by the Individuals with Disabilities Education Act.* 20 U.Dayton L.Rev. 243 (1994).

Greenwood, Christopher Dean. Student article. *Congress' new IDEA in special education: permitting a private right of action against state agencies.* 1992 B.Y.U.J.L.& Ed. 49.

Herring, Mary Lou. Note. *Model federal statute for the education of talented and gifted children.* 67 Chi.-Kent L.Rev. 1035 (1991).

Jaffe, Elizabeth M. Comment. *A structure for legal interpretation of the Individuals with Disabilities Education Act:* ...[Oberti v. Board of Education, 995 F.2d 1204 (3d Cir.1993)]. 46 Wash.U.J.Urb.& Contemp.L. 391 (1994).

Ketchum, Michelle Morgan. Note. *Academic decision-making: law schools' discretion under the Americans with Disabilities Act.* 62 UMKC L.Rev. 209 (1993).

Kidwell, Brent Edward. *The Americans with Disabilities Act of 1990: overview and analysis.* 26 Ind.L.Rev. 707 (1993).

Kotler, Martin A. *The Individuals with Disabilities Education Act: a parent's perspective and proposal for change.* 27 U.Mich.J.L.Ref. 331 (1994).

Lane, JoEllen. Note. *The use of the least restrictive environment principle in placement decisions affecting school-age students with disabilities.* 69 U.Det.Mercy L.Rev. 291 (1992).

Pokora, Leigh. Casenote. *Opening private schoolhouse doors to government aid.* [Zobrest v. Catalina Foothills School District, 113 S.Ct. 2462 (1993)]. 21 Ohio N.U.L.Rev. 331 (1994).

Schneider, R. Craig. Note. *Multi-factored analysis required for IEP reviews.* [Johnson v. Independent School Dist. No. 4 of Bixby, 921 F.2d 1022 (10th

Cir.1990), *per curiam, cert. denied,* 111 S.Ct. 1685 (1991)]. 18 J.Contemp.L. 177 (1992).

Stamps-Jones, Lisa. Note.*Accommodating students with disabilities: testing them on what they know.* 1994 B.Y.U.Educ.& L.J. 187.

Swygert, Jacob C., Jr. Casenote. *Constitutional law—Establishment Clause—state funding of sign language interpreter for deaf student attending parochial secondary school does not violate First Amendment. [Zobrest v. Catalina Foothills School District,* 113 S.Ct. 2462 (1993)]. 24 Cumb.L.Rev. 587 (1993-1994).

Zirkel, Perry A. *Over-due process revisions for the Individuals with Disabilities Education Act.* 55 Mont.L.Rev. 403 (1994).

Zirkel, Perry A. *The standard of review applicable to Pennsylvania's Special Education Appeals Panel.* 3 Widener J.Pub.L. 871 (1994).

TAXATION

Argrett, Loretta Collins. *Tax treatment of higher education expenditures: an unfair investment disincentive.* 41 Syracuse L.Rev. 621 (1990).

Bromell, John A. Comment. *An historical analysis of property taxes as a method of funding public education.* 10 St.Louis U.Pub.L.Rev. 615 (1991).

Dodge, Joseph M. *Taxing human capital acquisition costs — or why costs of higher education should not be deducted or amortized.* 54 Ohio St.L.J. 927 (1993).

Ginsburg, Martin D. *Teaching tax law after tax reform.* 65 Wash.L.Rev. 595 (1990).

Philipps, J. Timothy and Timothy G. Hatfield. *Uncle Sam gets the goldmine — students get the shaft: federal tax treatment of student loan indebtedness.* 15 Seton Hall Legis.J. 249 (1991).

Vari, Frank J. *The unrelated business income tax and its effects upon collegiate athletics.* 9 Akron Tax J. 111 (1992).

Williams, David II. *Foreign students and scholars and the United States tax system.* 23 J.L.& Educ. 1 (1994).

APPENDIX C

SUBJECT MATTER TABLE OF
EDUCATION CASES DECIDED BY THE
UNITED STATES SUPREME COURT

Note: Please see the Table of Cases (located at the front of this volume) for Supreme Court cases reported in this Volume.

<u>Subject</u> <u>Title & Citation</u>

Academic Freedom
>Univ. of Pennsylvania v. EEOC, 493 U.S. 182, 110 S.Ct. 577, 107 L.Ed.2d 571 (1990).
>Epperson v. Arkansas, 393 U.S. 97, 89 S.Ct. 266, 21 L.Ed.2d 228 (1968).
>Meyer v. Nebraska, 262 U.S. 390, 43 S.Ct. 625, 67 L.Ed.2d 1042 (1923).

Aliens
>Toll v. Moreno, 458 U.S. 1, 102 S.Ct. 2977, 73 L.Ed.2d 563 (1982).
>Plyler v. Doe, 457 U.S. 202, 102 S.Ct. 2382, 72 L.Ed.2d 786 (1982).
>Ambach v. Norwick, 441 U.S. 68, 99 S.Ct. 1589, 60 L.Ed.2d 49 (1979).
>Vlandis v. Kline, 412 U.S. 441, 93 S.Ct. 2230, 37 L.Ed.2d 63 (1973)

Arbitration
>Volt Information Sciences v. Bd. of Trustees of Stanford Univ., 489 U.S. 468, 109 S.Ct. 1248, 103 L.Ed.2d. 488 (1989).

Attorney's Fees
>Webb v. Board of Education, 471 U.S. 234, 105 S.Ct. 1923, 85 L.Ed.2d 233 (1985).
>Smith v. Robinson, 468 U.S. 992, 104 S.Ct. 3457, 82 L.Ed.2d 746 (1984).

Collective Bargaining
>Chicago Teachers Union v. Hudson, 475 U.S. 292, 106 S.Ct. 1066, 89 L.Ed.2d 232 (1986).
>Minnesota State Board for Community Colleges v. Knight, 465 U.S. 271, 104 S.Ct. 1058, 79 L.Ed.2d 299 (1984).
>Perry Education Association v. Perry Local Educators' Association, 460 U.S. 37, 103 S.Ct. 948, 74 L.Ed.2d 794 (1983).
>City of Madison Joint School District v. WERC, 429 U.S. 167, 97 S.Ct. 421, 50 L.Ed.2d 376 (1976).

Compulsory Attendance
>Wisconsin v. Yoder, 406 U.S. 205, 92 S.Ct. 526, 32 L.Ed.2d 15 (1972).
>Pierce v. Society of Sisters, 268 U.S. 510, 45 S.Ct. 571, 69 L.Ed. 1070 (1925).

Continuing Education

Austin ISD v. U.S., 443 U.S. 915, 99 S.Ct. 3106, 61 L.Ed.2d 879 (1979).
Harrah ISD v. Martin, 440 U.S. 194, 99 S.Ct. 1062, 59 L.Ed.2d 248 (1979).

Corporal Punishment

Ingraham v. Wright, 430 U.S. 651, 97 S.Ct. 1401, 51 L.Ed.2d 711 (1977).

Desegregation

U.S. v. Fordice, 505 U.S. —, 112 S.Ct. 2727, 120 L.Ed.2d 575 (1992).
Freeman v. Pitts, 503 U.S. 467, 112 S.Ct. 1430, 118 L.Ed.2d 108 (1992).
Bd. of Educ. of Oklahoma City Public Schools v. Dowell, 498 U.S. 237, 111 S.Ct. 630, 112 L.Ed.2d 715 (1991).
Missouri v. Jenkins, 495 U.S. 33, 110 S.Ct. 1651, 109 L.Ed.2d 31 (1990).
Crawford v. Bd. of Educ., 458 U.S. 527, 102 S.Ct. 3211, 73 L.Ed.2d 948 (1982).
Washington v. Seattle School Dist. No. 1, 458 U.S. 457, 102 S.Ct. 3187, 73 L.Ed.2d 896 (1982).
Board of Education v. Superior Court, 448 U.S. 1343, 101 S.Ct. 21, 65 L.Ed.2d 1166 (1980).
Columbus Board of Education v. Penick, 443 U.S. 449, 99 S.Ct. 2941, 61 L.Ed.2d 666 (1979).
Bustop v. Board of Education, 439 U.S. 1380, 99 S.Ct. 40, 58 L.Ed.2d 88 (1978).
Vetterli v. U.S. District Court, 435 U.S. 1304, 98 S.Ct. 1219, 55 L.Ed.2d 751 (1978).
Dayton Board of Education v. Brinkman, 433 U.S. 406, 97 S.Ct. 2766, 53 L.Ed.2d 851 (1977).
Milliken v. Bradley, 433 U.S. 267, 97 S.Ct. 2749, 53 L.Ed.2d 745 (1977).
Pasadena City Board of Education v. Spangler, 427 U.S. 424, 96 S.Ct. 2697, 49 L.Ed.2d 599 (1976).
Hills v. Gautreaux, 425 U.S. 284, 96 S.Ct. 1538, 47 L.Ed.2d 792 (1976).
Milliken v. Bradley, 418 U.S. 717, 94 S.Ct. 311, 41 L.Ed.2d 1069 (1974).
Gilmore v. City of Montgomery, 417 U.S. 556, 94 S.Ct. 2416, 41 L.Ed.2d 304 (1974).
Bradley v. School Board of City of Richmond, 416 U.S. 696, 94 S.Ct. 2006, 40 L.Ed.2d 476 (1974).
Keyes v. School District No. 1, 413 U.S. 189, 93 S.Ct. 2686, 37 L.Ed.2d 548 (1973).
Drummond v. Acree, 409 U.S. 1228, 93 S.Ct. 18, 34 L.Ed.2d 33 (1972).
U.S. v. Scotland Neck City Board of Education, 407 U.S. 484, 92 S.Ct. 2214, 33 L.Ed.2d 75 (1972).
Wright v. Council of City of Emporia, 407 U.S. 451, 92 S.Ct. 2196, 33 L.Ed.2d 51 (1972).
Winston-Salem/Forsyth County Board of Education v. Scott, 404 U.S. 1221, 92 S.Ct. 1236, 31 L.Ed.2d 441 (1971).
Dandridge v. Jefferson Parish School Board, 404 U.S. 1219, 92 S.Ct. 18, 30 L.Ed.2d 23 (1971).

Disabled Students

Honig v. Doe, 484 U.S. 305, 108 S.Ct. 592, 98 L.Ed.2d 686 (1988).

City of Cleburne, Texas v. Cleburne Living Center, 473 U.S. 432, 105 S.Ct. 3249, 87 L.Ed.2d 313 (1985).

Honig v. Students of Cal. School for the Blind, 471 U.S. 148, 105 S.Ct. 1820, 85 L.Ed.2d 114 (1985).

Burlington School Committee v. Department of Education, 471 U.S. 359, 105 S.Ct. 1996, 85 L.Ed.2d 385 (1985).

Smith v. Robinson, 468 U.S. 992, 104 S.Ct. 3457, 82 L.Ed.2d 746 (1984).

Irving Independent School District v. Tatro, 468 U.S. 883, 104 S.Ct. 3371, 82 L.Ed.2d 664 (1984).

Board of Education v. Rowley, 458 U.S. 176, 102 S.Ct. 3034, 73 L.Ed.2d 690 (1982).

University of Texas v. Camenisch, 451 U.S. 390, 101 S.Ct. 1830, 68 L.Ed.2d 175 (1981).

Pennhurst State School and Hosp. v. Halderman, 451 U.S. 1, 101 S.Ct. 1531, 67 L.Ed.2d 694 (1981).

Southeastern Community College v. Davis, 442 U.S. 397, 99 S.Ct. 2361, 60 L.Ed.2d 980 (1979).

Discrimination Generally

Jett v. Dallas Indep. School Dist., 491 U.S. 701, 109 S.Ct. 2702, 105 L.Ed.2d 598 (1989).

Carnegie-Mellon Univ. v. Cohill, 484 U.S. 343, 108 S.Ct. 614, 98 L.Ed.2d 720 (1988).

School Board of Nassau County v. Arline, 480 U.S. 273, 107 S.Ct. 1123, 94 L.Ed.2d 307 (1987).

Hazelwood School Dist. v. U.S., 433 U.S. 299, 97 S.Ct. 2736, 53 L.Ed.2d 768 (1977).

DeFunis v. Odegaard, 416 U.S. 312, 94 S.Ct. 1704, 40 L.Ed.2d 164 (1974).

Monell v. Dept. of Social Serv., 436 U.S. 658, 98 S.Ct. 2018, 56 L.Ed.2d 611 (1978).

Discrimination in Selection of Board Members

East Carroll Parish Board v. Marshall, 424 U.S. 636, 96 S.Ct. 1083, 47 L.Ed.2d 296 (1976).

Hadley v. Junior College District, 397 U.S. 50, 90 S.Ct. 791, 25 L.Ed.2d 45 (1970).

Turner v. Fouche, 396 U.S. 346, 90 S.Ct. 532, 24 L.Ed.2d 567 (1970).

Due Process

University of Tennessee v. Elliot, 478 U.S. 788, 106 S.Ct. 3220, 92 L.Ed.2d 635 (1986).

Memphis Community School District v. Stachura, 477 U.S. 299, 106 S.Ct. 2537, 91 L.Ed.2d 249 (1986).

Cleveland Board of Education v. Loudermill, 470 U.S. 532, 105 S.Ct. 1487, 84 L.Ed.2d 494 (1985).

Mathews v. Eldridge, 424 U.S. 319, 96 S.Ct. 893, 47 L.Ed.2d 18 (1976).

Perry v. Sindermann, 408 U.S. 593, 92 S.Ct. 2694, 33 L.Ed.2d 570 (1972).

Board of Regents v. Roth, 408 U.S. 564, 92 S.Ct. 2701, 33 L.Ed.2d 548 (1972).

Elections

Dougherty County Bd. of Educ. v. White, 439 U.S. 32, 99 S.Ct. 368, 58 L.Ed.2d 269 (1978).

Mayor of Philadelphia v. Educ. Equality League, 415 U.S. 605, 94 S.Ct. 1323, 39 L.Ed.2d 630 (1974).

Kramer v. Union Free School Dist. No. 15, 395 U.S. 621, 89 S.Ct. 1886, 23 L.Ed.2d 583 (1969).

Sailors v. Board of Education, 387 U.S. 105, 87 S.Ct. 1549, 18 L.Ed.2d 650 (1967).

Federal Aid

Traynor v. Turnage, 485 U.S. 535, 108 S.Ct. 1372, 99 L.Ed.2d 618 (1988).

Selective Service System v. MPIRG, 468 U.S. 841, 104 S.Ct. 3348, 82 L.Ed.2d 632 (1984).

Bell v. New Jersey and Pennsylvania, 461 U.S. 773, 103 S.Ct. 2187, 76 L.Ed.2d 312 (1984).

Valley Forge Christian College v. Americans United for Separation of Church and State, 454 U.S. 464, 102 S.Ct. 752, 70 L.Ed.2d 700 (1982).

Board of Education v. Harris, 444 U.S. 130, 100 S.Ct. 363, 62 L.Ed.2d 275 (1979).

Wheeler v. Barrera, 417 U.S. 402, 94 S.Ct. 2274, 41 L.Ed.2d 159 (1974).

Tilton v. Richardson, 403 U.S. 672, 91 S.Ct. 2091, 29 L.Ed.2d 790 (1971).

Financing

Papasan v. Allain, 478 U.S. 265, 106 S.Ct. 2932, 92 L.Ed.2d 209 (1986).

Bennett v. New Jersey, 470 U.S. 632, 105 S.Ct. 1555, 84 L.Ed.2d 572 (1985).

Bennett v. Kentucky Department of Education, 470 U.S. 656, 105 S.Ct. 1544, 84 L.Ed.2d 590 (1985).

Lawrence County v. Lead-Deadwood School Dist. No. 40-1, 469 U.S. 256, 105 S.Ct. 695, 83 L.Ed.2d 635 (1985).

Grove City College v. Bell, 465 U.S. 555, 104 S.Ct. 1211, 79 L.Ed.2d 516 (1984).

San Antonio v. Rodriguez, 411 U.S. 1, 93 S.Ct. 1278, 36 L.Ed.2d 16 (1973).

Freedom of Religion (see also Religious Activities)

Edwards v. Aguillard, 482 U.S. 578, 107 S.Ct. 2573, 96 L.Ed.2d 510 (1987).

Ansonia Board of Education v. Philbrook, 499 U.S. 60, 107 S.Ct. 367, 93 L.Ed.2d 305 (1986).

Freedom of Speech

Bd. of Educ. of Westside Com. Sch. v. Mergens, 496 U.S. 226, 110 S.Ct. 2356, 110 L.Ed.2d 191 (1990).

Bd. of Trustees of the State Univ. of New York v. Fox, 492 U.S. 469, 109 S.Ct. 3028, 106 L.Ed.2d 388 (1989).

Hazelwood School Dist. v. Kuhlmeier, 484 U.S. 261, 108 S.Ct. 562, 98 L.Ed.2d 592 (1988).

Bethel School District v. Fraser, 478 U.S. 675, 106 S.Ct. 3159, 92 L.Ed.2d 549 (1986).

Wayte v. U.S., 470 U.S. 598, 105 S.Ct. 1524, 84 L.Ed.2d 547 (1985).

Board of Education v. Pico, 457 U.S. 853, 102 S.Ct. 2799, 73 L.Ed.2d 435 (1982).

Givhan v. Western Line Consolidated School District, 439 U.S. 410, 99 S.Ct. 693, 58 L.Ed.2d 619 (1979).

Mt. Healthy City School v. Doyle, 429 U.S. 274, 97 S.Ct. 568, 50 L.Ed.2d 471 (1977).

Papish v. Board of Curators, 410 U.S. 667, 93 S.Ct. 1197, 35 L.Ed.2d 618 (1973).

Grayned v. City of Rockford, 408 U.S. 104, 92 S.Ct. 2294, 33 L.Ed.2d 222 (1972).

Police Dept. v. Mosley, 408 U.S. 92, 92 S.Ct. 2286, 33 L.Ed.2d 212 (1972).

Tinker v. Des Moines, 393 U.S. 503, 89 S.Ct. 733, 21 L.Ed.2d 733 (1969).

Pickering v. Board of Education, 391 U.S. 563, 88 S.Ct. 1731, 20 L.Ed.2d 811 (1968).

Keyishian v. Board of Regents, 385 U.S. 589, 87 S.Ct. 675, 17 L.Ed.2d 629 (1967).

Adler v. Bd. of Educ., 342 U.S. 485, 72 S.Ct. 380, 96 L.Ed. 517 (1952).

Labor Relations

Lehnert v. Ferris Faculty Assn., 500 U.S. 507, 111 S.Ct. 1950, 114 L.Ed.2d 572 (1991).

Fort Stewart Schools v. Federal Labor Relations Authority, 495 U.S. 641, 110 S.Ct. 2043, 109 L.Ed.2d 659 (1990).

Minnesota State Board for Community Colleges v. Knight, 465 U.S. 271, 104 S.Ct. 1058, 79 L.Ed.2d 299 (1984).

NLRB v. Yeshiva University, 444 U.S. 672, 100 S.Ct. 856, 63 L.Ed.2d 115 (1980).

NLRB v. Catholic Bishop of Chicago, 440 U.S. 490, 99 S.Ct. 1313, 59 L.Ed.2d 533 (1979).

Abood v. Detroit Bd. of Educ., 431 U.S. 209, 97 S.Ct. 1782, 52 L.Ed.2d 261 (1977).

Loyalty Oaths

Connell v. Higgenbotham, 403 U.S. 207, 91 S.Ct. 1772, 29 L.Ed.2d 418 (1971).

Whitehill v. Elkins, 389 U.S. 54, 88 S.Ct. 184, 19 L.Ed.2d 228 (1967).

Elfbrandt v. Russell, 384 U.S. 11, 86 S.Ct. 1238, 16 L.Ed.2d 321 (1966).

Baggett v. Bullitt, 377 U.S. 360, 84 S.Ct. 1316, 12 L.Ed.2d 377 (1964).

Cramp v. Bd. of Educ., 368 U.S. 278, 82 S.Ct. 275, 7 L.Ed.2d 285 (1961).

Slochower v. Bd. of Higher Educ., 350 U.S. 551, 76 S.Ct. 637, 100 L.Ed. 692 (1956).

Maternity Leave

Richmond Unified School Dist. v. Berg, 434 U.S. 158, 98 S.Ct. 623, 54 L.Ed.2d 375 (1977).

Cleveland Board of Education v. La Fleur, 414 U.S. 632, 94 S.Ct. 791, 39 L.Ed.2d 52 (1974).

Cohen v. Chesterfield, 414 U.S. 632, 94 S.Ct. 791, 39 L.Ed.2d 52 (1974).

Private Schools

Farrar v. Hobby, 506 U.S. —, 113 S.Ct. 566, 121 L.Ed.2d 494 (1992).

Corp. of the Presiding Bishop of the Church of Jesus Christ of Latter-Day Saints v. Amos, 483 U.S. 327, 107 S.Ct. 2862, 97 L.Ed.2d 273 (1987).

St. Francis College v. Al-Khazraji, 481 U.S. 604, 107 S.Ct. 2022, 97 L.Ed.2d 749 (1987).

Witters v. Washington Department of Services for the Blind, 474 U.S. 481, 106 S.Ct. 748, 88 L.Ed.2d 846 (1986).

Aguilar v. Felton, 473 U.S. 402, 105 S.Ct. 3232, 87 L.Ed.2d 290 (1985).

Grand Rapids School District v. Ball, 473 U.S. 373, 105 S.Ct. 3216, 87 L.Ed.2d 267 (1985).

Grove City College v. Bell, 465 U.S. 555, 104 S.Ct. 1211, 79 L.Ed.2d 516 (1984).

Mueller v. Allen, 463 U.S. 388, 103 S.Ct. 3062, 77 L.Ed.2d 721 (1983).

Valley Forge Christian College v. Americans United for Separation of Church and State, 454 U.S. 464, 102 S.Ct. 752, 70 L.Ed.2d 700 (1982).

St. Martin Evangelical Lutheran Church v. South Dakota, 451 U.S. 772, 101 S.Ct. 2142, 68 L.Ed.2d 612 (1981).

Committee v. Regan, 444 U.S. 646, 100 S.Ct. 840, 63 L.Ed.2d 94 (1980).

NLRB v. Catholic Bishop of Chicago, 440 U.S. 490, 99 S.Ct. 1313, 59 L.Ed.2d 533 (1979).

New York v. Cathedral Academy, 434 U.S. 125, 98 S.Ct. 340, 54 L.Ed.2d 346 (1977).

Wolman v. Walter, 433 U.S. 229, 97 S.Ct. 2593, 53 L.Ed.2d 714 (1977).

Runyon v. McCrary, 427 U.S. 160, 96 S.Ct. 2586, 49 L.Ed.2d 415 (1976).

Roemer v. Board of Public Works, 426 U.S. 736, 96 S.Ct. 2337, 49 L.Ed.2d 179 (1976).

Meek v. Pittenger, 421 U.S. 349, 95 S.Ct. 1753, 44 L.Ed.2d 217 (1975).

Wheeler v. Barrera, 417 U.S. 402, 94 S.Ct. 2274, 41 L.Ed.2d 159 (1974).

Sloan v. Lemon, 413 U.S. 825, 93 S.Ct. 2982, 37 L.Ed.2d 939 (1973).

Committee for Public Education and Religious Liberty v. Nyquist, 413 U.S. 756, 93 S.Ct. 2955, 37 L.Ed.2d 948 (1973).

Hunt v. McNair, 413 U.S. 734, 93 S.Ct. 2868, 37 L.Ed.2d 923 (1973).

Levitt v. Committee for Public Education and Religious Liberty, 413 U.S. 472, 93 S.Ct. 2814, 37 L.Ed.2d 736 (1973).

Early v. Di Censo, 403 U.S. 602, 91 S.Ct. 2105, 29 L.Ed.2d 745 (1971).

Lemon v. Kurtzman, 403 U.S. 602, 91 S.Ct. 2105, 29 L.Ed.2d 745 (1971).

Board of Education v. Allen, 392 U.S. 236, 88 S.Ct. 1923, 20 L.Ed.2d 1060 (1968).

Flast v. Cohen, 392 U.S. 83, 88 S.Ct. 1942, 20 L.Ed.2d 947 (1968).

Zorach v. Clauson, 343 U.S. 306, 72 S.Ct. 679, 96 L.Ed. 954 (1952).

McCollum v. Board of Education, 333 U.S. 203, 68 S.Ct. 461, 92 L.Ed. 649 (1948).

Everson v. Board of Education, 330 U.S. 1, 67 S.Ct. 504, 91 L.Ed. 711 (1947).

Farrington v. Tokushige, 273 U.S. 284, 47 S.Ct. 406, 71 L.Ed. 646 (1927).

Racial Discrimination

St. Francis College v. Al-Khazraji, 481 U.S. 604, 107 S.Ct. 2022, 97 L.Ed.2d 749 (1987).

City of Pleasant Grove v. United States, 479 U.S. 462, 107 S.Ct. 794, 93 L.Ed.2d 866 (1987).

Wygant v. Jackson Board of Education, 476 U.S. 267, 106 S.Ct. 1842, 90 L.Ed.2d 260 (1986).

Runyon v. McCrary, 427 U.S. 160, 96 S.Ct. 2586, 49 L.Ed.2d 415 (1976).

Lau v. Nichols, 414 U.S. 563, 94 S.Ct. 786, 39 L.Ed.2d 1 (1974).

Norwood v. Harrison, 413 U.S. 455, 93 S.Ct. 2804, 37 L.Ed.2d 723 (1973).

Recognition of Student Organizations

Healy v. James, 408 U.S. 169, 92 S.Ct. 2338, 33 L.Ed.2d 266 (1972).

Religious Activities in Public Schools

Bd. of Educ. of Kiryas Joel Village v. Grumet, 114 S.Ct. 2481, 129 L.Ed.2d 546 (1994).

Lamb's Chapel v. Center Moriches Union Free School District, 508 U.S.—, 113 S.Ct. 2141, 124 L.Ed.2d 352 (1993).

Lee v. Weisman, 505 U.S. —, 112 S.Ct. 2649, 120 L.Ed.2d 467 (1992).

Karcher v. May, 484 U.S. 72, 108 S.Ct. 388, 98 L.Ed.2d 327 (1987).

Bender v. Williamsport Area School District, 475 U.S. 534, 106 S.Ct. 1326, 89 L.Ed.2d 501 (1986).

Wallace v. Jaffree, 472 U.S. 38, 105 S.Ct. 2479, 96 L.Ed.2d 29 (1985).

Widmar v. Vincent, 454 U.S. 263, 102 S.Ct. 269, 70 L.Ed.2d 400 (1981).

Stone v. Graham, 449 U.S. 39, 101 S.Ct. 192, 66 L.Ed.2d 199 (1980).

Epperson v. Arkansas, 393 U.S. 97, 89 S.Ct. 266, 21 L.Ed.2d 228 (1968).

Chamberlin v. Dade County Board of Public Instruction, 377 U.S. 402, 84 S.Ct. 1272, 12 L.Ed.2d 407 (1964).

Abington School District v. Schempp, 374 U.S. 203, 83 S.Ct. 1560, 10 L.Ed.2d 844 (1963).

Engel v. Vitale, 370 U.S. 421, 82 S.Ct. 1261, 8 L.Ed.2d 601 (1962).

McCollum v. Bd. of Educ., 333 U.S. 203, 68 S.Ct. 461, 92 L.Ed. 649 (1948).

West Virginia Board of Education v. Barnette, 319 U.S. 624, 63 S.Ct. 1178, 87 L.Ed. 1628 (1943).

Residency

Martinez v. Bynum, 461 U.S. 321, 103 S.Ct. 1838, 75 L.Ed.2d 879 (1983).

Elgins v. Moreno, 435 U.S. 647, 98 S.Ct. 1338, 55 L.Ed.2d 614 (1978).

School Liability

Bradford Area School Dist. v. Stoneking, 489 U.S. 1062, 109 S.Ct. 1333, 103 L.Ed.2d 804 (1989).

Smith v. Sowers, 490 U.S. 1002, 109 S.Ct. 1634, 104 L.Ed.2d 150 (1989).

Deshaney v. Winnebago County DSS, 489 U.S. 189, 109 S.Ct. 998, 103 L.Ed.2d 249 (1989).

Sex Discrimination

Franklin v. Gwinnett County Public Schools, 503 U.S. 60, 112 S.Ct. 1028, 117 L.Ed.2d 208 (1992).

Ohio Civil Rights Commission v. Dayton Christian Schools, 477 U.S. 619, 106 S.Ct. 2718, 91 L.Ed.2d 512 (1986).

Mississippi University for Women v. Hogan, 458 U.S. 718, 102 S.Ct. 3331, 73 L.Ed.2d 1090 (1982).

Rendell-Baker v. Kohn, 457 U.S. 830, 102 S.Ct. 2764, 73 L.Ed.2d 418 (1982).

Cannon v. Univ. of Chicago, 441 U.S. 677, 99 S.Ct. 1946, 60 L.Ed.2d 560 (1979).

Bd. of Trustees v. Sweeney, 439 U.S. 24, 99 S.Ct. 295, 58 L.Ed.2d 216 (1978).

Striking Teachers

Hortonville Joint School District v. Hortonville Education Association, 426 U.S. 482, 96 S.Ct. 2308, 49 L.Ed.2d 1 (1976).

Student Searches

New Jersey v. T.L.O., 469 U.S. 325, 105 S.Ct. 733, 83 L.Ed.2d 720 (1985).

Student Suspensions

Regents v. Ewing, 474 U.S. 214, 106 S.Ct. 507, 88 L.Ed.2d 523 (1985).

Board of Education v. McCluskey, 458 U.S. 966, 103 S.Ct. 3469, 73 L.Ed.2d 1273 (1982).

Carey v. Piphus, 435 U.S. 247, 98 S.Ct. 1042, 55 L.Ed.2d 252 (1978).

Bd. of Curators v. Horowitz, 435 U.S. 78, 98 S.Ct. 948, 55 L.Ed.2d 124 (1978).

Wood v. Strickland, 420 U.S. 308, 95 S.Ct. 992, 43 L.Ed.2d 214 (1975).

Goss v. Lopez, 419 U.S. 565, 95 S.Ct. 729, 42 L.Ed.2d 725 (1975).

Taxation

Allen v. Wright, 468 U.S. 737, 104 S.Ct. 3315, 82 L.Ed.2d 556 (1984).

Bob Jones University v. United States, 461 U.S. 574, 103 S.Ct. 2017, 76 L.Ed.2d 157 (1983).

Mueller v. Allen, 463 U.S. 388, 103 S.Ct. 3062, 77 L.Ed.2d 721 (1983).

Ramah Navajo School Bd. v. Bureau of Revenue, 458 U.S. 832, 102 S.Ct. 3394, 73 L.Ed.2d 1174 (1982).

California v. Grace Brethren Church, 457 U.S. 393, 102 S.Ct. 2498, 73 L.Ed.2d 93 (1982).

Gordon v. Lance, 403 U.S. 1, 91 S.Ct. 1889, 29 L.Ed.2d 273 (1971).

Askew v. Hargrave, 401 U.S. 476, 91 S.Ct. 856, 28 L.Ed.2d 196 (1971).

Doremus v. Bd. of Educ., 342 U.S. 429, 72 S.Ct. 394, 96 L.Ed. 475 (1952).

Teacher Disclosure of Organization Memberships

Shelton v. Tucker, 364 U.S. 479, 81 S.Ct. 247, 5 L.Ed.2d 231 (1960).

Teacher Termination

Patsy v. Bd. of Regents, 457 U.S. 496, 102 S.Ct. 2557, 73 L.Ed.2d 172 (1982).

Chardon v. Fernandez, 454 U.S. 6, 102 S.Ct. 28, 70 L.Ed.2d 6 (1981).

Delaware State College v. Ricks, 449 U.S. 250, 101 S.Ct. 498, 66 L.Ed.2d 431 (1980).

Beilan v. Board of Public Education, 357 U.S. 399, 78 S.Ct. 1317, 2 L.Ed.2d 1414 (1958).

Textbooks

Norwood v. Harrison, 413 U.S. 455, 93 S.Ct. 2804, 37 L.Ed.2d 723 (1973).

Board of Education v. Allen, 392 U.S. 236, 88 S.Ct. 1923, 20 L.Ed.2d 1060 (1968).

Cochran v. Louisiana State Board of Education, 281 U.S. 370, 50 S.Ct. 335, 74 L.Ed.2d 1929 (1930).

Transportation Fees

Kadrmas v. Dickinson Pub. Schools, 487 U.S. 450, 108 S.Ct. 2481, 101 L.Ed.2d 399 (1988).

Use of School Facilities

Ellis v. Dixon, 349 U.S. 458, 75 S.Ct. 859, 99 L.Ed. 1231 (1955).

APPENDIX D

GLOSSARY

Age Discrimination in Employment Act (ADEA)- The ADEA, 29 U.S.C. § 621 *et seq.*, is part of the Fair Labor Standards Act. It prohibits discrimination against persons who are at least forty years old, and applies to employers which have twenty or more employees and which affect interstate commerce.

Americans With Disabilities Act (ADA)- The ADA, 42 U.S.C. § 12101 *et seq.*, went into effect on July 26, 1992. Among other things, it prohibits discrimination against a qualified individual with a disability because of that person's disability with respect to job application procedures, the hiring, advancement or discharge of employees, employee compensation, job training, and other terms, conditions and privileges of employment.

Bona fide Latin term meaning "good faith." Generally used to note a party's lack of bad intent or fraudulent purpose.

Class Action Suit- Federal Rule of Civil Procedure 23 allows members of a class to sue as representatives on behalf of the whole class provided that the class is so large that joinder of all parties is impractical, there are questions of law or fact common to the class, the claims or defenses of the representatives are typical of the claims or defenses of the class, and the representative parties will adequately protect the interests of the class. In addition, there must be some danger of inconsistent verdicts or adjudications if the class action were prosecuted as separate actions. Most states also allow class actions under the same or similar circumstances.

Collateral Estoppel - Also known as issue preclusion. The idea that once an issue has been litigated, it may not be re-tried. Similar to the doctrine of *Res Judicata* (see below).

Due Process Clause- The clauses of the Fifth and Fourteenth Amendments to the Constitution which guarantee the citizens of the United States "due process of law" (see below). The Fifth Amendment's Due Process Clause applies to the federal government, and the Fourteenth Amendment's Due Process Clause applies to the states.

Due Process of Law - The idea of "fair play" in the government's application of law to its citizens, guaranteed by the Fifth and Fourteenth Amendments. Substantive due process is just plain *fairness*, and procedural due process is accorded when the government utilizes adequate procedural safeguards for the protection of an individual's liberty or property interests.

Education for All Handicapped Children Act (EAHCA) - [see Individuals with Disabilities Education Act (IDEA).]

Education of the Handicapped Act (EHA) - [see Individuals with Disabilities Education Act (IDEA).]

Employee Retirement Income Security Act (ERISA) - Federal legislation which sets uniform standards for employee pension benefit plans and employee welfare benefit plans. It is codified at 29 U.S.C. § 1001 *et seq.*

Enjoin - (see Injunction).

Equal Pay Act - Federal legislation which is part of the Fair Labor Standards Act. It applies to discrimination in wages which is based on gender. For race discrimination, employees paid unequally must utilize Title VII or 42 U.S.C. § 1981. Unlike many labor statutes, there is no minimum number of employees necessary to invoke the act's protection.

Equal Protection Clause - The clause of the Fourteenth Amendment which prohibits a state from denying any person within its jurisdiction equal protection of its laws. Also, the Due Process Clause of the Fifth Amendment which pertains to the federal government. This has been interpreted by the Supreme Court to grant equal protection even though there is no explicit grant in the Constitution.

Establishment Clause - The clause of the First Amendment which prohibits Congress from making "any law respecting an establishment of religion." This clause has been interpreted as creating a "wall of separation" between church and state. The test now used to determine whether government action violates the Establishment Clause, referred to as the *Lemon* test, asks whether the action has a secular purpose, whether its primary effect promotes or inhibits religion, and whether it requires excessive entanglement between church and state.

Ex Post Facto Law - A law which punishes as criminal any action which was not a crime at the time it was performed. Prohibited by Article I, Section 9, of the Constitution.

Exclusionary Rule - Constitutional limitation on the introduction of evidence which states that evidence derived from a constitutional violation must be excluded from trial.

Fair Labor Standards Act (FLSA) - Federal legislation which mandates the payment of minimum wages and overtime compensation to covered employees. The overtime provisions require employers to pay at least time-and-one-half to employees who work more than 40 hours per week.

Federal Employers' Liability Act (FELA) - Legislation enacted to provide a federal remedy for railroad workers who are injured as a result of employer or co-employee negligence. It expressly prohibits covered carriers from adopting any regulation, or entering into any contract, which limits their FELA liability.

Federal Tort Claims Act - Federal legislation which determines the circumstances under which the United States waives its sovereign immunity (see below) and agrees to be sued in court for money damages. The government retains its immunity in cases of intentional torts committed by its employees or agents, and where the tort is the result of a "discretionary function" of a federal employee or agency. Many states have similar acts.

42 U.S.C. §§ 1981, 1983 - Section 1983 of the federal Civil Rights Act prohibits any person acting under color of state law from depriving any other person of rights protected by the Constitution or by federal laws. A vast majority of lawsuits claiming constitutional violations are brought under § 1983. Section 1981 provides that all persons enjoy the same right to make and enforce contracts as "white citizens." Section 1981 applies to employment contracts. Further, unlike § 1983, § 1981 applies even to private actors. It is not limited to those acting under color of state law. These sections do not apply to the federal government, though the government may be sued directly under the Constitution for any violations.

Free Exercise Clause - The clause of the First Amendment which prohibits Congress from interfering with citizens' rights to the free exercise of their religion. Through the Fourteenth Amendment, it has also been made applicable to the states and their sub-entities. The Supreme Court has held that laws of general applicability which have an incidental effect on persons' free exercise rights are not violative of the Free Exercise Clause.

Handicapped Children's Protection Act (HPCA) - [see also Individuals with Disabilities Education Act (IDEA).] The HPCA, enacted as an amendment to the EHA, provides for the payment of attorney's fees to a prevailing parent or guardian in a lawsuit brought under the EHA (and the IDEA).

Hearing Officer - Also known as an administrative law judge. The hearing officer decides disputes that arise *at the administrative level*, and has the power to administer oaths, take testimony, rule on evidentiary questions, and make determinations of fact.

Incorporation Doctrine - By its own terms, the Bill of Rights applies only to the federal government. The Incorporation Doctrine states that the Fourteenth Amendment makes the Bill of Rights applicable to the states.

Individualized Educational Program (IEP) - The IEP is designed to give children with disabilities a free, appropriate education. It is updated annually, with the participation of the child's parents or guardian.

Individuals with Disabilities Education Act (IDEA) - Also known as the Education of the Handicapped Act (EHA), the Education for All Handicapped Children Act (EAHCA), and the Handicapped Children's Protection Act (HPCA). Originally enacted as the EHA, the IDEA is the federal legislation which provides for the free, appropriate education of all children with disabilities.

Injunction - An equitable remedy (see Remedies) wherein a court orders a party to do or refrain from doing some particular action.

Issue Preclusion - (see Res Judicata).

Jurisdiction - The power of a court to determine cases and controversies. The Supreme Court's jurisdiction extends to cases arising under the Constitution and under federal law. Federal courts have the power to hear cases where there is diversity of citizenship or where a federal question is involved.

Labor Management Relations Act (LMRA) - Federal labor law which pre-empts state law with respect to controversies involving collective bargaining agreements. The most important provision of the LMRA is § 301, which is codified at 29 U.S.C. § 185.

Mainstreaming - Part of what is required for a free appropriate education is that each child with a disability be educated in the "least restrictive environment." To the extent that disabled children are educated with nondisabled children in regular education classes, those children are being mainstreamed.

National Labor Relations Act (NLRA) - Federal legislation which guarantees to employees the right to form and participate in labor organizations. It prohibits employers from interfering with employees in the exercise of their rights under the NLRA.

Negligence per se - Negligence on its face. Usually, the violation of an ordinance or statute will be treated as negligence per se because no careful person would have been guilty of it.

Occupational Safety and Health Act (OSHA) - Federal legislation which requires employers to provide a safe workplace. Employers have both general and specific duties under OSHA. The general duty is to provide a workplace which is free from recognized hazards that are likely to result in serious physical harm. The specific duty is to conform to the health and safety standards promulgated by the Secretary of Labor.

Overbroad - A government action is overbroad if, in an attempt to alleviate a specific evil, it impermissibly prohibits or chills a protected action. For example, attempting to deal with street litter by prohibiting the distribution of leaflets or handbills.

Per Curiam - Latin phrase meaning "by the court." Used in court reports to note an opinion written by the court rather than by a single judge or justice.

Placement - A special education student's placement must be appropriate (as well as responsive to the particular child's needs). Under the IDEA's "stay-put" provision, school officials may not remove a special education child from his or her "then current placement" over the parents' objections until the completion of administrative or judicial review proceedings.

Preemption Doctrine - Doctrine which states that when federal and state law attempt to regulate the same subject matter, federal law prevents the state law from operating. Based on the Supremacy Clause of Article VI, Clause 2, of the Constitution.

Prior Restraint - Restraining a publication before it is distributed. In general, constitutional law doctrine prohibits government from exercising prior restraint.

Pro Se - A party appearing in court, without the benefit of an attorney, is said to be appearing pro se.

Rehabilitation Act - Section 504 of the Rehabilitation Act prohibits employers who receive federal financial assistance from discriminating against otherwise qualified individuals with handicaps solely becuase of their handicaps. An otherwise qualified individual is one who can perform the "essential functions" of the job with "reasonable accomodation."

Related Services - As part of the free, appropriate education due to children with disabilities, school districts may have to provide related services such as transportation, physical and occupational therapy, and medical services which are for diagnostic or evaluative purposes relating to education.

Remand - The act of an appellate court in returning a case to the court from which it came for further action.

Remedies - There are two general categories of remedies, or relief: legal remedies, which consist of money damages, and equitable remedies, which consist of a court mandate that a specific action be prohibited or required. For example, a claim for compensatory and punitive damages seeks a legal remedy; a claim for an injunction seeks an equitable remedy. Equitable remedies are generally unavailable unless legal remedies are inadequate to address the harm.

Res Judicata - The judicial notion that a claim or action may not be tried twice or re-litigated, or that all causes of action arising out of the same set of operative facts should be tried at one time. Also known as claim preclusion.

Section 504 of the Rehabilitation Act of 1973 - Section 504 applies to public or private institutions receiving federal financial assistance. It requires that, in the employment context, an otherwise qualified individual cannot be denied employment based on his or her handicap. An otherwise qualified individual is one who can perform the "essential functions" of the job with "reasonable accomodation."

Section 1981 & Section 1983 - (see 42 U.S.C. §§ 1981, 1983).

Sovereign Immunity - The idea that the government cannot be sued without its consent. It stems from the English notion that the "King could do no wrong." This immunity from suit has been abrogated in most states and by the federal government through legislative acts known as "tort claims acts."

Standing - The judicial doctrine which states that in order to maintain a lawsuit a party must have some real interest at stake in the outcome of the trial.

Statute of Limitations - A statute of limitation provides the time period in which a specific cause of action may be brought.

Summary Judgment - Federal Rule of Civil Procedure 56 provides for the summary adjudication of a case if either party can show that there is no genuine issue as to any material fact and that, given the facts agreed upon, the party is entitled to judgment as a matter of law. In general, summary judgment is used to dispose of claims which do not support a legally recognized claim.

Supremacy Clause - Clause in Article VI of the Constitution which states that federal legislation is the supreme law of the land. This clause is used to support the Preemption Doctrine (see above).

Title VII, Civil Rights Act of 1964 (Title VII) - Title VII prohibits discrimination in employment based upon race, color, sex, national origin, or religion. It applies to any employer having fifteen or more employees. Under Title VII, where an employer intentionally discriminates, employees may obtain money damages unless the claim is for race discrimination. For those claims, monetary relief is available under 42 U.S.C. § 1981.

U.S. Equal Employment Opportunity Commission (EEOC) - The EEOC is the government entity which is empowered to enforce Title VII (see above) through investigation and/or lawsuits. Private individuals alleging discrimination must pursue administrative remedies within the EEOC before they are allowed to file suit under Title VII.

Vacate - The act of annulling the judgment of a court either by an appellate court or by the court itself. The Supreme Court will generally vacate a lower court's judgment without deciding the case itself, and remand the case to the lower court for further consideration in light of some recent controlling decision.

Void-for-Vagueness Doctrine - A judicial doctrine based on the Fourteenth Amendment's Due Process Clause. In order for a law which regulates speech, or any criminal statute, to pass muster under the doctrine, the law must make clear what actions are prohibited or made criminal. Under the principles of the Due Process Clause, people of average intelligence should not have to guess at the meaning of a law.

Writ of Certiorari - The device used by the Supreme Court to transfer cases from the appellate court's docket to its own. Since the Supreme Court's appellate jurisdiction is largely discretionary, it need only issue such a writ when it desires to rule in the case.

INDEX